D0674025

THE FIRST AND SECOND PRAYER BOOKS OF EDWARD VI

INTRODUCTION BY PROF. THE REVD CANON J.R. PORTER

THE FIRST AND SECOND PRAYER BOOKS OF EDWARD VI

INTRODUCTION BY PROF. THE REVD CANON J.R. PORTER

THE PRAYER BOOK SOCIETY

Published by

The Prayer Book Society
Registered Charity No. 1001783

St James Garlickhythe
Garlick Hill
London EC4V 2AF

ISBN 0 9535668 0 3

Introduction copyright © J.R. Porter 1999

First published 1549 and 1552
First published in the Everyman's Library by
J.M. Dent & Sons Ltd 1910

First published by the Prayer Book Society
with the co-operation of Everyman's Library May 1999
Second Inpression September 1999

Printed in Great Britain by
Short Run Press Ltd, Exeter

INTRODUCTION

The architect of the first English Prayer Book was Thomas Cranmer, Archbishop of Canterbury (1489-1556), who was probably mainly responsible for its actual composition, although, as the 1549 Act of Uniformity states, he was assisted by others. The origins of the Book are obscure but it represents a highly significant stage in the process of theological and liturgical reform towards which Cranmer had been working for a number of years, marking as it did a break with the long-established pattern of worship in England.

The principles underlying the work and the objects it was intended to achieve are set out in its Preface. In the first place, all public worship was now to be in English, in contrast to the Latin of the medieval services. This had been prepared for by the piecemeal introduction of the vernacular, even under the conservative regime of Henry VIII : an English Bible was introduced into all parish churches in 1536 and in 1543 it was directed that a chapter from it was to be read every Sunday and holy day at Mattins and Evensong after the Te Deum and the Magnificat, while the next year saw the appearance of an English Litany, one of the most impressive of Cranmer's liturgical achievements, which, with various modifications, was to survive in all successive versions of the Book of Common Prayer. After the death of Henry VIII, this development intensified and of particular importance, as the immediate predecessor of the 1549 Book, was the issue of an English Order of Communion in 1548. This was to be used in conjunction with the Latin Mass to enable the administration of communion in both kinds, which had been ordered by an Act of Parliament in the preceding year. The components of the Order were incorporated in the communion rite of the first Prayer Book and, though with some important changes, still remain in the present Prayer Book.

Equally significant, was the simplifying and unifying of the conduct of the Church's worship. The ordering of worship in the medieval church required at least half-a-dozen books to carry it out : now, as the Preface says, only one book, in addition to the Bible, would be required and that book was both 'short and plain'. Again, all this was Cranmer's particular response to widespread concerns in the early years of the sixteenth century. There were complaints from the clergy about the burden and complexity of the recitation of the daily office and, on the continent, there appeared efforts to remedy the situation, both in Catholic and Protestant circles. Especially notable were the two editions, in 1535 and 1537, of the Reformed Breviary of the Spanish Cardinal Quiñonez, the book produced by Hermann von Wied, Archbishop of Cologne in 1543, actually the work of Bucer and Melanchthon, translated into English two years later and known as the 'Simple and religious Consultation', and various Protestant Church Orders, particularly that of Brandenburg and Nüremberg. All these were well-known to Cranmer and his liturgical work borrowed extensively from them : a considerable part of the 1549 Preface is little more than a translation of the preface to the first edition of Quiñonez's work.

What Quiñonez stressed was that the elaboration of the medieval service books interrupted the continuous reading of the Bible, which both he and Cranmer saw as the original purpose and practice of divine service in the Church. According to the Preface of the first Prayer Book, this was proved by the evidence of the 'ancient fathers' and the appeal to the Early Fathers and the primitive Church is a constant theme in all of Cranmer's writings. He was a dedicated scholar, a voracious reader, with one of the best libraries of the time, and a representative of the New Learning of the Renaissance, with its patristic scholarship and rejection of medieval scholasticism : his liturgical work is to be seen in this light. The restoration of Scripture as the heart of worship was above all for edification both of the clergy and not least of the laity and here again is to be seen another of Cranmer's constant concerns. Whatever may be thought of his view of 'the first original and ground' of public worship, his ideal was that its central element should be the regular and comprehensive reading of the Bible, primarily by means of the two lessons at Mattins and Evensong. In this way, the daily offices, which had hitherto been the prerogative of the clergy, were made available to the laity also, a feature which has continued to be a distinctive characteristic of Anglican worship.

The Preface also refers to the diversity of worship in the country, exemplified by the 'Uses' of the great cathedral churches. No doubt Cranmer exaggerated the divergencies : the ordinary worshipper would hardly have noticed any great difference in the way the services were conducted in the various centres and there had already been moves towards a degree of uniformity, as when in 1542 the Convocation of Canterbury decreed that only the Sarum Breviary was to be used in the Southern Province. But the object of the first English Prayer Book that 'all the whole realm shall have but one use' went much further and marked a decisive step in the situation of worship in England. There is no evidence to indicate any great degree of discontent with the existing religious system and all the indications are that it continued to meet the needs and concerns of the majority of the population. The 1549 Prayer Book was the product of a carefully planned programme of change, set in motion, after Henry VIII's death, by a coalition between Cranmer and his associates, on the one hand, and Protector Somerset and the Privy Council on the other. It was thus the work of a comparatively small body, at the centre of state power, an establishment group which had a clear idea of what it wanted to achieve. Significantly, the first Prayer Book was authorized by Parliament in the first Act of Uniformity, a far-reaching innovation which brought matters of worship for the first time under the control of the central organs of the state.

The 1549 Book was much more than an attempt at liturgical simplifying and rationalizing. It embodied theological and doctrinal concepts intended to create a Church very different from the medieval institution. By 1548 at the latest, Cranmer's own theological development had led him to embrace the most important features characteristic of the continental Reformation. He now abandoned not only the doctrine of transubstantiation but any belief in a real presence of Christ in the eucharistic elements : Christ's presence was a spiritual one to the recipient of communion.

Further, he had moved to accept the great Reformation principle of justification by faith and this brought him to view the central medieval belief in the mass as a propitiatory sacrifice for the living and departed as a 'work' and to remove any notion of offering in connection with the eucharistic bread and wine. During this period, and later, Cranmer was greatly influenced not only by some of his English colleagues, such as Ridley, but also by his contacts with continental Reformers, notably Peter Martyr, who had settled in England in 1547, and especially Martin Bucer who also came here in 1549, both of whom Cranmer regularly consulted.

Cranmer thus had a clear programme which he was actively working to achieve in the first years of Edward VI's reign. However, he was always acutely aware of the advisability of caution and of the continuing strength of traditional beliefs and the need to conciliate those who still adhered to them, while always quietly moving in the direction of reform. Hence there is a certain Janus-like character about the 1549 Book. It has often been described as 'conservative' and certainly that is how it appears when compared with the service books of the continental Reformation. Its framework was the various services dispersed through the different medieval liturgical books : these were now revised and brought together in a single volume. Much of the traditional language was retained in the new Communion service, as were many of the old practices such as the eucharistic vestments, the chrism at Baptism and anointing with oil at Baptism and the Visitation of the Sick. The 1549 Book did not contain an Ordinal, which only appeared separately in the following year, and this stated the intention of continuing the apostolic threefold ministry of bishop, priest and deacon and the delivery of the instruments of office to those being ordained was still prescribed. At the conclusion of the first Book, there is a text headed 'Of Ceremonies', transferred to the introductory material in 1552, which illustrates the tight-rope that Cranmer had to walk. Against conservative opinion, it defends the abolition of various traditional rituals but equally the retention of others against those 'so new fangled that they would innovate all thing' : here Cranmer is taking on the more extreme Protestant reformers, who wished to proceed further and faster than he was prepared to do at this stage, and whose activities he had consistently opposed.

Hence there was a certain feasibility in the Council's message to the Western rebels against the 1549 Book, that 'it seemeth to you a new service, and indeed it is none other but the old : the selfsame words in English which were in Latin, saving a few things taken out'. But there was also a degree of disingenuousness in the claim, for the change from Latin to English, and the things omitted or modified from the old service, were intended to bring about a great change in the understanding and shape of worship which had hitherto prevailed in England. In the Middle Ages, with the Mass in Latin, the laity could take little verbal part in it and it became essentially a rite performed by the priest on their behalf, understood as a propitiatory sacrifice offered by him for the congregation : furthermore, the reception of the sacrament had become very infrequent, for many people rarely, if ever. In consequence, for the laity, the focus of the service became the elevation of the host, the sign of the real and corporal presence of Christ and the evidence that the miracle of transubstantiation had taken place. It could be said that the medieval church had developed a separation between the act of consecration and the act of communion.

It was Cranmer's aim, in his first Prayer Book and subsequently to reunite consecration and communion: Christ was to be seen not as an object on the altar but as spiritual food and drink to nourish the life of faith. Now the title of the Church's central service was to be 'the Supper of the Lord and Holy Communion' : the term 'Mass' was retained only as a concession to popular usage. A significant rubric at the end of the service ordered that 'there shall be no celebration of the Lord's Supper except there be some to communicate with the Priest.' Equally significant is the provision that the celebrant was to recite the narrative of the institution, the consecratory act in medieval thought, 'without any elevation, or showing the Sacrament to the people.' Even more important was the theology underlying the new rite which was fundamentally different from that of the medieval church, particularly with regard to the eucharistic sacrifice. First, the 1549 consecration prayer emphasizes the unrepeatable nature of Christ's offering, 'one oblation of himself once offered, a full, perfect and sufficient sacrifice, oblation and satisfaction for the sins of the whole world.' So, secondly, the eucharist is a 'perpetual memory' of that sacrifice, that is, it brings Christ's past sacrifice on Calvary into the present for worshippers, without adding anything to its eternal significance : there is an implicit denial of any offering for sin in the mass, given explicit expression in Article XXXI of the existing Thirty-Nine Articles, the original form of which was probably drafted by Cranmer himself as early as 1549. Thirdly, what is offered in the Communion service is 'our sacrifice of praise and thanksgiving' and 'ourselves, our souls and bodies, to be a reasonable, holy and lively sacrifice.' These expressions, with their echoes of Hebrews 13:15 and Romans 12:1 not only reflect the dominant Reformation appeal to Scripture, but also the particular understanding of the eucharistic sacrifice found in S. Augustine, Cranmer's favourite theologian.

Other changes in comparison with the medieval services move in the same generally Protestant direction. While the chasuble or vestment, the distinctive mark of the sacrificing priest, was still kept, the cope, which was not a distinctively sacerdotal garment, was allowed as an alternative. The use of oil was continued at Baptism and the Visitation of the Sick, but there was no requirement that it should be blessed and the anointing in Confirmation, which in Catholic theology constituted the matter of that sacrament, no longer appears. Many other 'ceremonies' hitherto characteristic of public worship also found no place in the new Book.

It is not surprizing that reactions to the first Book of Common Prayer varied greatly. Apart from peripheral attacks on it, such as the Western Rebellion, it appears to have been generally and quietly accepted : it was possible for the new Communion service to be celebrated in a way which, to the ordinary worshipper, would make it appear, apart from the language, much the same as the old mass.

The retention of so much of the phraseology and ceremonies of the medieval services enabled conservatives to argue that, as the Council had stated to the Western rebels, the new Book made no essential change in doctrine. In particular, Cranmer had to face the very able and convincing polemicist, Bishop Gardiner of Winchester, who claimed that the 1549 Book was ' not distant from the Catholic faith' with regard to transubstantiation and the mass as a propitiatory sacrifice. On the other hand, the changes did not go nearly far enough for the more radical Protestants, especially the foreign divines who had settled in England and with whom Cranmer at this period was becoming increasingly close. In any case, it would appear that Cranmer himself viewed the 1549 Book only as an interim measure, to be further revised as soon as opportunity allowed, and that, when Gardiner asserted that it diverged from the Archbishop's own beliefs, it was a shaft that went home. Bucer, who knew Cranmer well, was able to assure his correspondents at Strassburg, in a letter of April 1549, that the Catholic rituals of the new Book were only to be retained for a time, and represented merely 'a respect for antiquity and the infirmity of the present age.' and, in the section 'Of Ceremonies,' there was more than a strong hint that ceremonies 'upon just causes may be altered and changed.'

Various problems, not least troubles on the political scene, delayed the implementation of Cranmer's plans, and no more is known of the preparations for the second Prayer Book than is the case for the first, but Parliament finally authorized the new text by a further Act of Uniformity in April 1552. In the words of the Act, the first Prayer Book was 'made fully perfect' in the second and this no doubt represents how Cranmer viewed the matter. While it represents at least the partial realization of his long evolving plans, it seems likely that Cranmer took account of Gardiner's views, since the 1552 Book meets all Gardiner's claims, especially with respect to the Communion rite. Thus, if the 1549 Book can be described as 'conservative', the

1552 Book marked a much more radical break with the past.

In many ways, the 1552 Communion service can be seen as an outstanding example of Cranmer's liturgical skill, where, by drastically re-ordering the shape of the medieval canon, largely preserved in 1549, along with other changes, he created a vehicle which perfectly expressed the eucharistic theology which he now held. A rubric at the beginning of the Book proscribed the use of the traditional vestments, the altar, the site of sacrifice, was replaced by a table, the setting of a meal and for the opening Kyries a recitation of the Ten Commandments was substituted, another of Cranmer's borrowings from Protestant sources. Above all, the rite was careful to remove any connection of Christ's presence with the elements of bread and wine. The blessing of the elements, retained in 1549, is omitted and the petition that 'they may be unto us the body and blood' of Christ, which Gardiner had been able to interpret in a Catholic sense, is replaced by a prayer that, in receiving them, the communicants may be partakers of the body and blood. The central section has, since 1662, had the title 'The Prayer of Consecration' but this is not found in the second Prayer Book, which in fact avoids all notion of consecration : there are no Manual Acts and a concluding rubric directs that, if any of the bread and wine remain over at the end, 'the Curate shall have it to his own use'. The function of the eucharistic elements is to be received by the worshippers : so, after the recital of the words of institution, there is no 'Amen', and communion follows immediately with a new formula, exhorting the recipients to remember Christ's sacrifice, so avoiding the possibility that they might believe that they received Christ's body and blood in their mouths. Other traditional beliefs and practices which constituted a vital part of medieval religion were cut out entirely. Invocation of the saints, already much reduced in 1549, now disappeared entirely, as did all prayer for the departed : no provision was now made, as the first Prayer Book had done, for a celebration of Communion at funerals, and the great intercession in the service was to be only 'for the whole state of Christ's Church militant here in earth'. However the circumstances of the late inclusion of the so-called 'Black Rubric' are to be assessed, there can be little doubt that its rejection of any adoration of the eucharistic elements and its assertion that the natural body and blood of Christ 'are in heaven and not here' fully represent Cranmer's own sacramental understanding.

Characteristic of Reformation concerns was the emphasis on the instruction of the laity and the encouragement of the people to participate in public worship, where they would above all be exposed to Biblical doctrine. Homilectic elements, sermons designed to teach the congregation, were now much expanded. In particular, the offices of Morning and Evening Prayer, hitherto still primarily the preserve of the clergy, were considerably developed to permit greater congregational participation and an effort was made to bring the people as a whole to share in them day by day : so it was ordered that every incumbent was to say the offices daily and publicly in the parish church and to toll a bell to summon those so disposed to 'come to hear God's word and to pray with him'. Cranmer certainly wished that regular weekly communion should be the heart of public worship but his ideal, for whatever reasons, was never wholly realized. Instead, the abiding achievement of the second Prayer Book was to make Morning and Evening Prayer the staple of the religious life of Anglicans until at least comparatively modern times.

The Book of 1552 was in operation for less than twelve months, before it was repealed on the accession of Queen Mary, and the subsequent history of the English Prayer Book lies beyond the scope of this Introduction. It has been conjectured that had the Protestant Lady Jane Grey become queen and had Cranmer continued in office, he would in due course have produced a further revision, moving in an even more Reformed direction. This is not unlikely : after all, the Prayer Book was regularly revised until it reached its final form in 1662. It may be doubted, however, whether Cranmer would ever have wished to go as far as many Continental Reformers or the later English Puritans, who largely abandoned liturgical structures in favour of a service based on a long sermon, Scripture reading and metrical psalms, conducted by just one order of ministry. He was a scholar, with considerable reverence for antiquity, prepared to draw on Eastern Orthodox sources and even the obscure Mozarabic rite for certain of his liturgical projects. He was always greatly concerned with order and uniformity and he viewed the activities of the more radical Protestants as inevitably leading to anarchy, that great fear of Tudor England. Such were the grounds of his sharply worded opposition to Knox and his supporters who in 1552 wished to compel communicants to receive the sacrament seated. He described them as 'glorious and unquiet spirits which...cease not to make trouble and disquietness when things be most quiet and in good order'. He added that 'if such men should be heard, although the book were made every year anew, yet it should not lack faults in their opinion', which may suggest that, whatever some Marian exiles may later have believed, he would have been in no great hurry seriously to alter the second Prayer Book.

In any event, perhaps one of the most remarkable things about the Book of 1552 is that it survived. As the object of so much controversy and destined for so short a life, it might have seemed doomed. Yet it was brought back, with some comparatively small changes, under Queen Elizabeth and remains substantially, although again with significant modifications, the Prayer Book still in use today. It steadily made its way and, by the end of the sixteenth century, it had captured the hearts and minds of a large segment of the ordinary population. This was the result of Cranmer's literary genius, which infuses all his liturgical work and constitutes his greatest claim to be remembered : he borrowed freely from the work of others but the end product is always distinctively his own. He created an English liturgical language which ranks with the traditional Greek and Latin and it was the regular hearing of his words, with their easily memorable rhythms, which formed a structure of devotion and piety for successive generations. In the 1549 Preface, Cranmer had contrasted the way in which up until then the laity had simply learned various texts and prayers by heart with the great profit they were now to gain by 'daily reading upon the book'. The Prayer Book provided a short and simple resource not only for public celebration but also for private meditation, which would mould people's prayers and thoughts and instruct them in God's word. Further, even the 1552 Book retained much traditional language and many traditional elements, such as the collects, the great majority of which are translations from the Latin and have always been recognized as showing Cranmer at the height of his powers, and this made it possible to interpret the Book in a more Catholic and sacramental way than Cranmer himself might have wished : looked at in this light, the various changes over the next hundred years, which moved the second Prayer Book in that direction, do not jar and may be considered not wholly illegitimate developments. Doubtless they would not have gained Cranmer's approval but perhaps it may be said that he often wrote better than he knew.

Nor was the first Book of Common Prayer ever lost sight of. There is some evidence that Queen Elizabeth would have liked to restore it and a number of the bishops would have liked to introduce some of its features into the revision of 1662. In particular, the Scottish Prayer Book of 1637 re-arranged the Communion Service in a manner following that of 1549, employing much of its wording, and the resulting Communion Office not only remained as the basis of worship in Scotland but also, in its characteristic features, came to determine the liturgies of various other provinces of the Anglican Communion. It is the purpose of the present volume to make available again the two Edwardine Prayer Books, which for some time have been out of print, in the original spelling and punctuation, as important texts, not only for the history of the Prayer Book, but also for all students of English history, theology and literature.

J.R. PORTER

The first Edwardine Act of Uniformity was passed on January 21, 1549. It ordained that the new Prayer-Book, compiled by "the Archbishop of Canterbury, and certain of the most learned and discreet bishops, and other learned men of this realm," should be brought into use on "the Feast of Pentecost next coming" (June 9), or, if copies could be obtained earlier, three weeks after they had been obtained.

The earliest dated copies extant are those of March 7, 1549, printed by Edward Whitechurche. Other editions from the same printing house appeared in the following May and June. Richard Grafton, the King's Printer, issued editions of the Prayer-Book in March and June; and two editions, dated respectively May 23 and July 30, were printed at Worcester by John Oswen. These editions are not identical in detail.

In 1550, Grafton printed John Merbecke's musical edition of the new book, under the title *The booke of Common praier noted.*

The second Edwardine Act of Uniformity, passed on April 14, 1552, introduced the second Prayer-Book, which was attached to the Act as a schedule, and in which, according to the Act itself, the First Book was "explained and made fully perfect." The Act also added the Ordinal, which, in 1549, had been printed and published as a separate volume. The Second Prayer-Book came into use on All Saints' Day (November 1), 1552. It was abolished by Queen Mary's first Act of Repeal, passed in the autumn of 1553; but, with certain modifications, few though not unimportant, was restored by the Elizabethan Act of Uniformity of 1559. The Book of 1552, therefore, is the foundation of the existing Prayer-Book, which, the result of revision by a committee of bishops, and adopted by the Convocations in 1661, was enacted by the Restoration Parliament in the Act of Uniformity of May 19, 1662.

Several editions of the Second Book were printed by Whitechurche and Grafton; and at least one by Oswen. Earlier copies lack the "Declaration on Kneeling" or "Black Rubric" (see p. 392) which formed no part of the book passed by Parliament. The "Declaration" was issued on October 27, 1552, by an order in Council to the Lord Chancellor directing him "to cause to be joined unto the Book of Common Prayer lately set forth a certain declaration, signed by the King's Majesty and sent unto his Lordship, touching the Kneeling at the receiving of the Communion." In some copies, therefore, the "Declaration" appears upon a separate leaf, added to the book after printing.

No adaptation of Merbecke's *Common Prayer Noted* was made for the Book of 1552.

The Two Liturgies, A.D. 1549, and A.D. 1552, with other Documents. Parker Society, 1844, contains editions, with modernized spelling, of both books as printed by Whitechurche, the first being that dated May 4, 1549. *The First Book of Common Prayer of Edward VI. and the Ordinal of 1549 together with The Order of the Communion, 1548,* edited by H. B. Walton, with introduction by P. G. Medd, 1869, reprints Whitechurche's book of June 16. Cheap reprints of Whitechurche's First Book of May 4, 1549, and of his Second Book were issued by James Parker in 1883. *The First Prayer Book of King Edward VI., 1549, reprinted from a copy in the British Museum,* with an introduction by W. B., in the Ancient and Modern Library of Theological Literature, 1887, reproduces Whitechurche's first edition dated March 7, 1549. *The Second Prayer-Book of King Edward VI., 1552,* with an introduction by W. B., in the same series, is a reprint from a copy, also in the British Museum, of Whitechurche's book. Both these volumes were republished in the Westminster Library, 1891. Whitechurche's first edition of the First Book was also published under the care of Vernon Staley in the Library of Liturgiology and Ecclesiology, 1903. An almost exhaustive treatment of the sources, origins, and history of the two books, with their texts synoptically arranged, will be found in F. E. Brightman, *The English Rite,* 1915. J. E. Hunt, *Merbecke's Book of Common Prayer Noted,* 1939, contains a facsimile of the complete copy in the British Museum.

N.B.—In the present reprint, the original text of Whitechurche's first edition of the First Book and of his later issue of the Second Book is strictly followed, save that in the Second Book the Collects, Epistles, and Gospels, which are precisely the same with those of the first, are not repeated. (The Collect for St. Andrew's Day was, however, revised in 1552. See p. 375.) This measure is necessary to bring the two books into the compass of one volume.

St. John's College, Cambridge, *January 1949.* E. C. Ratcliff.

THE

BOOKE OF THE COMMON

PRAYER AND ADMI-

NISTRACION OF

THE

SACRAMENTES, AND OTHER

RITES AND CEREMONIES OF

THE CHURCHE AFTER THE

USE OF THE CHURCHE

OF ENGLAND.

Londini in Officina
Edouardi Whitchurche.
Cum privilegio ad imprimendum solum
Anno Do. 1549, *Mense* Martii.

THE CONTENTES OF THIS BOOKE.

THE PREFACE.

THERE was neuer any thing by the wit of man so well deuised, or so surely established, which (in continuãce of time) hath not been corrupted: as (emong other thinges) it may plainly appere by the common prayers in the Churche, commonlye called diuine seruice: the firste originall and grounde whereof, if a manne woulde searche out by the auncient fathers, he shall finde that the same was not ordeyned, but of a good purpose, and for a great aduauncement of godlines: For they so ordred the matter, that all the whole Bible (or the greatest parte thereof) should be read ouer once in the yeare, intendyng thereby, that the Cleargie, and specially suche as were Ministers of the congregacion, should (by often readyng and meditacion of Gods worde) be stirred up to godlines themselfes, and be more able also to exhorte other by wholsome doctrine, and to confute them that were aduersaries to the trueth. And further, that the people (by daily hearyng of holy scripture read in the Churche) should continuallye profite more and more in the knowledge of God, and bee the more inflamed with the loue of his true religion. But these many yeares passed this Godly and decent ordre of the auncient fathers, hath bee so altered, broken, and neglected, by planting in uncertein stories, Legēdes, Respondes, Verses, vaine repeticions, Commemoracions, and Synodalles, that commonly when any boke of the Bible was begon: before three or foure Chapiters were read out, all the rest were unread. And in this sorte the boke of Esaie was begon in Aduent, and the booke of Genesis in Septuagesima: but they were onely begon, and neuer read thorow. After a like sorte wer other bokes of holy scripture used. And moreouer, whereas s. Paule would haue suche language spoken to the people in the churche, as they mighte understande and haue profite by hearyng the same; the seruice in this Churche of England (these many yeares) hath been read in Latin to the people, whiche they understoode not; so that they haue heard with theyr eares onely; and their hartes, spirite, and minde, haue not been edified thereby. And furthermore, notwithstandyng that the auncient fathers had deuided the psalmes into seuen porcions,

3

wherof euery one was called a nocturne, now of late tyme a fewe of them haue been dailye sayed (and ofte repeated) and the rest utterly omitted. Moreouer the nōbre and hardnes of the rules called the pie, and the manifolde chaunginges of the seruice, was the cause, yᵗ to turne the boke onlye, was so hard and intricate a matter, that many times, there was more busines to fynd out what should be read, then to read it when it was founde out.

These inconueniences therfore considered: here is set furth suche an ordre, whereby the same shalbe redressed. And for a readines in this matter, here is drawen out a Kalendar for that purpose, whiche is plaine and easy to be understanded, wherin (so muche as maie be) the readyng of holy scripture is so set furthe, that all thynges shall bee doen in ordre, without break-yng one piece therof from another. For this cause be cut of Anthemes, Respondes, Inuitatories, and suche like thynges, as did breake the continuall course of the readyng of the scripture. Yet because there is no remedy, but that of necessitie there must be some rules: therfore certein rules are here set furth, whiche as they be fewe in nōbre; so they be plain and easy to be understanded. So yᵗ here you haue an ordre for praier (as touchyng the readyng of holy scripture) muche agreable to the mynde and purpose of the olde fathers, and a greate deale more profitable and commodious, than that whiche of late was used. It is more profitable, because here are left out many thynges, whereof some be untrue, some uncertein, some vain and super-sticious: and is ordeyned nothyng to be read, but the very pure worde of God, the holy scriptures, or that whiche is euidently grounded upon the same; and that in suche a language and ordre, as is moste easy and plain for the understandyng, bothe of the readers and hearers. It is also more cōmodious, bothe for the shortnes thereof, and for the plaines of the ordre, and for that the rules be fewe and easy. Furthermore by this ordre, the curates shal nede none other bookes for their publique seruice, but this boke and the Bible: by the meanes wherof, the people shall not be at so great charge for bookes, as in tyme past they haue been.

And where heretofore, there hath been great diuersitie in saying and synging in churches within this realme: some folowyng Salsbury use, some Herford use, some the use of Bangor, some of Yorke, and some of Lincolne: Now from hēcefurth, all the whole realme shall haue but one use. And if any would iudge this waye more painfull, because that all

thynges must be read upō the boke, whereas before, by the
reason of so often repeticion, they could saye many thinges by
heart: if those men will waye their labor, with the profite in
knowlege, whiche dayely they shal obtein by readyng upon the
boke, they will not refuse the payn, in consideracion of the greate
profite that shall ensue therof.

And forsomuche as nothyng can, almoste, be so plainly set
furth, but doubtes maie rise in the use and practisyng of the
same: to appease all suche diuersitie (if any arise), and for the
resolucion of all doubtes, concernyng the maner how to understande, do, and execute the thynges conteygned in this booke:
the parties that so doubt, or diuersly take any thyng, shall
alwaye resorte to the Bishop of the Diocese, who by his discrecion
shall take ordre for the quietyng and appeasyng of the same:
so that the same ordre be not contrary to any thyng conteigned
in this boke.

¶ Though it be appointed in the afore written preface, that al
thinges shalbe read and sōg in the churche, in the Englishe
tongue, to thende yᵗ the congregacion maie be therby edified:
yet it is not meant, but when men saye Matins and Euensong
priuatelye, they maye saie the same in any language that they
themselues do understande. Neither that anye man shalbe
bound to the saying of them, but suche as from tyme to tyme,
in Cathedrall and Collegiate Churches, Parishe Churches, and
Chapelles to the same annexed, shall serue the congregacion.

THE TABLE AND

KALENDER, EXPRESSING THE ORDRE OF THE PSALMES AND
LESSONS, TO BEE SAYED AT MATYNS AND EUENSONG,
THROUGHOUT THE YERE, EXCEPTE CERTAYNE
PROPER FEASTES, AS THE RULES
FOLOWYNG MORE PLAYNLYE
DECLARE.

THE ORDRE HOW THE PSALTER IS APPOYNTED TO BEE REDDE.

THE Psalter shalbe red through once euery Moneth, and because that some Moneths, be longer then some other be; it is thought good, to make thē euen by this meanes.

To euery Moneth, as concernyng this purpose, shall be appointed iust xxx dayes.

And because January and Marche hath one daye, aboue the sayd noumbre, and February, whiche is placed betwene them bothe, hath onely xxviii daies, February shall borowe of either of the Monethes of January and Marche one daie, and so the Psalter which shalbe red in February, muste bee begon the last daie of January, and ended the first daie of Marche.

And whereas Maie, July, August, October and December, haue xxxi dayes apeece, it is ordered that the same Psalmes shall be redde the laste daye of the saied Monethes, whiche were red the daie before: so that the Psalter maye bee begon agayne the firste daye of the nexte Moneths ensuyng.

Now to knowe what Psalmes shalbe red euery daye, loke in the Kalendar the nombre that is appoynted for the Psalmes, and then finde the same nombre in this Table, and upon that nombre shall you se, what Psalmes shalbe sayd at Matyns, and Euensong.

And where the Cxix. Psalme is deuided into xxii porcions, and is ouer long to be red at one tyme: it is so ordered, that at one tyme shall not be red aboue iiii. or v. of the saied porcions, as you shall perceiue to be noted in this Table.

And here is also to bee noted, that in this Table, and in all other partes of ye seruice, where any Psalmes are appoincted, the nombre is expressed after the greate English Bible, whiche from the ix. Psalme unto the Cxlviii. Psalme (folowyng the diuision of the Ebrues) doth vary in nombres from the comō Latyn translacion.

6

A TABLE FOR

	Matins.	Euensong.
i.	i, ii, ii, iv, v.	vi, vii, viii.
ii.	ix, x, xi.	xii, xiii, xiv.
iii.	xv, xvi, xvii.	xviii.
iv.	xix, xx, xxi.	xxii, xxiii.
v.	xxiv, xxv, xxvi.	xxvii, xxviii, xxix.
vi.	xxx, xxxi.	xxxii, xxxiii, xxxiv.
vii.	xxxv, xxxvi.	xxxvii.
viii.	xxxviii, xxxix, xl.	xli, xlii, xliii.
ix.	xliv, xlv, xlvi.	xlvii, xlviii, xlix.
x.	l, li, lii.	liii, liv, lv.
xi.	lvi, lvii, lviii.	lix, lx, lxi.
xii.	lxii, lxiii, lxiv.	lxv, lxvi, lxvii.
xiii.	lxviii.	lxix, lxx.
xiv.	lxxi, lxxii.	lxxiii, lxxiv.
xv.	lxxv, lxxvi, lxxvii.	lxxviii.
xvi.	lxxix, lxxx, lxxxi.	lxxxii, lxxxiii, lxxxiv, lxxxv.
xvii.	lxxxvi, lxxxvii, lxxxviii.	lxxxix.
xviii.	xc, xci, xcii.	xciii, xciv.
xix.	xcv, xcvi, xcvii.	xcviii, xcix, c, ci.
xx.	cii, ciii.	civ.
xxi.	cv.	cvi.
xxii.	cvii.	cviii, cix.
xxiii.	cx, cxi, cxii, cxiii.	cxiv, cxv.
xxiv.	cxvi, cxvii, cxviii.	cxix. Inde. iv.
xxv.	Inde. v.	Inde. iv.
xxvi.	Inde. v.	Inde. iv.
xxvii.	cxx, cxxi, cxxii, cxxiii, cxxiv, cxxv.	cxxvi, cxxvii, cxxviii, cxxix, cxxx, cxxxi.
xxviii.	cxxxii, cxxxiii, cxxxiv, cxxxv.	cxxxvi, cxxxvii, cxxxviii.
xxix.	cxxxix, cxl, cxli,	clxii, cxliii.
xxx.	cxliv, cxlv, cxlvi.	clxvii, clxviii, cxlix, cl.

7

THE ORDRE

The olde Testamēt.

THE olde Testament is appoynted for the first Lessons, at Matins and Euensong, and shal bee redde through euery yere once, except certain bokes and Chapiters, whiche bee least edifying, and might best be spared, and therfore are left unred.

The newe Testamēt.

The newe Testament is appoynted for the second Lessons, at Matins and Euensong, and shalbe red ouer orderly euery yere thrise, beside the Epistles and Gospelles: except the Apocalips, out of the whiche there be onely certain Lessons appoynted upon diuerse proper feastes.

Lessons.

And to knowe what Lessons shall bee red euery daye: finde the daye of the Moneth in the Kalendar folowyng: and there ye shal perceiue the bookes and Chapiters, that shalbe red for the Lessons, bothe at Matins and Euensong.

Proper Psalms.

And here is to be noted, that whensoeuer there bee any proper Psalmes or Lessōs appoynted for any feast, moueable or unmoueable; then the Psalmes and Lessons appoynted in the Kalendar shalbe omitted for that tyme.

Ye muste note also, that the Collect, Epistle, and Gospell, appoynted for the Sundaie, shall serue all the weeke after, except there fall some feast that hath his propre.

The Leape-Yeare.

This is also to bee noted, concernyng the leape yeres, that the xxv. daye of February, whiche in leape yeres is coumpted for twoo dayes, shall in those twoo dayes alter neither Psalme nor Lesson: but the same Psalmes and Lessons, whiche be sayed the first daye shall serue also for the seconde daye.

Also, wheresoeuer the beginnyng of any Lesson, Epistle, or Gospell is not expressed, there ye must begin at the beginnyng of the Chapiter.

JANUARY.

JANUARY.			Psalms	MATINS.		EUENSONG.	
				1 *Less.*	2 *Less.*	1 *Less.*	2 *Less.*
A	*Kalend.*	1 *Circumci.*	1	Gene. 17	Roma. 2	Deut. 10	Collos. 2
b	4 No.	2	2	Gene. 1	Math. 1	Gene. 2	Roma. 1
c	3 No.	3	3	3	2	4	2
d	Prid. No.	4	4	5	3	6	3
e	*Nonas.*	5	5	7	4	8	4
f	8 Id.	6 *Epiphani.*	6	Esai. 60	Luke 3	Esai. 49	John 2
g	7 Id.	7	7	Gen. 9	Math. 5	Gene. 11	Roma. 5
A	6 Id.	8	8	12	6	13	6
b	5 Id.	9	9	14	7	15	7
c	4 Id.	10	10	16	8	17	8
d	3 Id.	11	11	18	9	19	9
e	Prid. Id.	12	12	20	10	21	10
f	*Idus.*	13	13	22	11	23	11
g	19 kl.	14	14	24	12	25	12
A	18 kl.	15	15	26	13	27	13
b	17 kl.	16	16	28	14	29	14
c	16 kl.	17	17	30	15	31	15
d	15 kl.	18	18	32	16	33	16
e	14 kl.	19	19	34	17	35	1 Cor. 1
f	13 kl.	20	20	36	18	37	2
g	12 kl.	21	21	38	19	39	3
A	11 kl.	22	22	40	20	41	4
b	10 kl.	23	23	42	21	43	5
c	9 kl.	24	24	44	22	45	6
d	8 kl.	25 *Con. Pa*	25	46	Act. 22	47	Acte. 26
e	7 kl.	26	26	48	Mat. 23	49	1 Cor. 7
f	6 kl.	27	27	50	24	Exod. 1	8
g	5 kl.	28	28	Exod. 2	25	3	9
A	4 kl.	29	29	4	26	5	10
b	3 kl.	30	30	6	27	7	11
c	*Prid.* kl.	31	31	8	28	9	12

FEBRUARY.

FEBRUARY.			Psalms	MATINS.		EUENSONG.	
				1 Less.	2 Less.	1 Less.	2 Less.
d	*Kalend.*	1	*Puri. Ma.* 2	Exod. 10	Mark 1	Exod. 11	1 Cor. 13
e	4 No.	2	3	12	2	13	14
f	3 No.	3	4	14	3	15	15
g	Prid. No.	4	5	16	4	17	16
A	*Nonas.*	5	6	18	5	19	2 Cor. 1
b	8 Id.	6	7	20	6	21	2
c	7 Id.	7	8	22	7	23	3
d	6 Id.	8	9	24	8	32	4
e	5 Id.	9	10	33	9	34	5
f	4 Id.	10	11	35	10	40	6
g	3 Id.	11	12	Leui. 18	11	Leui. 19	7
A	Prid. Id.	12	13	20	12	Num. 10	8
b	*Idus.*	13	14	Num. 11	13	12	9
c	16 kl.	14	15	13	14	14	10
d	15 kl.	15	16	15	15	16	11
e	14 kl.	16	17	17	16	18	12
f	13 kl.	17	18	19	Luk. di. 1	20	13
g	12 kl.	18	19	21	di. 1	22	Galath. 1
A	11 kl.	19	20	23	2	24	2
b	10 kl.	20	21	25	3	26	3
c	9 kl.	21	22	27	4	28	4
d	8 kl.	22	23	29	5	30	5
e	7 kl.	23	24	31	6	32	6
f	6 kl.	24	*Mathias.* 25	33	7	34	Ephes. 1
g	5 kl.	25	26	35	8	36	2
A	4 kl.	26	27	Deut. 1	9	Deut. 2	3
b	3 kl.	27	28	3	10	4	4
c	Prid. kl.	28	29	5	11	6	5

MARCHE.

MARCHE.			Psalmes	MATINS.		EUENSONG.	
				1 *Less.*	2 *Less.*	1 *Less.*	2 *Less.*
d	*Kalend.*	1	30	Deu. 7	Luk. 12	Deu. 8	Ephe. 6
e	6 No.	2	1	9	13	10	Philip. 1
f	5 No.	3	2	11	14	12	2
g	4 No.	4	3	13	15	14	3
A	3 No.	5	4	15	16	16	4
b	Prid. No.	6	5	17	17	18	Collos. 1
c	*Nonas.*	7	6	19	18	20	2
d	8 Id.	8	7	21	19	22	3
e	7 Id.	9	8	23	20	24	4
f	6 Id.	10	9	25	21	26	1 Thes. 1
g	5 Id.	11	10	27	22	28	2
A	4 Id.	12	11	29	23	30	3
b	3 Id.	13	12	31	24	32	4
c	Prid. Id.	14	13	33	John 1	34	5
d	*Idus.*	15	14	Josue. 1	2	Josue. 2	2 Thes. 1
e	17 kl.	16	15	3	3	4	2
f	16 kl.	17	16	5	4	6	3
g	15 kl.	18	17	7	5	8	1 Timo. 1
A	14 kl.	19	18	9	6	10	2, 3
b	13 kl.	20	19	11	7	12	4
c	12 kl.	21	20	12	8	14	5
d	11 kl.	22	21	15	9	16	6
e	10 kl.	23	22	17	10	18	2 Tim. 1
f	9 kl.	24	23	19	11	20	2
g	8 kl.	25 *Annuncia*	24	21	12	22	3
A	7 kl.	26	25	23	13	24	4
b	6 kl.	27	26	Judic. 1	14	Judic. 2	Titus 1
c	5 kl.	28	27	3	15	4	2, 3
d	4 kl.	39	28	5	16	6	Phile. 1
e	3 kl.	20	29	7	17	8	Hebre. 1
f	*Prid.* kl.	31	30	9	18	10	2

APRILL.

APRYLL.			Psalmes	MATINS.		EUENSONG.	
				1 *Less.*	2 *Less.*	1 *Less.*	2 *Less.*
g	*Kalend.*	1	1	Judi. 11	John 19	Judi. 12	Hebre. 3
A	4 No.	2	2	13	20	14	4
b	3 No.	3	3	15	21	16	5
c	Prid. No.	4	4	17	Acts 1	18	6
d	*Nonas.*	5	5	19	2	20	7
e	8 Id.	6	6	21	3	Ruth 1	8
f	7 Id.	7	7	Ruth 2	4	3	9
g	6 Id.	8	8	4	5	1 Reg. 1	10
A	5 Id.	9	9	1 Reg. 2	6	3	11
b	4 Id.	10	10	4	7	5	12
c	3 Id.	11	11	6	8	7	13
d	Prid. Id.	12	12	8	9	9	Jacob. 1
e	*Idus.*	13	13	10	10	11	2
f	18 kl.	14	14	12	11	13	3
g	17 kl.	15	15	14	12	15	4
A	16 kl.	16	16	16	13	17	5
b	15 kl.	17	17	18	14	19	1 Peter. 1
c	14 kl.	18	18	20	15	21	2
d	13 kl.	19	19	22	16	23	3
e	12 kl.	20	20	24	17	25	4
f	11 kl.	21	21	26	18	27	5
g	10 kl.	22	22	28	19	29	2 Peter. 1
A	9 kl.	23	23	30	20	31	2
b	8 kl.	24	24	2 Reg. 1	21	2 Reg. 2	3
c	7 kl.	25 *Mar.Evan*	25	3	22	4	1 John. 1
d	6 kl.	26	26	5	23	6	2
e	5 kl.	27	27	7	24	8	3
f	4 kl.	28	28	9	25	10	4
g	3 kl.	29	29	11	26	12	5
A	*Prid.* kl.	30	30	13	27	14	2, 3. Joh.

MAYE.

	MAYE.			Psalmes	MATINS.		EUENSONG.	
					1 Less.	2 Less.	1 Less.	2 Less.
b	Kalend.	1	Phil.&Ja.	1	2 Re. 15	Acts 8	2 Re. 16	Judas. 1
c	6 No.	2		2	17	28	18	Roma. 1
d	5 No.	3		3	19	Math. 1	20	2
e	4 No.	4		4	21	2	22	3
f	3 No.	5		5	23	3	24	4
g	Prid. No.	6		6	3 Reg. 1	4	3 Reg. 2	5
A	Nonas.	7		7	3	5	4	6
b	8 Id.	8		8	5	6	6	7
c	7 Id.	9		9	7	7	8	8
d	6 Id.	10		10	9	8	10	9
e	5 Id.	11		11	11	9	12	10
f	4 Id.	12		12	13	10	14	11
g	3 Id.	13		13	15	11	16	12
A	Prid. Id.	14		14	17	12	18	13
b	Idus.	15		15	19	13	20	14
c	17 kl.	16		16	21	14	22	15
d	16 kl.	17		17	4 Reg. 1	15	4 Re. 2	16
e	15 kl.	18		18	3	16	4	1 Cor. 1
f	14 kl.	19		19	5	17	6	2
g	13 kl.	20		20	7	18	8	3
A	12 kl.	21		21	9	19	10	4
b	11 kl.	22		22	11	20	12	5
c	10 kl.	23		23	13	21	14	6
d	9 kl.	24		24	15	22	16	7
e	8 kl.	25		25	17	23	18	8
f	7 kl.	26		26	19	24	20	9
g	6 kl.	27		27	21	25	22	10
A	5 kl.	28		28	23	26	24	11
b	4 kl.	29		29	25	27	1 Esd. 2	12
c	3 kl.	30		30	1 Esd. 2	28	3	13
d	Prid. kl.	31		30	4	Mark 1	5	14

IUNE.

JUNE.			Psalms		MATINS.		EUENSONG.	
					1 *Less.*	2 *Less.*	1 *Less.*	2 *Less.*
e	*Kalend.*	1		1	1 Esd. 6	Mark 2	1 Esd. 7	1 Cor. 15
f	4 No.	2		2	8	3	9	16
g	3 No.	3		3	10	4	2 Esd. 1	2 Cor. 1
A	Prid. No.	4		4	2 Esd. 1	5	3	2
b	*Nonas.*	5		5	4	6	5	3
c	8 Id.	6		6	6	7	7	4
d	7 Id.	7		7	8	8	9	5
e	6 Id.	8		8	10	9	11	6
f	5 Id.	9		9	12	10	13	7
g	4 Id.	10		10	Hester 1	11	Hester 2	8
A	3 Id.	11	*Barna.ap.*	11	3	Act. 14	4	Acts 15
b	Prid. Id.	12		12	5	Mar. 12	6	2 Cor. 9
c	*Idus.*	13		13	7	13	8	10
d	18 kl.	14		14	9	14	Job 1	11
e	17 kl.	15		15	Job 2	15	3	12
f	16 kl.	16		16	4	16	5	13
g	15 kl.	17		17	6	Luke 1	7	Gala. 1
A	14 kl.	18		18	8	2	9	2
b	13 kl.	19		19	10	3	11	3
c	12 kl.	20		20	12	4	13	4
d	11 kl.	21		21	14	5	15	5
e	10 kl.	22		22	16	6	17, 18	6
f	9 kl.	23		23	19	7	20	Ephe. 1
g	8 kl.	24	*Na.Jo.Ba*	24	**Mala.** 3	Mat. 3	Mal. 3	Math. 14
A	7 kl.	25		25	Job 21	Lu. 8	Job 22	Ephe. 2
b	6 kl.	26		26	23	9	24, 25	3
c	5 kl.	27		27	26, 27	10	28	4
d	4 kl.	28		28	29	11	30	5
e	3 kl.	29	*S. Peter*	29	31	Acts 3	32	Acts 4
f	*Prid.* kl.	30		30	33	Luke 12	34	Ephe. 6

IULY.

	JULY.			Psalmes	MATINS.		EUENSONG.	
					1 *Less.*	2 *Less.*	1 *Less.*	2 *Less.*
g	*Kalend.*	1		1	Job 35	Luk. 13	Job 36	Philip. 1
A	6 No.	2		2	37	14	38	2
b	5 No.	3		3	39	15	40	3
c	4 No.	4		4	41	16	42	4
d	3 No.	5		5	Prov. 1	17	Prov. 2	Collos. 1
e	Prid. No.	6		6	3	18	4	2
f	*Nonas.*	7		7	5	19	6	3
g	8 Id.	8		8	7	20	8	4
A	7 Id.	9		9	9	21	10	1 Thes. 1
b	6 Id.	10		10	11	22	12	2
c	5 Id.	11		11	13	23	14	3
d	4 Id.	12		12	15	24	16	4
e	3 Id.	13		13	17	John 1	18	5
f	Prid. Id.	14		14	19	2	20	2 Thes. 1
g	*Idus.*	15		15	21	3	22	2
A	17 kl.	16		16	23	4	24	3
b	16 kl.	17		17	25	5	26	1 Timo. 1
c	15 kl.	18		18	27	6	28	2, 3
d	14 kl.	19		19	29	7	30	4
e	13 kl.	20		20	31	8	Eccles. 1	5
f	12 kl.	21		21	Eccles. 2	9	3	6
g	11 kl.	22	*Magdalen*	22	4	10	5	2 Tim. 1
A	10 kl.	23		23	6	11	7	2
b	9 kl.	24		24	8	12	9	3
c	8 kl.	25	*James Ap.*	25	10	13	11	4
d	7 kl.	26		26	12	14	Jere. 1	Titus. 1
e	6 kl.	27		27	Jere. 2	15	3	2, 3
f	5 kl.	28		28	4	16	5	Phile. 1
g	4 kl.	29		29	6	17	7	Hebre. 1
A	3 kl.	30		30	8	18	9	2
b	*Prid.* kl.	31		30	10	19	11	3

AUGUST.

AUGUST.			Psalmes	MATINS.		EUENSONG.	
				1 *Less.*	2 *Less.*	1 *Less.*	2 *Less.*
c	*Kalend.*	1	1	Jere. 12	John. 20	Jere. 13	Hebr. 4
d	4 No.	2	2	14	21	15	5
e	3 No.	3	3	16	Acts 1	17	6
f	Prid. No.	4	4	18	2	19	7
g	*Nonas.*	5	5	20	3	21	8
A	8 Id.	6	6	22	4	23	9
b	7 Id.	7	7	24	5	25	10
c	6 Id.	8	8	26	6	27	11
d	5 Id.	9	9	28	7	29	12
e	4 Id.	10	10	30	8	31	13
f	3 Id.	11	11	32	9	33	Jacob. 1
g	Prid. Id.	12	12	34	10	35	2
A	*Idus.*	13	13	36	11	37	3
b	19 kl.	14	14	38	12	39	4
c	18 kl.	15	15	40	13	41	5
d	17 kl.	16	16	42	14	43	Peter 1
e	16 kl.	17	17	44	15	45, 46	2
f	15 kl.	18	18	47	16	48	3
g	14 kl.	19	19	49	17	50	4
A	13 kl.	20	20	51	18	52	5
b	12 kl.	21	21	Lam. 1	19	Lam. 2	2 Peter 1
c	11 kl.	22	22	3	20	4	2
d	10 kl.	23	23	5	21	Ezech. 2	3
e	9 kl.	24 *Bart. Ap.*	24	Ezech. 3	22	6	1 John 1
f	8 kl.	25	25	7	23	13	2
g	7 kl.	26	26	14	24	18	3
A	6 kl.	27	27	33	25	34	4
b	3 kl.	28	28	Dani. 1	26	Dani. 2	5
c	4 kl.	29	29	3	27	4	2. 3 John
d	3 kl.	30	30	5	28	6	Jude 1
e	*Prid.* kl.	31	30	7	Math. 1	8	Roma. 1

SEPTEMBER.

	SEPTEMBER.			Psalmes	MATINS.		EUENSONG.	
					1 *Less.*	2 *Less.*	1 *Less.*	2 *Less.*
f	*Kalend.*	1		1	Dani. 9	Math. 2	Dani. 10	Roma. 2
g	4 No.	2		2	11	3	12	3
A	3 No.	3		3	13	4	14	4
b	Prid. No.	4		4	Ose. 1	5	Ose. 2, 3	5
c	*Nonas.*	5		5	4	6	5, 6	6
d	8 Id.	6		6	7	7	8	7
e	7 Id.	7		7	9	8	10	8
f	6 Id.	8		8	11	9	12	9
g	5 Id.	9		9	13	10	14	10
A	4 Id.	10		10	Joel 1	11	Joel 2	11
b	3 Id.	11		11	3	12	Amos 1	12
c	Prid. Id.	12		12	Amos 2	13	3	13
d	*Idus.*	13		13	4	14	5	14
e	18 kl.	14		14	6	15	7	15
f	17 kl.	15		15	8	16	9	16
g	16 kl.	16		16	Abdias. 1	17	Jonas. 1	1 Cor. 1
A	15 kl.	17		17	Jon. 2, 3	18	4	2
b	14 kl.	18		18	Miche. 1	19	Miche. 2	3
c	13 kl.	19		19	3	20	4	4
d	12 kl.	20		20	5	21	6	5
e	11 kl.	21	*Mathewe*	21	7	22	Naum. 1	6
f	10 kl.	22		22	Naum. 2	23	3	7
g	9 kl.	23		23	Abacu. 1	24	Abacu. 2	8
A	8 kl.	24		24	3	25	Sopho. 1	9
b	7 kl.	25		25	Soph. 2	26	3	10
c	6 kl.	26		26	Agge. 1	27	Agge. 2.	11
d	5 kl.	27		27	Zech. 1	28	Zech. 2, 3	12
e	4 kl.	28		28	4, 5	Marke 1	6	13
f	3 kl.	29	*Michael*	29	7	2	8	14
g	*Prid.* kl.	30		30	9	3	10	15

OCTOBER.

OCTOBER.			*Psalmes*	MATINS.		EUENSONG.	
				1 *Less.*	2 *Less.*	1 *Less.*	2 *Less.*
A	*Kalend.*	1		1	Zach. 11	Mark 4	Zach. 12	1 Cor. 16
b	6 No.	2		2	13	5	14	2 Cor. 1
c	5 No.	3		3	Mala. 1	6	Mala. 2	2
d	4 No.	4		4	3	7	4	3
e	3 No.	5		5	Toby. 1	8	Toby. 2	4
f	Prid. No.	6		6	3	9	4	5
g	*Nonas.*	7		7	5	10	6	6
A	8 Id.	8		8	7	11	8	7
b	7 Id.	9		9	9	12	10	8
c	6 Id.	10		10	11	13	12	9
d	5 Id.	11		11	13	14	14	10
e	4 Id.	12		12	Judith 1	15	Judit. 2	11
f	3 Id.	13		13	3	16	4	12
g	Prid. Id.	14		14	5	Lu. di. 1	6	13
A	*Idus.*	15		15	7	di. 1	8	Gala. 1
b	17 kl.	16		16	9	2	10	2
c	16 kl.	17		17	11	3	12	3
d	15 kl.	18	*Luc.Evan.*	18	13	4	14	4
e	14 kl.	19		19	15	5	16	5
f	13 kl.	20		20	Sap. 1	6	Sapi. 2	6
g	12 kl.	21		21	3	7	4	Ephe. 1
A	11 kl.	22		22	5	8	6	2
b	10 kl.	23		23	7	9	8	3
c	9 kl.	24		24	9	10	10	4
d	8 kl.	25		25	11	11	12	5
e	7 kl.	26		26	13	12	14	6
f	6 kl.	27		27	15	13	16	Philip. 1
g	5 kl.	28	*Sy. & Ju.*	28	17	14	18	2
A	4 kl.	29		29	19	15	Eccls. 1	3
b	3 kl.	30		30	Eccls. 2	16	3	4
c	*Prid.* kl.	31		30	4	17	5	Collos. 1

NOUEMBER.

	NOUEMBER.			Psalmes	MATINS.		EUENSONG.	
					1 *Less.*	2 *Less.*	1 *Less.*	2 *Less.*
d	*Kalend.*	1	*All Saints*	1	Sap. 3	He. 11,12	Sap. 5	Apoc. 1
e	4 No.	2		2	Eccle. 6	Lu. 18	Eccle. 7	Collos. 2
f	3 No.	3		3	8	19	9	3
g	Prid.	4		4	10	20	11	4
A	*Nonas.*	5		5	12	21	13	1 Thes. 1
b	8 Id.	6		6	14	22	15	2
c	7 Id.	7		7	16	23	17	3
d	6 Id.	8		8	18	24	19	4
e	5 Id.	9		9	20	John 1	21	5
f	4 Id.	10		10	22	2	23	2 Thes. 1
g	3 Id.	11		11	24	3	25	2
A	Prid. Id.	12		12	26	4	27	3
b	*Idus.*	13		13	28	5	29	1 Tim. 1
c	18 kl.	14		14	30	6	31	2, 3
d	17 kl.	15		15	32	7	33	4
e	16 kl.	16		16	34	8	35	5
f	15 kl.	17		17	36	9	37	6
g	14 kl.	18		18	38	10	39	2 Tim. 1
A	13 kl.	19		19	40	11	41	2
b	12 kl.	20		20	42	12	43	3
c	11 kl.	21		21	44	13	45	4
d	10 kl.	22		22	46	14	47	Titus 1
e	9 kl.	23		23	48	15	49	2, 3
f	8 kl.	24		24	50	16	51	Phile. 1
g	7 kl.	25		25	Baruc. 1	17	Baruc. 2	Hebre. 1
A	6 kl.	26		26	3	18	4	2
b	5 kl.	27		27	5	19	6	3
c	4 kl.	28		28	Esay. 1	20	Esay. 2	4
d	3 kl.	29		29	3	21	4	5
e	*Prid.* kl.	30	*Andr. Ap.*	30	5	Acts 1	6	6

DECEMBER.

DECEMBER.		Psalmes	MATINS.		EUENSONG.	
			1 *Less.*	2 *Less.*	1 *Less.*	2 *Less.*
f	*Kalend.* 1	1	Esai. 7	Actes 2	Esai. 8	Hebr. 7
g	4 No. 2	2	9	3	10	8
A	3 No. 3	3	11	4	12	9
b	Prid. No. 4	4	13	5	14	10
c	*Nonas.* 5	5	15	6	16	11
d	8 Id. 6	6	17	di. 7	18	12
e	7 Id. 7	7	19	di. 7	20, 21	13
f	6 Id. 8	8	22	8	23	Jacob. 1
g	5 Id. 9	9	24	9	25	2
A	4 Id. 10	10	26	10	27	3
b	3 Id. 11	11	28	11	29	4
c	Prid. Id. 12	12	30	12	31	5
d	*Idus.* 13	13	32	13	33	1 Peter. 1
e	19 kl. 14	14	34	14	35	2
f	18 kl. 15	15	36	15	37	3
g	17 kl. 16	16	38	16	39	4
A	16 kl. 17	17	40	17	41	5
b	15 kl. 18	18	42	18	43	2 Peter 1
c	14 kl. 19	19	44	19	45	2
d	13 kl. 20	20	46	20	47	3
e	12 kl. 21 *Tho.Apos.*	21	48	21	49	1 John. 1
f	11 kl. 22	22	50	22	51	2
g	10 kl. 23	23	52	23	53	3
A	9 kl. 24	24	54	24	55	4
b	8 kl. 25 *Nat. Dom.*	25	Esay. 9	Math. 1	Esay. 7	Tit. 3
c	7 kl. 26 *Stephan*	26	56	Act. 6. 7	57	Actes 7
d	6 kl. 27 *JohnEvan*	27	58	Apoc. 1	59	Apo. 22
e	5 kl. 28 *Innocen.*	28	Jer. 3	Acte 25	60	1 John 5
f	4 kl. 29	29	Esay. 61	26	62	2 John 1
g	3 kl. 30	30	63	27	64	3 John 1
A	*Prid.* kl. 31	30	65	28	66	Jude 1

AN ORDRE

The Priest beeyng in the quier, shall begynne with a loude voyce the Lordes prayer, called the Pater noster.

OURE father, whiche arte in heauen, hallowed by thy name. Thy kyngdom come. Thy wyll be done in earth as it is in heauen. Geue us this daye oure dayly bread. And forgeue us oure trespasses, as we forgeue them that trespasse agaynst us. And leade us not into temptacion. But deliuer us from euell. Amen.

Then lykewyse he shall saye,

O Lorde, open thou my lippes.
Aunswere. And my mouthe shall shewe forth thy prayse.
Priest. O God, make spede to saue me.
Aunswere. O Lorde make haste to helpe me.
Priest. Glory be to the father, and to the sonne, and to the holye ghost. As it was in the begynning, is now, and euer shalbe, world without ende. Amen.
Prayse ye the Lorde.

And from Easter to Trinitie Sondaye,

Alleluya.

Then shalbe saied or song without any Inuitatori this Psalme, Venite exultemus, *etc. in Englishe, followeth :*

Psal. xcv.

O COME lette us syng unto the Lorde : lette us hartely reioyce in the strengthe of oure salvacion.

Let us come before his presence with thankesgeuing : and shewe ourselfe glad in hym with Psalmes.

For the Lord is a great God : and a great kyng aboue all goddes.

In his hande are all the corners of the yearth : and the strength of the hylles is his also.

The sea is his, and he made it : and, his handes prepared the drye lande.

O come, let us worship and fall downe : and kneele before the Lorde oure maker.

For he is (the Lord) oure God : and we are the people of his pasture, and the shepe of his handes.

To daye, yf ye wyll heare his voyce, harden not your hartes : as in the prouocacion, and as in the daie of temptacion in the wildernes.

When your fathers tempted me : proued me, and sawe my workes.

Fourtye yeares long was I greued with this generacion, and sayed : it is a people that do erre in their hartes : for they haue not knowen my wayes.

Unto whom I sware in my wrath : that they shoulde not entre into my rest.

Glory be to the father, and to the sonne : and to the holy ghost.   As it was in the beginnyng, is nowe, and euer shalbe : worlde without end.   Amen.

Thē shal folow certaine Psalmes in ordre as they been appointed in a table made for ye purpose, except there be propre Psalmes appointed for that day.   And at the ende of euery Psalme throughout the yeare, and lyke-wyse in the ende of Benedictus, Benedicite, Magnificat, and Nunc Dimittis, shalbe repeated.

Glory be to the father and to the sonne, &c.

Then shalbe read ii. lessons distinctely with a loude voice, that the people maye heare.   The fyrst of the olde testament, the second of the newe.   Like as they be appoynted by the Kalender, excepte there be propre lessons assigned for that daye : The ministre that readeth the lesson, standing and turnyng hym so as he maye beste be hearde of all suche as be present.   And before euery lesson, the minister shall saye thus.
The fyrste, seconde, iii. or iiii. Chapter of Genesis, or Exodus, Matthewe. Marke, or other lyke as is appoynted in the Kalender.   And in the ende of euery Chapter, he shall saye.

¶ Here endeth suche a Chapter of suche a booke.

And (to thende the people may the better heare) in such places where they doe syng, there shall the lessons be songe in a playne tune after the maner of distincte readyng : and lykewyse the Epistle and Gospell.
After the fyrste lesson shall folowe Te Deum laudamus in Englishe, dayly throughout the yeare, excepte in Lente, all the which tyme in the place of Te Deum shalbe used Benedicite omnia Opera Domini Domino, in Englyshe as foloweth :

Te Deum Laudamus.

We praise the, O God, we knowlage thee to be the Lorde.

All the earth doeth wurship thee, the father euerlastyng.

To thee al Angels cry aloud, the heauens and all the powers therin.

To thee Cherubin, and Seraphin continually doe crye.

Holy, holy, holy, Lorde God of Sabaoth.

Heauen and earth are replenyshed with the maiestie of thy glory.

The gloryous company of the Apostles, praise thee.

The goodly felowshyp of the Prophetes, praise thee.

The noble armie of Martyrs, praise thee.

The holy churche throughout all the worlde doeth knowlage thee.

The father of an infinite maiestie.

Thy honourable, true, and onely sonne.

The holy gost also beeyng the coumforter.

Thou art the kyng of glory, O Christe.

Thou art the euerlastyng sonne of the father.

Whan thou tookest upon thee to delyuer manne, thou dyddest not abhorre the virgins wombe.

Whan thou haddest ouercomed the sharpenesse of death, thou diddest open the kyngdome of heauen to all beleuers.

Thou sittest on the ryght hande of God, in the glory of the father.

We beleue that thou shalt come to be our iudge.

We therfore praye thee, helpe thy seruauntes, whom thou haste redemed with thy precious bloud.

Make them to be noumbred with thy sainctes, in glory euerlastyng.

O Lorde, saue thy people: and blesse thyne heritage.

Gouerne them, and lift them up for euer.

Day by day we magnifie thee.

And we wurship thy name euer world without ende.

Vouchsafe, O Lorde, to kepe us this daye without synne.

O Lorde, haue mercy upon us : haue mercy upon us.

O Lorde, let thy mercy lighten upon us : as our trust is in thee.

O Lorde, in thee haue I trusted : let me neuer be confounded.

Benedicite omnia opera domini domino.

O ALL ye workes of the Lorde, speake good of the Lorde : prayse hym, and set hym up for euer.

O ye Angels of the Lorde, speake good of the Lorde : prayse hym, and set hym up for euer.

O ye heauens, speake good of the Lorde : prayse hym, and set him up for euer.

O ye waters that be aboue the fyrmamente, speake good of the Lorde : prayse hym, and set hym up for euer.

O all ye powers of the Lord, speake good of the Lord : prayse hym, and set hym up for euer.

O ye Sonne and Moone, speake good of the Lorde : prayse him, and set him up for euer.

O ye sterres of heauen, speake good of the lorde : prayse him, and set him up for euer.

O ye showers, and dewe, speake good of the lord : praise him, and set him up for euer.

O ye windes of God, speake good of the Lord : praise him, and set him up for euer.

O ye fier and heate, prayse ye the Lorde : praise him, and set him up for euer.

O ye winter and summer, speake good of the Lorde : praise him and set him up for euer.

O ye dewes and frostes, speake good of the Lord : praise him, and set him up for euer.

O ye frost and colde, speake good of the Lorde : prayse him, and set him up for euer.

O ye yse and snowe, speake good of the Lorde : prayse him, and set him up for euer.

O ye nyghtes and dayes, speake good of the Lorde : prayse him, and set him up for euer.

O ye light and darkenes, speake good of the Lorde : prayse him, and set him up for euer.

O ye lighteninges and cloudes, speake good of the Lord : prayse him, and set him up for euer.

O let the yearthe speake good of the Lord : yea, let it prayse him, and set him up for euer.

O ye mountaynes and hilles, speake good of the Lord : prayse him, and set him up for euer.

O all ye greene thynges upon the earth, speake good of the Lorde : praise him, and set him up for euer.

O ye welles, speake good of the Lorde : praise him, and set him up for euer.

O ye seas, and floudes, speake good of the Lord : praise him, and set him up for euer.

O ye whales, and all that moue in the waters, speake good of the Lorde : prayse hym, and set hym up for euer.

O all ye foules of the ayre, speake good of the lorde : prayse him, and set him up for euer.

O all ye beastes, and catell, speake ye good of the Lord : prayse him, and set him up for euer.

O ye children of men, speake good of the lorde : prayse him, and set him up for euer.

O let Israel speake good of the lorde : prayse him, and set him up for euer.

O ye priestes of the Lord, speake good of the Lorde : prayse him, and set him up for euer.

O ye seruauntes of the Lord, speake good of the Lord : prayse him, and set him up for euer.

O ye spirites and soules of the righteous, speake good of the Lorde : prayse him, and set him up for euer.

O ye holy and humble men of heart, speake ye good of the Lorde : prayse ye him, and set him up for euer.

O Ananias, Azarias, and Misael, speake ye good of the Lorde : prayse ye him, and set him up for euer.

Glory be to the father, and to the sonne : and to the holy gost.

As it was in the beginning, is now, and euer shalbe : worlde without ende.   Amen.

And after the seconde lesson, throughout the whole yere, shalbe used Benedictus dominus deus Israel, *etc. in Englishe as followeth :*

Benedictus.   Luc. i.

BLESSED be the lorde God of Israel : for he hath visited and redemed his people.

And hath lyfted up an horne of saluacyon to us : in the house of his seruaunt Dauid.

As he spake by the mouth of his holy Prophetes : which hath bene syns the world began.

That we shoulde be saued from our enemies : and from the handes of all that hate us.

To perfourme the mercy promised to our fathers : and to remember his holy couenaunt.

To perfourme the othe whiche he sware to our father Abraham : that he would geue us.

That we being deliuered out of the handes of our enemies : might serue him without feare,

In holynesse and ryghteousnes before him all the dayes of our lyfe.

And thou childe, shalte bee called the prophete of the highest : for thou shalte goe before the face of the Lord, to prepare his wayes.

To geue knowledge of saluacion unto his people : for the remission of their sinnes.

Through the tender mercie of our god : whereby the dayespryng from an hygh hath visited us;

To geue lighte to them that sitte in darkenes, and in the shadowe of death : and to guide our fete into the way of peace.

Glory be to the father, &c.
As it was in the beginnyng, &c.

Then shalbe said dailye through the yere the praiers folowing, as well at euensong as at Matins, all deuoutely kneelyng.

Lorde haue mercie upon us.   Christe haue mercie upon us.
Lorde, haue mercie upon us.

Then the minister s al say the Crede *and the Lordes praier in englishe, with a loude voice, &c.*

Answere. But deliuer us from eiuill.   Amen.
Prieste. O Lorde, shewe thy mercie upon us.
Answere. And graunt us thy saluacion.
Prieste. O Lorde saue the kyng.
Answere. And mercifully heare us when we cal upon thee.
Prieste. Indue thy ministers with righteousness.
Answere. And make thy chosen people ioyfull.
Prieste. O Lorde, saue thy people.
Answere. And blesse thyne inheritaunce.
Prieste. Geue peace in oure time, O Lorde.
Answere. Because there is none other that fyghteth for us, but only thou, O God.
Prieste. O God, make cleane our hartes within us.
Answere. And take not thyne holye spirite from us.
Prieste. The lorde be with you.
Answere. And with thy spirite.

Then shall dayly folowe three Collectes. The firste of the day, which shalbe the same that is appointed at the Communiō. The seconde for peace. The thirde for grace to lyue wel. And the two laste Collectes shall neuer alter, but dailye bee saide at Matins throughout al the yere as foloweth. The priest standyng up, and saiyng,

Let us praye.

¶ *Then the Collect of the daie.*

¶ *The second Collect : for peace.*

O GOD, which art author of peace, and louer of concorde, in knowledge of whome standeth oure eternall life, whose seruice is perfect fredome: defende us, thy humble seruautes, in al assaultes of our enemies, that wee surely trustyng in thy defence, maye not feare the power of any aduersaries: through the myght of Jesu Christ our lorde.   Amen.

The thyrde Collecte : for grace.

O LORDE oure heauenly father, almightye and euerliuyng God, whiche haste safelye brought us to the beginning of this day: defend us in the same with thy mighty power; and graunt that this daye wee fall into no synne, neyther runne into any kinde of daunger, but that al our doinges may be ordered by thy gouernaunce, to do alwaies that is righteous in thy sight: through Jesus Christe our lorde. Amen.

AN ORDRE

The prieste shall saye.

OURE FATHER, &c.

Then likewise he shall saye.

O God, make spede to saue me.

Answere. O Lorde, make haste to helpe me.

Prieste. Glory be to the father, and to the sonne: and to the holy ghost. As it was in the beginning, is now; and euer shall be: worlde without ende. Amen.

Prayse ye the lorde.

And from Easter to Trinitie Sonday.

Alleluya.

As before is appointed at Matins.

Then Psalmes in ordre as they bee appointed in the Table for Psalmes, except there be proper psalmes appointed for that daye. Then a lesson of the olde testamente, as it is appointed likewise in the Kalender, except there be proper Lessons appointed for that daye. After that, (Magnificat anima mea dominum) in Englishe, as foloweth.

Magnificat. Luc. i.

My soule doth magnifie the lorde.

And my spirite hath reioyced in God my sauioure.

For he hathe regarded the lowelinesse of hys handemaiden.

For beholde, from henceforth all generacions shal cal me blessed.

For he that is mightye hath magnified me : and holy is his name.

And his mercie is on thē that feare him throughoute all generacions.

He hath shewed strength with his arme, he hath scatered the proude in the imaginacion of their hartes.

He hath put down the mightie from their seate : and hath exalted the humble and meeke.

28

He hathe filled the hungrye with good thynges : and the riche he hath sente awaye emptye.

He remembring his mercie, hath holpen his seruaunt Israel : as he promised to oure fathers, Abraham and his seede, for euer.

Glory be to the father and to the sonne and to the holy gost.

As it was in the beginning, and is now and euer shall be, worlde without ende. Amen.

Then a lesson of the newe testamente. And after that (Nunc dimittis seruum tuum) *in Englishe as foloweth.*

Nunc Dimittis. Luc. ii.

LORDE, nowe lettest thou thy seruaunte departe in peace : accordyng to thy woorde.

For myne iyes haue sene thy saluacion.

Whiche thou haste prepared, before the face of all thy people;

To be a lyght for to lighten the Gentiles : and to bee the glorye of thy people of Israel.

Glorye be to the father, &c.

As it was in the beginnyng, &c.

Then the suffrages before assigned at Matins, the clerkes kneelyng likewise, with three Collectes. Fyrst of the daye : Seconde of peace : Thirde for ayde agaynste all perilles, as here foloweth. Whiche ii. laste collectes shall bee daylye saide at Euensong without alteracion.

The seconde Collecte at Euensong.

O GOD, from whom all holy desyres, all good counsayles, and all iuste workes do procede: Geue unto thy seruauntes that peace, which the world cannot geue; that both our hartes maye be sette to obey thy commaundementes, and also that by thee we being defended from the feare of oure enemies, may passe oure time in rest and quietnesse; throughe the merites of Jesu Christe our sauiour. Amen.

The thirde Collect for ayde agaynste all perils.

LYGHTEN our darkenes, we beseche thee, O lord, and by thy great mercy defende us from all perilles and daungers of thys nyght, for the loue of thy onely sonne, our sauiour Jesu Christ. Amen.

¶ *In the feastes of* Christmas, Thepiphanie, Easter, Thascencion, Pentecost, *and upon* Trinitie Sonday, *shalbe song or sayd immediatly after* Benedictus *this confession of our christian fayth.*

Quicunque vult, &c.

WHOSOEUER will be saued : before all thinges it is necessarye that he holde the Catholyke fayth.

Whiche fayth except euery one dooe kepe holy and undefyled : without doubt he shal perishe euerlastingly.

And the Catholike faith is this : that we wurship one God in Trinitie, and Trinitie in unitie.

Neyther confounding the persones : nor deuidyng the substaunce.

For there is one persone of the father, another of the sonne : and an other of the holy gost.

But the godhead of the father, of the sonne, and of the holy Goste, is all one : the glorye equall, the maiestie coeternall.

Such as the father is, suche is the sonne, and suche is the holy gost.

The father uncreate, the sonne uncreate : and the holy gost uncreate.

The father incomprehensible, the sonne incomprehensible : and the holy gost incomprehensible.

The father eternall, the sonne eternall : and the holy gost eternall.

And yet they are not three eternalles : but one eternall.

As also there be not three incomprehensibles, nor three un-created : but one uncreated, and one incomprehensible.

So lykewyse the father is almyghtie, the sonne almightie : and the holy gost almightie.

And yet are they not three almyghtyes : but one almightie.

So the father is God, the sonne God : and the holye gost God.

And yet are they not three Goddes : but one God.

So lykewise the father is Lord, the sonne Lord : and the holy gost Lorde.

And yet not three Lordes : but one Lorde.

For like as we be compelled by the christian veritie : to acknowlege euery persone by hymselfe to be god and lord:

So are we forbidden by the Catholike religion : to say there be three goddes, or three lordes.

The father is made of none : neyther created nor begotten.

The sonne is of the father alone : not made nor created, but begotten.

The holy gost is of the father and of the sonne : neyther made nor created, nor begotten, but proceding.

So there is one father, not three fathers; one sonne, not three sonnes : one holy gost, not three holy gostes.

And in thys trinitie none is afore nor after other : none is greater nor lesse then other.

But the whole three persones : be coeternall together and coequall.

So that in all thinges, as it is aforesayd : the unitie in trinitie, and the trinitie in unitie is to be wurshipped.

He therefore that will bee saued : must thus thinke of the trinitie.

Furthermore, it is necessary to euerlasting saluacion : that he also beleue ryghtly in the incarnacion of oure Lorde Jesu Christe.

For the ryght fayth is that we beleue and confesse : that our Lorde Jesus Christe the sonne of God, is God and man;

God of the substaunce of the father, begotten before the worldes : and man of the substaunce of his mother, borne in the worlde.

Perfecte God, and perfecte man : of a resonable soule, and humayne fleshe subsisting.

Equall to the father as touchyng his Godhead : and inferior to the father touchyng his manhoode.

Who although he be God and man : yet he is not two, but one Christe.

One, not by conuersion of the Godhead into flesh : but by takyng of the manhoode into God;

One altogether, not by confusion of substaunce : but by unitie of person.

For as the reasonable soule and fleshe is one man : So God and man is one Christe.

Who suffered for oure saluacion : descended into hell, rose agayne the third daye from the dead.

He ascended into heauen, he sytteth on the right hand of the father, God almighty : from whence he shall come to iudge the quicke and dead.

At whose commyng all men shall ryse agayne with theyr bodyes : and shall geue accompt of theyr owne workes.

And they that haue done good, shall goe into life euerlastyng : and they that haue done euyll, into euerlastyng fyre.

This is the Catholyke fayth : whiche excepte a man beleue faythfully, he cannot be saued.

Glory be to the father, and to the sonne, &c.

As it was in the begynnyng, &c.

Thus endeth the ordre of Matyns and Euensong, through the whole yere.

THE INTROITES,

COLLECTES, EPISTLES, AND GOSPELS, TO BE USED AT THE CELEBRACION OF THE LORDES SUPPER AND HOLYE COMMUNION THROUGHE THE YEARE: WITH PROPER PSALMES, AND LESSONS FOR DIUERS FEASTES AND DAYES.

¶ *The fyrst Sonday in Aduente.*

Beatus vir. Psalm i.

BLESSED is that manne that hath not walked in the counsayle of the ungodly, nor stand in the waye of synners : and hath not sate in the seate of the skornefull;

But his delight is in the law of the LORD : and in his law will he exercyse himself day and night.

And he shalbe like a tree planted by the watersyde : that will bring foorth his fruite in due season.

His leafe also shal not wither : and looke whatsoeuer he doth, it shall prospere.

As for the ungodly, it is not so with them : but they are like the chaffe whiche the wynde skatereth awaye (from the face of the yearth).

Therefore the ungodly shall not be hable to stand in the iudgement : neyther the synners in the congregacion of the righteous.

But the LORDE knoweth the waye of the righteous : and the waye of the ungodlye shal perishe.

Glory be to the father, and to the sonne : and to the holye ghoste.

As it was in the begynnyng, is nowe, and euer shalbe : worlde without ende. Amen.

And so must euery Introite be ended.

Let us pray.

The Collect.

ALMYGHTYE God, geue us grace, that we may cast awaye the workes of darknes, and put upon us the armour of light, now in the tyme of this mortall lyfe, (in the whiche thy sonne Jesus

32

Christe came to visite us in great humilitie;) that in the last daye whē he shal come again in his glorious maiestye to iudge bothe the quicke and the dead, we maye ryse to the lyfe immortal, through him who liueth and reigneth with thee and the holy ghoste now and euer. Amen.

The Epistle. Rom. xiii.

OWE nothing to any man but this, that ye loue one another. For he that loueth another, fulfilleth the law. For these commaundemētes, Thou shalt not commit adultry: Thou shalt not kyll: Thou shalte not steale: Thou shalte beare no false witnes: Thou shalt not luste: and so forth (if there be any other cōmaundemēte) it is al comprehended in this saiyng, namely, Loue thy neighbor as thyself. Loue hurteth not his neyghbor; therfore is loue the fulfillyng of the law. This also, we know the season, how that it is tyme that we should now awake out of slepe: for nowe is our saluacion nerer, then when we beleued. The nyght is passed, the day is come nye; let us therfore caste awaie the dedes of darkenes, and let us put on the armour of lyght. Let us walke honestlye, as it were in the day lyght; not in eating and drinking, neither in chambouryng and wantonnes, neither in stryfe nor enuiyng: but put ye on the lord Jesus Christe. And make not prouision for the fleshe, to fulfill the lustes of it.

The Gospell. Matt. xxi.

AND when they drew nigh to Jerusalem, and were com to Bethphage, unto Moūt Oliuet, then sente Jesus two disciples, saying unto them: Goe into the towne that lyeth ouer agaynst you, and anone ye shall fynde an Asse bound, and a Colte with her: looce them and bryng them unto me. And if any man say ought unto you, say ye, the lord hath neede of them; and straightway he wil let them goe. All this was done that it myghte bee fulfilled, whiche was spoken by the Prophete, saying: Tell ye the daughter of Sion, behold, thy kyng cummeth unto thee, meke, sitting upō an Asse, and a colt, the fole of the Asse used to the yoke. The disciples went and did as Jesus commaūded them; and brought the Asse, and the Colte, and put on them theyr clothes, and set him theron. And many of the people spred theyr garmentes in the waye. Other cut downe braunches from the trees, and strawed them in the way. Moreouer the people that wente beefore, and they that came after, cryed saying; *Hosanna* to the sonne of Dauid; Blessed is he that cummeth in the name of the lorde, *Hosanna* in the higheste.   And when he was come to Jerusalem all the citie was moued, saying: who is this?   And the people sayde, this is Jesus the Prophete of Nazareth a citie of Galile.   And Jesus went into the temple of god, and cast out al them that solde and boughte in the temple, and ouerthrew the tables of money-chaungers, and the seates of them that solde doues, and said unto them, It is written; My house shall be called the house of prayer, but ye haue made it a denne of theues.

The second sunday.

Ad Dominum cum tribularer.   Psalm cxx.

WHEN I was in trouble I called upon the Lorde : and he heard me.

Delyuer my soule (o Lorde) from lyinge lippes, and from a deceiptfull tongue.

What reward shal be geuen unto thee, thou false tong? euer mightie and sharpe arrowes, with hote burnyng coles.

Woe is me, that I am constrained to dwel with Mesech : and to haue mine habitacion amōg the tentes of Cedar.

My soule hath long dwelt among them : that be enemies unto peace.

I labour for peace, but when I speake unto them thereof : they make them to battayl.

Glory be to the father, &c.

As it was in the begynnyng, &c.

The Collect.

BLESSED lord, which hast caused all holy Scriptures to bee written for our learnyng; graunte us that we maye in suche wise heare them, read, marke, learne, and inwardly digeste them ; that by pacience, and coumfort of thy holy woorde, we may embrace, and euer holde fast the blessed hope of euerlasting life, which thou hast geuen us in our sauiour Jesus Christe.

The Epistle.   Rom. xv.

WHATSOEUER thinges are writtē aforetime, they are written for our learning, that we through pacience, and comfort of the scriptures, might haue hope.   The God of pacience and consolation graunt you to be like-minded one toward another, after the ensaumple of Christ Jesu: that ye all agreeyng together, may with one mouth prayse God the father of our lorde Jesus Christ :

wherfore receiue ye one another as Christ receiued us, to the prayse of God. And thys I say, that Jesus Christe is a minister of the circumcision for the trueth of God, to confirme the promises made unto the fathers, and that the Gentiles might praise God for his mercie, as it is written. For this cause I will praise thee among the Gentiles, and sing unto thy name. And agayne he sayeth: reioyce ye Gentiles with hys people. And againe; praise the Lorde, all ye Gentyles, and laude hym all ye nacyons together. And againe Esai sayeth: there shall be the rote of Jesse, and he that shall ryse to reigne over the Gentiles: in him shal the Gentiles trust. The God of hope fyll you with all ioy and peace in beleuyng, that ye may be riche in hope, through the power of the holy gost.

The Gospell. Luke xxi.

THERE shalbe signes in the Sunne, and in the Moone, and in the starres; and in the earth the people shalbe at their wittes ende, through despayre. The sea and the water shall roare, and mens heartes shall fayle them for feare, and for loking after those thinges which shall come on the earth. For the powers of heauen shall moue. And then shall they see the sonne of man come in a cloude, with power and great glorye. When these thynges begynne to come to passe, then loke up, and lyft up your heades, for your redempcion draweth nye. And he shewed them a similytude: beholde the fygge-tree, and all other trees, when they shote furth their buddes, ye see and knowe of your owne selues that sommer is then nye at hãde. So lykewyse ye also (whẽ ye see these thinges come to passe) be sure that the kyngdome of God is nye. Verely I saye unto you: this generacion shall not passe, tyll all be fulfylled: Heauen and earth shall passe: but my worde shall not passe.

¶ *The thirde sonday.*

Cum invocarem. Psalm iv.

HEARE me when I call, o God of my ryghteousnes : thou hast set me at libertie when I was in trouble; haue mercy upon me, and herken unto my prayer.

O ye sonnes of menne, howe long will ye blaspheme myne honor? and haue such pleasure in vanitie, and seke after leasing?

Know this also, that the Lord hath chosen to himselfe the manne that is godly : when I call upon the Lord, he will heare me.

Stande in awe, and synne not : common with your owne hearte, and in youre chambre, and be still.

Offer the sacrifice of righteousnes : and put your trust in the Lorde.

There be many that will saye : who wyll shewe us any good?

Lorde lift thou up : the light of thy countenaunce upon us.

Thou hast put gladnes in mine heart : sence the tyme that their corne and wyne, (and oyle) increased.

I will lay me downe in peace, and take my rest : for it is thou, Lorde, onely, that makest me to dwell in safetie.

Glory be to the Father, and to the Son, &c.

As it was in the beginning, is now, and euer &c.

The Collect.

LORD, we beseche thee, geue eare to our prayers, and by thy gracious visitacion lighten the darkenes of our hearte, by our Lorde Jesus Christe.

The Epistle.   1 Cor. iv.

LET a man this wise esteme us, euen as the ministers of Christ, and stewardes of the secretes of God.   Furthermore, it is required of the stewardes, that a man be founde faithfull: with me it is but a very small thing that I should be iudged of you, eyther of mannes iudgement: no I judge not mine owne selfe, for I know nought by myselfe, yet am I not therby iustified.   It is the Lorde that iudgeth me.   Therfore iudge nothing before the tyme, untyll the Lorde come, whiche wyll lighten thynges that are hydde in darkenesse, and open the counsayles of the heartes, and then shall euery manne haue prayse of God.

The Gospel.   Matt. xi.

WHEN John beeyng in pryson hearde the workes of Christe, he sente two of his disciples, and sayed unto hym; Art thou he that shall come? or doe we looke for another?   Jesus aunswered and sayd unto thē: Goe and shewe John agayne what ye haue hearde and seen: The blynde receiue their sight, the lame walke, the Lepers are clensed, and the deafe heare, the dead aryse up, and the poore receyue the gladde tydinges of the gospel, and happy is he that is not offended by me.   And as they departed, Jesus began to say unto the people cōcernyng John; What went ye out into the wildernes to see?   A rede that is shaken with the wynde?   Or what wēt ye out for to see?   A man clothed in soft rayment? behold, they that weare soft clothing, are in kinges houses. But what went ye out for to see? A prophete? verely I **saye** unto you, and more then a Prophete. For this is he of whom it is wrytten, beholde, I sende my messenger before thy face, whiche shall prepare thy waye before thee.

¶ *The fourth sonday.*

Verba mea auribus.   Psalm v.

PONDER my woordes, O Lorde : considre my meditacion.

O herken thou unto the voyce of my calling, my kyng, and my God : for unto thee wyll I make my prayer.

My voyce shalt thou heare betymes, o Lorde : early in the morning will I directe my prayer unto thee, and will looke up.

For thou art the God that hath no pleasure in wickednes : neither shall anye euill dwell with the.

Suche as be foolishe shalle not stande in thy sight : for thou hatest all them that worke vanitie.

Thou shalt destroy thē that speake leasing : the Lord will abhorre both the bloud-thirstie and deceiptfull man.

But as for me, I will come into thy house, euen upon the multitude of thy mercy : and in thy feare I wyl wurship towarde thy holy temple.

Leade me (o Lorde) in thy righteousnes, because of myne enemyes : make thy waye playne before my face.

For there is no faythfulnes in his mouthe : their inwarde partes are very wickednes.

Their throte is an open sepulchre : they flatter with their tongue.

Destroy thou them, O God; let them peryshe through their owne imaginacions : cast thē out in the multitude of their ungodlines; for they haue rebelled agaynst thee.

And let all them that put their trust in thee reioyce : they shall euer be geuyng of thankes, because thou defendest them; they that loue thy name shalbe ioyfull in thee.

For thou, Lord, wilt geue thy blessyng unto the righteous : and with thy fauorable kyndnes wylt thou defende him as his shelde.

Glory be to the father, and to the sonne, &c.

As it was in the begynnyng, is now, and euer &c.

The Collect.

LORDE rayse up (we pray the) thy power, and come among us, and with great might succour us; that whereas, through our

synnes and wickednes, we be soore lette and hindred, thy
bountifull grace and mercye, through the satisfaccion of thy
sonne our Lord, may spedily deliuer us; to whom with thee and
the holy gost be honor and glory, worlde without ende.

The Epistle. Philipp. iv.

REIOYCE in the Lord alway, and againe I saye, reioyce. Let
your softnes be knowen unto all men: the Lord is euen at hand.
Be careful for nothing: but in all praier and supplicacion, let
your peticions be manifest unto God, with geuyng of thankes.
And the peace of God (whiche passeth all understandyng) kepe
your heartes and myndes through Christe Jesu.

The Gospell. John i.

THIS is recorde of John, whē the Jewes sent priestes and
Leuites frō Jerusalem to aske him; what art thou? and he confessed, and denied not, and sayd playnly: I am not Christ.
And they asked him, what then? art thou Helyas? and he
sayeth: I am not. Art thou that Prophete? and he aunswered,
no. Then sayed they unto him; what art thou? that we may
geue an aūswer unto thē that sēt us? what sayest thou of thyselfe? he said: I am the voyce of a cryer in the wildernes, make
straight the way of the lorde, as said the prophete Esai. And
they whiche were sente were of the Phariseis, and they asked
hym, and sayde unto hym, why baptisest thou then, if thou be
not Christe, nor Helyas, neither that prophet? John aunswered
them, saying: I baptise with water: but there standeth one
among you, whome ye know not: he it is which though he came
after me, was before me, whose shooe-latchet, I am not woorthie
to unlooce. These thinges were doen at Bethabara beyond
Jordane, where John did baptise.

Proper Psalmes and lessons on Christmas day.

¶ At Mattins.

Psalms xix. xlv. lxxxv.

The First Lesson, Isa. ix. Unto the ende.

The Second Less, Matt. i. Unto the ende.

¶ At the First Communion.

Cantate Domino. Psalm xcviii.

O SING unto the Lorde a newe song : for he hath done maruaylous thinges.

With his owne right hande, and with his holy arme : hath he gotten himselfe the victorye.

The Lorde declared his saluacion : his righteousnes hath he openly shewed in the sight of the heathen.

He hath remembred his mercie and trueth toward the house of Israell : and all the endes the worlde haue seene the saluacion of our God.

Shewe youreselfes ioyfull unto the Lorde all ye landes : sing, reioyce, and geue thankes.

Prayse the Lorde upon the Harpe : syng to the Harpe with a Psalme of thankesgeuinge.

With trumpettes also and shawmes : O shewe youreselues ioyfull before the Lorde the kinge.

Let the sea make a noyse, and all that therein is : the round worlde, and they that dwell therein.

Let the fluddes clap theyr handes, and let the hilles bee ioyfull together before the Lorde : for he is come to iudge the yearth.

With righteousnes shall he iudge the worlde : and the people with equitie.

Glory be to the father, and to the sonne &c.

As it was in the begynnyng, is nowe, and euer &c.

The Collect.

GOD, whiche makest us glad with the yerely remembraunce of the birth of thy onely sonne Jesus Christ ; graunt that as we ioyfully receiue him for our redemer, so we may with sure confidence beholde hym, when he shall come to be our iudge, who liueth and reigneth &c.

The Epistle. Tit. ii.

THE grace of god that bringeth saluacion unto all men, hath appeared, and teacheth us that we should denye ungodlines and worldly lustes, and that we shoulde liue soberlye, and ryghteously, and godlye in this present world, looking for that blessed hope, and appering of the glory of the great god and of our sauiour Jesu Christ, which gaue himselfe for us, to redeme us from all unrighteousnes, and to purge us a peculiar people unto himselfe, feruently geuen unto good woorkes. These thynges speake, and exhorte, and rebuke with all feruentnes of commaundyng. See that no man despise thee.

The Gospel. Luke ii.

AND it chaunsed in those dayes, that there wente out a commaundemente from Augustus the Emperour, that all the worlde shoulde be taxed. And this taxing was the firste, and executed when Syrenius was lieutenaunt in Siria. And euery man wente unto hys owne citie to bee taxed. And Joseph also ascended frō Galile, out of a citie called Nazareth into Jury, unto the citie of Dauid, which is called Bethleem; because he was of the house and linage of Dauid, to be taxed wyth Mari his spoused wyfe, which was with childe. And it fortuned that while they were there, her tyme was come that she shoulde be deliuered. And she brought furth her first begotten sonne, and wrapped hym in swadlyng clothes and layde hym in a Maungier, because there was no roume for them in the Inne. And there were in the same region shepeherdes watchyng and kepyng theyr flocke by ngyht. And loe, the Angel of the Lorde stoode harde by them, and the bryghtenesse of the Lorde shone rounde about them, and they were sore affrayd. And the angel said unto them, Be not affraid, for behold, I bring you tidinges of great ioy, that shal come to al people: for unto you is borne this daie in the citie of Dauid a sauiour, which is Christ the lorde. And take this for a signe: ye shall fynde the childe wrapped in swadlyng clothes, and layde in a maungier. And strayghtwaye there was with the angel a multitude of heauenly souldiers, praisyng God, and saying: Glory to God on hye, and peace on the yearth, and unto men a good wyll.

¶ *At the Seconde Communion.*

Domine, Domenus noster. Ps. viii.

O LORDE oure gouernour, how excellente is thy name in al the worlde : thou that hast sette thy glorye aboue the heauens ?

Out of the mouth of very babes and sucklynges haste thou ordeined strength, because of thyne enemies : that thou mighteste styll the enemye and the auenger.

For I wyll consider thy heauens, euen the woorkes of thy fyngers : the Moone and the starres which thou hast ordeyned.

What is man, that thou art so mindefull of hym : and the sonne of man, that thou visitest him ?

Thou madest him lower then the angels : to croune him wyth glory and woorship.

Thou makeste hym to haue dominion of the workes of thy handes : and thou haste put all thynges in subieccion under his feete.

All shepe and oxen : yea and the beastes of the field.

The foules of the ayre and the fyshes of the sea : and what-soeuer walketh thorowe the pathes of the seas.

Lorde our gouernoure : how excellent is thy name in all the world.

Glory be to the father, and to the sonne &c.

As it was in the begynnyng, is now, and euer &c.

The Collect.

ALMYGHTYE God, whiche haste geuen us thy onlye begotten sonne to take our nature upon hym, and this daye to bee borne of a pure Vyrgyn; Graunte that we beyng regenerate, and made thy children by adoption and grace, maye dailye be renued by thy holy spirite, through the same our Lorde Jesus Christe who lyueth and reygneth &c.

The Epistle.   Heb. i.

GOD in tymes paste dyuerselye and manye waies spake unto the fathers by Prophetes: but in these laste dayes, he hathe spoken to us by his owne sonne, whome he hath made heyre of all thynges, by whome also he made the worlde. Whiche (sonne) beeing the brightenesse of his glorye, and the very image of his substaunce, rulying al thynges wyth the woorde of his power, hath by his owne person pourged our synnes, and sytteth on the righte hande of the Maiestye on hygh: being so much more excellēt then the Angels, as he hath by inheritaunce obtained a more excellent name then they. For unto which of the Angels said he at anye tyme? Thou arte my sonne, this daye haue I begotten thee. And agayne, I wilbe his father, and he shall bee my sonne. And agayne, when he bringeth in the first-begotten sonne into the worlde, he sayth: and let all the Angels of God wurship him. And unto the Angels he sayeth, He maketh his Angels spirites, and his ministers a flame of fyer. But unto the sonne he sayeth, thy seate (O God) shalbe for euer and euer. The scepter of thy kingdome is a ryghte scepter. Thou haste loued righteousnes and hated iniquitie; wherfore God, euen thy God, hath anointed thee with oyle of gladnes aboue thy felowes. And thou lorde in the beginning hast layde the foundacion of the yearth; and the heauens are the woorkes of thy handes. They shall perish, but thou endurest. But they al shal waxe old as doeth a garment, and as a vesture shalt thou chaunge them, and they shalbe chaunged. But thou art euen the same, and thy yeares shall not fayle.

The Gospel.   John i.

In the begynnyng was the woorde, and the woorde was with God: and God was the worde.   The same was in the beginning with God.   All thinges were made by it, and without it, was made nothyng that was made.   In it was life, and the lyfe was the light of men, and the light shineth in darkenes, and the darkenes cōprehended it not.   There was sente from God a manne, whose name was John.   The same came as a witnes to beare witnes of the light, that al mē through him might beleue. He was not that light, but was sent to beare witnes of the light. That light was the true lyghte, whiche lighteth euerye man that cometh into the worlde.   He was in the world, and the worlde was made by him; and the worlde knew him not.   He came among his owne, and his owne receiued him not: But as many as receiued him, to thē gaue he power to be the sonnes of god; euen thē that beleued on his name, whiche were borne, not of bloud, nor of the will of the fleshe, nor yet of the will of man; but of God.   And the same worde became fleshe, and dwelt among us; and we sawe the glory of it, as the glory of the onely-begotten sonne of the father, full of grace and trueth.

¶ *Proper Psalmes and lessons at Euensong.*

Psal. lxxxix. cx. cxxxii.

The First Lesson, Esa. vii. " God spake once agayne to Achas," &c. unto the ende.
The Seconde Lesson, Tit. iii. " The kyndnes and loue of our sauiour," &c. unto " Foolishe questions."

¶ *St. Stephin's Day.*

¶ *At Matins.*

The Seconde Lesson, Acts vi. vii. " Stephin full of fayth and power," (unto) " And when xl yeres."

At the Communion.
Quid gloriaris in malicia ?   Ps. lii.

WHY boastest thou thyself, thou tyraunt : that thou canst do mischiefe.
Whereas the goodnes of God : endureth yet dayly.
Thy tong imagineth wickednes : and with lyes thou cuttest lyke a sharp rasor.

Thou hast loued ungraciousnes more thã goodnes : and to talke of lyes more then righteousnes.

Thou hast loued to speake all woordes that may doe hurt : O thou false tongue.

Therfore shal God destroy thee for euer : he shall take thee, and plucke thee out of thy dwellyng, and roote thee out of the lande of the liuing.

The righteous also shall see this, and feare, and shall laugh him to skorne.

Loe, this is the man that toke not God for his strength : but trusted unto the multitude of his riches, and strengthed himselfe in his wickednes.

As for me, I am lyke a grene Oliue-tree in the house of God : my truste is in the tendre mercye of God for euer and euer.

I wyl alwaye geue thankes unto thee for that thou hast done : and I wyll hope in thy Name, for thy sainctes lyke it well.

Glory be to the father, and to the sonne &c.

As it was in the begynnyng, is nowe and euer &c.

The Collect.

GRAUNTE us, O Lorde, to learne to loue oure enemies, by the example of thy marter saincte Stephin, who prayed to thee for hys persecutors; whiche liuest and reignest, &c.

¶ Then shall folowe a Collect of the Natiuitie.

The Epistle. Acts vii.

AND Stephin, beyng ful of the holy goste, loked up stedfastly with his iyes into heauen, and sawe the glorye of God, and Jesus standyng on the ryght hande of God, and said: behold, I se the heauens open, and the sonne of man standyng on the ryght hande of God.   Then they gaue a shoute with a loude voice, and stopped their eares, and ran upon him al at once, and caste him out of the citie, and stoned him.   And the witnesses laide down their clothes at a young mannes fete, whose name was Saul. And thei stoned Stephin, calling on and saiyng; Lorde Jesus, receyue my spirite.   And he kneeled down, and cried with a loud voice, Lord, lay not this sinne to theyr charge.   And when he had thus spoken, he fell aslepe.

The Gospell. Matt. xxiii.

BEHOLD, I send unto you prophetes, and wise mē, and Scribes, and some of them ye shall kyll and crucifye; and some of them shall ye scourge in youre Sinagoges, and persecute them from citie to citie: that upon you maye come all the righteous bloude whiche hath bene shed upon the yearth, from the bloude of righteous Abel unto the bloud of Zacharias the sŏne of Barachias, whome ye slewe betwene the temple and the altare. Verelye I saye unto you, All these thynges shall come upon this generacion. O Jerusalem, Jerusalem, thou that killeste the prophetes and stonest them whiche are sent unto thee; how often would I haue gathered thy children together, euen as the henne gathereth her chickens under her wynges, and ye would not? Behold, your house is left unto you desolate. For I say unto you, Ye shall not se me henceforth, tyll that ye say: Blessed is he that commeth in the name of the Lord.

The Seconde lesson at Euensong.

Acts vii. ¶ "And when forty years were expired, there appeared unto Moses," unto "Stephin full of the holy ghost," &c.

¶ Sayncte John Euangelistes Daye.

At Matins.

¶ The Seconde Lesson, Apoc. i. unto the ende.

At the Communion.

In Domino confido. Psalm xi.

In the Lord put I my trust : how say ye thĕ to my soule, that she shoulde flye as a bird to the hyll?

For loe, the ungodly bend their bow, and make ready theyr arowes in the quiuer : that they maye prieuelye shote at them whiche are trew of hearte.

For the foundacions wil be cast downe : and what hath the righteous done?

The Lorde is in his holy temple : the Lordes seate is in heauen.

His iyes consider the poore : and his iyelyddes trieth the chyldren of men.

The Lord aloweth the ryghteous : but the ungodly, and hym that delyteth in wickednesse, doeth his soule abhorre.

Upon the ungodly he shall rayne snares, fyre and brymstone, storme and tempest : this shalbe their porcion to drinke.

For the righteous Lorde loueth righteousnes : his countenaunce wyll beholde the thynge that is just.

Glory be to the father, and to the sonne &c.

As it was in the beginnyng, is now, and euer &c.

The Collect.

MERCYFULL Lorde, we beseche thee to caste thy brygh†
beames of lyght upon thy Churche: that it beeyng lyghtened by
the doctryne of thy blessed Apostle and Euangelyste John may
attayne to thy euerlastyng gyftes; Through Jesus Christe our
Lorde.

The Epistle. 1 John i.

THAT whiche was from the begynnyng, whiche we haue
hearde, whiche we haue seen wyth our iyes, whiche we haue
looked upon, and oure handes haue handeled of the woorde of
lyfe. And the lyfe appeared, and we haue seen and beare
witnes, and shewe unto you that eternall lyfe, whiche was with
the father, and appered unto us. That whiche we haue seen
and heard, declare we unto you, that ye also may haue felowshyp
with us, and that oure felowshyp may be with the father and his
sonne Jesus Christe. And this wryte we unto you, that ye maye
reioyce, and that youre ioy maye bee full. And this is the
tydynges whiche we haue heard of him, and declare unto you,
that God is lyght, and in him is no darkenesse at all. If we saye
that we haue felowshyppe with hym, and walke in darkenes, we
lye, and do not saye the trueth. But and yf we walke in lyght,
euen as he is in light, then haue we felowshyp with him, and the
bloud of Jesus Christe hys sonne clenseth us from all synne. If
we saye we haue no synne, we deceyue ourselues, and the trueth
is not in us. If we knowlege our synnes, he is faythfull and iust
to forgeue us our synnes, and to clense us from all unrighteousnes.
If we saye we haue not synned, we make him a lyer, and his
woorde is not in us.

The Gospell. John xxi.

JESUS sayed unto Peter, folowe thou me. Peter turned about,
and sawe the disciple whome Jesus loued folowyng (whiche also
leaned on his breast at Supper, and sayed: Lorde, whiche is he
that betraieth the) when Peter therfore sawe hym, he sayed to
Jesus: Lord what shall he here do? Jesus sayed unto him; yf
I wyll haue him to tarye tyll I come, what is that to the?
Folowe thou me. Then went this saying abroade amonge the
brethren, that that disciple should not dye. Yet Jesus sayde not
to hym, he shall not dye; but if I wyll that he tarye tyll I come,
what is that to thee. The same disciple is he whiche testifyeth
of these thynges, and wrote these thinges, and we know that his
testimony is true. There are also many other thynges whiche

Jesus dyd, the whiche yf they should be wrytten euery one, I suppose the worlde coulde not conteyne the bookes that should be wrytten.

¶ *At Euensong.*

¶ The Seconde Lesson, Apoc. xxii. unto the ende.

¶ *The Innocentes Daye.*

¶ *At Mattyns.*

¶ The fyrste Lesson, Hiere. xxxi. unto, " Moreouer I heard Effraim."

Deus, venerunt gentes. Psalm lxxix.

O GOD, the Heathen are come into thyne inheritaunce : thy holy temple haue they defyled, and made Jerusalem an heape of stones.

The dead bodyes of thy seruauntes haue they geuen to bee meate unto the foules of the ayre; and the flesh of thy sainctes unto the beastes of the lande.

Theyr bloud haue they shed lyke water on euery syde of Jerusalem : and there was no man to bury them.

We are become an open shame to oure enemyes : a very skorne and derysyon unto them that are rounde aboute us.

Lorde, how longe wylt thou be angry? shall thy gelousye burne lyke fyre for euer?

Powre out thyne indignacion upon the Heathen that haue not knowen thee : and upon the kyngdomes that haue not called upon thy name.

For they haue deuoured Jacob : and layed waste hys dwellyng-place.

O remembre not oure olde synnes, but haue mercy upon us, and that soone : for we are come to greate myserye.

Helpe us, O God of oure saluacion, for the glory of thy Name : O delyuer us, and be mercyfull unto oure synnes, for thy names sake.

Wherfore shall the heathen saye : where is nowe theyr God?

O let the vengeaunce of thy seruauntes bloud that is shed : be openly shewed upon the heathen in oure syght.

O let the sorowfull syghyng of the prisoners come before the : acordinge unto the greatnesse of thy power, preserue thou those that are appoynted to dye.

And as for the blasphemye (wherewith oure neyghbours haue

blasphemed thee) : rewarde thou them, O Lorde, seuen-folde
into their bosome.

So we, that be thy people, and shepe of thy pasture, shall geue
thee thankes for euer : and will alwaye be shewing forth thy
prayse from generacion to generacion.

Glory be to the father, and to the sonne &c.

As it was in the begynning, is now, and euer &c.

The Collect.

ALMIGHTY God, whose prayse this daye the yong innocentes
thy witnesses hath confessed and shewed forth, not in speakyng
but in dying; Mortifye and kyll all vyces in us, that in oure con
uersacion oure lyfe maye expresse thy fayth, whiche with oure
tongues we doe confesse; through Jesus Christe oure Lord.

The Epistle.   Apoc. xiv.

I LOOKED, and loe, a lambe stode on the mounte Sion, and
with hym an hundred and xliiii thousande, hauyng his name and
his fathers name writtē in their forheades.   And I heard a voice
frō heauen, as the sounde of many waters, and as the voice of a
great thundre.   And I heard the voice of harpers harping with
their harpes.   And thei song as it were a new song before the
seate, and before the iiii beastes, and the elders, and no man
coulde learne the song, but the cxliiii thousande, whiche were
redemed from the earth.   These are they whiche were not defyled wyth weomen, for they are virgins.   These folowe the
lambe whethersoeuer he goeth.   These were redemed from mē,
being the firste fruites unto God, and to the lambe, and in their
mouthes was found no guile; for they are without spot before
the throne of God.

The Gospel.   Matt. ii.

THE Angel of the lorde appeared to Joseph in a slepe, saying:
aryse, and take the childe, and his mother, and flye into Egipt,
and be thou there til I bring thee worde.   For it wil come to
passe, that Herode shall seke the childe to destroy him.   So
when he awoke, he tooke the chylde and his mother by night,
and departed into Egipte, and was there unto the death of
Herode: that it myghte be fulfilled whiche was spoken of the
lorde by the prophete, saying: out of Egipt haue I called my
sonne.   Then Herode, when he sawe that he was mocked of the
wise men, he was exceding wroth, and sent furthe men of warre
and slewe all the chyldren that were in Bethleem, and in all the

coastes, (as many as were ii yere olde and under,) according to the time whiche he had diligently knowen out of the wise men. Then was fulfilled that whiche was spoken by the prophete Jeremie, where as he sayde: In Rama was there a voyce hearde, lamentacyon, weepyng, and great mourning, Rachel weepyng for her chyldren, and woulde not be conforted, because they were not.

¶ *The Sunday after Christmas Day.*

Levavi oculos.   Psalm cxxi.

I WIL lift up mine iyes unto the hilles : from whence cummeth my helpe.

My helpe cummeth euen from the Lorde : whiche hath made heauen and yearth.

He will not suffre thy foote to be moued : and he that kepeth thee will not slepe.

Beholde, he that kepeth Israell shall neyther slombre nor slepe.

The Lorde hymselfe is thy keper : the Lorde is thy defence upon thy ryght hande.

So that the Sunne shal not burne the by daye : neyther the Moone by nyght.

The Lord shall preserue thee from all eiuill : yea, it is euen he that shall kepe thy soule.

The Lorde shall preserue thy going out, and thy cummynge in : from this tyme forth for euermore.

Glory be to the father, and to the sonne &c.

As it was in the begynnyng, is now, and euer &c.

The Collect.

ALMIGHTY God, which hast geuen us, &c. as upon Christmas-day.

The Epistle.   Gal. iv.

AND I saye, that the heyre (as long as he is a child) differeth not from a seruaunt, though he be lorde of all, but is under tutors and gouernours, until the time that the father hath appoynted. Euen so wee also, when wee were chyldren, were in bondage under the ordinaunces of the worlde: But when the tyme was full come, God sente hys sonne, made of a woman, and made bonde unto the lawe, to redeme them which were bonde unto the lawe: that wee throughe eleccion myghte receyue the inheritaunce that belongeth unto the naturall sonnes. Because ye are sonnes, God hathe sente the spyryte of hys sonne into our hartes, which crieth Abba father. Wherfore nowe, thou art not a seruaunt, but a sonne: If thou bee a sonne, thou arte also an heyre of God throughe Christe.

The Gospel. Matt. i.

THYS is the booke of the generacyon of Jesus Christe, the sonne of Dauid, the sonne of Abraham. Abraham begat Isaac; Isaac begat Jacob; Jacob begat Judas and his brethren; Judas begat Phares and Zaram of Thamar; Phares begat Esrom; Esrom begat Aram; Aram begat Aminadab; Aminadab begat Naasson; Naasson begat Salmon; Salmon begat Boos of Rahab; Boos begat Obed of Ruth; Obed begat Jesse; Jesse begat Dauid the kyng; Dauid the king begat Salomon of her that was the wife of Urye; Salomon begat Roboam; Roboam begat Abia; Abia begat Asa; Asa begat Josaphat; Josaphat begat Joram; Joram begat Osias; Osias begat Joathan; Joathan begat Achas; Achas begat Ezechias; Ezechias begat Manasses; Manasses begat Amon; Amon begat Josias; Josias begat Jeconias and his brethren, about the time that they were caried awaye to Babilon. And after they were brought to Babilon, Jeconias begat Salathiell; Salathiell begat Zorobabel; Zorobabel begat Abiud; Abiud begat Eliachim; Eliachim begat Azor; Azor begat Sadoc; Sadoc begat Achyn; Achyn begat Eliud; Eliud begat Eliazar; Eliazar begat Matthan; Matthan begat Jacob; Jacob begat Joseph the husbande of Marie, of whome was borne Jesus, euen he that is called Christe. And so all the generacions from Abraham to Dauid are xiiii generacyons. And from Dauid unto the captiuitie of Babilon are xiiii generacions. And from the captiuitie of Babilon unto Christ, are xiiii generacions.

The birth of Jesus Christ was on this wise: When his mother Mary was maried to Joseph, (beefore they came to dwell together) she was founde with childe by the holy goste. Then Joseph her husbande (because he was a righteous man, and would not put her to shame) was minded prieuily to departe from her. But while he thus thought, beholde, the Angell of the lord appeared unto hym in slepe, saying: Joseph, thou sonne of Dauid, feare not to take unto the Mary thy wife: for that which is conceiued in her, cummeth of the holy gost. She shall bring furth a sonne, and thou shalt call his name JESUS: for he shall saue his people from theyr sinnes.

All this was doone, that it mighte be fulfilled which was spoken of the lorde by the prophet, saying: Beholde a mayde shall bee with chylde, and shall bryng foorth a sonne, and they shall call his name Emanuell, whiche, if a manne interprete, is as muche to saye, as God with us.   And Joseph as soone as he awoke out of slepe did as the Angel of the lorde had bidden him: and he toke his wife unto him, and knew her not, til she had broughte furth her firste begotten sonne, and called his name JESUS.

¶ The Circumcision of Christ.

At Mattins.

The Firste Lesson, Gen. xvii. unto the ende.
The Seconde Lesson, Rom. ii. unto the ende.

At the Communion.

Lætatus sum.   Ps. cxxii.

I WAS glad when they sayde unto me : We wil goe into the house of the Lorde.

Our fete shall stande in thy gates : O Jerusalem.

Jerusalem is builded as a citie : that is at unitie in itselfe.

For thither the tribes goe up, euen the tribes of the Lorde : to testifie unto Israell to geue thankes unto the Name of the Lorde.

For there is the seate of iudgement : euē the seate of the house of Dauid.

O pray for the peace of Jerusalem : they shall prosper that loue thee.

Peace be within thy walles, and plenteousnes within thy palaces.

For my brethren and companions sakes : I wishe thee prosperitie.

Yea, because of the house of the Lorde oure God : I wil seke to doe thee good.

Glory be to the father, &c.

As it was in the beginning, &c.

The Collect.

ALMYGHTIE God, whiche madeste thy blessed sonne to be circumcised, and obedyente to the law for man; Graunt us the true circumcision of thy spirite, that our hertes, and al our membres, being mortifyed from al worldly and carnal lustes, may in al thinges obey thy blessed wil; through the same thy sonne Jesus Christ our Lorde.

The Epistle. Rom. iv.

BLESSED is that mā to whom the lord will not impute sinne. Came this blessednes then upon the uncircūcisiō, or upon the circūcisiō also? for we say that faith was rekoned to Abrahā for righteousnes. How was it then rekoned? when he was in the circūcision, or whē he was in the uncircūcisiō? not in the time of circumcision; but when he was yet uncircūcised. And he receiued the signe of circumcision, as a seale of the righteousnes of fayth, whiche he had yet being uncircūcised; that he should be the father of al thē that belieue, though they be not circumcised, that righteousnes might be imputed to them also: and that he mighte be the father of circumcisiō, not unto them only which came of the circumcised, but unto them also that walke in the steppes of the faythe that was in our father Abraham, before the time of circumcision. For the promise (that he shoulde be the heyre of the worlde) happened not to Abraham, or to his seede, through the law, but through the righteousnes of faith. For if they which are of the law be heyres, then is faith but vayne, and the promise of none effect.

The Gospel. Luc. ii.

AND it fortuned, as soone as the Angels were gone away from the shepeheardes into heauen, they sayd one to another; let us goe now euen unto Bethleem, and se this thing that we heare say is happened, whiche the lorde hath shewed unto us. And they came with haste and foūd Mary and Joseph, and the Babe laid in a maūger. And when they had sene it, they published abrode the saying which was tolde them of that childe. And al they that heard it wondered at those thinges, whiche were tolde thē of the shepeheardes. But Mary kept all those sayinges, and pondered them in her hert. And the shepeherdes returned praisyng and laudyng God, for al the thynges that they had hearde and seene, euen as it was tolde unto them. And when the eyght day was come that the childe should be circumcised, his name was called JESUS, which was named of the Angel before he was cōceiued in the wombe.

¶ *At Euensong.*

The First Lesson, Deut. x. " And now Israel," unto the ende. The Seconde Lesson, Colloss. ii. unto the ende.

¶ *The Epiphanie.*

At Mattins.

The Firste Lesson, Isa. lx. unto the ende.
The ii Lesson, Luke iii. " And it fortuned," unto the ende.

At the Communion.

Cantate Domino.   Psalm xcvi.

O SYNG unto the Lorde a newe song : sing unto the Lorde all the whole yearth.

Syng unto the Lorde, and prayse his name : be tellyng of his saluacion from daye to daye.

Declare his honour unto the heathen : and his wonders unto all people.

For the Lord is great, and cannot worthely be praised : he is more to bee feared than all Goddes.

As for all the Goddes of the heathen, they bee but ydolles; but it is the Lorde that made the heauens.

Glory and woorshyp are before hym : power and honoure are in his Sanctuarie.

Ascribe unto the Lord, (O ye kinredes of the people) ascribe unto the Lorde woorship and power.

Ascribe unto the Lord the honour due unto his Name : brynge presentes, and come into his courtes.

O worshyp the Lorde in the beautie of holynes : let the whole earth stande in awe of hym.

Tell it out amonge the heathen that the Lord is Kinge : and that it is he whiche hathe made the rounde worlde so fast that it cannot be moued; and howe that he shall iudge the people righteouslye.

Let the heauens reioyse, and let the yearth be glad : let the sea make a noyse, and all that therein is.

Let the felde be ioyful and al that is in it : then shal all the trees of the wood reioyce before the Lorde.

For he commeth, for he commeth to iudge the yearth : and with rightuousnes to iudge the world, and the people with his trueth.

Glory be to the Father, &c.

As it was in the beginning, &c.

The Collect.

O GOD, which by the leading of a starre diddest manifest thy onelye begotten sonne to the Gentiles; Mercifully graūt, that we, which know thee now by faith, may after this life haue the fruicion of thy glorious Godhead; through Christe our Lorde.

The Epistle. Ephes. iii.

For thys cause I Paule am a priesoner of Jesus Christe for you heathen; yf ye haue heard of the ministracion of the grace of God, which is geuē me to you-ward. For by reuelacyon shewed he the misterie unto me, as I wrote afore in a few woordes, wherby when ye reade, ye maye understande my knowledge in the misterye of Christe; which misterie in times passed was not opened unto the sonnes of men, as it is nowe declared unto his holy apostles and prophetes by the spirite: that the Gentiles should be inheritors also, and of the same bodye, and partakers of his promise in Christ, by the meanes of the Gospei, whereof I am made a minister, accordyng to the gifte of the grace of god which is geuē unto me after the workyng of his power. Unto me the leaste of all saintes is this grace geuen, that I shoulde preache amonge the Gentiles the unsearcheable riches of Christe, and to make all men see what the felowship of the misterie is, whiche from the beginnyng of the worlde, hath bene hyd in God whiche made al thinges through Jesus Christe: to thentente, that nowe unto the rulers and powers in heauenly thinges, might be knowē, by the congregaciō the manifolde wisedome of God accordyng to the eternall purpose which he wrought in Christ Jesu our lord: by whō wee haue boldenesse and entraunce with the confidence which is by the faith of him.

The Gospel. Matt. ii.

When Jesus was borne in Bethleē a city of Jury, in the tyme of Herode the kyng: Behold there came wise men from the East to Jerusalē, saiyng: where is he that is borne king of Jewes? For we haue sene his starre in the East, and are come to worship him. When Herode the kyng had heard these thynges, he was troubled, and all the citie of Jerusalem with him. And when he had gathered al the chief priestes and scribes of the people together, he demaunded of them, where Christe shoulde be borne. And they said unto him, At Bethleem in Jurie. For thus it is written by the prophete; And thou, Bethleē, in the land of Jury, art not the least among the princes of Juda: for oute of thee there shall come unto me the capitain that shal gouerne my people Israel. Then Herode (when he had prieuely called the wise men) he inquired of them diligentlye what time the starre appeared, and he bad them go to Bethleem, and said;

go your waie thither, and serche diligentelye for the childe. And when ye haue found him, bring me woord again, that I maie come and worship him also. Whē they had heard the king, they departed; and loe, the starre whiche thei sawe in the Easte, wente beefore them, tyll it came and stoode ouer the place where the child was. When thei saw the starre thei were exceadyng glad, and wente into the house, and founde the child with Marie his mother, and fel downe flat and woorshipped him, and opened their treasures and offred unto hym gyftes: Golde, Frankinsence, and Mirre. And after they were warned of God in slepe, (that they shoulde not go again to Herode,) they returned into their owne countrey another waie.

At Euensong.

The Firste Lesson, Esai. xlix. unto the ende.
The ii Lesson, John ii. "After this he wente doune to Capernaum," unto the ende.

The firste Sonday after the Epiphanye.

Usquequo, Domine ?　Psalm xiii.

How long wilt thou forget me, O Lord, for euer? howe long wilt thou hide thy face from me?

How long shall I seke counsayle in my soule, and be so vexed in my heart : how long shal mine enemie triumph ouer me?

Consider, and heare me, o Lorde my God : lighten myne iyes, that I slepe not in death.

Lest myne enemie saie, I haue preuailed againste him : for if I be caste down, they that trouble me will reioyce at it.

But my trust is in thy mercye : and my harte is ioyful in thy saluacion.

I wil sing of the Lord, because he hath dealt so louingly with me : (ye I wyll prayse the name of the Lorde most Highest.)

Glory be to the father, &c.

As it was in the begynnyng, &c.

The Collect.

LORDE we beseche the mercyfullye to receiue the praiers of thy people which cal upō thee; and graūt that they maie both perceaue and knowe what thinges they ought to do, and also haue grace and power faithfully to fulfill the same.

The Epistle.　Rom. xii.

I BESECHE you therfore brethren, by the mercyfulnesse of God,

that ye make youre bodies a quicke sacrifice, holy, and acceptable
unto God, which is your resonable seruyng of god, and fashion
not yourselfes like unto this world; but be ye chaunged in your
shape by the renuing of your minde, that ye maie proue what
thing that good, and acceptable, and perfect wil of god is.   For
I saye (throughe the grace that unto me geuen is) to euerye man
amonge you, that no man stand hygh in his owne conceite, more
than it becommeth him to esteme of himself; but so iudge of
hymselfe, that he be gentle and sobre, accordyng as God hath
dealt to euery man the measure of faith: for as we haue many
membres in one body, and all membres haue not one office; so
we being many, are one body in Christ, and euery mā amōg
ourselues, one anothers members.

The Gospel. Luke ii.

THE father and mother of Jesus wente to Hierusalem after the
custome of the feast day.   And whē they had fulfilled the dayes;
as they returned home, the child Jesus abode stil in Jerusalē,
and his father and mother knewe not of it: but they supposyng
hym to haue beene in the cumpanye, came a dayes iourney, and
sought him among their kinsfolke and acquaintaūce.   And when
they found him not, they went backe agayn to Jerusalem, and
soughte him.   And it fortuned that after three dayes, they
founde him in the temple sitting in the middest of the doctours,
hearyng them, and posing them.   And all that heard him were
astonied at his understanding and answers.

And when they saw him, they merueiled, and his mother sayd
unto hym; Sonne why haste thou thus dealte with us?   Beholde,
thy father and I haue sought thee sorowing.   And he said unto
them: how happened it that ye sought me? wist ye not that I
must go about my fathers busines?   And they understode not
that saying, which he spake unto them.   And he went down
with them, and came to Nazareth, and was obedient unto them:
but his mother kept all these sayinges together in her heart.
And Jesus prospered in wisdō and age and in fauour with god
and mē.

¶ *The second Sonday.*

Dixit insipiens. Psalm xiiii.

THE foole hath sayd in his heart : there is no god.
They are corrupte, and become abhominable in theyr doinges :
there is not one that doth good, (no not one.)

The Lorde loked downe from heauen upon the children of men :
to see if there were any that woulde understande and seeke after
God.

But they are al gone out of the waye, they are altogether becū
abominable : there is none that doth good, (no not one.)

Their throte is an open sepulcre, with theyr tongues they haue
deceiued : the poyson of Aspes is under theyr lippes.

Theyr mouth is full of curssinge and bitternes : theyr feete
are swift to shed bloud.

Destruccion and unhappines is in theyr wayes, and the way
of peace haue they not knowē : there is no feare of God before
theyr iyes.

Haue they no knowlege, that they are all suche woorkers of
myschefe : eatinge up my people as it were bred, and call not
upō the Lorde?

There were they broughte in greate feare (euen where no feare
was) : for god is in the generacion of the righteous.

As for you, ye haue made a mocke at ꞌʰe counsaile of the
poore : because he putteth his truste in the Lorde.

Who shal geue saluacion unto Israell out of Syon? when the
Lorde turneth the captiuitie of his people : then shal Iacob
reioyce, and Israell be gladde.

Glory be to the father, &c.

As it was in the begynnyng, &c.

The Collect.

ALMIGHTIE and euerlasting God, whiche doest gouerne all
thynges in heauen and earthe: mercifully heare the supplicacions
of thy people, and graunt us thy peace all the dayes of our life.

The Epistle.   Rom. xii.

SEEYNG that we haue dyuerse gyftes, according to the grace
that is geuen unto us; if any mā haue yᵉ gift of prophecy, let
him haue it, that it be agreeing to the fayth. Let him that
hath an office waite on his office. Let him that teacheth, take
hede to hys doctryne. Let hym that exhorteth, geue attend-
aunce to hys exhortacion. If any mā geue, let him do it with
singlenes. Let him that ruleth, doe it with diligence. If any
man shew mercy, let him doe it with cherefulnes. Let loue be
without dissimulaciō. Hate that which is euil, and cleaue unto
yᵗ whiche is good. Be kynde one to another with brotherly
loue. In geuing honor goe one before another. Be not slothful
in the busines which ye haue in hād. Be feruēt in the spirite.

Apply yourselues to the time. Reioyce in hope; bee paciēt in tribulacion. Continue in praier, distribute unto the necessitie of the saintes. Be ready to harbour. Blesse them which persecute you; blesse, I say, and curse not. Be mery with thē that are merie; wepe also with them that wepe: be of like affeccion one towardes another. Bee not hie minded, but make youreselues equall to them of the lower sorte.

The Gospel. John ii.

AND the third daye was there a mariage in Cana, a citie of Galyle, and the mother of Jesus was there. And Jesus was called (and hys disciples) unto the mariage. And when the wine fayled, the mother of Jesus sayde unto hym: they haue no wine. Jesus said unto her, womā, what haue I to do with the? mine houre is not yet come. His mother said unto the ministers; whatsoeuer he saieth unto you, do it. And there were standing there vi waterpottes of stone, after the maner of the purifiyng of the Jewes, conteining ii or iii fyrkyns apeece. Jesus saide unto them: fil the waterpottes with water. And thei filled them up to the brimme. And he saide unto them: draw out now, and beare unto the Gouernour of the feast. And they bare it. Whē the ruler of the feast had tasted the water that was turned into wine, and knew not whence it was, (but the ministers, which drewe the water, knewe) he called the bridegrome, and said unto him; Euerie man at the beginning doth set forth good wine, and when men be dronke, then that whiche is woorse, but thou hast kepte the good wine until now. This beginning of miracles did Jesus in Cana of Galile, and shewed hys glorye, and his dysciples beleued on him.

¶ *The thirde Soondaye.*

Domine, quis habitabit ? Psalm xv.

LORDE who shall dwelle in thy tabernacle? who shall reste upon thy holye hyl?

Euen he that leadeth an uncorrupte lyfe, and doth the thing whiche is right, and speaketh the trueth from his harte.

He that hath used no deceite in his tōgue, nor done euil to his neighbour, and hath not slaundered his neighbours.

He that setteth not by hymselfe, but is lowelye in his own iyes : and maketh much of them that feare the lord.

He that sweareth unto his neighbour, and dissapointeth hym not : though it were to his owne hinderaunce.

He that hath not geuen his money unto usury : nor taken rewarde agaynst the innocente. Whoso dothe these thynges : shall neuer fall.

Glory be to the father, &c.

As it was in the beginnyng, &c.

The Collect.

ALMYGHTYE and euerlastyng God, mercifullye looke upon oure infirmities, and in al our daungiers and necessities, stretche foorth thy ryghte hande to helpe and defende us; through Christ our Lorde.

The Epistle.   Roma. xii.

BE not wise in your own opinions. Recompēce to no man eiuil for eiuil. Prouide aforehand thinges honest, not only before God, but also in the syghte of al mē. If it be possible, (as much as is in you) liue peaceablye with al men. Dearely beloued, auenge not youreselues, but rather geue place unto wrath. For it is written: Vengeaunce is myne; I will reward sayth the lorde. Therfore, if thyne enemie hunger, fede him, yf he thirst, geue hym drynke. For in so dooyng thou shalte heape coales of fyre on his head. Be not ouercome of eiuill, but ouercome eiuill with goodnes.

The Gospell.   Matt. viii.

WHEN he was come downe from the mountaine, muche people folowed him. And beholde, there came a Lepre and worshypped hym, saiyng, Maister, if thou wilte thou canst make me cleane. And Jesus putte foorth his hande, and touched hym, saying; I wil, bee thou cleane. And immediatelye hys Leprosye was cleansed. And Jesus saide unto hym, tell no manne, but goe and shew thyselfe to the priest, and offer the gift (that Moses commaunded to bee offered) for a witnesse unto them.

And when Jesus was entred into Capernaum, there came unto him a Cēturion, and besought him, saying: Maister, my seruaunt lyeth at home sicke of the palsey, and is greuously pained. And Jesus said, whē I come unto him, I wil heale him. The Centurion aunswered, and said: Sir I am not woorthie that thou shouldeste come under my roofe; but speake the woorde onely, and my seruaunt shalbe healed. For I also am a mā subiect to the autoritie of another, and haue souldiers under me: and I say to this man, goe, and he goeth; and to another man, come, and he cummeth; and to my seruaunt, doe thys, and he doeth it. When Jesus heard these wordes, he merueiled, and saide to them that folowed him: verely I say unto you, I haue not founde so great faith in Israel. I saye unto you, that many shal come from the East, and West, and shall reste with Abraham, and Isaac, and Jacob, in the kyngdome of heauen. But the children of the kyngdome shalbe caste out into utter darkenes, there shalbe weping and gnashing of teeth. And Jesus sayde unto the Centurion: Goe thy way, and as thou beleuest so be it unto thee: and his seruaunt was healed in the selfesame houre.

¶ *The iiii Sonday.*

Quare fremuerunt gentes ?   Psalm ii.

WHY do the heathen so furiously rage together : and why doe the people imagyn a vaine thing?

The kinges of the earth stande up, and the rulers take counsel together : against the lord, and against his anoynted.

Let us breake theyr bondes asunder : and cast away theyr coardes from us.

He that dwelleth in heauen, shall laugh them to scorne : the lorde shall haue them in derision.

Then shall he speake unto them in hys wrath, and vexe them in his sore dyspleasure.

Yet haue I set my kyng : upon my holy hill of Sion. I will preache the lawe, whereof the Lorde hath sayde unto me : thou art my sōne, this day haue I begottē thee.

Desyre of me, and I shall geue thee the heathen for thine inheritance : and the uttermost partes of the earth for thy possession.

Thou shalt bruse them with a rod of yron : and breake them in pieces lyke a potters vessel.

Be wise nowe therfore, o ye kinges : be learned, ye that are iudges of the yearth.

Serue the lorde in feare : and reioyse (unto him) with reuerence.

Kisse the sonne, lest he be angrie, and so ye perish from the righte way : if his wrath be kiendled, (yea but a litle,) blessed are all they that put their trust in him.

Glory be to the father, and to the sonne, and to the &c.

As it was in the beginning, is nowe and euer shalbe, worlde without ende. Amen.

The Collect.

GOD, whiche knoweste us to bee set in the middest of so many and great daungers, that for mannes fraylnes we cannot alwayes

stande uprightly; Graunt to us the health of body and soule
that al those thinges which we suffer for sinne, by thy helpe we
may wel passe and ouercome; through Christ our lorde.

The Epistle.   Rom. xiii.

LET euery soule submit hymselfe unto the auctoritie of the
higher powers; for there is no power but of God.   The powers
that be are ordeined of God, whosoeuer therefore resysteth
power, resisteth the ordinaunce of God: But they that resist,
shall receiue to themselues damnacion.

For rulers are not feareful to them that do good, but to them
that do euil.   Wilt thou be without feare of the power? do well
then, and so shalt thou be praysed of the same: for he is the
minister of God for thy wealth.   But and yf thou do that which
is euill, then feare, for he beareth not the swerde for naught: for
he is the minister of God to take vengeaunce on hym that doth
euill.   Wherfore, ye must nedes obey, not onely for feare of
vengeaunce, but also because of conscience: and euen for this
cause paye ye tribute; for they are Goddes ministers seruyng
for the same purpose.   Geue to euery man therefore his duetie;
tribute, to whom tribute belongeth: custome, to whom custome
is due: feare, to whom feare belongeth: honor to whom honor
pertaineth.

The Gospel.   Matt. viii.

AND when he entred into a ship, his disciples folowed him.
And behold, there arose a great tempest in the sea, insomuche
that the ship was couered with waues, but he was aslepe.   And
his disciples came to him, and awoke hym, saying, Maister, saue
us, we perishe.   And he sayeth unto them: Why are ye fearfull,
O ye of litle fayth?   Then he arose, and rebuked the wyndes
and the sea, and there folowed a great calme.   But the men
meruailed, saying, What maner of man is this, that both wyndes
and sea obey him?   And when he was come to the other syde
into the countrey of the Gergesites, there met hym ii possessed
of deuils, whiche came out of the graues, and were out of measure
fierce, so that no man might go by that way.   And beholde, they
cryed out, saying, O Jesu, thou sonne of God, what haue we to
do with thee?   Art thou come hither to torment us before the
tyme?   And there was a good way of from them a heerd of
many Swine, feding.   So the deuils besought him, saying, If
thou cast us out, suffre us to goe into the heerde of Swine.   And
he sayd unto thē, go your wayes.   Then went they out and

departed into the heerde of Swyne. And behold, the whole
heerde of swyne was caryed hedlong into the sea, and perished in
the waters. Then they that kept them, fled, and went theyr
wayes into the citie, and tolde euery thing, and what had
happened unto the possessed of the deuils. And behold, the
whole citie came out to mete Jesus : and when they sawe him,
they besought him that he would depart out of theyr coastes.

¶ *The v. Sonday.*

Exaudiat te Dominus. Psalm xx.

THE Lorde heare thee in the daye of trouble : the name of the
God of Jacob defende thee;

Sende thee helpe from the Sanctuary : and strength thee out
of Sion;

Remember all thy offeringes : and accept thy brent-sacrifice;

Graunt thee thy heartes desyre : and fulfyll all thy mynde.

We will reioyce in thy saluacion, and triumph in the Name of
the Lorde oure God : the Lorde perfourme all thy peticions.

Nowe knowe I that the Lorde helpeth his annoynted, and wil
heare him from his holy heauen : euen with the wholsome
strength of his right hand.

Some put their trust in Chariotes, and some in horsses : but we
wil remember the name of the lorde our God.

They are brought doune and fallen : but we are rysen, and
stand upright.

Saue, lorde, and heare us, O kyng of heauen : when we call
upon thee.

Glory be to the father, and to the sonne, and to the holy ghost.

As it was in the begynnyng, is nowe, and euer shalbe, worlde
withoute ende. Amen.

The Collect.

LORD, we beseche thee to kepe thy Churche and housholde continually in thy true religion; that they whiche do leane onlye
upon hope of thy heauenly grace may euermore bee defended by
thy mightie power; through Christ our lorde.

The Epistle. Coloss. iii.

PUT upon you as the electe of God, tendre mercy, kyndnes
humblenes of mynd, mekenes, long-suffryng, forbearyng one
another, and forgeuynge one another, if any man haue a querel
against another; as Christ forgaue you, euen so do ye. Aboue

all these thynges put on loue, which is the bond of perfectnes.
And the peace of God rule in your heartes, to the whiche peace
ye are called in one bodye; And see that ye bee thankefull.
Let the worde of Christe dwell in you plenteously with all wisedome.   Teache and exhorte your owne selues in Psalmes, and
Himnes, and spiritual songes, syngyng with grace in your hartes
to the lorde.   And whatsoeuer ye doe, in woorde or deede, doe
all in the name of the lorde Jesu, geuyng thankes to God the
father by him.

The Gospel. Matt. xiii.

THE kyngdome of heauen is like unto a manne whiche sowed
good sede in his felde: but while men slept, his enemy came,
and sowed tares amonge the wheat, and went his waye.   But
when the blade was sprong up, and had brought furth fruite, then
appeared the tares also.   So the seruauntes of the housholder
came, and said unto him: Sir, diddest not thou sowe good seede
in thy felde? from whence then hath it tares? he sayde unto
theim, the enuyous man hath done this.   The seruauntes sayd
unto him, Wilt thou then that we go and wede them up?   But
he saide, naye; leste whyle ye gather up the tares, ye plucke
up also the wheat with them: lette bothe growe together until
the haruest; and in tyme of haruest I will say to the reapers:
gather ye fyrste the tares, and bynde them together in sheues
to be brent: but gather the wheat into my barne.

The vi sonday (if there be so many) shall haue the same Psalme, Collect,
Epistle, and Gospel, that was upon the v.

¶ *The sonday called Septuagesima.*

Dominus regit. Psalm xxiii.

THE Lorde is my sheparde : therefore can I lacke nothyng.
He shall feede me in a grene pasture : and leade me foorth
beside the waters of comfort.
He shall conuerte my soule : and brynge me foorth in the
pathes of righteousnes, for his names sake.
Yea, though I walke thorough the valley of the shadowe of
death, I will feare no euill : for thou art wyth me; thy rod and
thy staffe comfort me.
Thou shalt prepare a table before me against them that trouble
me : thou haste annoynted my heade with oyle, and my cup
shalbe full.

But thy louyng-kyndnes and mercy shall folowe me all the dayes of my life : and I will dwell in the house of the lorde for euer.

Glory be to the father, and to the sonne : and to the holy ghost.

As it was in the beginnyng, is nowe and euer shall be : worlde without ende. Amen.

The Collect.

O LORD, we beseche thee fauourably to heare the praiers of thy people; that we whiche are iustly punished for our offences, may be mercifully deliuered by thy goodnes, for the glory of thy name, through Jesu Christ our sauior, who liueth and reigneth, &c.

The Epistle.   1 Cor. ix.

PERCEYUE ye not, how that they whiche runne in a course runne all, but one receiueth the reward? So runne that ye may obtayne: Euery man that proueth masteries, abstayneth from all thinges. And they do it to obtain a crowne that shall perishe, but we to obtayne an euerlastyng crowne. I therefore so runne not as at an uncertain thyng. So fight I, not as one that beateth the ayre: but I tame my body, and bryng it into subieccion, lest by any meanes it come to pass, that when I haue preached to other, I myselfe should be a cast-away.

The Gospell.   Matt. xx.

THE kyngdome of heauen is like unto a manne that is an housholder, whiche went out early in the mornyng to hyre laborers into his vyneyarde. And when the agrement was made with the laborers for a peny a day, he sent them into his vyneyarde. And he went out about the third houre and sawe other standyng idle in the marketplace, and sayd unto them: Go ye also into the vyneyarde, and whatsoeuer is right I will geue you. And they went theyr way. Againe he went out about the vi. and ix. houre, and did lykewise. And about the xi. houre he went out, and founde other standyng idle, and sayd unto them; why stande ye here all the day idle? They sayd unto hym; because no man hath hyred us. He sayeth unto them, Go ye also into the vineyarde, and whatsoeuer is right, that shall ye receyue.

So, when euen was come, the lorde of the vyneyarde sayd unto his steward: call the laborers and geue them their hyre, begin-

nyng at the last untill the first. And when they did come that
came about the xi. houre, they receiued euery man a penny:
But when the first came also, they supposed that they should
haue receyued more, and they lykewyse receyued euery man
a penny. And when they had receyued it, they murmured
against the good-man of the house, saying: these last haue
wrought but one houre, and thou hast made them equall with
us, whiche haue borne the burthen and heate of the day. But
he answered unto one of them, and sayd: Frende, I do thee no
wrong, diddest thou not agree with me for a penny? Take that
thyne is, and go thy way; I wyll geue unto this last, euen as
unto thee. Is it not lawfull for me to do as me lusteth with
myne owne goodes? Is thyne eye euill because I am good?
So the last shalbe first, and the first shalbe last. For many
be called, and fewe chosen.

¶ *The Sunday called Sexagesima.*

¶ *At the Communion.*

Domini est terra. Psalm xxiv.

The yearth is the lordes, and all that therin is : the compasse
of the worlde, and they that dwell therin.

For he hath founded it upon the seas : and prepared it upon
the fluddes.

Who shall ascende into the hyl of the Lorde? or who shall
rise up in his holy place?

Euen he that hath cleane handes, and a pure heart : and that
hath not lyft up his mynde unto vanitie, nor sworne to deceyue
his neyghbour.

He shall receyue the blessyng from the Lorde : and righteousnes from the God of his saluacion.

This is the generacion of them that seke hym : euen of them
that seke thy face, O Jacob.

Lyft up your heades O ye gates, and be ye lift up ye euerlastyng doores, and the kyng of glory shall come in.

Who is the kyng of glory : it is the Lord strong and mightie
euen the Lorde mightie in battail.

Lift up your heades (O ye gates) and be ye lift up ye euerlasting doores : and the kyng of glory shall come in.

Who is this kyng of glory : euen the lorde of hostes, he is the
kyng of glory.

Glory be to the father, and to the sonne, &c.

As it was in the begynning, is now, &c.

The Collect.

LORDE GOD, whiche seest that we put not our trust in any thyng that we do; mercyfully graunt that by thy power we may be defended against al aduersitie; through Jesus Christ our Lorde.

The Epistle. 2 Cor. xi.

YE suffre fooles gladly, seyng ye yourselues are wise. For ye suffre if a man bring you into bondage: yf a man deuoure: yf a man take: if a man exalte himselfe: if a man smite you on the face. I speake as concernyng rebuke, as though we had been weake in this behalfe. Howbeit, wherinsoeuer any man dare be bolde (I speake folishly) I dare be bolde also. They are Hebrues, euen so am I. They are Israelytes, euen so am I. They are the seede of Abraham, euen so am I. They are the ministers of Christ, (I speake as a foole) I am more: In labours more aboundaunt: In stripes aboue measure: In prison more plenteously: In death ofte: Of the Jewes fiue tymes receiued I xl. stripes saue one: Thrise was I beaten with roddes: I was once stoned. I suffered thrise shipwracke. Night and day haue I been in the depe sea. In iorneying often; in parels of waters, in parels of robbers; in ieopardyes of myne owne nacion; in ieopardyes among the heathen; in parels in the citie; in parels in wyldernes; in parels in the sea; in parels among false brethren; in labour and trauayle; in watchynges often; in hunger and thirst; in fastynges often; in colde and in nakednes; besyde the thynges whiche outwardly happen unto me. I am combred dayly, and do care for al congregacions. Who is weake, and I am not weake? who is offended, and I burne not? If I muste nedes boast, I wyl boast of the thynges that concerne myne infirmities. The God and father of our lorde Jesus Christ, whiche is blessed for euermore, knoweth that I lye not.

The Gospel. Luke viii.

WHEN muche people were gathered together, and were come to hym out of all cities, he spake by a similitude: The sower went out to sowe his seede: and as he sowed, some fell by the way-syde, and it was troden doune, and the foules of the ayre deuoured it up. And some fell on stones, and as sone as it was sprong up, it withered awaye, because it lacked moystnes. And some fell among thornes, and the thornes sprang up with it and choked it. And some fell on good ground, and sprong up, and bare fruite an hundreth-folde. And as he sayd these thinges, he cryed; he that hath eares to heare, let him heare. And his disciples asked hym, saying, what maner of similitude is this? And he sayd; unto you it is geuen to know the kyngdome of God, but to other by parables; that when they see, they should not see, and when they heare they should not understande. The parable is this: The seede is the worde of God: those that are beside the way, are they that heare: then commeth the deuil and taketh the worde out of their hartes, leste they should beleue, and be saued. They on the stones, are they whiche when they heare, receiue the woorde with ioye; and these haue no rotes, whiche for a while beleue, and in tyme of temptacion go away. And that whiche fell among thornes, are they whiche when they haue heard, go furth, and are choked with cares, and riches, and voluptuous lyuing, and bryng furth no fruite. That whiche fell in the good grounde, are they whiche with a pure and good heart, heare the woorde and kepe it, and bryng furth fruite through pacience.

¶ *The Sonday called Quinquagesima.*

Judica me Domine. Psalm xxvi.

Be thou my iudge, O lorde, for I haue walked innocently : my trust hath been also in the lorde, therfore shal I not fal.

Examyne me, O Lord, and proue me : trye out my reynes and my heart.

For thy louyng-kyndnes is before myne eyes : and I will walke in thy trueth.

I haue not dwelt with vaine persons : neither wil I haue felowship with the deceiptful.

I haue hated the congregacion of the wicked : and will not syt among the ungodly.

I will washe my handes in innocency, O lorde : and so will I go to thine aulter;

That I may shewe the voyce of thankesgeuyng : and tell of all thy wonderous workes.

Lorde, I haue loued the habitacion of thy house : and the place where thyne honor dwelleth.

O shut not up my soule with the synners : nor my life with the bloudthirsty;

In whose handes is wickednes : and their right hande is full of giftes.

But as for me I will walke innocently : O lorde deliuer me, and be mercyful unto me.

My foote standeth righte : I will praise the Lorde in the congregacions.

Glory be to the father, &c.

As it was in the &c.

The Collect.

O LORDE whiche doeste teache us that all our doynges withoute charitie are nothyng woorthe; sende thy holy ghost, and powre into our heartes that most excellent gyft of charitie, the very bond of peace and al vertues, without the whiche whosoeuer liueth is counted dead before thee: Graunte this for thy onlye sonne, Jesus Christes sake.

The Epistle. 1 Cor. xiii.

THOUGH I speake with the tongues of men and of angels, and haue no loue, I am euen as sounding brasse, or as a tynklyng Cimbal. And thoughe I could prophecy, and understande all secretes, and all knowlege; yea, if I haue al faith, so that I coulde moue mountaines out of their places, and yet haue no loue, I am nothyng. And thoughe I bestowe all my goodes to fede the poore, and thoughe I gaue my bodye euen that I burned, and yet haue no loue, it profyteth me nothyng. Loue suffreth longe, and is curteous; loue enuieth not; loue dothe not frowardely, swelleth not, dealeth not dishonestly, seketh not her owne, is not prouoked to anger, thynkethe none euyll, reioyseth not in iniquitie. But reioyseth in the trueth, suffreth all thynges, beleueth all thynges, hopeth all thynges, endureth all thyengs.

Thoughe that propheciyng fayle, either tongues cease, or knowlege vanishe awaye, yet loue falleth neuer awaye. For our knowlege is unperfecte, and our prophecying is unperfecte: But when that, which is perfect, is come, then that whiche is unperfect shalbee done awaye. When I was a childe I spake as a chylde; I understode as a childe, I imagined as a chylde. But as sone as I was a man, I put away childishnes. Nowe we see in a glasse, euen in a darke speakyng; but then shall wee see face to face. Nowe I knowe unperfectely, but then shall I know euen as I am knowen. Nowe abideth fayth, hope, and loue: euen these thre; but the chiefe of these is loue.

The Gospell.   Luke xviii.

JESUS toke unto him the xii, and sayd unto them: beholde, we go up to Jerusalem, and all shalbe fulfylled that are written by the Prophetes, of the sōne of man.   For he shalbe deliuered unto the gentyles, and shalbe mocked and despitefully intreated and spitted on.   And when they haue scourged him, they will put hym to death, and the third day he shall ryse again.   And they understode none of these thinges.   And this saying was hyd from them, so that they perceyued not the thynges whiche were spoken.   And it came to passe, that as he was come nigh unto Hierico, a certain blind mā sate by the hyewayside beggyng. And when he heard the people passe by, he asked what it meant. And they sayd unto him, that Jesus of Nazareth passed by.   And he cried, saying: Jesu thou sonne of Dauid haue mercy on me. And they whiche went before rebuked hym, that he shoulde holde his peace.   But he cryed so muche the more, thou sonne of Dauid haue mercy on me.   And Jesus stoode styll, and commaunded him to be brought unto hym.   And when he was come nere, he asked hym, saying, what wilt thou that I do unto the? and he sayd, Lord, that I may receyue my sight.   And Jesus sayd unto him, receiue thy syght, thy faith hath saued thee. And immediatly, he receyued his syght, and folowed hym, praysing God.   And all the people, when they saw it, gaue praise unto God.

¶ The fyrst day of Lent, commonly called Ash-Wednesday.

Domine ne.   Psalm vi.

O LORDE rebuke me not in thyne indignacion : neyther chasten me in thy displeasure.

Haue mercy upon me, O Lorde, for I am weake, O lorde, heale me, my bones are vexed.

My soule also is sore troubled : but Lorde, howe long wilt thou punishe me?

Turne thee, O Lorde, and delyuer my soul : Oh saue me for thy mercies sake.

For in death no man remembreth thee : and who will geue the thankes in the pyt?

I am wery of my gronyng; euery night washe I my bed : and water my couche with my teares.

My beautie is gone for very trouble : and worne away because of all myne enemyes.

Awaye fro me, all ye that worke vanitie : for the lorde hath hearde the voyce of my wepyng.

The Lorde hath heard my peticion : the Lorde wyll receiue my praier.

All mine enemies shalbee confounded, and sore vexed : they shalbe turned backe, and put to shame sodainly.

Glory be to the father, &c.

As it was in the beginnyng, &c.

The Collect.

ALMIGHTYE and euerlastyng God, whiche hatest nothyng that thou haste made, and doest forgeue the sinnes of all them that be penitente; Creat and make in us newe and contrite heartes, that wee worthely lamentyng oure synnes, and knowlegyng our wretchednes, maye obtaine of thee, the God of all mercye, perfect remission and forgeuenes; thorough Jesus Christ.

The Epistle. Joel ii.

TURNE you unto me with all your hartes, with fasting, wepyng, and mournyng: rent your heartes, and not your clothes. Turne you unto the Lorde your god: for he is gracious and mercyfull, long-sufferyng, and of greate compassion, and ready to pardō wickednes. Then (no doubt) he also shall turne and forgeue: and after his chastenyng, he shall let youre increase remaine for meat and drynke offerynges unto the Lorde your God. Blowe out with the Trompet in Sion, proclayme a fasting, call the congregacion, and gather the people together; warne the congregacion, gather the elders, brynge the children and sucklynges together. Let the brydgrome go furth of his chambre, and the bryde out of her closet. Let the priestes serue the Lorde betwene the Porche and the alter, wepyng and saiyng: be fauorable, O Lorde, bee fauorable unto thy people: let not thyne heritage be brought to suche confusion, leste the heathen be lordes thereof: Wherefore shoulde they say among the Heathen, Where is nowe their God.

The Gospell. Matt. vi.

WHEN ye fast, be not sad as the Hipocrites are, for they disfigure their faces, that it maye appeare unto men how that they fast. Verely I saye unto you, they haue their rewarde. But thou, when thou fastest. annointe thine head, and washe thy face, that it appeare not unto menne howe that thou fasteste, but unto thy father whiche is in secrete: and thy father, which seeth in secrete, shal reward thee openly.   Laye not uppe for yourselues treasure upõ earth, where the rust and moth doth corrupt, and where theues breake throughe and steale.   But Laye up for you treasures in heauen, where neither ruste nor moth dothe corrupte, and where theues doe not breake throughe nor steale.   For where your treasure is, there wil your heartes bee also.

¶ *The first Sonday in Lent.*

Beati, quorum.   Psalm xxxii.

BLESSED is he, whose unrighteousnes is forgeuen : and whose sinne is couered.

Blessed is the manne unto whome the Lord imputeth no sinne : and in whose spirite there is no guile.

For while I helde my toungue : my bones consumed awaye thoroughe my dayelye complainyng.

For thy hande is heauy upõ me both day and night : and my moysture is lyke the drougth is Somer.

I will knowlage my synne unto thee : and myne unryghteousnes haue I not hyd.

I sayde, I wyll confesse my sinnes unto the lorde : and so thou forgauest the wickednes of my synne.

For this shall euery one that is Godly, make his prayer unto thee, in a tyme when thou maiest bee found : but in the greate water-floudes, they shall not come nye hym.

Thou arte a place to hyde me in, thou shalte preserue me from trouble : thou shalte compasse me aboute wyth songes of deliueraunce.

I wyll enfourme thee and teache thee in the waye wherein thou shall go : and I will guyde thee wyth mine iye.

Be not ye like horsse and Mule, which haue no understandyng: whose mouthes must be holden with bitte and bridle, leste they fall upon thee.

Great plagues remaine for the ungodlye : but whoso putteth his truste in the lorde, mercye embraceth hym on euery side.

Be glad, O ye righteous, and reioyce in the Lord : and be ioyfull, all ye that are true of heart.

Glory be to the father, and to the sonne : and to the holy ghoste.

As it was in the beginnyng, and is nowe; and euer shalbe worlde without ende.   Amen.

The Collect.

O LORD, whiche for oure sake dyddeste faste fortye dayes and
fourtie nightes; Geue us grace to use suche abstinence, that, oure
fleshe beyng subdued to the spirite, wee maye euer obeye thy
Godlye mocions in righteousnesse, and true holinesse, to thy
honoure and glorye, whiche lyueste and reigneste, &c.

The Epistle. 2 Cor. vi.

WE, as helpers exhort you, that ye receiue not the grace of
God in vayne. For he sayeth, I haue heard thee in a tyme
accepted: and in the daye of saluacion haue I succoured thee.
Beholde nowe is that accepted time; beholde nowe is that day
of saluacion. Let us geue no occasion of euil, that in our office
be foūde no faute, but in all thynges let us behaue ourselues as
the ministers of God; In much pacience, in affliccions, in necessities, in anguyshes, in strypes, in prysonmentes, in strifes: in
labours, in watchynges, in fastinges, in purenes, in knowlege, in
long-suffring, in kindnes, in the holy goste, in loue unfayned, in
the woorde of trueth, in the power of God: by the armoure of
righteousnes of the ryghte hand and on the left; by honoure and
dyshonoure; by euill reporte and good reporte; as deceyuers and
yet true; as unknowen and yet knowen; as dying, and beholde
we lyue; as chastened and not killed; as sorowyng and yet
alway mery; as poore and yet make many riche: as hauing
nothyng, and yet possessyng all thynges.

The Gospell. Matt. iv.

THEN was Jesus led awaye of the spirite into wyldernesse, to
be tempted of the deuyll. And when he had fasted fourty dayes
and fourty nightes he was at the last an hungred. And when the
tempter came to hym, he sayed: Yf thou be the soonne of God,
commaunde that these stones be made bread. But he aunswered
and sayed: it is wrytten, man shall not lyue by bread only, but
by euery worde that procedeth out of the mouthe of God.
Then the deuill taketh hym up into the holy cytye and setteth
hym on a pynacle of the temple, and sayeth unto him, if thou be
the sōne of God, cast thyself downe hedlong. For it is wrytten,
he shall geue his Aungels charge ouer thee, and with their hādes
they shall holde thee up, leste at any tyme thou dashe thy foote
against a stone. And Jesus sayed unto hym, It is written
agayne: Thou shalt not tempte the Lorde thy God.
Agayne, the deuyll taketh hym up into an excedyng high

mountayne, and sheweth hym all the kyngdomes of the worlde, and the glory of them; and sayeth unto him: all these wyll I geue thee, if thou wylt fall downe and wurship me.   Then sayeth Jesus unto hym, Auoide, Sathã, for it is wrytten, Thou shalt wurshyp the Lord thy God, and hym onely shalt thou serue. Then the deuyll leaueth hym, and beholde, the Aungels came and ministred unto hym.

¶ The seconde Sonday.

De profundis.   Psalm. cxxx.

Out of the depe haue I called unto thee, O Lord : Lorde, heare my voyce.

Oh let thyne eares consyder well : the voyce of my complaynte.

If thou, Lord, wilt be extreme to marke what is done amysse : Oh Lord, who may abyde it?

For there is mercy with thee : therfore shalt thou be feared,

I looke for the Lord; my soule doth wayte for him : in his woorde is my trust.

My soule flyeth unto the Lorde, before the mornyng watche: I saye, before the mornyng watche.

O Israel trust in the Lorde, for with the Lorde there is mercy : and with hym is plenteous redempcion.

And he shall redeme Israell : from all his synnes.

Glory be to the father, and to the sonne and to the holy ghost.

As it was in the beginning, and is now and euer shal be worlde without ende.   Amen.

The Collect.

Almightye God, whiche doest see that we haue no power of oureselues to helpe ourselues; kepe thou us both outwardly in oure bodies, and inwardly in oure soules; that we maye be defended from all aduersities whiche maye happen to the body, and from all euel thoughtes which maye assault and hurte the soule; through Jesus Christ &c.

The Epistle.   1 Thess. iv.

We beseche you brethren, and exhorte you by the lorde Jesus, that ye increase more and more, euē as ye haue receiyued of us, howe ye oughte to walke and to please God.   For ye knowe what commaundemētes we gaue you by our lorde Jesu Christ. For this is the wyll of God, euen youre holynes, that ye should abstayne from fornicacion, and that euery one of you should

knowe howe to kepe his vessel in holines and honoure, and not
in the luste of concupiscence, as do the Heathen, whiche knowe
not God; that no man oppresse and defraude his brother in ber-
gaining; because that the lorde is the auenger of all suche
thynges, as we tolde you before and testified. For God hath
not called us unto unclennesse, but unto holines. He therfore
that despiseth, despiseth not man, but God, whiche hathe sente
his holye spirite among you.

The Gospell. Matt. xv.

JESUS went thence, and departed into the coastes of Tyre and
Sidon: and behold, a woman of Canaan (whiche came out of the
same coastes) cried unto hym, saying: haue mercye on me, O
Lorde, thou sonne of Dauid; My daughter is pyteously vexed
with a deuell. But he aunswered her nothing at all. And his
disciples came and besought hym, saying; sende her awaye, for
she cryeth after us. But he aunswered and saied; I am not sent,
but to the lost shepe of the house of Israell. Then came she
and worshipped hym, saying; Lorde, helpe me. He aunswered
and saied: it is not mete to take the childrens bread, and cast
it to dogges. She aunswered and saied: trueth Lorde, for the
dogges eate of the crummes whiche fall from their maisters
table. Then Jesus aunswered and sayed unto her: O woman
great is thy faith, be it unto thee, euen as thou wilt. And her
daughter was made whole euen at the same tyme.

¶ The iii. Sonday.

Judica me, Deus. Psalm xliii.

GEUE sentence with me, (O God,) and defende my cause
against the ungodly people : Oh delyuer me from the deceytfull
and wicked man.

For thou arte the God of my strength, why haste thou put me
from thee : and why go I so heuely, whyle the enemye oppresseth
me?

Oh, send out thy light and thy truthe, that they maye leade
me : and bring me unto thy holy hil, and to thy dwelling.

And that I maie go unto the aultare of God, euen unto the God
of my ioye and gladnes : and upon the harpe will I geue thankes
unto thee (O God) my God.

Why art thou so heauy, (O my soule) : and why arte thou so
disquieted within me?

O put thy trust in God : for I wyll yet geue him thankes whiche is the helpe of my countenaunce and my God.

Glory be to the father, and to the sonne.

As it was in the beginning, &c.

The Collect.

We beseche thee, almighty God, looke upon the hartye desires of thy humble seruauntes, and stretche foorth the right hande of thy maiestie, to bee oure defence against all oure enemies; through Jesus Christe oure Lorde.

The Epistle.   Ephes. v.

Be you the folowers of God as dere children and walke in loue, euen as Christe loued us, and gaue himselfe for us an offring and a sacrifyce of a swete sauour to god.   As for fornicacion, and all unclennes or couetousnes, let it not be once named among you, as it becommeth sainctes; or fylthynes, or folishe talking, or iesting, whiche are not comely, but rather geuing of thankes. For this ye knowe, that no whoremōger, either uncleane person, or couetous persō, (which is a worshipper of ymages,) hathe anye inheritaunce in the kingdome of Christ and of God.   Let no man deceue you with vaine wordes.   For because of suche thynges, commeth the wrath of God upon the chyldren of disobedience. Be not ye therfore companions of them.   Ye were sometime darckenes, but nowe ar ye light in the lorde: walke as children of light, for the fruite of the spirite consisteth in all goodness, and righteousnesse, and truthe.   Accepte that whiche is pleasyng unto the Lorde, and haue no felowship with the unfruitful workes of darcknes, but rather rebuke them.   For it is a shame euen to name those thynges, whiche are done of them in secrete: but all thinges when they are brought forth by the light are manifest. For whatsoeuer is manifest, the same is lyght: wherfore he sayeth, awake, thou that slepest, and stande up from death; and Christ shall geue thee light.

The Gospell.   Luke xi.

JESUS was casting out a deuel that was dōme.   And when he had cast the deuel, the dōme spake, and the people wondered. But other of them saied, He casteth out deuils through Belzebub, the chiefe of the deuels.   And other tempted him, and required of him a signe from heauen.   But he knowyng their thoughtes, sayed unto them; Euery kyngdome deuided against itselfe, is desolate; and one house doth fall upon another.   If Sathan also be deuided againste hymselfe, howe shall his kyngdome endure? Because ye saye that I cast out deuels through Belzebub: If I by the helpe of Belzebub caste oute deuels, by whose helpe do your chyldren caste them oute? Therfore shall they be youre iudges. But if I with the fynger of God caste out deuels, no doubt the kingdome of God is come upon you. When a strong man armed watcheth his house; the thinges that he possesseth are in peace. But when a stronger than he commeth upon hym, he taketh from hym all his harnes (wherin he trusted) and deuideth his goodes. He that is not with me, is against me. And he that gathereth not with me scattereth abrode. When the uncleane spirit is gone out of a man, he walketh through drye places, sekyng rest. And when he fyndeth none, he sayeth: I will returne agayne into my house whence I came out. And when he commeth, he fyndeth it swepte and garnisshed. Then goeth he and taketh to hym vii. other spirites worse then him-selfe; and they entre in and dwell there. And the ende of that man is worse than the beginning. And it fortuned that as he spake these thinges, a certaine woman of the company lifte up her voice, and saied unto hym: happy is the wombe that bare thee, and the pappes which gaue thee sucke. But he sayd: yea, happy are they that heare the woorde of God and kepe it.

¶ *The iiii. Sonday.*

Deus noster refugium. Psalm xlvi.

GOD is oure hope and strength : a very presente helpe in trouble.

Therfore wil not we feare, though the earth be moued : and though the hilles be caryed in the middest of the sea.

Though the waters therof rage and swell : and though the mountaines shake at the tempest of the same.

The ryuers of the floude therof shall make glad the citie of God : the holy place of the tabernacle of the moste highest.

God is in the middest of her, therfore shall she not be remoued : God shall helpe her, and that ryght early.

The heathen make muche adoe, and the kyngdomes are moued : but God hath shewed his voyce, and the earth shall mealte awaye.

The Lord of hostes is with us: the God of Jacob is oure refuge.

O come hither, and beholde the workes of the Lord : what destruccion he hath brought upon the earth.

He maketh warres to ceasse in all the worlde : he breaketh the bowe, and knappeth the speare in sunder, and burneth the Chariotes in the fyer.

Be styll then, and knowe that I am God : I wylbe exalted among the Heathen, and I wylbe exalted in the earth.

Glory be to the father, &c.

As it was in the begynnyng, &c.

The Collect.

GRAUNTE, we beseche thee, almyghtye God, that we, whiche for oure euill dedes are worthely punyshed, by the comforte of thy grace may mercyfully be releued; through our Lorde Jesus Christe.

The Epistle.   Gal. iv.

TELL me, (ye that desyre to be under the lawe) doe ye not heare of the lawe?   For it is written that Abraham had ii. sonnes, the one by a bondemayde, the other by a fre-woman.   Yea, and he which was borne of the bond-woman, was borne after the fleshe; but he whiche was borne of the fre-woman, was borne by promes: Whiche thinges are spoken by an allegory.   For these are two testamētes, the one from the mount Sina, whiche gendreth unto bondage, whiche is Agar: For Mount Sina is Agar in Arabia, and bordreth upon the citie, which is nowe called Jerusalem, and is in bondage with her children.   But Jerusalem, whiche is aboue, is free, whiche is the mother of us al.   For it is wrytten, reioyce thou barren that bearest no children; breake forthe and crye, thou that trauaylest not.   For the desolate hath many moe children than she whiche hath an husbande. Brethren, we are after Isaac the chyldren of promes.   But as then, he that was borne after the fleshe persecuted hym that was borne after the spirite; Euen so is it nowe.   Neuerthelesse, what sayeth the scripture? put away the bonde-woman and her sonne.   For the sonne of the bonde-woman shall not bee heire with the sonne of the fre-woman: So then brethren, we are not children of the bonde-woman, but of the fre-woman.

The Gospell.   John vi.

JESUS departed ouer the sea of Galile, which is the sea of Tiberias, and a great multitude folowed him, because thei sawe his miracles whiche he dyd on them that were diseased.   And Jesus went up into a mountayne, and there he sate with his disciples.   And Easter, a feaste of the Jewes, was nye.   Whē Jesus then lift up his iyes, and sawe a great company come unto him, he sayeth unto Philip; whence shall we bye bread that these may eate? Thys he sayd to proue him; for he himselfe knewe what he woulde dooe. Philip aunswered him; two hundreth peniwoorthe of bread are not sufficient for them, that euery manne may take a little. One of his disciples (Andrew, Simõ Peters brother) saith unto him; There is a lad here which hath fyue barley-loaues, and twoo fyshes: but what are they among so many? And Jesus sayde: make the people sit downe. There was muche grasse in the place: so the men sate downe, in number about fiue thousand. And Jesus toke the bread, and when he had geuen thankes, he gaue to the Discyples, and the Discyples to them that were set downe: and lykewyse of the fyshes as muche as they woulde. When they had eaten inough, he sayde unto his Discyples; gather up the broken meate whiche remayneth, that nothing be lost. And they gathered it together and filled xii. baskets with the broken meate of the fiue barley-loaues; which broken meate remayned unto them that had eaten. Then those men (when they had seene the miracle that Jesus did) sayde: this is of a trueth the same prophete that shoulde come into the worlde.

¶ *The v. Sonday.*

Deus, in nomine tuo. Psalm liv.

SAUE me (O god) for thy name's sake : and auenge me in thy strength.

Heare my prayer (O God) : and harken unto the woordes of my mouth.

For straungers are rysen up agaynste me : and Tirauntes (whiche haue not God before theyr iyes) seke after my soule.

Beholde, god is my helper: the Lorde is with them that upholde my soule.

He shall rewarde euell unto myne enemyes : destroye thou them in thy trueth.

An offering of a free hart will I geue thee, and praise thy Name (O lorde) : because it is so coumfortable.

For he hath delyuered me out of all my trouble : and myne iye hath seene his desire upon myne enemies.

Glory be to the father, and to the sonne, &c.

As it was in the beginning, &c.

The Collect.

WE beseche thee, almyghtie God, mercifullye to looke upon thy people; that by thy greate goodnesse they may be gouerned and preserued euermore, both in body and soule; through Jesus Christe our Lorde.

The Epistle. Heb. ix.

CHRISTE being an high prieste of good thynges to come, came by a greater and a more perfecte tabernacle, not made with handes, that is to saye, not of this building; neither by the bloud of goates and calues, but by his owne bloud he entred in once into the holy place, and founde eternall redempcion.   For if the bloude of oxen and of goates, and the ashes of a younge kowe, when it was sprynkled, purifyeth the uncleane as touching the purifying of the fleshe: howe muche more shal the bloud of Christ (which through the eternal spirite offred himselfe without spot to God) pourge your conscience from dead workes for to serue the liuing god?   And for this cause is he the mediatour of the new testamente; that through deathe whiche chaunsed for the redempcion of those transgressyons that were under the firste testamente, they whiche are called, might receyue the promes of eternall inheritaunce

The Gospell. John viii.

WHICHE of you can rebuke me of sinne?   If I saye the truthe, why doe ye not beleue me?   He that is of God, heareth Goddes wordes; ye therefore heare them not, because ye are not of God. Then answered the Jewes, and sayd unto him; saye we not wel, that thou art a Samaritan, and haste the deuil?   Jesus answered; I haue not the deuill, but I honor my father, and ye haue dishonored me.   I seke not myne owne prayse; there is one that seketh and iudgeth.   Verely, verely, I saye unto you; if a manne kepe my saiyng, he shall neuer see death.   Then sayd the Jewes unto hym, nowe knowe we that thou hast the deuil. Abrahā is dead, and the Prophetes, and thou sayeste: If a man kepe my saiyng, he shall neuer taste of deathe.   Art thou greater then our father Abrahā, whiche is deade, (And the Prophetes are dead:) whome makeste thou thyselfe?   Jesus aunswered: if I honor myselfe, myne honor is nothyng.   It is my father that honoreth me, which ye say is your god: and yet ye haue not knowen hym; but I knowe hym.   And if I saye I knowe hym not, I shalbe a lyer lyke unto you.   But I knowe him, and kepe his saiyng.   Your father Abraham was glad to see my daye: and he sawe it, and reioysed.   Then said the Jewes unto him, Thou art not yet l. yere olde, and haste thou seen Abrahā?   Jesus sayde unto them: Verely, verely, I saye unto you; yer Abraham was borne, I am. Then tooke they up stones to caste at hym: but Jesus hyd hymselfe, and went out of the temple.

¶ *The Sonday next before Easter.*

Exaudi, Deus deprecationem. Psalm lxi.

HEARE my criynge, O God : geue eare unto my prayer.

From the endes of the yearth wil I cal unto thee : when my heart is in heauynes.

Oh set me up upon the rocke that is higher then I : for thou haste been my hope, and a stronge tower for me against the enemy.

I will dwell in thy tabernacle for euer : and my truste shalbe under the coueryng of thy wynges.

For thou, O Lorde, hast hearde my desyres : and hast geuen an heritage unto those that feare thy Name.

Thou shalt graunt the kyng a long life : that his yeres may endure thoroughout all generacions.

He shall dwell before God for euer : O prepare thy louyng mercy and faythfulnes, that they maye preserue him.

So will I alwaye syng prayse unto thy name : that I may dayly performe my vowes.

Glory be to the father, &c.

As it was in the, &c.

The Collect.

ALMIGHTIE and euerlastynge God, whiche of thy tender loue towarde man, haste sente our sauior Jesus Christ, to take upon him oure fleshe, and to suffre death upon the crosse, that all mankynde shoulde folowe the example of his greate humilitie; mercifully graunte that we both folowe the example of his pacience, and be made partakers of his resurreccion; thoroughe the same Jesus Christ our lorde.

The Epistle. Philipp. ii.

LET the same mynde bee in you, that was also in Christ Jesu: which when he was in the shape of God, thought it no robbery to be equal wyth God; neuerthelesse he made himselfe of no reputacion, takyng on him the shape of a seruaunte, and beecame like unto men, and was founde in his apparel as a man. He humbled himselfe and became obediente to the death, euen the death of the crosse. Wherefore, God hath also exalted him on

high, and geuen him a name whiche is aboue all names; that in
the name of Jesus euery knee shoulde bowe, bothe of thinges
in heauen, and thynges in yearth, and thinges under the yearth;
and that all tõgues shoulde confesse that Jesus Christe is the
lorde, unto the prayse of God the father.

The Gospell. Matt. xxvi. xxvii.

AND it came to passe, when Jesus had finished all these
sayinges, he sayd unto his disciples: ye knowe that after two
dayes shalbe Easter, and the sonne of man shalbe delyuered
ouer to be crucified. Then assembled together the chiefe
Priestes, and the Scribes, and the Elders of the people unto the
palace of the high priest, (which was called Cayphas,) and helde
a counsayl that they might take Jesus by subteltie, and kill
him. But they sayd: not on the holy daye, leste there be an
uproare among the people.

When Jesus was in Bethany, in the house of Simon the Leper,
there came unto hym a woman hauyng an Alabaster boxe of
precious oyntment, and powred it on his head, as he sate at the
bourde. But when his disciples sawe it, they had indignacion,
saiyng, Whereto serueth this wast? This oynment might haue
been well solde and geuen to the poore. When Jesus understode that, he sayd unto them: why trouble ye the woman?
for she hath wrought a good worke upon me. For ye haue the
poore alwayes with you; but me ye shall not haue alwayes.
And in that she hath cast this oyntment on my body, she did
it to bury me. Verely I say unto you: whersoeuer this gospell
shalbe preached in al the worlde, there shall also this, that she
hath done, be tolde for a memoriall of her. Then one of the
xii (whiche was called Judas Iscarioth) went unto the chiefe
priestes, and sayd unto them, what will ye geue me, and I will
deliuer hym unto you? And they appointed unto him xxx
pieces of siluer. And from that tyme furth he sought oportunitie to betray hym. The first day of swete bread, the disciples came to Jesus, saying unto him; where wilt thou that
we prepare for thee, to eate the Passeouer? And he sayd; Go
into the citie, to suche a man, and say unto him, the Maister
sayth; my tyme is at hand, I will kepe my Easter by thee with
my disciples. And the disciples did as Jesus had appointed
them; and they made ready the passeouer. When the euen
was come, he sate doune with the xii. And as they did eate,
he sayd; Verely I say unto you, that one of you shall betray
me. And they were exceding sorowful, and began euery one

of them to say unto him; Lorde, is it I? he aunswered and sayd; he that dippeth his hād with me in the dishe, the same shal betraye me. The sonne of man truely goeth as it is written of him: but woe unto that man, by whom the sonne of man is betrayed. It had been good for that man if he had not been borne. Then Judas, which betraied him, answered and sayd; Maister, is it I? He said unto him, thou hast sayd. When they were eatyng, Jesus toke bread, and when he had geuen thankes, he brake it and gaue it to the disciples, and sayd, Take, eat, this is my body. And he tooke the cuppe and thanked, and gaue it them, saying; drinke ye all of this; For this is my bloud (whiche is of the newe testament) that is shed for many, for the remission of synnes. But I say unto you: I will not drinke hencefurth of this fruite of the vyne tree, untyll that day when I shall drynke it newe with you, in my fathers kyngdome. And when they had sayd grace, they went out unto mount Oliuete. Then sayth Jesus unto them; all ye shalbe offended because of me this night. For it is written; I will smyte the shepherde, and the shepe of the flocke shalbe scattered abroade: but after I am rysen again, I will go before you into Galilee. Peter answered and sayd unto him: though all men be offended because of thee, yet wil not I be offended. Jesus sayd unto him; verely I say unto thee, That in this same night before the cocke crowe; thou shalt deny me thrise. Peter sayd unto him: yea, though I should dye with thee, yet will I not deny thee: lykewyse also said all the disciples.

Then came Jesus with thē unto a farme place, (which is called Gethsemane,) and sayd unto the disciples; Syt ye here, whyle I go and pray yonder. And he tooke with him Peter and the two sonnes of Zebede, and began to waxe sorowful and heauy. Then sayd Jesus unto thē: My soule is heauy euen unto the death: Tary ye here and watche with me. And he went a litle farther, and fell flat on his face, and prayed, saying; O my father if it be possible, let this cup passe frome me: neuerthelesse not as I will, but as thou wilt. And he came unto the disciples, and found them aslepe, and sayd unto Peter, what, could ye not watche with me one houre? watche and praye, that ye entre not into temptacion: the spirite is willyng, but the fleshe is weake. He went away once againe and prayed, saying; O my father, yf this cup may not passe away frō me, except I drinke of it, thy wil be fulfylled: and he came and found them aslepe agayne, for their eyes were heauy. And he left them, and went againe and prayed the third tyme, saying the same

woordes. Then cōmeth he to his disciples, and sayth unto them,
Slepe on now, and take your rest. Behold, the houre is at hand,
and the sonne of man is betrayed into the handes of synners.
Ryse, let us be goyng: behold, he is at hand that doth betray me.

While he yet spake; lo, Judas one of the nombre of the xii,
came, and with him a great multitude with sweordes and staues
sent from the chief priestes and elders of the people. But he
that betrayed hym, gaue them a token, saying: whomsoeuer I
kisse, the same is he, holde him fast. And furthwith he came
to Jesus, and sayd, hayle Maister, and kyssed him. And Jesus
sayd unto hym, frend, wherfore art thou come? Then came
they, and layde handes on Jesus, and toke hym. And beholde,
one of them whiche were with Jesus, stretched out his hand and
drew his sworde, and stroke a seruaunt of the hye Priest, and
smote of his eare. Then sayd Jesus unto hym: put up thy
sworde into the sheath: for all they that take the sworde, shall
perishe with the sworde. Thynkest thou that I cannot nowe
pray to my father, and he shall geue me euen nowe more than
xii legions of Angelles? But howe then shall the scriptures bee
fulfylled? For thus must it be. In that same houre sayd
Jesus to the multitude: ye be come out as it were to a thefe
with swordes and staues, for to take me. I sate dayly with
you teaching in the temple, and ye tooke me not. But all this
is done, that the scriptures of the Prophets might be fulfilled.
Then all the disciples forsoke him, and fled. And they toke
Jesus and led him to Cayphas the hye Priest, where the Scribes
and the Elders were assembled.

But Peter folowed hym afar of unto the hye Priestes palace;
and went in and sate with the seruauntes, to see thende. The
chiefe priestes and the elders and all the counsail sought false
wytnesse against Jesus, (for to put hym to death,) but found
none: yea, when many false wytnesses came, yet found they
none. At the last came ii false wytnesses, and sayde: This
felow sayd: I am able to destroy the temple of God, and to buylde
it againe in iii days. And the chiefe priest arose, and sayd unto
hym; aunswerest thou nothing? Why do these beare wytnes
against thee? But Jesus helde his peace. And the chiefe
priest aunswered and sayd unto him I charge thee by the lyuing
God, that thou tel us, whether thou be Christ the sonne of God.
Jesus sayd unto him: thou hast sayd. Neuerthelesse I say
unto you: hereafter shall ye see the sonne of man sitting on the
right hand of power, and comming in the cloudes of the skye.
Then the hye priest rent his clothes, saying: he hath spoken

blasphemy; what nede we of any mo wytnesses? Beholde, now ye haue heard his blasphemy; what thynke ye? They aunswered and sayd: he is worthy to dye. Then did they spyt in his face, and buffeted him with fystes. And other smote him on the face with the palme of their handes, saying: tel us thou Christ, who is he that smote thee? Peter sate without in the palace, and a damosel came to him, saying: thou also wast with Jesus of Galile: but he denied before the al, saying; I wot not what thou sayest. When he was gone out into the porche, another wenche sawe him, and sayd unto them that were there; This felow was also with Jesus of Nazareth. And agayne he denyed with an othe, saying: I do not know the man. And after a while came unto him they that stode by, and sayd unto Peter: surely thou art euē one of thē; for thy speche bewrayeth thee. Then began he to cursse and to sweare, that he knewe not the man. And immediatly the cocke krewe. And Peter remembred the worde of Jesu, whiche sayd unto him; before the cocke krow, thou shalt deny me thrise: and he went out and wept bitterly.

When the mornyng was come, all the chiefe priestes and the elders of the people helde a coūsaill against Jesus, to put hym to death, and brought him bound, and deliuered hym unto Poncius Pylate the deputie. Then Judas (whiche had betrayed him) seyng that he was cōdemned, repēted himselfe, and brought againe the xxx plates of siluer to the chiefe priestes and elders, saying; I have synned, betraying the innocent bloud. And they sayd; what is that to us? Se thou to that. And he cast downe the siluer plates in the temple, and departed, and went and hāged himselfe. And the chief Priestes toke the siluer plates, and said: It is not lawfull for to put them into the treasure, because it is the price of bloud. And thei toke councell, and bought with them a potters felde, to burie straungers in. Wherefore the felde is called Haceldema, that is, the felde of bloud, untill this day. Then was fulfilled that whiche was spoken by Jeremie the prophet, saying: and thei toke xxx siluer plates, the price of him that was valued, whom they bought of the children of Israel, and gaue them for the potters felde, as the Lord appointed me.

Jesus stode before the deputie, and the deputie asked hym, saying, Art thou the king of the Jewes? Jesus sayed unto hym: thou sayest. And when he was accused of the chief priestes and elders, he answered nothyng. Then said Pilate unto hym: hearest thou not howe many witnesses they laye agaynste thee?

And he answered him to neuer a worde, insomuche that the deputie maruayled greatly. At that feaste, the deputie was woont to delyuer unto the people a prisoner, whom they would desire. He had then a notable prisoner, called Barrabas. Therfore, when they were gathered together, Pylate sayd; whether wyll ye that I geue loce unto you, Barrabas, or Jesus whiche is called Christ? For he knewe that for enuy they had deliuered hym. When he was set doune to geue iudgement, his wyfe sent unto him, saying, haue thou nothyng to do with that iust man: For I haue suffred many thynges this day in my slepe because of hym. But the chiefe priestes and Elders persuaded the people that they shoulde aske Barrabas, and destroy Jesus. The deputie answered, and sayd unto them: whether of the twayne wyll ye that I let loce unto you? They sayd, Barrabas. Pylate sayd unto them, what shal I do then with Jesus, which is called Christ? They all sayd unto hym, let hym be crucified. The deputie sayd: what euill hath he done? But they cried the more, saying; let hym be crucified. When Pylate sawe that he could preuayle nothyng, but that more busynes was made, he toke water and washed his handes before the people, saying; I am innocent of the bloud of this iust person, ye shall see. Then answered all the people and sayd; his bloud be on us, and on our children.

Then let he Barrabas loce unto them, and skourged Jesus, and deliuered hym to be crucified. Then the souldiers of the deputie toke Jesus into the common hall, and gathered unto hym all the company: and they stripped hym, and put on hym a purple robe, and platted a croune of thornes, ànd put it upon his head, and a rede in his right hãde, and bowed the knee before him, and mocked him, saying: hayle kyng of the Jewes: and when they had spyt upõ him, thei toke the rede, and smote him on the head. And after that they had mocked him, they toke the robe of him agayne, and put his owne rayment on him, and led him away to crucifie him. And as they came out, they found a mã of Cirene (named Symon) him they compelled to beare his crosse. And they came unto the place whiche is called Golgotha, that is to say (a place of dead men sculles) and gaue hym vynegar to drynke myngled with gall. And when he had tasted therof, he would not drynke. When they had crucified hym, they parted his garmentes, and did cast lottes: that it might be fulfilled which was spoken by the Prophet; They parted my garmentes among them, and upon my vesture did they cast lottes. And they sate, and watched hym there, and set up ouer hys head the cause of his death, written; This is Jesus the kyng of the Jewes. Then were there ii theues crucified with him, one on the right hand, and another on the left. They that passed by reuyled him waggyng their heades, and saying: thou that destroyedst the temple of God, and dyddest buylde it in thre daies, saue thyselfe. If thou be the sonne of God, come doune from the crosse. Likewise also the high Priestes, mockyng hym, with the Scribes and Elders, sayd; he saued other, hymselfe he cannot saue. If he be the kyng of Israel, let hym nowe come doune from the crosse, and we will beleue hym. He trusted in God, let him deliuer him nowe, if he wyll haue him, for he sayed; I am the sonne of God. The theues also, whiche were crucifyed with him, cast the same in his teethe. From the sixt houre was there darkenesse ouer all the lande, untill the nynth houre. And aboute the nynth houre, Jesus cryed with a loude voyce, saying, *Ely, Ely, lamasabathany?* that is to say, My God, my God, why hast thou forsaken me? Some of them that stoode there, when they heard that, sayd: This man calleth for Helias. And straightway one of them ranne and toke a sponge, and when he had fylled it full of vyneger, he put it on a reede, and gaue hym to drinke. Other sayd: let be, let us see whether Helias will come and deliuer hym. Jesus, when he had cried agayne with a loude voyce, yelded up the ghost. And beholde, the vayle of the temple did rent into two partes, from the top to the botome, and the yerth did quake, and the stones rent, and graues did open, and many bodies of saintes, whiche slept, arose and went out of the graues after his resurreccion, and came into the holy citie, and appeared unto many.

When the Centurion, and they that were with him watchyng Jesus, sawe the yerthquake and those thynges whiche happened, they feared greatly, saying; Truely, this was the sōne of God. And many women were there, (beholdyng him afarre of,) whiche folowed Jesus from Galilee, ministring unto him: Emong whiche was Mary Magdalene, and Mary the mother of James and Joses, and the mother of Zebedes children.

¶ Monday before Easter.

The Epistle. Isaiah lxiii.

WHAT is he this, that commeth from Edom, with red-colored clothes of Bosra? (whiche is so costly clothe) and commeth in so mightely with all his strength? I am he that teacheth righteousnes and am of power to help. Wherfore then is thy clothyng red, and thy rayment lyke his that treadeth in the wyne presse? I haue troden the presse myselfe alone, and of all people there is not one with me.

Thus will I tread doune myne enemies in my wrath, and sette my feete upon them in mine indignacion. And their bloud shall bespryng my clothes, and so wil I stayne all my rayment. For the day of vengeaunce is assigned in my heart, and the yere when my people shalbe deliuered is come. I loked aboute me, and there was no man to shewe me any helpe. I meruayled that no man helde me up. Then I helde me by myne owne arme, and my feruentnes sustayned me. And thus will I tread doune the people in my wrath, and bathe them in my displeasure, and upon the yearth will I lay their strength.

I wil declare the goodnes of the lorde, yea and the praise of the Lorde for all that he hath geuen us, for the great good that he hath done for Israel; whiche he hath geuen them of his owne fauour, and accordyng to the multitude of his louyng-kyndnesses. For he sayd: these no doubte are my people and no shrinkyng children; and so he was their sauior. In their troubles, he was also troubled with them: and the Angell that wente furth from his presence, deliuered them. Of very loue and kyndnes that he had unto them, he redemed them. He hath borne them and caried them up, euer sence the worlde began: But after they prouoked him to wrath and vexed his holy mynde, he was their enemy, and fought againste them himselfe. Yet remembred Israell the olde tyme of Moses and hys people, saiyng; where is he that broughte them from the water of the sea, with them that fedde his shepe? where is he that hath geuen his holy spirite among them? he led thē by the right hand of Moses, with his glorious arme: deuidyng the water before them, (whereby he gate hymselfe an euerlastyng name) he led them in the depe, as an horsse is led in the playne, that they shoulde not stumble, as a tame beast goeth in the felde: and the breath geuen of God, geueth him rest.

Thus (O God) hast thou led thy people, to make thyselfe a glorious name withall. Looke doune then from heauen, and beholde the dwellyngplace of thy sanctuary and thy glory. Howe is it that thy gelousy, thy strengthe, the multitude of thy mercyes, and thy louynge kyndnes, will not be intreated of us? yet art thou oure father. For Abraham knoweth us not, neither is Israell acquaynted with us: But thou Lord, art our father and redemer, and thy name is euerlastynge. O Lorde, wherfore haste thou led us out of thy way? wherfore hast thou hardened our heartes, that we feare thee not? Be at one with us againe, for thy seruauntes sake, and for the generacion of thyne heritage. Thy people haue had but a litle of thy Sanctuary in possession, for oure enemyes haue troden doune the holy place. And we were thyne from the beginnyng, when thou wast not their Lorde, for they haue not called upon thy name.

The Gospel. Mark xiv.

AFTER two daies was Easter, and the dayes of swet bread. And the hie Priestes and the Scribes sought how they might take him by crafte, and put him to death. But they sayde; not in the feaste daye, leste any busynes arise among the people. And when he was at Bethany, in the house of Symon the leper, euen as he sate at meat, there came a womā hauying an Alabaster boxe of oyntment called Narde, that was pure and costly; and she brake the boxe, and powred it upon his head. And there were some that were not contente within themselues, and sayde: what neded this waste of oyntment? for it mighte haue been solde for more than ccc pence, and haue been geuen unto the poore. And they grudged agaynste her. And Jesus sayde: let her alone, why trouble ye her? She hath done a good worke on me: for ye haue poore with you alwayes, and whensoeuer ye wyll ye may do them good; but me haue ye not alwayes. She hath done that she coulde, she came aforehād to anoynte my body to the buriyng. Verely I saye unto you; whersoeuer this Gospell shalbe preached throughout the whole worlde, this also that she hath done, shalbe rehearsed in remembraunce of her.

And Judas Iscarioth, one of the xii, went awaye unto the hye priestes to betraye hym unto them. When they hearde that they were glad, and promised that they woulde geue him money. And he soughte howe he mighte conueniently betraye him. And the fyrste daye of swete bread, (when they offered Passeouer,) his disciples sayde unto him: where wilt thou that we go and prepare, that thou maiest eat the Passeouer? And he sēt furth two of his disciples, and sayd unto them; go ye into the citie, and there shall mete you a man bearyng a pitcher of water, folowe him. And whithersoeuer he goeth in, saye ye unto the goodman of the house, the master sayth; where is the gest-chāber, where I shall eate Passeouer with my disciples? And he wil shew you a great parlour paued and prepared: there make ready for us. And hys Discyples wente furth, and came into the citie, and founde as he had sayd unto them: and they made

ready the passeouer. And whē it was now euentide he came
with the xii. And as they sate at boorde, and did eate, Jesus
sayd, verely I say unto you, one of you (that eateth with me)
shall betraye me. And they began to be sory, and to say to him
one by one; is it I? and another sayd, is it I? he aunswered
and sayd unto them: it is one of the xii, euen he that dippeth
with me in the platter. The sonne of man truely goeth, as it is
written of him, but woe to that man by whome the sonne of man
is betrayed: Good were it for that man if he had neuer bene
borne. And as they dyd eate, Jesus tooke breade, and when
he had geuen thankes, he brake it, and gaue to them, and sayd:
Take, eate, this is my bodye. And he toke the cup, and when
he had geuen thankes he tooke it to them, and they all dranke
of it. And he sayd unto them, Thys is my bloude of the new
testament, whiche is shed for many. Verelye I saye unto you,
I will drynke no more of the fruycte of the vyne, untyll that day
that I drinke it newe in the kingdome of God. And when they
had sayde grace, they wente oute to the mount Oliuete.

And Jesus sayeth unto them, all ye shall be offended because of
me, this night. For it is written; I will smite the shepeherd and
the shepe shall bee skatered: but after that I am risen agayn,
I will goe into Galile before you. Peter sayd unto him; and
though all men be offended, yet wil not I. And Jesus sayeth
unto him; verely I say unto the, that this day, euen in this night
before the Cocke krowe twise, thou shalt denie me thre times.
But he spake more vehementlye: no, if I shoulde dye with thee,
I will not deny thee. Lykewise also sayde they all. And they
came into a place whiche was named Gethsemany: and he sayd
to hys disciples; sit ye here, while I goe asyde and pray. And
he taketh with hym Peter, and James, and John, and began to
waxe abashed and to be in an agonye, and sayd unto them My
soule is heauy, euē unto the death; tary ye here, and watche.
And he wente furth a litle, and fell downe flat on the ground,
and prayed: that if it were possible, the houre might passe from
hym. And he sayd; Abba father, al thinges are possible unto
the, take away this cup from me; neuerthelesse, not that I will,
but that thou wilte bee doone. And he came and founde them
sleping, and sayth to Peter: Simon slepest thou? Couldeste
thou not watche one houre? watche ye and pray, leste ye enter
into temptacion, the spirite truely is ready, but the flesh is weake.
And again he went aside and praied, and spake the same wordes.
And he returned and found them aslepe agayne, for their iyes
were heauye, neyther wiste they what to aunswere him. And

he came the third time and sayde unto them: slepe hencefoorthe, and take your ease, it is enoughe. The houre is come, beholde, the sonne of man is betrayed into the handes of sinners: Rise up, let us goe; loe, he that betrayeth me is at hande. And immediately while he yet spake, cummeth Judas, (which was one of the xii,) and with him a great noumber of people with sweordes and staues, from the hye priestes, and Scribes, and elders. And he that betrayed hym, had geuen them a generall token, saiyng; whosoeuer I doe kysse, the same is he; take hym and leade hym awaye warely. And as sone as he was come, he goth streghtway to him, and saith unto him, Master, Master; and kissed him: and they laid their handes on hym, and toke hym. And one of them that stode by drewe out a sweord, and smote a seruaunte of the hye prieste, and cut of his eare. And Jesus aūswered, and said unto them; ye be come out as unto a thefe with sweordes and staues for to take me: I was dayly with you in the temple teachyng, and ye toke me not: but these thynges come to passe that the Scriptures shoulde be fulfilled. And they al forsooke hym, and ranne awaie. And there folowed him a certaine yong man clothed in linnen upon the bare, and the yong men caughte hym, and he left his linnen garmente and fled from them naked. And they led Jesus awaye to the higheste pryeste of all, and with hym came all the hie priestes and the Elders and the Scribes. And Peter folowed hym a greate waye of, (euen tyll he was come into the palace of the hye prieste,) and he sate with the seruauntes, and warmed hymselfe at the fyre. And the hie priestes and all the counsaile sought for witnes against Jesu to put hym to deathe, and founde none: for manye bare false witnesse againste hym, but theyr witnesses agreed not together. And there arose certayn, and brought false witnes against hym, saiyng; wee hearde hym saye, I wyll destroye this temple that is made with handes, and within iii daies I wyll buylde another made withoute handes. But yet their witnesses agreed not together. And the hye prieste stode uppe among them, and asked Jesus saying; aunswerest thou nothyng? Howe is it that these beare witnesse against the? But he helde his peace, and answered nothing. Againe the hie prieste asked him, and said unto him; art thou Christ the sonne of the blessed? And Jesus said; I am. And ye shal see the sonne of manne sitting on the righte hande of power, and comming in the cloudes of heauen. Then the hie priest rent his clothes, and said, what ned we any further of wytnesses? ye haue heard blasphemy, what thynke ye? And they all cōdemned him to be worthy of death. And some began to spyt at hym, and to couer his face, and to beate hym with fystes, and to saye unto hym; arede, and the seruauntes buffeted hym on the face. And as Peter was beneth in the palace, there came one of the wenches of the hieste prieste, and when she sawe Peter warmyng himselfe, she loked on hym, and said; waste not thou also with Jesus of Nazareth? And he deined, saying, I knowe hym not, neyther wote I what thou sayest. And he wĕt out into the porche, and the Cock krewe. And a damosel (when she sawe him) began again to saye to them that stode by: thys is one of them. And he denied it againe. And anone after they that stode by, said againe unto Peter: surely thou art one of them, for thou art of Galile, and thy speche agreeth therto. But he beganne to curse and to sweare, saying, I knowe not this man of whome ye speake. And agayne the Cocke krewe, and Peter remembred the worde that Jesus had sayd unto hym; before the Cocke crowe twyse, thou shalt deny me thre tymes. And he began to wepe.

¶ Tewesday before Easter.

The Epistle.   Esai. l.

THE Lorde God hath opened myne eare, therfore can I not saye naye, neither withdrawe myselfe: but I offre my backe unto the smiters, and my chekes to the nyppers: I turne not my face from shame and spittyng, and the Lorde God shall helpe me, therfore shall I not bee confounded. I haue hardened my face lyke a flynte stone, for I am sure that I shall not come to confusion. He is at hande that iustifyeth me, who will then go to lawe with me? Let us stande one against another; yf there be any that will reason with me, lette hym come here forth unto me. Beholde the Lorde God standeth by me, what is he then that can condemne me? loe, they shall bee all lyke as an olde clothe, the mothe shall eate them up.

Therfore, whoso feareth the Lorde among you, lette hym heare the voyce of his seruaunte. Whoso walketh in darkenesse, and no lyght shyneth upon him, lette him put his trust in the name of the Lorde, and holde hym by his God: but take hede, ye all kyndle a fyre of the wrathe of God, and steare up the coales: walke on in the glisteryng of youre owne fyre, and in the coales that ye haue kindled. This commeth unto you from my hande, namely that ye shall slepe in sorowe.

The Gospell. Mark xv.

AND anone in the dawnynge, the hye priestes helde a counsaile with the Elders and the Scribes, and the whole congregacion, and bounde Jesus, and led hym awaye, and delyuered hym to Pilate. And Pilate asked hym: art thou the kyng of the Jewes? and he answered and sayd to hym; thou saiest it. And the hie priestes accused him of many thynges. So Pilate asked him again, saiyng: aunswerest thou nothing? Beholde howe many thinges they lay to thy charge. Jesus aunswered yet nothyng, so that Pilate meruailed. At that feast Pilate dyd deliuer unto them a priesoner, whomsoeuer they woulde desire. And there was one that was named Barrabas, whiche laye bounde with them that made insurreccion: he had committed murther. And the people called unto him, and beganne to desyre him, that he woulde doe according as he had euer done unto them. Pilate answered them, saiyng: will ye that I lette loce unto you the King of the Jewes? For he knewe that the hye priestes had deliuered him of enuye. But the hye priestes moued the people, that he shoulde rather deliuer Barrabas unto them. Pilate answered againe, and saide unto them; what will ye that I then do unto hym, whom ye cal the kyng of the Jewes? And they cryed againe, crucifye hym. Pilate saide unto them: what eiuill hathe he doone? And they cryed the more feruentlye, crucifie hym. And so Pilate wyllyng to contente the people, lette loce Barrabas unto them, and deliuered up Jesus (when he had scorged him) for to be crucified. And the souldiours ledde hym awaye into the common hall, and called together the whole multitude, and they clothed hym wyth purple, and they platted a croune of thornes and crouned him withall, and began to salute him; Hayle kyng of the Jewes. And they smote hym on the heade with a reede, and did spit upon him, and bowed their knees and worshypped him. And when they had mocked him, they toke the purple of him, and put hys owne clothes on him, and led him out to crucify him. And they compelled one that passed by called Simon of Cirene, (the father of Alexander and Rufus,) whyche came out of the feld to beare his crosse. And they brought hym to a place named Golgotha (whiche if a manne interprete it, is the place of dead mens sculles) and they gaue him to drinke wyne mingled with mirre, but he receaued it not.

And when they had crucifyed hym, they parted hys garmentes, castyng lottes upon them what euery man should take. And it was about the third houre, and they crucyfied him. And the title of hys cause was wrytten, The kyng of the Jewes. And they crucified with hym two theues; the one on his right hand, and the other on hys left. And the scripture was fulfylled, which sayeth; he was coūted among the wicked. And they that went by, rayled on him; wagging their heades and saying; A wretche, thou that destroyest the temple and buildest it againe in thre dayes; saue thyselfe and come doune from the crosse. Lykewyse also mocked hym the hye priestes among themselues, with the scribes, and sayd; he saued other men, himself he cannot saue. Let Christ the king of Irsael descende nowe from the crosse, that we maye see and beleue. And they that were crucyfied with hym, checked hym also. And when the sixt houre was come, darcknes arose ouer all the earth until the ninth houre. And at the nynth houre Jesus cryed with a loude voyce, saying; *Eloy, Eloy, lamasabathany ?* whyche is, (if one interprete it,) my God, my God, why hast thou forsaken me? And some of them that stoode by, when they heard that, sayd; behold, he calleth for Helias. And one ranne and fylled a sponge full of vineger, and put it on a reede, and gaue hym to dryncke, saiyng; let him alone, let us se whether Helias will come and take hym downe. But Jesus cryed with a loude voyce, and gaue up the gost. And the vayle of the temple rente in ii peces, from the top to the bottom. And when the Centurion (which stoode before him) sawe that he so cryed, and gaue up the gost, he sayde: truely this man was the sonne of god. There were also weomen a good way of, beholding him; among whome was Marye Magdalene and Marye the mother of James the litle, and of Joses, and Mary Salome (which also whē he was in Galile had folowed him, and ministred unto him;) and many other weomē, which came up with him to Jerusalem. And nowe when the euen was come, (because it was the day of preparyng that goeth before the Sabboth,) Joseph of the citie of Aramathia, a noble coūsailor, whiche also loked for the kingdome of God, came and went in boldely unto Pilate, and begged of hym the body of Jesu. And Pilate marueiled that he was alredy dead, and called unto hym the Centurion, and asked of him, whether he had bene any while dead. And when he knewe the trueth of the Centurion, he gaue the bodye to Joseph. And he bought a linnen cloth, and toke him down, and wrapped him in the linnen cloth, and laied him in a sepulchre that was hewen out of a rocke, and rolled a stone before the dore of the sepulchre. And Mary Magdalene, and Mary Joses behelde where he was layde.

¶ *Wednesday before Easter.*

The Epistle. Heb. ix.

WHEREAS is a testament, there must also (of necessitie) be the death of him that maketh the testament. For the testament taketh aucthorite whē men are dead; for it is yet of no value, as long as he that maketh the testament is aliue, for whiche cause also, neither the first testament was ordayned without bloude. For when Moyses had declared all the commaundemente to all the people, according to the lawe, he tooke the bloude of calues and of Goates, with water, and purple wolle, and ysope, and sprinckled both the booke, and al the people, saying: this is the bloud of the testament, which god hath appoynted unto you. Moreouer, he sprinkled the tabernacle with bloude also, and all the ministring vessels. And almost all thinges are by the lawe purged with bloud, and without sheading of bloude is no remission. It is nede then, that the similitudes of heauenlye thynges bee purifyed with suche thinges; but that the heauenly thynges themselues, bee purifyed with better sacrifices thē are those. For Christ is not entred into the holye places that are made with handes, (whiche are similitudes of true thynges,) but is entred into very heauen, for to appeare now in the sight of god for us; not to offer himselfe often, as the hie priest entreth into the holye place euerye yere with strange bloud: for then must he haue oftē suffred sence the world began. But now in the end of the world hath he appeared once, to put sinne to flight by the offeryng up of hymselfe. And as it is appoynted unto al men that they shal once dye, and then cometh the iudgement: euen so Christ was once offered to take away the sinnes of many, and unto them that looke for hym shall he appeare agayne without sinne unto saluacion.

The Gospel. Luke xxii.

THE feast of swete bread drew nye, which is called Easter, and the hye priestes and Scribes sought howe they myght kill him; for they feared the people. Then entred Sathan into Judas, whose sirname was Iscarioth (whiche was of the numbre of the xii) and he went his waye and commoned with the hye priestes and officers, how he might betray hym unto them. And they were glad, and promysed to geue him moneye. And he consented, and sought oportunitie to betraye him unto them when the people were awaye. Then came the daye of swete breade, when of necessitie passeouer must be offred.   And he sent Peter and John, saying; go and prepare us the passeouer, that we maye eate.   They sayed unto him; where wilt thou that we prepare?   And he saied unto them; behold, when ye entre into the citie, there shall a man mete you bearing a pitcher of water, him folowe into the same house that he entreth in, and ye shall saye unto the good man of the house; the maister saieth unto the; where is the gest-chambre, where I shall eate the passeouer with my disciples?   And he shall shewe you a greate parlour paued; there make ready.   And they went, and found as he had sayed unto them, and they made ready the passeouer.   And when the houre was come, he sat doune, and the xii Apostles with him.   And he sayed unto them; I haue inwardly desired to eate this passeouer with you before that I suffre.   For I saye unto you; henceforth I wyll not eate of it any more, untill it be fulfilled in the kingdome of God.   And he tooke the cup, and gaue thankes, and sayed; Take this and deuide it amõg you. For I saye unto you; I wyll not drinke of the fruite of the vine, untill the kingdome of God come.   And he toke bread, and when he had geuen thankes, he brake it, and gaue unto them, saying; This is my body, whiche is geuen for you: This do in the re-membraunce of me.   Likewyse also when he had supped, he tooke the cup, saying; This cup is the new testamente in my bloude, whiche is shed for you.   Yet beholde, the hande of him that betraieth me is with me on the table.   And truely the sonne of man gooeth as it is appoynted; but woe unto that manne by whom he is betrayed.   And they began to enquire among them-selfes which of them it was that should do it.

And there was a striefe among them, whiche of them shoulde seme to bee greatteste.   And he sayde unto them; the kynges of nacions reigne ouer them, and they that haue authoritye upon them, are called gracious Lordes: but ye shall not so bee. But he that is greatteste among you, shal bee as the yonger, and he that is chiefe shalbe as he that doth minister.   For whether is greater, he that sitteth at meate, or he that serueth?   Is it not he that sitteth at meate?   But I am among you, as he that ministreth.   Ye are they which haue bydden with me in my temptacions.   And I appointe unto you a kyngdome, as my father hath apointed to me, that ye maye eate and drynke at my table in my kyngdome, and sitte on seates, iudgyng the xii tribes of Israell.   And the lorde said; Simon, Simon behold, Sathan hath desired to sift you, as it were wheat: But I haue praied for thee, that thy faith fayle not: And when thou arte

conuerted, strength thy brethren. And he saide unto hym;
Lorde, I am readye to go with thee into prieson, and to death.
And he said; I tel thee Peter, the Cocke shall not krow this
daye, tyl thou haue thrise denied that thou knoweste me. And
he sayde unto them; when I sent you without wallette, and
scrip, and shoes, lacked ye any thyng? And they said, no.
Then saide he unto them; but nowe he that hath a wallette,
lette him take it uppe, and lykewyse hys scrippe. And he that
hath no sworde, let hym sell his coate, and by one. For I saye
unto you, that yet the same whiche is written must be performed in me; euen among the wicked was he reputed: For
those thinges whiche are written of me haue an ende. And they
sayde: lorde, behold, here are ii swordes, and he saide unto them,
it is ynoughe. And he came oute, and wente (as he was wonte)
to Mounte Oliuete. And the disciples folowed hym. And
when he came to the place, he saide unto them; praye, leste ye
fal into temptacion. And he gate hymselfe from them aboute a
stones caste, and kneled doune and praied, saiyng; Father, if
thou wilte, remoue thys cup from me: Neuerthelesse, not my
will, but thyne bee fulfilled. And there appeared an Aungel
unto hym from heauen, coumfortyng hym. And he was in an
agony and prayed the lenger; and his sweate was like droppes of
bloud, trickling down to the groūd. And when he arose from
prayer, and was come to hys disciples, he founde them slepyng
for heauinesse, and he sayde unto them; why slepe ye? Ryse
and praye, leste ye fall into temptacion. Whyle he yet spake,
beholde, there came a company, and he that was called Judas,
one of the xii, went before them, and preased nye unto Jesus, to
kisse him. But Jesus sayde unto him; Judas, betrayeste thou
the sonne of man with a kysse? When they whiche were about
hym sawe what woulde folowe, they sayde unto him; Lorde,
shall we smyte with the sweorde? And one of them smote a
seruaunte of the hye prieste, and stroke of his right eare. Jesus
aunswered and sayde: suffre ye thus farre foorth. And when
he touched hys eare, he healed hym. Then Jesus sayde unto
the hye priestes, and rulers of the temple, and the Elders,
whiche were come to him. Ye be come out as unto a thefe, with
sweordes and staues. When I was dayly with you in the
temple, ye stretched foorth no handes agaynste me: but thys is
euen your very houre, and the power of darkenes. Then toke
they him and led hym, and brought him to the hye priestes
house. But Peter folowed afarre of. And when they had
kindled a fyer in the middes of the palace, and were set downe

together; Peter also sate downe among them. But when one of the wenches behelde him, as he sate by the fyer, (and loked upon him,) she sayd; this same felowe was also with hym. And he denyed him, saying: woman, I knowe him not. And after a litle whyle, another sawe him, and sayde: thou art also of them. And Peter sayd; man, I am not. And about the space of an houre after, another affirmed, saying; verely, thys felowe was with him also, for he is of Galile. And Peter said, man, I wot not what thou sayeste. And immediately whyle he yet spake, the Cocke krew. And the Lorde turned backe and looked upon Peter. And Peter remembred the word of the lord, how he had sayde unto him; before the Cocke krowe thou shalt denye me thrise: and Peter wente out and wept bitterly.

And the men that toke Jesus mocked him, and smote him: and whē they had blindfolded him, they stroke him on the face, and asked hym, saying; arede, who is he that smote thee? And many other thynges despitefully sayde they agaynst him. And as sone as it was daye, the Elders of the people, and the hye priestes and Scrybes, came together, and led hym into theyr counsell, saying; Art thou very Christ? tell us. And he sayd unto them, if I tell you ye will not beleue me, and if I aske you, you will not answer me, nor let me goe: hereafter shal the sonne of mā sit on the right hande of the power of god. Then sayd they all; Art thou then the sonne of god? He sayde: ye saye that I am. And they sayd; what nede we of any further witnes? for we ourselues haue heard of his owne mouth.

¶ *At Euensong.*

The First Lesson, Lamenta. i. unto the ende.

¶ *Thursday before Easter.*

At Mattins.

The First Lesson, Lamentations ii. unto the end.

The Epistle. 1 Cor. xi.

THIS I warne you of, and commende not, that ye come not together after a better maner, but after a woorse. For fyrste of all, when ye come together in the congregacyon; I heare that there is discencion among you, and I partly beleue it. For there muste bee sectes amonge you, that they whiche are perfecte among you maye be knowen. When ye come together therfore into one place, the lordes supper cānot be eaten, for euery man beginneth afore to eate his owne supper. And one is hungry, and another is dronken. Haue ye not houses to eate and drynke

in? despise ye the congregacion of God, and shame them that
haue not? what shall I say unto you? shall I praise you? In
this I praise you not. That whiche I deliuered unto you, I
receyued of the Lord. For the Lord Jesus, the same night in
whiche he was betrayed, tooke bread; and when he had geuen
thankes, he brake it, and sayd, Take ye and eate, this is my
body, which is broken for you. This do ye in the remembraunce of me. After the same maner also he tooke the cup
whē supper was done, saying; this cuppe is the new testament
in my bloud: This do, as oft as ye drynk it, in remembraunce of
me. For as often as ye shall eate this bread, and drinke this
cup, ye shall shewe the Lordes death tyll he come. Wherfore,
whosoeuer shall eate of this bread, or drynke of the cup of the
Lorde unworthely, shalbe giltie of the bodye and bloud of the
Lord. But let a man examine himselfe, and so let hym eate of
the bread, and drynke of the cuppe. For he that eateth and
drynketh unworthely, eateth and drynketh his own damnacion,
because he maketh no differēce of the Lordes body. For this
cause many are weake and sicke among you, and many slepe.
For if we had iudged ourselues, we should not haue been iudged.
But when we are iudged of the Lord, we are chastened, that we
should not be damned with the worlde. Wherfore my brethren,
when ye come together to eate, tary one for another. If any
mā hongre, let him eate at home; that ye come not together unto
condemnacion. Other thynges will I set in ordre when I come.

The Gospell. Luke xxiii.

THE whole multitude of them arose, and led hym unto Pylate.
And they began to accuse him, saying; we founde this felowe
peruertyng the people, and forbydding to paye tribute to Cesar;
saying that he is Christe a kyng. And Pylate apposed hym,
saying; art thou the king of the Jewes? he answered him and
sayd, thou sayest it. Then sayd Pilate to the hye priestes and
the people; I fynde no faute in this manne. And they were the
more fierce, saying; he moueth the people, teachyng throughout
all Jury, and began at Galile, euen to this place. When Pylate
heard mencion of Galile, he asked whether the manne were of
Galile. And as sone as he knew that he belonged unto Herodes
iurisdiccion, he sent hym to Herode, whiche was also at Jerusalem
at that tyme. And when Herode sawe Jesus he was excedyng
glad; for he was desirous to see hym of along season, because
he had heard many thinges of hym, and he trusted to haue
seen some myracle done by hym. Then he questioned with

hym many wordes. But he answered hym nothyng. The hye
priestes and Scribes stode furth and accused him straightly. And
Herode with his menne of warre despised hym. And when he
had mocked hym, he arayed hym in whyte clothing, and sente
him againe to Pylate. And the same daye Pylate and Herode
were made frendes together. For before thei were at variaüce.
And Pilate called together the hye priestes, and the rulers, and
the people, and sayd unto them; ye haue brought this mā unto
me, as one that peruerteth the people: and, behold, I examine
hym before you, and finde no faute in this mā of those thynges
wherof ye accuse him, no nor yet Herode: For I sent you unto
him, and loe, nothing worthy of death is done unto him: I will
therfore chasten him and let hym looce. For of necessitie he
must haue let one loce unto thē at that feast. And all the people
cryed at once, saying; away with him, and deliuer us Barrabas:
(whiche for a certayne insurreccion made in the citie, and for a
murther, was cast in prisō.) Pilate spake again unto thē, willing
to let Jesus looce. But they cryed, saying; crucifye hym,
crucifye hym. He sayed unto them the thirde tyme, what euyll
hath he done? I fynde no cause of death in hym: I will therfore chasten hym, and let him go. And they cried with loude
voices; requiring that he myght be crucifyed. And the voices
of them and of the hie priestes preuailed. And Pilate gaue
sentence that it shoulde be as they required, and he let loce unto
them him that (for insurreccion and murther) was cast into
pryson, whom they had desired; and he deliuered to them Jesus,
to do with hym what they would. And as they led him away,
they caught one Symon of Ciren, commyng out of the fielde:
and on him laide they the crosse, that he myght beare it after
Jesus. And there folowed him a great cōpanye of people, and
of womē, which bewayled and lamented him. But Jesus turned
backe unto them, and sayd; ye daughters of Jerusalem, wepe
not for me; but wepe for yourselfes, and for your children. For
beholde, the dayes wyll come, in the which they shall say;
Happy are the baren, and the wombes that neuer bare, and the
pappes which neuer gaue sucke. Then shaꝡ they begynne to
saye to the mountaynes; fall on us, and to the hylles, couer us.
For if they do this in a grene tree, what shalbe done in the drye?
And there were two euylldoers led with him to be slaine. And
after that they were come to the place (which is called Caluarie),
there they crucyfied him, and the euilldoers, one on the ryght
hand, and the other on the left. Then said Jesus, father forgeue
them, for they wote not what they do. And they parted hys

rayment, and cast lottes. And the people stoode and behelde. And the rulers mocked hym with them, saiyng: he saued other menne, lette hym saue hymselfe yf he be very Christ the chosen of God.

The souldiers also mocked him, and came and offred him vineger, and sayd; if thou be the kyng of the Jewes, saue thyselfe. And a superscripciõ was writtē ouer him with letters of Greke, and Latin, and Hebrue; this is the kyng of the Jewes. And one of the euildoers, which wer hanged, railed on him, saiyng; If thou be Christ, saue thyselfe and us. But the other answered and rebuked hym, saiyng; fearest thou not God, seyng thou art in the same damnacion? we are righteously punyshed, for we receiue according to our dedes: but this man hath done nothing amysse. And he sayd unto Jesus; Lorde, remembre me when thou commest into thy kyngdom. And Jesus sayd unto hym, verely I saye unto thee; to-daye shalt thou be with me in Paradise. And it was about the vi houre: and there was a darkenesse ouer all the earth untyll the ix houre, and the Sonne was darkened. And the vayle of the temple did rent, euē through the middes. And when Jesus had cryed with a loude voyce, he sayd: father, into thy handes I commende my spirite. And when he thus had said, he gaue up the ghost. When the Centurion saw what had happened, he gloryfied God, saiyng; verely this was a righteous man. And all the people that came together to that syght, and sawe the thynges which had happened, smote their brestes, and returned. And all his acquaintaunce, and the women that folowed him from Galilee, stoode afarre of beholdyng these thynges. And, behold, there was a man named Joseph a consailor, and he was a good man, and a iust: the same had not consented to the counsaill and dede of them, which was of Aramathia, a citie of the Jewes, which same also waited for the kyngdome of God: he went unto Pylate and begged the bodye of Jesus, and tooke it doune, and wrapped it in a lynnen cloth, and layd it in a sepulchre that was hewen in stone, wherin neuer man before had beene layde. And that daye was the preparyng of the sabboth, and the Sabboth drue on. The women that followed after, whyche had come with him from Galilee, behelde the sepulchre, and howe hys body was layde. And they returned and prepared swete Odours and ointmentes; But rested on the Sabboth daye, accordyng to the commaundement.

At Euensong.

The first Lesson, Lamentations iii. unto the end.

On good Fryday.

At Mattins.

The first Lesson, Gen. xxii.   Unto the ende.

The Collect.

ALMIGHTIE god, we beseche thee graciously to behold this thy famely, for the which our lord Jesus Christ was contented to bee betrayed, and geuen up into the handes of wicked men, and to suffre death upon the crosse: who liueth and reigneth, &c.

At the Communion.

Deus, Deus meus.   Psalm xxii.

My God, my God, (loke upō me;) why hast thou forsaken me : and art so farre from my health, and from the wordes of my complaint?

O my God, I cry in the daye-time, but thou hearest not : and in the night season also I take no reste.

And thou continuest holy : O thou worship of Israel.

Oure fathers hoped in thee : they trusted in thee, and thou diddest deliuer them.

They called upō thee, and were helped : they put their trust in thee, and were not confounded.

But as for me, I am a worme and no manne : a verye skorne of men, and the outcaste of the people.

All they that see me, laugh me to skorne : they shote out their lippes, and shake the head, saying.

He trusted in God that he would deliuer hym : let hym deliuer him, if he will haue hym.

But thou arte he that tooke me oute of my mothers wombe : thou waste my hope when I hanged yet upon my mother's brestes.

I haue been left unto thee euer sence I was borne : thou art my God, euen from my mothers wombe.

O, go not from me, for trouble is here at hande : and there is none to helpe me.

Many Oxen are come aboute me : fat Bulles of Basan close me in on euery syde.

They gape upon me with their mouthes : as it were a rampyng and roaryng Lyon.

I am powred out like water, and all my bones are out of ioynt : my heart also in the middes of my body is euen like meltyng waxe.

My strength is dryed up like a potsherd, and my tōgue cleaueth to my gummes : and thou shalte bryng me into the duste of death.

For (many) dogges are come aboute me : and the counsail of the wicked laye siege against me.

They pearsed my handes and my feete : I may tell all my bones, they stande staryng and lokyng upon me.

They parte my garmentes among them : and cast lottes upon my vesture.

But be not thou farre from me, O Lorde : thou art my succour, haste thee to helpe me.

Deliuer my soule from the sworde : my derlyng from the power of the dogge.

Saue me from the Lyons mouth : thou hast heard me also from among the hornes of Unicornes.

I will declare thy name unto my brethren : in the myddes of the congregacion will I prayse thee.

O prayse the Lorde, ye that feare hym : magnifie hym, all ye of the seede of Jacob, and feare ye hym, all ye seede of Israel.

For he hath not despised nor abhorred the lowe estate of the poore : he hath not hid his face from him, but when he called unto him, he heard him.

My prayse is of thee in the greate congregacion : my vowes will I performe in the sight of them that feare him.

The poore shall eate, and be satisfied : they that seke after the Lorde shall praise him, your hearte shall liue for euer.

All the endes of the worlde shal remembre themselues, and be turned unto the Lorde : and all the kynreds of the nacions shall woorship before him.

For the kyngdome is the Lordes : and he is the gouernour among the people.

All suche as be fat upon yearth : haue eaten, and woorshipped.

All they that go doune into the dust shal kneele before him : and no man hath quickened his owne soule.

My seede shal serue him : they shalbe counted unto the Lorde for a generacion.

They shall come, and the heauens shall declare his righteousnes : unto a people that bee borne, whome the Lorde hath made.

Glory be to the father, and to the sonne, &c.

As it was in the beginning, &c.

¶ After the ii Collectes at the Communion shalbe sayd these ii Collectes folowyng.

The Collecte.

ALMYGHTYE and euerlastyng God, by whose spirite the whole body of the Churche is gouerned and sanctified; receiue our supplicacions and prayers, whiche wee offre before thee for all estates of men in thy holye congregacion, that euerye membre of the same, in his vocacion and ministerye, maye truelye and godlye serue thee; thoroughe our Lord Jesus Christe.

MERCYFULL God, who hast made all men, and hatest nothyng that thou hast made, nor wouldest the deathe of a synner, but rather that he should be conuerted and liue; haue mercy upon all Jewes, Turkes, Infidels, and heretikes, and take from thē all ignoraunce, hardnes of heart, and contempt of thy word: and so fetche them home, blessed Lorde, to thy flocke, that they maye bee saued among the remnant of the true Israelites, and be made one folde under one shepeherde, Jesus Christ our Lord; who lyueth and reigneth, &c.

The Epistle. Heb. **x.**

THE lawe (whiche hathe but a shadowe of good thynges to come, and not the very fashion of thynges themselues) can neuer with those sacrifices, whiche they offre yere by yere continually, make the cōmers therunto perfite. For woulde not then those sacrifices haue ceased to haue been offred, because that the offerers once purged should haue had no more consciēce of sinnes? Neuertheles in those sacrifices is there mencion made of synnes euery yeare. For the bloud of Oxen and Goates cannot take away sinnes. Wherfore, when he commeth into the worlde, he sayeth, Sacrifice and offeryng thou wouldest not haue, but a body hast thou ordained me. Burnt-offeringes also for sinne hast thou not allowed. Then sayed I; lo, I am here. In the beginning of the booke it is written of me, that I should do thy wil, O God. Aboue, when he sayeth, Sacrifice and offeryng, and burnt sacrifices, and synne-offerynges thou wouldest not haue, neither hast thou allowed them, (whiche yet are offered by the lawe,) then sayed he; lo, I am here to do thy wyll, O God: he taketh awaye the first to establishe the later, by the which wille, we are made holye, euen by the offeryng of the bodye of Jesu Christ once for all.

And euery priest is ready daily ministring and offering often-tymes one manner of Oblacion, whiche can neuer take awaye sinnes. But this man, after he hath offered one sacrifice for sinnes, is set doune for euer on the righte hand of God; and from hencefoorth tarieth tyll his foes be made his footestoole. For with one offeryng hathe he made perfect for euer, them that are sanctified. The holye ghost himselfe also beareth us recorde, euen when he told before; This is the testament that I wil make unto thē: After those dayes (sayth the lord) I wil put my lawes in their heartes, and in their myndes wil I write them, and their sinnes and iniquities will I remember no more. And where remission of these thinges is, there is no more offeryng for sinnes. Seeing therfore brethren that by the meanes of the bloud of Jesu, we haue liberty to enter into the holy place by the newe and liuyng waye, which he hath prepared for us, through the vayle (that is to saye, by his fleshe): And seyng also that we haue an hie priest whiche is ruler ouer the house of God, let us drawe nye with a true heart in a sure fayth, sprinkeled in our heartes from an euil conscience, and washed in our bodies with pure water : Let us kepe the profession of our hope, without wauering; (for he is faythfull that promised) and let us considre one another, to the intent that we may prouoke unto loue, and to good weorkes, not forsakyng the felowshyp that we haue among ourselues, as the maner of some is; but lette us exhorte one another, and that so muche the more, because ye see that the day draweth nye.

The Gospel. John xviii. xix.

WHEN Jesus had spoken these woordes, he went furth with his disciples ouer the broke Cedron where was a garden, into the whiche he entred with his disciples. Judas also whiche betrayed him, knewe the place: for Jesus oftetymes resorted thither with hys disciples. Judas then, after he had receiued a bend of men, (and ministers of the hye priestes and Phariseis,) came thither with Lanterns and fyerbrandes and weapons. And Jesus, knowing al thinges that should come on him, went furth, and said unto thē, whome seke ye? They answered him; Jesus of Nazareth. Jesus sayeth unto them; I am he. Judas also whiche betrayed him, stoode with them. As sone then as he had sayde unto them; I am he, they went backeward, and fel to the ground. Then asked he them again; whome seke ye? They saide: Jesus of Nazareth. Jesus aunswered; I haue tolde you that I am he. If ye seke me therfore, let these goe theyr way: that the saying might be fulfilled, whiche he spake; Of them whiche thou gauest me, haue I not lost one. Then Simon Peter hauing a sword, drew it, and smote the hye priestes seruaunt, and cut of his right eare. The seruauntes name was

Malchus. Therfore sayeth Jesus unto Peter, put up thy sweorde into thy sheathe: shall I not drinke of the cup whiche my father hath geuen me? Then the cumpany and the capitayne, and the ministers of the Jewes, toke Jesus, and bound him, and led him away to Anna first; for he was father in law to Cayphas, whiche was the hye prieste the same yere. Cayphas was he that gaue coūsel to the Jewes, that it was expedient that one man shoulde dye for the people. And Simon Peter folowed Jesus, and so dyd another disciple: that disciple was knowen to the hye priest, and wēt in with Jesus into the palace of the hye priest. But Peter stoode at the doore without. Then wente out tha other disciple, (whiche was knowen to the hye priest,) and spake to the damosell that kept the doore, and broughte in Peter. Then said the damosel that kept the doore unto Peter; Art not thou also one of this mās disciples? he sayd, I am not. The seruauntes and ministers stode there, whiche had made a fyer of coales; for it was colde, and they warmed themselues. Peter also stode among them, and warmed himselfe. The hye priest then asked Jesus of his disciples, and of hys doctryne. Jesus aunswered him; I spake openly in the worlde, I euer taughte in the Sinagoge, and in the tēple, whither al the Jewes haue resorted, and in secrete haue I said nothyng. Why askest thou me? Aske them whiche heard me, what I sayde unto them. Beholde they can tell what I sayde. When he had thus spoken, one of the ministers, whiche stoode by, smote Jesus on the face, saying; Aunswerest thou the hie priest so? Jesus aunswered him; If I haue eiuill spoken, beare witnesse of the euill: But if I haue well spoken, why smitest thou me? And Annas sent him bounde unto Cayphas, the hye priest. Simon Peter stoode and warmed himselfe. Then sayde they unto him. Art not thou also one of his disciples? he denied it, and said; I am not. One of the seruantes of the hye priestes (his cosin whose eare Peter smote of) said unto him; did not I se thee in the garden with him? Peter therfore denied againe, and immediatly the Cocke krewe. Then led they Jesus from Cayphas into the hal of iudgement. It was in the morning; and they themselfes wēt not into the iudgement hall, leste thei should be defiled, but that thei might eate the Passeouer. Pylate then went out to them and sayd; what accusacion bryng you against this mā? They answered and sayd unto him; If he were not an euildoer, we would not have deliuered hym unto thee. Then sayed Pylate unto them; take ye him, and iudge him after your owne lawe. The Jewes therfore sayd unto him; It is not

lawful for us to put any man to death: that the woordes of
Jesus myght bee fulfilled, whiche he spake, signifying what
death he should dye. Then Pilate entred into the iudgemēt
hal again, and called Jesus, and sayd unto him; Art thou the
king of the Jewes? Jesus answered; sayest thou that of
thyself, or did other tel it thee of me? Pilate answered; am I
a Jew? Thine owne nacion and hye priestes haue deliuered
thee unto me: what hast thou done? Jesus āswered; my
kingdome is not of this worlde: if my kingdome were of this
worlde, then woulde my ministers surely fight, that I should not
be deliuered to the Jewes: but now is my kyngdom not frō
hence. Pilate therfore sayd unto hym; Art thou a kyng then?
Jesus answered; thou sayest that I am a kyng. For this cause
was I borne, and for this cause came I into the world, that I
shoulde bear wytnes unto the trueth. And all that are of the
trueth, heare my voyce. Pylate sayd unto hym, what thyng
is trueth? And whē he had sayd this, he wēt out again unto
the Jewes, and sayth unto thē; I finde in him no cause at al.
Ye haue a custome, that I should deliuer you one loce at Easter:
wil ye that I loce unto you the king of the Jewes? Then cryed
they all again, saying: Not him, but Barrabas: the same
Barrabas was a murtherer. Then Pilate toke Jesus therfore
and scourged hym. And the souldiers woūd a croune of thornes,
and put it on his head. And thei did on hym a purple garment,
and came unto hym and sayed; hayle kyng of the Jewes: and
they smote hym on the face. Pylate went furth agayne, and
sayed unto them; behold, I bring him furth to you, that ye
may knowe that I finde no faulte in hym. Then came Jesus
forth, wearyng a croune of thorne, and a robe of purple. And
he sayth unto them; beholde the man. When the hye priestes
therfore and ministers sawe hym, they cryed; crucifie hym,
crucifye him. Pylate sayeth unto them; take ye hym, and
crucifye him, for I fynde no cause in hym. The Jewes aunswered hym; we haue a lawe, and by oure lawe, he ought to
dye; because he made himselfe the sonne of God. When
Pilate heard that saying, he was the more afrayde: and went
agayne into the iudgement halle, and sayeth unto Jesus;
whence art thou? But Jesus gaue him none answer. Thē sayd
Pilate unto him; Speakest thou not unto me? knowest thou
not that I haue power to crucifie thee, and haue power to looce
thee? Jesus answered; Thou couldest haue no power at all
against me, except it were giuē thee frō aboue. Therfore he
that deliuered me unto thee, hath the more sinne. And from

thēcefurth sought Pilate meanes to looce him: but the Jews cryed, saying: yf thou let hym goe, thou arte not Cesar's frende: for whosoeuer maketh hymselfe a kyng is against Cesar. Whē Pilate heard that saying, he brought Jesus furth, and sate downe to geue sentence in a place that is called the Pauemēt, but in the Hebrue tong Gabbatha. It was the preparyng daye of Easter, aboute the vi houre. And he sayeth unto the Jewes; beholde your kyng. They cryed, saying; away with hym, away with hym, crucyfye hym. Pylate sayeth unto them; shall I crucyfy your king? The hye priestes aunswered; we haue no kyng but Cesar. Then deliuered he him unto them to be crucified. And they tooke Jesus, and ledde him away. And he bare his crosse, and wente furthe into a place whiche is called the place of dead mennes sculles, but in Hebrue, Golgotha: where they crucifyed hym, and two other with hym, on eyther syde one, and Jesus in the middest. And Pilate wrote a tytle, and put it on the crosse. The wrytyng was, Jesus of Nazareth kyng of the Jewes. This tytle read many of the Jewes: for the place where Jesus was crucified was nye to the cytie. And it was wrytten in Hebrue, Greke, and Latyn. Then sayed the hye priestes of the Jewes to Pilate; wryte not king of the Jewes, but that he sayed, I am kyng of the Jewes. Pylate aunswered; what I haue written, that haue I written. Then the souldiers, when they had crucifyed Jesus, toke his garmentes, and made iiii partes, to euery souldiour a part, and also his coate. The coate was without seme, wrought upon throughout: They sayed therfore among themselues; let us not deuyde it, but cast lottes for it, who shall haue it. That the scripture might be fulfylled, saying; They haue parted my raymente among them, and for my coate did they cast lottes. And the souldiours did suche thynges indede. There stoode by the crosse of Jesus, his mother and his mothers sister Mary the wyfe of Cleophas, and Mary Magdalene. When Jesus therfore sawe his mother, and the discyple standyng, whom he loued, he sayeth unto his mother; woman, behold thy sonne. Then sayd he to the disciple, beholde thy mother. And from that houre the disciple toke hir for his owne.

After these thynges, Jesus knowing that all thynges were nowe performed, that the scripture myght be fulfylled, he sayeth; I thirst. So there stoode a vessell by full of vineger: therfore they fylled a sponge with vineger, and wounde it aboute with Isope, and put it to his mouthe. As sone as Jesus then receyued of the vineger, he sayed; It is finished, and bowed his head, and gaue up the gost.

The Jewes therfore, because it was the preparyng of the Sabboth, that the bodyes should not remayne upon the crosse on the Sabboth daye (for that Sabboth daye was an hye daye) besought Pylate, that their legges might be broken, and that they might be taken downe. Then came the souldiours, and brake the legges of the firste and of the other whiche was crucified with hym. But when they came to Jesus, and sawe that he was dead already, they brake not his legges: but one of the souldiours with a speare thrust him into the syde, and forthwith there came out bloud and water. And he that sawe it bare recorde, and his recorde is true. And he knoweth that he sayeth true, that ye might beleue also. For these thynges were done that the scripture should be fulfilled; ye shall not breake a bone of hym.

And againe another scripture sayth; they shall loke upon him whom they haue pearced. After this Joseph of Aramathia (which was a disciple of Jesus, but secretly for feare of the Jewes) besought Pylate that he might take downe the bodye of Jesus. And Pylate gaue hym lycense: He came therfore and tooke the bodye of Jesus. And there came also Nicodemus, (whiche at the begynning came to Jesus by night) and brought of Myrre and Aloes mingled together, aboute an hundreth pounde weight. Then tooke they the body of Jesus, and wound it in lynnen clothes with the odoures, as the maner of the Jewes is to burye. And in the place where he was crucified, there was a garden; and in the garden a newe Sepulchre, wherein was neuer manne layde. There layde they Jesus therfore because of the preparyng of the Sabboth of the Jewes, for the Sepulchre was nye at hande.

At Euensong.

¶ The First Lesson, Isa. liii. unto the end.

Easter Euen.

At Matyns.

¶ The First Lesson, Lamentations iv. 5. unto the end.

At the Communion.

Domine Deus salutis. Ps. lxxxviii.

O Lorde God of my saluacion, I haue cryed day and nyght before thee : O lette my prayer entre into thy presence, incline thyne eare unto my callyng.

For my soule is ful of trouble : and my lyfe draweth nye unto hell.

I am counted as one of them that go downe unto the pytte : and I haue been euen as a man that hathe no strengthe.

Free among the deade, lyke unto them that bee wounded and lye in the graue, whiche be out of remembraunce; and are cut awaye from thy hande.

Thou hast layed me in the lowest pytte, in a place of darcknes; and in the depe.

Thyne indignacion lyeth harde upon me : and thou hast vexed me with all thy stormes.

Thou hast put awaye myne acquayntaunce far from me : and made me to be abhorred of them.

I am so fast in pryson : that I cannot get forth.

My sight fayleth for very trouble : lorde, I haue called dayly upon thee, I haue stretched oute my handes unto thee.

Doest thou shewe wonders among the deade? or shall the dead ryse up agayne and prayse thee?

Shal thy louyngkyndenes be shewed in the graue? or thy faithfulnes in destruccion?

Shal thy wonderous workes be knowen in the darke? and thy righteousnes in the land where all thinges are forgotten?

Unto thee haue I cried, O Lord : and earlye shall my praier come before thee.

Lorde, why abhorrest thou my soule? and hideste thou thy face from me?

I am in misery, and like unto him that is at the point to dye : (euen from my youth uppe) thy terrours haue I suffred with a troubled minde.

Thy wrathfull displeasure goeth ouer me : and the feare of thee, hath undone me.

They came rounde aboute me dayely lyke water : and compassed me together on euery syde.

My louers and frendes haste thou put awaye from me : and hyd myne acquayntaunce out of my syght.

Glory be to the father, and to the sonne : and to the holy ghost.

As it was in the beginning, is now, and euer shalbe : worlde without ende.   Amen.

The Epistle.   1 Peter iii.

It is better (if the wyll of God be so) that ye suffre for wel doing then for euil doing. Forasmuch as Christe hath once suffered for synnes, the Just for the uniust, to bring us to God; and was killed as partaynyng to the fleshe, but was quickened in the spirite. In which spirite he also went and preached to the spirites that were in pryson; which somtyme had bene disobedient, when the long-suffryng of God was once loked for in the dayes of Noe, whyle the Arke was a preparyng; wherin a fewe, that is to saye, eyght soules, were saued by the water, lyke as Baptysme also nowe saueth us; not the puttyng awaie of the fylth of the fleshe, but in that a good conscience consenteth to God by the resurreccion of Jesus Christ, whiche is on the right hand of God; and is gone into heauen; Angels, powers, and myght subdued unto hym.

The Gospel. Matt xxvii.

WHEN the Euen was come, there came a riche man of Aramathia named Joseph, whiche also was Jesus disciple. He went unto Pilate and begged the body of Jesus. Then Pilate commaūded the body to be deliuered. And when Joseph had taken the bodye, he wrapped it in a cleane lynnen clothe, and layde it in his newe Tombe, whiche he had hewen out euen in the rocke, and rolled a great stone to the doore of the Sepulchre, and departed. And there was Mary Magdalene, and the other Mary sytting ouer against the Sepulchre. The nexte day that foloweth the day of preparing, the high priestes and Phariseis came together unto Pilate, saying; Sir, we remembre that this deceyuer sayed whyle he was yet alyue; After iii dayes I wil rise agayne: Commaunde therfore that the Sepulchre be made sure untyll the thirde daye, leste his disciples come and steale hym awaye, and say unto the people, he is risen from the dead: and the last erroure shalbe worse then the firste. Pylate sayed unto thē: ye haue the watche, goe your way, make it as sure as ye can. So thei went and made the Sepulchre sure with the watchemenne, and sealed the stone.

¶ *Easter Daye.*

¶ In the mornyng, afore Mattyns, the people beyng assembled in the Churche, these Anthems shalbe fyrste solemnely song or sayed.

CHRIST rising again from the dead, nowe dieth not. Death from henceforth hath no power upon hym. For in that he dyed, he dyed but once to put away sinne: but in tha the liueth, he liueth unto God. And so lykewyse, counte yourselfes dead unto synne: but lyuyng unto God in Christe Jesus our Lorde. Alleluya, Alleluya.

CHRISTE is risen againe: the firste fruytes of them that slepe: for seyng that by man came death: by man also commeth the resurreccion of the dead. For as by Adam all men do dye, so by Christe all menne shalbe restored to lyfe. Alleluya.

The priest. Shewe forth to all nacions the glory of God.

The Answere. ¶ And among all people his wonderfull workes.

Let us praye.

O GOD, who for our redempciō dyddest geue thyne only begotten sonne to the death of the Crosse: and by his glorious resurreccion haste delyuered us from the power of our enemye: Graunte us so to dye daylye from synne, that we maye euermore lyue with hym in the ioy of hys resurreccion; through the same Christe our Lorde. Amen.

¶ Proper Psalmes and lessons.

At Matins.

The first lesson, Exod. xii. to thende.

Psalms ii. lvii. cxi.

The seconde lesson, Roma vi. to thende.

At the fyrst Communion.

Conserva me, Domine. Psalm xvi.

PRESERUE me, O God : for in thee haue I put my trust.

O my soule, thou haste sayed unto the Lorde : Thou art my God, my goodes are nothyng unto thee.

All my delight is upon the Sainctes that are in the yearth : and upon suche as excell in vertue.

But they that runne after another god : shall haue great trouble.

Their dryncke offerynges of bloud wyll not I offer : neither make mencion of their names within my lippes.

The Lord himselfe is the porcion of mine inheritaūce, and of my cuppe : thou shalt mayntayne my lotte.

The lotte is fallen unto me in a fayre grounde : yea, I haue a goodly heritage.

I will thanke the Lorde for geuing me warnyng : my reynes also chasten me in the nyght-season.

I haue sette God alwayes before me : for he is on my ryght hand, therfore I shall not fall.

Wherfore my harte was glad, and my glory reioysed : my fleshe also shall rest in hope.

For why? thou shalt not leaue my soule in helle : neyther shalt thou suffre thy holy one to see corrupcion.

Thou shalt shewe me the pathe of life; in thy presence is the fulnes of ioye : and at thy right hand there is pleasure for euermore.

Glory be to the father, and to the sonne, and to the &c.

As it was in the begynnyng, is nowe and euer &c.

The Collect.

ALMIGHTIE God, whiche through thy onely begotten sonne Jesus Christ hast ouercome death, and opened unto us the gate of euerlasting life; we humbly beseche thee, that, as by thy speciall grace, preuenting us, thou doest put in our mindes good desires, so by thy continuall help we may bring the same to good effect; through Jesus Christ our Lorde who lyueth and reigneth, &c.

The Epistle.   Coloss. iii.

IF ye be rysen agayne with Christe, seke those thynges whych are aboue, where Christ sytteth on the right hand of God.   Set your affeccion on heauenly thynges, and not on yearthy thynges. For ye are dead, and your life is hid with Christ in God.   Whensoeuer Christe (which is oure lyfe) shall shewe hymselfe, then shall ye also appeare with hym in glory.   Mortifie therfore your earthy membres, fornicacion, unclennes, unnaturall lust, euyll concupiscence, and couetousnes, whiche is worshyppyng of ydolles: for whiche thynges sake, the wrath of God useth to come on the disobedient chyldren, among whom ye walked sometime when ye lyued in them.

The Gospell.   John xx.

THE firste daye of the Sabbothes came Mary Magdalene earlye (when it was yet darcke) unto the Sepulchre, and sawe the stone taken awaye from the graue.   Then she ranne and came to Symon Peter, and to the other discyple whom Jesus loued, and sayeth unto them; they haue taken awaye the Lorde out of the graue, and we cannot tell where they haue layed hym.   Peter therfore wente foorth and that other disciple and came unto the Sepulchre.   They ranne both together, and that other disciple dyd outrūne Peter, and came first to the sepulchre.   And when he had stowped doune, he sawe the lynnen clothes liyng, yet went he not in.   Then came Symon Peter folowyng hym, and went into the sepulchre, and sawe the lynnen clothes lye, and the napkyn that was aboute his head, not liyng with the lynnen clothes, but wrapped together in a place by itselfe. Thē went in also that other disciple whyche came first to the sepulchre, and he sawe and beleued. For as yet they knewe not the scripture, that he shoulde ryse agayne from death. Then the disciples went awaye agayne unto their owne home.

At the second Communion.

Domine, quid multiplicati ? Ps. iii.

LORDE, howe are they encreased that trouble me? many are they that ryse agaynst me.

Many one there be that saye of my soule : There is no helpe for him in his God.

But thou, O Lorde, art my defender : thou art my worshyp, and the lifter up of my head.

I dyd call upon the Lord with my vioce : and he heard me out of his holy hyll.

I layde me doune and slept : and rose up agayne, for the lorde sustayned me.

I wil not be afrayd for ten thousādes of the people : that haue set themselues agaynst me round aboute.

Up Lord and helpe me, O my God : for thou smyteste all myne enemies upon the cheke bone, thou hast broken the teeth of the ungodly.

Saluacion belongeth unto the lorde : and thy blessyng is upon the people.

Glory be to the father and to the sonne : and to the holy ghost.

As it was in the beginning, is nowe and euer shalbe : worlde without ende. Amen.

The Collect.

ALMIGHTY father, whiche hast geuen thy only sonne to dye for our sinnes, and to rise againe for oure iustificacion; Graunte us so to putte awaye the leauen of malyce and wickednesse, that we maye alwaye serue thee in purenesse of liuing and trueth; through Jesus Christe oure Lorde.

The Epistle. 1 Cor. v.

KNOWE ye not that a lytle leauen sowreth the whole lompe of dowe? Pourge therfore the olde leauen, that ye maye be newe dowe, as ye are swete bread. For Christe our passeouer is offred up for us. Therfore let us kepe holye daye, not with olde

leaué, neither with the leauen of maliciousnes and wickednes;
but with the swete bread of purenes and trueth.

The Gospell.   Mark xvi.

WHEN the Sabboth was paste, Mary Magdalene, and Mary
Jacoby and Salome, bought swete odoures, that they myghte
come and annoynt him.   And early in the morning, the first
daye of the Saboth, they came unto the Sepulchre when the
sonne was risē.   And they saied omōg thēselues: who shall rolle
awaye the stone frō the dore of the Sepulchre?   And whē they
looked, they sawe howe that the stone was rolled awaye, for it
was a very great one.   And they wente into the Sepulchre, and
sawe a younge manne syttyng on the ryght syde, clothed in a
long white garmente, and they were afrayed.   And he sayed
unto them; Be not afrayed, ye seke Jesus of Nazareth whiche
was crucifyed.   He is risen, he is not here: Beholde the place
where they had put hym.   But goe your waye, and tell his
disciples, and Peter, that he goeth before you into Galile, there
shall ye see him, as he sayed unto you.   And they went out
quyckly and fledde from the Sepulchre, for they trembled, and
were amased, neyther sayed they any thyng to any man, for
they were afrayde.

At Euensong.

¶ *Proper Psalms and Lessons.*

Psalms cxiii. cxiv. cxviii.

The Second Lesson, Acts ii. unto the end.

¶ *Monedaye in Easter weke.*

At Mattyns.

¶ The ii. Lesson, Matt. xxviii. unto thende.

At the Communion.

Nonne Deo subiecta ?   Psalm lxii.

MY soule truly wayteth styll upon God : for of him commeth
my saluacion.

He verely is my strength and my saluaciō : he is my defence,
so that I shall not greatly fall.

Howe long will ye imagine mischiefe againste euery man? ye
shalbe slaine all the sorte of you, yea, as a totteryng wall shall
ye be, and lyke a broken hedge.

Their deuice is only howe to put him out whom God will

exalte : their delyght is in lyes; they geue good woordes with their mouth, but cursse with their harte.

Neuerthelesse, my soule, waite thou still upon God : for my hope is in hym.

He truly is my strength and my saluacion : he is my defence, so that I shall not fall.

In God is my health and my glory : the rocke of my myght, and in God is my trust.

O put your trust in hym alwaye, ye people : powre out your hartes before hym, for God is our hope.

As for the chyldren of men, they are but vayne, the children of men are deceiptfull : upon the weyghtes, they are altother lighter than vanitie itselfe.

O trust not in wrong and robbery, geue not yourselues unto vanitie : yf ryches encrease, sette not your harte upon them.

God spake once and twise : I haue also heard the same, that power belongeth unto God.

And that thou Lord art mercifull : for thou rewardest euery man accordyng to his worke.

Glory be to the father, and to the sonne, and to the holy goste.

As it was in the begynning, is nowe and euer shalbe : worlde without ende. Amen.

The Collect.

ALMIGHTYE God, whiche through thy onelye begotten sonne Jesus Christe hast ouercome deathe, and opened unto us the gate of euerlastyng lyfe; we humbly beseche thee, that as by thy speciall grace, preuentyng us, thou doest putte in our myndes good desyres, so by thy continuall helpe we may bryng the same to good effecte, through Jesus Christ our lorde, who lyueth and reigneth, etc.

The Epistle. Acts x.

PETER opened his mouth and sayed; of a trueth I perceyue that there is no respecte of persons with God; but in all people, he that feareth him, and worketh righteousnes, is accepted with him. Ye knowe the preaching that God sente unto the children of Israell, preachyng peace by Jesus Christe, whiche is lorde ouer all thinges; whiche preachyng was published throughout all Jewry, (and began in Galilee after the baptisme whiche John preached) howe God annoynted Jesus of Nazareth with the holy ghoste, and with power. Whiche Jesus went about doyng good, and healyng all that were oppressed of the deuell; for God was

with him.   And we are witnesses of al thinges which he did in
the lande of the Jewes, and at Jerusalem; whō they slewe and
hanged on tree.   Hym God reysed up the third daie, and shewed
hym openly, not to all the people, but unto us witnesses (chosen
before of God for the same intent,) whiche dyd eate and drinke
with him after he arose from death.   And he commaunded us
to preache unto the people, and to testify, that it is he whiche
was ordeyned of God to be the iudge of the quycke and deade.
To hym geue all the prophetes witnes, that through his name,
whosoeuer beleueth in hym, shall receyue remissiō of sinnes.

The Gospell.   Luke xxiv.

BEHOLDE two of the disciples wente that same daye to a
towne called Emaus, whyche was from Jerusalem about lx fur-
longes: and they talked together of all the thynges that had
happened.   And it chauncede while they commoned together
and reasoned; Jesus himselfe drue nere and went with them.
But their eyes were holden that they shoulde not knowe hym.
And he sayd unto them; what maner of cōmunicacions are
these that ye haue one to another as ye walke and are sad?
And the one of them (whose name was Cleophas) aunswered, and
saied unto hym; art thou onely a straunger in Jerusalem, and
haste not knowen the thynges which haue chaunced there in
these dayes? he saide unto them; what thynges?   And they
sayd unto hym, of Jesus of Nazareth, whyche was a Prophete,
mightie in dede and worde before God and all the people: and
how the hie priestes and oure rulers deliuered him to be condemned to death, and haue crucified him.   But we trusted that
it had been he whiche shoulde haue redemed Israel.   And as
touching all these thinges, to-daye is euen the third daye that
they were doen.   Yea, and certeyne women also of oure companye made us astonyed, whiche came earely unto the Sepulchre,
and founde not his body, and came, saying, that they had sene a
vision of Angels, whiche sayde that he was aliue.   And certeyne
of them whiche were with us, wente to the Sepulchre, and found
it euen so as the women had sayed; but hym they sawe not.

And he sayed unto them; O fooles and slowe of harte to
beleue al that the prophetes haue spoken.   Oughte not Christ to
haue suffred these thynges, and to entre into his glory?   And he
began at Moses and all the prophetes, and interpreted unto
them in all Scriptures which wer written of hym.

And it came to passe as he sate at meate with them, he tooke
bread and blessed it, and brake and gaue to them.   And their

eyes were opened, and they knewe hym, and he vanished out of their sight. And they sayed betwene themselues; did not oure heartes burne within us, whyle he talked with us by the waye, and opened to us the Scriptures? And they rose up the same houre and returned to Jerusalem, and founde the eleuen gathered together, and them that were with them, saying; the Lorde is rysen indede, and hath appered to Simon. And they tolde what thynges were dooen in the waye, and howe they knewe him in breakyng of bread.

At Euensong.

¶ The Second Lesson, Acts iii. unto the ende.

¶ *Tuisdaye in Easter weke.*

At Matins.

The ii Lesson, Luke xxiv. unto, " And behold ii of them."

At the Communion.

Laudate, pueri. Psalm cxiij.

Prayse the Lord (ye seruauntes) : O prayse the name of the Lorde.

Blessed is the name of the Lord : from this tyme furth for euermore.

The Lordes name is praysed : from the rysing up of the sonne unto the goyng doune of the same.

The lorde is hie aboue all heathen : and his glorie aboue the heauens.

Who is lyke unto the Lorde our God, that hathe his dwelling so hye : and yet humbleth himselfe, to beholde the thynges that are in heauen and earth?

He taketh up the symple oute of the duste : and lyfteth the poore out of the mier;

That he may set hym with the princes : euen wyth the princes of hys people.

He maketh the baren woman to kepe house : and to be a ioyful mother of children.

Glory be to the father and to the sonne : and to the holy ghost.

As it was in the beginning, is now, and euer shalbe : worlde without ende. Amen.

The Collect.

ALMYGHTY father, whiche haste geuen thy only sonne to dye for our synnes, and to ryse agayne for oure iustificacion; Graunt us so to put awaye the leuen of malyce and wyckednes, that we maye alwaye serue thee in purenes of lyuynge and truth; through Jesus Christe oure Lorde.

The Epistle. Acts xiii.

YE men and brethren, Children of the generacion of Abraham, and whosoeuer among you feareth God; to you is this word of saluacion sēt. For the inhabiters of Jerusalem, and their rulers, because they knew him not, nor yet the voyces of the prophetes which are read euery Sabboth day, thei haue fulfilled them in condemning him. And when they found no cause of death in him, yet desired they Pilate to kyll him. And when they hadde fulfilled all that were written of hym, they tooke hym downe from the tree, and put hym in a Sepulchre. But God raysed hym agayne from death the thirde daye, and he was seen manye dayes of them whiche wente with hym from Galile to Jerusalem; which are his witnesses unto the people. And we declare unto you, howe that the promes, (whiche was made unto the fathers,) GOD hath fulfilled unto their childrē, (euen unto us,) in that he raised up Jesus agayne : Euen as it is written in the seconde Psalme : Thou arte my sonne, this daye haue I begotten thee. As concernyng that he raised him up from death, now no more to return to corrupcion, he saied on this wyse; The holy promises made to Dauid will I geue faithfully to you. Wherefore he saieth also in another place, Thou shalte not suffre thyne holy to see corrupcion. For Dauid (after that he had in hys tyme fulfilled the will of GOD) fell on slepe, and was layed unto hys fathers, and sawe corrupcion. But he whome God raised agayne, sawe no corrupcion. Bee it knowen unto you therefore, (ye men and brethren,) that throughe thys man is preached unto you the forgeuenes of synnes, and that by hym all that beleue are iustified frome all thynges, frome whiche ye coulde not be iustified by the lawe of Moses. Beware therfore, lest that fall on you, which is spoken of in the Prophetes; beholde, ye despisers, and wonder, and perishe ye, for I doe a worke in your daies, whiche ye shall not beleue, thoughe a man declare it you.

The Gospell.   Luke xxiv.

JESUS stode in the middes of his disciples, and saied unto them; peace be unto you: It is I; feare not.   But thei were abashed and afraied, and supposed that they had seen a spirite And he saied unto them, why are ye troubled, and why doo thoughtes arise in your heartes?   Beholde my handes and my fete, that it is euen I myselfe.   Handle me, and see, for a spirite hath not flesh and bones, as ye see me haue.   And when he had thus spoken, he shewed them his handes and his fete.   And whyle they yet beleued not for ioye, and wondered, he saied unto them; Haue ye here any meate?   And they offered hym a pece of a broyled fishe, and of an Honyecombe.   And he tooke it, and did eate before them.   And he saied unto them; these are the wordes whiche I spake unto you, while I was yet with you; That all muste nedes be fulfilled, whiche were written of me in the Lawe of Moses, and in the Prophetes, and in the Psalmes.   Then opened he their wittes, that thei mighte understande the scriptures, and saied unto them; Thus it is written, and thus it behoued Christe to suffer, and to arise agayne from death the thirde daye, and that repentaunce and remission of synnes shoulde bee preached in his name emong all nacions, and muste begin at Jerusalem.   And ye are witnesses of these thynges.

At Euensong.

The seconde Lesson, 1 Cor. xv. unto the ende.

¶ *The first Sondaie after Easter.*

Beatus vir.   Psalm cxii.

BLESSED is the man that feareth the lorde : he hath greate delite in his commaundementes.

His seede shalbe mightie upon yearthe : the generacion of the faithefull shalbe blessed.

Riches and plēteousnes shalbe in his house : And hys righteousnes endureth for euer.

Unto the Godly there ariseth up light in the darkenes : he is mercifull, louyng and righteous.

A good man is mercifull and lendeth : and wil guyde his wordes with discrecion.

For he shal neuer be moued : and the righteous shalbe had in euerlastyng remembraunce.

He will not bee afraied for any euill tidynges : For hys heart standeth fast, and beleueth in the Lorde.

His hearte is stablished and will not shrinke : untill he se his desire upon his enemies.

He hath sparsed abroade and geuen to the poore : and his righteousnes remaineth for euer, his horne shalbee exalted with honor.

The ungodly shall se it, and it shall greue him : he shall gnashe with his teeth, and consume awaye, the desire of the ungodly shall perishe.

Glory be to the father, and to the sonne &c.

As it was in the beginnyng, is now, and euer &c.

The Collect.

ALMIGHTY Father, &c. *as at the second Communion on Easter day*.

The Epistle. 1 John v.

AL that is borne of GOD ouercommeth the world. And this is the victory that ouercommeth the world, euen our faith. Who is it that ouercommeth the worlde, but he whiche beleueth that Jesus is the sonne of God? This Jesus Christ is he that came by water and bloud; not by water onely, but by water and bloud. And it is the spirite that beareth witnes, because the spirite is truthe. For there are three whiche beare recorde in heauen, the father, the woorde and the holy Ghoste, and these three are one. And there are three whiche beare recorde in yearth, the spirite, and water, and bloud: and these iii are one. If wee receiue the witnes of menne, the witnes of God is greater. For this is the witnes of God that is greater, whiche he testified of his sonne. He that beleueth on the sonne of God, hath the witnes in hymselfe. He that beleueth not God, hath made him a lier, because he beleueth not the recorde that God gaue of his sonne. And this is the record, how that God hath geuē unto us eternall life, and this lyfe is in his sonne. He that hath the sonne, hath lyfe; and he that hath not the sonne of God, hath not lyfe.

The Gospell. John xx.

The same daye at nyghte; whiche was the firste daye of the Sabbothes, when the dores were shut (where the disciples were assembled together, for feare of the Jewes,) came Jesus and stode in the middes, and saide unto them; Peace bee unto you. And when he had so saide, he shewed unto them his handes and hys syde. Then were the disciples glad when thei sawe the lorde. Then saide Jesus to them againe: Peace be unto you. As my father sente me, euen so sende I you also. And when he had saide those wordes, he breathed on them, and saide unto them; receiue ye the holy ghoste. Whosoeuers synnes ye remitte, they are remitted unto them. And whosoeuers synnes ye retaine, they are retained.

¶ The second Sondaie after Easter.

Deus in adjutorium. Psalm lxx.

HASTE thee, O God, to deliuer me : Make haste to helpe me, O Lorde.

Let them bee ashamed and confounded that seke after my soule : let them bee turned backward and put to confusion, that wishe me euill.

Let them (for their reward) be sone brought to shame : that crye ouer me, there, there.

But let all those that seke thee be ioyfull and gladde in thee : and let all suche as delight in thy saluacion, saye allwaie, the Lorde be praised.

As for me, I am poore and in misery : Haste thee unto me, (O God.)

Thou art my helpe and my redemer : O lorde make no long tariyng.

Glory be to the father, &c.

As it was in the, &c.

The Collect.

ALMIGHTIE God, whiche haste geuen thy holy sonne to bee unto us, bothe a sacrifice for synne, and also an example of Godly life; Geue us the grace that we maie alwaies moste thankfully receiue that his inestimable benefite, and also dayely indeuour ourselfes to folow the blessed steppes of his moste holy lyfe.

The Epistle. 1 Peter ii.

THIS is thankeworthie, yf a man for conscience toward God endure griefe, and suffre wrong undeserued. For what praise is it yf when ye bee buffeted for your fautes, ye take it paciently? But and yf, when ye doo well, ye suffre wrong and take it paciently, then is there thanke with God. For herunto verely were ye called: For Christ also suffered for us, leauing us an ensample, that ye should folowe his steppes, whiche dyd no synne, neyther was there guyle found in his mouthe: whiche, when he was reuiled, reuiled not again; when he suffered, he threatned not; but committed the vengeaūce to him that iudgeth righteously, whiche his owne selfe bare our synnes in his body on the tree, that we beyng deliuered from sinne, should liue unto righteousnes. By whose stripes ye were healed. For ye were as shepe going astraie; But are now turned unto the shephard and bishop of your soules.

The Gospel.   John x.

CHRISTE sayed to his disciples, I am the good shephard, a good shephard geueth his lyfe for the shepe.   An hired seruaunt, and he which is not the shepharde, (neyther the shepe are his owne) seeth the wolfe commyng, and leaueth the shepe and flieth; and the woulfe catcheth, and skatereth the shepe.   The hired ser-uaūt flieth, because he is an hired seruaunt, and careth not for the shepe.   I am the good shepehard, and knowe my shepe, and am knowen of myne.   As my Father knoweth me, euen so knowe I also my Father.   And I geue my lyfe for the Shepe: and other Shepe I haue, whiche are not of this folde.   Them also must I bring, and they shall heare my voyce, and there shalbe one folde, and one shepeherde.

¶ *The iii Sondaye.*

Confitebimur.   Psalm lxxv.

UNTO thee (O God) doo we geue thankes : yea, unto thee do we geue thankes.

Thy name also is so nye : and that doe thy wonderous workes declare.

When I receyue the congregacion : I shall iudge according unto right.

The yearth is weake, and all the inhabitours therof : I beare up the pillers of it.

I sayed unto the fooles, deale not so madly : and to the un-godly, set not up your horne.

Set not up your horne on hye : and speake not with a stiffe necke.

For promocion commeth neyther from the East, nor from the west : nor yet from the Southe.

And why? GOD is the iudge : he putteth doune one, and setteth up another.

For in the hand of the lorde there is a cup, and the wine is red : It is full mixte, and he poureth out of the same.

As for the dregges thereof : all the ungodly of the yearth shall drynke them, and sucke them out.

But I will talk of the GOD of Jacob : and praise hym for euer.

All the hornes of the ungodly also will I breake : and the hornes of the righteous shalbe exalted.

Glory be to the father, and to the sonne, &c.

As it was in the beginnyng, &c.

The Collect.

ALMIGHTYE God, whiche shewest to all men that be in errour the light of thy truth, to the intent that they maie returne into the waye of righteousnes; Graunt unto all them that bee admitted into the felowship of Christes religion, that they maye exchew those thinges that be contrary to their profession, and folow all such thinges as be agreable to the same; through our Lorde Jesus Christ.

The Epistle. 1 Peter ii.

DERELY beloued, I beseche you as straungiers and pilgremes, abstain frō fleshly lustes, which fight against the soule: and see that ye haue honest conuersacion emong the Gentiles; that, whereas they backbite you as euilldoers, they maye see your good workes, and prayse God in the day of visitacion. Submit your-selfes therfore unto al maner ordinaunce of man, for the Lordes sake, whether it bee unto the kyng as unto the chief head; either unto rulers, as unto thē that are sent of him, for the punishment of euilldoers, but for the laude of them that do well. For so is the will of God, that with well-doing, ye maie stop the mouthes of foolishe and ignoraunt men: as free, and not as hauing the libertie for a cloke of maliciousnes, but euen as the seruauntes of God. Honor all men, loue brotherly felowship, feare God, honor the Kyng.

The Gospel. John xvi.

JESUS sayed to his disciples; After a while ye shall not see me, and again after a while ye shall se me; for I go to the father. Then saied some of his disciples betwene thēselfes; what is this that he sayth unto us, after a while ye shall not se me, and again, after a while ye shall se me, and that I go to the father? Thei saied therefore; what is this that he sayeth, after a whyle? We cānot tel what he saith. Jesus perceyued that they would aske hym, and saied unto them; ye inquire of this betwene yourselfes, because I sayed, after a whyle ye shall not se me, and again after a while ye shall se me. Verely, verely, I saye unto you, ye shall

wepe and lament; but contrarywyse, the worlde shall reioyse.
Ye shall sorowe, but your sorowe shalbee turned to ioye.   A
woman, when she trauayleth hath sorow; because her houre is
come.   But as sone as she is deliuered of the child, she remembreth no more the anguish, for ioye that a man is borne into
the world.   And ye now therfore haue sorowe: but I will se you
again, and your hartes shall reioyse, and your ioye shall no manne
take from you.

¶ *The iiii Sondaye.*

Deus stetit in synagoga.   Ps. lxxxii.

God standeth in the congregacion of princes : He is iudge
emong Goddes.

How long wyll ye geue wrong iudgement : and accept the
persones of the ungodly?

Defende the poore and fatherlesse : se that suche as be in nede
and necessitie haue right.

Deliuer the outcast and poore : Saue them from the hande of
the ungodly.

They will not be learned nor understande, but walke on still in
darkenes : all the foundacions of the yearth be out of course.

I haue sayd, ye are Goddes : and ye all are children of the
most highest.

But ye shall die like men : and fall like one of the princes.

Arise, O God, and iudge thou the yearth : For thou shalt take
all the Heathen to thyne inheritaunce.

Glory be to the father, and to the sonne, &c.

As it was in the beginnyng, is now, &c.

The Collect.

Almightie God, whiche doest make the myndes of all faythfull
men to be of one wil; graunt unto thy people, that they maye
loue the thyng, whiche thou commaundest, and desyre, that
whiche thou doest promes; that emong the sondery and manifold
chaunges of the worlde, oure heartes maye surely there bee fixed,
whereas true ioyes are to be founde; through Christe our Lorde.

The Epistle.   James i.

Euery good gift, and euery perfect gift, is from aboue, and
commeth doune from the father of lightes, with whom is no vari-
ablenes, nether is he chaunged unto darkenes.   Of his owne will
begat he us, with the worde of truthe, that we should be the first

fruites of his creatures.   Wherfore (dere brethren) let euery man be swift to heare, slowe to speake, slowe to wrath.   For the wrathe of man worketh not that whiche is righteous before God. Wherfore laye apart all filthines, and superfluitie of malicious-nes, and receiue with mekenes the worde that is graffed in you, whiche is able to saue your soules.

The Gospell.   John xvi.

JESUS saied unto his disciples; nowe I go my waie to him that sent me, and none of you asketh me whither I go.   But, because I haue sayed suche thinges unto you, youre heartes are ful of sorow.   Neuertheles I tel you the truth, it is expedient for you that I go awaye.   For if I go not away, that comforter will not come unto you.   But if I depart, I wil sende him unto you. And when he is come, he wil rebuke the worlde of sinne, and of righteousnes, and of iudgement.   Of sinne, because they beleue not on me: Of righteousnes, because I go to my father, and ye shall se me no more.   Of Judgement, because the Prince of this worlde is iudged already.   I haue yet many thynges to saye unto you, but ye cannot beare them awaye nowe: howbeit, when he is come, (whiche is the spirite of truth,) he will leade you into all truth.   He shall not speake of hymselfe, but whatsoeuer he shall heare, that shall he speake, and he wyll shewe you thynges to come.   He shall glorifie me: for he shall receyue of myne, and shall shewe unto you.   All thynges that the father hath, are mine: therfore sayed I unto you, that he shall take of myne, and shewe unto you.

¶ The v. Sondaie.

Quam dilecta tabernacula !   Psalm lxxxiv.

O HOWE amiable are thy dwellinges : Thou Lorde of Hostes?

My soule hath a desire and longing to entre into the courtes of the Lorde : My heart and my flesh reioise in the liuing God.

Yea, the Sparowe hath found her an house, and the Swalowe a neste where she maie laie her young : Euen thy altares, O Lorde of Hostes, my kyng and my God.

Blessed are thei that dwell in thy house : thei will be alwaie praisyng thee.

Blessed is that manne whose strength is in thee : In whose hearte are thy waies.

Whiche goyng throughe the vale of misery, use it for a well : and the pooles are filled with water.

Thei will go from strength to strength : and unto the God of Goddes appeareth euery one of them in Syon.

O Lorde God of Hostes, heare my praier : Harken, O God of Jacob.

Beholde, O God our defender : and loke upon the face of thyne annoynted.

For one daie in thy courtes : is better then a thousand.

I had rather be a dorekeper in the house of my God : then to dwell in the tentes of ungodlynes.

For the Lorde God is a light and defence : the Lorde will geue grace and worship, and no good thynge shall he withhold from them that liue a godly life.

O Lorde God of Hostes : blessed is the man that putteth his trust in thee.

Glory be to the father, and to the sonne, &c.

As it was in the beginnyng, &c.

The Collect.

LORDE from whom all good thynges do come; graunte us, thy humble seruauntes, that by thy holy inspiracion wee maie thynke those thynges that bee good, and by thy mercifull guydyng maye perfourme the same; thorow our Lorde Jesus Christ.

The Epistle.   James i.

SE that ye bee doers of the worde, and not hearers onely, deceiuyng youre owne selfes. For if any man heare the worde, and declareth not the same by his workes, he is like unto a man beholdyng his bodely face in a glasse. For as sone as he hath looked on hymselfe, he goeth his waie, and forgetteth immediatly what his fashion was. But whoso looketh in the perfect lawe of libertie, and continueth therin, (if he bee not a forgetfull hearer, but a dooer of the woorke,) the same shalbee happie in his deede. If any man emong you seme to be deuoute, and refraineth not his toungue but deceiueth his own harte, this mannes devocion is in vaine. Pure deuocion, and undefiled before God the father, is this; to viset the fatherles and widowes, in their aduersitie, and kepe hymselfe unspotted of the worlde.

The Gospell.   John xvi.

VERELY, verely, I saye unto you, whatsoeuer ye shall aske the father in my name, he will geue it you. Hitherto haue ye asked nothyng in my name. Aske, and ye shall receiue, that your ioye maye be full. These thinges haue I spokē unto you by prouerbes.

The tyme will come when I shall no more speake unto you by prouerbes; but I shall shewe you plainly from my father. At that daye shall ye aske in my name. And I saye not unto you that I wyll speake unto my father for you. For the father hymself loueth you, because ye haue loued me, and haue beleued that I came out from God. I wente out from the father, and came into the worlde. Againe, I leaue the world, and go to the father.

His disciples sayed unto hym; Loe nowe talkest thou plainly, and speakest no Prouerbe. Nowe are we sure that thou knowest all thinges, and nedest not that any man should aske thee any question: therefore beleue we that thou camest from God. Jesus aunswered them; now ye do beleue. Beholde, the houre draweth nye, and is already come, that ye shalbee skatered euery man to his owne, and shall leaue me alone. And yet am I not alone: for the father is with me. These woordes haue I spoken unto you, that in me ye might haue peace, for in the worlde shall ye haue tribulacion; but be of good chere, I haue ouercome the worlde.

¶ *The Assencion Day.*

¶ *Proper Psalmes and Lessons.*

At Matins.

Psalms viii. xv. xxi.

The Second Lesson, John xiv. unto the end.

¶ *At the Communion.*

Omnes gentes plaudite. Psalm xlvii.

O CLAP your handes together (all ye people) : O syng unto God with the voyce of melody.

For the Lorde is hye, and to bee feared : he is the greate kyng upon all the yearth.

He shall subdue the people under us : And the nacions under our fete.

He shall chose out an heritage for us : Euen the worship of Jacob whom he loued.

God is gone up with a mery noyse : And the Lorde with the sounde of the trompe.

O syng prayses, syng prayses unto oure God : O syng prayses, syng prayses unto our kyng.

For God is the kyng of al the yearth : syng ye praises with understandyng.

God reigneth ouer the heathen : god sitteth upō hıs holy seate.

The princes of the people are ioined to the people, of the God of Abraham : for God (whiche is very hye exalted) doth defende the earth, as it were with a shylde.

Glory be to the father, &c.

As it was in the begin : &c.

The Collect.

GRAUNTE we beseche thee, almightie god, that like as we doe beleue thy onely-begotten sonne our lorde to haue ascended into the heauens; so we may also in heart and mind thither ascende, and with him continually dwell.

The Epistle.   Acts i.

IN the former treatise (deare Theophilus) we haue spoken of all that Jesus began to dooe and teache, until the day in which he was takē up, after that he through the holy goste, had geuen commaundementes unto the Apostles, whome he had chosen: to whome he also shewed himselfe aliue after his passion, (and that by many tokens,) appearyng unto them xl dayes, and speaking of the kingdome of god; and gathered them together, and commaūded them that they should not depart from Jerusalem: but to wayte for the promes of the father, wherof (sayth he) ye haue heard of me. For John truely baptised with water; but ye shalbe baptised with the holy goste, after these fewe dayes. When they therfore were come together, they asked of him, saying; lord, wilt thou at this time restore agayn the kingdome of Israell? And he sayde unto them; it is not for you to knowe the times or the seasons, whiche the father hath put in hys owne power. But ye shall receyue power after that the holy gost is come upon you. And ye shall bee witnesses unto me, not onely in Jerusalem, but also in all Jewry, and in Samaria, and euen unto the worldes ende. And when he had spoken these thynges, while they behelde, he was taken up on hye, and a cloud receiued him up out of their sight. And while they loked stedfastly up toward heauen as he went, beholde, two men stoode by them in white apparel, whiche also sayde: ye men of Galile, why stand ye gasyng up into heauē? This same Jesus, which is taken up from you into heauen, shall so come, euen as ye haue sene him goe into heauen.

The Gospel. Matt. xvi.

JESUS appeared unto the eleuen as they sate at meate: and cast in their teth there unbelefe and hardnes of heart, because they beleued not them which had sene that he was risen agayn from the dead: and he sayd unto them; goe ye into all the world, and preache the gospel to all creatures: he that beleueth, and is baptised, shalbee saued; But he that beleueth not shalbee damned. And these tokens shal folowe them that beleue. In my name they shall cast out deuils, they shal speake with new tonges, they shall dryue away serpentes. And if they drinke any deadly thing, it shall not hurt them. They shall laye their handes on the sycke, and they shall recouer. So then when the lord had spoken unto thē, he was receiued into heauen, and is on the right hand of God. And they wente furth and preached euery where; The lord working with them, and confirming the word with miracles folowing.

¶ *Proper psalmes and lessons at Euensong.*

Psalms xxiv. lxviii. cxlviii.

The Seconde Lesson, Ephe. iv. unto the ende.

¶ *The Sonday after the Ascencion.*

Dominus regnavit. Psalm xciii.

THE lorde is king, and hath put on glorious apparel: the lord hath put on his apparell, and girded himselfe with strength.

He hath made the round world so sure : that it cannot be moued.

Euer sence the worlde began hath thy seate bene prepared : thou art from euerlasting.

The fluddes are risen, O Lorde, the fluddes haue lifte up theyr noyse : the fluddes lift up theyr waues.

The waues of the sea are mightie, and rage horrybly : but yet the Lorde that dwelleth on hygh is mightier.

Thy testimonies, O Lorde, are very sure : holynes becommeth thine house for euer.

Glory be to the father, &c.

As it was, &c.

The Collect.

O GOD, the kyng of glory, which hast exalted thine only sonne Jesus Christe, with great triumphe unto thy kingdom in heauē; we beseche thee, leaue us not comfortles; but sende to us thine holy ghost to comfort us, and exalte us unto the same place whither our sauiour Christe is gone before; who lyueth and reigneth &c.

The Epistle. 1 Peter iv.

THE ende of all thinges is at hand; be ye therfore sobre, and watch unto praier. But aboue all thinges haue feruent loue among yourselues: for loue shal couer the multitude of synnes. Be ye herberous one to another without grudgyng. As euery man hath receiued the gyfte, euen so minister the same one to another, as good ministers of the manifold grace of God. If any mã speake, let him talke as the wordes of God. If any man minister, let him do it as of the habilitie whiche God ministreth to him; that God in all thinges may be gloryfied through Jesus Christ; to whome be prayse and dominion for euer and euer. Amen.

The Gospell. John xv. xvi.

WHEN the comforter is come whom I will sende unto you from the father (euen the spirite of trueth, which procedeth of the father,) he shall testyfye of me. And ye shall beare witnes also, because ye haue bene with me from the begynnyng.

These thinges haue I said unto you, because ye should not be offended. They shall excommunicate you: yea the tyme shall come, that whosoeuer kylleth you, wyll thinke that he doeth God seruice. And such thinges will they do unto you, because they haue not knowen the father, neyther yet me. But these thinges I haue told you, that whan the tyme is come, ye may remembre then that I tolde you. These thinges sayde I not unto you at the beginning, because I was presente with you.

¶ Whit-Sunday.

¶ Proper Psalms and Lessons at Matins.

Psalm xlviii. lxvii. cxlv.

The Second Lesson, Acts x. " Then Peter opened his mouth," unto the end.

¶ At the Communion.

Exultate justi in Domino. Psalm xxxiii.

REIOICE in the Lorde, O ye righteous : for it becommeth well the iuste to be thankfull.

Prayse the Lorde with harpe : syng psalmes unto him wyth the lute and instrumente of ten stringes.

Syng unto the Lorde a new song : sing prayses lustely (unto him) with a good courage.

For the worde of the Lord is true : and al his workes are faythfull.

He loueth ryghteousnes and iudgement: the earth is full of the goodnes of the Lorde.

By the worde of the Lord were the heauens made: and all the hoostes of them, by the breath of hys mouth.

He gathereth the waters of the sea together, as it were upon a heap: and layeth up the depe as it were in a treasure-house.

Let all the earth feare the Lorde : stande in awe of him, all ye that dwell in the worlde.

For he spake and it was done : he commaunded, and it stoode faste.

The Lorde bringeth the counsayll of the heathen to noughte : and maketh the deuyses of the people to be of none effect, (and casteth out the counsailes of prynces.)

The counsaill of the Lord shal endure for euer : and the thoughtes of hys harte from generacion to generacion.

Blessed are the people whose God is the Lorde Jehouah : and blessed are the folke that haue chosen hym to be theyr inheritaunce.

The lorde loked downe from heauen, and beheld all the chyldren of menne : from the habitacion of hys dwelling, he considereth all them that dwell in the earth.

He fashyoneth all the heartes of them : and understandeth all theyr workes.

There is no king that can be saued by the multitude of an hoste : neyther is anye myghtye man delyuered by muche strength.

A horse is counted but a vayne thyng to saue a man : neither shall he deliuer any man by hys great strength.

Beholde, the eye of the lorde is upon them that feare him : and upon them that put theyr truste in his mercye.

To deliuer theyr soules from deathe : and to feade them in the tyme of derth.

Our soule hath paciently taryed for the lorde : for he is our helpe and our shielde.

For our heart shall reioyce in him : because we hoped in his holy name.

Let thy mercifull kyndnes, O lorde, be upon us : lyke as we haue put our trust in thee.

Glory be to the father, &c.
As it was in the beginning, &c.

The Collect.

GOD, whiche as upon this daye haste taughte the heartes of
thy faithful people, by the sending to them the lyght of thy holy
spirite; graunte us by the same spirite to haue a right iudgement
in al thinges, and euermore to reioyce in hys holy coumforte;
through the merites of Christ Jesus our sauiour; who liueth and
reigneth with thee, in the unitie of the same spirite, one God,
worlde without ende.

The Epistle.   Acts ii.

WHEN the fiftie dayes were come to an end, they were al with
one accorde together in one place.   And sodenly there came a
soūd from heauen, as it had bene the comming of a mighty wind,
and it filled al the house where they sate.   And there appered
unto them clouen tonges, like as they had bene of fyre, and it
sate upon eche one of them; and they were al filled with the holy
gost, and began to speake with other tonges, euen as the same
spirite gaue them utteraūce.   There were dwelling at Jerusalem
Jewes, deuout men out of euery nacion of them that are under
heauen.   When thys was noysed about, the multitude came together and were astonied, because that euery man heard them
speake with his owne language.   They wondred all, and
merueiled, saying among themselfes; behold, are not al these,
which speake, of Galile?   And how heare we euery mā his owne
tong, wherin we were borne?   Parthians, and Medes, and
Elamites, and the inhabiters of Mesopotamia, and of Jewry, and
of Capadocia, of Pontus and Asia, Phrigia and Pamphilia, of
Egipte, and of the parties of Libia, whiche is beside Siren, and
straungers of Rome, Jewes and Proselites, Grekes and Arrabians,
we haue heard them speake in our owne tongues the great
weorkes of God.

The Gospel.   John xiv.

JESUS sayde unto his disciples; If ye loue me kepe my commaundementes, and I wil pray the father, and he shall geue you
another câforter, that he maye abyde with you for euer; euen the
spirite of trueth, whome the worlde cannot receiue, because the
worlde seeth him not, neither knoweth hym.   But ye knowe
hym; for he dwelleth with you, and shalbe in you.   I will
not leaue you coumfortles; but will come to you.   Yet a

litle while, and the worlde seeth me no more; but ye se me.   For I lyue, and ye shall lyue.   That daye shall ye knowe that I am in my father, and you in me, and I in you.   He that hath my commaundementes, and kepeth them, the same is he that loueth me.   And he that loueth me, shalbe loued of my father; and I will loue him, and wil shewe mine owne selfe unto hym.

¶ *Proper psalmes and lessons at Euensong.*

Psalms ciiii. cxlv.

The ii Lesson, Actes xix. " It fortuned when Apollo wente to Corinthum," unto " After these thinges."

¶ *Monday in whitsonweke.*

Jubilate Deo.   Psalm c.

O BE ioyful in the Lorde (all ye landes) : serue the Lord with gladnes, and come before his presence with a song.

Be ye sure that the lord he is God : it is he that hath made us, and not we ourselfes; we are hys people, and the shepe of his pasture.

O goe your way into his gates with thankesgeuing, and into his courtes with praise : be thankeful unto him, and speake good of his name.

For the lorde is gracious, hys mercie is euerlasting : and his trueth endureth from generacion to generacion.

Glory be to the father, &c.

As it was in the be : &c.

The Collect.

¶ God, which, &c. *as upon witsonday.*

The Epistle.   Acts x.

THEN Peter opened his mouth and sayd; of a truth I perceyue that there is no respecte of persones with God, but in all people, he that feareth hym, and woorketh righteousnesse, is accepted with hym.   Ye knowe the preachyng that God sente unto the children of Israell, preachyng peace by Jesus Christe, whiche is Lorde ouer all thynges; whiche preachyng was published throughoute all Jewrye, (and began in Galile, after the baptisme whiche John preached) how God annointed Jesus of Nazareth with the holye goste, and with power.   Whiche Jesus went about doyng good, and healing all that were oppressed of the deuill.   For God was with hym.   And we are witnesses of all thynges whiche he did in the land of the Jewes and at Jeru-salem, whome they slewe and hanged on tree: Hym God raysed up the thirde day, and shewed him openly, not to all the people, but unto us witnesses, (chosen before of god for the same entente;) whiche dyd eate and drynke with hym, after he arose from deathe. And he commaunded us to preache unto the people, and to testifye that it is he, whiche was ordayned of God to be the iudge of quicke and dead. To hym geue all the Prophetes witnesse, that through his name whosoeuer beleueth in him, shall receyue remission of synnes.

Whyle Peter yet spake these woordes, the holy goste fel on all them whiche heard the preachyng. And they of the circum-cision which beleued, were astonied, as many as came with Peter, because that on the Gentyles also, was shed out the gift of the holy goste. For they hearde them speake with tongues, and magnifye God. Then aunswered Peter, can any man forbid water, that these shoulde not be baptised whiche haue receyued the holy goste as well as we? And he commaunded them to bee baptised in the name of the Lorde. Then prayed they him to tary a fewe dayes.

The Gospel.   John iii.

So God loued the worlde, that he gaue his only-begottē sonne, that whosoeuer beleueth in him, shoulde not perishe, but haue euerlastyng lyfe. For God sent not his sonne into the world to condemne the worlde, but that the worlde through him mighte be saued. He that beleueth on hym is not condemned. But he that beleueth not, is condemned already, because he hath not beleued in the name of the onelye-begotten sonne of God. And thys is the condemnacyon; that lyghte is come into the worlde, and menne loued darkenes more then lighte, because theyr dedes were euill. For euery one that euill doeth, hateth the light, neither cummeth to the lighte, leste his dedes shoulde bee reproued. But he that doth trueth cūmeth to the light, that his dedes may be knowen, how that they are wrought in God.

¶ Tuesday.

¶ At the Communion.

Misericordiam.   Psalm ci.

My song shall bee of mercye and iudgemente : unto thee (O Lorde) will I sing.

O let me haue understandyng : in the waye of Godlynes.

When wilte thou come unto me? I will walke in my house with a perfect heart.

I wil take no wicked thing in hand; I hate the sinnes of unfaythfulnes : there shall no such cleaue vnto me.

A frowarde hearte shall departe from me : I will not knowe a wicked persone.

Whoso prieuely slaundereth his neighbour : him wil I destroye.

Whoso hath also a proude looke and an hie stomake : I will not suffer him.

Myne eyes looke vnto such as be faythfull in the land : that they may dwell with me.

Whoso leadeth a godly lyfe : he shalbe my seruaunte.

There shal no deceiptfull persone dwell in my house : he that telleth lyes shall not tary in my syght.

I shall soone destroy all the vngodly that are in the lande : that I may roote out all wicked dooers from the citie of the Lorde.

Glory be to the father, &c.

As it was in the beginning, &c.

The Collect.

GOD, which &c., *as vpon witsonday.*

The Epistle. Acts viii.

WHEN the Apostles whiche were at Jerusalem heard saye, that Samaria had receyued the woord of god, they sent vnto them Peter and John. Whiche, when they were come downe, prayed for them, that they mighte receiue the holy goste: for as yet he was come on none of them; but they were baptised onely in the name of Christ Jesu. Then layde they theyr handes on them, and they receyued the holy gost.

The Gospell. John x.

VERELY, verily I say vnto you; he that entreth not in by the dore into the shepe folde, but climeth vp some other way, the same is a thefe and a murtherer. But he that entreth in by the doore, is the shepeheard of the shepe: To hym the porter openeth, and the shepe heare his voyce, and he calleth hys owne shepe by name, and leadeth them out. And whē he hath sent furth his owne shepe, he goeth beefore them, and the shepe folow him: for they knowe hys voyce. A straunger wil they not folowe; but will flye from hym; for they knowe not the voyce of straungers.

This prouerbe spake Jesus unto them, but they understoode not what thynges they were whiche he spake unto them. Then sayde Jesus unto them agayne: verely, verely, I saye unto you; I am the doore of the shepe. All (euen as many as came before me) are theues and murtherers, but the shepe did not heare them. I am the dore, by me if any enter in, he shalbe safe, and shall goe in and out, and fynde pasture. A thefe cummeth not but for to steale, kill, and destroy. I am come that they might haue lyfe, and that they mighte haue it more aboundauntlye.

¶ *Trinitie Sonday.*

¶ *At Mattins.*

The First Lesson, Gen. xviii. unto the ende.

The Seconde Lesson, Math. iii. unto the ende.

¶ *At the Communion.*

Deus misereatur. Psalm lxvii.

GOD bee mercyfull unto us, and blesse us : and shewe us the lyghte of his countenaunce, and be mercifull unto us.

That thy way may be knowen upon earth : thy sauing health among all nacions.

Let the people prayse thee, O God : yea let all the people prayse thee.

O let the nacions reioice and be glad : for thou shalte iudge the folke ryghteouslye, and gouerne the nacyons upon earth.

Let the people prayse thee, O God : let all the people prayse thee.

Then shall the yearthe bryng foorthe her increase : and God, euen oure owne God, shall geue us hys blessing.

God shall blesse us: and all the endes of the worlde shall feare hym.

Glorie bee to the father, and to the sonne, and to the holy gost.

As it was in the beginning, is nowe, and euer shalbe : worlde without ende. Amen.

The Collect.

ALMIGHTYE and euerlastyng Ood, whiche haste geuen unto us thy seruauntes grace by the confession of a true fayth to acknowlege the glorye of the eternall trinitie, and in the power of the diuyne maiestie to wurshippe the unitie: we beseche thee, that through the stedfastnes of thys fayth, me may euermore be defended from all aduersitie, whiche liueste and reignest, one God, worlde without end.

The Epistle.   Apoc. iv.

AFTER this I loked, and behold, a doore was open in heauen: and the first voice which I heard was as it wer of a trompet, talking with me, whiche sayd; come up hither, and I will shew thee thinges whiche must be fulfilled hereafter.   And immediately I was in the spirite: And behold, a seate was set in heauen, and one sate on the seate.   And he that sate was to loke upon, lyke unto a Jasper stone, and a Sardine stone.   And there was a raynebowe about the seate, in sight lyke unto an Emerauld. And about the seate were xxiiii seates.   And upon the seates xxiiii Elders sittyng, clothed in white raiment, and had on their heades crownes of golde.

And out of the seate proceded lightninges, and thunderynges, and voyces, and there were vii lampes of fire, burning before the seate, whiche are the vii spirites of God.   And beefore the seate there was a sea of glasse lyke unto Christall: and in the myddes of the seate, and rounde aboute the seate, were iiii beastes full of eyes, beefore and behynde.   And the fyrste beaste was like a Lion; and the second beast like a calfe; and the thirde beaste hadde a face as a manne: and the fourthe beaste was lyke a flying Egle.   And the iiii beastes had eche one of them syxe wynges aboute hym; and they were full of iyes within. And they had no rest day neyther night, saying; Holy, holy, holy, Lorde God almightie, whiche was, and is, and is to come. And when those beastes gaue glory and honour, and thankes to hym that sate on the seate (whiche lyueth for euer and euer,) the xxiiii elders fell doune before hym that sate on the throne, and worshipped hym that lyueth for euer, and cast their crounes before the throne, saying; thou art worthy, O Lorde, (our God,) to receyue glory, and honor, and power, for thou hast created all thinges, and for thy wylles sake they are, and were created.

The Gospel.   John iii.

THERE was a manne of the Phariseis, named Nicodemus, a ruler of the Jewes. The same came to Jesus by night, and sayd unto hym, Rabby, we knowe that thou art a teacher come from God: for no man could do suche miracles as thou doest, except God were with him. Jesus answered, and sayd unto him; Verely, verely, I saye unto thee; except a man be borne frō

aboue, he cannot see the kyngdom of god. Nicodemus sayd
unto him; how can a man be borne when he is olde? can he
entre into his mothers wombe, and be borne agayne? Jesus
answered; verely, verely, I saye unto thee; excepte a man be
borne of water, and of the spirite, he cannot entre into the
kyngdome of God.   That whiche is borne of the fleshe, is fleshe;
and that whiche is borne of the spirit, is spirit.   Maruayl not
thou that I sayd thee, ye must bee borne from aboue.   The
wynde bloweth where it lusteth, and thou hearest the sound
therof, but canst not tel whēce it commeth, and whither it goeth;
So is euery one that is borne of the spirite   Nicodemus answered,
and sayd unto him; how can these thinges be? Jesus answered,
and sayd unto him; arte thou a maister in Israell, and knowest
not these thinges?   Verely, verely I say unto thee; we speake
that we do know, and testifie that we haue seen; and ye receyue
not our wytnes.   If I haue tolde you yearthly thynges, and ye
beleue not; howe shall ye beleue yf I tell you of heauenly
thynges?   And no man ascendeth up to heauen, but he that came
doune from heauen, euen the sonne of man whiche is in heauen.
And as Moses lift up the serpent in the wilderness, euen so must
the Sonne of man be lift up, that whosoeuer beleueth in hym,
perishe not, but haue euerlastyng lyfe.

¶ *The first Sonday after Trinitie Sonday.*

Beati immaculati.   Psalm cxix.

BLESSED are those that bee undefiled in the way : and walke
in the lawe of the Lorde.

Blessed are they that kepe his testimonies : and seke him with
theyr whole heart.

For they whiche do no wickednesse : walke in his wayes.

Thou hast charged, that we shall diligently kepe thy commaundementes : O that my wayes were made so direct, that I
might kepe thy statutes.

So shall I not bee confounded : while I haue respect unto all
thy commaundementes.

I will thanke thee with an unfayned heart : when I shall haue
learned the iudgementes of thy righteousnes.

I will kepe thy cerimonies : O forsake me not utterly.

Glory be to the father, and to the sonne, &c.

As it was in the beginnyng, &c.

The Collect.

GOD, the strength of all theym that trust in thee, mercifully accept our prayers; and because the weakenes of oure mortall nature can do no good thyng without thee, graunt us the helpe of thy grace, that in kepyng of thy commaundementes we may please thee, both in will and dede; through Jesus Christ our lorde.

The Epistle. 1 John iv.

DEARELY beloued, let us loue one another: for loue commeth of God. And euery one that loueth, is borne of God, and knoweth God. He that loueth not, knoweth not God; for God is loue. In this appeared the loue of God to us-ward, because that God sent his onely-begotten sonne into the worlde, that we might lyue through him. Herein is loue, not that we loued God, but that he loued us, and sent his sonne to be the agrement for our synnes.

Dearely beloued, if God so loued us, we ought also to loue one another. No man hath seen God at any tyme. If we loue one another, God dwelleth in us, and his loue is perfect in us. Here-by knowe we that we dwel in hym, and he in us, because he hath geuen us of his spirite. And we haue seen, and do testify, that the father sent the sonne to be the sauiour of the worlde: whoso-euer cōfesseth that Jesus is the sonne of God, in hym dwelleth God, and he in God. And we haue knowen and beleued the loue that God hath to us.

God is loue; and he that dwelleth in loue dwelleth in God, and God in him. Herein is the loue perfect in us, that we should haue trust in the day of iudgemēt. For as he is, euen so are we in this worlde. There is no feare in loue, but perfecte loue casteth out feare, for feare hath paynefulnes. He that feareth is not perfect in loue. We loue him, for he loued us first. If a man say; I loue God, and yet hate his brother, he is a lyar. For how can he that loueth not his brother, whom he hath seen, loue God whom he hath not seen? And this commaundement haue we of hym: that he whiche loueth God, should loue his brother also.

The Gospell. Luke xvi.

THERE was a certaine riche man, whiche was clothed in purple and fyne white, and fared deliciously euery day: And there was a certaine begger named Lazarus whiche lay at his gate full of sores, desyring to be refreshed with the crummes whiche fell from the riche mans borde, and no mã gaue unto him. The dogges came also and licked his sores. And it fortuned, that the begger dyed, and was caried by the Angels into Abrahams bosome. The riche man also dyed, and was buried. And beyng in hell in tormētes, he lifte up his eyes and sawe Abraham afar of, and Lazarus in his bosome, and he cryed and sayd; father Abraham, haue mercy on me, and send Lazarus, that he may dippe the tippe of his finger in water, and coole my tongue, for I am tormented in this flame. But Abraham sayd; Sonne, remembre that thou in thy lyfetyme, receiuedst thy pleasure; and contrarywise Lazarus receiued payne: But nowe he is comforted, and thou art punished. Beyonde all this, betwene us and you there is a great space set, so that they whiche would go from hence to you cannot: neyther may come from thence to us. Then he sayd; I pray the therefore father, sende hym to my fathers house, (for I haue v brethren,) for to warne them, leste they also come into this place of torment. Abraham sayd unto hym; they haue Moses and the Prophetes, let them heare them. And he sayd, nay father Abraham; but if one come unto them from the deed, they will repent. He sayd unto him; If they heare not Moses and the Prophetes, neyther wyll they beleue, though one rose from death againe.

¶ *The second Sondaye.*

In quo corriget ?   Psalm cxix.

WHERWITH all shall a yong man clense his waye : euen by rulyng hymself after thy worde.

With my whole heart haue I sought thee : O let me not go wrong out of thy commaundementes.

Thy wordes haue I hyd within my heart : that I should not synne against thee.

Blessed art thou, O Lord : O teache me thy statutes.

With my lyppes haue I been tellyng : of all the iudgementes of thy mouth : I haue had as great delite in the way of thy testimonies as in all maner of riches.

I will talke of thy commaundementes : and haue respect unto thy wayes.

My delite shalbe in thy statutes : and I wil not forget thy worde.

Glory be to the father and to sonne, &c.

As it was in the begynning, &c.

The Collect.

LORD, make us to haue a perpetuall feare and loue of thy holy name: for thou neuer faillest to helpe and gouerne them whom thou doest bryng up in thy stedfast loue. Graunt this, &c.

The Epistle. 1 John iii.

MARUEIL not my brethren though the worlde hate you. We know that we are translated from death unto life, because we loue the brethren. He that loueth not his brother, abideth in death. Whosoeuer hateth his brother is a manslear. And ye knowe that no manslear hath eternall lyfe abyding in him. Hereby perceyue we loue, because he gaue his lyfe for us: and we ought to geue our lyues for the brethren. But whoso hath this worldes good, and seeth his brother haue nede, and shutteth up his compassion from him; howe dwelleth the loue of God in hym? My babes let us not loue in word, neyther in tongue; but in dede, and in veritie. Hereby we knowe that we are of the veritie, and can quiet our heartes before hym. For yf our heart condemne us, God is greater then our heart, and knoweth all thinges. Derely beloued, if oure heart condemne us not, then haue we trust to god-warde: And whatsoeuer we aske we receyue of hym, because we kepe his commaundementes, and do those thinges whiche are pleasaunt in his sight. And this is his commaundement, That we beleue on the name of his sonne Jesus Christ, and loue one another as he gaue commaundement. And he that kepeth his cōmaundementes dwelleth in him, and he in hym: and hereby we knowe that he abydeth in us, euen by the spirite whiche he hath geuen us.

The Gospel. Luke xiv.

A CERTAINE man ordayned a great supper, and bad many; and sent his seruaunt at supper-tyme to say to them that were bydden, come; for all thinges are nowe ready. And they all at once began to make excuse. The first sayd unto him, I haue bought a farme, and I must nedes go and see it; I pray thee haue me excused. And another sayd, I haue bought v. yoke of Oxen, and I go to proue them; I pray thee haue me excused. And another sayd, I haue maried a wife, and therfore I cannot come. And the seruaunt returned, and brought his maister worde againe therof. Then was the good man of the house displeased, and said to his seruaunt; go out quickely into the stretes and quarters of the citie, and bring in hither the poore

and the feble, and the halt and the blinde. And the seruaunt
sayd; Lord, it is done as thou hast commaunded, and yet there
is roume. And the Lorde sayd to the seruaunt; go out vnto
the hyewayes and hedges, and compell them to come in, that
my house maye bee fylled. For I say vnto you, that none of
those men which were bydden, shall tast of my supper.

¶ *The third sonday.*

Retribue servo tuo. Psalm cxix.

O DO well vnto thy seruaunt : that I may lyue, and kepe thy
worde.

Open thou myne eyes : that I may see the wonderous thinges
of thy lawe.

I am a straunger vpon yearth : O hyde not thy commaundementes from me.

My soule breaketh out for the very feruent desyre : that it
hath alway vnto thy iudgementes.

Thou hast rebuked the proude : and cursed are they that do
erre from thy commaundementes.

O turne from me shame and rebuke : for I haue kept thy
testimonies.

Princes also dyd sit and speake against me : but thy seruaunt
is occupied in thy statutes.

For thy testimonies are my delite : and my counsailours.

Glory be to the father, and to the sonne, &c.

As it was in the beginnyng, is now, &c.

The Collect.

LORDE, we beseche thee mercifully to heare vs, and vnto
whom thou hast geuen an heartie desyre to pray; graunt that
by thy mightie ayde we may be defended; through Jesus Christ
our Lorde.

The Epistle. 1 Peter v.

SUBMIT yourselues euery man one to another; knyt yourselues together in lowlynes of minde. For God resisteth the
proud, and geueth grace to the humble. Submit yourselues
therfore vnder the mightie hãd of God, that he may exalt you
when the tyme is come. Cast all your care vpon him, for he
careth for you. Be sober, and watche: for your aduersary the
deuil as a roaryng Lyon, walketh about, sekyng whom he may
deuour: whom resist stedfast in the fayth, knowyng that the
same affliccions are appointed vnto your brethren that are in

the worlde. But the God of all grace whiche hath called us unto his eternall glorye by Christ Jesu, shall his owne selfe (after that ye haue suffered a lytle affliccion) make you perfect, settle, strength, and stablishe you. To hym be glory and dominion for euer and euer.

The Gospel. Luke xv.

THEN resorted unto hym all the Publicans and synners for to heare hym. And the Phariseis and Scribes murmured, saying, He receyueth synners, and eateth with them. But he put furth this parable unto them, saying; what man among you hauyng an hundreth shepe (if he lose one of them,) doth not leaue nynty and nyne in the wyldernes, and goeth after that whiche is lost, untill he fynde it? And when he hath found it, he layeth it on his shoulders with ioy. And as sone as he commeth home, he calleth together his louers and neyghbours, saying unto theim; Reioyce with me, for I haue found my shepe whiche was lost. I say unto you, that lykewyse ioy shalbe in heauen ouer one synner that repenteth, more than ouer nynty and nyne iust persones whiche nede no repentaunce.

Either what woman hauing ten grotes, (if she lose one,) doth not light a candle, and swepe the house, and seke diligently till she fynd it? And when she hath found it, she calleth her louers and her neighbours together, saying; reioyce with me, for I haue founde the grote whiche I had lost. Lykewise I saye unto you, shall there be ioy in the presence of the Angels of god, ouer one synner that repenteth.

¶ *The fourth Sondaye.*

¶ *At the Communion.*

Adhæsit pavimento anima. Ps. cxix.

MY soule cleaueth to the dust : O quicken thou me, accordyng to thy worde.

I haue knowleged my wayes, and thou heardest me : O teache me thy statutes.

Make me to understande the waye of thy commaundmentes : and so shall I talke of thy wonderous workes.

My soule melteth away for very heauynes, comforte thou me accordyng unto thy worde.

Take frō me the way of lying : and cause thou me to make muche of thy lawe.

I haue chosen the way of truth : and thy iudgementes haue I layde before me.

I haue sticken unto thy testimonies : O Lorde confound me not.

I wil runne the way of thy commaundementes : when thou hast set my heart at libertie.

Glory be to the father, and to tne sonne, &c.

As it was in the beginning, is now, &c.

The Collect.

GOD the protector of all that trust in thee, without whom nothyng is strong, nothing is holy; increase and multiply upon us thy mercye; that thou being our ruler and guyde, we may so passe through thinges temporall, that we fynally lose not the thinges eternall: Graunt this heauenly father, for Jesu Christes sake our Lorde.

The Epistle. Rom. viii.

I SUPPOSE that the affliccions of this lyfe, are not worthy of the glory which shalbe shewed upon us. For the feruent desyre of the creature abydeth, lokyng when the sonnes of God shall appeare, because the creature is subdued to vanitie, against the will thereof, but for his will which hath subdued the same in hope. For the same creature shalbe deliuered from the bondage of corrupcion, into the glorious libertie of the sonnes of GOD. For we knowe that euery creature groneth with us also, and trauaileth in payne, euen unto this tyme: not onely it, but we also whiche haue the first-fruites of the spirite, mourne in ourselues also, and wayte for the adopcion, (of the children of God,) euen the deliueraunce of our bodyes.

The Gospel. Luke vi.

BE ye mercifull, as your father also is mercyful. Judge not and ye shall not be iudged: condemne not, and ye shall not be condemned. Forgeue, and ye shalbe forgeuen. Geue, and it shalbe geuen unto you, good measure, and pressed doune and shaken together, and runnyng ouer, shall menne geue into your bosomes. For with the same measure that ye mete withall, shall other men mete to you againe.

And he put furth a similitude unto thē. Can the blynd lead the blynd? do they not both fall into the diche? The disciple is not aboue his maister; Euery man shalbe perfect, euen as his Maister is. Why seest thou a mote in thy brothers eye, but considerest not the beame that is in thyne owne eye? Eyther how canst thou saye to thy brother? Brother, let me pull out the mote that is in thyne eye, when thou seest not the beame that is in thyne owne eye. Thou ypocrite, cast out the beame out of thyne owne eye first, and then shalt thou see perfectly to pul out the mote that is in thy brothers eye.

¶ The v Sunday.

Legem pone. Psalm cxix.

TEACHE me, O Lorde, the way of thy statutes : and I shall kepe it unto the ende.

Geue me understandyng, and I shall kepe thy lawe : yea, I shall kepe it with my whole heart.

Make me to goe in the path of thy commaundemētes : for therin is my desyre.

Encline my heart unto thy testimonies : and not to couetousnes.

O turne away myne eyes, leste they beholde vanitie : and quicken thou me in thy way.

O stablishe thy woorde in thy seruaunt : that I may feare thee.

Take away the rebuke that I am afrayde of : for thy iudgementes are good.

Beholde my delite is in thy commaundementes : O quicken me in thy righteousnes.

Glory be to the father, and to sonne, &c.

As it was in the begynning, &c.

The Collect.

GRAUNTE Lorde, wee besesche thee, that the course of thys worlde maye bee so peaceably ordred by thy gouernaunce, that thy congregacion may ioyfully serue thee in all godly quietnes; thoroughe Jesus Christe oure Lorde.

The Epistle. 1 Peter iii.

BE you all of one mynde and of one heart, loue as brethren, be pitifull, be courteous, (meke,) not rendring euil for euil, or rebuke for rebuke; but cōtrarywise blesse, knowyng that ye are therunto called, euen that ye shoulde bee heyres of the blessyng. For he that doeth long after life, and loueth to see good dayes, let him refrayne his tongue from euil, and his lippes that they speake no guile. Let hym eschewe euil and do good: let him seke peace, and ensue it. For the eyes of the Lorde are ouer the righteous, and his eares are open unto their prayers. Againe, the face of the Lorde is ouer them that do euil.

Moreouer, who is it that will harme you if ye folowe that whiche is good? yea, happye are ye, if any trouble happē unto you for righteousnes sake. Be not ye afrayed for any terror of them, neither be ye troubled, but sanctifie the Lorde God in your heartes.

The Gospel. Luke v.

IT came to passe that (when the people preased upon hym, to heare the worde of God) he stoode by the lake of Genezareth, and sawe two shippes stande by the lakes side; but the fishermen were gone out of them, and were washyng their nettes. And he entred into one of the shippes, (whiche pertained to Symon,) and praied him, that he would thrust out a litle from the land. And he sat doune and taught the people out of the shyp. When he had lefte speakyng, he sayd unto Symon: lanche out into the deepe, and let slippe your nettes to make a draughte. And Symon answered, and sayde unto hym; Master, we haue labored all nighte, and haue taken nothyng. Neuertheles, at thy commaundement, I will loce furth the nette. And when they had this done, they inclosed a great multitude of fishes. But their net brake, and they beckened to their felowes (whiche were in the other ship) that they shoulde come and helpe them. And they came, and fylled bothe the shippes, that they soncke againe.

When Symon Peter sawe this, he fell doune at Jesus' knees, saiyng; Lorde, goe from me, for I am a synnefull man. For he was astonyed, and all that were with hym, at the draughte of fyshes which they had taken; and so was also James and John the sonnes of Zebede, whyche were parteners wyth Symon. And Jesus said unto Symon; feare not, from hencefurth thou shalt catche men. And they brought the shippes to land, and forsoke all, and folowed him.

¶ *The vi Sondaie.*

Et veniat super me. Psalm cxix.

LET thy louyng mercie come also unto me, O Lorde : Euen thy saluacion, accordyng unto thy woorde.

So shall I make aunswere unto my blasphemers : For my truste is in thy woorde.

O take not the worde of truthe utterly out of my mouthe : For my hope is in thy iudgementes.

So shall I alwaye kepe thy lawe : yea, for euer and euer.

And I will walke at libertie : For I seke thy commaundementes.

I will speake of thy testimonies also, euē before kynges : and
will not be ashamed.

And my delight shalbe in thy commaundementes : whiche I
haue loued.

My handes also will I lift up unto thy commaundementes
whiche I haue loued : and my study shalbee in thy statutes.

Glory be to the father, and to the sonne, &c.

As it was in the beginning, is nowe, &c.

The Collect.

GOD, whiche haste prepared to them that loue thee suche good
thynges as passe all mannes understanding; Powre into our
hartes such loue toward thee, that we louyng thee in al thinges,
may obteine thy promises, whiche excede all that we canne
desyre; Through Jesus Christe our Lorde.

The Epistle.   Romans vi.

KNOWE ye not, that all we whiche are baptised in Jesu Christe,
are baptised to dye with hym? We are buryed then with hym
by baptisme for to dye; that likewise as Christ was raised from
death, by the glorye of the father, euen so we also should walke
in a newe life.   For if we be graft in death like unto him; euen
so shall we be partakers of the resurreccion: Knowing this, that
our olde man is crucified with hym also, that the body of synne
myght utterly be destroyed, that hencefurth we should not be
seruaūtes unto synne.   For he that is dead is iustified from
synne.

Wherfore, if we be dead with Christe, we beleue that we shall
also lyue with hym, knowyng that Christe beyng raysed from
death, dyeth no more.   Death hath no more power ouer hym.
For as touchyng that he dyed, he dyed concernyng synne once.
And as touching that he lyueth, he lyueth unto God: Likewise
consider ye also, that ye are dead as touchyng synne, but are
alyue unto God, through Jesus Christe our Lorde.

The Gospell.   Matt. v.

JESUS sayed unto his disciples; excepte youre ryghteousnesse
excede the ryghteousnesse of the Scribes and Phariseis, ye
cannot entre into the Kyngdome of heauen.   Ye haue heard
that it was sayed unto them of the olde tyme.   Thou shalt not

kill: whosoeuer killeth, shalbe in daunger of iudgement. But I saye unto you; that whosoeuer is angry with his brother un- aduisedly) shalbe in daunger of iudgement. And whosoeuer saye unto hys brother, Racha, shal be in daunger of a counsaill. But whosoeuer sayth, thou foole, shalbe in daunger of hell fire. Therfore, if thou offerest thy gift at the alter and there remem- brest that thy brother hath ought agaynst thee, leaue there thyne offeryng before the alter, and goe thy waye firste, and be recon- ciled to thy brother, and then come and offer thy gyfte.

Agree with thyne aduersarye quickly, whyles thou art in the waye with hym, leste at any tyme the aduersarye delyuer thee to the iudge, and the iudge delyuer thee to the minister, and then thou be cast into prison. Verelye I saye unto thee, thou shalt not come out thence, till thou haue payed the uttermoste farthyng.

¶ The vii Sonday.

Memor esto. Psalm cxix.

O THINKE upon thy seruaunte, as concerning thy worde : wherin thou hast caused me to put my trust.

The same is my comfort in my trouble : For thy worde hath quickened me.

The proude haue had me excedyngly in derision : yet haue I not shrynked from thy lawe.

For I remembred thyne euerlastyng iudgementes, O Lorde : and receyued comfort.

I am horribly afrayed : For the ungodly, that forsake thy lawe.

Thy statutes haue been my songes : In the house of my pilgrimage.

I haue thought upon thy name, O Lord, in the inght-season : and haue kept thy lawe.

This I had : because I kepte thy commaundementes.

Glory be to the father, and to the sonne : and to the holy gost.

As it was in the begynnyng, is nowe, and euer shalbe : worlde without ende. Amen.

The Collect.

LORDE of all power and might, whiche art the author and geuer of all good thynges; graffe in our hartes the loue of thy name, increase in us true religion, norishe us with all goodnes, and of thy great mercy kepe us in the same; Through Jesus Christe our Lorde.

The Epistle. Rom. vi.

I SPEAKE grosly, because of the infirmitie of your fleshe. As ye haue geuen your membres seruauntes to unclennes and to iniquitie (from one iniquitie to another); euen so now geue ouer your membres seruauntes unto righteousnes that ye may be sanctified. For when ye were the seruauntes of synne, ye were voyde of righteousnes. What fruite had you then in those thinges, wherof ye are nowe ashamed? for the ende of those thinges is death. But nowe are ye delyuered from synne, and made the seruauntes of God, and haue your fruite to be sāctified, and the ende euerlasting lyfe. For the rewarde of synne is death: but eternall lyfe is the gifte of God; Through Jesus Christe our Lorde.

The Gospel. Mark viii.

IN those dayes, when there was a verye great companie, and had nothyng to eate; Jesus called hys disciples unto hym, and sayed unto them: I haue compassion on the people, because they haue nowe been with me three dayes, and haue nothing to eate: And if I sende them awaye fasting to their owne houses, they shall faint by the waye; for diuerse of them came from farre. And his disciples answered him; where shoulde a manne haue bread here in the wildernessc, to satisfie these? And he asked them; howe manye loaues haue ye? They sayd, seuen. And he commaunded the people to sitte downe on the grounde. And he tooke the seuen loaues; And when he had geuen thankes, he brake and gaue to his disciples, to set before them. And they did set them before the people. And they had a fewe small fishes. And when he had blessed, he commaunded them also to be sette before them. And they did eate and were suffised. And they tooke up of the broken meate that was left, seuē baskettes ful. And they that did eate, were about foure thousande. And he sente them awaye.

¶ *The eight Sonday.*

¶ *At the Communion.*

Portio mea, Domine. Psalm cxix.

THOU art my porcion, O Lord : I haue promised to kepe thy lawe.

I made myne humble peticion in thy presēce with my whole heart : O be merciful unto me, according unto thy worde.

I call myne owne wayes to remembraunce : and turne my feete into thy testimonies.

I made hast : and prolonged not the tyme to kepe thy commaundementes.

The congregacions of the ungodly haue robbed me : but I haue not forgotten thy lawe.

At midnight will I rise, to geue thankes unto thee : because of thy righteous iudgementes.

I am a companion of all them that feare thee : and kepe thy commaundementes.

The earth, O Lorde, is full of thy mercye : O teache me thy statutes.

Glory be to the father, and to the sonne : and to the holy gost.

As it was in the beginning, is nowe, and euer shalbe : worlde without ende. Amen.

The Collect.

God, whose prouidence is neuer deceiued, we humbly beseche thee that thou wilt put away frō us al hurtfull thinges, and geue those thinges whiche be profitable for us; through Jesus Christe our Lorde.

The Epistle. Rom. viii.

Brethren, we are debters, not to the fleshe, to liue after the fleshe. For yf ye liue after the fleshe, ye shall dye. But yf ye (through the spirite) doe mortifie the deedes of the body, ye shall liue. For as many as are led by the spirite of God, they are the sonnes of God. For ye haue not receyued the spirite of bondage to feare any more, but ye haue receyued the spirite of adopcion, wherby we crye, Abba father. The same spirite certifieth our spirite, that we are the sonnes of God. If we be sōnes, then are we also heires, the heires I meane of God, and heires annexed with Christ: yf so be that we suffre with hym, that we may be also gloryfied together with hym.

The Gospell. Matt. vii.

Beware of false Prophetes, which come to you in shepes clothing, but inwardly they are rauenyng wolues. Ye shall knowe them by their fruites. Do men gather Grapes of Thornes? Or Figges of Thistles? Euen so euery good tree bryngeth furth good fruites: But a corrupte tree bryngeth furth euyll fruites. A good tree cannot bryng furth bad fruites, neythei can a bad tree bryng furth good fruites. Euery tree that bryngeth not furth good fruite, is hewen doune, and caste into the fire. Wherfore by their fruites ye shall knowe them. Not euery one that sayeth unto me, Lorde, Lorde, shall entre into the kyngdome of heauen; but he that doth the will of my father whiche is in heauen, he shall entre into the kyngdome of heauen.

¶ *The ix Sonday.*

Bonitatem. Psalm cxix.

O LORDE, thou hast delt graciously with thy seruaunt : accordyng unto thy worde.

O learne me true understanding and knowlege : For I haue beleued thy commaundementes.

Before I was troubled I went wrong : but nowe I haue kept thy worde.

Thou art good and gracious : O teache me thy statutes.

The proude haue imagined a lye againste me : but I wyll kepe thy commaundementes with my whole heart.

Their heart is as fat as braune : but my delite hath been in thy lawe.

It is good for me that I haue been in trouble : That I may learne thy statutes.

The lawe of thy mouth is derer unto me : then thousandes of golde and siluer.

Glory be to the father, and to the sonne : and to the holye gost.

As it was in the beginning, is nowe, and euer shalbe : worlde without ende. Amen.

The Collect.

GRAUNT to us Lorde we beseche thee, the spirite to thinke and doe alwayes suche thynges as be rightfull; that we, which cannot be without thee, may by thee be able to liue accordyng to thy wyll; Through Jesus Christe our Lorde.

The Epistle. 1 Cor. x.

BRETHREN, I would not that ye should be ignoraũt, how that our fathers were all under the cloude, and al passed through the sea, and were al baptised under Moses in the cloude, and in the sea, and did all eate of one spirituall meate, and did all drinke of one spirituall drinke. And they dranke of the spiritual rocke that folowed them, whiche Rocke was Christe. But in many of them hadde God no delight. For they were ouerthrowen in the wildernesse. These are ensamples to us, that we should not lust after euil thinges, as they lusted. And that ye should not be worshippers of ymages, as were some of them according as it is written. The people sate downe to eate, and drynke, and rose up to playe. Neither let us be defiled with fornicacion, as some of them were defiled with fornicacion, and fell in one daye thre and twentie thousand. Neither let us tempt Christe, as some of them tempted, and were destroyed of serpentes. Neither murmure ye, as some of them murmured, and were destroyed of the destroyer. All these thynges happened unto them for ensamples: But are written to put us in remembraunce, whom the endes of the world are come upon. Wherfore, let him that thinketh he standeth, take hede leste he fall. There hath none other temptacion taken you, but suche as foloweth the nature of manne. But God is faithful, whiche shall not suffer you to bee tempted aboue youre strength: but shal in the middes of the temptacion make a waye, that ye may be able to beare it.

The Gospel. Luke xvi.

JESUS sayd unto his disciples; There was a certaine riche man, which had a Steward, and the same was accused unto him, that he had wasted his goodes. And he called him, and sayed unto him; howe is it that I heare this of thee? Geue accomptes of thy stewardship, for thou maiest be no longer Steward. The Steward sayd within himselfe: what shal I do? For my Maister taketh away frō me the Stewardshippe. I cannot digge, and to begge I am ashamed. I wote what to doe, that when I am put out of the Stewardshippe, they may receyue me into their houses. So when he had called all his Masters debters together, he sayd unto the first; how much owest thou unto my Master? And he sayd; an hundred tunnes of oyle. And he sayed unto hym; take thy Bill, and sitte downe quickly, and write fiftie. Then sayd he to another; how muche owest thou? And he sayed; an hundred quarters of wheate. He sayed unto hym; take thy bill, and write foureskore. And the Lord commended the uniust Steward, because he had done wysely. For the children of this worlde are in their nacion, wiser than the children of light. And I saye unto you; Make you frendes of the unrighteous Mammon, that when ye shall haue nede, they may receyue you into euerlastyng Habitacions.

¶ *The x Sonday.*

Manus tuæ.   Psalm cxix.

THY handes haue made me and fashioned me : O geue me understandyng, that I maye learne thy commaundementes.

They that feare thee wyll bee glad, when they see me : because that I haue put my trust in thy worde.

I knowe, O Lorde, that thy iudgementes are ryght : and that thou of very faythfulnes, haste caused me to be troubled.

O let thy mercifull kyndnes be my comforte : Accordyng to thy worde unto thy seruaunt.

O let thy louyng mercies come unto me, that I may lyue : For thy lawe is my delight.

Let the proude be confounded, for they goe wickedly about to destroy me : But I will be occupied in thy commaundementes.

Let suche as feare thee, and haue knowen thy testimonies : be turned unto me.

O let my harte be sounde in thy statutes : that I be not ashamed.

Glory be to the father, and to the sonne, &c.

As it was in the beginning, &c.   Amen.

The Collect.

LET thy merciful eares, O Lord, be open to the praiers of thy humble seruauntes; and that they may obteine their peticions, make them to aske suche thinges as shal please thee; Through Jesus Christe our Lorde.

The Epistle.   1 Cor. xii.

CONCERNING spiritual thinges (brethren) I would not haue you ignoraunte. Ye knowe that ye were Gentiles, and wente youre wayes unto dumme ymages, euen as ye were ledde. Wherfore I declare unto you, that no manne, speakyng by the spirite of God, defyeth Jesus. Also no manne canne saye that Jesus is the Lorde, but by the holy gost. There are diuersities of gyftes, yet but one spirite. And there are differences of adminis-tracions, and yet but one Lorde. And there diuerse maners of operacions, and yet but one God, whiche worketh all in all.

The gift of the spirite is geuen to euery man to edifie withall. For to one is geuen through the spirite, the utteraunce of wise-dome: to another is geuen the utterauce of knowlege, by the same spirite. To another is geuen faith, by the same spirite.

To another the gift of healyng, by the same spirite.   To another, power to do miracles.   To another prophecie.   To another iudgemente to discerne spirites.   To another diuerse tongues. To another the interpretacion of tongues: But these al worketh euen the selfe same spirite, deuydyng to euery manne a seuerall gifte, euen as he will.

The Gospell.   Luke xix.

AND when he was come nere to Hierusalem, he behelde the citie, and wepte on it, saying; If thou haddest knowen those thinges, whiche belong unto thy peace, euen in this thy daye, thou wouldest take hede.   But nowe are they hid from thine iyes.   For the dayes shall come upon thee, that thy enemies also shall cast a banke aboute thee, and compasse thee rounde, and kepe thee in on euery syde, and make thee euen with the ground, and thy children whiche are in thee.   And they shall not leaue in thee one stone upon another, because thou knowest not the time of thy visitacion.   And he went into the Temple, and began to cast out thē that solde therin, and them that bought, saying unto them; It is written, my house is the house of prayer; but ye haue made it a denne of theues.   And he taught dayly in the Temple.

¶ The xi Sonday.

Defecit.   Psalm cxix.

MY soule hath longed for thy saluacion : and I haue a good hope, because of thy worde.

My iyes long soore for thy worde, saying; O when wilt thou comforte me?

For I am become like a botle in the smoke : yet doe I not forget thy statutes.

Howe many are the dayes of thy seruaunte? when wilt thou be auenged of them that persecute me?

The proude haue digged pittes for me : which are not after thy lawe.

All thy commaundementes are true : They persecute me falsely; O be thou my helpe.

They had almoste made an ende of me upon earthe : but I forsoke not thy commaundementes.

O quicken me after thy louyng-kyndnes : and so shall I kepe the testimonies of thy mouth.

Glory be to the father, and to the sonne, &c.
As it was in the beginning, is nowe, &c.

The Collect.

GOD, which declarest thy almighty power, most chiefly in shewyng mercy and pitie; Geue unto us abundauntly thy grace, that we, running to thy promises, may be made partakers of thy heauenly treasure; through Jesus Christe our Lorde.

The Epistle. 1 Cor. xv.

BRETHREN, as perteyning to the Gospell, whiche I preached unto you, whiche ye haue also accepted, and in the whiche ye continue, by the whiche also ye are saued; I doe you to wete after what maner I preached unto you, yf ye kepe it, excepte ye haue beleued in vayne. For fyrste of all I delyuered unto you that whiche I receyued, howe that Christe dyed for our synnes, agreyng to the scriptures; and that he was buryed; and that he arose agayne the thirde daye, accordyng to the scriptures; And that he was seen of Cephas, then of the xii. After that was he seen of moe than fyue hundreth brethren at once, of whiche many remaine unto this daye, and many are fallen aslepe.

After that appeared he to James, then to all the Apostles. And last of al he was seen of me, as of one that was borne out of duc time. For I am the least of the Apostles, whiche am not worthy to bee called an Apostle, because I haue persecuted the congregacion of God. But by the grace of God, I am that I am. And his grace whiche is in me; was not in vaine. But I labored more aboundātly then they all, yet not I, but the grace of God, whiche is with me. Therfore, whether it wer I or they, so we preached, and so ye haue beleued.

The Gospell. Luke xviii.

CHRISTE tolde this parable unto certaine whiche trusted in themselues, that they were perfect and despised other. Two men wente up into the temple to pray, the one a Pharise, and the other a Publican. The Pharise stode and prayed thus with himselfe. God, I thāke thee, that I am not as other mē are, extorcioners, uniust, adulterers, or as this Publicā. I fast twise in the weke: I geue tythe of al that I possesse. And the Publicā, standing afarre of, would not lyft up his eyes to heauen, but smote upon his brest, saying; God be mercifull to me a sinner. I tell you, this man departed home to his house iustifyed more then the other. For euery man that exalteth hymselfe shalbe brought lowe: And he that humbleth himselfe shalbe exalted.

¶ *The xii Sunday.*

In æternum, Domine.   Psalm cxix.

O LORDE, thy woorde : indureth for euer in heauen.

Thy trueth also remayneth from one generacion to another : thou haste layde the foundacion of the earth, and it abydeth.

They continue this daye accordyng to thyne ordinaunce : for all thynges serue thee.

If my delite had not been in thy lawe : I should haue peryshed in my trouble.

I will neuer forget thy commaundementes : for with them thou haste quickened me.

I am thyne, Oh saue me : For I haue sought thy commaundementes.

The ungodly layde wayte for me to destroy me : but I will considre thy testimonies.

I see that all thynges come to an ende : but thy commaundementes are excedyng broade.

Glory be to the father, and to the sonne, &c.

As it was in the beginning, &c.   Amen.

The Collect.

ALMIGHTIE and euerlastyng God, which art alwayes more ready to heare then we to praye, and art wont to geue more than eyther we desyre or deserue; Powre downe upon us the aboundance of thy mercy; forgeuing us those thynges wherof our conscience is afrayde, and geuyng unto us that that our prayer dare not presume to aske, through Jesus Christe our Lorde.

The Epistle.   2 Cor. iii.

SUCHE trust haue we through Christ to God-ward, not that we are sufficient of ourselues, to thynke any thyng as of ourselues, but if we be able unto any thyng, the same commeth of God; which hath made us able to minister the newe testament, not of the lettre, but of the spirite : For the letter kylleth, but the spirite geueth lyfe. If the ministraciō of death, through the letters figured in stones, was glorious, so that the children of Israel could not behold the face of Moses, for the glory of his countenaunce; (which glory is done away;) why shall not the ministracion of the spirite be muche more glorious? for if the ministracion of condemnacion be glorious, muche more doeth the ministracion of righteousnes excede in glory.

The Gospell. Mark vii.

JESUS departed from the coastes of Tyre and Sydon, and came unto the sea of Galile, through the middes of the coastes of the x cities. And they brought unto hym one that was deaffe, and had an impedimēt in his speche, and they prayed hym to put his hand upon him. And when he had taken him asyde from the people, he put his fingers into his eares; and did spit, and touched his tounge, and loked up to heauen, and sighed, and sayed unto him; Ephata, that is to say, be opened. And straightway his eares were opened, and the string of his tounge was looced, and he spake plaine. And he commaunded them that they should tel no man. But the more he forbad them, so muche the more a great deale they published, saying; He hath done all thynges well, he hath made bothe the deaffe to heare, and the dumme to speake.

The xiii Sonday.

Quomodo dilexi ! Psalm cxix.

LORDE what loue haue I unto thy lawe? all the day long is my study in it.

Thou thorough thy commaundementes haste made me wyser then my enemies : for they are euer with me.

I haue more understandyng then my teachers : for thy testimonies are my study.

I am wyser then the aged : because I kepte thy commaundementes.

I haue refrayned my feete from euery euill way : that I may kepe thy worde.

I haue not shrynked from thy iudgementes : for thou teachest me.

O howe swete are thy wordes unto my throte? yea, sweter than hony unto my mouth.

Through thy commaundementes I gette understandyng : therfore I hate all wicked wayes.

Glory be to the father, and to the sonne, &c.

As it was in the beginnyng, &c. Amen.

The Collect.

ALMYGHTIE and mercyfull God, of whose onely gifte it cometh that thy faythfull people doe unto thee true and laudable seruice; graunte we beseche thee, that we may so runne to thy heauenly promises, that we faile not finally to attayne the same; through Jesus Christe our Lorde.

The Epistle. Gal. iii.

To Abraham and his sede were the promises made. He sayeth not in the sedes, as manye; but in thy sede, as of one, which is Christ. This I say, that the lawe whyche began afterward, beyonde iiii. c. and xxx. yeres, doth not disanul the testament that was confirmed afore of God unto Christ-warde, to make the promise of none effect. For if the inheritaunce come of the lawe, it commeth not nowe of promise. But God gaue it to Abrahā by promyse. Wherfore then serueth the lawe? The lawe was added because of transgressiō, (till the sede came, to whome the promise was made,) and it was ordained by Angels in the hande of a mediator. A mediator is not a mediator of one; But God is one. Is the lawe then against the promise of God? God forbid. For if there had been a lawe geuen whiche could haue geuen lyfe; then no doubte righteousnes should haue come by the lawe. But the scripture concludeth all thinges under synne, that the promise, by the faythe of Jesus Christe, should be geuen unto them that beleue.

The Gospell. Luke x.

HAPPY are the iyes whiche see the thinges that ye see. For I tell you, that many Prophetes and kinges haue desired to see those thynges which ye see, and haue not seen them, and to heare those thynges whiche ye heare, and haue not heard thē.

And beholde, a certaine lawyer stode up, and tempted him, saying; Master, what shall I do to inherite eternall lyfe? he said unto him; what is written in the lawe? how readest thou? and he answered, and sayd; Loue the Lord thy God with al thy heart, and with al thy soule, and with all thy strength and with all thy mynde: and thy neighbour as thyselfe. And he sayed unto hym; Thou haste answered right. This do, and thou shalt liue: but he willyng to iustifie hymselfe, sayed unto Jesus; And who is my neighbor: Jesus answered and sayd. A certaine man descended from Jerusalem to Hierico, and fell among theues, whiche robbed him of his raymēt, and wounded him, and departed, leauyng him halfe dead. And it chaūsed that there came downe a certayne prieste that same waye, and when he sawe him, he passed by. And likewise a Leuite, when he went nye to the place came and loked on hym, and passed by. But a certaine Samaritane as he iorneyed, came unto hym; and when he sawe hym, he had compassion on hym, and went to, and bounde up his woundes, and powred in oyle and wyne, and set hym on his owne beast, and brought hym to a common inne, and made prouision for hym. And on the morowe, when he departed, he tooke out two pence, and gaue them to the hoste, and sayd unto hym; Take cure of hym, and whatsoeuer thou spendest more, when I come agayne, I wyll recompence thee. Which nowe of these thre thinkest thou was neighbour unto hym that fell among the theues? and he sayed; he that shewed mercy on hym. Then sayed Jesus unto him; goe, and doe thou lykewyse.

The xiiii Sonday.

Lucerna pedibus meis. Psalm cxix.

THY woorde is a Lanterne unto my feete : and a light unto my pathes.

I have sworne and am stedfastly purposed : to kepe thy righteous iudgementes.

I am troubled aboue measure : quicken me, O Lorde, accordyng unto thy woorde.

Let the freewill offeringes of my mouth please thee, O Lorde : and teache me thy iudgementes.

My soule is alwaye in my hande : yet doe not I forget thy lawe.

The ungodly haue layed a snare for me : but yet swarued not I from thy commaundementes.

Thy testimonies haue I claimed as mine heritage for euer : and why? they are the very ioy of my heart.

I haue applied my harte to fulfill thy statutes alway : euen unto the ende.

Glory be to the father, and to the sonne, &c.

As it was in the beginning, &c.

The Collect.

ALMIGHTYE and euerlastyng God, geue unto us the increase of faythe, hope, and charitie; and that we may obteine that whiche thou doest promise; make us to loue that whiche thou doest commaunde, through Jesus Christe our Lorde.

The Epistle. Gal. v.

I SAYE, walke in the spirite, and fulfyll not the lust of the fleshe. For the fleshe lusteth contrary to the spirite, and the spirite contrary to the fleshe; these are contrary one to the other, so that ye cannot doe whatsoeuer ye would. But and yf ye be led of the spirite, then are ye not under the lawe. The dedes of the fleshe are manyfest, whiche are these; adultry, fornicacion, unclennesse, wantonnesse, worshippyng of images, witchcraft, hatred, variance, zele, wrath, strife, sedicions, sectes, enuying, murder, dronkennes, gluttony, and suche like, of the whiche I tell you before, as I haue tolde you in tymes past, that they whiche commit suche thinges shall not be inheritors of the kingdome of God. Contrarily, the fruite of the spirite is loue, ioy, peace, long-sufferyng, gentlenes, goodnes, faithfulnes, mekenes, temperancie. Against suche there is no lawe. They truely th t are Christes, haue crucified the fleshe with the affeccions and lustes.

The Gospell. Luke xvii.

AND it chaunsed as Jesus went to Jerusalem, that he passed through Samaria and Galile. And as he entred into a certaine toune there met him x mē that were lepers. Which stode afarre of, and put furth their voyces, and sayed; Jesu master haue mercy upon us. When he sawe them, he sayed unto them; go, shewe yourselues unto the priestes. And it came to passe that as they went they were clensed. And one of them, when he sawe that he was clensed, turned backe agayne, and with a loude voyce praysed God, and fell downe on his face at his feete, and gaue him thankes. And the same was a Samaritane. And Jesus answered, and sayed; Are there not x clensed? but where are those ix? There are not founde that returned againe to geue God prayse, saue onely this straunger. And he sayed unto hym; arise, go thy waye, thy fayth hath made the whole.

The xv Sonday.

Iniquos odio habui. Psalm cxix.

I HATE them that imagine euill thinges : but thy lawe do I loue.

Thou art my defence and shylde : and my truste is in thy worde.

Awaye fro me ye wycked : I wyll kepe the commaundementes of my God.

O stablishe me accordyng unto thy worde, that I may liue : and let me not be disapointed of my hope.

Holde thou me up, and I shalbe safe : yea, my delite shall euer be in thy statutes.

Thou haste troden doune all them that depart from thy statutes : for they imagyne but deceipte.

Thou puttest awaye all the ungodly of the earth lyke drosse : therfore I loue thy testimonies.

My flesh trembleth for feare of thee : and I am afrayde of thy iudgementes.

Glory be to the father and to the sonne, &c.

As it was in the beginnyng, &c.

The Collect.

KEPE we beseche thee, O Lorde, thy Churche with thy perpetuall mercye: and because the frailtie of man without thee, cannot but fall: Kepe us euer by thy helpe, and leade us to al thynges profitable to our saluacion; through Jesus Christe our Lorde.

The Epistle. Gal. vi.

YE see howe large a letter I haue writtē unto you with mine owne hande. As many as desyre with outwarde apperaūce to please carnally, the same constraine you to be circumcised, only lest they should suffre persecucion for the crosse of Christ. For they thēselues whiche are circumcised kepe not the lawe; but desyre to haue you circūcised, that they might reioyce in your flesh. God forbyd that I should reioyce, but in the crosse of our Lorde Jesu Christ, whereby the worlde is crucified unto me, and I unto the world. For in Christ Jesu neither circumcision auaileth any thyng at all, nor uncircumcision; but a newe creature. And as many as walke accordyng unto this rule, peace be on them, and mercy, and upō Israel that pertayneth to God. From henceforth, lette no mā put me to busines; for I beare in my body the markes of the Lorde Jesu. Brethren, the grace of our Lorde Jesu Christ be with your spirite. Amen.

The Gospel Matt. vi.

No manne can serue two Maisters, for either he shall hate the one, and loue the other, or elles leane to the one, and despise the other: ye canne not serue God and Mammon. Therfore I saye unto you; be not carefull for your lyfe, what ye shall eate or dryncke: nor yet for your body, what raymente ye shall put on. Is not the life more worthe than meate? and the body more of value than rayment? Beholde the foules of the ayre, for they sowe not, neither do they reape, nor cary into the barnes; and your heauēly father fedeth them. Are ye not muche better than they? Whiche of you (by takyng carefull thought) can adde one cubite unto his stature? And why care ye for rayment: Consider the Lylies of the fielde how they growe. They laboure not; neither do they spynne. And yet I saye unto you, that euen Salamō in al his royaltie, was not clothed like one of these. Wherfore, if god so clothe the grasse of the fielde (whiche though it stād to-day, is to-morrow caste into the fornace;) shall he not muche more do the same for you, O ye of litle fayth? Therfore, take no thought, saying; what shall we eate, or what shal we drinke, or wherwith shall we be clothed? after all these thynges do the Gentyles seke. For youre heauenlye father knoweth that ye haue nede of all these thynges. But rather seeke ye first the kyngdome of god, and the righteousnes thereof, and all these thynges shalbe ministred unto you. Care not then for the morow, for the morow day shal care for itselfe: sufficient unto the daye is the trauayle thereof.

The xvi Sonday.

¶ At the Communion.

Feci judicium. Psalm cxix.

I DEALE with the thyng that is lawfull and right : O geue me not ouer unto myne oppressoures.

Make thou thy seruaūt to delite in that which is good : that the proude do me no wrong.

Myne iyes are wasted awaye with lookyng for thy health : and for the worde of thy righteousnes.

O deale with thy seruaūt accordyng unto thy louyng mercy : and teache me thy statutes.

I am thy seruaunt; O graunt me understandyng, that I maye knowe thy testimonies.

It is tyme for thee Lorde to laye to thyne hande : for they haue destroyed thy lawe.

For I loue thy commaundementes : aboue golde and precious stone.

Therfore holde I straight all thy commaundementes : and all false wayes I utterly abhorre.

Glory be to the father, and to the sonne, &c.

As it was in the beginnyng, &c. Amen.

The Collect.

LORD, we beseche thee, let thy continual pitie clense and defende thy congregacion; and, because it cannot continue in safetie without thy succoure, preserue it euermore by thy helpe and goodnes; through Jesus Christ our Lorde.

The Epistle. Ephes. iii.

I DESIRE that you faint not because of my tribulacions that I suffre for your sakes; whiche is youre praise. For this cause I bowe my knees unto the father of our lorde Jesus Christe, whiche is father ouer al that is called father in heauen and in yearth, that he would graunt you, accordyng to the riches of his glorye, that ye maie be strengthed with might by his spirite in the inner man; that Christ maye dwell in your heartes by faythe, that ye beyng rooted and grounded in loue, might be able to comprehend with all saintes, what is the bredthe and length, depth and height; and to know the excellent loue of the knowlege of Christ, that ye might be fulfilled with all fulnes, whiche commeth of God. Unto him that is able to do exceadyng aboundantly aboue all that we aske or thinke, according to the power that worketh in us, be praise in the congregacion by Christ Jesus, throughoute al generacions from time to time. Amen.

The Gospel. Luke vii.

AND it fortuned, that Jesus went into a Citie called Naim, and many of his disciples went with him, and muche people. When he came nye to the gate of the citie, beholde there was a deade man caried out, whiche was the only sonne of his mother, and she was a wydow; and muche people of the citie was with her. And when the lorde sawe her, he had compassion on her, and sayed unto her; wepe not. And he came nye, and touched the coffyn, and they that bare him stode stil. And he saied; yong man, I say unto thee, aryse. And he that was dead, sate up, and began to speake. And he deliuered hym to his mother. And there came a feare on them all. And they gaue the glorye unto God, saying; A great prophet is rysen up among us, and God hathe visited his people. And this rumor of hym went foorth throughout all Jewrye, and throughout all the regions which lye round about.

¶ *The xvii Sondaye.*

Mirabilia.   Psalm cxix.

THY testimonies are wonderful : therfore doeth my soule kepe them.

When thy word goeth forth : it geueth lighte and understandyng euen vnto the simple.

I opened my mouth, and drue in my breath : for my delite was in thy commaundementes.

O looke thou vpon me, and be mercifull vnto me : as thou usest to do vnto those that loue thy name.

Order my steppes in thy worde : and so shal no wickednes haue dominion ouer me.

O deliuer me from the wrongfull dealynges of men : and so shall I kepe thy commaundementes.

Shewe the light of thy countinaunce vpon thy seruaūt : and teache me thy statutes.

Myne iyes gushe out with water : because mē kepe not thy lawe.

Glory be to the father, and to the sonne, and to the &c.

As it was in the begynning, is nowe and euer &c.

The Collect.

LORD we praye thee that thy grace maye alwayes preuente and folowe us, and make us continuallye to be geuen to all good workes thorough Jesus Christe our Lorde.

The Epistle.   Ephes. iv.

I (WHICH am a prisoner of the Lordes) exhorte you that ye walke worthy of the vocacion wherwith ye are called, with al lowlines and mekenes, with humblenes of mynde, forbearyng one another through loue, and be dylygente to kepe the unytie of the spirite through the bonde of peace, beyng one bodye and one spirite, euen as ye are called in one hope of youre callyng. Let there be but one Lorde, one faith, one baptisme, one God and father of all, whiche is aboue all, and through all, and in you all.

The Gospel.   Luke xiv.

IT chaunced that Jesus went into the house of one of the chiefe Pharises, to eate breade on the Sabboth daye; and they watched him.   And behold, there was a certaine mā before him which had the dropsie.   And Jesus aunswered and spake vnto the lawiers

and pharises, saiyng.   Is it laweful to heale on the Sabboth day?
And they held theyr peace.   And he toke hym, and healed him,
and let him go; and answered them, saiyng; which of you shal
haue an Asse or an Oxe fallē into a pit, and wil not straightwaie
pul him oute on the Sabboth day?   And they could not aūswere
him again to these thinges.   He put forth also a similitude to the
gestes, wh† he marked how they preaced to bee in the hiest
roumes, and sayed unto them; when thou arte bidden of any
man to a weddyng, sit not doune in the highest roume, leste a
more honorable man than thou, be bidden of hym, and he (that
bad hym and thee) come and saye to thee; geue this man roume,
and thou then begin with shame to take the lowest roume.   But
rather when thou arte bidden, go and sit in the lowest roume,
that whē he that bad thee cometh, he maye saye unto thee,
frende, sit up hier.   Then shalte thou haue worship, in the
presēce of thē that sit at meate with thee.   For whosoeuer
exalteth himselfe, shalbe brought lowe, and he that humbleth
hymselfe, shalbe exalted.

¶ *The xviii Sondaye.*

Justus es, Domine.   Psalm cxix.

RIGHTEOUS arte thou, O Lorde : and true is thy iudgement.

The testimonies that thou hast commaūded : are excedyng
righteous and true.

My zeale hath euen consumed me : because mine enemyes
haue forgotten thy wordes.

Thy worde is tried to the uttermost : and thy seruaunt loueth
it.

I am small and of no reputacion : yet do not I forgette thy
commaundementes.

Thy righteousnesse is an euerlastyng righteousnesse : and thy
lawe is the truthe.

Trouble and heauines haue taken hold upon me : yet is my
delight in thy commaundementes.

The righteousnesse of thy testimonies is euerlastyng : O graunt
me understandyng, and I shall liue.

Glory be to the father, &c.

As it was in the begynning, &c.

The Collect.

LORDE we besche thee, graunt thy people grace to auoyde the

infeccions of the Deuil, and with pure harte and mynde to folowe thee the onelye God; Through Jesus Christ our Lorde.

The Epistle.   1 Cor. i.

I THANKE my god alwaies on your behalfe, for the grace of God, whych is gyuen you by Jesus Christe, that in all thynges ye are made riche by hym, in al utteraunce, and in al knowlege, by the whiche thynges, the testimonye of Jesus Christe, was confirmed in you, so that ye are behinde in no gift; waityng for the apperyng of oure Lorde Jesus Christe, which shall also strength you unto the ende, that ye maie be blameles, in the daye of the commyng of oure Lorde Jesus Christ.

The Gospell.   Matt. xxii.

WHEN the Phariseis had harde, that Jesus dyd put the Saduces to silence, they came together, and one of them (which was a doctor of lawe) asked hym a question, temptyng hym, and saying; Maister, whiche is the greatest Commaundement in the lawe? Jesus saied unto hym; Thou shalte loue the Lord thy God with all thy harte, and with all thy soule, and with all thy mynde. This is the firste and greatest commaundement. And the second is like unto it. Thou shalte loue thy neighbour as thyselfe. In these twoo commaundementes hang all the lawe and the prophetes. While the Phariseis were gathered together, Jesus asked them, saying; what thynke ye of Christ? whose sonne is he? They sayed unto him; the sonne of Dauid. He saied unto them; how then doeth Dauid in the spirite, call hym Lord? saying; The Lord sayed unto my Lord, sit thou on my right hand, till I make thyne enemies thy footestoole. If Dauid then call hym Lorde, how is he then his sonne? And no manne was able to aunswere hym any thyng, neither durst any man (from that daye furthe) aske hym any mo questions.

The xix Sundaie.

Clamavi.   Psalm cxix.

I CALL with my whole harte : heare me, O Lord, I wyll kepe thy statutes.

Yea, euen upon thee do I call : helpe me, and I shall kepe thy testimonies.

Early in the mornyng do I crye unto thee : For in thy worde is my trust.

Myne iyes preuente the night-watches : that I mighte be occupied in thy wordes.

Heare my voyce, (O lorde,) accordyng vnto thy louyngkynd-nesse : quicken me, according as thou art wont.

They drawe nye that of malice persecute me : and are farre from thy lawe.

Be thou nye at hande, O lorde : for all thy commaundementes are true.

As concernyng thy testimonies, I haue knowen long since : that thou hast grounded them for euer.

Glory be to the father, and to the sonne, &c.

As it was in the beginning, is now, &c.

The Collect.

O GOD, for asmuche as without thee, we are not able to please thee; Graunte that the workyng of thy mercie maye in all thynges directe and rule our heartes; Through Jesus Christ our Lorde.

The Epistle. Ephes. iv.

THIS I saye, and testifie through the Lord, that ye hencefoorth walke not as other Gentiles walke, in vanitie of their mynde; while they are blinded in their understandyng, being farre from a godly life, by the meanes of the ignorancie that is in them, and because of the blindnesse of their heartes, whiche, beyng past repentaunce, haue geuen themselues ouer vnto wātonnes, to woorke all manner of unclennes, euen with gredines.   But ye haue not so learned Christe.   If so bee that ye haue heard of hym, and haue been taught in him, as the trueth is in Jesu (as concernyng the conuersacion in time past) to laye from you that olde man, which is corrupt, accordyng to the deceiueable lustes.   To be renued also in the spirite of your mynde, and to putte on that newe man, whiche after God, is shapen in righteousnes and true holynes.   Wherfore put awaie lying, and speake euery man trueth vnto his neighbour, forasmuche as we are members one of another.   Be angery and synne not: Let not the Sunne go doune vpon your wrathe, neither geue place to the backbiter.   Lette hym that stole, steale no more, but lette him rather laboure with his handes the thing whiche is good, that he maye geue vnto hym that nedeth.   Let no filthy com-municacion procede out of your mouthe: But that whiche is good to edifie withall, as oft as nede is, that it maye minister grace vnto the hearers.   And greue not ye the holy spirite of

God, by whome ye are sealed unto the daie of redempcion. Let all bitternesse and fearsenesse, and wrath, and roaryng, and cursed speakyng, be put awaye from you, with all maliciousnes. Be ye curteous one to another, mercifull, forgeuing one another, euen as God for Christes sake hathe forgeuen you.

The Gospell. Matt. ix.

JESUS entred into a shippe and passed ouer, and came into his owne Citie: And beholde, they broughte to hym a manne sicke of the Palsey, lying in a bed. And when Jesus sawe the faith of them, he saied unto the sicke of the Palsey; Sonne bee of good chere, thy synnes be forgeuen thee. And behold, certaine of the Scribes saied within themselues; this manne blasphemeth. And when Jesus sawe their thoughtes, he saied; wherfore thinke ye euill in your heartes? Whether is it easyer to saye, they synnes be forgeuen thee? or to saye arise and walke? But that ye maye knowe that the sonne of manne hathe power to forgeue synnes in yearth; Then sayeth he unto the sick of the Palsey; Arise, take up thy bed, and go unto thyne house. And he arose, and departed to his house: But the people that sawe it, merueiled and glorified God, whiche had geuen suche power unto men.

The xx Sondaie.

Vide humilitatem meam. Ps. cxix.

O CONSIDRE myne aduersitie and deliuer me: For I do not forget thy lawe.

Auenge thou my cause and deliuer me : quicken me, accordyng unto thy worde.

Healthe is farre from the ungodly : For they regarde not thy statutes.

Great is thy mercie, O Lorde : quicken me, as thou art wont.

Many there are that trouble me, and persecute me : yet do not I swarue from thy testimonyes.

It greueth me when I se the trāsgressors : because they kepe not thy lawe.

Consider, O lord, how I loue thy commaundementes, O quicken me; accordyng to thy louyng-kyndnesse.

Thy worde is true from euerlastyng : All the iudgementes of thy righteousnes endure for euermore.

Glory be to the father, and to the sonne, &c.

As it was in the beginning, is now, &c.

The Collect.

ALMIGHTIE and merciful God, of thy bountiful goodnes, kepe us from all thynges that maye hurte us; that we, beyng ready bothe in body and soule, maye with free heartes accomplishe those thynges that thou wouldest haue doen; Through Jesus Christ our Lorde.

The Epistle. Ephes. v.

TAKE hede therefore, howe ye walke circumspectelye: not as unwise, but as wise menne, wynnyng occasion, because the dayes are euill. Wherfore be ye not unwise, but understand what the wyll of the Lorde is, and be not dronken with wine, wherin is excesse: But be filled with the spirite, speaking unto yourselues in Psalmes, and Hymnes, and spirituall songes, syngyng and makyng melody to the Lorde in your hartes, geuyng thankes alwayes for all thynges unto God the father, in the name of our Lorde Jesus Christe: submittyng yourselues one to another, in the feare of God.

The Gospell. Matt. xxii.

JESUS saied to his disciples; The kyngdome of heauen is lyke unto a man that was a Kyng, whiche made a Mariage for his sonne, and sēt furthe his seruauntes, to call them that were bid to the weddyng, and they would not come. Agayne he sent furth other seruauntes, saying; Tell thē whiche are bidden; beholde, I haue prepared my diner, myne Oxen and my fatlinges are kylled, and al thinges are redy, come unto the Mariage. But they made lighte of it, and wente their wayes; One to his farme place, another to his Marchaundise, and the remnaunte tooke his seruauntes, and intreated them shamefully, and slewe thē. But when the Kyng heard thereof, he was wrothe, and sente furthe his men of warre, and destroyed those murtherers, and brent up their citie. Then sayed he to his seruauntes; the Mariage indede is prepared, but they whiche were bidden, were not worthy: Go ye therfore out into the hyewayes: and as many as ye finde, bid thē to the mariage. And the seruauntes went furthe into the hyewayes, and gathered together all, as many as they could finde, bothe good and bad, and the weddyng was furnished with gestes. Then the King came in to see the gestes, and when he spied there a man, whiche had not on a wedding garment, he sayed unto hym; frende, howe cammest thou in hither not hauyng a wedding Garmēt? And he was euen speacheles. Then sayed the Kyng to the ministers; take and bynde hym hande and foote, and caste hym into utter darkenesse, there shalbe weping and gnashing of teeth. For many be called, but fewe are chosen.

¶ *The xxi Sondaie.*

Principes persecuti. Psalm cxix.

PRINCES haue persecuted me withoute cause : But my hart standeth in awe of thy wordes.

I am as glad of thy worde : as one that findeth great spoyles.

As for lies, I hate and abhorre them : But thy lawe do I loue.

Seuen tymes a daye do I prayse thee : Because of thy righteous iudgementes.

Greate is the peace that they haue whiche loue thy lawe : and they are not offended at it.

Lorde, I haue loked for thy sauyng healthe : and doen after thy commaundementes.

My soule hath kept thy testymonyes : and loued them excedingly.

I haue kept thy commaundementes and testimonies : for all my waies are before thee.

Glory be to the father, and to the sonne, &c.

As it was in the beginning, is now, &c.

The Collect.

GRAUNT we beseche thee, merciful Lord, to thy faithfull people pardon and peace, that they maye bee clensed from all their synnes, and serue thee with a quiet mynde. Through Jesus Christ our Lorde.

The Epistle. Ephes. vi.

MY brethren, be strong through the lord, and through the power of his might. Put on all the armoure of god, that ye may stande agaynst the assaultes of the deuill: for we wrestle not against bloude and fleshe, but againste rule, against power, against worldly rulers, euen gouernours of the darkenesse of this world, against spirituall craftinesse, in heauenly thynges. Wherfore, take unto you the whole armour of God, that ye maye be able to resist in the euill daie, and stande perfect in al thynges. Stande therfore and your loynes girde with the trueth, hauyng on the breste plate of righteousnesse, and hauyng shoes on your feete, that ye may be prepared for the gospel of peace. Aboue all, take to you the shilde of faith, wherwith ye maie quenche all the fiery dartes of the wicked; and take the helmet of saluacion, and the sworde of the spirite, whiche is the worde of God. And praie alwayes with all maner of prayer, and supplicacion in the spirite, and watch thereunto with all instaunce and supplicacion, for all sainctes, and for me; that utteraunce maye bee geuen unto me, that I maye open my mouthe frely, to utter the secretes of my Gospell (wherof I am a messenger in bondes,) that therein I maye speake frely, as I oughte to speake.

The Gospel.   John iv.

THERE was a certaine Ruler, whose sonne was sicke at Capernaum.   As sone as the same heard, that Jesus was come out of Jewry into Galile, he went unto him, and besought hym that he would come doune and heale his sonne.   For he was euen at the poinct of death.   Then saied Jesus unto him; except ye see signes and wōders, ye wil not beleue.   The Ruler saieth unto him; Sir, come doune or euer that my sonne dye.   Jesus sayeth unto hym; Go thy waye, thy sonne liueth.   The manne beleued the woorde that Jesus had spoken unto hym.   And he wente his waye.   And as he was goyng doune, the seruauntes mette hym, and told hym, saying; thy sonne liueth.   Then enquired he of them the houre, when he beganne to amende.   And thy saied unto hym; yesterdaie at the seuenth houre, the feuer left him. So the father knew that it was the same houre, in the whiche Jesus saied unto hym.   Thy sonne liueth, and he beleued, and all his boushold.   This is agayn the second miracle that Jesus did, when he was come out of Jewry into Galile.

¶ *The xxii Sondaye.*

Appropinquet deprecatio.   Ps. xcix.

LET my complainte come before thee, O Lorde : Geue me understandyng accordyng unto thy worde.

O let my supplicaciō come before thee : Deliuer me, according to thy worde.

My lippes shal speake of thy prayse : whē thou hast taught me thy statutes.

Yea, my toungue shall syng of thy worde : For all thy commaundementes are righteous.

Let thyne hand helpe me : For I haue chosen thy commaundementes.

I haue longed for thy sauyng health, O Lorde : And in thy lawe is my delight.

O lette my soule liue, and it shall praise thee : And thy iudgementes shall helpe me.

I haue gone astraie like a shepe that is loste : O seke thy seruaunte, for I do not forget thy commaundementes.

Glory be to the father, and to the sonne : and to the holy ghost.

As it was in the begynnyng, is nowe and euer shalbe : world without ende.   Amen.

The Collect.

LORDE we beseche thee to kepe thy housholde the churche in continuall godlines; that throughe thy proteccion it maye be free from al aduersities, and deuoutly geuen to serue thee in good workes, to the glory of thy name; Through Jesus Christ our Lorde.

The Epistle   Philipp. i.

I THANKE my God with all remembraunce of you alwayes in al my praiers for you, and praye with gladnes; Because ye are come into the felowship of the Gospell, from the firste daye unto nowe.   And am surelye certified of this, that he whiche hath begon a good worke in you, shall performe it untill the daie of Jesus Christe: as it becommeth me, so iudge I of you all, because I haue you in my heart; forasmuche as ye are all companions of grace with me, euen in my bondes, and in the defendyng and stablishyng of the Gospell: for god is my recorde, how greatly I long after you all from the very heart rote in Jesus Christ.   And this I praye, that your loue maye increase yet more and more in knowlege, and in al understandyng, that ye maye accept the thinges that are moste excellent, that ye maye be pure, and suche as offende no man, untill the daye of Christe, beyng filled with the fruite of righteousnes, whiche commeth by Jesus Christ, unto the glory and prayse of God.

The Gospell.   Matt. xviii.

PETER saied unto Jesus; lorde how oft shall I forgeue my brother, if he sinne against me, till seuen tymes?   Jesus sayeth unto hym; I saye not unto thee untill seuen tymes; but seuentie tymes seuē times.   Therfore is the kyngdome of heauen likened unto a certaine man that was a kyng, whiche would take accoumptes of his seruauntes.   And when he had begon to recken, one was brought unto hym, whiche ought hym tenne м talentes, but forasmuche as he was not able to paye, his lord commaunded hym to be solde, and his wife and children, and al that he had, and paiment to be made. The seruaunt fell doune, and besought hym, saying; syr, haue pacience with me, and I will paye thee all. Then had the lorde pitie on that seruaunt, and loced hym, and forgaue hym the debt. So the same seruaũt went out, and found one of his felowes, whiche ought him an c pence, and he layed handes on hym, and toke hym by the throte, saying; paye that thou owest. And his felowe fell doune, and besought hym, saying; haue pacience with me, and I will paye thee all. And he would not, but went and caste hym into pryson, till he shoulde paye the debt. So, when his felowes sawe what was doen, they were verye sorye, and came and tolde unto their Lorde all that had happened. Then his Lord called him and sayd unto hym. O thou ungracious seruaunt, I forgaue thee all that debte, when thou desiredst me: shouldest not thou also haue had compassion on thy felowe, euen as I had pitie on thee? And his lorde was wroth, and deliuered hym to the Jaylers, till he shoulde paye all that was due unto hym: So likewyse shall my heauenly father do also to you, yf ye from your hartes forgeue not (euery one his brother) their trespaces.

¶ *The xxiii Sondaye.*

Nisi quia Dominus. Psalm cxxiv.

IF the Lorde himselfe had not been on our side (now maye Israell saye) : if the Lorde hymselfe hadde not been on our side, when men rose up against us;

They had swalowed us up quicke : when they were so wrathfully displeased at us.

Yea, the waters had drouned us : and the streme had gone ouer our soule.

The depe waters of the proud : had gone euen ouer our soule.

But praysed be the Lorde : whiche hath not geuen us ouer for a praye unto theyr teethe.

Our soule is escaped, euen as a birde oute of the snare of the fouler : the snare is broken, and we are deliuered.

Oure helpe standeth in the name of the Lorde : whiche hath made heauen and yearth.

Glory be to the father, and to the sonne, and to the &c.

As it was in the begynning, is nowe and euer &c.

The Collect.

GOD, our refuge and strength, which art the author of all godlines, be ready to heare the deuoute prayers of thy churche; and graunt that those thynges which we aske faithfully we maye obteine effectually; through Jesu Christe our lorde.

The Epistle. Philipp. iii.

BRETHREN, be folowers together of me, and looke on them which walke euen so, as ye haue us for an example. For many walke (of whom I haue tolde you often and now tell you weping,) that they are the enemyes of the crosse of Christe, whose ende is damnacion, whose bely is theyr god, and glory to their shame, whiche are worldly mynded. But our conuersacion is in heauen, from whence we looke for the sauioure, euen the Lord Jesus Christ, which shal chaunge our vyle body, that he maye make it lyke unto his glorious body, accordyng to the working, whereby he is able also to subdue al thynges unto hymselfe.

The Gospell. Matt. xxii.

THEN the Phariseis went out and toke counsayl, howe they mighte tangle hym in his wordes. And they sent out unto hym their disciples with Herodes seruauntes, saying; Maister, we know that thou arte true, and teachest the waye of God truly, neither carest thou for any man: for thou regardest not the outward appearaunce of mē. Tel us therfore, how thinkest thou? Is it lawfull that tribute be geuen unto Cesar, or not? But Jesus perceyuing their wickednes, said; Why tempt ye me ye ypocrites? Shew me the tribute-money. And they tooke him a peny. And he sayed unto them; whose is this Image and superscripcion? they saied unto hym, Cesars: Then saied he unto them; geue therfore unto Cesar the thinges whiche are Cesars; and unto God, those thinges that are Goddes. When they had hearde these wordes, they meruayled, and left hym, and wente their waye.

¶ *The xxiiii Sondaye.*

Qui confidunt. Psalm cxxv.

THEY that pute their truste in the lord shalbe euen as the mount Syon : which maye not be remoued, but standeth fast for euer.

The hylles stande aboute Jerusalem : euen so standeth the

lorde rounde about his people, from this time foorth for euer-more.

For the rod of the ungodly commeth not into the lot of the righteous : leste the righteous put their hande unto wickednes.

Do well (O lorde) : unto those that be good and true of heart.

As for suche as turne backe unto their owne wickednes : the lorde shall lead them foorth with the euelldoers; but peace shalbe upon Israell.

Glory be to the father, and to the sonne, &c.

As it was in the beginning, &c.

The Collect.

LORD we beseche thee, assoyle thy people from their offences, that through thy bountiful goodnes we maye bee delyuered from the bandes of all those synnes, whiche by our frayltye we haue committed : Graunt this, &c.

The Epistle.　Coloss. i.

WE geue thankes to God, the father of our Lord Jesus Christe, alwayes for you in our prayers; for we haue heard of your fayth in Christ Jesu, and of the loue whiche ye beare to all saynctes; for the hopes sake whyche is layde up in store for you in heauen, of whych hope ye heard before by the true worde of the gospel, which is come unto you euen as it is, fruitfull, and groweth as it is also among you, from the daye in the whiche ye heard of it, and had experience in the grace of god through the truth, as ye learned of Epaphra, our deare fellowe seruaunt, which is for you a faythfull minister of Christe, whyche also declared unto us youre loue which ye haue in the spirite.　For this cause we also, euer sence the daye we heard of it, haue not ceased to pray for you, and to desyre that ye myght be fulfylled with the know-ledge of hys will in all wisdome and spiritual understandyng: that ye myght walke worthy of the Lorde, that in all thynges ye maye please, being fruitefull in all good workes, and encreasyng in the knowledge of God, strengthed with all myght, through his glorious power, unto al pacience and longsufferyng with ioiful-nesse, geuing thākes unto the father, which hath made us meete to be partakers of the inherytaunce of sainctes in lyght.

The Gospel.　Matt. ix.

WHYLE Jesus spake unto the people, beholde, there came a certaine ruler, and worshipped him, saiyng; my doughter is euen nowe disceased, but come and laye thy hande upon her, and she

shall lyue.   And Jesus arose and folowed hym, and so dyd hys
discyples.   And beholde, a woman whyche was diseased with
an issue of bloude twelue yeres, came behinde him and touched
the hemme of his vesture.   For she saide within herselfe: If I
maye touche but euen hys vesture only, I shalbe safe.   But
Jesus turned him about, and when he sawe her, he sayde :
doughter, be of good comfort, thy fayth hath made thee safe.
And the woman was made whole euen that same tyme.   And
when Jesus came into the rulers house, and sawe the mynstrelles
and the people makyng a noyse, he said unto them; get you
hence, for the maide is not dead but slepeth.   And they laughed
hym to scorne: But when the people were put furth he went in,
and toke her by the hande (and sayde: damosell aryse).   And
the damosell arose.   And thys noyse went abrode into all that
lande.

¶ *The xxv Sondaye.*

Nisi Dominus.   Psalm cxxvii.

EXCEPT the Lorde buylde the house : their labour is but loste
that buylde it.

Excepte the Lorde kepe the citye : the watchman waketh but
in vayne.

It is but lost labour that ye haste to ryse up early, and so late
take rest; and eate the bread of carefulnes, for so he geueth his
beloued slepe.

Lo, chyldren and the fruite of the wombe are an heritage and
gyfte : that commeth of the Lorde.

Lyke as the arrowes in the hand of the giaunt : euen so are the
yong chyldren.

Happye is the man, that hath hys quyuer full of them : they
shall not be ashamed when they speake with their enemies in
the gate.

Glory be to the father, and to the sonne, &c.

As it was in the begynning, is nowe, &c.

The Collect.

STIERE up we beseche thee, O Lord, the wylles of thy faythfull
people, that they, plenteously bringing furth the fruite of good
workes; may of thee, be plenteously rewarded; through Jesus
Christe our Lorde.

The Epistle.   Jer. xxiii.

BEHOLD, the tyme commeth, saith the Lord, that I wyll rayse
up the righteous braunche of Dauid, which kyng shall beare rule,

and he shall prosper with wysdome, and shall set up equite and
righteousnes againe in the earth. In his time shall Juda be
saued, and Israel shall dwell without feare. And this is the name
that they shal call him; euen the Lord our righteousnes: and
therfore behold, the time commeth, saith the Lord, that it shal no
more be saide: the Lorde lyueth, which brought the children of
Israel out of the lande of Egipt; But the Lorde lyueth which
brought furth and lead the seede of the house of Israel out of the
north lande, and from all contries where I had scatered them;
and they shall dwell in theyr owne lande agayne.

The Gospell. John vi.

WHEN Jesus lift up his eies, and sawe a great companie come
unto him, he saith unto Philip; whēce shall we bye bread that
these maye eate? This he sayd to proue him; for he himselfe
knewe what he wolde do. Phylyp aunswered hym; two
hundreth peniworth of bread are not sufficiente for thē, that
euery man may take a litle. One of hys dysciples (Andrewe,
Simon Peters brother) said unto hym; There is a ladde here,
whyche hath fiue barley-loues, and two fishes; but what are they
among so many? And Jesus sayd; make the people syt doune.
There was muche grasse in the place. So the mē sat doune, in
nombre about fiue thousand. And Jesus toke the breade, and
when he had geuen thankes, he gaue to the disciples, and the
dysciples to them that were set doune: And likewise of the fishes,
as much as thei wold. When they had eatē inough, he saith
unto his disciples; Gather up the broken meate which remayneth,
that nothing be lost. And they gathered it together, and fylled
twelue baskettes with the broken meate of the fyue barley
loaues, which broken meat remained unto them that had eaten.
Then those men (when they had seen the myracle that Jesus
did) said; this is of a truth the same Prophete that shoulde
come into the worlde.

Sainct Andrewes Daye.

At the Communion.

Sæpe expugnaverunt. Psalm cxxix.

MANY tymes they haue fought agaynst me fro my youth up :
may Israell nowe saye.

Yea, many a time haue thei vexed me from my youth up :
but thei haue not preuailed against me.

The plowers plowed upon my backe : and made long forowes.

But the righteous Lorde : hath hewen the snares of the ungodly in pieces.

Let them be confounded and turned backwarde : as many as haue euyll wyll at Sion.

Let them be euen as the grasse growyng upon the house-toppes : which withereth afore it be pluckt up.

Wherof the mower fylleth not hys hande : neither he that bindeth up the sheues, hys bosome.

So that they which go by, saye not so muche : as the Lord prospere you, we wish you good lucke in the name of the Lorde.

Glory be to the father, and to the sonne : and to the holy ghost.

As it was in the begynning, is nowe, and euer shalbe : worlde without ende. Amen.

The Collect.

ALMYGHTIE God, which hast geuen suche grace to thy Apostle saynct Andrew, that he counted the sharp and painful death of the crosse to be an high honour, and a great glory; Graunt us to take and esteme all troubles and aduersities which shal come unto us for thy sake, as thinges proffytable for us toward the obtaining of euerlasting life; through Jesus Christ our Lorde.

The Epistle. Rom. x.

IF thou knowledge with thy mouthe, that Jesus is the Lord, and beleue in thy heart that God raised him up from death, thou shalt be safe. For, to beleue with the hearte iustifyeth; and to knowledge with the mouth maketh a man safe. For the scripture saith; whosoeuer beleueth on hym shall not be confounded. There is no differēce betwene the Jewe and the Gentyle. For one is Lorde of all, whyche is ryche unto all that call upon hym. For whosoeuer doth cal on the name of the Lorde shalbe safe. Howe then shal they call on him, on whom they haue not beleued? How shal they beleue on him, of whom they haue not heard? How shal they heare, without a preacher? And how shal they preache except they be sent? As it is written; howe beutiful are the fete of thē which bring tidinges of peace, and bring tidynges of good thynges. But they haue not al obeyed to the gospel, for Esay sayeth; Lorde, who hath beleued our saiynges? So then, faith cōmeth by hearing, and hearing commeth by the worde of God. But I aske; haue they not heard? no doubt their sound went out into al landes, and their wordes into the endes of the world. But I demaunde whether Israell dyd knowe or not?

fyrst Moyses sayth; I wyll prouoke you to enuy, by them that
are no people, by a folysh nacion I wyll anger you.   Esaie after
that is bolde, and sayth; I am found of them that sought me not,
I am manyfest unto them that asked not after me.   But against
Israell he saith, all daye long haue I stretched furth my handes
unto a people that beleueth not, but speaketh agaynst me.

The Gospel.   Matt. iv.

As Jesus walked by the sea of Galilee, he sawe two brethren;
Simon, which was called Peter, and Andrew his brother, castyng
a net into the sea, (for they were fyshers) and he saieth unto
them; folowe me, and I will make you to become fishers of men.
And they streightway left their nettes, and folowed hym.

And when he was gone furth from thence, he sawe other two
brethren, James the sōne of Zebede, and John hys brother, in
the ship with Zebede theyr father, mending theyr nettes: and
he called them.   And they immediatly left the ship and their
father, and folowed hym.

Saynct Thomas the Apostle.

¶ At the Communion.

Beati omnes.   Psalm cxxviii.

BLESSED are all they that feare the Lorde : and walke in his
wayes.

For thou shalt eate the labours of thyne hādes : O well is thee,
and happy shalt thou be.

Thy wife shalbe as the fruitful vine : upon the walles of thyne
house.

Thy chyldren like the Olyue braunches : round about thy
table.

Lo, thus shal the man be blessed : that feareth the lorde.

The Lorde from out of Syon, shall so blesse thee : that thou
shalt see Jerusalem in prosperytie all thy lyfe long.

Yea, that thou shalt see thy chylders chyldren : and peace
upon Israell.

Glory be to the father, &c.

As it was in the beginning, &c.

The Collect.

ALMIGHTIE euerliuing God, whiche for the more confyrmacion
of the fayth didst suffer thy holy apostle Thomas to bee doubtfull
in thy sonnes resurreccyon; graunte us so perfectly, and without

all doubt, to beleue in thy sonne Jesus Christe, that our fayth in thy syghte neuer be reproued; here us, O Lorde, through the same Jesus Christe, to whome with thee and the holy goste be all honour, &c.

The Epistle. Ephes. ii.

Now ye are not straungers, nor foreners, but citezens with the saintes, and of the houshold of God, and are built upon the foundacion of the apostles and prophetes, Jesus Christ himselfe beeyng the head corner-stone, in whome what building soeuer is coupled together, it groweth unto an holy temple in the lord, in whome ye also are built together to be an habitacion of God through the holy gost.

The Gospell. John xx.

THOMAS one of the twelue, which is called Didimus, was not with them when Jesus came. The other disciples therfore sayed unto hym, we haue sene the lord. But he sayd unto them; except I see in hys handes the printe of the nayles, and put my finger into the print of the nayles, and thrust my hande into his syde, I will not beleue.

And after eighte dayes, agayne hys disciples were within, and Thomas with them. Then came Jesus when the doores were shut, and stode in the middes and sayd; peace be unto you. And after that he sayde to Thomas; bring thy finger hither, and see my handes, and reache hither thy hande, and thruste it into my syde, and be not faythlesse, but beleuing. Thomas aunswered and sayde unto hym; my lorde and my God. Jesus sayd unto him; Thomas, because thou hast sene me, thou hast beleued; blessed are they that haue not sene, and yet haue beleued. And many other sygnes truely dyd Jesus in the presence of his disciples, whiche are not written in thys booke. These are written, that ye myght beleue that Jesus is Christe the sonne of God, and that (in beleuing) ye myght haue lyfe through hys name.

¶ *The conuersion of sainct Paule.*
At Matins.

The Second Lesson, Acts xxii. unto " they heard him."

Confitebor tibi. Psalm cxxxviii.

I WILL geue thankes unto thee, O lord, with my whole hearte : euen before the Goddes, wil I syng prayse unto thee.

I will wurshyp towarde thy holye temple, and prayse thy name, because of thy louyng-kyndenesse and trueth : for thou haste magnifyed thy name, and thy woord aboue all thynges.

When I called upon thee, thou heardest me : and enduedst my soule with muche strength.

All the kinges of the earth shall prayse thee, O Lorde : for they haue hearde the woordes of thy mouth.

Yea, they shall syng in the wayes of the Lorde : that great is the glory of the Lorde.

For though the lorde be hye, yet hath he respecte unto the lowly : as for the proud, he beholdeth them afarre of.

Though I walke in the middes of trouble, yet shalte thou refreshe me : thou shalte stretche furth thyne hande upon the furiousnesse of myne enemyes, and thy ryghte hande shall saue me.

The Lorde shall make good hys louingkyndnes towarde me : yea thy mercie, O Lord, endureth for euer; despise not then the woorkes of thyne owne handes.

Glory be to the father, and to the sonne : and to the holy gost; As it was in the beginning, is nowe, and euer shalbe : world withoute ende.　Amen.

The Collect.

GOD, whiche haste taughte all the worlde, through the preachyng of thy blessed apostle saincte Paule; graunt, we beseche thee, that we whiche haue hys wonderfull conuersion in remembraunce, maye folowe and fulfill the holy doctryne that he taughte; through Jesus Christ our Lorde.

The Epistle.　Acts ix.

AND Saul yet breathyng out threatnynges, and slaughter agaynste the Disciples of the lord, went unto the hye prieste, and desired of him letters to cary to Damasco, to the Sinagoges; (that if he founde any of this waye, whether they were men or women, he might bring thē bound unto Jerusalē.)　And when he iorneied, it fortuned that as he was come nigh to Damasco, sodenly there shined roūd about him a light from heaven, and he fel to the earth, and heard a voyce, saying to him; Saul, Saul, why persecutest thou me?　And he sayde: what art thou Lorde. And the Lord sayd; I am Jesus whome thou persecuteste.　It is harde for thee to kicke agaynste the pricke.　And he both trembling and astonied, sayd; lorde, what wilt thou haue me to doe? And the lorde sayde unto hym; aryse, and goe into the citie, and it shalbe tolde thee what thou must doe.   The men whiche iourneyed with hym, stoode amased, hearing a voyce, but seeing no man.   And Saul arose frō the earth, and when he opened hys eyes, he saw no man; But they led him by the hād, and brought him into Damasco.   And he was three dayes without sight, and neyther did eate nor drynke.   And there was a certayn disciple at Damasco, named Ananias, and to him said the Lord in a vision; Ananias? and he sayd; beholde I am here lorde.   And the lord sayd unto him; arise and goe into the strete (whiche is called streighte) and seke in the house of Judas, after one called Saul of Tharsus.   For beholde, he prayeth, and hath seene in a vision a man, named Ananias, cummyng in to hym, and puttyng hys handes on hym, that he mighte receyue hys sighte.   Then Ananias aunswered; Lorde, I haue hearde by many of thys man, howe muche euill he hath doone to thy sainctes at Jerusalem; and here he hath aucthorytye of the hye pryestes, to bynde all that call on thy name.   The Lorde sayde unto hym; goe thy waye, for he is a chosen vessell unto me, to beare my name beefore the Gentyles, and kynges, and the chyldren of Israell. For I will shewe hym, howe great thynges he muste suffer for my names sake.   And Ananias wente hys way, and entred into the house, and put hys handes on hym, and sayde: brother Saul, the Lorde that appeared unto thee in the way as thou cameste, hath sent me, that thou mighteste receyue thy syghte, and be filled with the holy goste.   And immediately there fell from his eyes as it had bene scales, and he receyued syghte and arose, and was baptised, and receiued meate and was coumforted.   Then was Saul a certayne dayes with the discyples whiche were at Damasco.   And straightway he preached Christe in the Sina-goges, howe that he was the sonne of God.   But all that hearde hym were amased, and sayde: is not thys he that spoyled them whiche called on thys name in Hierusalem, and came hither for that entente that he mighte bring them bounde unto the hye priestes?   But Saul encreased the more in strength, and con-founded the Jewes whiche dwelte at Damasco, affirming that thys was very Christe.

The Gospell.   Matt. xix.

PETER aunswered and said unto Jesus; behold, we haue for-saken all, and folowed thee, what shall we haue therfore?   Jesus sayd unto them; verely I say unto you, that when the sonne of man shal sit in the seate of his Maiestie, ye that haue folowed me in the regeneracion shall sit also upon twelue seates, and iudge the twelue tribes of Israell. And euery one that forsaketh house, or brethren, or sisters, or father, or mother, or wyfe, or children, or landes, for my names sake, shall receiue an hundredfolde, and shall inherite euerlasting lyfe. But many that are first shalbe last, and the last shalbe first.

¶ *At Euensong.*

¶ The Second Lesson, Acts xxvi. unto the end.

¶ *The Purificacion of Saint Mary the Virgin.*

Ecce nunc benedicite. Psalm cxxxiv.

BEHOLDE (now) prayse the Lorde : all ye seruauntes of the lord; ye that by night stand in the house of the Lorde : (euen in the courtes of the house of our God.)

Lift up your handes in the Sanctuary : and prayse the Lorde.

The Lorde that made heauen and yearthe : geue thee blessing out of Sion.

Glory be to the father, and to the sonne, &c.

As it was in the beginning, is now, &c.

The Collect.

ALMYGHTYE and euerlastyng God, wc humbly beseche thy Maiestie, that as thy onelye begotten sonne was this day presented in the Temple in the substaunce of our fleshe; so graunte that we maie bee presented unto thee with pure and cleare myndes; By Jesus Christ our Lorde.

The Epistle.

The same that is appoynted for the Sondaye.

The Gospel. Luke ii.

WHEN the tyme of their Purificacion (after the lawe of Moses) was come, they brought him to Hierusalem, to present hym to the Lorde, (as it is written in the Lawe of the Lorde: euery manne child that first openeth the matrix, shalbe called holy to the lorde;) and to offre (as it is saied in the Lawe of the Lorde) a payre of turtle Dooues, or twoo young Pigions. And beholde, there was a man in Hierusalem, whose name was Simeon. And the same man was iust and godly, and loked for the consolacion of Israell, and the holy Goste was in hym. And an answere had he receiued of the holy Goste, that he should not see death, excepte he firste sawe the Lordes Christe. And he came by inspiracion into the temple.

¶ *Saint Mathies' daie.*

Eripe me. Psalm cxl.

DELYUER me, O lorde, from the euill manne : and preserue me from the wicked man.

Which imagine mischiefe in theyr heartes : and stirre up strife all the day long.

They haue sharpened theyr tongues lyke a Serpent : Adders poyson is under theyr lippes.

Kepe me, O lord, from the handes of the ungodly : preserue me from the wicked men, which are purposed to ouerthrowe my goynges.

The proude haue layed a snare for me, and spred a net abrode with cordes : yea, and set trappes in my way.

I sayde unto the Lorde, thou arte my God : heare the voyce of my prayers, O Lorde.

O Lorde God, thou strength of my health : thou haste couered my head in the day of battayl.

Let not the ungodly haue his desyre, O Lord : let not his mischeuous imaginacyon prosper, leste they bee too proude.

Let the myschiefe of theyr owne lippes fall upon the head of them : that compasse me about.

Let hote burning coales fall upon them : let them bee cast into the fyer, and into the pit, that they neuer rise up agayn.

A manne full of woordes shall not prosper upon the yearth : euill shall hunt the wicked person, to ouerthrowe hym.

Sure I am that the lorde will auenge the poore : and maynteyn the cause of the helpelesse.

The righteous also shal geue thankes unto thy name : and the iust shall continue in thy sight.

Glory be to the father, and to the sonne, &c.

As it was in the beginning, &c.

The Collect.

ALMYGHTYE God, whiche in the place of the traytor Judas, didst chose thy faythfull seruaunte Mathie to be of the number of thy twelue Apostles; Graunt that thy churche, being alway preserued from false Apostles, may be ordred and guided by faythfull and true pastors; Through Jesus Christ our Lorde.

The Epistle. Acts i.

IN those dayes, Peter stode up in the middes of the disciples, and sayd; (the numbre of names that were together, were about an cxx,) Ye men and brethren, thys scripture must nedes haue bene fulfilled, which the holye Ghoste, throughe the mouthe of Dauid, spake before of Judas, whiche was guyde to them that toke Jesus. For he was numbred with us, and had obteined felowship in this ministracion. And the same hath now possessed a plat of ground with the rewarde of iniquitie; and when he was hanged, he burst asunder in the middes, and all his bowels gusshed out: And it is knowen unto all the inhabiters of Hierusalem; insomuche that the same fielde is called, in theyr mother tongue, Acheldama, that is to saye, the bloude fielde. For it is written in the boke of Psalmes: his habitacion be voyde, and no man be dwelling therein, and his bishoprike let another take. Wherfore, of these menne whiche haue companyed with us (al the tyme that the lorde Jesus had al his conuersacion emong us, beginning at the baptisme of John unto that same day, that he was taken up from us) must one be ordayned, to be a witnes with us of his resurreccion. And they appoynted two, Joseph whiche is called Barsabas, (whose sirname was Justus,) and Matthias. And when they prayed, they sayde: Thou Lorde, which knowest the heartes of al menne, shew whether of these two thou haste chosen; That he may take the roume of this ministracion and Apostleship, from whiche Judas by transgression fel, that he might goe to his own place. And they gaue furth theyr lottes; and the lot fel on Matthias, and he was coumpted with the eleuen Apostles.

The Gospel. Matt. xi.

IN that tyme Jesus aunswered, and sayde: I thanke thee, (O father,) Lorde of heauen and yearth, because thou hast hyd these thynges from the wise and prudent, and hast shewed them unto babes: verely father, euen so was it thy good pleasure. All thynges are geuen ouer unto me of my father. And no manne knoweth the sonne, but the father; neither knoweth any man the father, saue the sonne, and he to whomesoeuer the sonne will open hym. Come unto me, all ye that labor, and are laden, and I wil ease you. Take my yoke upon you, and learne of me; for I am meke and lowly in heart: and ye shal fynd rest unto your soules, for my yoke is easie, and my burden is light.

The Annunciacion of the virgin Marie.

Domine, non est exal.   Psalm cxxxi.

LORDE, I am not hye-mynded : I haue no proude lookes.

I doe not exercise myselfe in great matters : whiche are to hye for me.

But I refrayne my soule, and kepe it low, lyke as a chyld that is weaned from hys mother : yea, my soule is euen as a weaned chylde.

O Israell, trust in the Lorde : from thys tyme foorth for euermore.

Glory be to the father, and to the sonne, &c.

As it was in the beginning, &c.   Amen.

The Collect.

WE beseche thee, Lorde, powre thy grace into our heartes; that, as we haue knowen Christ, thy sonnes incarnacion, by the message of an Angell: so by hys crosse and passion, we maye be brought unto the glory of his resurreccion; Through the same Christe our Lorde.

The Epistle.   Isaiah vii.

GOD spake once agayne unto Ahaz, saying; require a token of the Lorde thy God; whether it be towarde the depth beneth, or towarde the heigth aboue.   Then sayde Ahaz; I will require none, neyther will I tempte the Lorde.   And he sayed; hearken to, ye of the house of Dauyd; is it not ynoughe for you that ye bee greuous unto menne, but ye muste greue my God also?   And therefore the Lorde shall geue you a token; beholde a virgin shall conceiue, and beare a sonne, and his mother shall call hys name Emanuell.   Butter and Hony shall he eate, that he maye knowe to refuse the euill, and chose the good.

The Gospel.   Luke i.

AND in the sixth moneth the Angell Gabriell was sente from GOD unto a citie of Galile, named Nazareth, to a virgyn spoused to a manne, whose name was Joseph, of the house of Dauyd, and the virgins name was Mary.   And the Angel went in unto her, and sayd, Haile ful of grace, the Lorde is with thee; Blessed arte thou among weomen.   When she sawe hym, she was abasshed at hys saying, and caste in her mynde, what maner of salutacyon that shoulde be.   And the angel said unto her;

feare not Mary; for thou hast found grace with God. Beholde, thou shalt conceiue in thy wombe, and beare a sonne, and shalt call his name Jesus: He shall be greate, and shalbe called the sonne of the highest. And the Lorde God shall geue unto hym, the seat of his father Dauid, and he shall reigne ouer the house of Jacob for euer, and of hys kyngdome there shalbe none end. Then said Mary unto the angel; How shall this be, seeing I knowe not a man? And the Angel aunswered and sayde unto her, the holy gost shal come upon thee, and the power of the highest shal ouershadowe thee. Therfore also that holy thing which shal be borne, shall be called the sonne of God. And beholde, thy cosin Elizabeth, she hath also conceyued a sonne in her age. And this is her sixth moneth, which was called baren: for with god shal nothing be unpossible. And Mary sayde: beholde the handmayde of the lorde: be it unto me, according to thy woorde. And the Angell departed from her.

¶ *Sainct Markes day.*

Domine, clamavi. Psalm cxli.

LORDE I call upon thee, hast thee unto me : and considre my voyce when I crye unto thee.

Let my praycr bee set furth in thy sighte, as the incense : and let the lifting up of my handes be an euening Sacrifice.

Set a watche, O Lorde, beefore my mouth : and kepe the doore of my lippes.

O let not myne hearte be enclyned to any euill thyng : let me not be occupied in ungodly workes, with the men that woorke wickednesse, lest I eate of such thynges as please them.

Lette the ryghteous rather smyte me frendly : and reproue me.

But let not their precious Balmes breake mine head : yea, I will pray yet agaynst theyr wickednes.

Let theyr iudges be ouerthrowen in stony places : that they may heare my woordes, for they are swete.

Our bones lye scattered before the pit : Lyke as when one breaketh and heweth wood upon the earth.

But myne eyes looke unto thee, O lorde God : in thee is my trust, O cast not out my soule.

Kepe me from the snare, whiche they haue layed for me: and from the trappes of the wicked dooers.

Let the ungodly fall into theyr own nettes together: and let me euer escape them.

Glory bee to the father, and to the sonne : and to the holy Gost.

As it was in the begynnyng, is nowe, and euer shall be : world without ende. Amen.

The Collect.

ALMYGHTIE God, whiche haste instructed thy holy Church with the heauenly doctrine of thy Euangelist Sainct Marke: Geue us grace so to be established by thy holy Gospell, that we be not, lyke chyldren, caried away with euery blast of vaine Doctrine; through Jesus Christ our Lorde.

The Epistle. Ephes. iv.

UNTO euery one of us is geuen grace, according to the measure of the gift of Christe. Wherfore he sayeth; when he went up an hie, he led captiuitie captiue, and gaue giftes unto menne. That he ascended, what meaneth it, but that he also descended first into the lowest partes of the earth? he that descended, is euen the same also that ascended up aboue all heauens, to fulfill all thinges. And the verye same made some Apostles, some prophetes, some Euangelistes, some Shepheardes and teachers; to the edifying of the sainctes, to the worke and minystracyon, euen to the edifying of the body of Christ, till we all come to the unitie of fayth, and knowledge of the sonne of god, unto a perfecte man, unto the measure of the full perfect age of Christe. That we hencefurth should be no more children, wauering and caryed about with euery winde of doctrine, by the wylinesse of men, through craftines, wherby they lay awaite for us, to deceiue us. But let us folowe the trueth in loue, and in all thynges growe in him, which is the head, euen Christe, in whome if all the body be coupled and knit together, throughout euery ioint, wherwith one ministreth to another, (according to the operacion, as euerye parte hath his measure) he encreaseth the body, unto the edifying of itselfe thorow loue.

The Gospel. John xv.

I AM the true Vine, and my father is an housbandeman. Euery braunche that beareth not fruite in me, he will take awaye. And euerye braunche that beareth fruite, will he pourge, that it may bring furth more fruite. Nowe are ye cleane through the woordes whiche I haue spoken unto you. Bide in me, and I in you. As the braunche cannot beare fruite of itselfe, except it bide in the Vine; no more can ye, except ye abyde in me. I am the Vyne, ye are the braunches. He that abydeth in me, and I in him, the same bringeth furth muche fruite. For without me, can ye doe nothing. If a manne byde not in me, he is caste foorth as a braunche, and is withered; And menne gather them, and caste them into the fyer, and they burne. If ye byde in me, and my woordes abyde in you, aske what ye will, and it shalbe dooen for you. Herein is my father glorifyed, that ye beare muche fruite, and become my Disciples. As the father hath loued me, euē so haue I also loued you. Continue ye in my loue. If ye kepe my commaundementes, ye shall byde in my loue, euen as I haue kept my fathers commaundementes, and abyde in hys loue. These thynges haue I spoken unto you, that my ioye mighte remayne in you, and that your ioy might be full.

¶ *Sainct Philip and James.*

¶ *At Matins.*

The Second Lesson, Acts viii. unto " When the apostles."

¶ *At the Communion.*

Ecce, quam bonun ! Psalm cxxxiii.

BEHOLDE, how good and ioyfull a thing it is : brethren to dwell together in unitie.

It is lyke the precious oyntmente upon the head, that ran down unto the beard : euen unto Aarons bearde, and wente downe to the skirtes of hys clothing.

Lyke the dewe of Hermon : whiche fell upon the Hyll of Sion.

For there the Lorde promised hys blessyng : and lyfe for euermore.

Glory be to the father, and to the sonne, &c.

As it was in the beginning, is now, &c.

The Collect.

ALMIGHTIE God, whome truely to knowe is euerlasting lyfe; Graunt us perfectely to knowe thy sonne Jesus Christe to bee the way, the trueth, and the lyfe, as thou hast taught sainct Philip and other the Apostles; Through Jesus Christ our Lorde.

The Epistle. James i.

JAMES the seruaunt of God, andof the Lorde Jesus Christe, sendeth greeting to the twelue Tribes whiche are scattered abrode. My brethren, counte it for an excedynge ioye, when ye fall into diuerse temptacions; Knowyng thys, that the trying of youre faythe, gendreth pacyence: and lette pacience haue her perfecte woorke, that ye may bee perfecte and sounde, lackyng nothyng. If anye of you lacke wisedome, let him aske of him that geueth it; euen God, whiche geueth to all men indifferentley and casteth no man in the teeth, and it shalbe geuen hym. But let hym aske in fayth, and wauer not; for he that doubteth, is like a waue of the sea, whiche is tost of the windes, and caryed with violence. Neyther let that man thynke that he shall receyue any thing of the Lorde.

A waueryng-mynded manne is unstable in all hys wayes. Let the brother whiche is of lowe degree, reioyce when he is exalted. Agayne, let him that is ryche, reioyce when he is made lowe. For euen as the flower of the Grasse, shall he passe away. For as the sunne riseth with heate, and the grasse withereth, and his flower falleth away, and the beauty of the fashion of it perisheth; euen so shall the ryche man perishe in hys wayes. Happie is the man that endureth temptacyon; For when he is tryed, he shall receiue the croune of lyfe, which the Lorde hath promised to them that loue hym.

The Gospel. John xiv.

AND Jesus sayde unto hys disciples, let not your hearte bee troubled. Ye beleue in God, beleue also in me. In my fathers house are many Mansions. If it were not so, I woulde haue tolde you. I goe to prepare a place for you. And if I goe to prepare a place for you, I will come agayne, and receyue you, euen unto myselfe: that where I am, there may ye bee also. And whither I goe, ye knowe, and the waye ye knowe. Thomas sayeth unto hym. Lorde wee knowe not whither thou goeste. And howe is it possible for us to knowe the waye? Jesus sayeth unto hym; I am the way, and the truth, and the life: No man cometh unto the father but by me: if ye had knowen me, ye had knowen my father also: And nowe ye knowe hym, and haue seene hym. Philip sayeth unto him; Lord, shewe us the father, and it suffiseth us. Jesus sayeth unto him, haue I bene so long tyme with you; and yet haste thou not knowen me? Philip, he that hath sene me, hath sene my father, and how sayest thou then, shew us the Father? Beleuest thou not that I am in the father, and the Father in me? The woordes that I speake unto you, I speake not of myselfe: But the father that dwelleth in me, is he that dooeth the woorkes. Beleue me that I am in the father and the father in me. Orelles beleue me for the woorkes sake. Verely,

verely I say unto you; he that beleueth on me, the workes that I do, the same shal he doe also, and greater woorkes than these shall he do, because I goe unto my father.   And whatsoeuer ye aske in my name, that will I dooe, that the father may be glorifyed by the sonne.   If ye shall aske any thyng in my name, I will doe it.

Saint Barnabe Apostle.

At Matins.

¶ The Second Lesson, Acts xiv. unto the end.

¶ *At the Communion.*

Voce mea ad Dominum.   Ps. cxlii.

I CRYED unto the Lord with my voyce : yea euen unto the Lord did I make my supplicacion.

I powred out my complayntes before him : and shewed him of my trouble.

When my spirite was in heauines thou kneweste my path : in the waye wherein I walked, haue they pricuely layed a snare for me.

I loked also upon my right hande; and see, there was no man that would knowe me.

I had no place to flye unto : and no man cared for my soule.

I cryed unto thee, O Lorde, and sayd: Thou art my hope and my porcion in the lande of the liuing.

Consider my complaynt : for I am brought very low.

O delyuer me from my persecutours : for they are to strong for me.

Bryng my soule out of prieson, that I may geue thankes unto thy name : which thing if thou wilt graunt me, then shall the righteous resort unto my company.

Glory be to the father, and to the sonne, &c.

As it was in the beginning, is now, &c.

The Collect.

LORDE Almightie, whiche hast indued thy holy Apostle Barnabas with singuler giftes of thy holy goste; let us not be destytute of thy manyfold giftes, nor yet of grace to use them alway to thy honour and glory; through Jesus Christ our Lorde.

The Epistle. Acts xi.

TYDINGES of these thinges came unto the eares of the congregacyon which was in Hierusalem. And they sente furth Barnabas, that he should goe unto Antioche. Which when he came, and had seene the grace of God, was glad, and exhorted them all, that with purpose of heart, they would continually cleaue unto the Lorde. For he was a good man, and ful of the holy gost, and of fayth, and much people was added unto the Lorde. Then departed Barnabas to Tharsus, for to seke Saul. And when he had found him, he brought him unto Antioche. And it chaūsed, that a whole yere they had theyr conuersacyon with the congregacion there, and taught muche people, insomuche that the disciples of Antioche were the first that were called Christen. In those dayes came Prophetes from the citie of Hierusalem unto Antioche. And there stoode up one of them, named Agabus, and signifyed by the spirite, that there should be great dearth throughout al the world, which came to passe in the Emperour Claudius dayes. Then the disciples, euery man accordyng to his habilitie, purposed to send succour unto the brethren whiche dwelt in Jewry: which thyng they also dyd, and sent it to the elders by the handes of Barnabas and Saul.

The Gospel. John xv.

THIS is my commaundemente, that ye loue together, as I haue loued you. Greater loue hath no man, then thys; that a man bestowe his lyfe for hys frendes. Ye are my frendes, if ye doe whatsoeuer I commaunde you. Hencefurth call I you not seruauntes, for the seruaunt knoweth not what his Lorde doeth. But you haue I called frendes; for all thynges that I haue heard of my father, haue I opened to you: ye haue not chosen me, but I haue chosen you, and ordayned you to goe and bring furth fruit, and that your fruit shoulde remayn: that whatsoeuer ye aske of the father in my name, he may geue it you.

¶ *At Euensong.*

¶ The Second Lesson, Acts xv. (unto) " After certayne dayes."

¶ *Saint John Baptist.*

¶ *Proper Lessons at Matins.*

The First Lesson, Malachi iii. unto the end.
The Second Lesson, Matt. iii. unto the end.

At the Communion.

Domine, exaudi. Psalm cxliii.

HEARE my prayer, O Lord, and considre my desyre : herken unto me for thy trueth and righteousnes sake.

And entre not into iudgement with thy seruaunt : for in thy sighte shall no man liuing be iustifyed.

For the enemie hath persecuted my soule, he hath smitten my life down to the ground : he hath layed me in the darkenes, as the men that haue bene long dead.

Therfore is my spirite vexed within me : and my heart within me is desolate.

Yet doe I remember the time past, I muse upon al thy workes : yea I exercise myself in ye workes of thy hādes.

I stretche foorth my handes unto thee : my soule gaspeth unto thee as a thirstie lande.

Heare me, O Lord, and that soone, for my spirite wexeth faynt : hyde not thy face from me, lest I be lyke unto them that goe downe into the pit.

O let me heare thy louyng-kyndenesse betymes in the mornyng, for in thee is my trust : shewe thou me the way that I should walke in, for I lift up my soule unto thee.

Delyuer me, O Lorde, from myne enemyes : for I flye unto thee to hyde me.

Teache me to do the thing that pleaseth thee, for thou art my God : let thy louing spirite leade me foorth unto the land of righteousnes.

Quicken me O Lorde, for thy names sake : and for thy ryghteousnes sake, bryng my soule out of trouble.

And of thy goodnes slay myne enemyes : and destroye all them that vexe my soule, for I am thy seruaunt.

Glory be to the father, and to the sonne, &c.

As it was in the beginning, &c. Amen.

The Collect.

ALMIGHTIE God, by whose prouidence thy seruaunte John Baptiste was wonderfully borne, and sente to prepare the way of thy sonne our sauiour, by preaching of penaunce; make us so to folowe his doctrine and holy lyfe, that we may truely repent accordyng to his preachyng; and after his example constantly speake the trueth, boldly rebuke vice, and paciently suffre for the truethes sake; through Jesus Christ our Lorde.

The Epistle. Esai. xl.

BE of good chere my people, O ye Prophetes, comfort my people, sayeth your God, comfort Jerusalem at the heart, and tell her, that her trauayle is at an ende, that her offence is pardoned, that she hath receiued of the Lordes hand sufficiēt correccion for all her sinnes. A voyce crieth in wyldernes, Prepare the way of the Lorde in the wyldernes, make straight the path for oure God in the desert. Let all valleyes be exalted, and euery mountayne and hyll be layde lowe : whatso is croked, let it be made straight, and let the rough be made plain fieldes. For the glory of the lord shal appeare, and all fleshe shall at once se it: for why? the mouth of the Lorde hath spoken it.

The same voyce spake, Nowe crye. And the prophet answered; what shall I crye? that all fleshe is grasse, and that all the goodlynes therof is as the floure of the fedle. The grasse is withered, the floure falleth awaye. Euen so is the people as grasse, when the breath of the Lorde bloweth upon them. Neuerthelesse, whether the grasse wyther, or that the floure fade away, yet the worde of our God endureth for euer. Go up unto the hye hil (O Siõ,) thou that bringest good tydinges, lift up thy voyce with power, O thou preacher, Jerusalem; Lift it up without feare, and say unto the cities of Juda; Beholde your God: behold, the lorde God shall come with power, and beare rule with his arme. Beholde, he bryngeth his treasure with hym, and his workes go before hym. He shall feede his flocke lyke an herdman. He shall gather the lambes together with his arme, and carye them in his bosome, and shall kyndely entreat those that beare yong.

The Gospel. Luke i.

ELIZABETHES tyme came that she should be deliuered, and she brought furth a sonne. And her neighbours and her cosyns heard howe the Lorde had shewed great mercy upõ her, and they reioysed with her. And it fortuned, that in the eight day they came to circūcise the child; and called his name Zacharias, after the name of his father. And his mother answered and sayd; not so, but he shalbe called John. And they sayd unto her.   There is none in thy kynred that is named with this name. And they made signes to his father, how he would haue hym called.   And he asked for writyng tables, and wrote, saying; his name is Jhon.   And they meruayled all.   And his mouth was opened immediatly, and his tongue also, and he spake and praysed God.   And feare came on all them that dwelt nye unto them.   And al these sayinges were noysed abrode throughout all the hyll countrey of Jury : and all they that heard thē layd thē up in their heartes, saying; what maner of childe shal this be?   And the hand of the Lorde was with hym.   And his father Zacharias was fylled with the holy ghost, and prophecied, saying; Praysed be the lorde God of Israell, for he hath visited and redemed his people.   And hath raysed up an horne of saluacion unto us, in the house of his seruaunt Dauid.   Euen as he promised by the mouth of his holy prophetes, which were sence the worlde begā.   That we should be saued from our enemies, and from the hand of all that hate us.   That he would deale mercifully with our fathers, and remēbre his holy coue- naunt.   And that he would perfourm the othe which he sware to our father Abrahā for to geue us.   That we deliuered out of the hādes of our enemies, might serue hym without feare, all the daies of our life in suche holines and righteousnes as arc acceptable before him.   And thou child shalt be called the prophet of the highest, for thou shalt go before the face of the Lorde to prepare his wayes; to geue knowledge of saluacion unto his people, for the remission of synnes.   Thorough the tendre mercy of our God, whereby the day-spring from an hye hath visited us.   To geue light to them that sate in darkenes and in the shadow of death, to guide our fete into the waye of peace.   And the childe grewe, and weaxed strong in spirit, and was in wyldernes till the day came, when he shoulde shewe himselfe unto the Israelites.

Proper Lessons at Euensong.

The First Lesson, Malachi iii. unto the end.

The Second Lesson, Matt. xiv. (unto) " When Jesus heard."

¶ *Saint Peter's Day.*

At Matins.

The Second Lesson, Acts iii. unto the end.

At the Communion.

Benedictus Dominus. Psalm cxliv.

BLESSED be the Lorde my strengthe : whiche teacheth my handes to warre, and my fyngers to fight;

My hope and my fortresse, my castle, and deliuerer, my defender in whome I truste : whiche subdueth my people that is under me.

Lord, what is man that thou hast suche respecte unto him? or the sonne of man, that thou so regardest him?

Man is lyke a thyng of noughte : his tyme passeth away like a shadow.

Bowe thy heauens, O Lorde, and come downe : touche the mountaines, and they shall smoke.

Caste furth the lightnyng, and teare theim : shote out thyne arrowes, and consume them.

Sende doune thyne hand from aboue : deliuer me and take me out of the great waters, frō the hand of straunge children;

Whose mouth talketh of vanitie : and their right hande is a ryght hand of wikednes.

I will syng a newe song unto thee, O God : and syng praises unto thee upon a ten-strynged Lute.

Thou that geuest victorye unto kynges : and hast deliuered Dauid thy seruaunte from the peril of the sworde.

Saue me, and deliuer me from the hande of straunge children : whose mouth talketh of vanitie, and their righte hand is a right hand of iniquitie.

That our sonnes maye growe up as the yong plantes : and that oure daughters maie bee as the pollished corners of the temple.

That our garners may be ful and plenteous with al maner of store : that our shepe may bring furth thousandes and ten thousandes in our stretes.

That our Oxen may be strong to labor, that there be no decay : no leadyng into captiuitie and no complainyng in our stretes.

Happy are the people that bee in suche a case : yea, blessed are the people whiche haue the Lorde for their God.

Glory be to the father, and to the sonne, &c.

As it was in the beginnyng, &c.

The Collect.

ALMIGHTIE God, whiche by thy sonne Jesus Christe haste geuen to thy Apostle saincte Peter many excellente giftes, and commaundeste him earnestly to feede thy flocke; make, wee beseche thee, all bishops and pastors diligently to preache thy holy woorde and the people obediently to folowe the same, that they maye receiue the croune of euerlasting glory; through Jesus Christ our Lord.

The Epistle.   Acts xii.

AT the same tyme Herode the kynge stretched furthe his handes to vexe certaine of the congregacion.   And he kylled James the brother of John wyth the sworde.   And because he sawe that it pleased the Jewes, he proceded farther and tooke Peter also.   Then were the dayes of swete breade.   And when he had caught him, he put him in prison also, and deliuered hym to foure quaternions of souldiers to be kept, entending after Easter to bring him furth to the people.   And Peter was kepte in prison; but prayer was made without ceassyng, of the cōgregacion unto God for him.   And when Herode would haue brought him out unto the people, the same night slept Peter betwene two souldiers bound with two chaynes; And the kepers before the doore, kept the prison.   And beholde, the angel of the Lord was there present, and a light shyned in the habitacion. And he smote Peter on the syde, and stiered him up, saying; arise up quickly.   And his chaynes fell of from his handes.   And the angel sayd unto hym, gyrde thyselfe, and binde on thy sandales.   And so he did.   And he sayth unto hym: cast thy garment about thee, and folowe me.   And he came out, and folowed him, and wyst not that it was truth whiche was done by the angel, but thought he had seen a vision.   When they were past the first and the secōd watche, they came unto the yron gate, that leadeth unto the citie, whiche opened to them by the owne accorde.   And they went out, and passed thorough one strete, and furthwith the angel departed from him.   And when Peter was come to himselfe, he sayd; nowe I knowe of a suertie that the Lord hath sent his angell, and hath deliuered me out of the hande of Herode, and from all the waityng for of the people of the Jewes.

The Gospell.   Matt. xvi.

WHEN Jesus came into the coastes of the citie whiche is called Cesarea Philippi, he asked his disciples, saying; whom do men say that I the sonne of man am? They sayd; some say that thou art Jhon Baptiste, some Helias, some Jeremias, or one of the noumbre of the prophetes. He sayeth unto them; but whō say ye that I am? Simon Peter answered, and sayd; Thou art Christ the sonne of the lyuing God. And Jesus answered, and said unto him; happy art thou Simon the sonne of Jonas, for fleshe and bloud hath not opened that unto thee; but my father whiche is in heauen. And I say unto thee, that thou art Peter; and upon this rocke I will buylde my congregacion. And the gates of hel shall not preuail against it. And I wil geue unto thee the keyes of the kingdom of heauen. And whatsoeuer thou byndest in earth, shalbe bound in heauen; and whatsoeuer thou locest in earth, shalbe loced in heauen.

At Euensong.

The Second Lesson, Act iiii unto the ende.

¶ *Sainct Mary Magdalene.*

Lauda, anima mea. Psalm cxlvi.

PRAYSE the Lorde, O my soule : whyle I lyue will I praise the Lord, yea as long as I haue any being, I will syng prayses unto my God.

O put not your trust in princes; nor in any childe of man, for there is no helpe in them.

For when the breath of man goeth furth : he shal turne againe to his yearth, and then all his thoughtes perish.

Blessed is he that hath the God of Jacob for his helpe; and whose hope is in the Lorde his God;

Whiche made heauen and yearth, the sea and all that therin is : whiche kepeth his promyse for euer;

Which helpeth them to right that suffre wrong : which fedeth the hungry.

The Lorde loceth menne out of prison : the Lorde geueth sight to the blynde.

The Lord helpeth theim up that are fallen : the Lorde careth for the righteous.

The Lorde careth for the straungers; he defendeth the father-les and wydowe : as for the waye of the ungodly, he turneth it upsyde doune.

The Lorde thy God, O Sion, shalbe kyng for euermore : and throughout all generacions.

Glory be to the father, &c.

As it was in the &c. Amen.

The Collect.

MERCYFUL father, geue us grace, that we neuer presume to synne thorough the example of any creature; but if it shall chaunce us at any tyme to offende thy diuine maiestie; that then we may truely repent, and lament the same, after the example of Mary Magdalene, and by lyuely fayth obtaine remission of all our sinnes; through the only merites of thy sonne our sauiour Christ.

The Epistle.   Prov. xxxi.

WHOSOEUER findeth an honest faithful woman, she is muche more worth then perles.   The heart of her husband may safely trust in her, so that he shall fall in no pouertie.   She will do hym good and not euill, all the dayes of her lyfe.   She occupieth woll and flaxe, and laboureth gladly with her handes.   She is lyke a marchauntes ship that bringeth her vitayles from afarre.   She is up in the night season to prouide meate for her housholde, and fode for her maydens.   She considereth land and byeth it, and with the fruites of her handes she planteth a vyneyarde.   She girdeth her loynes with strength, and courageth her armes.   And yf she perceyue that her huswifery doeth good, her candle goth not out by night.   She layeth her fyngers to the spindle; and her hand taketh holde of the distaffe.   She openeth her hande to the poore, yea she stretcheth furth her handes to suche as haue nede.   She feareth not that the colde of wynter shall hurt her house, for all her houshold folkes are clothed with skarlet.   She maketh herselfe fayre ornamentes, her clothing is white silke and purple.   Her husband is muche set by in the gates, when he sytteth among the rulers of the land.   She maketh clothe of silke, and selleth it, and deliuereth gyrdles unto the marchaunt.   Strength and honour is her clothyng, and in the latter day she shall reioyce.   She openeth her mouth with wisdome and in her tongue is the lawe of grace.   She loketh well to the wayes of her housholde, and eateth not her bread with idlenes.   Her children shall aryse, and call her blessed; and her husbãd shal make muche of her.   Many daughters there be that gather riches together; but thou goest aboue them all.   As for fauour it is deceiptful, and beutie is a vayne thyng: but a woman that feareth the Lorde, she is worthy to bee praised.   Geue her of the fruite of her handes, and let her owne workes prayse her in the gates.

The Gospell.   Luke vii.

AND one of the Phariseis desyred Jesus that he would eate with
him.   And he wēt into the Phariseis house, and sate doune to
meate.   And behold, a woman in that citie (which was a synner,)
as sone as she knew that Jesus sate at meate in the Phariseis
house, she brought an Alabaster boxe of oyntment, and stode at
his fete behynde hym wepyng, and began to washe his fete with
teares, and did wipe them with the heares of her head, and
kyssed his fete, and anoynted them with the oyntment.   When
the Pharisee (which had bydden hym) sawe that, he spake within
hymselfe, saying; if this man were a prophet, he would surely
know who and what maner of woman this is that touched hym,
for she is a synner.   Jesus answered and sayd unto him; Simon,
I haue somewhat to say unto thee.   And he sayd; Maister, say
on.   There was a certaine lender whiche had two debters, the
one ought hym fiue hundreth pence, and the other fiftie.   When
they had nothing to pay, he forguave thē both.   Tel me therfore,
whiche of them will loue him most?   Simon answered and sayd;
I suppose that he to whom he forgaue most.   And he sayd unto
hym; thou hast truely iudged.   And he turned to the woman,
and sayd unto Symon; Seest thou this woman?   I entred into
thy house, thou gauest me no water for my fete: but she hath
washed my feete with teares, and wyped them with the heeres of
her head.   Thou gauest me no kysse: but she sence the tyme
I came in, hath not ceased to kysse my feete.   My head with oyle
thou diddest not anoynt, but she hath anoynted my fete with
oyntment.   Wherfore I say unto thee, many synnes are forgeuen her; for she loued muche.   To whom lesse is forgeuen,
the same doth lesse loue.   And he sayd unto her; thy synnnes
are forgeuen thee.   And they that sate at meate with him, began
to saye within themselues.   Who is this whiche forgeueth synnes
also?   And he sayd to the woman.   Thy fayth hath saued thee;
go in peace.

¶ *Sainct James the Apostle.*

Laudate Dominum de cœlis.   Psalm cxlviii.

O PRAISE the Lord of heauen : prayse hym in the heigth.
Praise hym all ye Angels of his : praise him all his host.
Prayse hym, Sonne and Moone : prayse ye him all ye starres
and light.
Prayse hym all ye heauens : and ye waters that be aboue the
heauens.

Let them prayse the name of the Lorde : for (he spake the worde, and they were made;) he commaunded, and they were created.

He hath made them fast for euer and euer : he hath geuen them a lawe, whiche shall not be broken.

Prayse the Lorde upon the yearth : ye dragons, and all depes.

Fyer and hayle, snow and vapours, winde and storme : fulfillyng his worde.

Mountaynes and all hylles : fruitfull trees and all Cedres.

Beastes and all cattel : wormes and fethered foules.

Kynges of the yearth and all people : princes and all the Judges of the worlde.

Yong men and maydens, olde men and children, praise the name of the Lorde : for his name only is excellent, and his prayse aboue heauen and yearth.

He shall exalt the horne of his people, all his sainctes shall praise hym : euen the children of Israel, euen the people that serueth him.

Glory be to the father, &c.

As it was in the &c. Amen.

The Collect.

GRAUNT, O mercifull God, that as thyne holy apostle James, leauyng his father and all that he had, without delay was obedient unto the calling of thy sonne Jesus Christ, and folowed hym; So we, forsakyng all worldly and carnal affeccions, may be euermore ready to folowe thy cōmaundementes; thorough Jesus Christ our lorde.

The Epistle. Acts xi. xii.

IN those daies came prophetes frō the citie of Jerusalem unto Antioche. And there stode up one of thē, named Agabus, and signified by the spirite, that there shoulde be great derth thoroughout all the world, whiche came to passe in the Emperour Claudius daies. Then the disciples, euery man accordyng to his habilitie, purposed to send succour unto the brethren which dwelt in Jury, which thing they also dyd, and sēt it to the elders, by the handes of Barnabas and Saul. At the same tyme Herode the kyng stretched furth his handes to vexe certain of the congregaciō. And he kylled James the brother of John with the sworde. And because he sawe that it pleased the Jewes, he proceded farther and toke Peter also.

The Gospell. Matt. xx.

THEN came to him the mother of Zebedes children, with her sonnes, worshippyng hym, and desyryng a certain thing of hym. And he sayd unto her; what wilt thou? She sayd unto him; Graunt that these my two sonnes may sit, the one on thy right hand, and the other on thy lefte, in thy kingedome. But Jesus answered and sayd; ye wot not what ye aske. Are ye able to drynke of the cup that I shall drynke of, and to bee baptised with the baptisme, that I am baptised with? They sayde unto hym, we are: He sayde unto them; ye shal drynke in deede of my cuppe, and be baptized with the baptisme that I am baptised with: but to syt on my right hand and on my left, is not myne to geue; but it shall chaunce unto them that it is prepared for of my father. And when the ten heard this, they disdayned at the two brethren. But Jesus called them unto hym, and sayde: ye knowe that the princes of the nacions haue dominion ouer them, and they that are greate menne, exercise authoritie upon them. It shall not be so amonge you. But whosoeuer will be great among you, let him be your minister, and whosoeuer wilbe chiefe amonge you, let hym be your seruaunte. Euen as the sonne of man came not to bee ministred unto, but to minister, and to geue his life a redempcion for many.

Sainct Bartholomewe.

Non nobis, Domine. Psalm cxv.

NOT unto us, (O Lorde) not unto us, but unto thy name geue the praise : for thy louyng mercy, and for thy truthes sake.

Wherefore shall the heathen say : Where is nowe their God?

As for our God he is in heauen : he hath none whatsoeuer pleased him.

Their Idoles are syluer and gold : euen the woorke of mens handes.

They haue mouthes, and speake not : eyes haue they and see not.

They haue eares, and heare not : noses haue they, and smel not.

They haue handes, and handle not : feete haue they, and walke not, neither speake they thorough their throte.

They that make them are lyke unto them : and so are all suche as put their trust in them.

But the house of Israel, trust thou in the Lorde : he is their succour and defence.

Ye house of Aaron put your trust in the Lorde : he is their helper and defender.

Ye that feare the Lorde, truste ye in the Lorde : he is their helper and defender.

The lorde hath been myndefull of us, and he shall blesse us : euen he shall blesse the house of Israell, he shall blesse the house of Aaron.

He shall blesse them that feare the Lorde : both small and great.

The Lorde shall increace you more and more : you and your children.

Ye are the blessed of the Lorde : whiche made heauen and yearth.

All the whole heauens are the lordes : the yerthe hath he geuen unto the children of men.

The dead prayse not thee (O lorde) : neither all they that go doune into the silence.

But we will prayse the Lorde : from this tyme furth for euermore.

Glory be to the father, and to the sonne, &c.

As it was in the beginnyng, &c.   Amen.

The Collect.

O ALMIGHTIE and euerlastyng God, whiche haste geuen grace to thy apostle Bartholomewe truly to beleue and to preache thy worde; graūt, we beseche thee, unto thy Churche, both to loue that he beleued, and to preache that he taught; thorough Christ our Lorde.

The Epistle.   Acts v.

By the handes of the Apostles were many signes and wonders shewed among the people.   And they were altogether with one accorde in Salomous porch.   And of other durste no man ioyne himselfe to them: neuertheles the people magnified them.   The nombre of them that beleued in the Lord, both of men and women, grewe more and more: insomuche that they brought the sicke into the stretes, and layde them on beddes and couches, that at the leaste waye the shadowe of Peter, whē he came by, might shadowe some of them, (and that they might all be deliuered from their infirmities.)   There came also a multitude out of the cities rounde about unto Jerusalem, bringing sicke folkes, and them which were vexed with uncleane spirites.   And they were healed euery one.

The Gospell. Luke xxii.

AND there was a strife among them, which of them should seme
to be the greatest. And he sayd unto them; the kinges of nacions
reigne ouer them; and they that haue authoritie upon them
are called gracious Lordes: But ye shall not be so. But he
that is greatest among you, shalbe as the yonger; and he that is
chiefe, shalbe as he that doth minister. For whether is greater
he that sytteth at meate, or he that serueth? Is not he that
sitteth at meate? But I amōg you, as he that ministreth. Ye
are they, which haue bidden with me in my temptacions. And
I appoynt unto you a kyngdome, as my father hath appointed
to me, that ye may eate and drynke at my table in my kingdome,
and sytte on seates iudging the xii tribes of Israel.

¶ *Sayncte Matthewe.*

Laudate Dominum omnes gentes. Psalm cxvii.

O PRAISE the Lord all ye heathen : prayse hym all ye nacions.
For hys mercifull kyndnes is euer more and more towarde us :
and the trueth of the Lorde endureth for euer.
Glory be to the father, and to the sonne, &c.
As it was in the beginning, &c. Amen.

The Collect.

ALMIGHTIE God, whiche by thy blessed sonne dyddest call
Mathewe from the receipte of custome to be an Apostle and
Euangelist; Graunt us grace to forsake all couetous desires, and
inordinate loue of riches, and to folowe thy sayed sonne Jesus
Christ; who lyueth and reigneth, &c.

The Epistle. 2 Cor. iv.

SEYNG that we haue suche an office, euen as God hath had
mercye on us, we go not out of kynde, but haue cast from us the
clokes of unhonestye, and walke not in craftines, neither handle
we the worde of God deceiptfully, but open the trueth, and
reporte ourselues to euery mans conscience in the sight of God.
If our gospel be yet hid, it is hid among them that are lost: in
whom the god of this world hath blinded the mindes of them
whiche beleue not, leste the light of the gospell of the glory of
Christe (whiche is the image of God) should shyne unto them.
For we preache not ourselues, but Christe Jesus to be the Lorde,
and oureselues youre seruauntes for Jesus sake. For it is God,

that commaunded the light to shyne out of darkenes, whiche
hath shyned in our heartes, for to geue the light of the knowlege
of the glory of God, in the face of Jesus Christe.

The Gospell.   Matt. ix.

AND as Jesus passed forth frō thence, he sawe a mā (named
Mathewe) sitting at the receipt of custome, and he sayd unto
him, folowe me: and he arose, and folowed him.   And it came
to passe as Jesus sate at meate in his house; beholde, many
Publicans also and synners that came, sate downe with Jesus
and his disciples.   And when the Phariseis sawe it, they sayd
unto his disciples; why eateth your Master with Publicanes
and synners?   But when Jesus heard that, he sayed unto them;
They that be strong nede not the phisicion, but they that are
sicke.   Goe ye rather and learne what that meaneth; I will
haue mercy, and not sacrifice, for I am not come to cal the
righteous, but synners to repentaunce.

¶ *Saynte Michaell and all Angels.*

¶ *At the Communion.*

Laudate, pueri.   Psalm cxiii.

PRAYSE the Lorde (ye seruauntes) : O prayse the name of
the Lorde.

Blessed be the name of the Lorde : from this tyme furth
for euermore.

The Lordes name is praysed : from the risyng up of the Sunne,
unto the goyng downe of the same.

The Lorde is hye aboue all heathen : and his glory aboue the
heauens.

Who is lyke unto the Lorde our God, that hath his dwellyng
so hye : and yet humbleth himselfe to beholde the thynges
that are in heauen and earth?

He taketh up the simple out of the dust : and lifteth the poore
out of the myre;

That he may set him with the princes : euen with the princes
of his people.

He maketh the baren woman to kepe house : and to be a
ioyfull mother of children.

Glory be to the father, and to the sonne, &c.

As it was in the beginning, &c.

The Collect.

EUERLASTYNG God, which haste ordayned and constituted the seruices of all Angels and mē in a wonderfull ordre: mercifully graunt, that they whiche alwaye doe thee seruice in heauen, may by thy appoyntment succour and defende us in earth: through Jesus Christe our Lorde, &c.

The Epistle. Apoc. xii.

THERE was a great battaile in heauen: Michael and his Angels foughte with the Dragon, and the Dragon fought and his Angels, and preuailed not, neither was their place found any more in heauen. And the great dragon that olde serpente, called the deuill and Sathanas, was cast out, whiche deceiueth all the worlde. And he was cast into the earth, and his Angels were cast out also with him. And I heard a loude voyce, saying; in heauen is nowe made saluacion, and strength, and the kingdom of our God, and the power of his Christ. For the accuser of our brethren is cast downe, whiche accused them before our God day and night. And they ouercame him by the bloud of the lambe, and by the word of their testimony, and they loued not their liues unto the death. Therfore reioyce, heauens, and ye that dwell in them. Woe unto the inhabitors of the earth, and of the sea: for the deuill is come downe unto you, whiche hath great wrathe, because he knoweth that he hathe but a shorte tyme.

The Gospell. Matt. xviii.

AT the same tyme came the disciples unto Jesus, saying, who is the greatest in the kyngdome of heauen? Jesus called a childe unto hym, and sette hym in the myddest of them, and sayed; Verely I saye unto you, excepte ye turne and become as children, ye shall not entre into the kyngdome of heauen. Whosoeuer therfore humbleth hymselfe as this childe, tnat same is the greatest in the kyngdome of heauen. And whosoeuer receyueth such a childe in my name, receyueth me. But whoso doth offende one of these lytle ons which beleue in me, it were better for him that a milstone were hanged aboute his necke, and that he were drowned in the depth of the sea. Woe unto the worlde, because of offences: necessary it is that offences come: But woe unto the manne, by whom the offence cometh. Wherfore, yf thy hande or thy foote hynder thee, cut him of, and cast it from thee: it is better for thee to entre into life halt or maimed, rather thē thou shouldest (hauing two handes or two fete) be cast into euerlasting fyer.   And yf thine iye offende thee, plucke it out, and cast it from thee.   It is better for thee to entre into life with one iye, rather then (hauing ii iyes) to be cast into hell fyer.   Take hede that ye despise not one of these lytle ons.   For I saye unto you; that in heauen their Angels doe alwayes beholde the face of my father, whiche is in heauen.

¶ Sainct Luke euangelist.

Super flumina.   Psalm cxxxvii.

By the waters of Babylon we sate downe and wept : when we remembred (thee O) Syon.

As for our harpes we hanged them up : upon the trees that are therin.

For they that led us away captiue, required of us then a song and melodye in our heauines : sing us one of the songes of Sion.

Howe shall we syng the Lordes song : in a straunge lande?

If I forget thee, O Jerusalem : let my ryght hande forget her cunnyng.

If I doe not remembre thee, let my tong cleaue to the rofe of my mouth : yea if I preferre not Jerusalem in my myrth.

Remembre the chyldren of Edom, O Lord : in the day of Jerusalem, howe they sayed; downe with it, downe with it euen to the grounde.

O daughter of Babylon, wasted with miserie : yea happye shall he be that rewardeth thee, as thou hast serued us.

Blessed shall he be, that taketh thy chyldren : and throweth them against the stones.

Glory be to the &c.

As it was in the begynnyng, &c.

The Collect.

ALMIGHTIE God whiche calledst Luke the phisicion, whose prayse is in the gospell, to be a phisicion of the soule ; it may please thee, by the holsome medicines of his doctryne, to heale all the diseases of our soules; through thy sonne Jesus Christe our Lorde.

The Epistle.   2 Tim. iv.

WATCHE thou in all thinges, suffre affliccions, doe the worke throughly of an Euangelyst, fulfyll thyne office unto the utmoste, be sobre.   For I am nowe ready to be offred, and the tyme of my departing is at hand. I haue fought a good fight, I haue fulfilled my course, I haue kept the fayth. From hencefurth there is layed up for me a crowne of righteousnes, whiche the Lorde (that is a righteous iudge) shall geue me at that day: not to me only, but unto all them also that loue his commyng. Doe thy dylygence that thou mayst come shortly unto me. For Demas hath forsaken me, and loueth this presente worlde, and is departed unto Thessalonica. Crescens is gone to Galacia, Titus unto Dalmacia, only Lucas is with me. Take Marke and bring him with thee, for he is profytable unto me for the ministracion. And Tichicus haue I sent to Ephesus: The cloke that I left at Troada with Carpus, when thou commest, bryng with thee, and the bookes, but specially the parchemēt. Alexander the copper-smith did me muche euyll; the Lorde rewarde him accordyng to his dedes, of whom be thou ware also. For he hath greatly withstande our wordes.

The Gospel. Luke x.

THE Lorde appointed other seuenty (and two) also, and sente them two and two before hym into euery citie and place, whither he himselfe would come. Therfore sayd he unto them; the haruest is great, but the labourers are fewe. Praye ye therfore the Lorde of the haruest, to sende furthe labourers into the haruest. Go your wayes; beholde, I sende you foorth as lambes among wolues. Beare no wallet, neither scrip, nor shoes, and salute no man by the waye: into whatsoeuer house ye entre, fyrst saie, peace be to this house. And if the sonne of peace be there, your peace shall rest upon him: if not, it shall returne to you againe. And in the same house tary styll, eatyng and drinking suche as they geue. For the labourer is worthy of his reward.

¶ *Symon and Jude Apostles.*

Laudate Dominum. Psalm cl.

O PRAYSE God in his holynes : praise him in the fyrmament of his power.

Prayse him in his noble actes : prayse him accordyng to his excellent greatnesse.

Prayse him in the sounde of the trumpet : prayse hym upon the lute and harpe.

Prayse hym in the cymbales and daunse : praise him upon the stringes and pipe.

Prayse hym upon the wel-tuned cymbales : prayse hym upon the loud cymbales.

Let euery thyng that hath breth prayse the lord.

Glory be to the father, and to the sonne, &c.

As it was in the beginning, &c.

The Collect.

ALMIGHTIE God, whiche hast builded the congregacion upon the foundacion of the Apostles and prophetes, Jesu Christ himselfe beyng the head corner-stone; graunte us so to bee ioyned together in unitie of spirite by their doctrine, that we maye be made an holye temple acceptable to thee; throughe Jesu Christe our Lorde.

The Epistle.   Jude i.

JUDAS, the seruaunte of Jesu Christe, the brother of James, to them whiche are called and sanctifyed in God the father, and preserued in Jesu Christe: Mercy unto you and peace, and loue be multiplied. Beloued, when I gaue all diligence to wryte unto you of the common saluacion, it was nedeful for me to wryte unto you, to exhort you that ye shoulde continuallye laboure in the faith, which was once geuen unto the saintes. For there are certain ungodly men craftely crept in, of which it was written aforetyme unto suche iudgement. They turne the grace of our God unto wantonnes, and denye God, (which is the only lorde) and our lord Jesus Christ. My mynde is therfore to putte you in remembraunce, forasmuche as ye once knowe this, how that the lord (after that he had deliuered the people out of Egypt) destroyed them which afterward beleued not. The Angels also which kept not their firste estate, but left their own habitaciō, he hath reserued in euerlastig chaines under darknes, unto the iudgement of the great daye: euen as Sodom and Gomor, and the Cities aboute them, whiche in like maner defiled themselues with fornicacion, and folowed straunge fleshe, are set furth for an example, and suffre the paine of eternall fyre: likewyse these beyng deceyued by dreames, defyle the fleshe, despise rulers, and speake euell of them that are in aucthoritie.

The Gospel.   John xv.

THIS commaunde I you, that ye loue together. If the world hate you, ye know yt it hated me before it hated you. If ye were of the worlde, the world would loue his owne: Howbeit because ye are not of the worlde, but I haue chosen you out of

the worlde, therfore the worlde hateth you. Remembre the
worde that I sayed unto you, the seruaunt is not greater than
the lorde. If they haue persecuted me, they will also persecute
you. If they haue kepte my saying, they wil kepe yours also.
But al these thinges will they doe unto you for my names sake,
because they haue not knowen him that sente me. If I had not
come and spoken unto them, they should haue had no synne:
but nowe haue they nothyng to cloke their synne withall. He
that hateth me hateth my father also. If I had not done among
them the workes which none other mā did, they should haue had
no synne. But nowe haue they both seen and hated: not only
me but also my father. But this happeneth that the saying
myght be fulfilled that is writen in their lawe. They hated me
without a cause. But when the comforter is come, whom I
wyll sende unto you from the father, euen the spirite of trueth,
(whiche procedeth of the father,) he shall testifie of me. And
ye shal beare witnes also, because ye haue been with me from
the beginnyng.

¶ All Saynctes.

Propre lessons at Mattyns.

The first lesson, Sapi. iii. unto " Blessed is rather the Baren."
The second lesson, Hebrews xi. xii. " Saynctes by fayth
subdued," unto, " If ye indure chastising."

At the Communion.

Cantate Domino. Psalm cxlix.

O syng unto the Lorde a newe song : let the congregacion of
saynctes prayse hym.

Let Israel reioyce in him that made him : and let the children
of Syon be ioyful in their kyng.

Let them prayse his name in the daunce : let them syng
prayses unto him with tabret and harpe.

For the lord hath pleasure in his people : and helpeth the
meke-hearted.

Let the saynctes be ioyfull with glory : let them reioyce in
their beddes.

Let the prayses of God be in their mouth : and a two-edged
sworde in their handes;

To be auenged of the heathen : and to rebuke the people.

To bynde their kinges in chaynes : and their nobles with
lynkes of yron.

That they may be auenged of them, as it is written : suche honor haue all his Saynctes.

Glory be to the father, and to the sonne, &c.

As it was in the beginnyng, &c.

The Collect.

ALMIGHTIE God, whiche haste knitte together thy electe in one Communion and felowship, in the misticall body of thy sonne Christe our Lord; graunt us grace so to folow thy holy Saynctes in all virtues, and godly liuyng, that we maye come to those inspeakeable ioyes, whiche thou hast prepared for all them that unfaynedly loue thee; through Jesus Christe.

The Epistle. Apoc. vii.

BEHOLDE, I John sawe another Angell ascende from the rising of the Sūne, whiche had the seale of the lyuyng God, and he cryed with a loude voyce to the foure Angels, (to whom power was geuen to hurt the earth and the sea,) saying; Hurt not the earth neither the sea, neither the trees, tyll we haue sealed the seruauntes of our God in their foreheades. And I heard the nombre of them whiche were sealed; and there were sealed an C. and xliiii.M., of all the tribes of the children of Israel.

Of the tribe of Juda were sealed xii.M.

Of the tribe of Ruben were sealed xii.M.

Of the tribe of Gad were sealed xii.M.

Of the tribe of Aser were sealed xii.M.

Of the tribe of Neptalim were sealed xii.M.

Of the tribe of Manasses were sealed xii.M.

Of the tribe of Symeon were sealed xii.M.

Of the tribe of Leuy were sealed xii.M.

Of the tribe of Isachar were sealed xii.M.

Of the tribe of Zabulon were sealed xii.M.

Of the tribe of Joseph were sealed xii.M.

Of the tribe of Beniamin were sealed xii.M.

After this I behelde, and loe, a great multitude, (whiche no manne could nombre) of all nacions and people, and tongues stode before the seate and before the lambe, clothed with long white garmentes, and Palmes in theyr handes, and cried with a loude voyce, saying; saluacion be ascribed to him that sitteth upon the seate of our god, and unto the lambe. And al the Angels stode in the compasse of the seate, and of the elders, and of the foure beastes, and fell before the seate on their faces, and worshipped God, saying; Amen. Blessyng and glory, and wisedome, and thankes, and honour, and power, and might, be unto our God for euermore. Amen.

The Gospell.   Matt. **v.**

Jesus seing the people, went up into the mountaine: and when he was set, his disciples came to hym, and after that he hadde opened his mouth, he taught them, saying; Blessed are the poore in spirite, for theirs is the kyngdome of heauen. Blessed are they that morne; for they shall receyue comfort. Blessed are the meke: for they shall receyue the enheritaunce of the earth. Blessed are they whiche hunger and thirst after righteousnes: for they shall be satisfied. Blessed are the mercyfull: for they shall obtaine mercy. Blessed are the pure in heart, for they shal see God. Blessed are the peacemakers: for they shalbe called the children of God. Blessed are they whiche suffre persecucion for righteousnes sake: for theirs is the kyngdome of heauen. Blessed are ye when men reuile you, and persecute you, and shall falsly saye all maner of euill sayinges against you for my sake: reioice, and be glad; for great is youre rewarde in heauen. For so persecuted they the Prophetes whiche were before you.

¶ *Proper Lessons at Euensong.*

The First Lesson, Sap. **v.** (unto) " His jealousy also."

The Second Lesson, Apoc. **xix.** (unto) " And I saw an angel stand."

THE

SUPPER OF THE LORDE

AND

THE HOLY COMMUNION,

COMMONLY CALLED THE MASSE.

¶ *SO many as intende to bee partakers of the holy Communion, shall sygnifie their names to the Curate, ouer night : or els in the morning, afore the beginning of Matins, or immediatly after.*

¶ *And if any of those be an open and notorious euill liuer, so that the congregacion by hym is offended, or haue doen any wrong to his neighbours by worde or dede : The Curate shall call hym, and aduertise hym, in any wise not to presume to the lordes table, untill he haue openly declared hymselfe to haue truly repented, and amended his former naughtie life : that the congregacion maie thereby be satisfied, whiche afore were offended : and that he haue recompensed the parties, whom he hath dooen wrong unto, or at the least bee in full purpose so to doo, as sone as he conueniently maie.*

¶ *The same ordre shall the Curate use, with those betwixt whom he perceiueth malice, and hatred to reigne, not suffering them to bee partakers of the Lordes table, untill he knowe them to bee reconciled. And yf one of the parties so at variaunce, be content to forgeue from the botome of his harte all that the other hath trespaced against hym, and to make amendes for that he hymself hath offended : and the other partie will not bee perswaded to a godly unitie, but remaigne still in his frowardnes and malice : The Minister in that case, ought to admit the penitent persone to the holy Communion, and not hym that is obstinate.*

¶ *Upon the daie and at the tyme appoincted for the ministracion of the holy Communion, the Priest that shal execute the holy ministery, shall put upon hym the vesture appoincted for that ministracion, that is to saye : a white Albe plain, with a vestement or Cope. And where there be many Priestes, or Decons, there so many shalbe ready to helpe the Priest, in the ministracion, as shalbee requisite : And shall haue upon them lykewise the vestures appointed for their ministery, that is to saye, Albes with tunacles. Then shall the Clerkes syng in Englishe for the office, or Introite, (as they call it,) a Psalme appointed for that daie.*

The Priest standing humbly afore the middes of the Altar, shall saie the Lordes praier, with this Collect.

ALMIGHTIE God, unto whom all hartes bee open, and all desyres knowen, and from whom no secretes are hid: clense the thoughtes of our hartes, by the inspiracion of thy holy spirite: that we may perfectly loue thee, and worthely magnifie thy holy name: through Christ our Lorde.   Amen.

Then shall he saie a Psalme appointed for the introite: whiche Psalme ended the Priest shall saye, or els the Clerkes shal syng,

    iii. Lorde haue mercie upon us.
    iii. Christ haue mercie upon us.
    iii. Lorde haue mercie upon us.

Then the Prieste standyng at Goddes borde shall begin,

Glory be to God on high.

The Clerkes. And in yearth peace, good will towardes men.

We praise thee, we blesse thee, we worship thee, we glorifie thee, wee geue tankes to thee for thy greate glory, O Lorde GOD, heauenly kyng, God the father almightie.

O Lorde the onely begotten sonne Jesu Christe, O Lorde GOD, Lambe of GOD, sonne of the father, that takest awaye the synnes of the worlde, haue mercie upon us: thou that takest awaye the synnes of the worlde, receiue our praier.

Thou that sittest at the right hande of God the father, haue mercie upon us: For thou onely art holy, thou onely art the Lorde. Thou onely (O Christ) with the holy Ghoste, are moste high in the glory of God the father. Amen.

Then the priest shall turne him to the people and saye,

The Lorde be with you.

The Aunswere. And with thy spirite.

The Priest. Let us praie.

Then shall folowe the Collect of the daie, with one of these two Collectes folowynge, for the kyng.

ALMIGHTIE God, whose kingdom is euerlasting, and power infinite, haue mercie upon the whole congregacion, and so rule the heart of thy chosen seruaunt Edward the sixt, our kyng and gouernour: that he (knowyng whose minister he is) maie aboue al thinges, seke thy honour and glory, and that we his subiectes (duely consyderyng whose auctoritie he hath) maye faithfully serue, honour, and humbly obeye him, in thee, and for thee, according to thy blessed word and ordinaunce: Through Jesus Christe oure Lorde, who with thee, and the holy ghoste, liueth and reigneth, euer one God, worlde without ende. Amen.

ALMIGHTIE and euerlasting GOD, wee bee taught by thy holy worde, that the heartes of Kynges are in thy rule and gouernaunce, and that thou doest dispose, and turne them as it semeth best to thy godly wisedom: We humbly beseche thee, so to dispose and gouerne, the heart of Edward the sixt, thy seruaunt, our Kyng and gouernour, that in all his thoughtes, wordes, and workes, he maye euer seke thy honour and glory, and study to preserue thy people, committed to his charge, in wealth, peace, and Godlynes: Graunt this, O mercifull father, for thy dere sonnes sake, Jesus Christ our Lorde. Amen.

The Collectes ended, the priest, or he that is appointed, shall reade the Epistle, in a place assigned for the purpose, saying,

The Epistle of sainct Paule, written in the   Chapter of   to the

The Minister then shall reade thepistle. Immediatly after the Epistle ended, the priest, or one appointed to reade the Gospel, shall saie,

The holy Gospell, written in the   Chapter of

The Clearkes and people shall aunswere,

Glory be to thee, O Lorde.

The priest or deacon then shall reade the Gospel: After the Gospell ended, the Priest shall begin,

I BELEUE in one God.

The clerkes shall syng the rest.

The father almightie, maker of heauen and yearth, and of all thinges visible, and inuisible: And in one Lorde Jesu Christ, the onely begotten sonne of GOD, begotten of his father before all worldes, God of GOD, light of light, very God of very God, begotten, not made, beeyng of one substaunce with the father, by whom all thinges were made, who for us men, and for our saluacion, came doune from heauen, and was incarnate by the holy Ghoste, of the Virgin Mary, and was made manne, and was Crucified also for us under Poncius Pilate, he suffered and was buried, and the thirde daye he arose again according to the scriptures, and ascended into heauen, and sitteth at the right hande of the father: and he shall come again with glory, to iudge both the quicke and the dead.

And I beleue in the holy ghost, the Lorde and geuer of life, who precedeth from the father and the sonne, who with the father and the sonne together, is worshipped and glorified, who spake by the Prophetes. And I beleue one Catholike and Apostolike Churche. I acknowlege one Baptisme, for the remission of synnes. And I loke for the resurreccion of the deade: and the lyfe of the worlde to come. Amen.

¶ *After the Crede ended, shall folowe the Sermon or Homely, or some portiõ of one of the Homelyes, as thei shalbe herafter deuided : wherein if the people bee not exhorted to the worthy recciuyng of the holy Sacrament of the bodye and bloude of our sauior Christ : then shal the Curate geue this exhortaciõ, to those yt be minded to receiue ye same.*

DERELY beloued in the Lord, ye that mynde to come to the

holy Communiō of the bodye and bloude of our sauior Christe, must considre what S. Paule writeth to the Corinthiās, how he exhorteth all persones diligently to trie and examine thēselues, before they presume to eate of that breade, and drinke of that cup: for as the benefite is great, if with a truly penitent heart, and liuely faith, we receiue that holy Sacramēt; (for then we spiritually eate the fleshe of Christ, and drinke his bloude, then we dwell in Christ and Christ in us, wee bee made one with Christ, and Christ with us;) so is the daunger great, yf wee receyue the same unworthely; for then wee become gyltie of the body and bloud of Christ our sauior, we eate and drinke our owne damnacion, not considering the Lordes bodye. We kyndle Gods wrathe ouer us, we prouoke him to plague us with diuerse dyseases, and sondery kyndes of death. Therefore if any here be a blasphemer, aduouterer, or bee in malyce, or enuie, or in any other greuous cryme (excepte he bee truly sory therefore, and earnestly mynded to leaue the same vices, and do trust him-selfe to be reconciled to almightie God, and in Charitie with all the worlde), lette him bewayle his synnes, and not come to that holy table; lest after the taking of that most blessed breade, the deuyll enter into him, as he dyd into Judas, to fyll him full of all iniquitie, and brynge him to destruccion, bothe of body and soule.

Judge therfore yourselfes (brethren) that ye bee not iudged of the Lorde. Let your mynde be without desire to synne, repent you truely for your synnes past, haue an earnest and lyuely faith in Christ our sauior, be in perfect charitie with all men, so shall ye be mete partakers of those holy misteries. And aboue all thynges: ye must geue moste humble and hartie thankes to God the father, the sonne, and the holy ghost, for the redempcion of the worlde, by the death and passion of our sauior Christ, both God and man, who did humble himself euen to the death upon the crosse, for us miserable synners, whiche laie in darknes and shadowe of death, that he myghte make us the children of God: and exalt us to euerlasting life. And to thende that wee should alwaye remembre the excedyng loue of our master, and onely sauior Jesu Christe, thus diyng for us, and the innumerable benefites (whiche by his precious bloud-shedyng) he hath ob-teigned to us, he hath left in those holy Misteries, as a pledge of his loue, and a continuall remēbraunce of the same his owne blessed body, and precious bloud, for us to fede upon spiritually, to our endles comfort and consolacion. To him therfore, with the father and the holy ghost, let us geue (as we are most bounden) continual thankes, submittyng ourselfes wholy to hys holy wil and pleasure, and studying to serue hym in true holines and righteousnes, al the daies of our life.   Amen.

¶ *In Cathedral churches or other places, where there is dailie Communion, it shall be sufficient to read this exhortacion aboue written, once in a moneth.   And in parish churches, upon the weke daies it may be lefte unsayed.*

¶ *And if upon the Sunday or holydaye the people be negligent to come to the Communion : Then shall the Priest earnestly exhorte his parishoners, to dispose themselfes to the receiuing of the holy cōmunion more diligētly, saiyng these or like wordes unto thē.*

DERE frendes, and you especially upon whose soules I haue cure and charge, on   next, I do intende by Gods grace, to offre to all suche as shalbe godlye disposed, the moste comfortable Sacrament of the body and bloud of Christ, to be taken of them in the remembraunce of his moste fruitfull and glorious Passyon : by the whiche passion we have obteigned remission of our synnes, and be made partakers of the kyngdom of heauen, whereof wee bee assured and asserteigned, yf wee come to the sayde Sacrament, with hartie repentaunce for our offences, stedfast faithe in Goddes mercye, and earnest mynde to obeye Goddes will, and to offende no more.   Wherefore our duetie is, to come to these holy misteries, with moste heartie thankes to bee geuen to almightie GOD, for his infinite mercie and benefites geuen and bestowed upon us his unworthye seruauntes, for whom he hath not onely geuen his body to death, and shed his bloude, but also doothe vouchesaue in a Sacrament and Mistery, to geue us his sayed bodye and bloud to feede upon spiritually.   The whyche Sacrament beyng so Diuine and holy a thyng, and so comfortable to them whiche receyue it worthilye, and so daungerous to them that wyll presume to take the same unworthely :   My duetie is to exhorte you in the meane season, to consider the greatnes of the thing, and to serche and examine your owne consciences, and that not lyghtly nor after the maner of dissimulers with GOD :   But as they whiche shoulde come to a moste Godly and heauenly Banket, not to come but in the mariage garment required of God in scripture, that you may (so muche as lieth in you) be founde worthie to come to suche a table.   The waies and meanes thereto is,

First, that you be truly repentaūt of your former euill life, and that you confesse with an unfained hearte to almightie God, youre synnes and unkyndnes towardes his Maiestie committed, either by will, worde or dede, infirmitie or ignoraunce : and that with inwarde sorowe and teares you bewaile your offences, and require of almightie God mercie and pardon, promising to him

(from the botome of your hartes) thamendment of your former
lyfe. And emonges all others, I am commaunded of God,
especially to moue and exhorte you to reconcile yourselfes to
your neighbors, whom you haue offended, or who hath offended
you, putting out of your heartes al hatred and malice against
them, and to be in loue and charitie with all the worlde, and to
forgeue other, as you woulde that god should forgeue you. And
yf any mā haue doen wrōg to any other: let him make satisfaccion, and due restitucion of all landes and goodes, wronfully
taken awaye or withholden, before he come to Goddes borde,
or at the least be in ful minde and purpose so to do, as sone as
he is able, or els let him not come to this holy table, thinking
to deceyue God, who seeth all mēnes hartes. For neither the
absolucion of the priest, can any thing auayle them, nor the
receiuyng of this holy sacrament doth any thing but increase
their damnacion. And yf there bee any of you, whose conscience is troubled and greued in any thing, lackyng comforte
or counsaill, let him come to me, or to some other dyscrete and
learned priest, taught in the law of God, and confesse and open
his synne and griefe secretly, that he may receiue suche ghostly
counsaill, aduyse, and comfort, that his conscience maye be
releued, and that of us (as of the ministers of GOD and of the
churche) he may receiue comfort and absolucion, to the satisfaccion of his mynde, and auoyding of all scruple and doubtfulnes: requiryng suche as shalbe satisfied with a generall
confession, not to be offended with them that doe use, to their
further satisfiyng, the auriculer and secret confession to the
Priest : nor those also whiche thinke nedefull or conuenient,
for the quietnes of their awne cōsciences, particuliarly to open
their sinnes to the Priest: to bee offended with them that are
satisfied, with their humble confession to GOD, and the generall
confession to the churche. But in all thinges to folowe and kepe
the rule of charitie, and euery man to be satisfied with his owne
conscience, not iudgyng other mennes myndes or consciences;
where as he hath no warrant of Goddes word to the same.

¶ *Then shall folowe for the Offertory, one or mo, of these Sentences of holy*
scripture, to bee song whiles the people doo offer, or els one of theim to bee
saied by the minister, immediatly afore the offeryng.

LET your light so shine before men, that they maye see your
good woorkes, and glorify your father whiche is in heauen.
Math. v.
Laie not up for yourselfes treasure upon the yearth, where the

rust and mothe doth corrupt, and where theues breake through and steale: But laie up for yourselfes treasures in heauen, where neyther ruste nor mothe doth corrupt, and where theues do not breake through nor steale. *Math*. vi.

Whatsoeuer you would that menne should do unto you, euen so do you unto them: for this is the Lawe and the Prophetes. *Math*. vii.

Not euery one that saieth unto me, lorde, lorde, shall entre into the kyngdom of heauen, but he that doth the will of my father whiche is in heauen. *Math*. vii.

Zache stode furthe, and saied unto the Lorde: Beholde, Lord, the halfe of my goodes I geue to the poore, and if I haue doen any wrong to any man, I restore fourefold. *Luc*. xix.

Who goeth a warfare at any tyme at his owne cost? Who planteth a vineyarde, and eateth not of the fruite thereof? Or who fedeth a flocke, and eateth not of the milke of the flocke? i *Cor*. ix.

If we have sowen unto you spirituall thinges, is it a great matter yf we shall reape your worldly thynges? i *Cor*. ix.

Dooe ye not knowe, that they whiche minister aboute holy thinges, lyue of the Sacrifice? They whiche waite of the alter are partakers with the alter? euen so hath the lorde also ordained: that they whiche preache the Gospell, should lyue of the Gospell. i *Cor*. ix.

He whiche soweth litle, shall reape litle, and he that soweth plenteously, shall reape plenteously. Let euery manne do accordyng as he is disposed in his hearte, not grudgyngly, or of necessitie; for God loueth a cherefull geuer. 2 *Cor*. ix.

Let him that is taught in the woorde, minister unto hym that teacheth, in all good thinges. Be not deceiued; GOD is not mocked. For whatsoeuer a man soweth, that shall he reape. *Gala*. vi.

While we haue tyme, let us do good unto all men, and specially unto them, whiche are of the houshold of fayth. *Gala*. vi.

Godlynes is greate riches, if a man be contented with that he hath: For we brought nothing into the worlde, neither maie we cary anything out. i *Timo*. vi.

Charge them whiche are riche in this worlde, that they bee ready to geue, and glad to distribute, laying up in stoare for themselfes a good foundacion, against the time to come, that they maie attain eternall lyfe. i *Timo*. vi.

GOD is not unrighteous, that he will forget youre woorkes and labor, that procedeth of loue, whiche loue ye haue shewed for his names sake, whiche haue ministred vnto the sainctes, and yet do minister. *Hebre.* vi.

To do good, and to distribute, forget not, for with suche Sacrifices God is pleased. *Hebre.* xiii.

Whoso hath this worldes good, and seeth his brother haue nede, and shutteth vp his compassion from hym, how dwelleth the loue of God in him? i *John* iii.

Geue almose of thy goodes, and turne neuer thy face from any poore man, and then the face of the lorde shall not be turned awaye from thee. *Toby* iv.

Bee mercifull after thy power: if thou hast muche, geue plenteously, if thou hast litle, do thy diligence gladly to geue of that litle: for so gathereste thou thyselfe a good reward, in the daie of necessitie. *Toby* iv.

He that hath pitie vpon the poore, lendeth vnto the Lorde; and loke what he laieth out, it shal be paied hym again. *Prov.* xix.

Blessed be the man that prouideth for the sicke and nedy, the lorde shall deliuer hym, in the tyme of trouble. *Psalm* xli.

Where there be Clerkes, thei shall syng one, or many of the sentences aboue written, accordyng to the length and shortenesse of the tyme, that the people be offeryng.

In the meane time, whyles the Clerkes do syng the Offertory, so many as are disposed, shall offer vnto the poore mennes boxe euery one accordynge to his habilitie and charitable mynde. And at the offeryng daies appoynted, euery manne and woman shall paie to the Curate, the due and accustomed offerynges.

Then so manye as shalbe partakers of the holy Communion, shall tary still in the quire, or in some conuenient place nigh the quire, the men on the one side, and the women on the other syde. All other (that mynde not to receiue the said holy Communion) shall departe out of the quire, except the ministers and Clerkes.

Than shall the minister take so muche Bread and Wine, as shall suffice for the persons appoynted to receiue the holy Communion, laiyng the breade vpon the corporas, or els in the paten, or in some other comely thyng, prepared for that purpose. And puttyng ye wyne into the Chalice, or els in some faire or conuenient cup, prepared for that vse (if the Chalice will not serue), puttyng thereto a litle pure and cleane water: And settyng both the breade and wyne vpon the Alter: then the Priest shall saye.

The Lorde be with you.

Aunswere. And with thy spirite.

Priest. Lift up your heartes.

Aunswere. We lift them up vnto the Lorde.

Priest. Let us geue thankes to our Lorde God.

Aunswere. It is mete and right so to do.

The Priest. It is very mete, righte, and our boūden dutie, that wee shoulde at all tymes, and in all places, geue thankes to thee, O Lorde holy father, almightie euerlastyng God.

¶ Here shall folowe the proper preface accordyng to the tyme (if there bee any specially appoynted), or els immediatly shall folowe,

Therefore with Angelles, &c.

PROPRE PREFACES.

¶ *Upon Christmas Daie.*

BECAUSE thou diddeste geue Jesus Christe, thyne onely sonne, to bee borne as this daye for us, who by the operacion of the holy ghoste, was made very man, of the substaunce of the Virgin Mari his mother, and that without spot of sinne to make us cleane from all synne.　Therefore &c.

¶ *Upon Easter daie.*

BUT chiefly are we bound to praise thee, for the glorious resurreccion of thy sonne Jesus Christe, our Lorde, for he is the very Pascall Lambe, whiche was offered for us, and hath taken awaie the synne of the worlde, who by his death hath destroyed death, and by his risyng to life againe, hath restored to us euerlastynge life.　Therefore &c.

¶ *Upon the Assencion Day.*

THROUGH thy most dere beloued sonne, Jesus Christ our Lorde, who after his moste glorious resurreccion manifestly appered to all his disciples, and in their sight ascended up into heauen, to prepare a place for us, that where he is, thither mighte we also ascende, and reigne with hym in glory.　Therfore &c.

¶ *Upon Whitsondaye.*

THROUGH Jesus Christe our Lorde, accordyng to whose moste true promise, the holy Ghoste came doune this daye frō heauen, with a sodain great sound, as it had been a mightie wynde, in the likenes of fiery toungues, lightyng upon the Apostles, to teache them, and to leade them to all trueth, geuyng them bothe the gifte of diuerse languages, and also boldnes with feruent zeale, constantly to preache the Gospell unto all nacions, whereby we are brought out of darkenes and error, into the cleare light and true knowlege of thee, and of thy sonne Jesus Christ.　Therfore &c.

¶ *Upon the feast of the Trinitie.*

IT is very meete, righte, and oure bounden duetie, that we should at al tymes, and in al places, geue thankes to thee O Lorde, almightye euerlasting God, whiche arte one God, one Lorde, not one onely person, but three persones in one substaunce: For that which we beleue of the glory of the father, the same we beleue of the sōne, and of the holy ghost, without any difference, or inequalitie: whom the Angels &c.

After whiche preface shall folowe immediatly,

Therfore with Angels and Archangels, and with all the holy companye of heauen, we laude and magnify thy glorious name, euermore praisyng thee, and saying,

¶ Holy, holy, holy, Lorde God of Hostes: heauen and earth are full of thy glory: Osanna in the highest. Blessed is he that commeth in the name of the Lorde: Glory to thee, O lorde in the highest.

This the Clerkes shall also syng.

¶ *When the Clerkes have dooen syngyng, then shall the Priest, or Deacon, turne hym to the people, and saye,*

Let us praie for the whole state of Christes churche.

¶ *Then the Priest, turnyng hym to the Altar, shall saye or syng, playnly and distinctly, this prayer folowyng:*

ALMIGHTIE and euerliuyng GOD, whiche by thy holy Apostle haste taught us to make prayers and supplicacions, and to geue thankes for al menne: We humbly beseche thee moste mercyfully to receiue these our praiers, which we offre unto thy diuine Maiestie, beseching thee to inspire cōtinually the uniuersal churche with the spirite of trueth, unitie, and concorde: And graunt that al they that do cōfesse thy holy name, maye agree in the trueth of thy holye worde, and liue in unitie and godly loue. Speciallye we beseche thee to saue and defende thy seruaunt Edwarde our Kyng, that under hym we maye be Godly and quietly gouerned. And graunt unto his whole coūsaile, and to all that he put in auctoritie under hym, that they maye truely and indifferently minister iustice, to the punishemente of wickednesse and vice, and to the maintenaunce of Goddes true religion and vertue. Geue grace (O heauenly father) to all Bishoppes, Pastors, and Curates, that thei maie bothe by their life and doctrine set furthe thy true and liuely worde, and rightely and duely administer thy holy Sacramentes: and to al thy people geue thy heauenly grace, that with meke heart and due reuerence they may heare and receiue thy holy worde, truely seruyng thee in holynes and righteousnes all the dayes of their life: And we most hūbly beseche thee of thy goodnes (O Lorde) to coumfort and succour all them, whyche in thys transytory life be in trouble, sorowe, nede, syckenes, or any other aduersitie. And especially we commend unto thy mercifull goodnes, this congregacion which is here assembled in thy name, to celebrate the commemoracion of the most glorious death of thy sonne: And here we do geue unto thee moste high praise, and heartie thankes, for the wonderfull grace and vertue, declared in all thy sainctes, from the begynning of the worlde: And chiefly in the glorious and moste blessed virgin Mary, mother of thy sonne Jesu Christe our Lorde and God, and in the holy Patriarches, Prophetes, Apostles and Martyrs, whose examples (o Lorde) and stedfastnes in thy fayth, and kepyng thy holy commaundementes, graunt us to folowe. We commend unto thy mercye (O Lorde) all other thy seruauntes, which are departed hence from us, with the signe of faith, and nowe do reste in the slepe of peace: Graūt unto them, we beseche thee, thy mercy, and euerlasting peace, and that, at the day of the generall resurreccion, we and all they which bee of the misticall body of thy sonne, may altogether be set on his right hand, and heare that his most ioyfull voyce: Come unto me, O ye that be blessed of my father, and possesse the kingdom, whiche is prepared for you from the begynning of the worlde: Graunt this, O father, for Jesus Christes sake, our onely mediatour and aduocate.

O God heauenly father, which of thy tender mercie diddest geue thine only sonne Jesu Christ to suffre death upon the crosse for our redempcion, who made there (by his one oblacion once offered) a full, perfect, and sufficient sacrifyce, oblacion, and satysfaccyon, for the sinnes of the whole worlde, and did institute, and in his holy Gospell commaund us, to celebrate a perpetuall memory of that his precious death, untyll his comming again: Heare us (o merciful father) we besech thee; and with thy holy spirite and worde, vouchsafe to bl✠esse and sanc✠tifie these thy gyftes, and creatures of bread and wyne, that they maie be unto us the bodye and bloude of thy moste derely beloued sonne Jesus Christe. Who in the same nyght that he

Here the priest must take the bread into his hādes.

was betrayed: tooke breade, and when he had blessed, and geuen thankes: he brake it, and gaue it to his disciples, saiyng: Take, eate, this is my bodye which is geuen for you, do this in remembraunce of me.

Likewyse after supper he toke the cuppe, and when he had geuen thankes, he gaue it to them, saiyng: drynk ye all of this, for this is my bloude of the newe Testament, whyche is shed for you and for many, for remission of synnes: do this as oft as you shall drinke it, in remembraunce of me.

Here the priest shall take the Cuppe into his hãdes.

These wordes before rehersed are to be saied, turning still to the Altar, without any eleuacion, or shewing the Sacrament to the people.

WHERFORE, O Lorde and heauenly father, accordyng to the Instytucyon of thy derely beloued sonne, our sauiour Jesu Christ, we thy humble seruauntes do celebrate, and make here before thy diuine Maiestie, with these thy holy giftes, the memoryall whyche thy sonne hath wylled us to make, hauyng in remembraunce his blessed passion, mightie resurreccyon, and gloryous ascencion, renderyng unto thee most hartie thankes, for the innumerable benefites procured unto us by the same, entierely desiryng thy fatherly goodnes, mercifully to accepte this our Sacrifice of praise and thankes geuing: most humbly beseching thee to graunt, that by the merites and death of thy sõne Jesus Christ, and through faith in his bloud, we and al thy whole church, may obteigne remission of our sinnes, and all other benefites of hys passyon. And here wee offre and present unto thee (O Lorde) oure selfe, oure soules, and bodies, to be a reasonable, holy, and liuely sacrifice unto thee: humbly besechyng thee, that whosoeuer shalbee partakers of thys holy Communion, maye worthely receiue the most precious body and bloude of thy sonne Jesus Christe: and bee fulfilled with thy grace and heauenly benediccion, and made one bodye with thy sonne Jesu Christe, that he maye dwell in them, and they in hym. And although we be unworthy (through our manyfolde synnes) to offre unto thee any Sacryfice: Yet we besECHE thee to accepte thys our bounden duetie and seruice, and commaunde these our prayers and supplicacions, by the Ministery of thy holy Angels, to be brought up into thy holy Tabernacle before the syght of thy dyuine maiestie; not waiyng our merites, but pardonyng our offences, through Christe our Lorde, by whome, and with whome, in the unitie of the holy Ghost: all honour and glory, be unto thee, O father almightie, world without ende. Amen.

Let us praye.

As our sauiour Christe hath commaunded and taught us, we are bolde to saye. Our father, whyche art in heauen, halowed

be thy name. Thy Kyngdome come. Thy wyll be doen in
yearth, as it is in heauen.   Geue us this daye our dayly breade.
And forgeue us our trespaces, as wee forgeue them that trespasse agaynst us.   And leade us not into temptacion.

The aunswere. But deliuer us from euill.   Amen.

Then shall the priest saye.

The peace of the Lorde be alwaye with you.

The Clerkes. And with thy spirite.

The Priest. Christ our Pascall lambe is offred up for us, once
for al, when he bare our sinnes on hys body upon the crosse, for
he is the very lambe of God, that taketh away the sinnes of the
worlde: wherfore let us kepe a ioyfull and holy feast with the
Lorde.

*Here the priest shall turne hym toward those that come to the holy Communion,
and shall saye.*

YOu that do truly and earnestly repent you of your synnes to
almightie God, and be in loue and charitie with your neighbors,
and entende to lede a newe life, folowyng the commaundementes
of God, and walkyng from hencefurth in his holy wayes: drawe
nere and take this holy Sacrament to your comforte, make your
humble confession to almightie God, and to his holy church here
gathered together in hys name, mekely knelyng upon your
knees.

*Then shall thys generall Confession bee made, in the name of al those that
are minded to receiue the holy Communion, either by one of them, or els
by one of the ministers, or by the prieste himselfe, all kneeling humbly upon
their knees.*

ALMYGHTIE GOD father of oure Lord Jesus Christ, maker of
all thynges, iudge of all men, we knowlege and bewaile our
manyfold synnes and wyckednes, which we from tyme to tyme,
most greuously haue committed, by thought, word and dede,
agaynst thy diuine maiestie, prouokyng moste iustely thy wrath
and indignacion against us, we do earnestly repent and be
hartely sory for these our misdoinges, the remembraunce of
them is greuous unto us, the burthen of them is intollerable:
haue mercye upon us, haue mercie upon us, moste mercyfull
father, for thy sonne our Lorde Jesus Christes sake, forgeue us
all that is past, and graunt that we may euer hereafter, serue
and please thee in neunes of life, to the honor and glory of thy
name: Through Jesus Christe our Lorde.

*Then shall the Prieste stande up, and turnyng himselfe to the people,
say thus,*

ALMIGHTIE GOD, our heauenly father, who of his great mercie

hath promysed forgeuenesse of synnes to all them, whiche with hartye repentaunce and true fayth, turne unto him: haue mercy upon you, pardon and delyuer you from all youre sinnes, confirme and strēgthen you in all goodnes, and bring you to euerlasting lyfe: through Jesus Christ our Lord. Amen.

Then shall the Priest also say,

Heare what coumfortable woordes our sauiour Christ sayeth, to all that truely turne to him.

Come unto me all that trauell, and bee heauy laden, and I shall refreshe you. So God loued the worlde that he gaue his onely begotten sonne, to the ende that al that beleue in hym, shoulde not perishe, but haue lyfe euerlasting.

Heare also what saint Paul sayeth.

This is a true saying, and woorthie of all men to bee receiued, that Jesus Christe came into thys worlde to saue sinners.

Heare also what saint John sayeth.

If any man sinne, we haue an aduocate with the father, Jesus Christ the righteous, and he is the propiciacion for our sinnes.

Then shall the Priest turnyng him to gods boord, knele down, and say in the name of all them, that shall receyue the Communion, this prayer folowing.

WE do not presume to come to this thy table (o mercifull lord) trusting in our owne righteousnes, but in thy manifold and great mercies: we be not woorthie so much as to gather up the cromes under thy table: but thou art the same lorde whose propertie is alwayes to haue mercie: Graunt us therefore (gracious lorde) so to eate the fleshe of thy dere sonne Jesus Christ, and to drynke his bloud in these holy Misteries, that we may continuallye dwell in hym, and he in us, that our synfull bodyes may bee made cleane by his body, and our soules washed through hys most precious bloud. Amen.

¶ *Then shall the Prieste firste receiue the Communion in both kindes himselfe, and next deliuer it to other Ministers, if any be there present, (that they may bee ready to helpe the chiefe Minister,) and after to the people.*

¶ *And when he deliuereth the Sacramente of the body of Christe, he shall say to euery one these woordes.*

The body of our Lorde Jesus Christe whiche was geuen for thee, preserue thy bodye and soule unto euerlasting lyfe.

And the Minister deliuering the Sacramēt of the bloud, and geuing euery one to drinke once and no more, shall say,

The bloud of our Lorde Jesus Christe which was shed for thee, preserue thy bodye and soule unto euerlastyng lyfe.

If there be a Deacon or other Priest, then shal he folow with the Chalice: and as the Priest ministereth the Sacramēt of the body, so shal he (for more expeditiō) minister the Sacrament of the bloud, in fourme before written.

In the Communion tyme the Clarkes shall syng,

ii. O lambe of god, that takeste away the sinnes of the worlde: haue mercie upon us.

O lambe of god, that takeste away the synnes of the worlde : graunt us thy peace.

Beginning so soone as the Prieste doeth receyue the holy Communion, and when the Communion is ended, then shall the Clarkes syng the post Communion.

¶ *Sentences of holy Scripture, to be sayd or song euery daye one, after the holy Communion, called the post Communion.*

IF any man will folowe me, let him forsake hymselfe, and take up his crosse and folowe me. *Math.* xvi.

Whosoeuer shall indure unto thende, he shalbe saued. *Mar.* xiii.

Praysed be the Lorde god of Israell, for he hath visited and redemed hys people : therefore let us serue hym all the dayes of our lyfe, in holines and righteousnes accepted before hym. *Luc.* i.

Happie are those seruauntes, whome the Lord (when he cummeth) shall fynde waking. *Luc.* xii.

Be ye readye, for the sonne of manne will come at an hower when ye thinke not. *Luc.* xii.

The seruaunte that knoweth hys maisters will, and hath not prepared himself, neither hath doen according to his will, shalbe beaten with many stripes. *Luc.* xii.

The howre cummeth, and now it is, when true woorshippers shall wurship the father in spirite and trueth. *John* iiii.

Beholde, thou art made whole, sinne no more, lest any wurse thing happen unto thee. *John* v.

If ye shall continue in my woorde, then are ye my very disciples, and ye shall knowe the truth, and the truth shall make you free. *John* viii.

While ye haue lighte, beleue on the lyght, that ye may be the children of light. *John* xii.

He that hath my commaundemētes, and kepeth them, the same is he that loueth me. *John* xiiii.

If any man loue me, he will kepe my woorde, and my father will loue hym, and wee will come unto hym, and dwell with hym. *John* xiiii.

If ye shall byde in me, and my woorde shall abyde in you, ye shall aske what ye will, and it shall bee doen to you. *John* xv.

Herein is my father gloryfyed, that ye beare much fruite, and become my disciples. *John* xv.

This is my commaundement, that you loue together as I haue loued you. *John* xv.

If God be on our syde, who can be agaynst us? which did not spare his owne sonne, but gaue him for us all. *Roma.* viii.

Who shall lay any thing to the charge of Goddes chosen? it is GOD that iustifyeth, who is he that can condemne? *Roma.* viii.

The nyght is passed and the day is at hande, let us therfore cast away the dedes of darkenes, and put on the armour of light. *Rom.* xiii.

Christe Jesus is made of GOD, unto us wisedome, and right-eousnes, and sanctifying, and redempcion, that (according as it is written) he whiche reioyceth shoulde reioyce in the Lorde. *i Corin.* i.

Knowe ye not that ye are the temple of GOD, and that the spirite of GOD dwelleth in you? If any manne defile the temple of GOD, him shall God destroy. *i Corin.* iii.

Ye are derely bought, therfore glorifye God in your bodies, and in your spirites, for they belong to God. *i Cor.* vi.

Be you folowers of God as deare children, and walke in loue, euen as Christe loued us, and gaue himselfe for us an offeryng and a Sacrifyce of a sweete sauoure to God. *Ephes.* v.

Then the Priest shall geue thankes to God, in the name af all them that haue communicated, turning him first to the people, and saying.

The Lorde be with you.

The aunswere. And with thy spirite.

The priest. Let us pray.

ALMIGHTYE and euerlyuyng GOD, we moste hartely thanke thee, for that thou hast vouchsafed to feede us in these holy Misteries, with the spirituall foode of the moste precious body and bloud of thy sonne, our sauiour Jesus Christ, and haste assured us (duely receiuing the same) of thy fauour and goodnes toward us, an that we be very membres incorporate in thy Misticall bodye, whiche is the blessed companye of all faythfull people, and heyres through hope of thy euerlasting kingdome, by the merites of the most precious death and passion, of thy deare sonne. We therfore most humbly beseche thee, O heauenly father, so to assist us with thy grace, that we may continue in that holy felowship, and doe all suche good woorkes, as thou hast prepared for us to walke in: through Jesus Christe our Lorde, to whome with thee and the holy gost, bee all honour and glory, world without ende.

Then the Priest turning hym to the people, shall let them depart with this blessing :

The peace of GOD (which passeth all understanding) kepe your hartes and mindes in the knowledge and loue of GOD, and of his sonne Jesus Christ our Lorde: And the blessing of God Almighty, the father, the sonne, and the holy Ghost, be amongst you and remain with you alwaye.

Then the people shall aunswere.

Amen.

Where there are no clerkes, there the Priest shall say al thinges appoynted here for them to sing.
When the holy Communion is celebrate on the workeday, or in priuate howses : Then may be omitted, the Gloria in exceisis, the Crede, the Homily, and the exhortacion, beginning.

DEARELY beloued, &c.

¶ *Collectes to bee sayed after the Offertory, when there is no Communion, euery such day one.*

ASSIST us mercifully, O Lord, in these our supplicacions and praiers, and dispose the way of thy seruauntes, toward the attainement of euerlasting saluacion, that emong all the chaunges and chaunces of thys mortall lyfe, they maye euer bee defended by thy moste gracious and readye helpe; throughe Christe our Lorde. Amen.

O ALMIGHTIE Lorde and euerlyuyng GOD, vouchesafe, we besече thee, to direct, sanctifye, and gouerne, both our heartes and bodies, in the wayes of thy lawes, and in the workes of thy cōmaundementes: that through thy most mightie proteccion, both here and euer, we may be preserued in body and soule: Through our Lorde and sauiour Jesus Christ. Amen.

GRAUNT we beseche thee almightie god, that the wordes whiche we haue hearde this day with our outwarde eares, may throughe thy grace, bee so grafted inwardly in our heartes, that they may bring foorth in us the fruite of good liuing, to the honour and prayse of thy name: through Jesus Christe our Lorde. Amen.

PREUENT us, O lorde, in all our doinges, with thy most gracious fauour, and further us with thy continuall helpe, that in al our woorkes begonne, continued, and ended in thee: we may glorifye thy holy name, and finally by thy mercy obteine euerlasting life: Through, &c.

ALMIGHTIE God, the fountayn of all wisdome, which knowest our necessities beefore we aske, and our ignoraunce in asking: we beseche thee to haue compassion upon our infirmities, and those thynges, whiche for our unwoorthines we dare not, and

for our blindnes we cannot aske, vouchsaue to geue us for the
woorthines of thy sonne Jesu Christ our Lorde.   Amen.

ALMIGHTIE god, which hast promised to heare the peticions of
them that aske in thy sonnes name, we beseche thee mercifully
to inclyne thyne eares to us that haue made nowe our prayers
and supplicacions unto thee, and graunt that those thynges
whiche we haue faythfullye asked accordyng to thy will, maye
effectually bee obteyned to the reliefe of oure necessitye, and
to the settyng foorth of thy glorye: Through Jesus Christ our
Lorde.

¶ *For rayne.*

O GOD heauenly father, whiche by thy sonne Jesu Christ,
hast promised to al thē that seke thy kingdom, and the righteousnes therof, al thinges necessary to the bodely sustenaunce:
send us (we beseche thee) in this our necessitie, such moderate
rayne and showers, that we may receiue the fruites of the earth,
to our comfort and to thy honor; Through Jesus Christ our
Lord.

For fayre wether.

O LORDE God, whiche for the sinne of manne didst once
drowne all the worlde, except eight persons, and afterwarde of
thy great mercye, didste promise neuer to destroy it so agayn:
We hūbly beseche thee, that although we for oure iniquities
haue woorthelye deserued this plague of rayne and waters, yet,
upon our true repentaunce, thou wilt sende us suche wether
wherby we may receiue the fruites of the earth in due season,
and learne both by the punishment to amende our liues, and by
the graunting of our peticion to geue thee prayse and glory:
Through Jesu Christ our Lorde.

¶ *Upon wednesdaies and frydaies the English Letany shalbe said or song
in all places, after suche forme as is appoynted by the kynges maiesties
Iniunccions : Or as is or shal bee otherwyse appoynted by his highnes.
And thoughe there be none to cōmunicate with the Prieste, yet these dayes
(after the Litany ended) the Priest shall put upon him a playn Albe or
surplesse, with a cope, and say al thinges at the Altar (appoynted to be
sayed at the celebracyon of the lordes supper), untill after the offertory.
And then shall adde one or two of the Collectes aforewritten, as occasion
shall serue by his discrecion. And then turning him to the people shall
let them depart with the accustomed blessing. And the same order shall
be used all other dayes whensoeuer the people be customably assembled to
pray in the churche, and none disposed to communicate with the Priest.*

*Lykewyse in Chapelles annexed, and all other places, there shalbe no cele-
bracion of the Lordes supper, except there be some to communicate with
the Priest. And in suche Chapelles annexed where ye people hath not
bene accustomed to pay any holy bread, there they must either make some
charitable prouision for the bering of the charges of the Communion, or
elles (for receyuying of the same) resort to theyr Parish Churche.*

For aduoyding of all matters and occasyon of dyscencyon, it is mete that the breade prepared for the Communion, bee made, through all thys realme, after one sort and fashion : that is to say, unleauened, and rounde, as it was afore, but without all maner of printe, and somethyng more larger and thicker than it was, so that it may be aptly deuided in diuers pieces : and euery one shall be deuided in two pieces, at the leaste, or more, by the discrecion of the minister, and so distributed. And menne muste not thynke lesse to be receyued in parte then in the whole, but in eache of them the whole body of our saulour Jesu Christ.

And forsomuche as the Pastours and Curates within thys realme shal continually fynd at theyr costes and charges in theyr cures, sufficient Breade and Wyne for the holy Communion (as oft as theyr Parishioners shalbe disposed for theyr spiritual comfort to receyue the same) it is therefore ordred, that in recompence of suche costes and charges, the Parishioners of euery Parishe shall offer euery Sonday, at the tyme of the Offertory, the iuste valour and price of the holy lofe (with all suche money, and other thinges as were wont to be offered with the same) to the use of theyr Pastours and Curates, and that in suche ordre and course, as they were woont to fynde and pay the sayd holy lofe.

Also, that the receiuing of the Sacrament of the blessed body and bloud of Christ, may be most agreable to the instituciō thereof, and to the usage of the primitiue Churche : In all Cathederall and Collegiate Churches, there shal alwaies some Communicate with the Prieste that ministreth. And that the same may bee also obserued euery where abrode in the countrey : Some one at the least of that house in euery Parishe to whome by course after the ordinaunce herein made, it apperteyneth to offer for the charges of the Communiō, or some other whom they shall prouide to offer for them, shall receiue the holy Communion with the Prieste : the whiche may be the better doen, for that they knowe before, when theyr course commeth, and maie therfore dispose thēselues to the worthie receiuyng of the Sacramente. And with hym or them who doeth so offre the charges of the Communion ; all other, who be then Godly disposed thereunto, shall lykewyse receiue the Communion. And by this meanes the Minister hauyng alwaies some to communicate with him, maie accordingly solempnise so high and holy misteries, with all the suffrages and due ordre appoynted for the same. And the Priest on the weke daie shall forbeare to celebrate the Communion, excepte he haue some that will communicate with hym.

Furthermore, euery man and womā to be bound to heare and be at the diuine seruice, in the Parishe churche where they be resident, and there with deuout prayer, or Godlye silence and meditacion, to occupie themselues. There to paie their dueties, to communicate once in the yeare at the least, and there to receyue, and take all other Sacramentes and rites, in this booke appoynted. And whosoeuer willyngly upon no iust cause, doeth absent themselues, or doeth ungodly in the Parishe churche occupie thēselues : upon profe therof, by the Ecclesiasticall lawes of the Realme to bee excommunicate, or suffre other punishement, as shall to the Ecclesiastical iudge (accordyng to his discrecion) seme conuenient.

And although it bee redde in aunciente writers, that the people many yeares past receiued at the priestes hādes the Sacrament of the body of Christ in theyr owne handes, and no commaundemēt of Christ to the contrary : Yet forasmuche as they many tymes conueyghed the same secretelye awaye, kept it with them, and diuersly abused it to supersticion and wickednes : lest any suche thynge hereafter should be attempted, and that an uniformitie might be used, throughoute the whole Realme : it is thought conuenient the people commōly receiue the Sacramēt of Christes body, in their mouthes, at the Priestes hande.

THE LETANY AND SUFFRAGES.

O GOD the father of heauen : haue mercy upon us miserable synners.

O God the father of heauen : haue mercy upon us miserable sinners.

O God the sonne, redemer of the world : haue mercy upon us miserable sinners.

O God the sonne, redemer of the world : haue mercy upon us miserable sinners.

O God the holy ghost, procedyng from the father and the sonne : haue mercy upon us miserable sinners.

O God the holy ghost, procedyng from the father and the sonne : haue mercy upon us miserable sinners.

O holy, blessed, and glorious Trinitie, three persons and one God : haue mercye upon us miserable synners.

O holy, blessed, and glorious Trinitie, three persons and one God : haue mercye upon us miserable synners.

Remember not lorde, our offences, nor the offences of our forefathers, neither take thou vengeaunce of our sinnes : spare us good lord, spare thy people, whom thou hast redemed with thy moost precious bloude, and be not angry with us for euer.

Spare us, good Lorde.

From al euill and mischiefe, from synne, from the craftes and assaultes of the deuyll, from thy wrathe, and from euerlastyng damnacion :

Good lorde deliuer us.

From blyndnes of heart, from pryde, vainglory, and Hypocrisy, from enuy, hatred, and malice, and all uncharitablenes :

Good lorde deliuer us.

From fornicacion, and all other deadlye synne, and from al the deceytes of the worlde, the fleshe, and the deuill :

Good lorde deliuer us.

From lightning and tempest, from plage, pestilence, and famine, from battaile and murther, and from sodain death :

Good lorde deliuer us.

From all sedicion and priuye conspiracie, from the tyrannye of the bishop of Rome and all his detestable enormities, from al false doctrine and herisy, from hardnes of heart, and contempte of thy word and commaundemente:

Good lorde deliuer us.

By the mistery of thy holy incarnacion, by thy holy Natiuitie and Circumcision, by thy Baptisme, fastyng, and temptacion:

Good lorde deliuer us.

By thyne agony and bloudy sweate, by thy crosse and passion, by thy precious death and burial, by thy glorious resurrecciō and ascencion, by the cōming of the holy gost:

Good lorde deliuer us.

In all tyme of our tribulacion, in all time of our wealth, in the houre of death, in the daye of iudgement:

Good lorde deliuer us.

We synners do beseche thee to heare us (O Lorde God) and that it maye please thee to rule and gouern thy holy Churche uniuersall in the right waye:

We beseche thee to heare us good lorde.

That it maye please thee to kepe Edward the vi., thy seruaunt our kyng and gouernour:

We beseche thee to heure us good lorde.

That it maye please thee to rule his heart in thy faythe, feare, and loue, that he maye alwayes haue affiaunce in thee, and euer seke thy honour and glory:

We beseche thee to heare us good lorde.

That it maye please thee to be his defendour and keper, geuyng hym the victorye ouer all his enemyes:

We beseche thee to heare us good lorde.

That it maye please thee to illuminate all Bishops, pastours and ministers of the churche, with true knowlege and understandyng of thy word, and that bothe by theyr preachyng and liuing, they maye set it foorth, and shewe it accordyngly:

We beseche thee to heare us good lorde.

That it may please thee to endue the Lordes of the counsaile and all the nobilitie, with grace, wisedome, and understandyng:

We beseche thee to heare us good lorde.

That it may please thee to blesse and kepe the magistrates, geuyng them grace to execute iustice, and to mayntayne trueth:

We beseche thee to heare us good lorde.

That it may please thee to blesse and kepe al thy people:
We beseche thee to heare us good lorde.

That it may please thee to geue to all nacions unitie, peace, and concorde:
We beseche thee to heare us good lorde.

That it may please thee to geue us an heart to loue and dread thee, and diligently to lyue after thy commaundementes:
We beseche thee to heare us good lorde.

That it may please thee to geue all thy people increase of grace, to heare mekely thy worde, and to receyue it with pure affeccion, and to bryng forth the fruites of the spirite:
We beseche thee to heare us good lorde.

That it may please thee to bryng into the way of trueth all suche as haue erred and are deceyued:
We beseche thee to heare us good lorde.

That it may please thee to strengthen suche as do stand, and to comfort and helpe the weake hearted, and to raise up them that fall, and finally to beate downe Sathan under our feete:
We beseche thee to heare us good lorde.

That it may please thee to succoure, helpe, and comfort all that be in daunger, necessitie, and tribulacion:
We beseche thee to heare us good lorde.

That it may please thee to preserue all that trauayle by lande or by water, all women labouryng of chylde, all sicke persons, and yong chyldren, and to shewe the pytie upon all prisoners and captyues:
We beseche thee to heare us good lorde.

That it may please thee to defende and prouide for the father-les children and wyddowes, and all that be desolate and oppressed:
We beseche thee to heare us good lorde.

That it may please thee to haue mercy upon all menne:
We beseche thee to heare us good lorde.

That it may please thee to forgeue our enemies, persecutours, and sclaunderers, and to turne their heartes:
We beseche thee to heare us good lorde.

That it may please thee to geue and preserue to our use the kyndly fruytes of the earth, so as in due tyme we may enioy them:
We beseche thee to heare us good lorde.

That it may please thee to geue us true repentaunce, to forgeue us all our synnes, negligences, and ignoraunces, and to endue us with the grace of thy holy spirite to amende our lyues accordyng to thy holy worde:
We beseche thee to heare us good lorde.

Sonne of God: we beseche thee to heare us.
Sonne of God : we beseche thee to heare us.

O lãbe of God, that takest away the sinnes of the world:
Graunt us thy peace.

O lãbe of God, that takest away the sinnes of the world:
Haue mercy upon us.

O Christe heare us.
O Christe heare us.

Lorde haue mercy upon us.
Lorde haue mercy upon us.

Christe haue mercy upon us.
Christe haue mercy upon us.

Lorde haue mercy upon us.
Lorde haue mercy upon us.

Our father whiche art in heauen. *With the residue of the Paternoster.*

And leade us not into temptacion.
But deliuer us from euyll.

The versicle. O Lorde, deale not with us after our synnes.
The aunswere. Neither rewarde us after our iniquities.

Let us praye.

O God mercifull father, that despisest not the syghyng of a contrite heart, nor the desire of such as be sorowfull, mercifully assyste our prayers, that we make before the in all our troubles and aduersities, whensoeuer they oppresse us: And graciousely heare us, that those euyls, whiche the crafte and subteltie of the deuyll or man worketh against us, be brought to nought, and by the prouidence of thy goodnes, they maye be dyspersed, that we thy seruauntes, beyng hurte by no persecucions, maye euermore geue thãkes unto thee, in thy holy churche, thorough Jesu Christe our Lorde.
O Lorde, aryse, helpe us, and delyuer us for thy names sake.
O God, we haue heard with our eares, and our fathers haue

declared unto us the noble workes that thou dyddest in theyr dayes, and in the olde tyme before them.

O Lorde, aryse, helpe us, and deliuer us for thy honour.

Glory be to the father, the sonne, and to the holy ghoste; as it was in the begynning, is nowe, and euer shall be worlde without ende.   Amen.

From our enemies defende us, O Chryste.
Graciously loke upon our afflyctions.

Pytifully beholde the sorowes of our heart.
Mercifully forgeue the synnes of thy people.

Fauourably with mercy heare our prayers.
O sonne of Dauid haue mercy upon us.

Both nowe and euer vouchsafe to here us Christe.
Graciousely heare us, O Christ.
Graciousely heare us, O lord Christ.

The versicle.   O Lorde, let thy mercy be shewed upon us.
The Aunswere.   As we do put our truste in thee.

Let us praye.

WE humbly besche thee, O father, mercifully to loke upon our infirmities, and for the glory of thy name sake, turne from us all those euilles that we moste righteously haue deserued; and graunte that in all oure troubles we maye put our whole trust and confidence in thy mercy, and euermore serue thee in purenes of liuyng, to thy honour and glory: through our onely mediator and aduocate Jesus Christ our Lorde.   Amen.

ALMIGHTIE God, whiche hast geuen us grace at this tyme with
one accorde to make our commune supplicacions unto thee,
and doest promise, that whan two or three bee
gathered in thy name, thou wylt graunt theyr
requestes: fulfill now, O lorde, the desires
and peticions of thy seruauntes, as
maye bee moste expediente for them,
grauntyng us in this worlde knowlege of thy trueth, and in
the worlde to come,
lyfe euerlasting.
Amen.

ADMINISTRACION OF PUBLYKE BAPTISME

TO BE USED IN THE CHURCHE

It appeareth by aũcient wryters, that the Sacramente of Baptisme in the olde tyme was not commonly ministred, but at two tymes in the yeare, at Easter and whytsontyde, at whiche tymes it was openly mynistred in the presence of all the congregacion: Whiche custome (now beeyng growen out of use) although it cannot for many consideracions be wel restored again, yet it is thought good to folowe the same as nere as conueniently maybe be: Wherfore the people are to bee admonished, that it is moste con- ueniente that baptisme shoulde not be ministred but upon Sondayes and other holy dayes, when the most numbre of people maye come together. As well for that the congregacion there presente may testifie the receyuyng of them, that be newly baptysed, into the noumbre of Christes Churche, as also because in the Baptisme of Infantes, euery manne presente maye be put in remembraunce of his owne profession made to God in his Baptisme. For whiche cause also, it is expediente that Baptisme be ministred in the Englishe tounge. Neuerthelesse (yf necessitie so requyre) children ought at all tymes to be baptised, eyther at the churche or els at home.

PUBLIKE BAPTISME.

When there are children to be Baptised upon the Sonday, or holy daye, the parentes shall geue knowledge ouer nyght or in the mornyng, afore the begin- ning of Mattens, to the curate. And then the Godfathers, Godmothers, and people, with the children muste be ready at the Church dore, either im- mediatly afore the laste Canticle at Mattens or els immediatly afore the last Canticle at Euensong, as the Curate by his discrecion shall appoynte. And then, standyng there, the prieste shall aske whether the chyldren be baptised on no. If they aunswere No, then shall the priest saye thus.

DEARE beloued, forasmuche as all men bee conceyued and borne in sinne, and that no manne borne in synne, can entre into the kingdom of God (except he be regenerate, and borne anewe of water, and the holy ghost) I beseche you to call upon God the father through our Lord Jesus Christ, that of his bounteouse mercy he wil graunt to these children that thing, which by nature they cannot haue, that is to saye, they may be baptised with the holy ghost, and receyued into Christes holy Church, and be made lyuely membres of the same.

Then the prieste shall saye.

Let us praye.

ALMYGHTIE and euerlastyng God, whiche of thy iustice dydest

destroy by fluddes of water the whole worlde for synne, excepte
viii persones, whome of thy mercy (the same tyme) thou didest
saue in the Arke: And when thou didest drowne in the read sea
wycked kyng Pharao with al his armie, yet (at the same time)
thou didest leade thy people the chyldren of Israel safely through
the myddes therof: wherby thou didest fygure the washyng of
thy holy Baptisme: and by the Baptisme of thy wel beloued
sonne Jesus Christe, thou dydest sanctifie the fludde Jordan, and
al other waters to this misticall washing away of synne: We
beseche thee (for thy infinite mercies) that thou wilt mercifully
looke upon these children, and sanctifie them with thy holy gost,
that by this holesome lauer of regeneracion, whatsoeuer synne is
in them, may be washed cleane away, that they, being deliuered
from thy wrathe, may be receiued into tharke of Christes churche,
and so saued from peryshyng: and beeyng feruente in spirite,
stedfaste in fayth, ioyfull through hope, rooted in charitie, maye
euer serue thee: And finally attayne to euerlastyng lyfe, with
all thy holy and chosen people. This graunte us we beseche the,
for Jesus Christes sake our Lorde. Amen.

¶ *Here shall the priest aske what shall be the name of the childe, and when
the Godfathers and Godmothers haue tolde the name, then shall he make
a crosse upon the childes forehead and breste, saying.*

¶ N. Receyue the signe of the holy Crosse, both in thy forehead, and in thy breste, in token that thou shalt not be ashamed
to confesse thy fayth in Christe crucifyed, and manfully to fyght
under his banner against synne, the worlde, and the deuill, and to
continewe his faythfull soldiour and seruaunt unto thy lyfes
ende. Amen.

*And this he shall doe and saye to as many children as bee presented to be
Baptised, one after another.*

Let us praye.

ALMIGHTIE and immortall God, the ayde of all that nede, the
helper of all that flee to thee for succour, the life of them that
beleue, and the resurreccion of the dead: we call upon the for
these infantes, that they cummyng to thy holy Baptisme, may
receyue remission of theyr sinnes, by spirituall regeneracion.
Receyue them (o Lorde) as thou haste promysed by thy welbeloued sonne, saying: Aske, and you shall haue: seke, and you
shall fynde: knocke, and it shalbe opened unto you. So geue
nowe unto us that aske: Lette us that seke, fynde: open thy gate
unto us that knocke: that these infantes maye enioy the euer-

lastyng benediccion of thy heauenly washing, and may come to the eternall kyngdome whiche thou haste promysed, by Christe our Lorde.   Amen.

Then let the priest lokyng upon the chyldren, saye.

I COMMAŪDE thee, uncleane spirite, in the name of the father, of the sonne, and of the holy ghost, that thou come out, and departe from these infantes, whom our Lord Jesus Christe hath vouchsaued, to call to his holy Baptisme, to be made membres of his body, and of his holy congregacion.   Therfore thou cursed spirite, remember thy sentence, remember thy iudgemente, remember the daye to be at hande, wherin thou shalt burne in fyre euerlasting, prepared for the and thy Angels.   And presume not hereafter to exercise any tyrannye towarde these infantes, whom Christe hathe bought with his precious bloud, and by this his holy Baptisme calleth to be of his flocke.

Then shall the priest saye.

The Lorde be with you.
The people.   And with thy spirite.
The Minister. ¶ Heare nowe the gospell written by S. Marke.

Marke x.

At a certayne tyme they brought children to Christe that he should touche them, and hys disciples rebuked those that brought them.   But when Jesus sawe it, he was displeased, and sayed unto them: Suffre lytle children to come unto me, and forbyd them not; for to suche belongeth the kingdom of God. Verely I say unto you: whosoeuer doeth not receyue the kyngdom of God, as a lytle chylde: he shall not entre therin.   And when he had taken them up in his armes: he put his handes upon them, and blessed them.

After the gospell is red, the Minister shall make this briefe exhortacion upon the woordes of the gospell.

FRENDES you heare in this gospell the woordes of our Sauiour Christe, that he commaunded the children to be brought unto him: howe he blamed those that would haue kept them from hym: howe he exhorteth all men to folowe their innocencie. Ye perceyue howe by his outwarde gesture and dede he declared his good wyll towarde them.   For he embraced thē in his armes, he layed his handes upon them, and blessed them: doubte ye not therfore, but earnestly beleue, that he wyll lykewyse fauourably receyue these present infantes, that he wyll embrace them with the arms of his mercy, that he wyll geue unto them the blessyng of eternall lyfe: and make them partakers of his euer-lasting kingdome. Wherfore we beyng thus perswaded of the good wyll of our heauenly father towarde these infantes, declared by his sonne Jesus Christe; and nothyng doubtyng but that he fauourably alloweth this charitable worke of ours, in bringing these children to his holy baptisme: let us faythfully and deuoutly geue thankes unto him; And say the prayer which the Lorde himselfe taught. And in declaracion of our fayth, let us also recyte the articles conteyned in our Crede.

Here the minister with the Godfathers, Godmothers, and people presente, shall saye.

¶ Our father whiche art in heauen, halowed bee thy name, &c.

And then shall saye openly.

I beleue in God the father almightie, &c.

The priest shall adde also this prayer.

ALMIGHTIE and euerlastyng God, heauenly father, we geue the humble thankes, that thou haste vouchesaued to call us to know-ledge of thy grace, and fayth in thee: Increase and confyrme this fayth in us euermore: Geue thy holy spirite to these infantes, that they may be borne agayne, and be made heyres of euerlast-ing saluacion, through our Lord Jesus Christ: Who lyueth and reigneth with thee and the holy spirite, nowe end for euer. Amen.

Then let the priest take one of the children by the ryght hande, thother being brought after him. And cūming into the Churche towarde the fonte, saye.

THE Lorde vouchesafe to receyue you into his holy housholde, and to kepe and gouerne you alwaye in the same, that you may haue euerlasting lyfe. Amen.

Then standyng at the fonte the priest shall speake to the Godfathers and Godmothers, on this wyse.

Wel beloued frendes, ye haue brought these childrē here to bee Baptized, ye haue prayed that our Lorde Jesus Christ would vouchsafe to receyue them, to lay his handes upon them, to blesse them, to release them of theyr sinnes, to geue them the kyngdome of heauen, and euerlastyng life. Ye haue heard also that our Lorde Jesus Christe hath promysed in his gospel, to graunte all these thynges that ye haue prayed for: whiche promyse he for his parte, will moste suerly kepe and perfourme. Wherfore, after this promyse made by Christe, these infantes muste also faythfully for theyr parte promise by you, that be theyr suerties, that they wyll forsake the deuyll and all his workes, and constantly beleue Gods holy woorde, and obediently kepe his commaundementes.

Then shall the priest demaunde of the childe (which shalbe first Baptized) these questiōs folowing : first naming the childe, and saying.

N. Doest thou forsake the deuill and all his workes?

Aunswere. I forsake them.

Minister. Doest thou forsake the vaine pompe, and glory of the worlde, with all the couetouse desyres of the same?

Aunswere. I forsake them.

Minister. Doest thou forsake the carnall desyres of the flesh, so that thou wilt not folowe, nor be ledde by them?

Aunswere. I forsake them.

Minister. Doest thou beleue in God the father almightie, maker of heauen and earth?

Aunswere. I beleue.

Minister. Doest thou beleue in Jesus Christe his only begotten sonne our Lorde, and that he was conceyued by the holy gost, borne of the virgin Mary, that he suffered under Poncius Pilate, was crucified, dead, and buryed, that he went downe into hell, and also dyd ryse agayne the thyrde daye; that he ascended into heauen, and sitteth on the ryght hande of God the father almighty: And from thence shall come agayne at the ende of the worlde, to iudge the quicke and the dead: Doest thou beleue this?

Aunswere. I beleue.

Minister. Doest thou beleue in the holy gost, the holy Catholike Churche, the cōmuniō of sainctes, remissiō of Sinnes, resurreccion of the fleshe, and euerlastyng lyfe after death?

Aunswere. I beleue.

Minister. What doest thou desyre?

Aunswere. Baptisme.

Minister. Wilt thou be baptized?

Aunswere. I wyll.

¶ *Then the prieste shall take the childe in his handes, and aske the name. And naming the childe, shall dyppe it in the water thryse. First dypping the ryght syde : Seconde the left syde : The thryd tyme dippyng the face towarde the fonte : So it be discretly and warely done, saying.*

¶ *N.* I Baptize thee in the name of the father, and of the sonne, and of the holy gost.   Amen.

¶ *And if the childe be weake, it shall suffice to powre water upon it, saying the foresayed woordes.   N. I baptize thee, &c.*

Then the Godfathers and Godmothers shall take and lay theyr handes upon the childe, and the minister shall put upon him his white vesture, commonly called the Crisome : and saye.

TAKE this white vesture for a tokē of the innocencie, whiche by Gods grace in this holy sacramente of Baptisme, is giuen unto t̄e: and for a signe wherby thou art admonished, so long as thou lyuest, to geue thyselfe to innocencie of liuing, that, after this transitorye lyfe, thou mayest be partaker of the lyfe euerlasting. Amen.

Then the prieste shall annoynt the infant upon the head, saying.

ALMIGHTY God the father of our lorde Jesus Christ, who hath regenerate thee by water and the holy gost, and hath geuē unto t̄ee remissiō of al thy sinnes: he vouchsaue to annoynte thee with the unccion of his holy spirite, and bryng thee to the inheritaunce of euerlasting lyfe. Amen.

When there are many to be Baptized, this ordre of demaunding, Baptizing, puttyng on the Crysome, and enoyntyng, shalbe used seuerally with euery chylde. Those that be firste Baptized departing from the fonte, and remaynyng in some conuenient place within the Churche untill all be Baptized. At the laste ende, the priest calling the Godfathers and Godmothers together : shall saye this shorte exhortacion folowing :

FORASMUCH as these children haue promised by you to forsake the deuill and al his workes, to beleue in God, and to serue him: you must remēbre that it is your partes and duetie to see that these infantes be taught, so soone as they shalbe able to learne, what a solemne vowe, promyse, and profession, they haue made by you. And that they maye knowe these thynges the better: ye shall call upon them to heare sermons, and chiefly you shal prouide that thei may learne the Crede, the Lordes prayer, and the ten commaundementes, in thenglish tounge: and all other thinges which a christian manne ought to knowe and beleue to his soules health. And that these children may be vertuously brought up to leade a godly and christiā life; remēbring alwayes that Baptisme doeth represent unto us our professiō, which is to folow thexample of our Sauiour Christe, and to be made lyke unto him, that as he dyed and rose againe for us: so should we (whiche are Baptised) dye from synne, and ryse agayne unto righteousnesse, continually mortifying all our euyll and corrupte affeccions, and dayly procedyng in all vertue and godlynesse of lyuyng.

¶ *The minister shall commaunde that the Crisomes be brought to the churche, and delyuered to the priestes after the accustomed maner, at the purificacion of the mother of euery chylde. And that the children be brought to the Bushop to bee confirmed of hym, so soone as they can saye in theyr vulgare tounge the articles of the fayth, the Lordes prayer, and the ten*

commaūdementes, and be further instructed in the Catechisme, set furth for that purpose, accordingly as it is there expressed.
And so lette the congregacion departe in the name of the Lorde.

¶ *Note that yf the numbre of children to be Baptized, and multitude of people presente bee so great that they cannot conueniently stand at the Churche doore: then let them stand within the Churche in some conuenient place, nygh unto the Churche doore; And there all thynges be sayed and done, appoynted to be sayed and done at the Churche doore.*

OF THEM THAT BE

BAPTIZED IN PRIUATE HOUSES

IN TYME OF NECESSITIE

¶ *The pastours and curates shall oft admonyshe the people, that they differ not the Baptisme of infantes any longer then the Sondaye, or other holy daye, nexte after the chylde bee borne, onlesse upon a great and reasonable cause declared to the curate and by hym approued.*

And also they shal warne them that without great cause, and necessitie, they Baptise not children at home in theyr houses. And when great nede shall compell them so to doe, that then they minister it on this fashion.

¶ *First let them that be present cal upon God for his grace, and saye the Lordes prayer, yf the tyme will suffre. And then one of them shal name the childe, and dippe him in the water, or poure water upon him, saying these woordes.*

¶ *N.* I Baptise the in the name of the father, and of the sonne and of the holy ghoste. Amen.

And let them not doubt, but that the childe so Baptised, is lawfully and suffi-ciently Baptised, and ought not to be Baptised againe, in the Churche. But yet neuerthelesse if the childe whiche is after this sorte Baptised, doe afterwarde lyue: it is expedient that he be brought into the Churche, to thentent the prieste maye examine and trye, whether the childe be lawfully Baptised or no. And yf those that bryng any childe to the Churche doe aunswere that he is alreadye Baptised: Then shall the priest examin them, further.

¶ By whom the childe was Baptised?

Who was presente when the childe was baptised?

Whether they called upon God for grace and succoure in that necessitie?

With what thyng, or what matter they dyd Baptise the childe?

With what woordes the childe was Baptised?

Whether they thinke the childe to be lawfully and perfectly Baptised?

And if the ministers shall proue by the aunswers of suche as brought the childe, that all thynges were done, as they ought to be: Then shall not he christen the childe agayne, but shall receyue hym, as one of the flocke of the true christian people, saying thus.

I CERTIFIE you, that in this case ye haue doen wel, and according unto due ordre concerning the baptising of this child, which being borne in original synne, and in the wrathe of God, is nowe by the lauer of regeneracion in Baptisme, made the childe of God, and heire of euerlastyng life: for oure Lorde Jesus Christe doeth not denye hys grace and mercie unto such infantes, but most louingly doeth call them unto him. As the holy ghospell doeth witnesse to our coumforte on this wyse.

Marke x.

AT a certaine time thei brought children unto Christ that he should touch them, and his disciples rebuked those that brought them. But when Jesus sawe it, he was displeased, and sayed unto them: Suffre lytle chyldren to come unto me, and forbidde them not, for to suche belongeth the kingdome of God. Verely I saye unto you, whosoeuer doeth not receyue the kingdom of God as a lytle chylde, he shall not enter therin. And when he had taken them up in his armes, he put his handes upon them, and blissed them.

After the ghospell is read: the minister shall make this exhortacion upon the woordes of the ghospell.

FRENDES ye heare in this ghospell the woordes of our Saueoure Christ, that he cōmaunded the children to be brought unto him, how he blamed those that would haue kept them from hym, howe he exhorted all men to folowe their innocencie: Ye perceiue how by his outward gesture and dede he declared his good wyll towarde them, for he embraced them in his armes, he layed his handes upon them, and blessed them. Doubt you not therfore, but earnestly beleue, that he hath lykewyse fauourably receyued this presente infante, that he hath embraced him with the armes of his mercy, that he hath geuen unto him the blessing of eternal lyfe, and made him partaker of his euerlasting kingdom. Wherfore we beyng thus persuaded of the good will of oure heauenly father, declared by his sonne Jesus Christ towardes this infante: Let us faythfully and deuoutly geue thankes unto him, and saye the prayer whiche the Lorde himselfe taught; and in declaracion of our fayth, let us also recyte the articles conteined in our Crede.

Here the minister with the Godfathers and Godmothers shall saye.

OUR father whiche arte in heauen, halowed be thy name, &c.

Then shall they saye the Crede, and then the prieste shall demaund the name of the childe, whiche beyng by the Godfathers and Godmothers pronounced, the minister shall saye.

¶ *N.* Doest thou forsake the deuill and all his workes?

Aunswere. I forsake them.

Minister. Doest thou forsake the vaine pompe and glory of the worlde, with all the couetous desyres of the same?

Aunswere. I forsake them.

Minister. Doest thou forsake the carnall desyres of the flesh, so that thou wilt not folowe and be led by them?

Aunswere. I forsake them.

Minister. Doest thou beleue in God the father almyghtie, maker of heauen and yearth?

Aunswere. I beleue.

Minister. Doest thou beleue in Jesus Christe hys onely begotten sonne our lorde, and that he was conceyued by the holy Gost, borne of the virgin Marie, that he suffered under Pontius Pilate, was crucifyed, dead, and buried, that he went downe into hel, and also did arise againe the third day, that he ascended into heauen, and sitteth on the righte hande of god the father almightie: And from thence shal come agayn at the ende of the world to iudge the quicke and the dead, doest thou beleue thus?

Aunswere. I beleue.

Minister. Doest thou beleue in the holy goste, the holy catholyke Churche, the Communion of Saintes, Remission of sinnes, Resurrecciō of the flesh, and euerlasting life after deth?

Aunswere. I beleue.

Then the minister shal put the white vesture, commonly called the Crysome, upon the childe, saying.

TAKE thys whyte vesture for a token of the innocencie whiche by goddes grace in the holy sacramente of baptysme is geuen unto thee, and for a signe wherby thou art admonished so lōg as thou shalt lyue, to geue thyselfe to innocencye of liuyng, that after this transitory life, thou maiest be partaker of the life euerlasting. Amen.

¶ Let us pray.

ALMIGHTIE and euerlasting god heauenly father, wee geue thee humble thankes that thou hast vouchesafed to cal us to the knowlege of thy grace, and faith in thee: Increase and confirme this fayth in us euermore: Geue thy holy spirite to this infant, that he being borne agayne, and beeing made heyre of euerlasting saluacion through our lord Jesus Christ, may cōtinue thy seruaūt, and attein thy promises through the same our lorde Jesus Christe thy sonne, who liueth and reigneth with the in unitie of the same holy spirite euerlastinglye. Amen.

Then shall the minister make this exhortacion, to the Godfathers, and Godmothers.

FORASMUCHE as this chylde hath promised by you to forsake the deuil and al his workes, to beleue in god, and to serue him, you must remember that it is your partes and duetie to see that this infant be taught, so sone as he shalbe able to learne, what a solemne vowe, promise, and profession he hath made by you, and that he may know these thinges the better, ye shall call upon hym to heare sermons: and chiefly ye shal prouide that he may learne the Crede, the Lordes prayer, and the ten commaunde-mentes in the english tong, and al other thinges which a christian man ought to know and beleue to his soules health, and that this childe may bee vertuously brought up, to leade a godly and a christian life. Remembring alway that baptisme doeth repre-sent unto us our profession, which is to folow thexample of our sauiour Christe, and to be made like unto him, that as he died and rose again for us: so should we whiche are baptized, dye from sin, and ryse againe unto righteousnes, continually morti-fying al our euil and corrupt affeccions, and dayly proceding in al vertue and godlines of liuing.

&c. As in Publike Baptisme.

¶ *But if they which bring the infantes to the church, do make an uncertain answere to the priestes questions, and say that they cannot tel what they thought, did, or sayde in that great feare and trouble of mynde (as often-tymes it chaunseth) : Then let the priest Baptize him in forme aboue written, concernyng publyke Baptisme, sauyng that at the dyppyng of the childe in the fonte, he shall use this forme of woordes.*

IF thou be not Baptized already, *N.* I Baptize thee in the name of the father, and of the sonne, and of the holy gost. Amen.

The water in the fonte shalbe chaunged euery moneth once at the lest, and afore any child be Baptized in the water so chaunged, the priest shall say at the font these prayers folowing.

O MOSTE mercifull god our sauioure Jesu Christ, who hast ordeyned the element of water for the regeneraciō of thy faythful people, upon whom, beyng baptised in the riuer of Jordane, the holye ghoste came down in the likenesse of a dooue: Sende down we beseche thee the same thy holye spirite to assiste us, and to bee present at this our inuocacion of thy holy name: Sanctifie ✠ this foūtaine of baptisme, thou that art the sanctifier of al thynges, that by the power of thy worde, all those that shall be baptized therein, maye be spirituallye regenerated, and made the children of euerlasting adopcion. Amen.

O MERCIFULL God, graunte that the olde Adam, in them that

shalbe baptized in this fountayne, maye so be buried, that the newe man may be raised up agayne. Amen.

GRAUNT that all carnal affeccions maie die in them; and that all thynges, belongyng to the spirite maye liue and growe in them. Amen.

GRAUNT to all them which at this fountayne forsake the deuill and all his workes: that they maye haue power and strength to haue victorye and to triumph againste hym, the worlde, and the fleshe. Amen.

WHOSOEUER shal confesse the, o lorde: recognise him also in thy kingdome. Amen.

GRAUNT that al sinne and vice here maie bee so extinct: that thei neuer haue power to raigne in thy seruaūtes. Amen.

GRAUNTE that whosoeuer here shall begynne to be of thy flocke: maie euermore continue in the same. Amen.

GRAUNT that all they which for thy sake in this life doe denie and forsake themselfes: may winne and purchase thee, o lord, which art euerlasting treasure. Amen.

GRAUNT that whosoeuer is here dedicated to thee by our office and ministerie: maye also bee endewed with heauenly vertues, and euerlastinglye rewarded through thy mercie, O Blessed lorde God, who doest liue and gouerne al thinges world without ende. Amen.

The Lorde be with you.
Answere. And with thy spirite.

ALMIGHTVE euerliuing God, whose moste derely beloued sonne Jesus Christe, for the forgeuenesse of our sinnes did shead out of his moste precious side bothe water and bloude, and gaue commaundemente to his disciples that they shoulde goe teache all nacions, and baptise them in the name of the father, the sonne, and the holye ghoste: Regarde, we beseche thee, the supplicacions of thy congregacion, and graunte that all thy seruauntes which shall bee baptized in this water prepared for the mynystracion of thy holy sacrament, maye receiue the fulnesse of thy grace, and euer remaine in the noumbre of thy faithful, and elect childrē, through Jesus Christ our Lord.

CONFIRMACION,

WHERIN IS CONTEINED A CATECHISME FOR CHILDREN.

To thende that confirmacion may be ministred to the more edifying of suche as shall receiue it (according to Saint Paules doctrine, who teacheth that all thynges should be doen in the churche to the edificacion of the same) it is thought good that none hereafter shall be confirmed, but suche as can say in theyr mother tong, tharticles of the faith the lordes prayer, and the tenne commaundementes; And can also aunswere to suche questions of this shorte Catechisme, as the Busshop (or suche as he shall appoynte) shall by his discrecion appose them in. And this ordre is most conuenient to be obserued for diuers consideracions.

¶ *First because that whan children come to the yeres of discrecion and haue learned what theyr Godfathers and Godmothers promised for them in Baptisme, they may then theselfes with their owne mouth, and with theyr owne consent, openly before the churche ratifie and confesse the same, and also promise that by the grace of God, they will euermore endeuour themselues faithfully to obserue and kepe such thinges, as they by theyre owne mouth and confession haue assented vnto.*

¶ *Secondly, forasmuch as confirmacion is ministred to them that be Baptised, that by imposicion of handes, and praier they may receiue strength and defence against all temptacions to sin, and the assautes of the worlde, and the deuill: it is most mete to be ministred, when children come to that age, that partly by the frayltie of theyr owne fleshe, partly by the assautes of the world and the deuil, they begin to be in daungier to fall into sinne.*

¶ *Thirdly, for that it is agreeable with the usage of the churche in tymes past, wherby it was ordeined, that Confirmacion should bee ministred to them that were of perfecte age, that they beyng instructed in Christes religion, should openly professe theyr owne fayth, and promise to be obedient unto the will of God.*

¶ *And that no manne shall thynke that anye detrimente shall come to children by differryng of theyr confirmacion: he shall knowe for trueth, that it is certayn by Goddes woorde, that children beeyng Baptized (if they departe out of thys lyfe in theyr infancie) are undoubtedly saued.*

A CATECHISME,

THAT IS TO SAY,

AN INSTRUCCION TO BEE LEARNED OF EUERY CHILDE, BEFORE HE BE BROUGHT TO BE CONFIRMED OF THE BUSHOP.

Question. What is your name?

Aunswere. N or M.

Question. Who gaue you this name?

Aunswere. My Godfathers and Godmothers in my Baptisme, wherein I was made a member of Christe, the childe of God, and inheritour of the kingdome of heauen.

Question. What did your Godfathers and Godmothers then for you?

Aunswere. They did promise and vowe three thinges in my name. First, that I should forsake the deuil and all his workes and pompes, the vanities of the wicked worlde, and all the sinnefull lustes of the fleshe. Secondly, that I should beleue all the articles of the Christian fayth. And thirdly, that I should kepe Goddes holy will and commaundementes and walke in the same al the daies of my life.

Question. Dooest thou not thinke that thou arte bound to beleue, and to doe as they haue promised for thee?

Aunswere. Yes verely. And by Gods helpe so I wil. And I hartily thanke our heauenly father, that he hath called me to thys state of saluacion, through Jesus Christe our Saueour And I pray God to geue me hys grace, that I may continue in the same unto my liues ende.

Question. Rehearse the articles of thy beliefe.

Aunswere. I beleue in God the father almightie, maker of heauen and earth. And in Jesus Christ his only sonne our lord. Whiche was conceiued by the holy gost, borne of the virgin Marie. Suffered under Ponce Pilate, was crucified, dead, and buried, he descended into hel. The third day he rose agayn from the dead. He ascended into heauen, and sitteth on the right hande of God the father almightie. From thence shal he come to iudge the quicke and the dead. I beleue in the holy goste. The holye catholike church. The communion of saintes. The forgeuenes of sinnes. The resurreccion of the bodie. And the lyfe euerlasting. Amen.

Question. What dooest thou chiefely learne in these articles of thy beliefe?

Aunswere. Firste, I learne to beleue in God the father, who hath made me and all the worlde.

Secondely, in God the sonne who hath redemed me and all mankinde.

Thirdly, in god the holy goste, who sanctifyeth me and all the electe people of god.

Question. You sayde that your Godfathers and Godmothers dyd promyse for you that ye should kepe Goddes commaundementes. Tell me how many there bee.

Aunswere. Tenne.

Question. Whiche be they?

Aunswere. Thou shalte haue none other Gods but me.

II. Thou shalte not make to thyselfe anye grauen image, nor

the likenesse of any thyng that is in heauen aboue, or in the earth beneath, nor in the water under the earth: thou shalt not bowe downe to them, nor wurship them.

III. Thou shalt not take the name of the lord thy God in vayne.

IV. Remember that thou kepe holy the Sabboth day.

V. Honor thy father and thy mother.

VI. Thou shalt doe no murdre.

VII. Thou shalt not commit adultry.

VIII. Thou shalt not steale.

IX. Thou shalt not beare false witnes against thy neighbour.

X. Thou shalt not couet thy neighbours wife, nor his seruaunt, nor his mayde, nor his Oxe, nor his Asse, nor any thing that is his.

Question. What dooest thou chiefely learne by these commaundementes?

Aunswere. I learne two thinges: My duetie towardes god, and my duetie towardes my neighbour.

Question. What is thy duetie towardes god?

Aunswere. My duetie towardes God is, to beleue in him. To feare him. And to loue him with al my hart, with al my mind, with al my soule, and with all my strength. To wurship him. To geue him thankes. To put my whole truste in hym. To call upon him. To honor his holy name and his word, and to serue him truely all the daies of my life.

Question. What is thy dutie towardes thy neighboure?

Answere. My duetie towardes my neighbour is, to loue hym as myselfe. And to do to al men as I would they should do to me. To loue, honour, and succoure my father and mother. To honour and obey the kyng and his ministers. To submitte myselfe to all my gouernours, teachers, spirituall pastours, and maisters. To ordre myselfe lowlye and reuerentelye to al my betters. To hurte no bodie by woorde nor dede. To bee true and iust in al my dealing. To beare no malice nor hatred in my heart. To kepe my handes from picking and stealing, and my tongue from euill speaking, liyng, and slaundring. To kepe my bodie in temperaunce, sobreness, and chastitie. Not to couet nor desire other mennes goodes. But learne and laboure truely to geate my owne liuing, and to doe my duetie in that state of life: unto which it shal please God to cal me.

Question. My good sonne, knowe this, that thou arte not hable to do these thinges of thyself, nor to walke in the cōmaundementes of God and to serue him, without his speciall grace, which thou muste learne at all times to cal for by diligent prayer. Leat me heare therfore if thou canst say the Lordes prayer.

Answere. Our father whiche art in heauen, halowed bee thy name. Thy kyngdome come. Thy wil bee done in earth as it is in heauē. Geue us this day our dailye breade. And forgeue us our trespasses, as we forgeue them that trespasse againste us. And leade us not into temptacion, but deliuer us from euil. Amen.

Question. What desireste thou of God in this prayer?

Answere. I desire my lord god our heuēly father, who is the geuer of al goodnes, to send his grace unto me, and to all people, that we may wurship him, serue hym, and obey him, as we ought to doe. And I praye unto God, that he will sende us al thynges that be nedeful both for our soules and bodies: And that he wil bee mercifull unto us, and forgeue us our sinnes: And that it will please him to saue and defende us in al daungers gostly and bodily: And that he wil kepe us from al sinne and wickednes, and from our gostly enemye, and from euerlastyng death. And this I truste he wil doe of his mercie and goodnes, through our lorde Jesu Christe. And therefore I say, Amen. So be it.

¶ *So soone as the children can say in their mother tongue tharticles of the faith, the lordes praier, the ten commaundementes, and also can aunswere to such questions of this short Cathechisme as the Bushop (or suche as he shall appointe) shal by hys discrecion appose them in : then shall they bee brought to the Bushop by one that shalbee his godfather or godmother, that euerye childe maye haue a wittenesse of hys confirmacion.*

¶ *And the Bushop shal confirme them on this wyse.*

¶ CONFIRMACION.

Our helpe is in the name of the Lorde.

Answere. Whiche hath made both heauen and yearth.

Minister. Blessed is the name of the lorde.

Answere. Henceforth worlde without ende.

Minister. The lorde be with you.

Answere. And with thy spirite.

Let us praye.

ALMIGHTY and euerliuing God, who hast vouchesafed to re-generate these thy seruauntes of water and the holy goste: And haste geuen unto them forgeuenesse of all their sinnes: Sende downe from heauen we beseche thee, (O lorde) upon them thy holy gost the coumforter, with the manifold giftes of grace, the spirite of wisdom and understandyng; the spirite of counsell and gostly strength; The spirite of knowledge and true godlinesse, and fulfil them, (o lord) with the spirite of thy holy feare.

Aunswere. Amen.

Minister. Signe them (o lorde) and marke them to be thyne for euer, by the vertue of thy holye crosse and passion. Confirme and strength them with the inward unccion of thy holy gost, mercifully unto euerlasting life. Amen.

Then the Bushop shal crosse them in the forehead, and lay his handes upon theyr heades, saying

N. I signe thee with the signe of the crosse, and laye my hande upon thee. In the name of the father, and of the sonne, and of the holy gost. Amen.

And thus shall he doe to euery childe one after another. And whan he hath layed hys hande upon euery chylde, then shall he say.

The peace of the lorde abide with you.

Aunswere. And with thy spirite.

¶ Let us pray.

ALMIGHTIE euerliuing god, which makest us both to will and to doe those thinges that bee good and acceptable unto thy maiestie: we make our humble supplicacions unto thee for these children, upon whome (after thexample of thy holy apostles) we haue laied our handes, to certify them (by this signe) of thy fauour and gracious goodnes toward them: leat thy fatherly hand (we beseche thee) euer be ouer them, let thy holy spirite euer bee with them, and so leade them in the knowledge and obedience of thy woord, that in the end they may obtein the life euerlasting, through our lord Jesus Christ, who with thee and the holy goste liueth and reyneth one god world without ende. Amen.

Then shall the Busshop blisse the children, thus saying.

The blissing of god almightie, the father, the sonne, and the holy goste, be upon you, and remayne with you fore euer. Amen.

The curate of euery parish once in sixe wekes at the least upon warnyng by him geuen, shal upon some Soonday or holy day, half an houre before euensong opēly in the churche instructe and examine so many childrē of his parish sent unto him, as the time wil serue, and as he shal thynke conueniente, in some parte of this Cathechisme. And all fathers, mothers, maisters, and dames, shall cause theyr children, seruauntes, and prentises (whiche are not yet confirmed), to come to the churche at the date appoynted, and obediently heare and be ordered by the curate, until suche time as they haue learned all that is here appointed for them to learne.

¶ *And whansoeuer the Bushop shal geue knowlage for childrē to be brought afore him to any conueniēt place, for their confirmacion : Then shal the curate of euery parish either bring or send in writing, ye names of al those children of his parish which can say tharticles of theyr faith, the lordes praier, and the ten cōmaundementes. And also how many of them can answere to thother questions conteined in this Cathechisme.*

¶ *And there shal none be admitted to the holye communion : until suche time as he be confirmed.*

SOLEMNIZACION OF MATRIMONIE.

¶ *First the bannes must be asked three seueral Soondaies or holye dayes, in the seruice tyme, the people beeyng presente, after the accustomed maner*

And if the persones that woulde bee maried dwel in diuers parishes, the bannes muste bee asked in bothe parishes, and the Curate of thone parish shall not solemnize matrimonie betwixt them, withoute a certificate of the bannes beeyng thrise asked from the Curate of thother parishe.

At the daye appointed for Solemnizacion of Matrimonie, the persones to be maried shal come into the bodie of ye churche, with theyr frendes and neighbours. And there the priest shal thus saye.

DEERELY beloued frendes, we are gathered together here in the syght of God, and in the face of his congregacion, to ioyne together this man and this woman in holy matrimonie, which is an honorable estate instituted of God in paradise, in the time of mannes innocencie, signifying unto us the misticall union that is betwixte Christe and his Churche: whiche holy estate, Christe adorned and beutified with his presence, and first miracle that he wrought in Cana of Galile, and is commended of Sainct Paule to be honourable emong all men; and therefore is not to bee enterprised, nor taken in hande unaduisedlye, lightelye, or wantonly, to satisfie mens carnal lustes and appetites, like brute beastes that haue no understanding: but reuerentely, discretely, aduisedly, soberly, and in the feare of God. Duely consideryng the causes for the whiche matrimonie was ordeined. One cause was the procreacion of children, to be brought up in the feare and nurture of the Lord, and prayse of God. Secondly it was ordeined for a remedie agaynst sinne, and to auoide fornicacion, that suche persones as bee maried, might liue chastlie in matrimonie, and kepe themselues undefiled membres of Christes bodye. Thirdelye for the mutuall societie, helpe, and coumfort, that the one oughte to haue of thother, both in prosperitie and aduersitie. Into the whiche holy estate these two persones present: come nowe to be ioyned. Therefore if any man can shewe any iuste cause why they maie not lawfully be ioyned so together: Leat him now speake, or els hereafter for euer hold his peace.

And also speakyng to the persones that shalbe maried, he shall saie.

I REQUIRE and charge you (as you will aunswere at the dreadefull daye of iudgemente, when the secretes of all hartes shalbee disclosed) that if either of you doe knowe any impedimente, why ye maie not bee lawfully ioyned together in matrimonie, that ye confesse it. For be ye wel assured, that so manye as bee coupled together otherwaies then Goddes woord doeth allowe: are not ioyned of God, neither is their matrimonie lawful.

At which daye of mariage yf any man doe allege any impediment why they maye not be coupled together in matrimonie; And will be bound, and sureties with hym, to the parties, or els put in a caution to the full value of suche charges as the persones to bee maried dooe susteyne to proue his allegacion: then the Solemnizacion muste bee differred, unto suche tyme as the trueth bee tried. Yf no impedimente bee alleged, then shall the Curate saye unto the man.

N. WILTE thou haue this woman to thy wedded wife, to liue together after Goddes ordeinaūce in the holy estate of matrimonie? Wilt thou loue her, coumforte her, honor, and kepe her in sickenesse and in health? And forsaking all other kepe thee only to her, so long as you both shall liue?

The man shall aunswere,

I will.

Then shall the priest saye to the woman.

N. Wilt thou haue this man to thy wedded houseband, to liue together after Goddes ordeinaunce, ni the holy estate of matrimonie? Wilt thou obey him, and serue him, loue, honor, and kepe him in sickenes and in health? And forsaking al other kepe thee onely to him, so long as you bothe shall liue?

The woman shall aunswere,

I will.

Then shall the Minister say,

Who geueth this woman to be maried to this man?

And the minister receiuing the woman at her father or frendes handes: shall cause the man to take the woman by the right hande, and so either to geue their trouth to other: The man first saying.

I *N.* take thee *N.* to my wedded wife, to haue and to holde from this day forwarde, for better, for wurse, for richer, for poorer, in sickenes, and in health, to loue and to cherishe, til death us departe: according to Goddes holy ordeinaunce: And therto I plight thee my trouth.

Then shall they looce theyr handes, and the woman taking again the man by the right hande shall say,

I *N.* take thee *N.* to my wedded husbande, to haue and to holde from this day forwarde, for better, for woorse, for richer, for poorer, in sickenes, and in health, to loue, cherishe, and to obey, till death us departe: accordyng to Goddes holy ordeinaunce: And thereto I geue thee my trouth.

Then shall they agayne looce theyr handes, and the manne shall geue unto the womanne a ring, and other tokens of spousage, as golde or siluer, laying the same upon the boke: And the Priest taking the ring shall deliuer it unto the man: to put it upon the fowerth finger of the womans left hande. And the man taught by the priest, shall say.

¶ With thys ring I thee wed: Thys golde and siluer I thee geue: with my body I thee wurship: and withal my worldly Goodes I thee endowe. In the name of the father, and of the sonne, and of the holy goste. Amen.

Then the man leauyng the ring upon the fowerth finger of the womans lef hande, the minister shal say,

¶ Let us pray.

O ETERNAL God creator and preseruer of al mankinde, geuer of al spiritual grace, the author of euerlasting life: Sende thy blessing upon these thy seruauntes, thys manne, and this woman, whome we blesse in thy name, that as Isaac and Rebecca (after bracellets and Jewels of golde geuen of thone to thother for tokēs of their matrimonie) liued faithfully together; So these persōs may surely perfourme and kepe the vowe and couenaunt betwixt them made, wherof this ring geuen, and receiued, is a token and pledge. And may euer remayne in perfite loue and peace together; And lyue accordyng to thy lawes; through Jesus Christe our lorde. Amen.

Then shal the prieste ioyne theyr ryght handes together, and say.

¶ Those whome god hath ioyned together: let no man put a sundre.

Then shall the minister speake unto the people.

FORASMUCHE as *N.* and *N.* haue consented together in holye wedlocke, and haue witnessed the same here before god and this cūpany; And therto haue geuē and pledged theyr trouth eyther to other, and haue declared the same by geuyng and receyuyng golde and syluer, and by ioyning of handes: I pronounce that they bee man and wyfe together. In the name of the father, of the sonne, and of the holy gost. Amen.

¶ God the father blesse you. ✠ God the sōne kepe you: god the holye gost lightē your understāding: The lorde mercifully with his fauour loke upō you, and so fil you with al spiritual benediction, and grace, that you may haue remissiō of your sinnes in this life, and in the worlde to come lyfe euerlastyng. Amen.

Then shal they goe into the quier, and the ministers or clerkes shal saye or syng, this psalme folowyng.

Beati omnes. cxxviii.

BLESSED are al they that feare the lord, and walke in his wayes.

For thou shalte eate the laboure of thy handes. O wel is thee, and happie shalt thou bee.

Thy wife shalbee as the fruitful vine, upon the walles of thy house.

Thy children like the olife braunches rounde about thy table.

Loe, thus shal the man be blessed, that feareth the lord.

The lord from out of Sion, shall so blesse thee : that thou shalt see Hierusalem in prosperitie, al thy life long.

Yea that thou shalt see thy childers children : and peace upon Israel.

Glory to the father, &c.

As it was in the beginning, &c.

Or els this psalme folowyng.

Deus misereatur nostri. Psalm lxvii.

GOD be merciful unto us, and blesse us, and shew us the lighte of his countenaunce : and bee mercifull unto us.

That thy waye maye bee knowen upon yearth, thy sauing health emong all nacions.

Leate the people praise thee (o god) yea leate all people prayse thee.

O leate the nacions reioyce and bee glad, for thou shalte iudge the folke righteously, and gouerne the nacions upon yearth.

Leat the people prayse thee (o god) leat al people prayse the.

Then shal the yearth bring foorth her increase : and god, euen our owne God, shal geue us his blessyng.

God shal blesse us, and all the endes of the worlde shall feare hym.

Glory to the father, &c.

As it was in the beginning, &c.

*The psalme ended, and the manne and woman knelyng afore the aulter :
the prieste standyng at the aulter, and turnyng his face towarde them,
shall saye.*

Lorde haue mercie upon us.

Answere. Christe haue mercie upon us.

Minister. Lorde haue mercie upon us.

¶ Our father whiche art in heauen, &c.

And leade us not into temptacion.

Answere. But deliuer us from euill.   Amen.

Minister. O lorde saue thy seruaunte, and thy hand-maide.

Answere. Whiche put theyr truste in the.

Minister. O lorde sende them helpe from thy holy place.

Answere. And euermore defende them.

Minister. Bee unto them a tower of strength.

Answere. From the face of their enemie.

Minister. O lorde heare my prayer.

Answere. And leate my crie come unto the.

The Minister. Leat us praye.

O GOD of Abraham, God of Isaac, God of Jacob, blesse these
thy seruauntes, and sowe the seede of eternall life in their
mindes, that whatsoeuer in thy holy woorde they shall profit-
ablye learne: they may in dede fulfill the same.   Looke, O
Lord, mercifully upon them from heauen, and blesse them:
And as thou diddest sende thy Aungell Raphaell to Thobie,
and Sara, the daughter of Raguel, to their great comfort; so
vouchsafe to send thy blessyng upon these thy seruauntes, that
thei obeyng thy wil, and alwaye beyng in safetie under thy proteccion: may abyde in thy loue unto theyr lyues ende: throughe
Jesu Christe our Lorde.   Amen.

This prayer folowing shalbe omitted where the woman is past childe byrth.

O MERCIFUL Lord, and heauēly father, by whose gracious
gifte mākind is increased: We besech thee assiste with thy
blessing these two persones, that they may both be fruictful in
procreacion of children; and also liue together so long in godlye
loue and honestie, that they may see their childers children,
unto the thirde and fourth generacion, unto thy prayse and
honour: through Jesus Christe our Lorde.   Amen.

O God whiche by thy myghtye power haste made all thinges
of naughte, whiche also after other thinges set in order diddeste
appoint that out of man (created after thine own image and
similitude) womā should take her beginning: and, knitting
them together, diddest teache, that it should neuer be lawful
to put a sondre those, whome thou by matrimonie haddeste

made one: O god, whiche hast consecrated the state of matrimonie to such an excellent misterie, that in it is signified and
represēted the spirituall mariage and unitie betwixte Christe and
his churche: Loke mercifully upō these thy seruaunts, that both
this manne may loue his wyfe, accordyng to thy woord, (as
Christ did loue his spouse the churche, who gaue himself for it,
louing and cherishing it euen as his own flesh;) And also that
this womā may be louing and amiable to her houseband as
Rachel, wise as Rebecca, faithful and obediēt as Sara; And in
al quietnes, sobrietie, and peace, bee a folower of holy and
godlye matrones. O lorde, blesse them bothe, and graunte
them to inherite thy euerlastyng kyngdome, throughe Jesu
Christe our Lorde. Amen.

Then shall the prieste blesse the man and the woman, saiyng

ALMIGHTY god, which at the beginnyng did create oure
firste parentes Adam and Eue, and dyd sanctifie and ioyne thē
together in mariage: Powre upon you the rychesse of his grace,
sanctifie and ✠ blisse you, that ye may please him bothe in
bodye and soule; and liue together in holy loue unto your liues
ende. Amen.

*Then shalbee sayed after the gospell a sermon, wherein ordinarily (so oft as
there is any mariage) thoffice of man and wife shall bee declared according
to holy scripture. Or if there be no sermon, the minister shall reade this
that foloweth.*

AL ye whiche bee maried, or whiche entende to take the holye
estate of matrimonie upon you: heare what holye scripture
dooeth saye, as touchyng the duetye of housebandes towarde
their wiues, and wiues towarde their housebandes.

Saincte Paule (in his epistle to the Ephesians the fyfth
chapter) doeth geue this commaundement to al maried men.

Ye housebandes loue your wiues, euen as Christ loued the
churche, and hathe geuen hymselfe for it, to sanctifie it, purge-
yng it in the fountayne of water, throughe the word, that he
might make it unto himself, a glorious cōgregacion, not hauing
spot or wrincle, or any such thing; but that it should be holy
and blameles. So mē are bounde to loue their owne wiues as
their owne bodies: he that loueth his owne wife, loueth himse'f.
For neuer did any man hate his owne flesh, but nourisheth and
cherisheth it, euen as the lorde doeth the congregacion, for wee
are membres of his bodie, of his fleshe, and of his bones. For
this cause shal a man leaue father and mother, and shalbe ioyned
unto his wife, and they two shalbe one fleshe. This mistery is
great, but I speake of Christ and of the congregacion. Neuer-

thelesse let euery one of you so loue his owne wife, euen as himselfe.

Likewise the same Saint Paule (writing to the Colossians) speaketh thus to al menne that be maried: Ye men, loue your wiues and be not bitter unto them. Coloss. iii.

Heare also what saint Peter thapostle of Christ, (which was himselfe a maried man,) sayeth unto al menne that are maried. Ye husbandes, dwel with your wiues according to knowledge: Geuyng honor unto the wife, as unto the weaker vessel, and as heyres together of the grace of lyfe, so that your prayers be not hindred. 1 *Pet*. iii.

> Hitherto ye haue heard the duetie of the husbande towarde the wife.

> Nowe lykewise, ye wiues, heare and lerne your duetie toward your husbandes, euen as it is playnely set furth in holy scripture.

Saint Paul (in the forenamed epistle to the Ephesians) teacheth you thus: Ye weomen submit yourselues unto your own husbandes as unto the lord: for the husbād is the wiues head, euen as Christ is the head of the church: And he also is the sauiour of the whole bodye. Therefore as the Churche, or congregacyon, is subiecte unto Christe: So lykewise let the wiues also be in subieccyon unto theyr owne husbandes in all thynges. *Ephes*. v. And agayn he sayeth: Let the wife reuerence her husbande. And (in his epistle to the Colossians) Saincte Paule geueth you this short lesson. Ye wiues, submit yourselues unto your owne husbandes, as it is conueniente in the Lorde. *Coloss*. iii.

Saincte Peter also doeth instructe you very godly, thus saying, Let wiues be subiect to theyr owne husbandes, so that if any obey not the woorde, they may bee wonne without the woorde, by the conuersacyon of the wiues; Whyle they beholde your chaste conuersacyon, coupled with feare, whose apparell let it not bee outwarde, with broyded heare, and trymmyng about with golde, either in putting on of gorgeous apparell: But leat the hyd man whiche is in the hearte, be without all corrupcion, so that the spirite be milde and quiete, which is a precious thing in the sight of god. For after this manèr (in the olde tyme) did the holy women, which trusted in God, apparell themselues, beeing subiecte to theyr own husbandes: as Sara obeied Abraham calling him lorde, whose daughters ye are made, doing wel, and being not dismaied with any feare. 1 *Pet*. iii.

The newe maried persones (the same daye of their mariage)
must receiue the holy communion.

VISITACION OF THE SICKE,

AND THE COMMUNION OF THE SAME.

¶ *The Prieste entring into the sicke persones house, shall saye.*

PEACE be in this house, and to all that dwell in it.

Wh..n he commeth into the sicke mannes presence, he shall saye this psalme

Domine exaudi. Psalm cxliii.

HEARE my prayer, (o lorde,) and consider my desire : herken unto me for thy trueth and righteousnes sake.

And entre not into iudgemente with thy seruaunt : for in thy sight shal no man liuing be iustified.

For the enemie hath persecuted my soule : he hath smittē my life downe to the grounde : he hath laied me in the darkenesse, as the men that haue bene long dead.

Therefore is my spirite vexed within me : and my hartē within me is desolate.

Yet doe I remember the time paste, I muse upon all thy woorkes : yea, I exercise myselfe in the workes of thy handes.

I stretche forth mine handes unto the : my soule gaspeth unto the as a thyrstie lande.

Heare me, (o lorde) and that soone : for my spirite weaxeth faint : hide not thy face from me, lest I be like unto them that goe downe into the pitte.

O leate me heare thy louyng-kyndenesse betimes in the morning, for in thee is my trust : shewe thou me the waie that I should walke in for I lift up soule unto thee.

Deliuer me, (o lorde,) from myne enemies : for I flye unto thee to hide me.

Teache me to dooe the thynge, that pleaseth thee, for thou art my god, leate thy louing spirite leade me foorth unto the lande of righteousnesse.

Quicken me, (o lorde) for thy names sake, and for thy righteousnesse sake bring my soule out of trouble.

And of thy goodnesse slaie my enemies : and destroye all them that vexe my soule, for I am thy seruaunt.

Glory to the father and to the sonne, &c.

As it was in the beginning, &c.

¶ *With this antheme.*

REMEMBRE not Lord our iniquities, nor the iniquities of our forefathers. Spare us good Lord, spare thy people, whom thou hast redemed with thy most precious bloud, and be not angry with us for euer.

Lorde haue mercye upon us.

Christe haue mercie upon us.

Lorde haue mercie upon us.

Our father, whiche art in heauen, &c.

And leade us not into temptacion.

Answere. But deliuer us from euill.   Amen.

The Minister. O lorde saue thy seruaunte.

Answere. Whiche putteth his trust in the.

Minister. Sende hym helpe from thy holy place.

Answere. And euermore mightily defende hym.

Minister. Leat the enemie have none aduauntage of hym.

Answere. Nor the wicked approche to hurte hym.

Minister. Bee unto hym, o lorde, a strong tower.

Answere. From the face of his enemie.

Minister. Lord heare my prayer.

Answer. And let my crye come unto thee.

Minister.   Let us praye.

O LORD looke downe from heauen, beholde, visite, and releue this thy seruaunte: Looke upon hym with the iyes of thy mercy, geue hym coumforte, and sure cōfidence in thee: Defende him from the daunger of the enemie, and kepe hym in perpetual peace, and safetie: through Jesus Christe our Lorde.   Amen.

Heare us, almightie and moste merciful God, and Sauiour: Extende thy accustomed goodnesse to this thy seruaunt, which is greued with sickenesse: Visite hym, o Lorde, as thou diddest visite Peters wifes mother, and the Capitaines seruaunt.   And as thou preseruedst Thobie and Sara by thy Aūgel from daunger: So restore unto this sicke person his former helth, (if it be thy will), or els geue hym grace so to take thy correccion, that after this painfull lyfe ended, he maye dwell with thee in lyfe euerlastyng.   Amen.

Then shall the Minister exhorte the sicke person after this fourme,
or other lyke.

DERELY beloued, know this that almighty God is the Lorde ouer lyfe, and death, and ouer all thynges to them perteyning, as yougth, strength, helth, age, weakenesse, and sickenesse.   Wherfore, whatsoeuer your sickenes is, knowe you certaynly, that it is Gods visitacion. And for what cause soeuer this sickenesse is sent unto you; whether it bee to trye your pacience for the example of other, and that your fayth may be founde, in the day of the Lorde, laudable, glorious, and honourable, to the encrease of glory, and endelesse felicitie: Orels it be sent unto you to correcte and amende in you, whatsoeuer doeth offende the iyes of our heauenly father: knowe you certainly, that if you truely repent you of your synnes, and beare your sickenes paciently, trusting in Gods mercy, for his dere sōne Jesus Christes sake, and rēdre unto him humble thankes for his fatherly visitacion, submytting yourselfe wholy to his wil; it shal turne to your profite, and helpe you forewarde in the ryght waye that leadeth unto euerlastyng lyfe.* Take therfore in good worthe, the chastement of the lorde: For whom the lorde loueth he chastiseth. Yea, (as saincte Paul sayth,) he scourgeth euery sōne, which he receiueth: yf you indure chastisemēt, he offereth himselfe unto you as unto his owne children. What sōne is he that the father chastiseth not? Yf ye be not under correccion (wherof all the true children are partakers), then are ye bastardes, and not children. Therfore seyng that whā our carnal fathers doe correct us, we reuerently obey thē, shall we not now much rather be obediēt to our spirituall father, and so liue? And they for a fewe daies doe chastise us after theyr owne pleasure: but he doeth chastise us for our profite, to thentente he maye make us partakers of his holines. These wordes, good brother, are Gods wordes, and wryten in holy scripture for our coumfort and instruccion, that we should paciently and with thankesgeuyng, beare our heauēly fathers correccion: whansoeuer by any maner of aduersitie it shall please his gracious goodnesse to visite us. And there should be no greater coumfort to christian persons, then to be made lyke unto Christ, by sufferyng paciently aduersities, troubles, and sickenesses. For he himselfe wente not up to ioy, but firste he suffered payne: he entred not into his glory, before he was crucified. So truely our waye to eternall ioy is to suffre here with Christe, and our doore to entre into eternal life: is gladly to dye with Christe, that we may ryse againe from death, and dwell with him in euerlasting life. Now therfore taking your sickenesse, which is thus profitable for you, paciently: I exhorte you in the name of God, to remēbre the profession, which you made unto God in your Baptisme. And forasmuch as after

*If the person visited bee very sicke, then the curate may end his exhortacion at this place.

this lyfe, there is accompte to be geuen vnto the ryghteous iudge, of whom all must be iudged without respecte of persons: I require you to examine yourselfe, and your state, both towarde God and man, so that accusyng and condemnyng yourselfe for your owne faultes, you may fynde mercy at our heauenly fathers hande, for Christes sake, and not be accused and condemned in that fearfull iudgemēt.   Therfore I shall shortely rehearse the articles of our fayth, that ye maye knowe whether you doe beleue as a christian manne should beleue, or no.

Here the minister shall rehearse the articles of the fayth saying thus.

DOEST thou beleue in God the father almyghtie?

And so forth as it is in Baptisme.

Then shall the minister examine whether he be in charitie with all the worlde . Exhortyng hym to forgeue frō the botome of his herte al persons, that haue offended hym, and yf he haue offended other, to aske them forgeuenesse : and where he hathe done iniurye or wrong to any manne, that he make amendes to hys uttermoste power.   And if he haue not afore disposed his goodes, let him then make his will.   (But mē must be oft admonished that they set an ordre for their temporall goodes and landes whan they be in helth.)   And also to declare his debtes, what he oweth, and what is owing to him : for discharging of his conscience, and quietnesse of his executours.   The minister may not forget nor omitte to moue the sicke person (and that moste earnestly) to lyberalitie towarde the poore.*

* *This may be done before the minister begyn his prayers, as he shal see cause.*

¶ *Here shall the sicke person make a speciall confession, yf he fele his conscience troubled with any weightie matter.   After which confession, the priest shall absolue hym after this forme : and the same forme of absolucion shalbe used in all pryuate confessions.*

OUR Lord Jesus Christ, who hath lefte power to his Churche to absolue all sinners, which truely repent and beleue in hym: of his great mercy forgeue thee thyne offences: and by his autoritie committed to me, I absolue thee frō all thy synnes, in the name of the father, and of the sonne, and of the holy gost.   Amen.

And then the priest shall saye the collette folowyng.

Let us praye.

O MOST mercifull God, which according to the multitude of thy mercies, doest so putte away the synnes of those which truely repent, that thou remēbrest them no more: open thy iye of mercy vpon this thy seruaunt, who moste earnestly desireth pardon and forgeuenesse: Renue in hym, moste louyng father, whatsoeuer hath been decayed by the fraude and malice of the deuil, or by his owne carnall wyll, and frailnesse: preserue and continue this sicke membre in the vnitie of thy Churche, cōsyder his contricion, accepte his teares, aswage his payne, as shalbe seen to thee moste expedient for him. And forasmuch as he putteth his full trust only in thy mercy: Impute not unto him his former sinnes, but take him unto thy fauour: through the merites of thy moste derely beloued sonne Jesus Christe. Amen.

Then the minister shall saye this psalme.

In te Domine speravi. Psal. lxxi.

In thee, O Lorde haue I put my trust, let me neuer be put to confusion, but ridde me, and deliuer me into thy righteousnes: enclyne thyne eare unto me, and saue me.

Be thou my strong holde (wherunto I may alwaye resorte) thou haste promysed to helpe me : for thou art my house of defence, and my castell.

Deliuer me (O my God) out of the hande of the ungodly, out of the hande of the unrighteous and cruell man.

For thou (O Lord God) art the thyng that I long for, thou art my hope, euen fro my youth.

Through the haue I been holden up euer since I was borne, thou art he that tooke me out of my mothers wombe; my prayse shalbe alwaye of thee.

I am become as it were a monster unto many : but my sure trust is in thee.

Oh let my mouth be filled with thy prayse (that I may syng of thy glory) and honour all the daye long.

Cast me not awaye in the tyme of age, forsake me not when my strength fayleth me.

For mine enemies speake against me : and they that lay waite for my soule take their cousayle together, saying : God hath forsaken hym, persecute hym, and take hym, for there is none to delyuer hym.

Goe not ferre fro me, O God : my God, haste thee to helpe me.

Let them be confounded and perishe, that are againste my soule : let them be couered with shame and dishonour, that seke to doe me euill.

As for me, I will paciently abyde alwaye, and wyll prayse thee more and more.

My mouth shall dayly speake of thy righteousnes and saluacion, for I knowe no ende therof.

I will goe forth in the strength of the Lorde God : and will make mencion of thy righteousnesse onely.

Thou (O God) haste taught me from my youth up until now, therfore wil I tel of thy wonderous workes.

Forsake me not (O God) in myne olde age, when I am gray-headed, untill I haue shewed thy strength unto this generacion, and thy power to all them that are yet for to come.

Thy righteousnesse (O God) is very high, and great thinges are they that thou haste doen : O God who is lyke unto thee?

O what great troubles and aduersities hast thou shewed me? and yet diddest thou turne and refreshe me : yea, and broughtest me from the depe of the earth agayne.

Thou haste brought me to great honour, and coumforted me on euery side.

Therfore will I prayse thee and thy faithfulnes (O God) playing upon an instrument of musicke, unto thee will I syng upon the harpe, O thou holy one of Israel.

My lippes will be fayne, when I syng unto thee: and so will my soule whom thou haste delyuered.

My tounge also shall talke of thy righteousnesse all the daye long, for they are confounded and brought unto shame that seke to doe me euyll.

Glory to the father, &c.

As it was in the beginnyng, &c.

Addyng this Anthem.

O Saueour of the world saue us, which by thy crosse and precious bloud hast redemed us, helpe us we beseche the, O God.

Then shall the minister saye.

The almighty Lord, whiche is a moste strong tower to all them that put their trust in hym, to whom all thynges in heauen, in earth, and under earth, doe bowe and obey: be now and euer-more thy defence, and make thee knowe and fele, that there is no other name under heauen geuen to man, in whom and through whom thou mayest receyue helth and saluacion, but only the name of our Lorde Jesus Christe. Amen.

¶ *If the sicke person desyre to be annoynted, then shal the priest annoynte him upon the forehead or breast only, makyng the signe of the crosse, saying thus,*

As with this visible oyle thy body outwardly is annoynted: so our heauenly father almyghtye God, graunt of his infinite goodnesse, that thy soule inwardly may be annoynted with the holy gost, who is the spirite of al strength, coumforte, reliefe, and gladnesse. And vouchesafe for his great mercy (yf it be his blessed will) to restore unto thee thy bodely helth, and strength, to serue him, and sende thee release of al thy paines, troubles, and diseases, both in body and minde. And howsoeuer his goodnesse (by his diuyne and unserchable prouidēce) shall dispose of thee: we, his unworthy ministers and seruaūts, humbly beseche the eternall maiestie, to doe with thee according to the multitude of his innumerable mercies, and to pardon thee all thy sinnes and offences, committed by all thy bodily senses, passions, and carnall affeccions: who also vouchsafe mercifully to graūt unto thee gostely strēgth, by his holy spirite, to withstād and ouercome al temptacions and assaultes of thine aduersarye, that in no wise he preuaile against thee, but that thou mayest haue perfit victory and triumph against the deuil, sinne, and death, through Christ our Lord: Who by his death hath ouercomed the Prince of death, and with the father, and the holy gost euermore liueth and reigneth God, worlde without ende. Amen.

Usque quo, Domine. Psalm xiii.

How long wilt thou forget me, (O Lord,) for euer? how lōg wilt thou hyde thy face fro me? How long shall I seke counsell in my soule? and be so vexed in myne herte? how long shall myne enemye triumph ouer me? Consydre, and heare me, (O lord my God): lighten myne iyes, that I slepe not in death. Leste myne enemy saye: I haue preuayled against hym: for yf I be cast downe, they that trouble me will reioyce at it. But my trust is in thy mercy: and my herte is ioyfull in thy saluacion. I will sing of the lord, because he hath delte so louingly with me. Yea, I wyll prayse the name of the Lord the most highest. Glory be to the, &c. As it was in the, &c.

COMMUNION OF THE SICKE.

*Forasmuche as all mortal men be subiect to many sodaine perils, diseases,
and sickenesses, and euer uncertaine what time they shall departe out of
this lyfe: Therfore to thentent they may be alwayes in a readinesse to
dye, whensoeuer it shall please almighty God to call them: The curates
shall diligently from tyme to tyme, but specially in the plague tyme, exhorte
theyr paryshoners to the ofte receyuyng (in the churche) of the holy communion of the body and bloud of oure Sauioure Christe: whiche (yf they
doe) they shall haue no cause in theyr sodaine visitacion, to be unquyeted
for lacke of the same. But if the sicke persō be not hable to come to the
churche, and yet is desirous to receyue the communion in his house, then
he must geue knowlage ouer night, or els early in the morning to the curate,
signifying also howe many he appoynted to communicate with hym. And
yf the same daye there be a celebracion of the holy cōmunion in the churche,
then shall the priest reserue (at the open communion) so muche of the
sacrament of the body and bloud, as shall serue the sicke person, and so
many as shall communicate with hym (yf there be any.) And so soone
as he conueniently may, after the open communion ended in the church,
shall goe and minister the same, firste to those that are appoynted to communicate with the sicke (yf there be any), and last of all to the sicke person
himselfe. But before the curate distribute the holy communion: the
appoynted generall confession must be made in the name of the communi-
cantes, the curate addyng the absolucion with the coumfortable sentences
of scripture folowyng in the open communion, and after the communion
ended, the collecte.*

ALMIGHTIE and euerlyuyng God, we moste hertely thanke
thee, &c.

¶ *But yf the daye be not appoynted for the open communion in the churche,
then (upon conuenient warning geuen) the curate shal come and visite
the sick person afore noone. And hauing a conueniēt place in the sicke
mans house (where he may reuerētly celebrate) with all thinges necessary
for the same, and not beyng otherwyse letted with the publike seruice, or
any other iust impedimēt; he shal there celebrate ye holy communion
after suche forme and sorte as hereafter is appoynted.*

THE CELEBRACION

of the holy communion for the sicke.

O PRAYSE the Lorde, all ye nacions, laude hym, all ye people:
for his mercifull kyndenesse is confyrmed towarde us, and the
trueth of the Lorde endureth for euer.

Glory be to the father, &c.

> Lord, haue mercy upon us.   ⎞   Without any
> Christ, haue mercy upon us.   ⎬   more repeticion.
> Lord, haue mercy upon us.   ⎠

The Priest. The Lorde be with you.

Aunswere. And with thy spirite.

Let us pray.

ALMIGHTIE euerlyuing God, maker of mankynde, which doest correcte those whom thou doest loue, and chatisest euery one whome thou doest receyue: we beseche the to haue mercy upon this thy seruaunte visited with thy hande, and to graunt that he may take his sickenesse paciently, and recouer his bodily helth (if it be thy gracious will), and whansoeuer his soule shall departe from the body, it may without spotte be presented unto thee: through Jesus Christe our Lord. Amen.

The Epistle.   Heb. xii.

MY sonne, despise not the correccion of the Lorde, neyther fainte when thou art rebuked of hym: for whom the Lorde loueth, hym he correcteth, yea and he scourgeth euery sonne whom he receyueth.

The gospell.   John v.

VERELY, verely I saye unto you, he that heareth my woorde, and beleueth on hym that sente me, hath euerlasting life, and shall not come unto damnacion, but he passeth from death unto life.

The Preface.

The Lorde be with you.

Aunswere. And with thy spirite.

¶ Lifte up your hertes, &c.

Unto the ende of the Canon.

¶ *At the tyme of the distribucion of the holy sacrament, the prieste shall firste receyue the communion hymselfe, and after minister to them that be appoynted to communicate with the sicke (yf there be any), and then to the sicke person. And the sicke person shall all wayes desyre some, eyther of his owne house, or els of his neyghbours, to receyue the holy communion with hym; for that shall be to hym a singuler great coumforte, and of theyr parte a great token of charitie.*

¶ *And yf there be moe sicke persons to be visited the same day that the curate doth celebrate in any sicke mās house; then shall the curate (there) reserue so muche of the sacramente of the body and bloud: as shall serue the other sicke persons, and suche as be appoynted to communicate with them (yf there be any).   And shall immediatly cary it, and minister it unto them.*

¶ *But yf any man eyther by reason of extremitie of sickenesse, or for lacke of warnyng geuen in due tyme, to the curate, or by any other iust impediment, doe not receyue the sacramente of Christes bodye and bloud : then the curate shall instruct hym, that yf he doe truely repent hym of his sinnes, and stedfastly beleue that Jesus Christ hath suffered death upon the crosse for hym, and shed his bloud for his redempcion, earnestly remembring the benefites he hath therby, and geuing hym hertie thankes therfore ; he doeth eate and drynke spiritually the bodye and bloud of our sauioure Christe, profitably to his soules helth, although he doe not receyue the sacrament with his mouth.*

¶ *When the sicke persone is visited and receiueth the holy communion, all at one tyme : then the priest for more expedicion shall use this ordre at the visitacion.*

The Anthem.

Remembre not Lorde, &c.

Lorde haue mercy upon us.
Christe haue mercy upon us.
Lorde haue mercy upon us.

¶ Our father whiche art in heauen, &c.
And leade us not into temptacion.
Aunswere. But deliuer us from euyll.   Amen.

Let us praye.

O Lorde, looke downe from heauen, &c.

With the firste parte of the exhortacion and all other thynges unto the Psalme :

In thee o Lorde haue I put my trust, &c.

And yf the sicke desyre to be annoyncted, then shall the priest use thappoynted prayer without any Psalme.

BURIALL OF THE DEAD.

The priest metyng the Corps at the Churche style, shall say : Or els the priestes and clerkes shall sing, and so goe either into the Churche, or towardes the graue.

I AM the resurrecciō and the life (sayth the Lord): he that beleueth in me, yea though he were dead, yet shall he liue. And whosoeuer lyueth and beleueth in me: shall not dye for euer. *John* xi.

I KNOWE that my redemer lyueth, and that I shall ryse out of the yearth in the last daye, and shalbe couered again with my skinne and shall see God in my flesh: yea and I myselfe shall beholde hym, not with other but with these same iyes. *Job* xix.

WE brought nothyng into this worlde, neyther may we carye any thyng out of this worlde. The Lord geueth, and the Lord taketh awaie. Euen as it pleaseth the Lorde, so cummeth thynges to passe: blessed be the name of the Lorde. 1 *Tim.* vi. ♭ i.

When they come at the graue, whyles the Corps is made readie to be layed into the earth, the priest shall saye, or els the priest and clerkes shall syng.

MAN that is borne of a woman, hath but a shorte tyme to lyue, and is full of miserye : he cummeth up and is cut downe lyke a floure; he flyeth as it were a shadowe, and neuer continueth in one staye. *Job* ix.

¶ In the myddest of lyfe we be in death, of whom may we seke for succour but of thee, o Lorde, whiche for our synnes iustly art moued? yet o Lord God moste holy, o Lord moste mighty, o holy and moste merciful sauiour, delyuer us not into the bitter paines of eternal death. Thou knowest, Lord, the secretes of our hartes : shutte not up thy mercyfull iyes to our praiers : But spare us, Lord most holy, o God moste mighty, o holy and mercifull sauiour, thou moste worthy iudge eternal, suffre us not at our last houre for any paines of death to fal frō the.

Then the priest castyng earth upon the Corps, shall saye.

I COMMENDE thy soule to God the father almighty, and thy body to the grounde, earth to earth, asshes to asshes, dust to dust, in sure and certayne hope of resurreccion to eternall lyfe, through our Lord Jesus Christ, who shall chaunge our vile body, that it may be lyke to his glorious body, accordyng to the myghtie workyng wherby he is hable to subdue all thynges to himselfe.

Then shalbe sayed or song.

I HEARDE a voyce from heauen saying, unto me: Wryte, blessed are the dead whiche dye in the Lorde. Euen so sayeth the spirite, that they rest from theyr labours. *Apoca.* xiiii.

Let us praye.

WE commende into thy handes of mercy (moste mercifull father) the soule of this our brother departed, *N.* And his body we commit to the earth, besechyng thyne infinite goodnesse, to geue us grace to lyue in thy feare and loue, and to dye in thy fauoure: that when the iudgmente shall come which thou haste commytted to thy welbeloued sonne, both this our brother, and we, may be found acceptable in thy sight, and receiue that blessing, whiche thy welbeloued sōne shall then pronounce to all that loue and feare thee, saying: Come ye blessed children of my Father: Receyue the kingdome prepared for you before the beginning of the worlde. Graunt this, mercifull father, for the honour of Jesu Christe our onely sauior, mediator, and aduocate. Amen.

This praier shall also be added.

ALMIGHTIE God, we geue thee hertie thankes for this thy seruaunte, whom thou haste delyuered frō the miseries of this wretched world, from the body of death and all temptacion. And, as we trust, hast brought his soule whiche he committed into thy holye handes, into sure consolacion and reste: Graunte, we beseche thee, that at the daye of iudgement his soule and all the soules of thy electe, departed out of this lyfe, may with us and we with them, fully receiue thy promisses, and be made perfite altogether thorow the glorious resurreccion of thy sonne Jesus Christ our Lorde.

These psalmes with other suffrages folowyng are to be sayed in the churche either before or after the buriall of the corps

Dilexi, quoniam. Psalm cxvi.

I AM well pleased that the lorde hath hearde the voyce of my prayer.

That he hath enclined his eare unto me, therefore wil I call upon him as long as I liue.

The snares of death compased me round about, and the paynes of hel gatte holde upon me : I shal finde trouble and heauines, and I shal cal upon the name of the lorde, (O Lorde,) I beseche thee deliuer my soule.

Gracious is the lord, and righteous, yea, our god is mercifull.

The lord preserueth the simple : I was in misery and he helped me.

Turne agayn then unto thy rest, o my soule, for the lord hath rewarded thee.

And why? thou hast deliuered my soule frō death, mine iyes from teares, and my feete from fallyng.

I will walke before the lorde in the lande of the liuing.

I beleued, and therfore wil I speake : but I was sore troubled. I sayd in my haste : all menne are lyers.

What rewarde shall I geue unto the lorde, for al the benefites that he hath doen unto me?

I wil receiue the cup of saluacion, and call upon the name of the lorde.

I will pay my vowes now in the presence of all his people: right dere in the sight of the lord is the death of hys Saintes.

Beholde (O lorde) how that I am thy seruaunte : I am thy seruaunt, and the sonne of thy handmayde, thou hast broken my bondes in sunder.

I will offer to thee the sacrifice of thankesgeuyng, and will call upon the Name of the Lorde.

I will pay my vowes unto the lorde, in the syghte of all his people, in the courtes of the lordes house, euen in the middest of thee, O Hierusalem.

Glorie to the father, &c.

As it was in the beginning, &c.

Lauda, anima, mea. Psal. cxlvi.

PRAYSE the lorde, (o my soule), while I liue wil I prayse the lorde : yea, as long as I haue any being, I wil sing prayses unto my god.

☞ *Note that this psalme is to be saied after the others that foloweth.*

O put not your trust in princes, nor in any childe of man, for there is no helpe in them.

For when the breath of man goeth furth, he shall turne agayn to his yearth, and then all his thoughtes perish.

Blessed is he that hath the God of Jacob for hys helpe : and whose hope is in the lorde hys god.

Which made heauen and earth, the sea, and al that therein is : whiche kepeth his promise for euer.

Whiche helpeth them to right that suffer wrong, which feedeth the hungrie.

The lorde looceth men out of prieson, the lorde geueth sight to the blynde.

The lorde helpeth them up that are fallen, the lorde careth for the righteous.

The lord careth for the straungers, he defendeth the father-lesse and widdowe : as for the waye of the ungodly, he turneth it upsyde downe.

The lorde thy God, O Sion, shalbe kyng for euermore, and throughout all generacions.

Glory to the father, &c.

As it was in the beginning, &c.

Domine, probasti.　Psalm cxxxix.

O LORD, thou hast searched me out, and knowe me.

Thou knowest my down-sitting, and mine up-rising : thou understandest my thoughtes long before.

Thou art about my pathe, and about my bed, and spiest out al my waies.

For loe, there is not a woord in my toungue, but thou (o lorde) knoweste it altogether.

Thou hast fashioned me, behinde and before, and layed thine hande upon me.

Such knowelage is to woonderfull and excellente for me : I cannot attaine unto it.

Whither shall I goe then from thy spirite? or whither shal I goe then from thy presence?

If I clime up into heauē, thou art there : If I goe down to hel, thou art there also.

If I take the winges of the morning, and remaine in the utter-moste partes of the sea;

Euen there also shal thy hande leade me, and thy righte hande shall holde me.

If I saye : paraduenture the darkenesse shall couer me, then shall my night bee turned to daye.

Yea the darkenesse is no darkenesse with thee : but the night is all clere as the daye, the darkenesse and lyghte to thee are bothe alike.

For my reynes are thine, thou hast coured me in my mothers wombe : I wyll geue thankes unto thee, for I am fearefully and woonderously made: meruailous are thy woorkes, and that my soule knoweth right well.

My bones are not hidde from thee, though I bee made secretely, and fashioned beneath in the yearth.

Thine eyes did see my substaunce, yet being unperfecte : and in thy booke were al my membres written.

Whiche daye by daye were fashioned, when as yet there was none of them.

Howe dere are thy councels unto me, O God? O howe greate is the summe of them?

If I tell them, they are moe in noumbre then the sande : when I wake up, I am present with thee.

Wilt thou not sley the wicked, O God? departe from me, ye bloudethristie men.

For they speake unrighteously againste thee : and thyne enemies take thy name in vaine.

Dooe not I hate them, O Lord, that hate thee : and am not I greued with those that ryse up against thee?

Yea I hate them righte sore, euen as thoughe they were myne enemies.

Trye me, O God, and seeke the grounde of myne harte : proue me and examine my thoughtes.

Looke well if there be any way of wickednes in me, and leade me in the waye euerlasting.

Glory to the father, &c.

As it was in the beginning, &c.

Then shall folowe this lesson, taken out of the XV. Chapter to the Corinthians, the firste Epistle.

CHRISTE is risen from the dead, and become the firstfruictes of them that slepte. For by a man came death, and by a man came the resurreccion of the deade. For as by Adam all dye : euen so by Christ shal al be made aliue, but euery manne in his owne ordre. The firste is Christe, then they that are Christes, at hys comming. Then commeth the ende, when he hath de-liuered up the kyngdome to God the father, when he hath put downe al rule and al authoritie and power. For he must reygne til he haue putte al his enemies under his feete. The laste enemie that shal bee destroyed, is death. For he hath putte all thinges under his feete. But when he sayeth al thinges are put under him, it is manifeste that he is excepted, whiche dyd putte all thinges under him. When all thynges are subdued unto hym, then shall the soonne also hymselfe bee subiecte unto hym that put all thynges under him, that god mai be all in all. Elles what

doe they, whiche are baptized ouer the dead, if the dead ryse not
at all? Why are they then baptized ouer them? yea, and why
stand we alway then in ieoperdie? By our reioysing whiche I
haue in Christ Jesu oure lorde, I dye dayly. That I haue fought
with beastes at Ephesus after the maner of men, what auaūtageth
it me, if the dead ryse not agayn? Let us eate and drynke, for
to-morowe we shall dye. Be not ye deceiued: eiuill wordes
corrupt good maners. Awake truly out of slepe, and sinne not.
For some haue not the knowledge of God. I speake this to your
shame. But some mā will say: how aryse the dead? with
what bodye shall they come? Thou foole, that whiche thou
sowest, is not quickened, except it dye. And what sowest thou?
Thou sowest not that body that thall be; but bare corne as of
wheate, or of some other: but god geueth it a bodie at hys
pleasure, to euery seede his owne body. All fleshe is not one
maner of fleshe: but there is one maner of fleshe of men, another
maner of fleshe of beastes, another of fishes, another of birdes.
There are also celestiall bodies, and there are bodies terrestriall.
But the glorye of the celestiall is one, and the glorye of the terrestrial is another. There is one maner glory of the sonne, and
another glorye of the moone, and another glorye of the sterres.
For one sterre differeth from another in glorie. So is the resurreccyon of the dead. It is sowen in corrupcion, it ryseth again
in incorrupcion. It is sowē in dishonour, it rysethe agayne in
honour. It is sowen in weakenesse, it ryseth agayn in power.
It is sowen a naturiall bodie, it ryseth agayn a spirituall bodie.
There is a naturall bodie, and there is a spirituall bodye: as it is
also written: The firste manne Adam was made a liuing soule,
and the last Adam was made a quickning spirite. Howebeit,
that is not firste which is spiritual: but that which is naturall,
and then that whiche is spirituall. The firste man is of the
earthe, yearthy: The seconde manne is the Lorde from heauen
(heauenly). As is the earthy, such are they that are yearthy.
And as is the heauenly, such are they that are heauenly. And
as we haue borne the image of the yearthy, so shal we beare the
image of the heauenly. This say I brethren, that fleshe and
bloud cannot enherite the kyngdome of God: Neyther doeth
corrupcion enherite uncorrupcion. Behold, I shewe you a
mistery. We shall not all slepe: but we shal al be chaunged,
and that in a momente, in the twynkeling of an iye by the last
trumpe. For the trumpe shall blowe, and the dead shall ryse
incorruptible, and we shall be chaunged. For this corruptible
must put on incorrupcion: and this mortall must put on im-

mortalitie. When this corruptible hath put on incorruption, and this mortall hath put on immortalitie: then shall bee brought to passe the saying that is written: Death is swalowed up in victorye: Death where is thy styng? Hell where is thy victorye? The styng of deathe is sinne: and the strength of sinne is the lawe. But thankes be unto god, whiche hath geuen us victory, through our Lorde Jesus Christ. Therefore, my dere brethren, be ye stedfast and unmouable, alwaies ryche in the woorke of the lorde, forasmuch as ye know that your labour is not in vayne, in the lorde.

The Lesson ended then shall the Priest say.

Lorde, haue mercie upon us.

Christe, haue mercie upon us.

Lorde, haue mercie upon us.

Our father whiche art in heauen, &c.

And leade us not into temptacion.

Aunswere. But deliuer us from euil. Amen.

Priest. Entre not (o lorde) into iudgement with thy seruaunt.

Aunswere. For in thy sight no liuing creature shalbe iustifyed.

Priest. From the gates of hell.

Aunswere. Deliuer theyr soules, o lorde.

Priest. I beleue to see the goodnes of the lorde.

Aunswere. In the lande of the liuing.

Prieste. O lorde, graciously heare my prayer.

Aunswere. And let my crye come unto thee.

Let us pray.

O Lorde, with whome dooe lyue the spirites of them that be dead: and in whome the soules of them that bee elected, after they be deliuered from the burden of the fleshe, be in ioy and felicitie: Graunte unto us thy seruaunte, that the sinnes whiche he committed in this world be not imputed unto him, but that he, escaping the gates of hell and paynes of eternall derkenesse: may euer dwel in the region of lighte, with Abraham, Isaac, and Jacob, in the place where is no wepyng, sorowe, nor heauinesse: and when that dredeful day of the generall resurreccion shall come, make him to ryse also with the iust and righteous, and receiue this bodie agayn to glory, then made pure and incorruptible, set him on the right hand of thy sone Jesus Christ, emong thy holy and elect, that then he may heare with them these most swete and coumfortable wordes: Come to me ye blessed of my father, possesse the kingdome whiche hath bene prepared for you from the beginning of the worlde: Graunte thys we beseche thee, o mercifull father: through Jesus Christe our mediatour and redemer. Amen.

THE CELEBRACION

of the holy communion when there is a burial of the dead.

Quemadmodum. Psalm xlii.

LIKE as the hart desireth the water-brookes, so longeth my soule after thee, o God.

My soule is athirst for god, yea, euen for the liuing god : when shal I come to appeare before the presence of god?

My teares haue beene my meate day and nighte, whyle they dayly say unto me, Where is now thy god?

Nowe when I thinke thereupon, I powre out my hart by my-selfe : for I went with the multitude, and brought them furth unto the house of god, in the voyce of praise and thankesgeuing, emong suche as kepe holyday.

Why art thou so full of heauines, (O my soule) : and why art thou so unquiete within me?

Put thy trust in god, for I wil yet geue him thankes for the helpe of his countenaunce.

My God, my soule is vexed within me : therefore will I remember thee concerning the land of Jordane, and the litle hill of Hermonim.

One deepe calleth another, beecause of the noyse of thy water-pypes, all thy waues and stormes are gone ouer me.

The lorde hath graunted his louing-kyndenesse on the daye tyme, and in the nighte season dyd I syng of hym, and made my prayer unto the god of my lyfe.

I wil say unto the God of my strength, why haste thou forgotten me? why goe I thus heuelye, whyle the enemie oppresseth me?

My bones are smitten asoonder, whyle myne enemies (that trouble me) cast me in the teeth, namely while they say dayly unto me : where is nowe thy God?

Why art thou so vexed, (O my soule) and why arte thou so disquieted within me?

O put thy trust in god, for I will yet thanke him which is the helpe of my countenaunce, and my God.

Glorie to the Father, &c.

As it was in the beginning, &c.

Collette.

O MERCIFULL god the father of oure lorde Jesu Christ, who is the resurreccion and the life: In whom whosoeuer beleueth shall liue thoughe he dye: And whosoeuer liueth, and beleueth in hym, shal not dye eternallye: who also hath taughte us (by his holye Apostle Paule) not to bee sory as men without hope for them that slepe in him: We mekely beseche thee (o father) to raise us frō the death of sin, unto the life of righteousnes, that when we shall departe this lyfe, we maye slepe in him (as our hope is this our brother doeth), and at the general resurreccion in the laste daie, bothe we and this oure brother departed, receiuyng agayne oure bodies, and rising againe in thy moste gracious fauoure: maye with all thine elect Saynctes, obteine eternall ioye. Graunte this, o Lorde god, by the meanes of our aduocate Jesus Christ: which with thee and the holy ghoste, liueth and reigneth one God for euer. Amen.

The Epistle. 1 Thess. iv.

I WOULDE not brethren that ye shoulde bee ignoraunt concernyng them which are fallen aslepe, that ye sorowe not as other doe, whiche haue no hope. For if we beleue that Jesus dyed, and rose againe: euen so them also whiche slepe by Jesus, will God bring again with him. For thys saye we unto you in the word of the Lorde: that we whiche shall lyue, and shal remain in the comyng of the Lord, shal not come ere they which slepe. For the Lorde himselfe shal descende from heauē with a shoute, and the voice of the Archangell, and troump of God. And the deade in Christe shal arise first: then we whiche shall lyue (euen wee whiche shal remayne) shal bee caughte up wyth them also in the cloudes, to meete the Lorde in the ayre. And so shall wee euer be with the Lorde. Wherefore coumforte youreselues one another wyth these woordes.

¶ *The gospell.* John vi.

Jesus saied to his disciples and to the Jewes: Al that the father geueth me, shall come to me: and he that cōmeth to me, I cast not away. For I came down from heauen: not to do that I wil, but that he wil, which hath sent me. And this is the fathers wyll whiche hath sente me, that of all whiche he hath geuē me, I shal lose nothing: but raise them up again at the last day. And this is the wil of him that sent me: that euery one which seeth the sonne and beleueth on him, haue euerlasting life: And I wil raise him up at the laste daye.

PURIFICACION OF WEOMEN.

The woman shall come into the churche, and there shal knele downe in some conueniente place, nygh unto the quier doore : and the prieste standyng by her shall saye these woordes, or suche lyke, as the case shall require.

FORASMUCHE as it hath pleased almightie god of hys goodnes to geue you safe deliueraunce, and your childe baptisme, and hath preserued you in the greate daunger of childebirth: ye shal therefore geue hartie thankes unto god, and pray.

Then shall the prieste saye this psalme.

Leuaui oculos. Psalm cxxi.

I HAUE lifted up mine iyes unto the hilles, from whence cummeth my helpe?

My help cummeth euen from the lord, which hath made heauen and earth.

He will not suffer thy foote to be moued, and he that kepeth thee wil not slepe.

Beholde he that kepeth Israel, shal neither slumber nor slepe.

The lorde himselfe is thy keper, the lorde is thy defence upon thy right hande.

So that the sonne shall not burne thee by daye, neyther the moone by nyght.

The lord shal preserue thee from al euil, yea it is euen he that shal kepe thy soule.

The lord shal preserue thy going out, and thy cumming in, from this tyme furth for euermore.

Glorye to the father, &c.

As it was in the beginning, &c.

      Lord haue mercie upon us.

      Christ haue mercie upon us.

      Lord haue mercie upon us.

      ¶ Our father whiche art in heauen, &c.

And leade us not into temptacion.

Aunswere. But deliuer us from euil.   Amen.

Priest. O lord saue this woman thy seruaunt.

Aunswere. Whiche putteth her trust in thee.

Priest. Bee thou to her a strong tower.
Aunswere. From the face of her enemie.
Priest. O Lorde heare our prayer.
Aunswere. And let our crye come to thee.

Priest. ¶ Let us pray.

O ALMIGHTIE God, which hast deliuered this woman thy seruant from the great payne and peril of childbirth: Graūt, we beseche thee (most mercifull father), that she through thy helpe may both faithfully lyue, and walke in her vocacyon accordynge to thy will in thys lyfe presente; and also may be partaker of euerlastyng glorye in the lyfe to come: through Jesus Christ our lorde.   Amen.

The woman that is purifyed, must offer her Crysome and other accustomed offeringes.   And if there be a communion, it is conuenient that she receiue the holy communion.

THE FIRSTE DAIE OF LENTE

ASHE-WEDNISDAYE.

¶ *After mattens ended, the people beeyng called together by the ryngyng of*
a bel, and assembled in the churche : Thinglyshe letanye shall be sayed
after thaccustomed maner : whiche ended, the prieste shal goe into the
pulpitte and saye thus :

BRETHREN, in the prymitiue churche there was a godlye disciplyne, that at the begynnyng of lente suche persones as were notorious synners, were put to open penaunce, and punished in this worlde, that theyr soules myght bee saued in the day of the lord. And that other admonished by theyr example, might he more afrayed to offende. In the steede whereof until the saide disciplyne maye bee restored agayne; (whiche thynge is muche to bee wyshed,) it is thoughte good, that at thys tyme (in your presence) shoulde bee read the general sentences of goddes cursyng agaynste impenitente sinners, gathered out of the xxvii Chapter of Deuteronomie, and other places of scripture. And that ye shoulde aunswere to euery sentence, Amen: To thentente that you beeyng admonished of the greate indignacion of God agaynste sinners: may the rather be called to earneste and true repentaunce, and maye walke more warely in these daungerous dayes, fleyng from suche vices, for the whiche ye affirme with your owne mouthes: the curse of god to be due.

¶ CURSED is the mā that maketh any carued or molten image, an abominacion to the Lorde, the woorke of the handes of the craftesmanne, and putteth it in a secrete place, to wurship it.

And the people shal aunswere, and saye,

Amen.

Minister. Cursed is he that curseth his father, and mother.
Answere. Amen.
Minister. Cursed is he that remoueth awaye the marke of hys neighbours land.
Answere. Amen.
Minister. Cursed is he that maketh the blinde to goe oute of hys waye.
Aunswere. Amen.

Minister. Cursed is he that letteth in iudgemente the right of the straungier, of them that be fatherlesse, and of widowes.

Answere. Amen.

Minister. Cursed is he that smiteth his neighbour secretely.

Answere. Amen.

Minister. Cursed is he that lieth with his neighbour's wyfe.

Answere. Amen.

Minister. Cursed is he that taketh rewarde to slea the soule of innocent bloude.

Answere. Amen.

Minister. Cursed is he that putteth his truste in man, and taketh manne for his defence, and in his harte goeth from the Lorde.

Aunswere. Amen.

Minister. Cursed are the unmercifull, the fornicators and aduouterers, the couetous persones, the wurshyppers of images, slaunderers, drunkardes, and extorcioners.

Aunswere. Amen.

The minister. Nowe seeing that all they bee accursed (as the Prophete Dauid beareth witnesse) whiche doe erre and goe astray from the commaundementes of God, let us (remembring the dredefull iudgement hanging ouer our heades, and beyng alwayes at hande) returne unto our lorde God, with all contricion and mekenes of heart, bewailing and lamenting our sinful life, knowlaging and confessing our offences, and seekyng to bring furth worthie fruites of penance. For euen now is the axe put unto the roote of the trees, so that euery tree whiche bryngeth not furth good fruite, is hewen downe and cast into the fyer. It is a fearefull thing to fall into the handes of the liuing God: he shal powre downe rayne upon the sinners, snares, fyer and brimstone, storme and tempest: this shalbe theyr porcion to drynke. For loe, the lorde is cummen out of his place, to visite the wickednes of such as dwell upon the earth. But who may abyde the daye of his cumming? Who shalbe hable to endure whan he appeareth? His fanne is in his hande, and he wil pourge his floore, and gather his wheate into the barne, but he will burne the chaffe with unquencheable fier. The day of the lorde cummeth as a thiefe upon the night, and when men shall say peace, and all thynges are safe, then shall sodayne destruccion come upon them, as sorowe cometh upon a woman trauaylyng with chylde, and they shall not escape: then shall appeare the wrathe

Psal. cxviii.

Mat. iii.

Hebru. x.
Psal. x.
Esai.
xxvi.

Mal. iii.
Mat. iii.

i Thess. v.

of God in the daye of vengeaunce, whiche obstinate synners, through the stubbernes of theyr hearte, haue heaped unto themselfe, which despised the goodnesse, pacience and long-sufferaunce of god, whē he called them continually to repentaunce. Then shall they cal upō me (sayth the lorde), but I wil not heare: they shal seke me early, but thei shal not finde me, and that because they hated knowlage, and receiued not the feare of the lord, but abhorred my coūsell and despised my correcciō: then shal it be to late to knocke, whē the doore shalbe shut, and to late to cry for mercy, whē it is the tyme ofiustice. O terrible voice of most iust iudgement, which shalbe pronounced upon thē when it shalbe sayde unto thē. Go ye cursed into the fyer euerlasting, which is prepared for the deuil and his angels. Therfore, brethrē, take we hede by time, while the day of saluaciō lasteth, for the night cometh whē none can worke: but let us while we haue the light, beleue in the light, and walke as the childrē of the light, that we be not cast into the utter derkenes, where is weping and gnashing of teeth. Let us not abuse the goodnes of god, whiche calleth us mercifully to amēdement, and of his endlesse pitie, promiseth us forgeuenes of that which is past: if (with a whole mind and a true hert) we returne unto him: for though our sinnes be red as scarlet, they shalbe as white as snowe, and though they be lyke purple, yet shall they be as whyte as woolle. Turne you cleane (sayth ye lord) frō all your wickednes, and your synne shall not be your destrucciō. Cast away from you all your ungodlines that ye haue doen, make you new hertes, and a new spirite: wherfore will ye dye, O ye house of Israel? seing I haue no pleasure in the death of him that dieth (sayth the Lord God). Turne you thē, and you shall lyue. Although we haue sinned yet haue we an aduocate with the father Jesus Christ the righteous, and he it is that obteyneth grace for our sinnes; for he was wounded for our offences, and smitten for our wickednes: let us therfore returne unto him, who is the merciful receiuer of al true penitent sinners, assuring ourselfe that he is ready to receiue us, and most willing to pardon us, if we come to him with faithful repentaūce: if we wil submit ourselues unto him, and from hēceforth walke in hys waies: if we wil take his easy yoke and light burdē upō us to folowe hym in lowlynesse, pacience, and charitie, and bee ordred by the gouernaunce of his holy spirite, seking alwayes

Rom. ii.

Prouer. i.

Mat. xxv.

ii. Cor. vi.
John ix.

Mat. xxv.

Esai. i.
Esech
xviii.

1 John ii.

Esai. liii.

Mat. xi.

his glorye, and seruing him duely in our vocacion with thankesgeuyng. This yf we doe, Christe wil deliuer us from the curse
of the law, and frō the extreme malediccion whiche shall lyght
upon them that shalbee set on the left hand: and he Math.
wyl set us on his right hand, and geue us the blessed xxv.
benediccion of hys father, commaundyng us to take possessions
of hys glorious kyngdome, unto the whiche he vouchsafe to
bryng us al, for hys infinite mercye. Amen.

¶ *Then shall they all kneele upon theyr knees : And the prieste and clerkes
    kneelyng (where they are accustomed to saye the letanye) shall saye this
    psalme.*

Miserere mei Deus. Psal. li.

HAUE mercye upon me, (O God,) after thy great goodnesse :
according to the multitude of thy mercies, do away mine offences.

Washe me throwly fro my wickednes, and clense me from
my synne.

For I knowlage my faultes, and my sinne is euer before me.

Agaynst thee only haue I synned, and done this euyl in thy
syght : that thou myghtest bee iustified in thy saying, and clere
when thou art iudged.

Behold, I was shapen in wickednes, and in synne hath my
mother conceiued me.

But loe, thou requirest trueth in the inward partes, and shalte
make me to understande wysedome secretelye.

Thou shalt pourge me with Isope, and I shall bee cleane :
thou shalt washe me, and I shal bee whyter then snowe.

Thou shalte make me heare of ioye and gladnesse, that the
bones whiche thou haste broken, maye reioyce.

Turne thy face from my synnes, and putte out all my mys-
dedes.

Make me a cleane herte, (O God) and renue a ryght spyrite
within me.

Caste me not awaye from thy presence, and take not thy
holy spirite from me.

O geue me the coumforte of thy helpe agayne, and stablishe
me wyth thy free spirite.

Then shal I teache thy waies unto the wicked, and sinners
shal bee conuerted unto thee.

Deliuer me from bloud-giltinesse, (O God,) thou that art the
god of my health : and my toungue shall syng of thy righteousnesse.

Thou shalt open my lippes, (O Lorde) my mouthe shal shewe
thy prayse.

For thou desyreste no sacrifice, els would I geue it thee : but thou deliteste not in burnt offeryng.

The sacrifice of God is a troubled spirite, a brokē and contrite herte, (O God), shalt thou not despise.

O bee fauourable and gracious unto Syon, build thou the walles of Hierusalem.

Then shalt thou be pleased with the sacrifice of righteousnesse, wyth the burnt-offeringes and oblacions : then shall they offre young bullockes upon thyne aultare.

Glorye to the father, &c.

As it was in the beginning, &c.

¶ Lorde haue mercie upon us.

¶ Christe haue mercye upon us.

¶ Lorde haue mercye upon us.

Our father whiche art in heauen, &c.

And leade us not into temptacion.

Answere. But deliuer us from euyll.   Amen.

Minister. O Lorde saue thy seruauntes.

Answere. Whiche put theyr truste in thee.

Minister. Sende unto them helpe from aboue.

Aunswere. And euermore mightily defende them.

Minister. Helpe us O God our sauiour.

Aunswere. And for the glory of thy names sake delyuer us, be mercifull unto us synners for thy names sake.

Minister. O Lorde heare my prayer.

Aunswere. And let my crye come to thee.

Let us praye.

O LORD, we beseche thee mercifully heare our prayers, and spare all those which confesse theyr synnes to thee, that they (whose consciences by synne are accused), by thy mercyfull pardon may be absoluled, through Christe our Lorde.   Amen.

O MOST mightie god and mercifull father, which hast compassion of all menne, and hateste nothyng that thou haste made: whiche wouldeste not the deathe of a sinner, but that he shoulde rather turne from sinne and bee saued: mercifully forgeue us oure trespasses, receyue and coumforte us, whiche bee grieued and weried with the burden of our sinne: Thy propertie is to haue mercie, to thee onely it apperteineth to forgeue sinnes: spare us therfore, good Lorde, spare thy people whome thou hast redemed.   Enter not into iudgemente with thy seruauntes, which be vile yearthe, and miserable sinners: But so turne thy ire from us, which mekely knowlage our vilenes, and truely repent us of our fautes: so make hast to helpe us in this worlde: that wee may euer liue with thee in the worlde to come: through Jesus Christe our Lorde. Amen.

Then shal this antheme be sayed or song.

TURNE thou us, good Lord, and so shall we be turned: bee fauourable (O Lorde) be fauourable to thy people, whiche turne to thee in wepyng, fasting and praying: for thou art a mercifull God, full of compassion, long sufferyng, and of a great pietie. Thou sparest when we deserue punishement, and in thy wrathe thynkest upon mercy. Spare thy people, good Lorde, spare them, and lette not thy heritage bee brought to confusion: Heare us (O Lorde) for thy mercy is great, and after the multitude of thy mercyes looke upon us.

OF CEREMONIES,

OF suche Ceremonies as be used in the Church, and haue had their beginning by thinstitucion of man: Some at the first were of godly intent and purpose deuised, and yet at length turned to vanitie and supersticiō: Some entred into the Churche by undiscrete deuocion, and suche a zele as was without knowlage, and for because they were winked at in the beginning, they grewe dayly to more and more abuses, which not onely for their unprofitablenesse, but also because they haue muche blynded the people, and obscured the glory of God, are worthy to be cut awaye, and cleane reiected. Other there be, which although they haue been deuised by mã: yet it is thought good to reserue thẽ still, as well for a decent ordre in the Churche (for the which they were first deuised) as because they pertayne to edificacion: Wherunto all thynges doen in the Churche (as the Apostle teacheth) ought to be referred. And although the keping or omytting of a ceremonie (in itselfe considered) is but a small thyng: Yet the wilfull and contemptuous transgression, and breakyng of a common ordre, and disciplyne, is no small offence before God. Let all thynges bee done emong you (sayeth Sainte Paule) in a semely and due ordre. The appoyntemente of the whiche ordre pertayneth not to pryuate menne: Therfore no manne ought to take in hande nor presume to appoynte or alter any publyke or common ordre in Christes Churche, excepte he be lawfully called and autorized thereunto. And whereas in this our tyme, the myndes of menne bee so diuerse, that some thynke it a greate matter of conscience to departe from a peece of the leaste of theyr Ceremonies (they bee so addicted to their olde customes), and agayne on the other syde, some bee so newe fangle that they woulde innouate all thyng, and so doe despyse the olde that nothyng canne lyke them, but that is newe: It was thought expediente not so muche to haue respecte howe to please and satisfie eyther of these partyes, as howe to please God, and profitte them bothe. And yet leste any manne should bee offended (whom good reason might satisfie), here be certayne causes rendered, why some of the accustomed Ceremonies be put awaye, and some be retayned and kept still.

Some are put awaye, because the great excesse and multytude of them hathe so encreased in these latter dayes, that the burden of them was intollerable: wherof saincte Augustine in his tyme complayned, that they were growen to suche a noumbre: that the state of christian people was in wurse case (concernyng that matter) then were the Jewes. And he counsayled that suche yocke and burden should be taken awaye: as tyme woulde serue quietely to doe it. But what woulde saincte Augustine haue sayed if he hadde seen the Ceremonies of late dayes used among us? Wherunto the multitude used in his time was not to bee compared. This our excessiue multitude of Ceremonies, was so great, and many of them so darke: that they dyd more confounde and darken, then declare and sette forth Christes benefites unto us. And besides this, Christes Gospell is not a Ceremoniall lawe (as muche of Moses lawe was), but it is a relygion to serue God, not in bondage of the figure or shadowe: but in the freedome of spirite, beeyng contente onely wyth those ceremonyes whyche dooe serue to a decente ordre and godlye discipline, and suche as bee apte to stirre uppe the dulle mynde of manne to the remembraunce of his duetie to God, by some notable and speciall significacion, whereby he myght bee edified.

¶ Furthermore, the most weightye cause of the abolishement of certayne Ceremonies was, that they were so farre abused, partely by the supersticious blyndenes of the rude and unlearned, and partelye by the unsaciable auarice of suche as soughte more theyr owne lucre than the glorye of God; that the abuses coulde not well bee taken awaye, the thyng remaynyng styll. But nowe as concernyng those persones, whiche peraduenture will bee offended for that some of the olde Ceremonies are retayned still: Yf they consyder, that wythoute some Ceremonies it is not possible to kepe anye ordre or quyete dyscyplyne in the churche: they shall easilye perceyue iuste cause to refourme theyr iudgementes. And yf they thynke muche that anye of the olde dooe remayne, and woulde rather haue all deuised anewe: then such menne (grauntyng some Ceremonyes conueniente to bee hadde), surelye where the olde maye bee well used: there they cannot reasonablye reproue the olde (onelye for theyr age) wythoute bewraiyng of theyr owne folye. For in suche a case they oughte rather to haue reuerence unto them for theyr antyquitye, yf they wyll declare themselues to bee more studious of unitie and concorde, then of innouacions and newefanglenesse, whiche (as muche as maye bee wyth the trewe settyng foorthe of Christes religion) is alwayes to bee eschewed. Furthermore, suche shall haue no iuste cause wyth the Ceremonies reserued, to bee offended: for as those bee taken awaye whiche were moste abused, and dydde burden mennes consciences wythoute any cause: So the other that remaine are retained for a discipline and ordre, which (upon iust causes) may be altered and chaūged, and therfore are not to be estemed equal with goddes lawe. And moreouer they be neyther darke nor dumme ceremonies, but are so set forth that euery man may understande what they dooe meane, and to what use they do serue. So that it is not like that thei, in time to come, shoulde bee abused as the other haue been. And in these all our dooynges wee condemne no other nacions, nor prescribe anye thyng, but to oure owne people onelye. For we thinke it conueniente that euery countreye should use such ceremonies, as thei shal thynke beste to the settyng foorth of goddes honor, and glorye: and to the reducyng of the people to a moste perfecte and Godly liuing, without errour or supersticion: and that they shoulde putte awaye other thynges, which from time to time they perceiue to be most abused, as in mennes ordinaunces it often chaūceth diuerselye in diuerse countreyes.

CERTAYNE NOTES FOR THE MORE PLAYNE EXPLICACION AND DECENT MINISTRACION OF THINGES, CONTEINED IN THYS BOOKE.

In the saying or singing of Matens and Euensong, Baptizyng and Burying, the minister, in paryshe churches and chapels annexed to the same, shall use a Surples. And in all Cathedral churches and Colledges, tharchdeacons, Deanes, Prouestes, Maisters, Prebendaryes, and fellowes, being Graduates, may use in the quiere, beside theyr Surplesses, such hoodes as pertaineth to their seuerall degrees, which they haue taken in any uniuersitie within this realme. But in all other places, euery minister shall be at libertie to use any Surples or no. It is also seemely that Graduates, when they dooe preache, shoulde use such hoodes as pertayneth to theyr seuerall degrees.

¶ And whensoeuer the Bushop shall celebrate the holye communion in the churche, or execute any other publique mynystracyon, he shall haue upon hym, besyde his rochette, a Surples or albe, and a cope or vestment, and also his pastorall staffe in his hande, or elles borne or holden by his chapeleyne.

¶ *As touching kneeling, crossing, holding up of handes, knocking upon the brest, and other gestures : they may be used or left as euery mans deuocion serueth without blame.*

¶ *Also upon Christmas day, Ester day, the Ascension daye, whit-Soonday, and the feaste of the Trinitie, may bee used anye parte of holye scripture hereafter to be certaynly limited and appoynted, in the stede of the Letany.*

¶ *If there bee a sermone, or for other greate cause, the Curate by his discrecion may leaue out the Letanye, Gloria in excelsis, the Crede, thomely, and the exhortacion to the communion.*

FINIS.

Imprinted at London in
Fletestrete, at the signe of the Sunne ouer against
the conduyte, by EdVVarde VVhitchurche.
The seuenth daye of Marche, the
yeare of our Lorde,
1549.

The Kinges Maiestie, by
the aduyse of his moste deare uncle the Lord Protector and other his highnes Counsell, streightly
chargeth and commaundeth, that no maner
of person do sell this present booke un-
bounde, aboue the price of ii. Shyllynges the piece. And the
same bounde in paste or
in boordes, not aboue
the price of three
shyllynges and
fourepence
the piece.

GOD SAUE THE KYNG.

The Forme
and maner of makyng
and consecratyng of
Archebishoppes
Bishoppes
Priestes
and
Deacons
M.D.XLIX.

This Ordinal was not printed as part of the first issues of the Prayer-Book of 1549, but as the colophons of some copies shew, it was intended to be bound up with copies of the Prayer-Book.

THE PREFACE.

Iᴛ is euident unto all men, diligently readinge holye scripture, and auncient aucthours, that frõ the Apostles tyme, there hathe bene these orders of Ministers in Christes church, Bisshoppes, Priestes, and Deacons, which Offices were euermore had in suche reuerent estimacion, that no mã by his own priuate aucthoritie, might presume to execute any of them, except he were first called, tried, examined, and knowen, to haue such equalities, as were requisite for the same. And also by publique prayer, with imposicion of handes, approued, and admitted thereunto. And therfore to the entent these orders shoulde bee continued, and reuerentlye used, and estemed in this Church of England, it is requysite, that no man (not beynge at thys presente Bisshop, Priest, nor Deacon) shall execute anye of them, excepte he be called, tryed, examined, and admitted, accordynge to the forme hereafter folowinge. And none shalbe admitted a Deacon, except he be xxi yeres of age at the least. And euery man, which is to be admitted a Priest, shalbe full xxiiii yeres olde. And euery man, which is to be consecrated a Bishop, shalbe fully thyrtie yeres of age. And the Bisshop knowinge, eyther by hymself, or by sufficient testimonye, any person to be a man of vertuous conuersacion, and wythoute cryme, and after examinacion and triall, fyndynge hym learned in the Latyne tongue, and sufficientlye instructed in holye Scripture, maye upon a Sondaye or Holyday, in the face of the church, admitte hym a Deacon in suche maner and fourme, as hereafter foloweth.

FOURME AND MANER

OF

ORDERINGE OF DEACONS.

¶ *Fyrst, when the daye appoynted by the Bisshoppe is come, there shalbe an exhortaciō, declaring the duetie and office, of suche as come to be admitted Ministers, howe necessarie suche Orders are in the Churche of Christe, and also howe the people oughte to esteme them in theyr vocacion.*

¶ *After the exhortacion ended, the Archedeacon, or his deputie, shal present such as come to be admitted to the Bisshop euery one of them, that are presented, hauing upon hym a playne Albe; and the Archedeacon or his deputie shal saye these wordes.*

REUERENDE Father in GOD, I presente unto you, these persones presente, to bee admitted Deacons.

¶ *The Bisshoppe.* Take hede that the persones whom ye presente unto us, be apte and mete, for theyr learninge and godlye conuersacion, to exercyse theyr ministerye duely, to the honoure of God, and edifyinge of hys Church.

The Archedeacon shall aunswere.

I haue enquyred of them, and also examined them, and thynke them so to be.

¶ *And then the Bisshop shal saye unto the people.*

BRETHREN, yf there bee anye of you, who knoweth anye impediment, or notable crime, in any of these persones presented to bee ordered Deacons, for the whych he oughte not to bee admitted to the same, lette hym come foorthe in the name of God, and shewe what the cryme, or impediment is.

¶ *And yf any great cryme, or impediment be obiected, the Bisshoppe shal surcease, from ordering that person, untyl suche tyme as the partie accused, shal trye himself clere of that cryme.*

Then the Bisshop, commending suche as shalbe found mete to be ordered to the prayers of the congregacion, wyth the Clerkes, and people present, shall saye or synge the Letany as foloweth wyth the prayers.

The Letanie and Suffrages.

O GOD the father of heauen : haue mercye upon us myserable synners.

O God the father of heauen : haue mercie upon us miserable synners.

O God the sonne, redemer of the world : haue mercye upon us myserable synners.

O God the Sonne, redemer of the world : haue mercy upon us miserable synners.

O God the holy Ghost, proceding from the father and the sonne : haue mercye upon us myserable synners.

O God the holy gost, proceding from the Father and the sonne : haue mercye upon us miserable synners.

O holy, blessed, and glorious Trinitie, thre persons and one God : haue mercie upon us miserable synners.

O holy, blessed, and glorious Trinitie, thre persons and one God : haue mercie upon us miserable synners.

Remembre not Lorde our offences, nor the offences of oure forefathers, neyther take thou vengeaunce of oure synnes : spare us good Lorde, spare thy people, whō thou hast redemed with thy most precious bloud, and be not angry wyth us for euer.

Spare us good Lorde.

From all euyll and mischiefe, from synne, from the craftes and assaultes of the deuyll, from thy wrath, and from euerlasting damnacion.

Good Lorde deliuer us.

Frō al blyndnes of hearte, from pryde, vayneglory, and hypocrisie, from enuie, hatred, and malice, and all uncharitablenes.

Good lord, deliuer us.

From fornicacion, and all other deadlye synne, and from all the deceyptes of the worlde, the fleshe, and the deuyll.

Good lord, deliuer us.

From lighteninges and tempestes, from plague, pestilence, and famine, from battayle and murther, and from sodeyne death.

Good lord, deliuer us.

From all sedicion and pryuie conspiracie, from the tyrannye of the Bysshop of Rome, and al hys detestable enormities, from al false doctryne and heresy, from hardnes of hearte, and contempte of thy worde and commaundement.

Good lord, deliuer us.

By the misterye of thy holy incarnacion, by thy holy natiuitie and circumcisiō, by thy baptisme, fastynge, and temptacion.

Good lord, deliuer us.

By thyne agonye and bloudie sweate, by thy crosse, and

passion, by thy precious death and buriall, by thy glorious resurrection and ascension, and by the cominge of the holy Ghost.

Good lord, deliuer us.

In al time of our tribulaciõ, in al tyme of our welth, in the houre of death, and in the daye of iudgement.

Good Lorde delyuer us.

We synners doe beseche thee to heare us (O Lorde God), and that it may please thee to rule and gouerne thy holy Church uniuersally, in the ryghte waye.

We beseche thee to heare us good Lorde.

That it may please thee, to kepe EDWARD the sixth thy seruaunt, our Kynge and gouernour.

We beseche thee to heare us good lord.

That it may please thee, to rule his heart in thy fayth feare and loue, that he may alwayes haue affiaunce in thee, and euer seke thy honour and glory.

We beseche thee to heare us good Lorde.

That it may please thee, to be his defendour and keper, geuyng hym the victorie ouer all his enemies.

We beseche thee to heare us good Lord.

That it may please thee, to illuminate al Bisshops, Pastours, and Ministers of the Churche, wyth true knowledge, and understanding of thy worde, and that both by theyr preachynge and lyuing, they may sette it forth and shewe it accordingly.

We beseche thee to heare us good Lorde.

That it may please thee, to blesse these men, and send thy grace upon them, that they maye duelye execute the offyce nowe to bee commytted unto them, to the edifyinge of thy Churche, and to thy honoure, prayse, and glorye.

We beseche thee to heare us good Lorde.

That it may please thee to endue the Lordes of the Counsayle and al the nobilitie wyth grace, wysdome, and understanding.

We beseche thee to heare us good Lord.

That it may please thee, to blesse and kepe the Magistrates, geuing them grace to execute Justice, and to maynteyne trueth.

We beseche thee to heare us good Lorde.

That it may please thee, to blesse and kepe al thy people.

We beseche thee to heare us good Lorde.

That it may please thee, to geue to al nacions, unitie, peace, and concorde.

We beseche thee to heare us good Lorde.

That it may please thee to geue us an heart, to loue and dreade thee, and dyligently to lyue after thy commaundementes.
We beseche thee to heare us good Lorde.

That it maye please thee to geue all thy people encrease of grace, to heare mekely thy woorde, and to receyue it wyth pure affection, and to brynge foorth the fruytes of the spirite.
We beseche thee to heare us good Lorde.

That it maye please thee, to bringe into the waye of trueth, al suche as haue erred, and are deceyued.
We beseche thee to heare us good Lorde.

That it may please thee, to strengthen suche as doe stande, and to comforte and helpe the weake hearted, and to rayse them up that fall, and finallye to beate downe Sathan under our feete.
We beseche thee to heare us good Lorde.

That it may please thee, to succoure, helpe and comforte, al that be in daunger, necessitie, and tribulacion.
We beseche thee to heare us good Lorde.

That it may please thee, to preserue al that trauayl by lande, or by water, al women labouringe of chylde, al sycke persons and yonge chyldren, and to shewe thy pytie upon al prysoners and captyues.
We beseche thee to heare us good lorde.

That it may please thee, to defende and prouide for the father-les chyldren and wyddowes, and all that be desolate and oppressed.
We beseche thee to heare us good lorde.

That it may please thee, to haue mercie upō al men.
We beseche thee to heare us good lorde.

That it may please thee, to forgeue oure enemyes, persecutours, and slaunderers, and to turne theyr heartes.
We beseche thee to heare us good Lorde.

That it may please thee, to geue and preserue to our use, the kyndly fruytes of the yearth, so as in due tyme we may enioye them.
We beseche thee to heare us good Lorde.

That it may please thee to geue us true repentaunce, to forgeue us all oure synnes, negligences, and ignoraunces, and to endue us wyth the grace of thy holye spirite, to amende oure lyues accordinge to thy holye worde.
We beseche thee to heare us good Lorde.

Sonne of God: we beseche thee to heare us.
Sonne of God : we beseche thee to heare us.

O Lambe of God, that takeste awaye the synnnes of the worlde.
Graunt us thy peace.

O Lambe of God, that takest awaye the synnes of the worlde.
Haue mercie upon us.

O Christe heare us.
O Christe, heare us.

Lorde haue mercy upon us.
Lorde haue mercy upon us.

Christ haue mercy upon us.
Christ haue mercy upon us.

Lorde haue mercy upon us.
Lorde haue mercy upon us.

Our father which art in heauen, etc.
And leade us not into temptacion.
But deliuer us from euill.

The Versicle. O lorde deale not with us after our sinnes.
The aunswere. Neither reward us after our iniquities.

Let us pray.

O God mercyfull father, that despyseste not the sighinge of a contryte hearte, nor the desyre of suche as be sorowfull, mercyfully assiste oure prayers that we make before thee, in all oure troubles and aduersities, whensoeuer they oppresse us: and graciously heare us, that those euyls, which the craft and subteltie of the deuyl, or man worketh agaynst us, be brought to naught, and by the prouidence of thy goodnes, they may be dispersed, that we thy seruauntes, beyng hurte by no persecutiõs, may euermore geue thankes unto thee, in thy holy Church, through Jesu Christ oure Lorde.
O Lorde aryse, help us, and delyuer us, for thy names sake.

O God, we haue heard with our eares, and oure fathers haue declared unto us, the noble workes, that thou dyddeste in their dayes, and in the olde tyme before them.
O Lorde aryse, help us, and delyuer us, for thyne honour.

Glorye be to the father, the sonne, and to the holy ghost. As it was in the begynning, is now, and euer shal be, world without ende. Amen.

From our enemies defende us, O Christ.
Graciously loke upon our afflictions.

Pitifully beholde the sorowes of our heart.
Mercifully forgeue the synnes of thy people.

Fauourably with mercy heare our prayers.
O sonne of Dauid haue mercy upon us.

Both nowe and euer vouchesafe to heare us, O Christ.
Graciously heare us, O Christe, Graciously heare us,
O Lord Christe.

¶ *The Versicle.* O Lorde let thy mercy be shewed upon us.
The Aunswere. As we do put our trust in thee.

¶ Let us praye.

WE humbly beseche thee, O father, mercyfully to looke upon oure infirmities, and for the glory of thy names sake, tourne from us all those euylles, that we moste ryghteouslye haue deserued: And graunte that in all oure troubles, we maye put oure whole trust, and confidence in thy mercye, and euermore serue thee, in holynes and purenesse of lyuinge, to thy honour and glorye, through our onely mediatour and aduocate Jesus Christ our lord. Amen.

ALMYGHTIE God, which hast geuen us grace at this tyme with one accorde, to make our cōmon supplicacions unto the, and doest promise that when two, or three be gathered in thy name, thou wilt graunt their requestes, fulfyll nowe, O Lorde, the desyres and peticions of thy seruauntes, as may be moste expediente for them, grauntynge us in thys worlde, knowledge of thy trueth, and in the worlde to come lyfe euerlastynge.   Amen.

Then shalbe sayde also thys that foloweth.

ALMYGHTIE God, whiche by thy deuyne prouidence, haste appoynted dyuerse Orders of ministers in the Churche: and dyddeste enspyre thyne holy Apostles to chose unto this Ordre of Deacons, the fyrste Martyr sainct Stephyn, wyth other: mercyfully beholde these thy seruauntes, now called to the lyke office and adminꞏistraciō; replenishe them so wyth the trueth of thy doctryne, and innocencie of lyfe, that, both by worde and good example, they may faithfully serue thee in this office, to the glory of thy name, and profyte of the congregacion, through the merites of our sauiour Jesu Christ, who lyueth and reygneth wyth thee, and the holy Ghost, nowe and euer.   Amen.

*Then shal be songe or sayd, the Communion of the daye, sauyng the Epistle
shalbe read out of Timothe, as foloweth.*

LIKEWYSE muste the ministers be honest, not double-tongued,
not geuen vnto muche wyne, neyther gredy of fylthy lucre, but
holding the mistery of the fayth, wyth a pure conscience. And
let them first be proued, and thē let them minister, so that no
man be able to reproue them. Euen so must theyr wiues be
honest, not euyll speakers, but sobre and faythfull in all thinges.
Lette the Deacons bee the husbandes of one wyfe, and suche as
rule theyr chyldren well, and theyr owne housholdes. For they
that minister well, geat themselues a good degre, and a greate
lybertie in the fayth, whych is in Christ Jesu.

These thinges wryte I vnto thee trusting to come shortely
vnto thee; but and yf I tarye longe, that then thou mayst yet
haue knowledge, howe thou oughteste to behaue thyselfe, in
the house of God, whiche is the congregacion of the lyuinge God,
the pyller and grounde of trueth. And without doubt, greate
is that misterie of Godlynesse. God was shewed in the fleshe,
was iustifyed in the spirite, was sene amonge the Angels, was
preached vnto the Gentyles, was beleued on in the worlde, and
receyued up in glory.

Or els thys out of the sixth of the Actes.

THEN the twelue called the multitude of the disciples together,
and sayde: it is not mete that we shoulde leaue the worde of
God, and serue tables. Wherefore brethren, looke ye oute
amonge you, seuen men of honest report and full of the holy
goste and wysdome, to whome we maye committe thys busynesse: but we wyll geue oureselues continually to prayer, and
to the administraciō of the word. And that saying pleased the
whole multitude. And they chose Stephin, a man ful of fayth,
and ful of the holy ghoste, and Philip, and Procorus, and
Nichanor, and Tymon, and Permenas, and Nicholas a conuert
of Antioche. These they set before the Apostles: and whē they
had prayed, they layed theyr handes on them. And the worde
of God increased, and the nombre of the Disciples multiplied in
Jerusalē greatly, and a great companie of the Priestes, were
obedient vnto the fayth.

¶ *And before the Gospel, the Bisshop sitting in a Chaire, shal cause the
Othe of the Kinges supremacie, and against the usurped power and
aucthoritie of the Bishop of Rome, to be ministred vnto euery of them
that are to be Ordred.*

¶ *The Othe of the* Kynges Supremacie.

I FRō henceforth shal utterly renoūce, refuse, relinquisshe and forsake the Bysshop of Rome, and hys aucthoritie, power, and iurisdiction. And I shal neuer consent nor agree, that the Bysshop of Rome shall practyse, exercyse, or haue any maner of aucthoritie, Jurisdiction, or Power wythin thys Realme, or anye other the Kynges dominions, but shall resyste the same at all tymes, to the uttermoste of my power. And I from hence-foorth wyll accepte, repute, and take the Kynges Maiestie, to be the onelye Supreme head in earth, of the Church of Englande: And to my connynge, wytte, and uttermoste of my power, wythoute guyle, fraude, or other undue meane, I wyll obserue, kepe, maynteyne and defende, the whole effectes and contentes, of al, and synguler actes and Statutes made, and to be made wythin thys realme in derogacion, extirpacion, and extinguish-mēt of the Bisshop of Rome and his aucthoritie, and al other Actes and Statutes, made or to be made, in confirmacion and corroboracion of the Kynges power, of the supreme head in earth, of the Church of Englande: and this I wyll do agaynst all maner of persones, of what estate, dignitie or degree, or condicion they be, and in no wise do nor attempt, nor to my power, suffre to be done or attempted, directely or indirectly, any thing or thinges, priuely or appertelye, to the let, hinder-aunce, dammage, or derogacion thereof, or any part thereof, by any maner of meanes, or for any maner of pretence. And in case any othe bee made, or hath been made by me, to any person or persones, in mayntenaunce, defence, or fauoure of the Bisshoppe of Rome, or hys aucthoritie, iurisdiction, or power, I repute the same, as vayne and adnichilate: so help me God, ali Saints and the holy Evangelist.

Then shall the Bisshop examine euery one of them that are to be ordered, in the presence of the people, after thys maner folowynge.

Do you trust that you are inwardely moued by the holy Ghoste, to take upon you thys offyce and ministracion, to serue God, for the promotinge of hys glorye, and the edyfyinge of hys people?

Aunswere. I truste so.

The Bisshop. Do ye thinke, that ye truely be called according to the wyll of our Lord Jesus Christe, and the due ordre of thys realme to the ministery of the Church?

Aunswere. I thinke so.

The Bisshop. Doe ye unfeynedly beleue all the Canonicall scriptures, of the olde and newe Testament?

Aunswere. I doe beleue.

The Bisshoppe. Will you diligētly reade the same unto the

people assembled in the Churche, where you shalbe appoynted to serue?

Aunswere. I wyll.

The Bisshoppe. It perteyneth to the office of a Deacō in the Churche where he shalbe appoynted to assiste the Prieste in deuine seruice, and speciallye when he ministreth the holye Communion, and to helpe him in distribuciō thereof, and to reade holye scriptures and Homelies in the congregacion, and to instructe the youth in the Cathechisme, to Baptise and to preache yf he be admitted therto by the Bisshop. And furthermore, it is his office where prouision is so made to searche for the sicke, poore, and impotente people of the parishe, and to intimate theyr estates, names, and places where thei dwel to the Curate, that by his exhortacion they maye bee relieued by the parishe or other conueniēt almose: wil you do this gladly and wyllingly?

Aunswere. I wyll so do by the helpe of God.

The Bisshoppe. Will you applye all youre diligence to frame and fasshion youre owne lyues, and the liues of all your familie according to the doctrine of Christ, and to make bothe your-selues and them as muche as in you lieth, wholesome examples of the flocke of Christ?

Aunswere. I wyll so do, the Lorde beyng my helper.

The Bisshoppe. Will you reuerently obeye your ordinary and other chiefe Ministers of the Church, and them to whō the gouernemente and charge is committed ouer you, folowyng wyth a gladde mynde and wyll theyr godly admonicions?

Aunswere. I wyl thus endeuor myself, the lord beyng my helper.

¶ *Then the Bishop layinge his handes seuerally upon the head of euery of them, shall saye.*

Take thou aucthoritic to execute the office of a Deacon in the Church of God committed unto thee: in the name of the father, the sonne, and the holy ghost. Amen.

Then shal the Bisshop delyuer to euery one of them the newe Testamente, sayinge.

Take thou aucthoritie to reade the Gospell in the Church of God, and to preache the same, yf thou bee thereunto ordinarely commaunded.

Then one of them appoynted by the Bisshop, shal reade the Gospel of that daye. Then shal the Bisshop procede to the Communion, and al that be ordered, shal tarye and receyue the holy Communion the same daye wyth the Bisshop. The Communion ended, after the laste Collecte and immediatly before the benedictiō, shalbe sayed this Collecte folowynge.

ALMYGHTIE God, geuer of al good thinges, which of thy great goodnes hast vouchsafed to accepte and take these thy seruauntes unto the office of Deacons in thy church: make thē we besebe thee, O Lorde, to bee modest, hūble, and constant in their ministracion, to haue a ready wyl to obserue al spiritual discipline, that they hauinge alwayes the testimonie of a good conscience, and continuing euer stable and strong in thy sonne Christ, may so wel use themselues in thys inferior offyce, that they may be found worthi to be called unto the higher ministeries in thy Church: through the same thy sonne our Sauiour Christ, to whom be glorye and honoure, worlde wythout ende. Amen.

¶ *And here it must be shewed unto the Deacon that he must continue in that office of a Deacõ, the space of a whole yeare at the least (excepte for reasonable causes, it bee otherwyse seen to his ordenarie) to thentent he may be perfecte, and wel expert in the thinges apperteyning to the Ecclesiasticall administraciõ, in executing whereof, yf he be found faithful and diligent, he may be admitted by his Diocesan to the ordre of Priesthode.*

THE FOURME

OF

ORDERING PRIESTES.

Whē the exhortacion is ended, then shall be song, for the introyte to the Com muniō, this psalme—Expectans expectavi Dominum, Psal. xl. Or els this psalme—Memento Domine Dauid, Psalm cxxxii. Or els this Psalme— Laudate nomen Domini, Psalm cxxxv.

Then shalbe read for the Epistle this out of the twentieth Chapter of the Actes of the Apostles.

FROM Mileto Paule sent messengers to Ephesus, and called the Elders of the congregacion; which when they were come to him, he sayde unto thē. Ye know, that from the first day that I came into Asia, after what maner I haue been wyth you at al seasons, seruynge the Lord wyth al humblenes of mynde, and wyth many teares and temptacions which happened unto me by the layinges awayte of the Jewes, because I would kepe backe nothinge that was profitable unto you, but to shewe you and teache you openly throughout euery house: witnessing bothe to the Jewes, and also to the Grekes, the repentaunce that is towarde God, and the fayth whiche is towarde oure Lorde Jesus. And now behold, I goe bound in the spyryte unto Jerusalem, not knowing the thinges that shall come on me there; but that the holy ghost witnesseth in euery citie, saying that bandes and trouble abyde me. But none of these thynges moue me, nether is my lyfe deare unto myselfe, that I might fulfyll my course with ioye and the ministracion of the worde whiche I haue receyued of the Lord Jesu to testifye the Gospell of the grace of God. And now behold, I am sure that henceforth ye al (through whom I haue gone preaching the kingdom of God) shall see my face no more. Wherefore I take you to recorde thys daye, that I am pure frō the bloud of all men. For I haue spared no labor, but haue shewed you all the counsayle of God. Take hede therefore unto yourselues, and to all the flocke amonge whom the holy ghost hath made you ouerseers to rule the cōgregacion of God, whiche he hathe purchased wyth hys bloud. For I am sure of this, that after my departing, shal greuous wolues entre in among you, not sparing the flocke.

Moreouer, of your owne selues shall men aryse, speaking per-uerse thinges, to drawe disciples after them. Therefore awake, and remembre that by the space of three yeares I ceassed not to warne euery one of you nyght and daye, wyth teares.

And now brethren, I commende you to God and to the woorde of his grace, whiche is able to buylde further, and to gyue you an inheritaunce among al them which are sanctified. I haue de-syred no mans syluer, golde or vesture. Yea, you knowe youre-selues, that these handes haue ministred unto my necessities, and to them that were wyth me. I haue shewed you all thynges, howe that so labouring ye oughte to receyue the weake, and to remembre the wordes of the Lorde Jesu, howe that he sayd; it is more blessed to geue than to receyue.

Or els thys thyrde Chapter, of the fyrst Epistle to Timothe.

THYS is a true sayinge; yf any man desyre the offyce of a Bisshoppe, he desyreth an honeste worke. A Bisshop therfore must be blamelesse, the husbãd of one wyfe, vigilant, sobre, discrete, a keper of hospitalitie, apte to teache, not geuẽ to ouer-much wyne, no fyghter, nor gredye of filthye lucre; but gentle, abhorring fyghting, abhorringe couetousnes; one that ruleth wel his owne house, one that hath children in subiection with al reuerence. For yf a man cannot rule hys owne house, how shall he care for the congregacion of God? He may not be a yong scholer, leste he swell, and fall into the Judgement of the euyl speaker. He must also haue a good reporte of them whiche are without; leste he fall into rebuke, and snare of the euyll speaker.

Likewise must the Ministers be honest, not double-tongued, not geuen unto muche wyne, nether gredy of filthie lucre; But holding the mistery of the fayth, with a pure consciẽce; and let them first be proued, and then let them minister so that no man be able to reproue them.

Euẽ so must their wyues be honest, not euil-speakers; but sobre and faithful in al thinges. Let the Deacons be the husbandes of one wyfe, and such as rule their chyldren wel, and theyr owne housholdes, For they that minister wel geat them-selues a good degre, and great libertie in the fayth which is in Christe Jesu.

These thinges wryte I unto thee, trusting to come shortly unto thee; but and yf I tary longe, that then thou mayst haue yet knowledge, howe thou oughtest to behaue thy self in the house of God, which is the cógregacion of the liuinge God, the Piller and ground of trueth. And without doubt, greate is that misterie of

Godlynes: God was shewed in the flesh, was Justified in the spirite, was seen among the Angelles, was Preached unto the Gentyles, was beleued on in the worlde, and receyued up in glory.

After thys shalbe read for the Gospell a pece of the laste Chapter of Mathew, as foloweth.

JESUS came and spake unto them, saying: All power is geuen unto me in heauen and in earth. Goe ye therefore and teache all nacions, baptising them in the name of the father, and of the sonne, and of the holy gost. Teachyng them to obserue all thinges, whatsoeuer I haue commaunded you. And loe, I am with you alway, euen untill the end of the worlde.

Or els this that foloweth, of the tenth Chapter of John.

VERELY, verely, I saye unto you; He that entreth not in by the dore into the sheepe folde, but climbeth up some other way, the same is a thefe and a murtherer. But he that entereth in by the doore, is the shepeheard of the shepe, to hym the Porter openeth, and the Shepe heareth hys voyce, and he calleth hys owne shepe by name, and leadeth them out. And when he hath sente forth his owne shepe, he goeth before them, and the shepe folowe hym, for they knowe his voyce. A straunger wyll they not folow, but wyll flee from hym, for they knowe not the voyce of straungers. Thys Prouerbe spake Jesus unto them, but they understoode not what thynges they were, whyche he spake unto them. Then sayde Jesus unto them agayne: verely, verely, I saye unto you, I am the doore of the shepe. All (euen as manye as come before me) are theues and murtherers: but the shepe dyd not heare them. I am the doore, by me yf any man entre in, he shall be safe, and goe in and out, and fynde pasture. A thefe cometh not but for to steale, kyll and to destroye. I am come that they myght haue lyfe, and that they myghte haue it more aboundauntlye. I am the good shepeheard: a good shepehearde geueth his lyfe for the shepe. An hired seruaunt, and he whiche is not the shepeheard (neyther the shepe are hys owne) seeth the wolfe comming, and leaueth the shepe and fleeth, and the wolfe catcheth and scattereth the shepe. The hyred seruaunt fleeth, because he is an hyred seruaunte, and careth not for the shepe. I am the good shepeherd and knowe my shepe, and am knowen of myne. As my father knoweth me, euen so know I also my father. And I geue my lyfe for the shepe, and other shepe I haue, which are not of this folde. Them also must I bring, and they shall heare my voyce, and there shall be one folde and one shepehearde.

Or els thys, of the xx. Chapter of John.

THE same daye at night, which was the fyrst daye of the Sabbothes, when the doores were shutte (where the Disciples were assembled together, for feare of the Jewes) came Jesus and stode in the middes, and sayde unto them; peace be unto you. And whē he had so sayd, he shewed unto them hys handes and his syde. Then were the disciples glad, when they sawe the Lord. Then sayd Jesus unto them agayne, peace bee unto you. As my father sent me, euen so send I you also. And when he had sayd those wordes, he breathed on them and said unto them, receyue ye the holy ghost: whosoeuers synnes ye remytte, they are remytted unto them: and whosoeuers synnes ye retayne, they are retayned.

When the Gospel is ended, then shalbe sayd or songe.

COME holy ghost eternall God procedinge from aboue,
Both from the father and the sonne, the God of peace and loue:
Vysyte oure myndes, and into us, thy heauenly grace inspyre;
That in all trueth and godlynesse, we maye haue true desyre.
Thou art the very comforter, in al wo and distresse:
The heauenly gyfte of God moste highe, whych no tongue can expresse.
The foūtayne and the liuely springe, of ioye celestiall:
The fyre so brighte, the loue so clere, and Unction spirituall.
Thou in thy gyftes arte manifolde, whereby Christes Churche doeth stande:
In faythfull heartes wrytinge thy lawe, the fynger of Goddes hande.
According to thy promes made, thou geuest speache of grace;
That throughe thy helpe, the prayse of God, may sounde in euery place.
O holy ghoste, into oure wittes, sende downe thyne heauenly lyght;
Kyndle our heartes wyth feruent loue, to serue God daye and nyght.
Strength and stablishe all oure weakenes, so feble and so frayle:
That neyther fleshe, the worlde, nor deuyl, agaynste us do preuayle.
Put backe oure enemie farre from us, and graunte us to obtayne:
Peace in our heartes with God and man, withoute grudge or disdayne.
And graunt O Lorde that thou beyng, oure leader and oure guyde;

We may eschewe the snares of synne, and from thee neuer slyde.
To us such plentie of thy grace, good Lord graunt we thee praye:
That thou mayest bee oure comforter, at the laste dreadfull daye.
Of all stryfe and dissencion, O Lorde, dissolue the bandes:
And make the knottes of peace and loue, throughoute all
    Christien landes.
Graunte us O Lorde, throughe thee to knowe the father most of
    myght;
That of hys deare beloued sonne we may attayne the syght.
And that wyth perfect fayth also, we may acknowledge thee;
The Spirite of them both alwaye, one God in persones three.
Laude and prayse be to the father, and to the sonne equall:
And to the holy spyryte also, one God coeternall.
And praye we that the onely sonne, vouchesafe hys spyryte to
    sende;
To all that do professe hys name, unto the worldes ende.   Amen.

*And then the Archedeacon shall present unto the Bisshop, all them that shall
    receyue the order of Priesthode that daye, euery of them hauing upon hym
    a playne Albe—The Archedeacon sayinge.*

REUERENDE Father in GOD, I presente unto you, these
persones presente, to bee admitted to the ordre of Priesthode,
Cum interrogatione et responsione, ut in ordine Diaconatus.

And then the Bisshop shal saye to the people.

GOOD people, these bee they whome we purpose God wyllyng,
to receyue this daye, unto the holye offyce of Priesthode. For
after due examinacion, we fynd not the contrary but that they
be lawfully called to theyr functiō and ministery, and that they
be persones mete for the same: but yet yf there be any of you
whyche knoweth any impediment, or notable cryme in any of
thē, for the whyche he oughte not to bee receyued into this holy
ministery, nowe in the name of God declare the same.

¶ *And yf any great cryme or impediment be obiected, &c.* Ut supra in
    Ordine Diaconatus usque ad finem Litanie cum hac Collecta.

ALMYGHTIE GOD, geuer of all good thinges, which by thy holy
spirit has appoynted dyuerse orders of Ministers in thy church,
mercifully behold these thy seruātes, now called to the Office of
Priesthode, and replenish thē so wyth the trueth of thy doctryne,
and innocencie of lyfe, that both by worde and good example,
they may faythfully serue thee in thys office, to the glorye of thy
name, and profyte of the congregacion, through the merites of
oure sauiour Jesu Christ, who lyueth and reygneth, wyth thee
and the holy Ghoste, worlde wythout ende.   Amen.

¶ *Then the Bisshop shal minister unto euery of them the othe, concernıng the Kinges Supremacie, as it is set oute in the ordre of Deacons. And that done, he shall saye unto them, which are appoynted to receyue the sayde Office, as hereafter foloweth.*

You haue hearde brethren, as well in youre priuate examinacion, as in the exhortaciō, and in the holy lessons taken out of the Gospel, and of the writinges of the Apostles, of what dignitie, and of how great importaunce thys offyce is, (whereunto ye be called). And nowe we exhorte you, in the name of oure LORDE Jesus Christe, to haue in remembraunce, into howe hyghe a dignitie, and to howe chargeable an offyce ye bee called, that is to saye, to be the messengers, the watchemen, the Pastours, and the stewardes of the LORDE to teache to premonisshe, to feede, and prouyde for the Lordes famylye: to seeke for Christes shepe that be dispersed abrode, and for hys children whiche bee in the myddest of thys naughtye worlde, to be saued through Christe for euer. Haue alwayes therfore printed in your remembraunce, howe great a treasure is committed to your charge, for they be the shepe of Chryste, whiche he boughte with hys death, and for whom he shed his bloud. The churche and congregacion whom you must serue, is his spouse and his body. And if it shall chaunce the same churche, or any membre therof, to take any hurt or hinderaūce, by reason of youre negligence, ye knowe the greatnesse of the faulte, and also of the horrible punishment which will ensue. Wherfore, consider with yourselues the end of your ministery, towardes the chyldren of God, towarde the spouse and body of Christ, and see that ye neuer cease your laboure, your care and dilygence, untill you haue doen all that lieth in you, accordynge to your bounden dutie, to bryng all suche as are, or shalbe commytted to youre charge, unto that agremente in faith, and knowledge of God, and to that ripenes, and perfectnesse of age in Christe, that there be no place left emong them, either for errour in Religion, or for viciousnesse in lyfe.

Then, forasmuche as your office is both of so greate excellencye, and of so great difficultie, ye se with howe greate care and study ye oughte to apply yourselues, as well that you maye shewe yourselues kinde to that Lorde, who hath placed you in so high a dignitie, as also to beware, that neyther you yourselues offende, neither be occasion that other offende. Howbeit, ye cannot haue a mynde and a wyll thereto of yourselues, for that power and abilitie is geuen of God alone. Therfore ye se how ye ought and haue nede earnestly to praye for hys holy spirit. And seyng that ye cannot by any other meanes compasse the doyng

of so weightie a woorke perteining to the saluacion of man, but
with doctryne and exhortacion, taken out of holy scripture and
with a life agreable unto the same. Ye perceyue how studyous
ye oughte to be in readyng and learnyng the holy scriptures,
and in framyng the maners, both of yourselues, and of them that
specially partein unto you, accordyng to the rule of the same
scriptures. And for this selfesame cause, ye see how you oughte
to forsake and set aside (as much as you maye) all worldly cares
and studyes.

We haue a good hope, that you haue well weighed and pondred
these thynges with yourselues, long before thys tyme, and that
you haue clerely determyned, by goddes grace, to geue yourselues
wholy to this vocacyon, wherunto it hath pleased God to call
you, so that (as muche as lieth in you) you apply youreselues
wholy to this one thing, and drawe al your cares and studies this
way, and to thys ende. And that you wyll continually praye
for the heauenly assistaunce of the holy goste, from God the
father, by the mediacion of our only mediatour and sauiour Jesus
Chryste, that by dayly readyng and weighing of the scriptures,
ye may waxe riper and stronger in your ministerie. And that
ye may so endeuour yourselfes from time to time to sanctifie the
liues of you and yours, and to fashion them after the rule and
doctrine of Christ. And that ye maye be wholesome and godly
examples and paternes, for the reste of the congregacyon to folowe.
And that this present congregaciō of Christ here assembled, may
also understande youre myndes and wylles, in these thynges:
And that this your promes, shall more moue you to doe your
dueties, ye shal answer plainly to these thinges, whiche we in
the name of the congregacyon shal demaunde of you, touchyng
the same

Doe you thynke in your heart, that you be truly called accordyng to the will of our Lorde Jesus Chyrste, and the ordre of this
Churche of Englande, to the ministerie of Priesthode?

Aunswere. I thinke it.

The Bishoppe. Be you perswaded that the holy Scriptures
cōtein sufficiently al doctrine required of necessitie for eternal
saluacion, throughe the saied faith in Jesu Christe? And are you determined with the saied scriptures, to enstructe the people cōmitted
to your charge, and to teache nothyng, as required of necessitie,
to eternal saluacion, but that you shalbe perswaded may be concluded, and proued by the scripture?

Aunswere. I am so perswaded, and haue so determyned by
Gods grace.

The Bishoppe. Will you then geue your faythfull dylygence alwayes, so to mynister the doctryne and Sacramentes, and the discipline of Christ, as the lord hath commaunded, and as thys realme hath receiued the same, accordyng to the commaunde- mentes of God, so that you may teache the people committed to youre cure and charge, with al diligence to kepe and obserue the same?

Aunswere. I wil so doe, by the helpe of the Lord.

The Bishoppe. Wil you be ready with al faithful diligence, to banishe and driue away al erronious and straunge doctrines, con- trarye to gods worde, and to use both publyke and priuate monycyons and exhortacyons, as well to the sicke as to the whole, within youre cures, as nede shall require and occasion be geuen?

Aunswere. I wyll, the Lorde beyng my helper.

The Bisshoppe. Wil you be diligent in praiers, and in reading of the holy scriptures, and in such studies as help to the know- ledge of the same, laying aside the study of the world and the fleshe?

Aunswere. I wyll endeuour myself so to doe, the Lord beyng my helper.

The Bisshoppe. Wil you be diligent to frame and fashion youre own selues, and your families, according to the doctrine of Christe, and to make bothe youreselues and them (as muche as in you lieth) wholsome examples and spectacles to the flocke of Chryst?

Aunswere. I wyll so apply myselfe, the lorde beyng my helper.

The Bisshoppe. Wil you maintein and set forwardes (as much as lieth in you) quietnes, peace, and loue emonges al christian people, and specially emong them that are, or sha be committed to your charge?

Aunswere. I will so do, the Lorde being my helper.

The Bisshoppe. Will you reuerentlye obeye your Ordinarie, and other chiefe ministers, unto whom the gouernement and charge is commytted ouer you, folowing with a glad mynde and will, their godly admonicion, and submyttyng youreselues to theyr godlye iudgementes?

Aunswere. I wyll so doe, the Lorde beyng my helper.

¶ *Then shal the Bisshoppe saye.*

ALMIGHTIE god, who hath geuen you this wyl to doe al these thynges, graunt also unto you strength and power to performe the same, that he may accomplishe his worke which he hath begon in you, until the tyme he shal come at the latter day, to iudge the quicke and the dead.

¶ *After this, the congregaciō shalbe desired, secretly in their praiers, to make humble supplicacions to God for the foresaied thinges ; for the whiche praiers, there shalbe a certaine space kept in silence.*

That doen, the Bisshoppe shall praye in this wyse.

THE Lorde be with you.
Aunswere. And with thy spirite.

¶ Let us praye.

ALMIGHTIE god and heauenly father, which of thy infinite loue and goodnes towardes us, hast geuen to us thy onely and moste deare beloued sonne Jesus Christe, to be our redemer and aucthour of euerlasting life: who after he had made perfecte our redempcion by hys death, and was ascended into heauen, sent abrode into the worlde hys Apostles, Prophetes, Euangelistes, Doctours and Pastours, by whose labour and minister e, he gathered together a greate flocke in al the partes of the worlde, to set furth the eternal praise of thy holy name.   For these so greate benefites of thy eternal goodnes, and for that thou hast vouchsafed to cal these thy seruauntes here present, to the same office and ministerie of the saluacion of mankynde; we render unto thee moste hartie thankes, we worship and praise thee, and we humbly beseche thee by the same thy sonne, to graunt unto al us which either here, or elswhere cal upon thy name, that we maye shewe ourselues thankefull to thee for these and all other thy benefites, and that we maye daily encrease and goe forwardes, in the knowledge and faith of thee, and thy sonne, by the holy spirite.   So that as well by these thy ministers, as by them to whom thei shalbe appointed ministers, thy holy name may be alwaies glorified, and thy blessed kyngdom enlarged, throughe the same thy sonne our Lorde Jesus Christe; which liueth and reigneth with thee, in the unitie of the same holy spirite, world without ende.   Amen.

¶ *When this praier is done, the Bisshoppe with the priestes present, shal lay theyr handes seuerally upon the head of euery one that receiueth orders. The receiuers humbly knelyng upon their knees, and the Bisshop saying.*

RECEIUE the holy goste, whose synnes thou doest forgeue, they are forgeuen: and whose sinnes thou doest retaine, thei are retained: and be thou a faithful despensor of the word of god, and of his holy Sacramentes.   In the name of the father, and of the sonne, and of the holy gost.   Amen.

The Bisshop shall deliuer to euery one of them, the Bible in the one hande, and the Chalice or cuppe with the breade, in the other hande, and saying.

TAKE thou aucthoritie to preache the word of god, and to minister the holy Sacramentes in thys congregacion, where thou shalt be so appointed.

¶ *When thys is doen, the Congregacyon shall syng the Crede, and also they shal goe to the Communion which al they that receiue orders shal take together, and remaine in the same place where the handes were layd upon the̅, untyl suche time as thei haue receiued the Communion.*

¶ *The Communion beyng doen, after the last Collecte, and immediatly before the benediccion, shalbe sayed thys Collecte.*

MOST mercifull father, we beseche thee so to sende upon these thy seruauntes thy heauenly blessyng, that they maye be cladde about with all iustice, and that thy worde spoken by theyr mouthes may haue such successe, that it may neuer be spoken in vain. Graunt also that we may haue grace to heare, and receiue the same as thy moste holy worde and the meane of our saluacion, that in all our wordes and dedes we may seke thy glory, and the encrease of thy kingdom, thorow Jesus Christ our lord.   Amen.

¶ *If the orders of Deacon and Priesthood, be geuen both upon one day, then shal the Psalme for the Introyte and other thinges at the holy Communion, be used as they are appointed at the orderyng of Priestes. Sauing that for the Epistle, the whole thirde Chapiter of the first to Timothe shalbe read, as it is sette out before in the order of Priestes. And immediatly after the Epistle, the Deacons shalbe ordered. And it shall suffice, the Letany to be sayed once.*

THE FOURME OF CONSECRATING

ARCHEBISSHOPPE OR BISSHOPPE.

The Psalme for the Introyte at the Communion, as at the orderyng of Priestes.

The Epistle. 1 Tim. iii.

THIS is a true saying, if a man desire the office of a Bisshoppe, he desireth an honest woorke. A Bishoppe therefore muste bee blamelesse, the husbande of one wyfe, dilygent, sober, discrete, a keper of hospitalitie, apte to teache, not geuen to ouermuche wyne, no fyghter, not gredy of filthy lucre, but gentle, abhorring fightynge, abhorrynge couetousnesse, one that ruleth wel his own house, one that hath children in subieccion with al reuerence. For if a mā cannot rule his own house, howe shal he care for the congregacion of God? He may not be a yong scholer, lest he swel and fal into the iudgemente of the euil speaker. He must also haue a good report of them whiche are without, leste he fall into rebuke and snare of the euil speaker.

The Gospell. John xxi.

JESUS saied to Symon Peter, Symon Johanna, loueste thou me more than these? He said unto him, yea, lorde, thou knowest that I loue thee: he said unto him, fede my lambes. He said to him againe the seconde time: Simon Johanna, louest thou me? He saied unto him, yea lorde, thou knowest that I loue thee: he saied unto him, feede my shepe. He said unto him the thirde time; Simō Johanna, louest thou me? Peter was sory, because he said unto hym the third time, louest thou me, and he said unto him: lord thou knowest al thinges, thou knowest that I loue thee. Jesus said unto hym, fede my shepe.

¶ *Or els out of the tenth Chapiter of John, as before in thorder of Priestes.*

¶ *After the gospel and Credo ended, firste the elected Bisshoppe hauyng upon hym a Surples and Cope shall bee presented by two Bisshoppes (beeyng also in surplesses and copes, and hauing theyr pastorall staues in their handes) unto the Archebisshoppe of that Prouince, or to some other Bysshoppe appoynted by his commission : The Bisshoppes that present hym saying.*

MOST reuerend father in god, we presente unto you this godly and wel learned man to be consecrated Bisshoppe.

¶ *And then the Kynges mandate to the Archebisshoppe for the consecracion shalbe read. And the othe touching the knowledging of the kinges supremacie, shalbe ministred to the person elected, as it is set oute in the Order of Deacons. And then shalbe ministred also, the othe of due obedience unto the Archebisshoppe, as foloweth.*

¶ THE OTHE OF DUE OBE-
dience to the Archebisshoppe.

IN the name of GOD, Amen.   I, *N.* chosen Bisshoppe of the Churche and sie of *N.* doe professe and promesse, al due reuerence and obedience to the Archebisshoppe, and to the Metropoliticall churche of *N.* and to their successours: so helpe me God, and his holy gospell.

¶ *Then the Archebisshoppe shal moue the congregacion present to praye; saying thus to them.*

BRETHREN, it is written in the gospel of saincte Luke, that our sauioure Christe continued the whole night in praier, or euer that he did chose and sende furth his xii. Apostles.   It is written also in the Actes of the Apostles, that the disciples whiche were at Antioche did fast and pray, or euer they layed handes upon, or sent furth Paul and Barnabas.   Let us therefore, folowyng the example of oure sauioure Christ and his Apostles, first fal to prayer, or that we admit and send furth thys person presented unto us, to the worke wherunto we truste the holy goste hath called hym.

¶ *And then shalbe saied the Letany, as afore in the order of Deacons, And after this place: That it may please the to illuminate al Bisshoppes. &c. he shal saye.*

THAT it maye please thee to blesse this our brother elected, and to sende thy grace upon him, they he may duely execute the office wherunto he is called, to the edifying of thy Churche, and to the honour, prayse and glory of thy name.

Aunswere. We beseche thee to heare us good Lorde.

Concluding the Letanye in thende, with this prayer.

ALMIGHTIE God, geuer of all good thynges, which by thy holy spirite hast appointed diuerse orders of ministers in thy Church: mercifully beholde this thy seruaunt, now called to the worke and ministerie of a Bisshoppe, and replenishe him so with the trueth of thy doctryne, and innocencie of life, that both by worde and dede, he may faithfully serue thee in this office, to the glorye of thy name, and profite of thy congregacyon: Through the merites of our sauioure Jesu Christe, who lyueth and reigneth with thee and the holy gost, worlde without ende.   Amen.

Then the Archebisshoppe sittyng in a chaire, shall saye this to hym that is to be consecrated.

BROTHER, forasmuche as holy scripture and the olde Canons commaundeth, that we should not be hastie in laying on handes and admyttynge of any person to the gouernement of the congregacion of Christe, whiche he hath purchased with no lesse price than the effusion of hys owne bloud; afore that I admit you to this administracion wherunto ye are called, I wil examyne you in certaine articles, to thende the congregacion present, may haue a trial and beare witnes how ye be minded to behaue yourself in the churche of god.

Are you perswaded that you be truely called to thys ministracion according to the will of oure Lorde Jesus Christ, and the order of this realme?

Aunswere. I am so perswaded.

The Archebisshoppe. Are you perswaded that the holy Scriptures conteine sufficiently all doctryne, requyred of necessitie for eternall saluacyon, through the faith in Jesu Christe? And are you determyned with the same holy scriptures, to enstruct the people committed to your charge, and to teache or maintein nothyng, as required of necessitie to eternall saluacion, but that you shall bee perswaded may be concluded, and proued by the same?

Aunswere. I am so perswaded and determined by gods grace.

The Archebisshoppe. Wil you then faithfully exercise yourselfe in the said holy scriptures, and call upon god by prayer for the true understanding of the same, so as ye may be able by them to teache and exhorte with wholesome doctrine, and to withstande and conuince the gainsaiers?

Aunswere. I wyll so doe, by the helpe of God.

The Archebisshoppe. Be you ready with al faithful diligence, to banishe and driue away al erronious and straunge doctryne, contrary to god's worde, and both priuately and openly to call upon, and encourage other to the same?

Aunswere. I am ready, the lord beyng my helper.

The Archebisshoppe. Wil you deny al ungodlinesse and worldly lustes, and liue soberly, ryghteouslye, and godly in thys world, that you may shewe yourself in all thinges an example of good workes unto other, that the aduersary maye be ashamed, hauynge nothing to lay agaynst you?

Aunswere. I wyll so doe, the lorde beyng my helper.

The Archebisshoppe. Wil you maintain and set forward (as muche as shal lie in you) quietnesse, peace, and loue, emonge al men? And suche as be unquiete, disobedyente, and criminous within your Diocesse, correcte and punishe, accordyng to suche aucthoritie, as ye haue by gods worde, and as to you shalbe committed, by the ordinaunce of thys realme?

Aunswere. I wyll so doe by the helpe of god.

The Archebisshoppe. Wil you shewe yourself gentle, and be mercifull for Christes sake to poore and nedy people, and to all straungers destitute of helpe?

Aunswere. I wyll so shewe myselfe by gods helpe.

The Archebisshoppe. Almightie God oure heauenly father, who hath geuē you a good wil to doe all these thinges, graūt also unto you, strengthe and power to performe the same, that he accomplishing in you, the good worke which he hath begon, ye may be found perfecte, and irreprehensible at the latter day, through Jesu Chryst our Lord. Amen.

Then shal be song or sayd, Cum holy gost, *&c. as it is set out in the Order of Priestes.*

That ended, the Archebisshoppe shall saye.

THE Lord be with you.

Aunswere. And with thy spirite.

¶ Let us praye.

ALMIGHTIE God and moste mercyfull father, which of thy infinite goodnesse haste geuen to us thy only and most dere beloued sonne Jesus Chryst, to be our redemer and aucthour of euerlasting life; who after that he had made perfecte our redempcion by his deathe, and was ascended into heauen, powred downe his gyftes aboundauntly upon men, making some Apostles, some Prophetes, some Euangelistes, some Pastours and doctours, to the edifying and makyng perfecte of his congregacion: graunt we beseche the, to this thy seruaūt suche grace, that he may be euermore ready to spreade abrode thy gospell, and glad tidinges of reconcilement to God, and to use the aucthoritie geuen unto him, not to destroie, but to saue, not to hurt, but to helpe: so that he as a wise and a faithfull seruaunt, geuing to thy family meate in due season, may at the last daye be receiued into ioye, through Jesu Christ our lorde, who with thee, and the holy goste liueth and reigneth one God, world without ende. Amen.

Then the Archebisshoppe and Bisshoppes present, shal lay their handes upon the head of the elect Bisshop, the Archebisshoppe saying.

TAKE the holy gost, and remember that thou stirre up the grace of god, whiche is in thee, by imposicion of handes: for god hath not geuen us the spirite of feare, but of power, and loue, and of sobernesse.

Then the Archebisshoppe shal lay the Bible upon hys necke, saying.

GEUE hede unto reading, exhortacion and doctrine. Thinke upon these thinges conteined in this boke, be diligent in them, that the encrease comyng therby, may be manyfest unto all men. Take hede unto thyselfe, and unto teaching, and be diligent in doing them, for by doing this thou shalt saue thyselfe, and them that heare thee: through Jesus Christe our Lorde.

Then shal the Archebisshoppe putte into his hande the pastorall staffe, saying.

BE to the flocke of Christ a shepeheard, not a wolfe: feede them, deuoure them not; holde up the weake, heale the sicke, binde together the broken, bryng againe the outcastes, seke the lost. Be so mercifull, that you be not to remisse, so minister discipline, that ye forgeat not mercy; that whē the chief shepheard shal come, ye may receyue the immarcessible croune of glory, through Jesus Christ our lord. Amen.

¶ *Then the Archebisshoppe shal procede to the Communion, with whom the newe consecrated Bysshopp shal also communicate. And after the laste Collecte, immediatlye afore the benediccyon, shall bee sayed thys prayer :*

MOST merciful father, we beseche thee to send down upon this thy seruaunt, thy heauenly blessynge, and so endue hym with thy holy spirite, that he preaching thy worde, may not only be earneste to reproue, beseche, and rebuke with al pacience and doctryne, but also may be to such as beleue, an wholesome example in worde, in conuersacion, in loue, in faith, in chastitie, and puritie, that faythfully fulfilling his course, at the latter day he may receiue the croune of righteousnesse, laied up by the Lord, the righteous iudge, who liueth and reigneth, one god with the father and holy gost, worlde withoute ende. Amen.

THE BOKE OF
COMMON PRAYER AND AD-
MINISTRACION OF THE
SACRAMENTES,
AND OTHER
RITES
AND CEREMONIES IN
THE CHURCHE OF
ENGLAND.

Londini, in Officina
Edvvardi Whytchurche.
Cum privilegio ad imprimendum solum.
Anno 1552.

THE CONTENTS OF THIS BOOK.

THE PREFACE

[In several copies the Act of Uniformity is printed before this Preface]

THERE was neuer anye thynge by the wytte of man so wel deuised, or so sure established, whiche (in continuance of tyme) hath not been corrupted: as (emong other thynges) it may playnlye appeare by the common prayers in the Churche commonlye called diuine seruyce: the firste originall and grounde whereof yf a manne woulde searche out by auncient fathers, he shall fynde that the same was not ordayned but of a good purpose, and for a great aduancemente of godlynesse. For they so ordered the matter, that all the whole Bible (or the greatest part thereof) shoulde be readde ouer once in the yeare entendynge thereby, that the clergie and speciallye suche as were ministers of the congregacion, should (by often readynge and meditacion of Godde's woorde) be stirred up to godlynesse themselues, and be more able also to exhorte other by wholesome doctrine, and to confute them that were aduersaries to the trueth. And further, that the people (by dayly hearynge of holye scripture read in the Churche) should continuallye profyte more and more in the knowledge of God, and be the more inflamed with the loue of hys true religion. But these manye yeres passed, this godly and decent order of the auncient fathers hath been so altered, broken, and neglected, by plantinge in uncertayn Stories, Legendes, Respondes, Verses, vayne repeticions, Commemoracions, and Sinodalles, that commonlye when anye boke of the Bible was begonne, before three or foure Chapters were read out, al the rest were unread. And in thys sorte the boke of Esay was begonne in Aduent, and the boke of Genesis in Septuagesima: but they were onely begonne, and never read through. After a lyke sorte were other bokes of holy scripture used. And moreouer, where as Sainct Paule woulde haue such language spoken to the people in the Churche, as thei might understande, and haue profite by hearing the same; the seruice in this Churche of Englande (these manye yeres) hath been read in Latyn to the people, whiche they understode not: so that they haue heard with their eares onely; and their heartes, spirite, and mynde, haue not been edified thereby.

And furthermore, notwithstandynge that the auncient fathers haue diuided the Psalmes into seuen porcions, whereof euerye one was called a Nocturne; nowe of late tyme, a fewe of them haue been dayly sayd (and ofte repeated) and the rest utterlye omitted. Moreover, the numbre and hardnesse of the rules, called the Pie, and the manyfolde chaungynges of the seruyce, was the cause, that to tourne the boke onely was so harde and intricate a matter, that manye tymes there was more busynesse to fynde out what shoulde be read, then to reade it when it was founde out.

These inconueniences therefore consydered, here is set furthe suche an order, whereby the same shalbe redressed. And for a redynesse in thys matter, here is drawen out a kalendar for that purpose, whiche is playne and easye to be understanden: wherin (so muche as may be) the readynge of holye scriptures is so set furthe, that all thynges shalbe doen in order, without breakynge one pyece thereof from another. For thys cause be cut of Anthemes, Respondes, Inuitatories, and suche lyke thynges, as dyd breake the continuall course of the readynge of the scripture. Yet because there is no remedye, but that of necessitie there must be some rules, therefore certayn rules are here sette furth, whiche as they be fewe in numbre, so they be playn and easie to be understanden. So that here you haue an order for prayer (as touchynge the readynge of holye scripture) muche agreable to the mynde and purpose of thold fathers, and a great deale more profitable and commodious, then that which of late was used. It is more profitable, because here are lefte out manye thynges, where of some be untrue, some uncertayn, some vayne and supersticious, and is ordeined nothynge to be read, but the very pure worde of God, the holye scriptures, or that which is euidentlye grounded upon the same, and that in such a language and order, as is most easy and playne for the understandynge bothe of the readers and hearers. It is also more commodious, bothe for the shortness thereof, and for the playnnesse of the order, and for that the rules be fewe and easye. Furthermore, by thys order, the curates shall nede none other bokes for their publyke seruice, but thys boke, and the Bible: By the meanse whereof, the people shall not be at so greate charge for bokes, as in tyme paste they haue been.

And where heretofore there hath been great diuersitie in sayeng and syngyng in Churches within this realme, some folowynge Salisbury use, some of Herford use, some the use of Bangor, some of Yorke, and some of Lincolne. Nowe from hence furthe, all the whole realme shall haue but one use. And yf any woulde judge thys way more painfull, because that all thynges muste be read upon the booke where as before by the reason of so often repeticion, they could saye many thynges by heart; yf those men wyl weygh their laboure, with the profyte and knowledge, which dayly they shal obtayne by readyng upon the boke, they wyl not refuse the payne, in cõsideracion of the great profite that shal ensue therof.

And for asmuche as nothynge can almoste be so playnly set furthe, but doubtes may ryse in the use and practisynge of the same: To appease all suche diuersitie (yf any aryse), and for the resolucion of all doubtes concernynge the maner howe to understande doe and execute the thynges conteyned in this boke: the partes that so doubt, or diuersly take any thyng, shall alway resorte to the Byshoppe of the Diocesse, who by hys discrecion shall take order for the quietynge and appeasyng of the same: so that the same order be not contrarye to anye thynge conteyned in thys boke. And yf the Byshoppe of the Diocesse be in anye doubte, then maye he sende for the resolution thereof unto the Archebyshoppe.

Though it be appoynted in the afore wrytten Preface, that all thynges shalbe read and songe in the Churche in the Englyshe tongue, to the ende that the congregacion maye be thereby edified: yet it is not ment, but when menne say Mornyng and Euenynge prayer priuatly, they may saie the same in anye language that they themselues do understande.

And all Priestes and Deacons shalbe bounde to say dayly the Mornynge and Euenyng prayer, either priuatly or openly, excepte they be letted by preaching, studeing of diuinityie, or by some other urgent cause.

And the Curate that ministreth in every Parish Churche or Chapell, beyng at home, and not beyng otherwise reasonably letted, shall say the same in the Parishe Churche or Chapell where he ministreth, and shall tolle a belle thereto, a convenient tyme before he begyn, that suche as be disposed maye come to heare Goddes worde, and to praie with hym.

OF CEREMONIES,

OF suche ceremonies as be used in the church, and haue had their beginning by ye institutiō of man: some at the first were of Godly entent and purpose deuised, and yet at length turned to vanitie and superstitiō: some entred into the church by undiscrete deuotiō, and such a zeale as was without knowledge: and for because thei were winked at in the beginning, thei grewe daily to more and more abuses: whiche not onely for their unprofitablenesse, but also because thei haue much blinded the people, and obscured the glory of God, are worthy to be cut awaie, and clene reiected. Other there be, which although thei haue been deuised by man, yet it is thought good to reserue them still, aswel for a decent order in the churche (for the whiche thei were first deuised) as because thei pertein to edification: whereunto all thynges doen in the churche (as the Apostle teacheth) ought to be referred. And although the kepyng or omittyng of a ceremonie (in it self considered) is but a small thynge: yet the wilful and contempteous transgression, and breakynge of a common order and discipline, is no small offence before God.

Let al thynges be doen emonge you (saith S. Paule) in a semely and due order. The appointmēt of the which order, perteineth not to priuate men: therefore no man ought to take in hand, nor presume to appoynt or alter any publique or common order in Christes church, except he be lawfully called and authorized thereunto.

And whereas as in this our tyme, the mindes of menne are so diuerse, that some thynke it a greate matter of conscience to departe from a pece of the least of their Ceremonies (thei be so addicted to their old customs:) and again on the other side, some be so new fāgled, that thei would innouate all thyng, and so do despise the old, that nothyng can like them, but that is new: it was thought expediēt, not so much to haue respect how to please and satisfie either of these parties, as how to please God, and profyte them both. And yet lest any man should be offēded (whom good reasone might satisfie) here be certain causes rēdred why some of the accustomed Ceremonies be put away, and some retayned and kept styll.

Some are put away, because the great excess and multitude of thē hath so encreased in these latter daies, that the burthen of them was intolerable: whereof S. Augustine in his tyme complayned, that they were growen to such a numbre, that the state of Christian-people was in worse case (concernyng that matter) then were the Jewes. And he counsayled yt such yoke and burthē should be taken away, as tyme woulde serue quietly to doe it.

But what would S. Augustine haue sayed, if he had seen the ceremonies of late daies used among us? whereunto the multitude used in his time was not to be compared. This oure excessiue multitude of Ceremonies was so great, and many of them so darke: that they did more confounde and darken, then declare and set furth Christes benefites unto us.

And besides thys, Christes Gospell is not a Ceremonial lawe (as much of Moses lawe was) but it is a religion to serue God, not in bondage of the figure or shadowe but in the fredome of spirite beynge content only with those Ceremonies, which do serue to a decent ordre and godly discipline, and such as be apte to stirre up the dull mynde of man, to the remembraunce of his duety to God, by some not able and speciall significacion, whereby he myght be edified.

Furthermore, the most weightie cause of thabolishemēt of certayn Ceremonies was, that thei were so farre abused, partly by the supersticious blyndnes of the rude and unlearned, and partly by the unsaciable auarice of suche as sought more their owne lucre, then the glory of God; that the abuses could not well be taken away, the thing remayning stil. But now as cōcerning those persones, which peraduenture wylbe offended, for that some of thold ceremonies are reteyned styl: if they cōsider, that without some Ceremonies it is not possible to kepe any ordre or quiete discipline in the churche, they shal easely perceyue iust cause to reforme their judgemētes. And yf thei thinke much that any of thold do remain, and would rather have all deuised anewe. Then suche men graunting some ceremonies conueniēt to be had, surely where the old may be well used, there thei cannot reasonably reproue the old only for their age without bewraying of their owne foly. For in suche a case, they ought rather to have reuerēce unto them for their antiquitie, if they wyl declare themselves to be more studious of unitie and concord, then of innouacions and newe fanglenes, which (asmuche as may be with the true setting furth of Christes Religion) is alwayes to be eschewed.   Furthermore, such shall haue no just cause with the ceremonies reserued to be offended: For as those be taken away, which were moste abused, and dyd burthen men's consciences without any cause: so the other that remain are retayned for a Discipline and order, whiche (upon just causes) may be altered and chaunged, and therefore are not to be estemed equal with god's law.   And moreouer they be neither darke nor dombe ceremonies: but are so sette forth, that euery man may understand what they doe mean, and to what use thei do serve.   So that it is not like that thei in time to come, should be abused as the other haue been.   And in these our doinges, we condemne no other nacions, nor prescribe any thing, but to our owne people only.   For we think it côuenient that every country should use such ceremonies, as they shal think best to the settyng furth of Goddes honour or glory, and to the reducyng of the people to a most perfecte and godly lyuyng, without errour or Supersticion.   And that they shoulde put awaye other thynges, whiche from tyme to tyme they perceyue to be moste abused, as in mennes ordinances it often chaunceth diuersely in diuerse countreyes.

THE TABLE AND KALENDAR

EXPRESSYNGE THE ORDRE OF THE PSALMES AND LESSONS,
TO BE SAYED AT THE MORNYNG AND EUENING PRAIER
THROUGHOUT THE YERE, EXCEPTE CERTAYN PROPER
FEASTES, AS THE RULES FOLLOWYNGE
MORE PLAINLYE DECLARE.

THE ORDER HOWE THE PSALTER IS APPOYNTED TO BE READDE.

THE Psalter shalbe readde through once euery Moneth. And because that some Monethes be longer than some other be, it is thought good to make them euen by thys meanes.

To everye Moneth shalbe appoynted (as concernynge thys purpose) just xxx dayes.

And because January and Marche hath one daie aboue the sayed numbre, and February whiche is placed betwene them bothe hath onely xxviii days: February shal borowe of either of the Monethes (of January and Marche) one daye. And so the Psalter which shalbe readde in February, muste begyn the last daye of January, and ende the first daye of Marche.

And where as May, July, August, October and December, have xxxi days a piece, it is ordered that the same Psalms shalbe read the laste daye of the sayed Monethes, whiche were reade the daye before. So that the Psalter may begyn agayn the fyrst day of the nexte Monethes ensuynge.

Nowe to know whate Psalms shalbe read euerye daye, loke in the Kalendar, the numbre that is appointed for the Psalmes, and then finde the same numbre in thys table, and upon that numbre shal you see, what Psalmes shalbe sayed at Mornyng and Euenyng prayer.

And where the cxix Psalme is diuided into xxii porcions, and is ouerlonge to be read at one tyme: it is so ordered, that at one tyme shall not be read aboue foure or fyve of the sayed porcions, as you shall perceyue to be noted in thys Table folowyng.

And here is also to be noted, that in thys table, and in all other partes of the Seruyce, where anye Psalmes are appoynted, the numbre is expressed after the great Englyshe Bible, which from the ix Psalme unto the cxlviiithe Psalm (folowyng the division of the Hebrues) doth varie in numbres from the common Latyn translacion.

327

THE TABLE

For the Order of the Psalms, to be sayed at Mornyng and Evening Praier.

	¶ Morning Praier.	¶ Evening Praier.
i.	i, ii, ii, iv, v.	vi, vii, viii.
ii.	ix, x, xi.	xii, xiii, xiv.
iii.	xv, xvi, xvii.	xviii.
iv.	xix, xx, xxi.	xxii, xxiii.
v.	xxiv, xxv, xxvi.	xxvii, xxviii, xxix.
vi.	xxx, xxxi.	xxxii, xxxiii, xxxiv.
vii.	xxxv, xxxvi.	xxxvii.
viii.	xxxviii, xxxix, xl.	xli, xlii, xliii.
ix.	xliv, xlv, xlvi.	xlvii, xlviii, xlix.
x.	l, li, lii.	liii, liv, lv.
xi.	lvi, lvii, lviii.	lix, lx, lxi.
xii.	lxii, lxiii, lxiv.	lxv, lxvi, lxvii.
xiii.	lxviii.	lxix, lxx.
xiv.	lxxi, lxxii.	lxxiii, lxxiv.
xv.	lxxv, lxxvi, lxxvii.	lxxviii.
xvi.	lxxix, lxxx, lxxxi.	lxxxii, lxxxiii, lxxxiv, lxxxv.
xvii.	lxxxvi, lxxxvii, lxxxviii.	lxxxix.
xviii.	xc, xci, xcii.	xciii, xciv.
xix.	xcvi, xcvii.	xcviii, xcix, c, ci.
xx.	cii, ciii.	civ.
xxi.	cv.	cvi.
xxii.	cvii.	cviii, cix.
xxiii.	cx, cxi, cxii, cxiii.	cxiv, cxv.
xxiv.	cxvi, cxvii, cxviii.	cxix. Inde. iv.
xxv.	Inde. v.	Inde. iv.
xxvi.	Inde. v.	Inde. iv.
xxvii.	cxx, cxxi, cxxii, cxxiii, cxxiv, cxxv.	cxxvi, cxxvii, cxxviii, cxxix, cxxx, cxxxi.
xxviii.	cxxxii, cxxxiii, cxxxiv, cxxxv.	cxxxvi, cxxxvii, cxxxviii.
xxix.	cxxxix, cxl, cxli,	clxii, cxliii.
xxx.	cxliv, cxlv, cxlvi.	clxvii, clxviii, cxlix, cl.

THE ORDER

THOLD Testament is appointed for the firste lessons, at Morning and Evening praier, and shalbe read throughe every yere once, except certain bokes and chapiters, whiche be least edifyeng, and might best be spared, and therefore be lefte unread.

The Newe Testament is appoynted for the seconde Lessons, at Mornyng and Evenyng praier, and shalbe read over orderlye everye yere thrise, beside the Epistles and Gospelles: excepte the Apocalips, out of the whiche there be onelye certain Lessons appoynted, upon diuers proper feastes.

And to knowe what Lessons shalbe read everye daie: finde the daie of the Monethe in the Kalendar folowyng: and there ye shall perceiue the bokes and Chapiters, that shalbe read for the Lessons, both at Morning and Evening praier.

And here is to be noted, that whensoeuer there be any proper Psalmes or Lessons appoynted for anye feaste moveable or unmoveable: then the Psalms and Lessons appointed in the Kalendar, shall be omitted for that tyme.

Ye muste note also, that the Collect, Epistle, and Gospell, appoynted for the Sundai, shall serve all the wiek after, excepte there fall some feast that hath hys proper.

This is also to be noted, concernyng the Leape yeres, that the xxv daie of February, whiche in Leap year is compted for two daies, shall in those two daies alter neither Psalme nor Lesson: but the same Psalmes and Lessons, whiche be sayed the firste daye shall also serve for the seconde daie.

Also, wheresoever the begynnynge of any Lesson, Epistle, or Gospell is not expressed: there ye must begyn at the begynnyng of the Chapiter.

And wheresoever is not expressed howe farre shalbe read, there shall you reade to the ende of the Chapiter.

PROPER PSALMES AND LESSONS FOR DIVERSE FEASTES, AND DAYES,

AT MORNYNG AND EVENYNG PRAIER

On Christemas dai at Mornyng praier.	Psalm xix. Psalm xlv. Psalm lxxxv.	The first Lesson. Esay. ix. The ii. Lesson. Luke ii. *unto* And unto mē a good wyl.
At Evenyng praier.	Psalm lxxxix. Psalm cx. Psalm cxxxii.	The first Lesson. Esa. vii. God spake once again to Achas. &c., *unto the end.* The second Lesson. Tit. iii. The kindness and love &c.. *unto* foolyshe questions.
On Sainct Stephenes day, at Mornyng praier.		The seconde Lesson. Actes vi. and vii. Stephen ful of fayth and power, *unto* And when fourtie yeres were. &c.
At Evening prayer.		The second Lesson. Acts vii. And when fourtie yeres were expired, there appeared unto Moses, &c. *unto* Stephen full of the holy ghost.
On Sainct John the Evāgelistes day, at Mornyng praier.		The secōd Lesson. Apocalips i. The whole Chapter.
At Evening prayer.		The seconde Lesson. Apocalips. xxii.
On the Innocēts' day, at morning prayer.		The firste Lesson. Jeremie. xxxi. *unto* Moreover I heard Ephraim.
On the Circumcision day, at morning prayer		The first Lesson. Genesis. xvii. The seconde Lesson. Roma. ii.
At Evening prayer.		The i. Lesson. Deut. x. And now Israel. &c. The second Lesson. Collos. ii.

On the Epiphanie, at Morning Prayer.	The firste Lesson. Esay. lx. The seconde Lesson. Luke iii. And it for-turned, &c.
At Evening Prayer.	The first lesson. Esay. xlix. The seconde lesson. John ii. After thys he went doune to Capernaum.
On Wednesdaie before Easter, at Evening prayer.	The first lesson. Ozee. xiii. xiiii.
On Thursdaye before Easter, at Morning prayer.	The first Lesson. Daniel. ix.
At Evening prayer.	The first Lesson. Jeremie. xxxi.
On Good Friday, at Morning prayer.	The first lesson. Genesis. xxii.
At Evening prayer.	The first lesson. Esay. liii.
On Easter Even, at Morning prayer.	The first lesson. Zachary. ix.
On Easter day, at Morning prayer.	Psalm ii. Psalm lvii. Psalm cxi. } The first lesson. Exodi. xii. The seconde lesson. Ro. vi.
At Evening prayer.	Psalm cxiii. Psalm cxiiii. Psalm cxviii. } The second lesson. Act. ii.
On Monday in Easter wiek, at Morning prayer.	The seconde lesson. Math. xxviii
At Evening prayer.	The seconde lesson. Actes. iii.
On Tuesday in Easter wieke, at Morning prayer.	The seconde lesson. Luke xxiiii. *unto* And beholde two of them.

At Evening prayer.	The seconde Lesson. 1 Corin. xv.

On the Ascencion day, at Morning prayer.
Psalm viii.
Psalm xv.
Psalm xxi.
The ii. Lesson. John. xiiii.

At Evening prayer.
Psalm xxiiii.
Psalm lxviii.
Psalm cviii.
The ii. Lesson. Ephe. iiii.

On Whitsonday, at Morning prayer.
Psalm xlviii.
Psalm xlvii. (*sic.*)
The seconde lesson. Act. x. Then Peter opened his. &c.

At Evening prayer.
Psalm ciiii.
Psalm cxlv.
The second Lesson. Act. xix. It fortuned when Apollo went to Corinthū, &c. *unto* After these thyngs.

⁋ On Trinitie Sonday, at Morning prayer.
The first lesson. Gene. xviii.
The seconde lesson. Math. iii.

Conversion of Saynct Paule, at Morning prayer.
The second lesson. Actes. xxii. *unto* They heard hym.

At Evening prayer.
The second lesson. Acts. xxvi.

Sainct Barnabie's day, at Morning prayer.
The seconde lesson. Acts. xiiii.

At Evening prayer.
The second Lesson. Acts. xv. *unto* After certayne dayes.

St. John baptistes day, at Morning prayer.
The first lesson. Malachi. iii.
The seconde lesson. Math. iii.

At Evening prayer.
The first lesson. Malachi. iiii.
The seconde lesson. Math. xiv. *unto* When Jesus heard.

Saincte Peter's day, at Morning prayer.	The seconde Lesson. Acts. iii.
At Evening prayer.	The seconde Lesson. Acts. iiii.
Al saincts' day at Morning prayer.	The first Lesson. Sapien. iii. *unto* Blessed is rather the barrayne. The second Lessō. Hebr. xi. xii. Sainctes by faith subdued. *unto* If you endure chastisyng.
At Evening prayer.	The fyrst Lesson. Sapience. v. *unto* Hys jealosie also. The second Lesson. Apocalips xix. *unto* An I sawe an Angell stande.

AN ALMANACK FOR NINETEEN YEARS.

The year of our Lord.	The Golden Number.	The epact.	The Cycle of the sun.	Dominical letter.	Easter day.
1552	xiv	iv.	xxi	C. B.	xvii April.
1553	xv	xv	xxii	A.	ii April.
1554	xvi	xxvi	xxiii	G.	xxv March.
1555	xvii	vii	xxiv.	F.	xiv April.
1556	xviii	xviii	xxv	E. D.	v April.
1557	xix	xxix	xxvi	C.	xviii April.
1558	i	xi	xxvii	B.	x April.
1559	ii	xxii	xxviii	A.	xxvi March
1560	iii	iii	i	G. F.	xiv April.
1561	iv	xiv	ii	E.	vi April.
1562	v	xxv	iii	D.	22 Mar.
1563	vi	xxvi	iv	C.	11 April.
1564	vii	xvii	v	B. A.	3 April.
1565	viii	xxvii	vi	G.	22 April.
1566	ix	ix	vii	F.	7 April.
1567	x	xx	viii	E.	30 Mar.
1568	xi	i	ix	D. C.	8 Mar.
1569	xii	xii	x	B.	10 April.
1570	xiii	xxiii	xi	A.	26 Mar.

JANUARY HATH XXXI. DAYS.

				Psalms.	MORNING PRAYER		EVENING PRAYER	
					1 *Lesson.*	2 *Lesson.*	1 *Lesson.*	2 *Lesson.*
3	A	*Kalend.*	*Circumci.*	1	Gen. 17	Roma. 2	Deut. 10	Collos. 2
	b	4 No.		2	Gen. 1	Math. 1	Gene. 2	Roman 1
11	c	3 No.		3	3	2	4	2
	d	Prid. No.		4	5	3	6	3
19	e	*Nonas.*		5	7	4	8	4
8	f	8 Id.	*Epiphani.*	6	Esai. 60	Luke 3	Esai. 49	Jhon 2
	g	7 Id.		7	Genesi 9	Math. 5	Gene. 11	Roma. 5
16	A	6 Id.		8	12	6	13	6
5	b	5 Id.		9	14	7	15	7
	c	4 Id.		10	16	8	17	8
10	d	3 Id.		11	18	9	19	9
2	e	Prid. Id.	*Sol in aqua*	12	20	10	21	10
	f	*Idus.*		13	22	11	23	11
10	g	19 kl.	Februarii	14	24	12	25	12
	A	18 kl.		15	26	13	27	13
18	b	17 kl.	Term beg.	16	28	14	29	14
7	c	16 kl.		17	30	15	31	15
	d	15 kl.		18	32	16	33	16
15	e	14 kl.		19	34	17	35	1 Corin. 1
4	f	13 kl.		20	36	18	37	2
	g	12 kl.		21	39	19	39	3
12	A	11 kl.		22	40	20	41	4
1	b	10 kl.		23	42	21	43	5
	c	9 kl.		24	44	22	45	6
9	d	8 kl.	*Con. Pau.*	25	46	Act. 22	47	Acte. 26
	e	7 kl.		26	48	Mat. 23	49	1 Cor. 7
17	f	6 kl.		27	50	24	Exod. 1	8
6	g	5 kl.		28	Exodi 2	25	3	9
	A	4 kl.		29	4	26	5	10
14	b	3 kl.		30	6	27	7	11
3	c	*Prid.* kl.		1	8	28	9	12

FEBRUARY HATH XXVIII. DAYS.

				Psalms.	MORNING PRAYER		EVENING PRAYER	
					1 Lesson.	2 Lesson.	1 Lesson.	2 Lesson.
	d	Kalend.	Pur. Mary	2	Exod. 10	Marke 1	Exod. 11	1 Cor. 13
11	e	4 No.		3	12	2	13	14
19	f	3 No.		4	14	3	15	15
8	g	Prid. No.		5	16	4	17	16
	A	Nonas.		6	18	5	19	2 Cor. 1
16	b	8 Id.		7	20	6	21	2
5	c	7 Id.		8	22	7	23	3
	d	6 Id.		9	24	8	32	4
13	e	5 Id.		10	33	9	34	5
2	f	4 Id.	Sol in pis	11	35	10	40	6
	g	3 Id.		12	Lev. 18	11	Lev. 19	7
10	A	Prid. Id.		13	20	12	Nume 10	8
	b	Idus.		14	Nume 11	13	12	9
18	c	16 kl.	March.	15	13	14	14	10
7	d	15 kl.		16	15	15	16	11
	e	14 kl.		17	17	16	18	12
15	f	13 kl.		18	19	Luk.di. 1	20	13
4	g	12 kl.		19	21	di. 1	22	Galath. 1
	A	11 kl.		20	23	2	24	2
12	b	10 kl.		21	25	3	26	3
1	c	9 kl.		22	27	4	28	4
	d	8 kl.		23	29	5	30	5
9	e	7 kl.		24	31	6	32	6
	f	6 kl.	Mathias.	25	33	7	34	Ephesi. 1
17	g	5 kl.		26	35	8	36	2
6	A	4 kl.		27	Deut. 1	9	Deut. 2	3
	b	3 kl.		28	3	10	4	4
14	c	Prid. kl.		29	5	11	6	5

MARCH HATH XXXI. DAYS.

			Psalms.	MORNING PRAYER		EVENING PRAYER	
				1 *Lesson.*	2 *Lesson.*	1 *Lesson.*	2 *Lesson.*
3	d	*Kalend.*	30	Deut. 7.	Luke 12	Deut. 8	Ephe. 6
	e	6 No.	1	9	13	10	Philip. 1
11	f	5 No.	2	11	14	12	2
	g	4 No.	3	13	15	14	3
19	A	3 No.	4	15	16	16	4
8	b	Prid. No.	5	17	17	18	Collo. 1
	c	*Nonas.*	6	19	18	20	2
16	d	8 Id.	7	21	19	22	3
5	e	7 Id.	8	23	20	24	4
	f	6 Id.	9	25	21	26	1 Thes. 1
13	g	5 Id.	Equinoct. 10	27	22	28	2
2	A	4 Id.	*Solin ariete* 11	29	23	30	3
	b	3 Id.	12	31	24	32	4
10	c	Prid. Id.	13	33	Jhon. 1	34	5
	d	*Idus.*	14	Josue. 1.	2	Josue. 2.	2 Thes. 1
18	e	17 kl.	Aprilis. 15	3	3	3	2
7	f	16 kl.	16	4	4	4	3
	g	15 kl.	17	5	5	5	1 Timo. 1
15	A	14 kl.	18	6	6	6	2. 3
4	b	13 kl.	19	7	7	7	4
	c	12 kl.	20	8	8	8	5
12	d	11 kl.	21	9	9	9	6
1	e	10 kl.	22	10	10	11	2 Tim. 1
	f	9 kl.	23	12	11	20	2
9	g	8 kl.	*Annuncia.* 24	21	12	22	3
	A	7 kl.	25	23	13	24	4
17	b	6 kl.	26	Judic. 1	14	Judic. 2	Titus 1
6	c	5 kl.	27	3	15	4	2. 3
	d	4 kl.	28	5	16	6	Phile. 1
14	e	3 kl.	29	7	17	8	Hebreo. 1
3	f	*Prid.* kl.	30	9	18	10	2

APRIL HATH XXX. DAYS.

				Psalms.	MORNING PRAYER		EVENING PRAYER	
					1 _Lesson._	2 _Lesson._	1 _Lesson._	2 _Lesson._
	g	_Kalend._		1	Judic. 11	Jhon 19	Judi. 12	Hebre. 3
11	A	4 No.		2	13	20	14	4
	b	3 No.		3	15	21	16	5
19	c	Prid. No.		4	17	Acts 1	18	6
8	d	_Nonas._		5	19	2	20	7
16	e	8 Id.		6	21	3	Ruth 1	8
5	f	7 Id.		7	Ruth 2	4	3	9
	g	6 Id.		8	4	5	1 Reg. 1	10
13	A	5 Id.		9	1 Regū.2	6	3	11
2	b	4 Id.		10	4	7	5	12
	c	3 Id.		11	6	8	7	13
10	d	Prid. Id.	_Sol in tau_	12	8	9	9	Jacob. 1
	e	_Idus._		13	10	10	11	2
18	f	18 kl.	Maii.	14	12	11	13	3
7	g	17 kl.		15	14	12	15	4
	A	16 kl.		16	16	13	17	5
15	b	15 kl.		17	18	14	19	1 Petr. 1
4	c	14 kl.		18	20	15	21	2
	d	13 kl.		19	22	16	23	3
12	e	12 kl.		20	24	17	25	4
1	f	11 kl.		21	26	18	27	5
	g	10 kl.		22	28	19	29	2 Petr. 1
9	A	9 kl.	_S. George_	23	30	20	31	2
	b	8 kl.		24	2 Regū.1	21	2 Re. 2	3
17	c	7 kl.	_Mark Eva_	25	3	22	4	1 Jhon. 1
6	d	6 kl.		26	5	23	6	2
	e	5 kl.		27	7	24	8	3
14	f	4 kl.		28	9	25	10	4
3	g	3 kl.		29	11	26	12	5
	A	_Prid._ kl.		30	13	27	14	2. 3. Jhō

MAY HATH XXXI. DAYS.

				Psalms.	MORNING PRAYER		EVENING PRAYER	
					1 *Lesson.*	2 *Lesson.*	1 *Lesson.*	2 *Lesson.*
11	b	*Kalend.*	*Phil. & Jac*	1	2 Re. 15	Acte 8	2 re. 6	Judas. 1
	c	6 No.		2	17	28	18	Roma. 1
19	d	5 No.		3	19	Matth. 1	20	2
8	e	4 No.		4	21	2	22	3
	f	3 No.		5	23	3	24	4
16	g	Prid. No.		6	3 Regū. 1	4	3 Re. 2	5
5	A	*Nonas.*		7	3	5	4	6
	b	8 Id.		8	5	6	6	7
13	c	7 Id.		9	7	7	8	8
2	d	6 Id.		10	9	8	10	9
	e	5 Id.	*Sol in gem*	11	11	9	12	10
10	f	4 Id.		12	13	10	14	11
	g	3 Id.		13	15	11	16	12
18	A	Prid. Id.		14	17	12	18	13
7	b	*Idus.*		15	19	13	20	14
	c	17 kl.	*Junii.*	16	21	14	22	15
15	d	16 kl.		17	4 Reg. 1	15	4 re. 2	16
4	e	15 kl.		18	3	16	4	1 Cor. 1
	f	14 kl.		19	5	17	6	2
12	g	13 kl.		20	7	18	8	3
1	A	12 kl.		21	9	19	10	4
	b	11 kl.		22	11	20	12	5
9	c	10 kl.		23	13	21	14	6
	d	9 kl.		24	15	22	16	7
17	e	8 kl.		25	17	23	18	8
6	f	7 kl.		26	19	24	20	9
	g	6 kl.		27	21	25	22	10
14	A	5 kl.		28	23	26	24	11
3	b	4 kl.		29	25	27	25	12
	c	3 kl.		30	1 Esdra 1	28	1 Esd. 2	13
11	d	*Prid.* kl.		30	3	Marke 1	4	14

JUNE HATH XXX. DAYS.

				Psalms.	MORNING PRAYER		EVENING PRAYER	
					1 Lesson.	2 Lesson.	1 Lesson.	2 Lesson.
	e	*Kalend.*		1	1 Esd. 4	Mark 2	1 Esd. 5	1 Cor. 15
19	f	4 No.		2	6	3	6	16
8	g	3 No.		3	7	4	7	2 Corin. 1
15	A	Prid. No.		4	8	5	8	2
5	b	*Nonas.*		5	9	6	10	3
	c	8 Id.		6	2 Esd. 1	7	3	4
4	d	7 Id.		7	4	8	5	5
2	e	6 Id.		8	6	9	8	6
	f	5 Id.		9	9	10	13	7
10	g	4 Id.		10	Hester 1	11	Hest. 2	8
	A	3 Id.		11	3	Acte 14	4	Actes 15
18	b	Prid. Id.		12	5	Mark 12	6	2 Cor. 9
7	c	*Idus.*	*Sol.in Can.*	13	7	13	8	10
	d	18 kl.	*Julii.*	14	9	14	Job. 1	11
15	e	17 kl.		15	Job. 2	15	3	12
4	f	16 kl.		16	4	16	5	13
	g	15 kl.	*Term beg.*	17	6	Luke 1	7	Galath. 1
12	A	14 kl.		18	8	2	9	2
1	b	13 kl.		19	10	3	11	3
	c	12 kl.		20	12	4	13	4
9	d	11 kl.		21	14	5	15	5
	e	10 kl.		22	16	6	17. 18	6
17	f	9 kl.		23	19	7	20	Ephesi. 1
6	g	8 kl.	*Jhon bapt.*	24	Mala. 3	Matth. 3	Mal. 3	Mat. 14
	A	7 kl.		25	Job 21	Luke 8	Job 22	Ephe. 2
14	b	6 kl.		26	23	9	24. 25	3
3	c	5 kl.		27	26. 27	10	28	4
	d	4 kl.		28	29	11	30	5
11	e	3 kl.	*S.Peter ap.*	29	31	Actes 3	32	Actes 4
	f	*Prid.* kl.		30	33	Luke 12	34	Ephes. 6

JULY HATH XXXI. DAYS.

				Psalms.	MORNING PRAYER		EVENING PRAYER	
					1 *Lesson.*	2 *Lesson.*	1 *Lesson.*	2 *Lesson.*
19	g	*Kalend.*		1	Job 35	Luk. 13	Job 36	Philip. 1
8	A	6 No.		2	37	14	38	2
	b	5 No.		3	39	15	40	3
16	c	4 No.		4	41	16	42	4
5	d	3 No.		5	Prover. 1	17	Prov. 2	Collos. 1
	e	Prid. No.	*Term.ende.*	6	3	18	4	2
13	f	*Nonas.*	Dog daies.	7	5	19	6	3
2	g	8 Id.		8	7	20	8	4
	A	7 Id.		9	9	21	10	1 Tessa.1
10	b	6 Id.		10	11	22	12	2
	c	5 Id.		11	13	23	14	3
18	d	4 Id.		12	15	24	16	4
7	e	3 Id.		13	17	Ihon 1	18	5
	f	Prid. Id.	*Sol in Leo.*	14	19	2	20	2 Thess.1
15	g	*Idus.*		15	21	3	22	2
4	A	17 kl.	Augusti.	16	23	4	24	3
	b	16 kl.		17	25	5	26	1 Timo. 1
12	c	15 kl.		18	27	6	28	2. 3
1	d	14 kl.		19	29	7	30	4
	e	13 kl.		20	31	8	Eccle. 1	5
9	f	12 kl.		21	Eccles. 2	9	3	6
	g	11 kl.		22	4	10	5	2 Tim. 1
17	A	10 kl.		23	6	11	7	2
6	b	9 kl.		24	8	12	9	3
	c	8 kl.	*James Apo*	25	10	13	11	4
14	d	7 kl.		26	12	14	Jere. 1	Titus. 1
3	e	6 kl.		27	Jerem. 2	15	3	2. 3
	f	5 kl.		28	4	16	5	Philem.1
11	g	4 kl.		29	6	17	7	Hebreo.1
	A	3 kl.		30	8	18	9	2
14	b	*Prid.* kl.		30	10	19	11	3

AUGUST HATH XXXI. DAYS.

				Psalms.	MORNING PRAYER		EVENING PRAYER	
					1 *Lesson.*	2 *Lesson.*	1 *Lesson.*	2 *Lesson.*
8	c	*Kalend.*	Lammas	1	Jere. 12	Iohn. 20	Jer. 13	Hebr. 4
16	d	4 No.		2	14	21	15	5
5	e	3 No.		3	16	Actes 1	17	6
	f	Prid. No.		4	18	2	19	7
13	g	*Nonas.*		5	20	3	21	8
2	A	8 Id.		6	22	4	23	9
	b	7 Id.		7	24	5	25	10
10	c	6 Id.		8	26	6	27	11
	d	5 Id.		9	28	7	29	12
18	e	4 Id.	S. Laur.	10	30	8	31	13
7	f	3 Id.		11	32	9	33	Jacobi. 1
	g	Prid. Id.		12	34	10	35	2
15	A	*Idus.*		13	36	11	37	3
4	b	19 kl.	Septemb.	14	38	12	39	4
	c	18 kl.	*Sol in virgo*	15	40	13	41	5
12	d	17 kl.		16	42	14	43	1 Peter 1
1	e	16 kl.		17	44	15	45. 46	2
	f	15 kl.		18	47	16	48	3
9	g	14 kl.		19	49	17	50	4
	A	13 kl.		20	51	18	52	5
17	b	12 kl.		21	Lam. 1	19	Lam. 2	2 Peter 1
6	c	11 kl.		22	3	20	4	2
	d	10 kl.		23	5	21	Ezech. 2	3
13	e	9 kl.	*Bartho. ap.*	24	Ezech. 3	22	6	1 Iohn 1
3	f	8 kl.		25	7	23	13	2
	g	7 kl.		26	14	24	18	3
11	A	6 kl.		27	33	25	34	4
	b	5 kl.		28	Daniel 1	26	Dani. 2	5
19	c	4 kl.		29	3	27	4	2. 3 Ihon
8	d	3 kl.		30	5	28	6	Jude 1
	e	*Prid.* kl.		30	7	Matth. 1	8	Roma. 1

SEPTEMBER HATH XXX. DAYS.

				Psalms.	MORNING PRAYER		EVENING PRAYER	
					1 Lesson.	2 Lesson.	1 Lesson.	2 Lesson
16	f	Kalend.		1	Daniel 9	Matth. 2	Dani. 10	Roma..2
5	g	4 No.		2	11	3	12	3
	A	3 No.		3	13	4	14	4
13	b	Prid. No.		4	Ozee. 1	5	Oz. 2. 3	5
2	c	Nonas.	Dog daie en	5	4	6	5. 6	6
	d	8 Id.		6	7	7	8	7
10	e	7 Id.		7	9	8	10	8
	f	6 Id.		8	11	9	12	9
18	g	5 Id.		9	13	10	14	10
7	A	4 Id.		10	Joel 1	11	Joel 2	11
	b	3 Id.		11	3	12	Amos 1	12
15	c	Prid. Id.		12	Amos 2	13	3	13
4	d	Idus.		13	4	14	5	14
	e	18 kl.	Octobris	14	6	15	7	15
12	f	17 kl.	Sol in Libr.	15	8	16	9	16
1	g	16 kl.		16	Abdias.1	17	Jonas. 1	1 Corin.1
	A	15 kl.		17	Ihon.2. 3	18	4	2
9	b	14 kl.		18	Miche. 1	19	Mich. 2	3
	c	13 kl.		19	3	20	4	4
17	d	12 kl.		20	5	21	6	5
6	e	11 kl.	S. Matthew	21	7	22	Naum. 1	6
	f	10 kl.		22	Naum. 2	23	3	7
14	g	9 kl.		23	Abacuc.1	24	Abac. 2	8
3	A	8 kl.		24	3	25	Soph. 1	9
	b	7 kl.		25	Soph. 2	26	3	10
11	c	6 kl.		26	Agge. 1	27	Agge. 2	11
	d	5 kl.		27	Zachari 1	28	Zac. 2. 3	12
19	e	4 kl.		28	4. 5	Marke 1	6	13
8	f	3 kl.	S. Michael	29	7	2	8	14
	g	Prid. kl.		30	9	3	10	15

OCTOBER HATH XXXI. DAYS.

				Psalms.	MORNING PRAYER		EVENING PRAYER	
					1 *Lesson.*	2 *Lesson.*	1 *Lesson.*	2 *Lesson.*
16	A	*Kalend.*		1	zachar 11	Mark 4	Zach. 12	1 Cor. 16
5	b	6 No.		2	13	5	14	2 Cor. 1
13	c	5 No.		3	Malach. 1	6	Mala. 2	2
2	d	4 No.		4	3	7	4	3
	e	3 No.		5	Toby. 1	8	Toby. 2	4
10	f	Prid. No.		6	3	9	4	5
	g	*Nonas.*		7	5	10	6	6
18	A	8 Id.		8	7	11	8	7
7	b	7 Id.	*Terme beg.*	9	9	12	10	8
	c	6 Id.		10	11	13	12	9
15	d	5 Id.		11	13	14	14	10
4	e	4 Id.		12	Judith. 1	15	Judit. 2	11
	f	3 Id.		13	3	16	4	12
12	g	Prid. Id	*Sol. in Scor*	14	5	Luke di.1	6	13
1	A	*Idus.*		15	7	di. 1	8	Gala. 1
	b	17 kl.	*Nov'mbris*	16	9	2	10	2
9	c	16 kl.		17	11	3	12	3
	d	15 kl.	*LukeEvan.*	18	13	4	14	4
17	e	14 kl.		19	15	5	16	5
6	f	13 kl.		20	Sapien. 1	6	Sapi. 2	6
	g	12 kl.		21	3	7	4	Ephesi.1
14	A	11 kl.		22	5	8	6	2
3	b	10 kl.		23	7	9	8	3
	c	9 kl.		24	9	10	10	4
11	d	8 kl.		25	11	11	12	5
	e	7 kl.		26	13	12	14	6
19	f	6 kl.		27	15	13	16	Philip. 1
8	g	5 kl.	*Sim. & Ju.*	28	17	14	18	2
	A	4 kl.		29	19	15	Eccls. 1	3
16	b	3 kl.		30	Eccle. 2	16	3	4
5	c	*Prid.* kl.		30	4	17	5	Collos. 1

NOVEMBER ʜᴀᴛʜ XXX. DAYS.

				Psalms.	MORNING PRAYER		EVENING PRAYER	
					1 Lesson.	2 Lesson.	1 Lesson.	2 Lesson.
	d	Kalend.	All Sainct.	1	Sapie. 3	Heb 11 12	Sapi. 5	Apoc. 19
13	e	4 No.		2	Eccles. 6	Luk. 18	Eccl. 7	Collo. 2
2	f	3 No.		3	8	19	9	3
	g	Prid. No.		4	10	20	11	4
10	A	Nonas.		5	12	21	13	1 Thes. 1
	b	8 Id.		6	14	22	15	2
18	c	7 Id.		7	16	23	17	3
7	d	6 Id.		8	18	24	19	4
	e	5 Id.		9	20	Ihon 1	21	5
15	f	4 Id.		10	22	2	23	2 Thes. 1
4	g	3 Id.		11	24	3	25	2
	A	Prid. Id.		12	26	4	27	3
12	b	Idus.	Sol. in Sag.	13	28	5	29	1 Timo. 1
	c	18 kl.	December	14	30	6	31	2. 3
	d	17 kl.		15	32	7	33	4
9	e	16 kl.		16	34	8	35	5
	f	15 kl.		17	36	9	37	6
17	g	14 kl.		18	38	10	39	2 Tim. 1
6	A	13 kl.		19	40	11	41	2
	b	12 kl.		20	42	12	43	3
14	c	11 kl.		21	44	13	45	4
3	d	10 kl.		22	46	14	47	Titus 1
	e	9 kl.	S. Clement	23	48	15	49	2. 3
11	f	8 kl.		24	50	16	51	Phile. 1
	g	7 kl.		25	Baruch 1	17	Baru. 2	Hebr. 1
19	A	6 kl.		26	3	18	4	2
8	b	5 kl.		27	5	19	6	3
	c	4 kl.	Terme ende	28	Esay. 1	20	Esay. 2	4
16	d	3 kl.		29	3	21	4	5
5	e	Prid. kl.	And. Apo.	30	5	Actes 1	6	6

DECEMBER HATH XXXI. DAYS.

			Psalms.	MORNING PRAYER		EVENING PRAYER	
				1 _Lesson._	2 _Lesson._	1 _Lesson._	2 _Lesson_
	f	_Kalend._	1	Esay. 7	Actes 2	Esai. 8	Hebr.
13	g	4 No.	2	9	3	10	8
2	A	3 No.	3	11	4	12	9
10	b	Prid. No.	4	13	5	14	10
	c	_Nonas._	5	15	6	16	11
18	d	8 Id.	6	17	di. 7	18	12
7	e	7 Id.	7	19	di. 7	20. 21	13
	f	6 Id.	8	22	8	23	James. 1
15	g	5 Id.	9	24	9	25	2
4	A	4 Id.	10	26	10	27	3
	b	3 Id.	11	28	11	29	4
12	c	Prid. Id. _Sol.in Cap._	12	30	12	31	5
1	d	_Idus._	13	32	13	33	1 Peter. 1
	e	19 kl. _Januarii._	14	34	14	35	2
9	f	18 kl.	15	36	15	37	3
	g	17 kl.	16	38	16	39	4
17	A	16 kl.	17	40	17	41	5
6	b	15 kl.	18	42	18	43	2 Peter. 1
	c	14 kl.	19	44	19	45	2
14	d	13 kl.	20	46	20	47	3
3	e	12 kl. _Thos. Apo._	21	48	21	49	1 Ihon. 1
	f	11 kl.	22	50	22	51	2
11	g	10 kl.	23	52	23	53	3
	A	9 kl.	24	54	24	55	4
19	b	8 kl. _Christmas_	25	Esay. 9	Luke 22	Esay. 7	Titus. 3
8	c	7 kl. _S. Stephan_	26	56	Ac. 6. 7	57	Actes. 7
	d	6 kl. _S JhonEv._	27	58	Apocali 1	59	Apo22
16	e	5 kl. _Innocentes_	28	Jere. 31	Acte 25	Esay. 60	1 Ihon. 5
5	f	4 kl.	29	Esaie 61	26	62	2 Ihon. 1
	g	3 kl.	30	63	27	64	3 Ihon. 1
13	A	_Prid._ kl.	30	65	28	66	Jude. 1

AN ORDER FOR MORNING

PRAYER DAYLY THROUGHOUT THE YEARE.

The order where mornynge and euenynge prayer shalbe used and sayed.

¶ *The morning and euening prayer, shalbe used in suche place of the Churche, Chapell, or Chauncel, and the minister shal so turne him, as ye people maye best heare. And if there be any cõtroversie therein, the matter shalbe referred to the ordenarie, and he or his deputie shal appoynte the place, and the Chauncels shal remayne, as they have done in times past.*

And here is to be noted, that the minister at the tyme of the Cõmunion and all other tymes in his ministracion, shall use neither albe, vestment, nor cope : but being archbishop or bishop, he shall have and wear a rochet ; and being a preest or deacon, he shall have and wear a surplice onely.

At the beginning both of Morning Prayer, and likewyse of Evening Prayer, the minister shal reade with a loud voyce some one of these sentences of the scriptures that folow. And then he shal say that, which is written after the said sentences.

At what time soever a synner doeth repente hym of hys synne from the bottome of hys heart: I wyl put all his wickedness oute of my remembraunce, sayth the Lorde. Ezechiel xviii.

I do know mine owne wickednes, and my synnne is alway against me. Psalm li.

Turn thy face away from our sinnes (O Lorde) and blot out all our offences. Psalm li.

A sorowfull spyryt is a Sacrifice to God: despise not (O Lord) humble and contrite hearts. Psalm li.

Rente your heartes, and not your garmentes, and turne to the lord your God: because he is gentle and mercyful, he is pacient and of muche mercy, and suche a one that is sory for your afflictions. Joel ii.

To thee, O lord God belongeth mercy and forgeuenes: for we have gone away from thee, and have not harkened to thy voyce, whereby we myght walke in thy lawes, which thou has appoynted for us. Dan. ix.

Correct us, O Lord, and yet in thy judgemente, not in thy furie, lest we should be consumed and broughte to nothinge. Jerem. ii.

Amende your lyues, for the kingdom of God is at hand. Math. iii.

I wyl goe to my father and saye to hym: father, I have synned agaynst heaven, and against thee, I am no more worthy to be called thy son. Luke xv.

Enter not into judgemente with thy servaunts, O Lord, for no fleshe is righteous in thy syght.   Psa. cxliii.

Yf we saye that we have no synne, we deceyve ourselves, and there is no trueth in us.   i John i.

DEARELY beloved brethren, the scripture moveth us in sundry places, to acknowledge and confess our manifold synnes and wickedness, and that we should not dissemble nor cloke them before the face of almighty God our heavenly father, but confess them with an humble, lowely, penitent and obedient heart: to thende that we may obtayn forgeueness of the same by hys infinite goodness and mercie.   And although we ought at al times humbly to knowledge our synnes before God: yet ought we most chiefly so to doe, when we assemble and mete together, to rendre thanks for the great benefytes that we have receyved at his hands, to set foorth hys moste worthy prayse, to hear his most holy word, and to aske those things which be requisite and necessarye, as well for the body as the soule.   Wherfore I praye and beseche you, as many as be here present, to accompany me wyth a pure heart and humble voyce, unto the throne of the heavenly grace, saying after me.

A generall confession, to be sayd of the whole congregacion after the minister, knelynge.

ALMIGHTY and most mercyfull father, we have erred and strayed from thy wayes, lyke lost shepe.   We have folowed too much the devises and desyres of oure owne hearts.   We have offended against thy holy lawes.   We have left undone those things whiche we oughte to have done, and we have done those thinges which we ought not to have done, and there is no health in us: but thou, O Lord, have mercy upon us miserable offendors. Spare thou them, O God, which confesse theyr faultes.   Restore thou them that be penitent, according to thy promyses declared unto mankynde, in Christe Jesu oure Lorde.   And graunt, O most merciful father, for his sake, that we may hereafter live a godly, righteous, and sobre life, to the glory of thy holy name. Amen.

The absolucion to be pronounced by the minister alone.

ALMIGHTY God, the father of oure Lord Jesus Christ, which desireth not the death of a synner, but rather that he maye turne from his wickednesse and live: and hath geuen power and commaundment to hys ministers, to declare and pronounce to his people, beinge penitent, the absolution and remission of their synnnes: he pardoneth and absolveth all them which truely repent, and unfeynedly believe his holy Gospel. Wherefore we beseche him to graunt us true repentaunce and his holy Spirite, that those thinges may please him, which we do at this present, and that the rest of our life hereafter may be pure and holy: so that at the last we may come to hys eternall joye, through Jesus Christ our Lord.

The people shal answere.

Amen.

Then shal the Minister begin the Lordes Prayer wyth a loude voyce.

OUR Father, which art in heaven, hallowed by thy name. Thy kingdom come. Thy wylle be done in earth as it is in heaven. Geue us this daye oure daylye bread. And forgeue us our trespasses, as we forgeue them that trespass against us. And leade us not into temptacion. But delyver us from evyll. Amen.

Then lykewyse he shall saye.

O Lord, open thou our lyppes.

Aunswer.

And our mouth shal shewe forth thy prayse.

Prieste.

O God, make spede to save us.

Answere.

O Lord, make haste to help us.

Prieste.

Glory be to the father, and to the sonne, and to the holy ghost. As it was in the beginning, is now, and ever shal be: worlde wythout ende. Amen.

Prayse ye the Lorde.

Then shal be said or song thys Psalme folowinge.

O COME let us syng unto the Lord : let us heartely rejoice in the strength of our salvation.

Lette us come before hys presence with thanksgeuing : and shew ourselves glad in hym wyth Psalms.

For the lord is a greate God : and a great King, above all Goddes.

In hys hand are al the corners of the earth : and the strength of the hylles is his also.

The sea is his, and he made it : and hys hands prepared the drye land.

O come, lette us worship and fal downe : and knele before the Lord our maker.

For he is the lord our God : and we are the people of his pasture, and the shepe of his hands.

To day yf ye will hear hys voice, harden not your heartes : as in the provocation, and as in the day of temptacion in the wyldernesse.

When your fathers tempted me : proved me, and saw my works.

Forty yeres long was I grieved with this generation, and said : it is a people that do erre in their hearts, for they have not known my wayes.

Unto whom I sware in my wrath : that they should not entre into my rest.

Glory be to the father, and to the sonne : and to &c.

As it was in the beginning, is now, &c. Amen.

Then shal folowe certain Psalms in order, as they bee appointed in a Table, made for that purpose, except there be proper Psalms appoynted for that day. And at thend of every Psalme throughout the yere, and lykewyse in thend of Benedictus, Benedicite, Magnificat, and Nunc Dimittis, shall be repeated.

Glory be to the father, and to the sonne, &c.

Then shall be read two lessons distinctlye wyth a loude voice, that the people maye heare. The fyrst of the old Testament, the second of the new, lyke as they be appointed by the Kalendar, except there be proper lessons assigned for that daye : the minister that readeth the Lesson, standing and turning him so, as he may best be heard of al such as be present. And before every lesson, the minister shall say thus. The first, second, third, or fourth Chapiter of Genesis or Exodus, Matthew, Mark, or other like, as is appointed in the Kalendar. And in the ende of every Chapter, he shall say.

¶ Here endeth such a Chapiter of such a Boke.

And (to thend the people may the better hear) in such places where thei do sing, there shal the lessons be song in a plain tune after the maner of distinct reading : and likewise the Epistle and Gospell.

After the fyrst lesson shall folow Te Deum laudamus, in English, dayly through the whole yeare.

Te Deum.

We prayse thee, O God, we knowledge thee to be the Lord.

All the earth doeth worship thee, the father everlasting.

To thee all Aungels cry aloud, the heavens and al the powers therein.

To thee Cherubin, and Seraphin continually do cry,

Holy, holy, holy, Lord God of Sabaoth.

Heaven and earth are ful of the Majestie of thy glorye.

The glorious company of the Apostles, praise thee.

The goodly fellowship of the prophets, praise thee.

The noble army of Martyrs, praise thee.

The holy Church throughout al the world doeth knowledge thee.

The Father of an infinite Majesty.

Thy honourable, true, and onely son.

Also the holy ghost the comforter.

Thou art the king of glory, O Christ.

Thou art the everlasting son of the father.

When thou tookest upon thee to deliver man, thou dyddest not abhor the virgin's womb.

When thou hadst overcomed the sharpness of death, thou diddest open the kingdom of heaven to all beleeuers.

Thou sittest on the right hand of God, in the Glory of the father.

We believe that thou shalt come to be our judge.

We therefore pray thee, help thy servants, whom thou hast redemed with thy precious bloud.

Make them to be numbered with thy saints, in glory euerlasting.

O lord, save thy people : and bless thine heritage.

Govern them, and lift them up for ever.

Day by day we magnify thee.

And we worship thy name euer world without end.

Vouchsafe, O Lord, to kepe us this day without sinne.

O lord, have mercy upon us : have mercy upon us.

O Lord, let thy mercy lighten upon us : as our trust is in thee.

O Lord, in thee have I trusted : lette me never be confounded.

Or this canticle, Benedicite omnia opera domini domino.

O ALL ye workes of the Lord, blesse ye the Lorde : prayse hym, and magnifye hym for euer.

O ye Aungelles of the Lorde, blesse ye the Lorde : praise ye hym, and magnifye hym for euer.

O ye heauens, blesse ye the Lorde : prayse hym, and magnifye hym for euer.

O ye waters that be aboue the firmament, blesse ye the Lorde : prayse hym, and magnifye hym for euer.

O all ye powers of the Lorde, blesse ye the Lorde : prayse hym, and magnifye hym for euer.

O ye Sunne, and Moone, blesse ye the Lord : prayse hym, and magnifye hym for euer.

O ye starres of heauē, blesse ye the Lord : prayse hym, and magnifye hym for euer.

O ye showres, and dewe, blesse ye the lorde : prayse him, and magnifie hym for euer.

O ye wyndes of God, blesse ye the Lord : prayse him, and magnifye hym for euer.

O ye fyre and heate, blesse ye the Lord : prayse hym, and magnifie him for euer.

O ye wynter and sommer, blesse ye the Lorde : praise hym, and magnifye hym for euer.

O ye dewes and frostes, blesse ye the Lorde : prayse him, and magnifye hym for euer.

O ye froste and colde, blesse ye the Lorde : prayse hym, and magnifye hym for euer.

O ye Ice and snowe, blesse ye the Lord : prayse hym, and magnifye hym for euer.

O ye nightes and dayes, blesse ye the Lorde : prayse hym, and magnifye hym for euer.

O ye lyght and darkenesse, blesse ye the Lord : praise hym, and magnifye hym for euer.

O ye lighteninges and cloudes, blesse ye the Lord : praise hym, and magnifye hym for euer.

O let the yearth blesse the Lorde : yes, lette it prayse hym, and magnifye hym for euer.

O ye Mountaynes and hylles, blesse ye the Lorde : praise hym, and magnifye hym for euer.

O all ye grene thinges upon the earth, blesse ye the Lord : prayse him, and magnifye hym for euer.

O ye welles, blesse ye the Lorde : prayse hym, and magnyfye hym for euer.

O ye Seas, and fluddes, blesse ye the Lorde : prayse him, and magnyfye him for feuer.

O ye whales, and al that moue in the waters, blesse ye the lorde : prayse him, and magnifye hym for euer.

O al ye foules of the ayre, blesse ye the lorde : prayse hym, and magnifie him for euer.

O al ye beastes, and cattell, blesse ye the Lord : praise hym, and magnifye hym for euer.

O ye children of men, blesse ye the Lord : prayse him, and magnifye hym for euer.

O let Israel blesse the Lorde : prayse him, and magnifye hym for euer.

O ye priestes of the Lord, blesse ye the Lord : prayse hym, and magnifye hym for euer.

O ye seruauntes of the Lorde, blesse ye the Lorde : prayse hym, and magnifye hym for euer.

O ye spyrites and soules of the righteous, blesse ye the Lord : prayse him, and magnifye him for euer.

O ye holye and humble men of hearte, blesse ye the Lord : prayse him, and magnifye him for euer.

O Ananias, Azarias, and Misael, blesse ye the lord : prayse him, and magnifye hym for euer.

Glory bee to the father, and to the sonne : and to the holy ghoste.

As it was in the beginning, is nowe, and euer shalbe : worlde wythout ende. Amen.

And after the second lesson shalbe used and sayde, Benedictus, *in Englishe as foloweth :*

Benedictus.

BLESSED be the Lorde God of Israell : for he hath visyted and redemed hys people;

And hathe raysed up a mightie saluacion for us : in the house of hys seruaunt Dauid;

As he spake by the mouthe of hys holy Prophetes : whyche haue been sence the worlde beganne;

That we should be saued from our enemies : and from the handes of al that hate us;

To perfourme the mercye promysed to oure forefathers : and to remembre hys holy couenaunt;

To perfourme the othe which he sware to our forefather Abraham : that he would geue us;

That we beyng deliuered out of the handes of oure enemies: might serue hym wythoute feare;

In holynesse and righteousnesse before hym : all the dayes of oure lyfe.

And thou chyld, shalte be called the Prophet of the highest : for thou shalt go before the face of the Lorde, to prepare hys wayes;

To geue knowledge of saluacion unto hys people : for the remission of theyr sinnes,

Through the tender mercye of oure God : whereby the daye spring from an hyghe hath vysited us;

To geue lyghte to them that syt in darkenes, and in the shadowe of death : and to guyde our fete into the waye of peace.

Glory be to the father, and to the sonne, and to the holy ghoste.
As it was in the beginning, is now, and euer shalbe : worlde
wythout ende. Amen.

Or els thys Psalme.

Jubilate Deo.　Ps. c

Then shall be sayd the Crede, *by the Minister and the people, standinge.*

I BELEUE in God the father almightie, maker of heauen and
earth.　And in Jesus Christ his onely sonne our Lord, whiche
was conceued by the holy gost, borne of the virgin Mary ; Suffred
under Ponce Pilate, was crucifyed, dead and buried, he descended
into hell.　The thyrd daye he rose agayn frō the dead.　He
ascended into heauen, and sytteth on the ryght hande of God
the father almighty.　From thence shall he come to judge the
quicke and the dead.　I beleue in the holy ghost.　The holy
Catholique Church.　The communion of saincts.　The forgeueness of synnes.　The resurrection of the bodye.　And the lyfe
euerlastinge.　Amen.

*And after that, these prayers folowing, aswell at Euening prayer as at Morning
　prayer : all devoutly kneeling.　The Minister first pronouncinge with a
　loude voyce.*

The Lorde be wyth you.
Answer. And wyth thy spyryte.
The Minister. Let us praye.
Lorde, haue mercy upon us.
　Christ, haue mercy upon us.
Lorde, haue mercy upon us.

*Then the Minister, Clerkes, and people, shall saye the Lordes prayer in
　Englishe, with a loude voyce.*

Oure Father which art, &c.

Then the Minister standing up shall saye.

O Lord, shewe thy mercy upon us.
Aunswere. And graunt us thy saluacion.
Priest. O Lorde, saue the kynge.
Aunswere. And mercyfully hear us, when we call upon thee.
Priest. Indue thy ministers with righteousnes.
Aunswere. And make thy chosen people joyeful.
Priset. O Lorde, saue thy people.
Aunswere. And blesse thine enheritaunce.
Priest. Geue peace in oure time, O Lorde.
Aunswere. Because there is none other that fyghteth for us,
but onely thou, O God.

Priest. O God, make clean our heartes within us.

Aunswere. And take not thyne holy spyryte from us.

Then shal folow three Collectes. The fyrst of the daye, whyche shalbe the same that is appoynted at the Communion. The second for peace. The thyrd for Grace to lyue well. And the two last Collects shal neuer alter, but dayly be sayd at Morning prayer, throughout al the yere as foloweth.

¶ *The seconde Collecte for Peace.*

O GOD, whiche art aucthor of peace, and louer of concorde, in knowledge of whome standeth our eternal lyfe, whose seruice is perfecte freedome; defend us, thy humble seruants, in al assaults of our enemies, that we surely trusting in thy defence, may not feare the power of any aduersaries: through the might of Jesu Christ our Lord. Amen.

The thyrde Collecte for Grace.

O LORD, our heauenly father, almighty and euerlasting God, which hast safely broughte us to the beginninge of this daye: defend us in the same wyth thy mightie power, and graunt that this day we fall into no synne, nether runne into any kind of daunger: but that al our doynges may be ordred by thy gouernaunce, to doe alwayes that is righteous in thy syght: through Jesus Christe our Lorde. Amen.

AN ORDRE

The Priest shall saye.

OUR Father which, &c.

Then lykewyse he shal saye.

O Lord, open thou our lippes.

Aunswere. And our mouth shal shewe furth thy prayse.

Priest. O God, make spede to saue us.

Aunswere. Lord, make haste to helpe us.

Priest.

Glory be to the father, and to the sonne: and to the holy gost;

As it was in the beginning, is now, and euer shall be: world without ende. Amen.

Prayse ye the Lorde.

Then Psalmes in ordre as they be appointed in ye Table for Psalmes, except there be proper Psalmes appointed for that day. Then a Lesson of the Old Testament, as it is appointed likewise in the Kalendar, except there be propre lessons appointed for that day. After that, Magnificat *in Englishe, as foloweth.*

Magnificat.

My soule doth magnifie the Lord :

And my spirite hath rejoyced in god my Sauiour.

For he hath regarded the lowelyness of hys handmayden.

For beholde from henceforth all generacions shall call me blessed.

For he that is mightie, hath magnified me : and holy is his name.

And his mercy is on them that feare him : throughout all generacions.

He hath shewed strength with hys arm : he hath scatered the proud, in the imaginacion of their hearts.

He hath put down the mighty from their seate : and hath exalted the humble and meke.

He hath filled the hungrye with good thyngs : and the riche he hath sent emptie away.

He rememberynge hys mercy, hath holpen hys servaunt Israel : as he promised to our forefathers, Abraham and his sede, for euer.

Glory be to the father, &c.

As it was in the, &c.

Or els thys Psalme.

Cantate Dominio. Ps. xcviii.

O SING unto the Lorde a newe song : for he hath done maruaylous thynges.

With his own right hande, and with hys holy arme : hath he gotten himselfe the victorye.

The lord declared his saluacion : his rightousnes hath he openly shewed in the sight of the heathen.

He hath remembred his mercy and trueth toward the house of Israel: and all the endes of the world haue seen the saluation of our God.

Shewe your selfes ioiful unto the lord al ye lands : syng, rejoyce and geue thankes.

Prayse the Lord upon the harpe : sing to the harpe with a Psalme of thankesgeuing.

With trompettes also and shawmes : O shewe your selfes joyful before the Lord the king.

Let the sea make a noise, and all that therin is : the rounde world, and they that dwel therin.

Let the flouds clappe their hands, and let the hilles be ioiful together before the Lorde : for he is come to judge the yearth.

With righteousnes shal he iudge the world : and the people with equitie.

Glory be to the father, &c.

As it was in the, &c.

Then a Lesson of the newe Testament. And after that (Nunc dimittis) *in Englishe, as foloweth.*

LORD, now lettest thou thy seruant depart in peace : accordyng to thy worde.

For mine iyes haue seen : thy saluacion.

Whiche thou hast prepared : before the face of al people;

To be a light to lighten the Gentiles : and to be the glory of thy people Israel.

Glory be to the father, &c.

As it was in the, &c.

Or els thys Psalme.

Deus misereatur. Ps. lxvii.

Then shal folowe the Crede, with other prayers as is before appointed at Morning prayer after Benedictus. And with three Collects : First of the day : the second of peace : Third for aide against al perilles, as hereafter foloweth : whiche two laste Collectes shalbe daiely said at Euening praier without alteracion.

The second Collecte at Euening Prayer.

O GOD, from whom all holy desyres, all good counsayls, and all just woorks doe procede. Geue unto thy servaunts that peace, which the worlde cannot geue; that both our heartes maie be set to obeye thy commaundments, and also that by thee we beeing defended from the feare of our enemies, may passe our tyme in reste and quietnes through the merites of Jesus Chryste our Sauioure. Amen.

The third Collecte for ayde agaynst al perilles.

LIGHTEN our darkenes, we beseche thee, O Lorde, and by thy greate mercye, defend us from al perilles and daungers of thys nyghte, for the loue of thy onely Sonne, our Sauyoure Jesus Christe. Amen.

In the feastes of Christmas, the Epiphanie, Saincte Mathie, Easter, Thassencion, Pentecost, Saint John Baptist, Sainct James, Sainct Bartholomew, Saint Matthew, Sainct Symon and Jude, Sainct Andrewe, and Trinitie Sunday ; shalbe song or sayd immediatly after Benedictus, this confession of our Christen fayth.

WHOSOEUER will be saued : before al thinges it is necessarye that he holde the Catholyke fayth.

Which faith except euery one doe kepe holy and undefiled : without doubte he shall perishe euerlastyngly.

And the Catholyke fayth is thys : that we worshyp one God in Trinitie, and Trinitie in unity;

Neither confounding the persons : nor diuiding the substance.

For there is one person of the father, another of the sonne : and an other of the holy gost.

But the Godhed of the father, of the sonne, and of the holy goste, is all one : the glory equall, the maiestye coeternall.

Such as the father is, suche is the sonne : and such is the holy gost.

The father uncreate, the sonne uncreate : and the holy gost uncreate.

The father incomprehensible, the sonne incomprehensible : and the holy gost incomprehensible.

The father eternall, the sonne eternall : and the holy gost eternall.

And yet they are not three eternalls : but one eternall.

As also there be not three incomprehensibles, nor three uncreated, but one uncreated, and one incomprehensible.

So likewyse the father is almightie, the sonne almighty : and the holy gost almightie.

And yet they are not three almighties : but one almightie.

So the father is God, the sonne is God : and the holy gost is God.

And yet are they not three Goddes : but one God.

So likewise the father is lorde, the sonne lorde : and the holy gost lord.

And yet not three lordes : but one Lord.

For like as we be compelled by the Christian verytie : to acknowledge every person by himself, to be God and lorde.

So are we forbidden by the Catholyke religion : to saye there be three Goddes, or three Lordes.

The father is made of none : neyther created nor begotten.

The son is of the father alone : not made nor created, but begotten.

The holy gost is of the father and of the sonne neither made, nor created, nor begotten, but procedyng.

So there is one father, not three fathers, one sonne not three sonnes : one holy gost, not three holy gostes.

And in this Trinitie none is afore nor after other : none is greater nor lesse then an other.

But the whole three persons : be coeternal together and coequal.

So that in all thyngs, as is aforesaid : the unitie in Trinitie, and the Trinitie in unitie, is to be worshypped.

He therefore that wilbe saued : muste thus thynk of the Trinitie.

Furthurmore, it is necessary to euerlasting saluacion : that he also beleue rightely in the incarnacion of our Lord Jesu Christ.

For the ryght fayth is, that we beleue and confesse : that our lorde Jesus Christe, the sonne of God, is God and man ;

God of the Substaunce of the father, begotten before the worldes : and man of the substaunce of his mother, borne in the worlde.

Perfecte god, and perfect man : of a reasonable soule, and humaine flesh subsistyng.

Equall to the father, as touchyng hys Godhead : and inferiour to the father, touchyng hys manhode.

Who although he be god and man : yet he is not two, but one Christ.

One, not by conuersion of the Godhead into fleshe : but by takyng of the manhode into God;

One altogether, not by confusion of substaunce : but by unitie of person.

For as the reasonable soule and fleshe is one man : so God and man is one Christ.

Who suffred for our saluacion : descended into hell, rose agayn the thirde daye from the dead.

He ascended into heauen, he sytteth on the ryghte hand of the father, god almighty : from whence he shal come to iudge the quicke and the dead.

At whose coming all men shall ryse agayn with their bodyes : and shall geue accoumpte for their own woorks.

And they that have done good, shall goe into lyfe euerlasting : and they that have done euill, into euerlasting fyre.

This is the Catholike fayth : whiche except a man beleue faythfully, he cannot be saued.

Glory be to the father, and to the sonne : and to the holy goste.

As it was in the beginning, is now, and euer shall bee : worlde without ende.   Amen.

Thus endeth the ordre of Morning and Euening Prayer through the whole yeare.

LETANY

UPON SUNDAYES, WEDNESDAYES, AND FRIDAYES,

AND AT OTHER TIMES, WHEN IT SHALBE COMMANDED BY THE ORDENARY.

O God the father of heauen : haue mercye upon us miserable synners.

O God the father of heauen : haue mercie upon us miserable synners.

O God the sonne, redemer of the world : haue mercye upon us miserable synners.

O God the sonne, redemer of the world : haue mercy upon us miserable synners.

O God the holy Ghost, proceding from the father and the sonne : haue mercye upon us miserable synners.

O God the holy ghost, proceding from the father and the sonne : haue mercye upon us miserable synners.

O holy, blessed and glorious Trinitie, three persones and one God : haue mercy upon us miserable synners.

O holy, blessed, and glorious Trinitie, three persons and one God : haue mercie upon us miserable synners.

Remember not, Lorde, our offences, nor the offences of oure forefathers, neyther take thou vengeaunce of our sinnes : spare us, good lord, spare thy people, whom thou hast redemed with thy most precious bloud, and be not angry with us for ever.

Spare us, good Lorde.

From all euill and myschiefe, from synne, from the craftes and assaultes of the deuill, from thy wrath, and from euerlasting damnacion.

Good Lorde, deliuer us.

From all blyndnes of heart, from pryde, vaynglorye, and hipocricie, from enuy, hatred, and malice, and all uncharitable-ness.

Good lord, deliuer us.

From fornicacion, and al other deadly synne, and from all the disceites of the world, the fleshe, and the deuill.

Good lord, deliuer us.

From lightninges and tempestes, from plage, pestilence, and famine, from battayle and murther, and from sodayne death.

Good lord, deliuer us.

From all sedicion and prieuie conspiracie, from the tyranny of the Bysshop of Rome and al hys detestable enormities, from all false doctrine and heresy, from hardnesse of hearte, and contempte of thy woorde and commaundemente.

Good lord, deliuer us.

By the mistery of thy holy incarnacion, by thy holy Nativitie and Circumcision, by thy baptisme, fastyng, and temptacion.

Good lord, deliuer us.

By thyne agonye and bloudy sweate, by thy crosse and passion, by thy precious death and buriall, by thy gloryous resurrecyon and ascensyon, and by the cumming of the holy gost.

Good lord, deliuer us.

In all tyme of our tribulacion, in all time of our wealth, in the houre of death, and in the daye of judgemente.

Good Lorde, delyuer us.

We sinners doe beseche thee to heare us (O lord god) and that it maye please thee to rule and gouerne thy holy churche universally in the ryght way.

We beseche thee to heare us, good Lorde.

That it maye please thee to kepe Edward the sixth, thy servaunt, our King and gouernour.

We beseche thee to heare us, good Lorde.

That it may please thee to rule his hearte in thy faith, feare, and loue, that he maye alwayes haue affiaunce in thee, and euer seke thy honour and glory.

We beseche thee to heare us good Lorde.

That it may please thee to bee his defendoure and keper, geuing him the victory ouer all hys enemies.

We beseche thee to heare us good Lorde.

That it may please thee to illuminate al Bisshops, Pastours, and ministers of the Churche with true knowledge and understanding of thy worde, and that both by theyr preaching and liuing they maye sette it furth, and shewe it accordyngly.

We beseche thee to heare us, good Lord.

That it maye please thee to endue the Lordes of the counsayle, and all the nobilitie, with grace, wysedome, and understanding.
We beseche thee to heare us, good Lorde.

That it may please thee to blesse and kepe the Magistrates, geuing them grace to execute justice, and to mainteine truth.
We beseche thee to heare us, good Lorde.

That it may please thee to bless and kepe all thy people.
We beseche thee to heare us, good Lorde.

That it may please thee to geue to al nacions unitie, peace, and concorde.
We beseche thee to heare us, good Lorde.

That it may please thee to geue us an hearte to loue and dreade thee, and diligently to lyue after thy commaundementes.
We beseche thee to heare us, good Lorde.

That it may please thee to geue all thy people encrease of grace, to here mekely thy worde, and to receiue it with pure affeccion, and to bryng furth the fruites of the Spirite.
We beseche thee to heare us, good Lorde.

That it may please thee to bryng into the way of trueth all suche as have erred and are deceiued.
We beseche thee to heare us, good Lorde.

That it may please thee to strengthen suche as doe stand, and to comfort and helpe the weake harted, and to raise them up that fall, and finally to beate down Satan under our fete.
We beseche thee to heare us, good Lorde.

That it may please thee to succoure, helpe, and comforte al that be in daunger, necessitie, and tribulacion.
We beseche thee to heare us, good Lorde.

That it may please thee to preserue all that trauaile by lande or by water, al women labouringe of chyld, al sycke persons, and yong chyldren, and to shewe thy pietie upon al prysoners and captiues.
We beseche thee to heare us, good lorde.

That it may please thee to defende and prouide for the fatherles chyldren and wyddowes, and all that be desolate and oppressed.
We beseche thee to heare us, good lorde.

That it may please thee to have mercie upon al men.
We beseche thee to heare us, good lorde.

That it may please thee to forgeue our enemyes, persecutours and slaunderers, and to turne their heartes.

We beseche thee to heare us, good Lorde.

That it may please thee to geue and preserue to our use the kyndly fruites of the yearth, so as in due tyme we may enjoie them.

We beseche thee to heare us, good Lorde.

That it may please thee to geue us true repentaunce, to forgeue us all our synnes, neglygences, and ignoraunces, and to endue us with the grace of thy holy spirite to amende oure lyues accord-ynge to thy holy worde.

We beseche thee to heare us, good Lorde.

Sonne of God: we beseche thee to heare us.
Sonne of God : we beseche thee to heare us.

O lambe of god, that takest away the synnes of the worlde.
Graunt us thy peace.

O Lambe of god, that takest away the synnes of the worlde.
Haue mercie upon us.

O Christe heare us.
O Christe heare us.

Lorde, haue mercy upon us.
Lorde, haue mercy upon us.

Christ, haue mercy upon us.
Christ, haue mercy upon us.

Lorde, haue mercy upon us.
Lorde, haue mercy upon us.

Our Father, which art in heauen, &c.
And lead us not into temptacion.

But deliuer us from euill.
The versicle. O lord, deale not with us after our sinnes.
The answere. Neither reward us after our iniquities.

Let us pray.

O GOD merciful father, that despisest not the sighing of a con-trite hearte, nor the desyre of such as be sorowful, mercifully assist our prayers, that we make before thee in al our troubles and aduersities, whensoeuer they oppresse us: And graciouslye heare us, that those euils, whiche the craft and subtiltie of the deuil or man worketh againste us, be brought to naught, and by the prouidence of thy goodnes they may be dispersed, that we thy seruaunts, beeing hurte by no persecucions, maye euermore geue thankes unto thee, in thy holy Churche: through Jesu Chryste our Lorde.

O Lord, aryse, help us, and deliuer us for thy names sake.

O god, we have heard with our eares, and our fathers haue declared unto us, the noble woorks that thou didst in theyr dayes, and in the olde tyme before them.

O Lord, aryse, helpe us, and deliuer us for thyne honor.

Glory be to the father, and to the sonne, and to the holy gost: as it was in the beginning, is nowe, and euer shalbe: worlde wythout ende. Amen.

From our enemyes defende us, O Christe.

Graciously loke upon our affliccions.

Pitifully beholde the sorowes of our heart.

Mercifully forgeue the synnes of thy people.

Favourably with mercy heare our prayers.

O sonne of Dauid haue mercy upon us.

Both nowe and euer vouchesafe to heare us, O Christ.

Graciousely heare us, O Christe, graciously hear us, O Lorde Christe.

The Versicle. O Lorde, let thy mercy be shewed upon us.
The Aunswere. As we do put our trust in thee.

Let us praye.

We humbly beseche thee, O father, mercifully to loke upon our infirmities, and for the glory of thy names sake turne from us all those euills that we most righteously haue deserued; and graunte that in all our troubles we may put our whole trust and confidence in thy mercye and euermore serue thee in holynesse and pure-nesse of lyuinge, to thy honour and glory: through our only mediatour and aduocate Jesus Christ our lord. Amen.

For rayne yf the tyme require.

O GOD, heauenly Father, which by thy sonne Jesu Christ haste promised to all them that seke thy kingdom and the righteousnes therof, all thyngs necessarie to their bodily sustenance: sende us, we beseche thee, in this our necessitie, such moderate raine and showers, that we may receiue the fruites of the yearth to oure comforte and to thy honoure: throughe Jesus Christ our Lorde. Amen.

¶ *For faire weather.*

O Lord god, which for the sinne of man didst once drown all
the world, excepte eighte persons, and afterward of thye greate
mercy didst promise neuer to destroie it so again: we humbly
beseche thee, that although we for our iniquities haue worthely
deserued this plague of rayne and waters, yet upon our true
repentaunce thou wilt send us such weather whereby we may
receiue the fruites of the earth in due season, and learne bothe
by thy punishment to amende our liues, and for thy clemency
to geue thee prayse and glory: through Jesus Christ our Lord.
Amen.

¶ *In the tyme of dearth and famine.*

O God heauenly father, whose gift it is that the raine doeth
fall, the yearth is fruitfull, beastes increase, and fishes doe
multiplye: beholde, we beseche thee, the afflictions of thy
people, and graunte that the scarcitie and dearth (which we doe
now most justly suffer for our iniquitie) may throughe thy goodness be mercifully turned into cheapnes and plentie, for the loue
of Jesu Christ our lorde, to whom wyth thee and the holy
gost, &c.

¶ *Or thus.*

O God merciful father, which, in the tyme of Heliseus the
Prophete, didst suddynly turne in Samaria great scarcitie and
dearth into plentie and cheapnes, and extreme famine into
abundance of vyctuall: Haue pietie upon us, that nowe bee
punished for oure sinnes with like adversitie, encrease the fruites
of the yearth by thy heauenly benediction: And grant, that we
receuyng thy bountyful lyberalytye, maye use the same to thy
glorye, oure comforte, and reliefe of our nedy neyghbours:
through Jesu Christ our lord. Amen.

In the tyme of Warre.

O Almightie God, kyng of al kinges, and governour of all
thyngs, whose power no creature is able to resiste, to whom it
belongeth justly to punishe sinners, and to be merciful to them
that truly repent: saue and deliuer us (we humbly beseche thee)
from the handes of our enemies: abate their pride, assuage their
malice, and confound their deuises, that we beeing armed with
thy defence, may be preserued euermore from al periles to glorifie
thee, whiche art the onely geuer of all victory, through the
merites of thy only sonne Jesu Christ our Lord.

¶ *In the tyme of any common plague or sickness.*

O ALMIGHTY god, which in thy wrath, in the time of king David, did slea with the plague of pestilence lx and ten thousande, and yet remembryng thy mercye dyddest saue the rest: have pietie upon us miserable synners, that nowe are visited with great sickenes and mortalitie, that like as thou diddest then command thy angel to ceasse from punishing : So it maye now please thee to withdrawe from us thys plague and greuous sickenesse, throughe Jesu Chryste oure Lorde.

¶ *And the Letany shall euer ende with thys Collecte folowyng :*

ALMIGHTIE god, which hast geuen us grace at this time with one accorde to make oure common supplicacions unto thee, and doest promyse that when two or three be gathered in thy name, thou wilt graunte their requestes: fulfil now, O Lorde, the desires and peticions of thy seruaunts, as may be most expediente for them, grauntynge us in thys worlde knowledge of thy trueth, and in the worlde to come life euerlastyng. Amen.

¶ *The fyrst Sundaye of Aduent.*

*The Collecte.**

ALMIGHTY God, geue us grace that we may cast away the
workes of darkenes.

The Epistle. Rom. xiii.*

OWE nothing to any man but this, that ye loue one another.

The Gospell. Matt. xxi.*

AND when they drew nigh unto Jerusalem.

The Second Sundaye.

The Collecte. *The Epistle.* Roma. xv. *The Gospell.* Luc. xxi.*

The Thirde Sundaye.

The Collect. *The Epistle.* i Cor. iv. *The Gospel.* Matt. xi.*

¶ *The Fourth Sundaye.*

The Collect. *The Epistle.* Philipp. iv. *The Gospell.* John i.*

Christmas Day.

The Collect. *The Epistle.* Heb. i. *The Gospel.* John i.*

¶ *Sainct Stephin's Day.*

The Collecte.

¶ Then shal folow a Collect of the Natiuitie, which shalbe sayd continually
unto newe yeares daye.

The Epistle. Acts vii. *The Gospell.* Matt. xxiii.*

* In the Second Prayer-Book, the Introit is omitted throughout; while
the Collect, Epistle, and Gospel repeat those of the First Prayer-Book with
occasional slight change of spelling. The asterisk denotes in each case
that these are the same as in 1549 (for the one exception see p. 375).

¶ *Sainct John Euangelistes Daye.*

The Collecte. *The Epistle.* 1 John i. *The Gospell.* John xxi.*

¶ *Thinnocentes Daye.*

The Collecte. *The Epistle.* Apoc. xiv. *The Gospel.* Matt. ii.*

¶ *The Sundaye after Christmas Daye.*

The Collect. *The Epistle.* Gal. iv. *The Gospel.* Matt. i.*

¶ *The Circumcision of Christ.*

The Collecte. *The Epistle.* Rom. iv. *The Gospel.* Luc. ii.*

¶ *The Epiphany.*

The Collect. *The Epistle.* Ephes. iii. *The Gospel.* Matt. ii.*

The first Sunday after the Epiphanie.

The Collect. *The Epistle.* Rom. xii. *The Gospel.* Luke ii.*

¶ *The second Sunday after the Epiphanie.*

The Collecte. *The Epistle.* Rom. xii. *The Gospel.* John ii.*

¶ *The third Sundaye.*

The Collecte. *The Epistle.* Roma. xii. *The Gospell.* Matt. viii.*

¶ *The fourth Sonday.*

The Collect. *The Epistle.* Rom. xiii. *The Gospel.* Matt. viii.*

¶ *The fifth Sundaye.*

The Collecte. *The Epistle.* Coloss. iii. *The Gospel.* Matt. xiii.*

¶ *The Sundaye called Septuagesima.*

The Collecte. *The Epistle.* 1 Cor. ix. *The Gospel.* Matt. xx.*

¶ *The Sunday called Sexagesima.*

The Collecte. *The Epistle.* 2 Cor. xi. *The Gospel.* Luke viii.*

¶ *The Sunday called Quinquagesima.*

The Collecte. *The Epistle.* 1 Cor. xiii. *The Gospell.* Luke xviii.*

¶ *The first day of Lent.*

The Collect. *The Epistle.* Joel ii. *The Gospell.* Matt. vi.*

The first Sunday in Lent.

The Collect. *The Epistle.* 2 Cor. vi. *The Gospell.* Matt. iv.*

¶ *The second Sunday.*

The Collect. *The Epistle.* 1 Thess. iv. *The Gospell.* Matt. xv.*

¶ *The third Sunday.*

The Collect. *The Epistle.* Ephes. v. *The Gospell.* Luke xi.*

¶ *The fourth Sunday.*

The Collect. *The Epistle.* Gal. iv. *The Gospell.* John vi.*

¶ *The fifth Sunday.*

The Collect. *The Epistle.* Heb. ix. *The Gospell.* John viii.*

¶ *The Sundaye next before Easter.*

The Collecte. *The Epistle.* Philipp. ii. *The Gospell.* Matt. xxvi. xxvii.*

¶ *Monday before Easter.*

The Epistle. Isaiah lxiii. *The Gospel.* Mark xiv.*

¶ *Tuesdaye before Easter.*

The Epistle. Esai. i. *The Gospell.* Mark xv.*

¶ *Wednesday before Easter.*

The Epistle. Heb. ix. *The Gospell.* Luke xxii.*

¶ *At Euensong.*

The First Lesson, Lamenta. i. unto the ende.

¶ *Thursday before Easter.*

The Epistle. 1 Cor. xi. *The Gospell.* Luke xxiii.*

On good Fryday.

The Collect. *The Epistle.* Heb. x. *The Gospel.* John xviii. xix.*

Easter Euen.

The Epistle. 1 Peter iii. *The Gospel.* Matt. xxvii.*

¶ Easter Daye.

¶ At Morning Prayer, insted of the Psalm, O come let us, &c. These Anthems shalbe song or sayed.

CHRIST rysing agayn from the dead, nowe dyeth not. Death from henceforth hath no power upon him. For in that he dyed, he dyed but once to put awaye sinne: but in that he lyueth, he lyueth unto God. And so lykewyse, counte youreselues dead unto synne: but lyuyng unto God in Christ Jesus our Lorde.

CHRISTE is risen againe: the fyrste fruites of them that slepe: for seeng that by man came death: by man also cometh the resurreccion of the dead. For as by Adam all men doe die, so by Christe all men shalbe restored to lyfe.

The Collect. *The Epistle.* Coloss. iii. *The Gospell.* John xx.*

Mondaye in Easter weke.

The Collect. *The Epistle.* Acts x. *The Gospell.* Luke xxiv.*

¶ Tuesdaye in Easter weke.

The Collecte. *The Epistle.* Acts xiii. *The Gospell.* Luke xxiv.*

¶ The first Sunday after Easter.

The Collect.

ALMIGHTY God, &c., *as at the Communion on Easter daye.*

The Epistle. 1 John v. *The Gospell.* John xx.*

¶ The second Sunday after Easter.

The Collect. *The Epistle.* 1 Peter ii. *The Gospel.* John x.*

The third Sunday.

The Collect.   The Epistle.   1 Peter ii.   *The Gospel.*   John xvi.*

¶ The fourth Sunday.

The Collecte.   The Epistle.   James i.   *The Gospell.*   John xvi.*

¶ The fifth Sunday.

The Collect.   The Epistle.   James i.   *The Gospell.*   John xvi.*

¶ The Ascencion Day.

The Collecte.   The Epistle.   Acts. i.   *The Gospel.*   Mark xvi.*

¶ The Sunday after the Ascencion day.

The Collect.   The Epistle.   1 Peter iv.   *The Gospell.*   John
xv. xvi.*

¶ Whitsundaye.

The Collecte.   The Epistle.   Acts ii.   *The Gospell.*   John xiv.*

¶ Monday in Whitsonweke.

The Collect.

¶ God, which, &c. *as upon Whitsondaye.*

The Epistle.   Acts x.   *The Gospel.*   John iii.*

¶ The tuesday after Whitsondaye

The Collect.

God, which &c., *as upon whitsonday.*

The Epistle.   Acts viii.   *The Gospell.*   John x.*

¶ Trinitie Sonday.

The Collect.   The Epistle.   Apoc. iv.   *The Gospel.*   John iii.*

¶ The first Sunday after Trinitie Sundaye.

The Collecte.   The Epistle.   1 John iv.   *The Gospel.*   Luke xvi.*

¶ *The second Sundaye.*

The Collect. *The Epistle.* 1 John iii. *The Gospel.* Luke xiv.*

¶ *The third Sunday.*

The Collect. *The Epistle.* 1 Peter v. *The Gospel.* Luke xv.*

¶ *The fourth Sunday.*

The Collect. *The Epistle.* Rom. viii. *The Gospel.* Luke vi.*

¶ *The fifth Sunday.*

The Collect. *The Epistle.* 1 Peter iii. *The Gospel.* Luke v.*

¶ *The sixth Sunday.*

The Collect. *The Epistle.* Romans vi. *The Gospell.* Matt. v.*

¶ *The seuenth Sunday.*

The Collect. *The Epistle.* Rom. vi. *The Gospel.* Mark viii.*

¶ *The eighth Sunday.*

The Collect. *The Epistle.* Rom. viii. *The Gospell.* Matt. vii.*

¶ *The ninth Sunday.*

The Collect. *The Epistle.* *The Gospel.* Luke xvi.*

The tenth Sundaye.

The Collect. *The Epistle.* 1 Cor. xii. *The Gospell.* Luke xix.*

The eleuenth Sunday.

The Collect. *The Epistle.* 1 Cor. xv. *The Gospell.* Luke xviii.*

The twelfth Sunday.

The Collect. *The Epistle.* 2 Cor. iii. *The Gospell.* Mark vii.*

The thirteenth Sunday.

The Collect. *The Epistle.* Gal. iii. *The Gospell.* Luke. x.*

The fourteenth Sundaye.

The Collecte. *The Epistle.* Gal. v. *The Gospell.* Luke xvii.*

The fifteenth Sunday.

The Collecte. *The Epistle.* Gal. vi. *The Gospel.* Matt. vi.*

The xvi Sundaye.

The Collect. *The Epistle.* Ephes. iii. *The Gospel.* Luke vii.*

¶ The xvii Sundaye.

The Collect. *The Epistle.* Ephes. iv. *The Gospel.* Luke xiv.*

¶ The xviii Sundaye.

The Collect. *The Epistle.* 1 Cor. i. *The Gospell.* Matt. xxii.*

The xix Sundaye

The Collect. *The Epistle.* Ephes. iv. *The Gospell.* Matt. ix.*

The xx Sundaye.

The Collect. *The Epistle.* Ephes. v. *The Gospell.* Matt. xxii.*

¶ The xxi Sundaye.

The Collect. *The Epistle.* Ephes. vi. *The Gospel.* John iv.*

¶ The xxii Sundaye.

The Collect. *The Epistle.* Philipp. i. *The Gospell.* Matt. xviii.*

¶ The xxiii Sundaye.

The Collecte. *The Epistle.* Philipp. iii. *The Gospell.* Matt. xxii.*

The xxiiii Sundaye.

The Collect. *The Epistle.* Coloss. i. *The Gospel.* Matt. ix.*

¶ The xxv. Sunday.

The Collect. *The Epistle.* Jer. xxiii. *The Gospell.* John vi.*

Sainct Andrewes Daye.

*The Collecte.*** *The Epistle.* Rom. x.   *The Gospel.*   Matt. iv.*

Saynct Thomas the Apostle.

The Collect.   *The Epistle.* Ephes. ii.   *The Gospell.* John xx.*

¶ *The conuersion of sainct Paule.*

The Collect.   *The Epistle.* Acts ix.   *The Gospell.* Matt. xix.*

¶ *The Purification of Sainct Mary the virgin.*

The Collecte.

The Epistle.
¶ *The same that is appoynted for the Sundaye.*
The Gospel. Luke ii.

¶ *Saint Mathies' daie.*

The Collect.   *The Epistle.* Acts i.   *The Gospel.* Matt. xi.*

The Annunciacion of the vyrgyn Mary.

The Collect.   *The Epistle.* Isaiah vii.   *The Gospel.* Luke i.*

¶ *Sainct Markes Day.*

The Collecte.   *The Epistle.* Ephes. iv.   *The Gospel.* John xv.*

¶ *Sainct Philip and James.*

The Collecte.   *The Epistle.* James i.   *The Gospel.* John xiv.*

St Barnabe Apostle.

The Collecte.   *The Epistle.* Acts xi.   *The Gospel.* John xv.*

** The Collect for St. Andrew's Day was revised in 1552, as follows:

ALMIGHTY GOD, which didst give such grace unto thy holy apostle St. Andrew, that he readily obeyed the calling of thy Son, Jesus Christ, and followed him without delay: Grant unto us all, that we being called by thy holy word, may forthwith give over ourselves obediently to follow thy holy commandments: through the same Jesus Christ our Lord.

¶ *Sainct John Baptist.*

The Collect. *The Epistle.* Esai. xl. *The Gospel.* Luke i.*

¶ *Sainct Peter's Daye.*

The Collect. *The Epistle.* Acts xii. *The Gospell.* Matt. xvi.*

¶ *Sainct James the Apostle.*

The Collect. *The Epistle.* Acts xi. xii. *The Gospel.* Matt. xx.*

Sainct Bartholomewe.

The Collect. *The Epistle.* Acts v. *The Gospell.* Luke xxii.*

¶ *Sayncte Mathewe.*

The Collect. *The Epistle.* 2 Cor. iv. *The Gospell.* Matt. ix.*

¶ *Saynte Michaell and all Aungels.*

The Collect. *The Epistle.* Apoc. xii. *The Gospel.* Matt. xviii.*

¶ *Sainct Luke the Euangeliste.*

The Collect. *The Epistle.* 2 Tim. iv. *The Gospel.* Luke x.*

¶ *Simon and Jude Apostles.*

The Collect. *The Epistle.* Jude i. *The Gospel.* John xv.*

¶ *All Sainctes.*

The Collect.

ALMIGHTIE God, whiche haste knitte together thy electe in one Communion and felowship.

The Epistle. Apoc. vii.

BEHOLDE, I John sawe another Angell ascende from the rising of the Sūne.

The Gospell. Matt. v.*

JESUS seeing the people, went up into the mountaine.

ORDER FOR THE ADMINISTRACION

OF THE

LORDES SUPPER,

OR

HOLYE COMMUNION.

SO many as entend to be partakers of the holye Communion, shall sygnifye theyr names to the Curate ouer nyghte, or els in the morning, afore the begynninge of mornynge prayer, or immediatly after.

And yf any of those be an open and notorious euyll lyuer, so that the congregacion by hym is offended, or haue done anye wronge to his neyghbours, by woord or deede: The Curate hauinge knowledge thereof, shall call hym, and aduertyse him, in anye wyse not to presume to the Lordes Table, untyll he haue openly declared hymselfe to haue truely repented, and amended hys former naughtye lyfe, that the congregacion maye thereby be satisfyed, whyche afore were offended: and that he haue recompensed the parties, whome he hathe done wronge unto, or at the least declare hym selfe to be in full purpose so to doe, as soone as he conueniently maye.

¶ *The same ordre shall the Curate use with those, betwyxte whome he perceyueth malyce and hatred to rayne, not sufferinge them to be partakers of the LORDES table, untyll he know them to be reconcyled. And yf one of the parties so at variaunce be content to forgeue, from the bottome of hys hearte, all that the other hathe trespassed agaynst hym, and to make amendes for that he hym selfe hath offended: and the other partie wyll not be persuaded to a godly unitie, but remayne styll in hys frowardnesse and malyce: The Minister in that case, ought to admytte the penitent person to the holy Communion, and not hym that is obstinate.*

¶ *The Table hauyng at the Communion tyme a fayre white lynnen clothe upon it, shall stande in the body of the Churche, or in the chauncell, where Morning prayer and Euening prayer be appoynted to bee sayde. And the Priest standing at the north syde of the Table, shall saye the Lordes prayer, with thys Collecte folowinge.*

Almightie God, unto whom all heartes be open, all desyres knowen, and from whom no secretes are hyd: clense the thoughtes of our heartes by the inspiracion of thy holy spirit, that we maye perfectlye loue thee, and worthely magnify thy holy name: through Christ our Lorde. Amen.

¶ *Then shal the Priest rehearse distinctly all the Ten Commaundments: and the people knelyng, shal after euery Commaundment aske Gods mercy for theyr transgression of the same, after thys sorte.*

Ministre. God spake these wordes, and sayd: I am the Lord thy God. Thou shalt haue none other Goddes but me.

People. Lord, haue mercye upon us, and encline our heartes to kepe this lawe.

Ministre. Thou shalt not make to thy selfe any grauen ymage nor the likeness of any thyng that is in heauen aboue, or in the yearthe beneath, nor in the water under the yearth   Thou shalte not bowe downe to them, nor worshyppe them: for I the lord thy God am a gelous God, and visite the sinne of the fathers upon the children, unto the thyrde and fourth generacion of them that hate me, and shewe mercye unto thousandes in them that loue me and kepe my commaundments.

People. Lord, haue mercye upon us, and encline our heartes to kepe thys lawe.

Ministre. Thou shalte not take the name of the lord thy God in vayne: for the lord wil not holde him gilteles that taketh his name in vayne.

People. Lord, haue mercye upon us, and encline our. &c.

Ministre. Remembre that thou kepe holy the Sabboth day. Vi dayes shalt thou laboure and doe all that thou haste to doe, but the seuenth day is the sabboth of the lorde thy god.   In it thou shalte doe no maner of woork, thou and thy sonne and thy daughter, thy man seruaunt, and thy maidseruant, thy Catel, and the straunger that is within thy gates: for in vi days the lord made heauen and earth, the Sea, and al that in them is, and rested the seuenth daye.   Wherefore the Lorde blessed the seuenth day, and halowed it.

People. Lorde, haue mercye upon us, and encline our. &c.

Ministre. Honoure thy father and thy mother, that thy dayes may be long in the land which the lord thy god geueth thee.

People. Lorde, haue mercye upon us, and encline our. &c.

Minister. Thou shalt doe no murther.

People. Lorde, haue mercye upon us, and encline our. &c.

Minister. Thou shalt not commit adulterie.

People. Lorde, haue mercye upon us, and encline our. &c.

Minister. Thou shalt not steale.

People. Lorde, haue mercye upon us, and encline our. &c.

Ministre. Thou shalt not beare false witnesse agaynste thy neighboure.

People. Lorde, haue mercye upon us, and encline our heartes to kepe thys lawe.

Ministre. Thou shalt not couet thy neighbours house.   Thou shalt not couet thy neighbours wife, nor his seruaunt, nor his maid, nor his oxe, nor his asse, nor any thing that is his.

People. Lorde, haue mercye upon us, and write al these thy lawes in our heartes we beseche thee.

¶ *Then shall folowe the Collecte of the daye with one of these two Collectes folowynge for the king : the Priest standing up and saying.*

¶ Let us praye.

Priest.

ALMIGHTIE God, whose kingdome is euerlasting, and power infinite: haue mercye upon the whole congregacion, and so rule the heart of thy chosen seruaunt Edwarde the sixth, our king and gouernoure, that he (knowing whose minister he is) may aboue al thynges seek thy honoure and glory: and that we his subjectes (duely considering whose aucthoritie he hath) may faythfully serue, honour, and humbly obey him, in thee, and for thee, accordyng to thy blessed worde and ordinaunce: Throughe Jesus Christ our lord, who with thee, and the holy ghost, liueth, and reigneth euer one god, world without end.   Amen.

ALMIGHTIE and euerlastyng god, we be taughte by thy holy word, that the heartes of kinges are in thy rule and gouernaunce, and that thou dooeste dispose, and turne them as it semeth best to thy godly wysedome: we humbly beeseche thee, so to dispose and gouerne the heart of Edwarde the sixth, thy seruaunt, our king and gouernoure that in al his thoughts, wordes, and workes, he may euer seke thy honor and glory, and study to preserue thy people committed to his charge, in wealth, peace, and godlynes. Graunt this, O mercifull father, for thy deare sonnes sake Jesus Christ our Lorde.   Amen.

¶ *Immediatly after the Collectes, the Priest shal reade the Epistle, begynnyng thus.*

¶ The Epistle written in the.   Chapter of.

And the Epistle ended, he shal saye the Gospel, beginning thus.

The Gospell wrytten in the.   Chapter of.

And the Epistle and Gospel beyng ended, shal be sayd the Crede.

I BELEUE in one God, the father almighty, maker of heauen and earth, and of al things visible, and inuisible: And in one lorde Jesu Christ, the only begotten sonne of God, begotten of his father before al worldes: God of goddes, light of lyght, very God of very God: begotten, not made, beeyng of one sub-staunce with the father, by whom al thynges were made: who for us men and for our saluacion, came downe from heauen, and was incarnate by the holy gost, of the virgyn Mary, and was made man: and was crucified also for us, under Poncius Pilate.

He suffred and was buried, and the thyrd day he rose againe accordyng to the scriptures: and ascended into heauen, and sytteth at the ryght hand of the father.   And he shal come agayne with glory, to judge both the quicke and the dead: Whose kyngdome shal haue none ende.   And I beleue in the holy gost, the Lord and geuer of lyfe, who procedeth from the father and the sonne, who with the father and the sonne together, is worshipped and glorifyed, who spake by the Prophetes.   And I beleue one Catholike and Apostolike churche.   I acknowledge one Baptisme for the remission of synnes.   And I loke for the resurreccion of the dead, and the life of the world to come. Amen.

After the Crede, if there be no sermon, shal follow one of the homelies already set forth, or hereafter to be set forth by commune aucthoritie.

¶ *After suche sermon, homelie, or exhortacion, the Curate shal declare unto the people whether there be any holye dayes or fasting dayes the weke folowing: and earnestly exhort them to remember the poore, saying one or moe of these Sentences folowing, as he thinketh most conuenient by his discrecion.*

LET your light so shine before men, that they may see your good workes, and glorifie your father whiche is in heauen. *Math.* v.

Laye not up for your selues treasure upon the earth, where the rust and moth doeth corrupt, and where theues break through and steal: But laye up for yourselues treasure in heauen, where neither rust nor mothe doth corrupte, and where theues do not break through and steale.   *Math.* vi.

Whatsoeuer you woulde that men shoulde doe unto you, euen so do unto them: for thys is the lawe and the Prophetes. *Math.* vii.

Not euery one that sayth unto me, lord, lord, shal entre into the kingdom of heauen, but he that doth the wil of my father which is in heauen.   *Math.* vii.

Zache stode forth, and said unto the lord, Behold, lord, the half of my goodes I geue to the poore, and if I haue done any wrong to any man, I restore fourefolde.   *Luke* xix.

Who goeth a warre fare at any tyme at his owne coste?   Who planteth a vineyarde, and eateth not of the fruite thereof?   Or who fedeth a flock, and eateth not of the milke of the flocke? i *Cor.* ix.

If we have sowen unto you spiritual thinges, is it a great matter yf we shal reape your worldly thynges?   i *Cor.* ix.

Do ye not know, that they which minister about holy thynges, liue of the sacrifice? They which waite of the altare are partakers with the altare? Euen so hath the lord also ordained: that they whiche preache the gospel, should lyue of the gospel. ı *Cor*. ix.

He which soweth little, shal reape little, and he that soweth plenteously, shal reape plenteously. Let euery man do according as he is disposed in his hearte; not grudgeing, or of necessitie; for God loueth a cherefull geuer. 2 *Cor*. ix.

Let him that is taught in the word, minister unto him that teacheth, in all good thinges. Be not deceiued; God is not mocked. For whatsoeuer a man soweth, that shall he reape. *Gal*. vi.

Whyle we haue time, let us doe good unto al men, and specially unto them, which are of the household of faith. *Gal*. vi.

Godliness is greate riches, yf a man be contented with that he hath: For we brought nothing into the world, neither may we cary any thyng out. ı *Tim*. vi.

Charge them which are riche in this world, that they be ready to geue, and glad to distribute, laying up in store for themselues a good foundacion, againste the time to come, that they may attayne eternall lyfe. ı *Tim*. vi.

God is not unrighteous, that he wyll forgette youre workes and labour, that procedeth of loue, which loue ye haue shewed for his names sake, which haue ministred unto saincts, and yet doe ministre.

To doe good, and to distribute, forgeat not, for with such sacrifices god is pleased. *Heb*. xiii.

Whoso hath this worldes good, and seeth his brother haue nede, and shutteth up his compassion from him, how dwelleth the loue of god in him? ı *John* iii.

Geue almose of thy goods, and turne neuer thy face from any poore man, and then the face of the lorde shall not be turned away from thee. *Job* iiii.

Be merciful after thy power. If thou hast much, geue plenteously: Yf thou hast litle, do thy dylygence gladly to geue of that litle: for so gatherest thou thy selfe a good rewarde in the day of necessitie. *Job* iiii.

He that hath pietie upon the poore lendeth unto the lord; and loke, what he laieth out, it shall be paied him again. *Pro*. xix.

Blessed be the man that prouideth for the sicke and nedy; the lord shal deliuer him, in the tyme of trouble. *Psal*. xli.

¶ *Then shal the Churche wardens, or some other by them appointed, gather the deuocion of the people, and put the same into the poremens boxe: and*

*upon the offering daies appointed, euery man and woman shall paye to
the curate the due and accustomed offeringes : after whiche done the priest
shal saye.*

Let us pray for the whole state of Christes Church militant
here in earth.

ALMIGHTIE and euerliuing God, which by the holye Apostle
hast taught us to make prayers and supplicacions, and to geue
thankes for all menne. We humbly beseche thee
most mercifullye to accepte our almose and to
receiue these our prayers, which we offer unto thy
diuine Majestie, beseching thee to inspire continually the uniuersall churche with the spirite of
trueth, unitie, and concorde: And graunt that all
they that dooe confesse thy holye name, may agree
in the trueth of thy holy woord, and liue in unitie and godlye loue.
We beseche thee also to saue and defende all Christian Kynges,
Princes, and Gouernoures, and speciallye thy seruaunt, Edward
our Kyng, that under hym we maye bee godlye and quietly
gouerned: and graunt unto hys whole counsayle, and to all that
bee putte in aucthoritie under hym, that they may truely and
indifferently minister justice, to the punishement of wickednes
and vice, and to the mayntenaunce of God's true religion and
vertue. Geue grace (O heauenly father) to all Bisshops,
Pastours, and Curates, that they maye bothe by their lyfe and
doctrine sette foorth thy true and lyuely woord, and rightly and
duely administer thy holye Sacramentes: and to all thy people
geue thy heauenly grace, and especiallye to thys congregacion
here present, that with meke hearte and due reuerence they may
heare and receiue thy holy woord, truely seruing thee in holynesse and ryghteousnesse all the dayes of theyr lyfe. And we
most humbly beseche thee of thy goodnesse (O Lord) to coumfort and succour all them, whiche in this transitory lyfe bee
in trouble, sorowe, nede, sickenes, or anye other aduersitie:
Graunt this, O father, for Jesus Christes sake, oure onely
mediatour and aduocate. Amen.

*Yf there be
none almosen
geuen unto the
poore, then shal
the wordes of
acceptyng our
almes be lefte
out unsayde.*

¶ *Then shal folowe this exhortacion at certaine tymes when the Curate shal
see the people negligent to come to the holy Communion.*

WE be come together at this time, derely beloued brethren,
to fede at the Lord's supper, unto the whiche in Goddes behalf
I bydde you all that be here present, and beseche you for the
Lord Jesus Christes sake, that ye will not refuse to come thereto,
being so louingly called and bidden of god hymselfe. Ye knowe
how greuouse and unkynde a thing it is, when a man hath

prepared a riche feaste, decked his table with al kinde of prouision, so that there lacketh nothing but the geastes to sit down: and yet they which be called, without any cause most unthankefully refuse to come. Which of you, in such a case, would not be moued? Who would not thynke a great injury and wrong done unto him? Wherfore, most derely beloued in Christ, take ye good hede, lest ye with drawyng yourselues from this holy supper, prouoke god's indignacion against you. It is an easy matter for a man to saye, I wyll not communicate, because I am otherwyse letted with worldly busines: but suche excuses be not so easily accepted and allowed beefore god. If any man saye, I am a greuous sinner, and therefore am afraied to come: wherefore then doe you not repent and amend? When god calleth you, be you not ashamed to saye you will not come? When you shoulde returne to god, wyll you excuse your selfe, and saye that you be not ready? Consydre earnestly with youreselues howe lytle such feyned excuses shall auayl before God. They that refused the feaste in the gospell, because they had boughte a farme, or would trie theyr yokes of oxen, or because they were maried, were not so excused, but counted unworthy of the heauenly feast. I for my part am here present, and according to mine office, I bidde you in the name of God, I call you in Christ's behalf, I exhort you, as you loue your owne saluacion, that ye wilbe partakers of thys holy Communion. And as the sonne of God did vouchesafe to yelde up hys soule by death upon the Crosse for youre health: euen so it is youre duetie to receyue the Communion together in the remembraunce of hys death, as he himself commaunded. Nowe if you wyll in nowyse thus doe, considre with youreselues howe greate injurye you do unto God, and howe sore punishmente hangeth ouer your heades for the same. And whereas ye offend god so sore in refusing this holy Banquet, I admonishe, exhort, and beseche you, that unto this unkindnes ye wyll not adde any more. Which thing ye shal doe, if ye stande by as gazers and lokers on them that doe communicate, and be no partakers of the same youreselues. For what thing can this be accoumpted els, then a further contempt and unkindness unto god. Truely it is a great unthankfulnes to saye naye when ye be called: but the faulte is muche greater when men stand by, and yet wyll neither eate nor drynke this holy Communion with other. I pray you what can this be els, but euen to haue the mysteries of Christ in derision? It is said unto all: Take ye and eate. Take and drinke ye all of thys: doe this in remembraunce of me. With what face then, or with what countenaunce shal ye hear these words? What wil this be els but a neglecting, a despysing, and mocking of the Testament of Christ? Wherefore, rather then you should so doe, depart you hence and geue place to them that be godly disposed. But when you depart, I beseche you, pondre with yourselues from whom you depart: ye depart from the lordes table, ye depart from your brethren, and from the banquete of moste heauenly fode. These thynges if ye earnestly considre, ye shal by gods grace returne to a better mynd, for the obteyning whereof, we shal make our humble peticions while we shall receiue the holy Communion.

¶ *And some tyme shal be sayd this also, at the discrecion of the Curate.*

DERELY beloued, forasmuche as our duetie is to rendre to Almightie god our heauenly father most harty thankes, for that he hath geuen his sonne our sauioure Jesus Christ, not only to die for us, but also to be our spiritual fode and sustenaunce, as it is declared unto us, as wel by goddes word as by the holy Sacramentes of his blessed body and bloud, the whiche being so comfortable a thyng to them whiche receiue it worthely, and so daungerous to them that wyl presume to receiue it unworthely: My duetie is to exhort you to consider the dignitie of the holy mistery, and the greate perel of the unworthy receiuing thereof, and so to searche and examine your own consciences, as you should come holy and cleane to a moste Godly and heauenly feaste: so that in no wise you come but in the mariage garment, required of god in holy scripture; and so come and be receiued, as worthy partakers of suche a heauenly table. The way and meanes thereto is: First to examine your liues and conuersacion by the rule of goddes commaundements, and whereinsoeuer ye shall perceiue your selues to have offended, either by wil, word, or dede, there beewaile your owne sinful liues, confess your selfes to almightie god with ful purpose of amendment of life. And yf ye shal perceiue your offences to be such, as be not only against god, but also againste your neighbours: then ye shal reconcile your selues unto them, ready to make restitucion and satisfaccion, accordyng to the uttermost of your powers, for all injuries and wronges done by you to any other: and likewise beeyng ready to forgeue other that have offended you, as you would have forgeuenesse of your offences at gods hande: for otherwyse the receiuing of the holy Communion doth nothyng els, but encrease your damnacion. And because it is requisite that no man shoulde come to the holy Communion but with a full truste in God's mercy, and with a quiet conscience: therefore if there be any of you which by the meanes afore said cannot quiet his own conscience, but requireth further comfort or counsel; then let him come to me, or some other discreet and learned minister of god's word, and open his griefe, that he may receiue such gostlye counsail, aduise, and coumfort, as his conscience maye be relieued; and that by the ministery of god's word he may receiue coumfort and the benefite of absolucion, to the quietting of his conscience, and auoiding of al Scruple and doubtfulnes.

¶ *Then shal the Priest say thys exhortacion.*

DERELY beloued in the Lord: ye that mynde to come to the holy Communion of the body and bloud of our sauiour Christ, muste considre what St. Paul writeth to the Corinthians, how he exhorteth all persons diligently to trye and examine themselues, before they presume to eate of that bread, and drinke of that cup: for as the benefite is great, if with a truly penitent heart and liuely fayth, we receiue that holy Sacrament (for then we spirituallye eate the fleshe of Christ, and drynke hys bloud, then we dwel in Christ and Christ in us, we be one with Christ, and Christ with us;) so is the daunger great, if we receiue the same unworthely. For then we be giltie of the bodye and bloud of Christ our sauiour. We eate and drynke our own damnacion, not consideryng the Lordes body. We kindle Goddes wrath againste us, we prouoke hym to plague us with diuers diseases, and sundry kynds of death. Therfore, yf any of you be a blasphemer of God, an hynderer or slaunderer of his worde, an adulturer, or be in malice or enuie, or in any other greuous cryme, bewayle your sinnes, and come not to thys holy Table; lest after the takyng of that holy Sacrament, the Deuill entre into you, as he entred into Judas, and fyll you ful of al iniquities, and bryng you to destruccion, both of bodye and soule. Judge therefore your selues (brethren) that ye bee not judged of the Lorde. Repent you truely for your sinnes paste haue a liuely and stedfaste fayth in Christe our sauioure. Amende youre lyues, and be in perfecte charitie with al men, so shall ye be meete partakers of those holy misteries. And aboue all thynges, ye muste geue most humble and hartie thankes to God the father, the sonne, and the holy ghost, for the redempcyon of the worlde by the death and passyon of our Sauiour Chryst, both God and man, who did humble hymself, euen to the death upon the Crosse for us miserable synners, which laye in darkenesse and shadowe of death, that he myght make us the chyldren of God, and exalte us to euerlastinge lyfe. And to thend that we shoulde alway remembre the exceding great loue of our Maister, and onely Sauioure Jesu Christ, thus dying for us, and the innumerable benefites, (whiche by his precyous bloud-sheding) he hath obteined to us, he hath instituted and ordayned holy misteries, as pledges of his loue, and continual remem-braunce of hys death, to our great and endles comforte. To hym therefore, with the father and the holy ghost, let us geue (as we are most bounden) continuall thankes: submitting our-selues wholy to hys holy wil and pleasure, and studying to serue him in true holyness and righteousnesse, all the dayes of oure lyfe. Amen.

¶ *Then shal the Priest saye to them that come to receiue the holy Communion.*

You that doe truly and earnestly repente you of youre synnes, and bee in loue and charitie with your neighbours, and entende to leade a newe lyfe, folowyng the commaundments of god, and walking from henceforth in his holy waies: Drawe nere and take this holy Sacramente to youre comfort: make your humble con-fession to almightie god, before this congregacion here gathered together in his holy name, mekely knelyng upon your knees.

¶ *Then shal this general confession be made, in the name of al those that are mynded to receiue the holy Communion, eyther by one of them, or els by one of the ministers, or by the Priest himself, al kneling humbly upon theyr knees.*

ALMIGHTIE God, father of our Lorde Jesus Christe, maker of all thyngs, Judge of all men, we knowledge and bewayle oure manyfolde synnes and wyckednes, whiche we from tyme to tyme moste greuously have committed, by thoughte, woord and dede, agaynst thy deuine Majestie: prouokyng most justely thy wrath and indignacion agaynste us: we doe earnestlye repente, and be hartely sory for these our misdoynges: the remem-braunce of them is grieuouse unto us, the burthen of them is in-tollerable: haue mercye upon us, haue mercye upon us, moste mercifull father, for thy sonne oure Lorde Jesus Chrystes sake: forgeue us all that is past, and graunt that we maye euer here-after serue and please thee, in newnesse of lyfe, to the honoure and glory of thy name: Through Jesus Christ our Lord.

¶ *Then shal the Priest or the Bisshop (being present) stand up, and turning himselfe to the people, say thus,*

ALMIGHTIE god, our heauenly father, who of his great mercy, hath promised forgeueness of synnes to all them, whiche with hartie repentaunce and true fayth turne unto hym: haue mercye upon you, pardon and deliuer you from all your synnes, confirme and strength you in all goodnesse and bring you to euerlasting life: through Jesus Christe our Lorde. Amen.

¶ Then shal the Priest also saye,

Heare what comfortable woords our sauioure Christe sayeth, to al that truly turne to hym.

Come unto me all that trauaile, and be heauye laden, and I shal refreshe you. So god loued the world, that he gaue his onely begotten sonne to thend that al that beleue in him, should not perishe, but haue life euerlasting.

Heare also what Sainct Paul sayeth.

This is a true saying, and worthy of all men to be receiued, that Jesus Christe came into the world to saue synners.

Heare also what Sainct John sayeth.

If any man sinne, we have an aduocate with the father, Jesus Christ the righteous, and he is the propiciacion for our synnes.

¶ After the whiche the Priest shall procede, saying,

Lyfte up your heartes.

Answer. We lyfte them up unto the Lorde.

Priest. Let us geue thankes unto our Lorde God.

Answer. It is mete and right so to doe.

Priest. It is very mete, ryght, and oure bounden duetie, that we should at al times, and in al places, geue thankes unto thee, O lord holy father, almightie euerlastyng God.

¶ Here shal folowe the proper Preface accordinge to the tyme (yf there be any specially appointed,) or els immediatly shal folowe. Therefore with Angelles, &c.

PROPRE PREFACES.

¶ Upon Christmas daye, and seuen dayes after.

BECAUSE thou diddest geue Jesus Christ, thine onely sonne, to be borne as this daye for us, who by the operacion of the holy goste, was made very man, of the substaunce of the Virgin Mary his mother, and that without spot of synne, to make us cleane from al synne. Therefore, &c.

¶ Upon Easter daye, and seuen dayes after.

BUT chiefly are we bounde to prayse thee, for the glorious resurreccion of Thy sonne Jesus Christ our Lorde; for he is the very Paschall lambe which was offered for us, and hath taken away the sinne of the worlde, who by his death hath destroyed

death, and by his rysing to lyfe agayne hath restored to us euerlasting lyfe.   Therefore, &c.

¶ *Upon the Ascencion daye, and seuen dayes after.*

THROUGHE thy moste dere beloued sonne, Jesus Christ our
lorde, who after his moste glorious resurreccion manifestlye
appeared to all hys Apostles, and in their sighte ascended up
into heauen, to prepare a place for us, that where he is, thether
might we also ascend, and reigne with him in glorye.   Therefore, &c.

¶ *Upon Whitsondaye, and six dayes after.*

THROUGH Jesus Christ our Lorde, accordyng to whose most
true promise, the holye ghoste came downe thys daye from
heauen, with a sodayne great sound, as it had been a myghty
wynde, in the lykenesse of fyery tongues, lyghting upon the
Apostles, to teache them, and to leade them to all trueth, geuing
them both the gyft of diuerse languages, and also boldnes with
feruent zeale, constantly to preache the gospell unto all nacions,
whereby we are brought out of darknesse and errour, into the
cleare lyghte and true knowledge of thee, and of thy sonne Jesus
Christ.   Therefore with. &c.

¶ *Upon the feast of Trinitie onely.*

IT is very mete, ryght, and our bounden duetie, that we shoulde
at all tymes, and in all places, geue thanks to thee, O Lord,
almightie and euerlasting God, whi he art one God, one Lorde,
not one onely person, but three persons in one substaunce: For
that which we beleue of the glorye of the father, the same we
beleue of the sonne, and of the holye ghoste without anye
dyfference, or inequalitie.   Therefore with. &c.

¶ *After whiche preface, shal folowe immediatly,*

Therefore with Angelles and Archangelles, and with al the
companye of heauen, we laude and magnifye thy glorious name,
euermore praysing thee, and saying:

Holye, holye, holye, Lorde God of hostes: heauen and yearthe
are full of thy glory: glory be to thee, O lord, most high.

¶ *Then shal the Priest, kneling down at Goddes borde, say in the name of all
them that shal receiue the Communion, this praier folowyng.*

WE doe not presume to come to this thy table (O mercyfull
Lorde) trusting in our owne righteousnesse, but in thy manifolde
and greate mercies: we bee not worthye, so much as to gather up
the crommes under thy table: but thou art the same Lorde whose

propertie is alwayes to haue mercye: graunt us therfore (gracious lord) so to eate the fleshe of thy dere sonne Jesus Christe, and to drinke his bloud, that our synfulle bodyes maye be made cleane by his body, and our soules wasched through his most precious bloud, and that we may euermore dwel in him, and he in us. Amen.

¶ *Then the Priest standing up shal saye, as foloweth.*

ALMIGHTY God oure heauenly father, whiche of thy tender mercye dyddest geue thine onely sonne Jesus Christ, to suffre death upon the crosse for our redempcion, who made there (by hys one oblacion of hymselfe once offered) a full, perfecte and sufficiente sacrifice, oblacion, and satisfaccion, for the synnes of the whole worlde, and dyd institute, and in hys holye Gospell commaund us to continue, a perpetuall memorye of that his precious death, untyll hys comynge agayne: Heare us O mercyefull father wee beeseche thee; and graunt that wee, receyuing these thy creatures of bread and wyne, accordinge to thy sonne our Sauioure Jesus Christ's holy institucion, in remembraunce of his death and passion, maye be partakers of his most blessed body and bloud: who, in the same night that he was betrayed, tooke bread, and when he had geuen thanks, he brake it, and gaue it to his Disciples, sayinge: Take, eate, this is my bodye which is geuen for you. Doe this in remembraunce of me. Lykewyse after supper he tooke the cup, and when he had geuen thankes, he gaue it to them, sayinge: Drink ye all of this, for this is my bloud of the new Testament, whiche is shed for you and for many, for remission of synnes: do this as oft as ye shal drinke it in remembraunce of me.

¶ *Then shal the minister first receyue the Communion in both kyndes hymselfe, and next deliuer it to other ministers, yf any be there present (that they may help the chief minister,) and after to the people in their handes kneling.*

¶ *And when he delyuereth the bread, he shall saye.*

Take and eate this, in remembraunce that Christ dyed for thee, and feede on him in thy hearte by faythe, with thankesgeuing.

And the Minister that delyuereth the cup, shal saye,

Drinke this in remembraunce that Christ's bloude was shed for thee, and be thankefull.

¶ *Then shall the Priest saye the Lordes prayer, the people repeating after him euery peticion.*

¶ *After shalbe sayde as foloweth.*

O LORDE and heauenly father, we thy humble seruaunts entierly desire thy fatherly goodnes, mercifully to accept this our

Sacrifice of prayse and thanks geuing: most humbly beseching thee to graunt, that by the merites and death of thy sonne Jesus Christe, and through fayth in his bloud, we and al thy whole church may obtayne remission of oure synnes, and all other benefytes of his Passion. And here we offre and presente unto thee, O lord, our selfes, our soules, and bodies, to be a reasonable, holy, and liuely Sacrifice unto thee: humbly beseching thee, that al we which be partakers of this holy Communion, maye bee fulfylled with thy grace and heauenly benediccion. And although we bee unworthy throughe oure manifolde sinnes to offre unto thee any Sacrifice: yet we beseche thee to accept this our bounden duetie and seruice, not weighing our merites, but pardoning our offences, through Jesus Christ our Lord; by whom and with whom, in the unitie of the holy ghost, all honour and glory bee unto thee, O father almightie, world without ende. Amen.

¶ *Or this.*

ALMIGHTIE and euerliuing God, we most hartely thank thee, for that thou dooest vouchsafe to fede us, whiche haue duely receyued these holye misteries, with the spirituall foode of the most precious body and bloud of thy sonne our sauiour Jesus Christ, and doest assure us thereby of thy fauoure and goodnes towarde us, and that we bee verye membres incorporate in thy mistical body, which is the blessed companie of all faythfull people, and be also heyrs, through hope, of thy euerlasting kingdom, by the merites of the most precious death and Passion of thy deare sonne. We now most humbly beseche thee, O heauenly father, so to assiste us with thy grace, that we may continue in that holy felowship, and do al such good workes, as thou hast prepared for us to walk in: through Jesus Christ our Lord, to whom, with thee and the holy ghost, be all honour and glorye, world without ende. Amen.

¶ *Then shalbe sayd or song.*

GLORYE bee to God on hyghe. And in yearth peace, good wyll towardes men. We prayse thee, we blesse thee, we worshippe thee, we glorifye thee, we geue thanks to thee for thy greate glorye, O Lorde God heauenly kyng, God the father almightie. O lord the onely begotten sonne Jesu Christ: O lord God, Lambe of god, sonne of the father, that takest away the sinnes of the worlde, haue mercye upon us: Thou that takest away the sinnes of the world, haue mercye upon us. Thou that takest awaye the sinnes of the world, receyue oure prayer. Thou that syttest at the ryght hande of God the father, haue mercye upon us: For thou only art holy, Thou only arte the Lord. Thou only, (O Christ,) with the holy ghost, art most high in the glory of god the father. Amen.

¶ *Then the Priest or the Bishop, if he be present, shal let them depart with thys blessyng :*

THE peace of GOD which passeth al understanding kepe youre heartes and mynds in the knowledge and loue of GOD, and of his sonne Jesus Christ our Lord: And the blessing of god almightye, the father, the sonne, and the holy ghost, be amongest you and remayne with you always. Amen.

¶ *Collectes to be saide after the Offertorie, when there is no Communyon, euery suche daye one. And the same maye be sayd also as often as occasion shal serue, after the Collectes, eyther of Morning and Euening prayer, Communion or Letany, by the discrecion of the minister.*

ASSIST us mercyfully, O lord, in these our supplicacions and prayers, and dispose the waye of thy seruaunts toward the attaynment of euerlasting saluacion: that among al the chaunges and chaunces of this mortall lyfe, they may euer be defended by thy most gracious and ready helpe; throughe Christ our Lorde. Amen.

O ALMIGHTIE Lord and euerliuing god, vouchsafe, we beseche thee, to directe, sanctifye, and gouerne, both oure heartes and bodies, in the wayes of thy lawes, and in the woorks of thy commaundments: that through thy most mightie proteccion, both here and euer, we may be preserued in body and soule: through our lorde and sauioure Jesus Christ. Amen.

GRAUNT, we beseche thee, Almightie God, that the wordes which we haue heard this daye, with our outward eares, may through thy grace be so grafted inwardly in oure heartes, that they may bring forth in us the fruite of good liuing, to the honour and prayse of thy name: through Jesus Christ our Lorde. Amen.

PREUENT us, O Lord, in al our doinges, with thy most gracious fauoure, and further us with thy continual helpe, that in all our works begon, continued, and ended in thee, we may glorifye thy holy name, and finallye by thy mercie obtayne euerlasting lyfe: through Jesus Christ our Lorde. Amen.

ALMIGHTY God, the fountayn of al wisdom, which knowest our necessities before we ask, and oure ignoraunce in asking: we beseche thee to haue compassion upon our infirmities, and those things, whiche for our unworthinesse we dare not, and for oure blindnesse we cannot aske, vouchsafe to geue us for the worthines of thy sonne Jesus Christe our Lord.   Amen.

ALMIGHTYE God, whiche haste promysed to heare the peticions of them that aske in thy sonnes name: we beseche thee mercyfully to enclyne thyne eares to us that haue made nowe oure prayers and supplicacions unto thee: and graunt that those things which we faythfully asked according to thy wyll, may effectually be obteyned to the reliefe of our necessitie, and to the setting foorth of thy glory: Through Jesus Christ our Lord. Amen.

¶ *Upon the holy dayes, yf there be no Communion, shalbe said al that is appoynted at the Communion, untyl the ende of the Homelie, concluding with the general prayer,* ' for the whole state of Christ's churche militante here in earth: ' *and one or moe of these Collectes before rehearsed, as occasyon shal serue.*

¶ *And there shalbe no celebracion of the lordes Supper, except there be a good noumbre to communicate wyth the Priest, accordynge to hys discrecion.*

¶ *And yf there be not aboue twentie persons in the Parishe of discretion to receiue the Communion · yet there shalbe no Communion, excepte foure, or three at the least communicate wyth the Prieste.   And in Cathedrall and Collegiate churches, where be many Priestes and Deacons, they shall al receyue the Communion wyth the minister euery Sonday at the least, excepte they haue a reasonable cause to the contrary.*

¶ *And to take away the supersticion, whiche any person hathe, or myghte haue in the bread and wyne, it shall suffyse that the bread bee such, as is usuall to bee eaten at the Table wyth other meates, but the best and purest wheate bread, that conueniently maye be gotten.   And yf any of the bread or wine remayne, the Curate shal haue it to hys owne use.*

¶ *The bread and wyne for the Communion shall be prouyded by the Curate, and the churchwardens, at the charges of the Parishe, and the Parishe shalbe discharged of such summes of money, or other dueties, which hetherto they haue payde for the same, by order of theyr houses euery Sondaye.*

¶ *And note, that euery Parishioner shall communicate, at the least thre tymes in the yere: of which, Easter to be one : and shal also receyue the Sacramentes, and other rytes, according to the order in this boke appointed. And verely at Easter, euery Parishioner shal reken with his Person, Vicare, or Curate, or his, or their deputie or deputies, and paye to them or hym all Ecclesiasticall dueties, accustomably due, then and at that tyme to be payde.*

Although no ordre can be so perfectlye deuised, but it may be of some, eyther for theyr ignoraunce and infirmitie, or els of malice and obstinacie, misconstrued, depraued, and interpreted in a wrong part : And yet because brotherly charitie willeth, that so much as conueniently may be, offences shoulde be taken awaye : therefore we willing to doe the same.   Whereas it is ordeyned in the booke of common prayer, in the administracion of the Lord's Supper, that the Communicants knelyng shoulde receyue the holye Communion : whiche thynge beyng well mente, for a sygnificacion of the humble and gratefull acknowledgyng of the benefites of Chryst, geuen unto the woorthye receyuer, and to auoyde the prophanacion and dysordre, which about the holy Communion myght els ensue : Leste yet the same kneelyng myght be thought or taken otherwyse, we dooe declare that it is not ment thereby, that any adoracion is doone, or oughte to bee doone, eyther unto the Sacramentall bread or wyne there bodily receyued, or unto anye reall and essencial presence there beeyng of Christ's naturall fleshe and bloude. For as concernynge the Sacramentall bread and wyne, they remayne styll in theyr verye naturall substaunces, and therefore may not be adored, for that were Idolatrye to be abhorred of all faythfull christians. And as concernynge the naturall body and blood of our sauiour Christ, they are in heauen and not here. For it is agaynst the trueth of Christes true natural bodye, to be in moe places then in one, at one tyme.

MINISTRACION OF BAPTISME

TO BE USED IN THE CHURCHE.

It appeareth by auncient wryters, that the Sacramente of Baptisme in the olde tyme was not commonlye ministred but at two tymes in the yeare: at Easter and Whytsontyde At which tymes it was openly ministred in the presence of all the congregacion: whiche custome (nowe being growen out of use) althoughe it cannot for many consideracions be well restored agayne, yet it is thoughte good to folowe the same as nere as conueniently may be: wherefore the people are to be admonished, that it is most conueniente that Baptisme should not be ministred but upon Sundayes, and other holy dayes, when the moste noumbre of people maye come together, as well for that the congregacion there present may testifye the receyuing of them, that be newely Baptyzed, into the noumbre of Christes Churche, as also because in the Baptisme of infantes, euery man present may be put in remembraunce of hys owne profession made to God in hys Baptisme. For whyche cause also, it is expediente that Baptisme be ministred in the Englishe tongue. Neuerthelesse (yf necessitie so requyre) chyldren maye at all tymes be Baptized at home.

PUBLIQUE BAPTISME.

¶ *When there are chyldren to be Baptized upon the Sunday or holy day, the Parentes shall geue knowledge ouer nyght or in the morning, afore the beginning of Morning prayer, to the Curate. And then the Godfathers, Godmothers, and people, with the children, muste be ready at the Fonte, eyther immediatly after the laste Lesson at Morning prayer, or els immediatly after the last Lesson at Euening prayer, as the Curate by his discretion shall appoynte. And then standing there, the Priest shall aske whether the children be Baptyzed or no. If they answere, no; then shall the Prieste saye thus.*

DEARELY beloued, for asmuche as all men bee conceyued and borne in synne, and that oure Sauiour Christ saith, none can entre into the kingdom of God (except he be regenerate and borne a newe of water and the holy Ghost); I beseche you to call upon God the father through our Lord Jesus Christ, that of his bounteous mercie, he will graunt to these children, that thing which by nature they cannot haue, that they may be Baptized with water and the holy ghoste, and receyued into Christes holy church, and be made lyuely membres of the same.

Then the Priest shal saye.

¶ Let us praye.

ALMIGHTY and euerlasting God, which of thy great merce

diddest saue Noe and his familie in the Arke from perishing by water: and also dyddest safely leade the chyldren of Israel, thy people throughe the redde Sea: figuring thereby thy holy Baptisme; and by the Baptisme of thy welbeloued sonne Jesus Christe, dyddest sanctifye the floud Jordane, and al other waters, to the mistical washing away of sinne: We beseche thee for thy infinite mercies, that thou wylt mercyfully loke upon these chyldren, sanctifie them and washe them with thy holy ghoste, that they, beyng deliuered from thy wrath, may be receyued into the Arke of Christes Church, and beyng stedfast in fayth, ioyeful through hope, and rooted in charitie, may so passe the waues of this troublesome world, that finally they maye come to the lande of euerlasting lyfe, there to reygne wyth thee, worlde without ende, through Jesus Christ our Lord. Amen.

ALMIGHTIE and immortall God, the ayde of all that nede, the helper of all that flee to thee for succour, the lyfe of them that beleue, and the resurreccion of the dead: We call upon thee for these infantes, that they coming to thy holye Baptisme, may receyue remission of theyre sinnes by spirituall regeneracion. Receyue them (O Lord) as thou hast promysed by thy wel beloued sonne, sayinge: Aske, and you shal haue, seke, and you shal fynd, knocke, and it shal be opened unto you. So geue now unto us that aske. Let us that seke fynde. Open the gate unto us that knocke, that these infantes may enioye the euerlasting benediccion of thy heauenly washing, and may come to the eternall Kingdom, which thou haste promysed by Christe our Lorde. Amen.

Then shal the Priest say : Heare the wordes of the Gospell, wrytten by Sainct Marke in the tenth Chapter.

AT a certayne tyme they broughte chyldren to Chryste that he shoulde touche them, and his Disciples rebuked those that broughte them. But when Jesus sawe it, he was displeased, and sayde unto them: Suffre lyttle children to come unto me, and forbid them not; for to suche belongeth the kingdom of God. Verely I saye unto you: whosoever doeth not receyue the kingdom of God, as a lyttle chyld, he shall not entre therein. And when he hadde taken them up in his armes, he put his handes upon them, and blessed them. *Mark x.*

After the Gospel is read, the Minister shal make this brief exhortacion upon the woords of the Gospell.

FRENDES, you heare in this Gospell the wordes of oure

sauiour Christe, that he commaunded the children to be brought
unto him: how he blamed those that would have kept them
from him: how he exhorteth al men to follow their innocencie.
You perceyue how by his outward gesture and dede he declared
his good wyl toward them.   For he embrased them in his arms,
he laide his handes upon them, and blessed them.   Doubt not
ye therefore, but earnestly belieue, that he wyll lykewise
fauourably receyue these presente infantes, that he wyl em-
brase them with the armes of his mercie, that he wyll geue unto
them the blessinge of eternal life, and make them partakers
of his euerlasting kingdome.   Wherefore we beeing thus perswaded of the good will of our heauenly father towards these
infantes, declared by his sonne Jesus Christ; and nothinge
doubtinge but that he fauourably alloweth this charitable
worke of ours, in bringinge these children to his holy Baptisme:
let us faythfullye and deuoutlye geue thankes unto hym, and
saye.

ALMIGHTIE and euerlasting God, heauenly father, we geue
thee humble thankes, that thou haste vouchsafed to call us to
the knowledge of thy grace, and faith in thee: encrease this
knowledge, and confirme this fayth in us euermore: Geue thy
holy spirite to these infantes, that they maye bee borne agayne,
and bee made heyres of euerlastinge saluacion, through our Lord
Jesus Christ: who lyueth and reygneth with thee and the holy
spirite, now and for euer.   Amen.

¶ *Then the priest shal speake unto the Godfathers and Godmothers,
on this wyse.*

WELBELOUED frends, ye haue broughte these children here to
bee Baptyzed; ye haue prayed that oure Lorde Jesus Christ
would vouchsafe to receiue them, to laye his hands upon them,
to blesse them, to release them of theyre sinnes, to geue them
the kingdome of heauen, and euerlasting lyfe.   Ye haue heard
also that our Lorde Jesus Christ hath promysed in his Gospell,
to graunte all these thinges that ye haue prayed for: which
promyse he for his part wyl most surely kepe and perfourme.
Wherfore after this promise made by Christ, these infants must
also faithfully for their part promise by you that be their suerties,
that they wil forsake the deuil and al his workes, and constantly beleue gods holy worde, and obediently kepe his commaundmentes.

¶ *Then shall the Priest demaunde of the Godfathers and Godmothers
these questions folowynge.*

DOEST thou forsake the deuyl and al his workes, the vayne

pompe and glorye of the worlde, with al couetouse desyres of the same, the carnall desyres of the flessh, so that thou wylt not folow, nor be led by them?

Aunswere. I forsake them all.

Minister. Doest thou beleue in God the father almightie, maker of heauen and earth? and in Jesus Christ his onely begotten sonne our Lorde, and that he was conceyued by the holy ghoste, borne of the vyrgin Mary, that he suffred under Poncius Pylate, was crucified, dead, and buried, that he went downe into hell, and also dyd ryse again the thyrd daye; that he ascended into heauen, and sytteth at the right hande of God the father almightie, and from thence shal come agayne at the end of the worlde, to iudge the quicke and the dead:

And doest thou beleue in the holy ghost, the holye Catholique Churche, the Communion of Sainctes, the remission of sinnes, the resurreccion of the flesh, and euerlasting lyfe after death?

Aunswere. All this I stedfastly beleue.

Ministre. Wylt thou be baptyzed in this fayth?

Aunswere. That is my desyre.

Then shall the Priest saye.

O MERCYFULL God, graunt that the olde Adam in these chyldren maye be so buried, that the newe man maye be raysed up in them. Amen.

Graunt that al carnall affeccions maye dye in them, and that all things belonginge to the spirite may lyue and growe in them. Amen.

Graunt that they maye haue power and strength to haue victorie and to triumphe agaynste the deuyll, the worlde, and the fleshe. Amen.

Graunt that whosoeuer is here dedicated to thee by our office and ministerie, may also be endued with heauenly vertues, and euerlastingly rewarded throughe thy mercye, O blessed Lord God, who doest lyue and gouerne al thinges worlde without ende. Amen.

ALMIGHTIE euerliuing God, whose most dearely beloued sonne Jesus Christ, for the forgeuenesse of our sinnes, did shead out of his most precious syde bothe water and bloud, and gaue commaundement to his disciples that they shoulde goe teache all nacions, and baptize them in the name of the father, the sonne, and of the holy ghost: Regarde, we beseche thee, the supplicacions of thy congregacion, and graunte that al thy seruauntes which shalbe baptyzed in this water, may receyue the fulnesse of thy grace, and euer remayne in the noumbre of thy faythfull and electe chyldren, throughe Jesus Christ our Lorde.   Amen.

¶ *Then the Priest shal take the childe in his handes, and aske the name : and naming the chyld, shal dippe it in the water, so it be discretely and warely done, sayinge.*

¶ *N.* I Baptyse thee in the name of the father, and of the sonne, and of the holy ghost.   Amen.

¶ *And yf the child be weke, it shall suffyce to power water upon it sayinge the foresayde wordes.*

N. I Baptyse thee in the name of the father, and of the sonne, and of the holy ghost.   Amen.

Then the Priest shall make a crosse upon the chyld's forehead, sayinge.

WE receyue this child into the congregacion of Christes flocke, and doe signe him with the signe of the crosse, in token that hereafter he shal not be ashamed to confesse the fayth of Christ crucified, and manfully to fight under his banner agaynst synne, the world, and the deuyll, and to continue Christ's faythfull souldiour and seruaunt unto his lyues end.   Amen.

Then shall the Priest saye.

SEEYNG nowe, derely beloued brethren, that these chyldren be regenerate and grafted into the bodye of Christes congregacion: lette us geue thankes unto God for these benefites, and with one accorde make our praiers unto almighty god, that they may leade the rest of theyr lyfe according to this beginninge.

Then shall be sayde.

¶ OUR father which art in heauen, &c.

Then shall the Priest saye.

WE yelde thee heartie thankes, most merciful father, that it hathe pleased thee to regenerate this infant with thy holy spirite, to receyue him for thy owne chylde by adopcion, and to incorporate him into thy holy congregacion.   And humbly we beseche thee to graunt that he, being dead unto sinne, and lyuing unto righteousnes, and beeinge buried with Christ in his death, may crucify the old man, and utterly abolishe the whole body of sinne: that as he is made partaker of the death of thy sonne, so he may be partaker of his resurreccion: so that finalli, with the residue of thy holy congregacion, he may be enheritour of thine euerlasting kingdom: through Christ our lord.   Amen.

¶ *At the last ende, the Priest, calling the Godfathers and Godmothers together, shall saye this short exhortacion folowinge.*

FORASMUCHE as these chyldren haue promysed by you to forsake the Deuyl and all hys workes, to beleue in God, and to serue him; you must remembre that it is youre partes and dueties to see these infantes be taught, so sone as they shalbe hable to learne, what a solemne vowe, promise, and profession they haue made by you. And that they maye knowe these thinges the better, ye shal call upon them to heare sermons: And chiefly ye shal prouyde that they may learne the Crede, the Lordes prayer, and the ten Commaundements, in the Englishe tongue, and all other thyngs whiche a Chrystian man ought to knowe and beleue, to his soules health: and that these children may be vertuously brought up to leade a godlye and Christen lyfe; Remembryng alwaye that Baptism doeth represente unto us our profession, which is, to folowe the example of our sauiour Christe, and to be made lyke unto hym; that as he dyed and rose agayne for us, so should we which are baptized die from sinne, and ryse agayne unto righteousnesse, continually mortyfying al our euill and corrupte affeccions, and dayly proceding in all vertue, and godlynes of lyuing.

¶ *The Minister shal commaunde that the chyldren be brought to the Bisshop to be confirmed of him, so sone as they can saie in theyr vulgare tongue the articles of the fayth, the lord's prayer, and the x commaundements, and be further instructed in the Catechisme, set forth for that purpose, accordingly as it is there expressed.*

OF THEM THAT BE
BAPTYSED IN PRIUATE HOUSES
IN TYME OF NECESSITIE.

¶ *The Pastours and Curates shall oft admonishe the people that they deferre not the Baptisme of Infantes anye longer than the Sondaye, or other holye daye nexte after the chyld bee borne, unlesse upon a great and reasonable cause declared to the Curate and by him approued.*

And also they shal warne them, that without great cause and necessitie, they baptyse not chyldren at home in theyre houses. And when great nede shal compel them so to do, that then they minister it on this fashion.

First let them that be present cal upon God for his grace, and saye the Lordes prayer, yf the tyme wyl suffre. And then one of them shall name the chyld, and dippe him in the water, or powre water upon him, saying these wordes.

¶ N. I Baptyse thee in the name of the father, and of the sonne, and of the holy ghost.   Amen.

And let them not doubt, but that the child so Baptised, is lawfully and sufficiently Baptised, and ought not to be Baptised agayne, in the Church. But yet neuerthelesse, yf the child which is after this sorte Baptised, do afterward lyue, it is expedient that he be brought into the churche, to the entent the Priest may examine and trie, whether the child be lawfully Baptised or no. And yf those that bringe any child to the church do answere that he is already baptysed, then shall the Priest examine them further.

¶ By whom the chyld was Baptysed?

Who was present when the chyld was Baptysed?

Whether they called upon God for grace and succour in that necessitie?

With what thing, or what matter, they dyd Baptyse the chylde.

With what wordes the childe was Baptised?

Whether they thinke the childe to bee lawefully and perfectly Baptysed?

And yf the ministers shall proue by the aunswercs of suche as brought the childe, that al thinges were done as they ought to be: Then shall not he Christen the chylde agayne, but shal receyue him, as one of the flocke of the true Christian people, sayinge thus.

I CERTIFIE you, that in this case ye haue done well, and according unto due order concerning the baptysing of this child, which beynge born in original synne and in the wrathe of God, is nowe by the lauer of regeneracion in Baptisme receyued into the noumbre of the children of God, and heyres of euerlasting lyfe: for our Lorde Jesus Christ doeth not denie his grace and mercie unto such infantes, but most lovingly doth cal them unto him, as the holy gospel doeth witnesse to our comfort, on this wyse.

AT a certayne tyme they brought chyldren unto Christ that he should touche them, and his disciples rebuked those that brought them. But when Jesus saw it, he was displeased, and sayde unto them: Suffre litle chyldren to come unto me, and forbid them not, for to such belongeth the kingdom of God. Verely I saye unto you, whosoeuer doeth not receyue the kyngdome of God as a litle chyld, he shal not entre therein. And when he had taken them up in his arms, he put his handes upon them and blessed them. *Mark* x.

¶ *After the Gospell is read, the Minister shall make this exhortacion upon the words of the Gospel.*

FRENDES, youe heare in this Gospell the wordes of our Sauiour Christe, that he commaunded the chyldren to bee broughte unto him: howe he blamed those that woulde haue kepte them from him: howe he exhorted all men to folow their innocencie: ye perceyue howe by his outwarde gesture and dede he declared his good wyll toward them. For he embrased them in his arms, he layde his handes upon them, and blessed them. Doubt ye not therefore, but earnestly belieue, that he hath lykewise fauourably receyued thys present infante, that he hath embrased him with the armes of his mercie, that he hath geuen unto him the blessinge of eternall lyfe, and made him partaker of his euerlasting kyngdome. Wherfore we beeing thus perswaded of the good wyll of our heauenly father, declared by hys sonne Jesus Christ towardes this infant: Let us faythfully and deuoutly geue thankes unto hym, and saye the prayer which the Lorde himselfe taught; and in declaracion of our fayth, let us recyte the articles conteyned in our Crede.

Here the Ministre with the Godfathers and Godmothers shall say.

OUR father which art in heauen, &c.

¶ *Then shal the Priest demaund the name of the chyld, which beyng by the Godfathers and Godmothers pronounced, the Ministre shall saye.*

N. Doest thou in the name of this childe forsake the Deuill and all hys woorks, the vayne pompe and glorye of the worlde, with all the couetous desyres of the same, the carnall desyres of the flesh, and not to folow, and be ledde by them?

Answere. I forsake them all.

Minister. Doest thou in the name of this childe professe thys fayth, to beleue in God the father almightye, maker of heauen and earth.   And in Jesus Christ his onely begotten sonne our Lorde: and that he was conceiued by the holy ghoste, borne of the vyrgin Marye, that he suffred under Poncius Pilate, was crucifyed, dead and buried, that he went downe into hell, and also dyd ryse agayne the thyrde day: that he ascended into heauen, and sytteth at the ryght hande of God the father almightie: and from thence he shall come agayne at the ende of the worlde to iudge the quicke and the dead?

And doe you in hys name beleue in the holy gost.   The holy catholique Churche.   The Communion of saincts.   The remission of synnes.   Resurreccion, and euerlasting lyfe after death?

Aunswere. All this I stedfastly believe.

¶ Let us praye.

ALMIGHTIE and euerlastyng God, heauenly father, we geue thee humble thankes, for that thou hast vouchsafed to cal us to the knowledge of thy grace, and fayth in thee: increase this knowledge and confyrme this fayth in us euermore: Geue thy holy spirit to this infante, that he beyng borne agayne, and beeyng made heyre of euerlasting saluacion, through oure Lorde Jesus Christe, maye continue thy seruaunt, and attayne thy promyse, through the same oure Lord Jesus Christ thy sonne: who lyueth and reygneth with thee in unitie of the same holy spirite euerlastingly.   Amen.

Then shal the minister make this exhortacion to the Godfathers, and Godmothers.

FORASMUCHE as thys chylde hath promysed by you to forsake the deuill and all his works, to beleue in God, and to serue him: you must remembre that it is youre parte and duetie to see that this infante be taughte so soone as he shalbe able to learne, what a solemne vowe, promyse, and profession he hath made by you: and that he maye knowe these thyngs the better, ye shall call upon hym to heare sermons: And chieflye ye shall prouyde that he maye learne the Crede, the Lordes Prayer, and the ten Commaundements in the Englishe tongue, and all other thyngs whiche a Chrystian man ought to knowe, and beleue, to his soules health, and that thys childe maye be vertuously broughte up, to leade a godly and a Christen lyfe: Remembryng alwaye that Baptisme doeth represent unto us our profession, which is to folowe the example of our sauiour Christe, and be made lyke unto hym: that as he dyed and rose agayne for us, so should we, which are baptized, die from synne, and ryse agayne unto righteousnesse, continually mortyfyyng al our euill and corrupte affeccions, and dayly proceding in all vertue, and godlynes of lyuing.

¶ And so forth, as in Publique Baptisme

¶ *But yf they which bring the infantes to the Churche, doe make an uncertayn aunswere to the Priestes questions, and saye that they cannot tel what they thoughte, dyd, or sayde, in that greate feare and trouble of mynd (as oftentymes it chaunceth) : then lette the Priest baptyse him in forme aboue wrytten concernynge Publique Baptysme, sauyng that at the dypping of the Chyld in the Fonte, he shal use this forme of wordes.*

IF thou be not baptysed already, *N.* I baptise thee in the name of the father, and of the sonne, and of the holy goste.   Amen.

CONFIRMACION

WHEREIN IS CONTEYNED A CATECHISME FOR CHILDREN.

To the ende that Confirmacion maye be ministred to the more edifying of such as shal receyue it (according unto saincte Paules doctrine, who teaches that al things should be done in the Churche to the edificacion of the same) it is thought good that none hereafter shalbe confirmed, but such as can say in their mother tongue the articles of the fayth, the Lord's prayer, and the x commaundementes; And can also answere to suche questions of this short Catechism, as the Bisshop (or such as he shal appointe) shal by his discrecion appose them in. And this ordre is most conueniente to be observed for dyuers consideracions.

First, because that when children come to the yeres of discrecion, and haue learned what their godfathers and godmothers promised for them in baptisme, they may then themselues with their own mouth, and with their own consent, openly before the Churche, ratifie and confirme the same: and also promise that by the grace of god they wil euermore endeuoure themselfes faithfully to obserue and kepe suche thynges, as they by their owne mouth and confession haue assented unto.

Secondly, forasmuche as Confirmacion is ministred to them that be Baptized, that by imposicion of handes and prayer they maye receyue strength and defence against all temptacions to sinne and the assaultes of the worlde, and the Deuyll: it is most mete to be ministred when children come to that age, that partly by the frailtie of their own flesh, partly by the assaultes of the world and the Deuil, they begyn to be in daunger to fall into sondry kindes of synne.

Thirdly, for that it is agreable with the usage of the Churche in times past, whereby it was ordeined that Confirmacion should be ministred to them that were of perfect age, that thei being instructed in Christes religion, shoulde openly professe their owne fayth, and promise to be obedyent unto the wyll of God.

And that noman shal think that any detriment shall come to children by deferryng of their Confirmacion; he shal knowe for truth, that it is certeyne by Goddes woord, that children beyng baptysed, haue al thynges necessary for their saluacion, and be undoubtedly saued.

A CATECHISME,

THAT IS TO SAYE,

AN INSTRUCCION TO BE LEARNED OF EUERY CHYLD,
BEFORE HE BE BROUGHT TO BE CONFYRMED OF THE BISSHOPPE.

Question. What is your name?
Aunswere. N. or M.
Question. Who gaue you thys name?
Aunswere. My Godfathers and Godmothers in my baptisme,

404

wherein I was made a member of Christe, the childe of god, and an inheritour of the kingdome of heauen.

Question. What dyd your godfathers and godmothers then for you?

Aunswere. They did promise and vowe three thinges in my name. First, that I should forsake the deuil and all his woorks and pompes, the vanities of the wycked worlde, and all the synfull lustes of the fleshe. Secondly, that I shoulde belieue al the articles of the christen fayth. And thirdly, that I shoulde kepe Goddes holy wyll and commaundements, and walke in the same all the dayes of my lyfe.

Question. Doest thou not thinke that thou art bounde to beleue and to doe as they haue promised for thee?

Aunswere. Yes verely. And by Gods helpe so I wyl. And I hertely thank our heauenly father, that he hath called me to thys state of saluacion, through Jesus Christe our sauiour. And I pray god to geue me his grace, that I may continue in the same unto my lyues ende.

Question. Rehearse the articles of thy beliefe.

Aunswere. I beleue in god the father almightie, maker of heauen and of earth. And in Jesus Chryst hys onely sonne our lord. Which was conceyued of the holy gost, borne of the vyrgin Mary. Suffred under Ponce Pilate, was crucyfyed, dead and buried, he descended into hel. The thirde day he rose againe from the dead. He ascended into heauen, and sitteth at the right hande of God the father almightie. From thence he shall come to iudge the quicke and the dead. I beleue in the holy gost. The holy Catholyke Churche. The communion of Sainctes. The forgiueness of synnes. The resurreccion of the bodye. And the lyfe euerlastyng. Amen.

Question. What doest thou chiefely learne in these articles of thy beliefe?

Aunswere. Firste I learne to beleue in God the father, who hath made me and al the worlde.

Secondly, in god the sonne who hath redemed me and all mankynde.

Thirdly, in god the holy gost, who sanctifieth me and all the electe people of God.

Question. You sayed that your godfathers and godmothers dyd promise for you that you should kepe goddes commaundementes. Tel me how many there be.

Aunswere. Tenne.

Question. Whiche be they?

Aunswere. The same whiche God spake in the xx. Chapter of Exodus, saying: I am the lord thy god which haue brought thee out of the lande of Egipte, out of the house of bondage.

I. Thou shalt haue noné other goddes but me.

II. Thou shalt not make to thyself any grauen ymage, nor the likeness of any thyng that is in heauen aboue, or in the earth beneath, nor in the water under the yearth: thou shalte not bowe downe to them, nor woorshippe them. For I the Lorde thy God am a gelous God, and visite the synnes of the fathers upon the children, unto the thirde and fourth generacion of them that hate me, and shew mercy unto thousandes in them that loue me, and kepe my commaundementes.

III. Thou shalt not take the name of the lord thy god in vayne: for the Lord will not holde hym giltlesse that taketh hys name in vayne.

IV. Remembre thou kepe holy the Sabboth daye. Sixe dayes shalte thou laboure and doe all that thou hast to doe: but the seuenth daye is the Sabboth of the lorde thy God. In it thou shalte doe no maner of worke, thou, and thy sonne and thy daughter, thy man seruaunt, and thy maide seruaunt, thy catell, and the straunger that is within thy gates: for in sixe dayes the Lorde made heauen and earth, the Sea, and all that in them is, and rested the seuenth daye. Wherefore the lord blessed the seuenth daye and halowed it.

V. Honour thy father and thy mother, that thy dayes may be long in the lande which the lord thy god geueth thee.

VI. Thou shalt doe no murthur.

VII. Thou shalt not commit adulterye.

VIII. Thou shalt not steale.

IX. Thou shalt not bear false witnesse agaynste thy neighbour.

X. Thou shalt not couite thy neighbour's house, thou shalt not couite thy neighbour's wife, nor his seruaunt, nor his maide, nor his oxe, nor hys asse, nor any thyng that is hys.

Question. What doest thou chieflye learne by these commaundementes?

Aunswere. I learne two thinges: My duetie towardes God, and my duetie towardes my neighbour.

Question. What is thy duetie towards god?

Answer. My duetie towards god is, to beleue in hym, to feare hym, and to loue hym with all my hearte, with all my mynde, with al my soule, and with all my strength. To worship him. To geue him thankes. To put my whole truste in him. To call upon him. To honoure his holy name and his word, and to serue hym truely all the daies of my lyfe.

Question. What is thy duetie towardes thy neyghbour?

Answer. My duetie towards my neighboure is, to loue hym as myself. And to doe to al men as I would they should do unto me. To loue, honour and succour my father and mother. To honour and obey the kyng and hys ministers. To submit my self to all my gouernours, teachers, spiritual Pastours, and maisters. To ordre myself lowly and reuerently to al my betters. To hurte no body by worde nor dede. To be true and iuste in al my dealynge. To beare no malice nor hatred in my heart. To kepe my handes from pickyng and stealing, and my tongue from euil speaking, lying, and slaunderyng. To kepe my body in temperaunce, soberness, and chastitie. Not to couet nor desyre other men's goodes. But learne and labour truly to geat myne owne liuing, and to do my duetie in that state of lyfe, unto which it shall please god to call me.

Question. My good chylde, knowe this, that thou art not able to doe these thyngs of thy selfe, nor to walke in the commaundementes of god, and to serue him, without hys speciall grace, which thou must learne at all tymes to cal for by diligent praier. Let me heare therefore if thou canst say the Lordes prayer.

Aunswere. Our father, which art in heauen, hallowed be thy name. Thy kyngdome come. Thy wyll be doen in earth as it is in heauen. Geue us thys daye our dayly bread. And forgeue us oure trespasses, as we forgeue them that trespasse against us. And leade us not into temptacyon. But delyuer us from euill. Amen.

Question. What desirest thou of god in thys prayer?

Aunswere. I desire my Lord God oure heauenly father, who is the geuer of all goodnes, to send hys grace unto me and to al people, that we may worshyp him, serue hym, and obey hym as we ought to doe. And I praye unto God, that he wyll sende us all thynges that be nedeful both for our soules and bodyes: And that he will be mercyful unto us, and forgeue us oure synnes: and that it wyll please him to saue and defende us in all daungers gostly and bodyly. And that he will kepe us from all synne and wyckednes, and from our gostly enemye, and from euerlasting death. And thys I truste he wyll doe of hys mercy and goodnes, through our lord Jesus Christ. And therefore I saye, Amen. So be it.

¶ *So sone as the children can say in theyr mother tongue the artycles of the fayth, the Lordes prayer, the x Commaundementes : and also can answer to such questions of this shorte Catechisme, as the Bisshop (or such as he shal appoynt) shall by his discrecion appose them in : then shall they be broughte to the Bisshop by one that shalbe hys Godfather, or Godmother, that euery childe maye haue a witnes of his confirmacion.*

¶ *And the Bisshop shall confyrm them on this wise.*

¶ CONFIRMACYON.

Our helpe is in the name of the Lord.
Aunswere. Which hath made both heauen and earth.
Minister. Blessed is the name of the Lord.
Aunswere. Hencefurth world without ende.
Minister. Lord heare our prayer.
Aunswere. And let out crye come to thee.

Let us praye.

ALMIGHTIE and euerliuinge God, who haste vouchesafed to regenerate these thy seruaunts by water and the holy gost, and hast geuen unto them forgyuenes of all theyr synnes: strengthen them, we beseche thee, (O Lord,) with the holy gost the comforter, and daily encrease in them thy manifold giftes of grace, the spirite of wisdome and understanding; the spirite of counsel and gostly strength, the spirite of knowledge and true godlynes: and fulfil them, (O lord,) with the spirit of thy holy feare. Amen.

Then the Bisshoppe shal laye hys hande upon euery chylde seuerally, saying,

DEFENDE, O lord, this child with thy heauenly grace, that he may continue thine for euer, and dayly encrease in thy holy spirite more and more, until he come unto thy euerlastyng kyngdom. Amen.

Then shall the Bisshoppe saye.

¶ Let us pray.

ALMIGHTIE euerliuing God, whiche makeste us both to will, and to doe those thyngs that be good and acceptable unto thy Maiestie: we make oure humble supplycacyons unto thee for these children, upon whom (after the example of thy holy Apostles) we haue layed our handes, to certifie them (by thys sygne) of thy fauoure and gracious goodnes towarde them: lette thy fatherly hande we beseche thee euer be ouer them, let thy holy spirite euer be with them, and so leade them in the knowledge and obedience of thy woord, that in the ende they may obteine the euerlastyng lyfe, through our Lord Jesus Chryst, who with thee and the holy goste, lyueth and reygneth one god, world without ende. Amen.

Then the Bisshoppe shall bless the children, thus saying.

THE blessyng of god Almightie, the father, the sonne, and the holy goste, be upon you, and remayne with you for euer. Amen.

The Curate of euery Parishe, or some other at his appoynctmente, shall diligently upon Sundaies, and holy daies halfe an hour before Euensong, openly in the Churche instruct and examine so many children of his parishe sente unto him, as the time wil serue, and as he shal thinke conuenient, in some parte of this Catechisme

And all Fathers, Mothers, Maisters, and Dames, shall cause theyr chyldren, seruaunts, and prentises (whiche haue not earned theyr Catechisme), to come to the church at the time appoynted, and obediently to heare and be ordered by the Curate, until such time as they haue learned all that is here appointed for them to learne. And whensoeuer the Bisshop shall geue knowledge for children to be brought afore him to any conuenient place, for theyr confirmacion : Then shall the Curate of euery parish either bryng, or send in writing, the names of al those children of his parishe which can say the Articles of their fayth, the Lordes praier, and the x commaundementes : and also howe many of them can aunswere to thother questions conteined in this Catechisme.

And there shal none be admitted to the holy Communion, until suche tyme as he can saye the Catechisme, and bee confirmed.

THE FOURME OF
SOLEMNIZACYON OF MATRYMONYE.

First the bannes must be asked three seuerall Sundayes or holy daies, in the time of seruice, the people being present after the accustomed maner.

And if the persons that woulde be maryed dwell in diuers Parishes, the bannes must be asked in both Parishes, and the Curate of thone Parish shall not solemnize Matrimonie betwixt them, without a certificat of the bannes beeyng thryce asked, from the Curate of the other Parishe. At the daye appoynted for Solemnizacion of Matrimonye, the persones to be maryed shal come into the bodye of the churche, with theyr frendes and neyghbours. And there the Priest shall thus saye.

DEARELY beloued frendes, we are gathered together here in the syght of God, and in the face of his congregacion, to ioyne together thys man and this woman in holy matrimonie, which is an honorable estate, instituted of god in Paradise, in the time of man's innocency, signifying unto us the misticall union that is betwixte Chryste and hys Churche: whiche holy estate Chryst adourned and beutified with his presence, and fyrst miracle that he wrought, in Cana of Galile, and is commended of Saincte Paul to bee honourable among all men; and therefore is not to bee enterprised, nor taken in hande unaduisedly, lightely, or wantonly, to satisfie mennes carnall lustes and appetites, lyke brute beastes that haue no understandynge: but reuerently, discretely, aduisedly, soberly, and in the feare of God: Duely consideryng the causes for whiche Matrymonye was ordayned. One was the procreacion of children, to be broughte up in the feare and nurtoure of the Lorde, and prayse of God. Secondlye it was ordeined for a remedye agaynste synne, and to auoide fornicacion, that suche persons as haue not the gyfte of continencie myght marye, and kepe themselues undefiled members of Christes body. Thirdly, for the mutuall societie, helpe, and coumforte, that the one ought to haue of the other, both in prosperitie and aduersitie; into the whiche holy estate these two persons present come now to be ioyned. Therefore if any man can shew any iust cause, why they may not lawfully be ioined together: let him now speake, or els hereafter for euer holde hys peace.

And also speakyng to the persones that shalbe maried, he shall saye.

I require and charge you (as you wil aunswere at the dreadful day of iudgment, when the secretes of al hearts shalbe disclosed) that if either of you doe knowe any impediment, why ye may not be lawfully ioyned together in Matrimonie, that ye confesse it. For be ye wel assured, that so many as be coupled together otherwyse then god's word doth allowe, are not ioyned together by god, neither is there Matrimonye lawfull.

At whiche daye, of mariage if any man doe allege and declare any impediment why thei may not be coupled together in Matrimony by god's law or the lawes of this Realme, and wyl be bounde, and sufficient suerties with him, to the parties, or elles put in a caucion to the full value of such charges as the persons to be maried doeth susteine to proue his allegacion: then the Solemnizacion must be deferred, unto such tyme as the trueth be tryed. If no impedimente bee alleged, then shal the Curate saye unto the man.

N. Wilt thou haue this woman to thy wedded wife, to liue together after god's ordinaunce in the holy estate of matrimonie? Wilte thou loue her, coumfort her, honour, and kepe her in sickenes and in health? And forsaking al other kepe thee onely to her, so long as you both shall lyue?

The man shall aunswere,

I wyll.

Then shal the Priest saye to the woman.

N. Wilte thou haue this man to thy wedded housband, To lyue together after god's ordynaunce, in the holy estate of matrimony? Wylte thou obey him, and serue him, loue, honor, and kepe him, in sickenes and in health? and forsakyng al other kepe thee onely unto him, so long as you both shall lyue?

The woman shall aunswere,

I wyll.

Then shall the Minister saye,

Who geueth this woman to be maryed unto thys man?

And the Ministre receiuing the woman at her father or frendes handes, shal cause the man to take the woman by the ryght hande, and so either to geue their trouth to other. The man first saying,

I *N.* take thee *N.* to my wedded wife, to haue and to hold from this day foreward, for better, for worse, for rycher, for poorer, in sickenes, and in health, to loue, and to cherish, till death us depart, according to goddes holy ordynaunce: And thereto I plight thee my troth.

Then shall they loose theyr handes, and the woman takyng again the man by the ryght hand shall saye.

I *N.* take thee *N.* to my wedded husbande, to haue and to holde from this day forewarde, for better, for worse, for richer, for poorer, in sickenes, and in health, to loue, cherish, and to obeye, tyl death us depart, according to goddes holy ordynaunce: And thereto I geue thee my troth.

Then shall they agayne loose their handes, and the man shal geue unto the woman a ryng, laying the same upon the boke, with the accustomed duty to the priest and clerke. And the priest taking the ring shall delyuer it unto the man, to put it upon the fourth finger of the woman's left hand. And the man taught by the priest, shal say,

With this ring I thee wedde: with my body I thee worship: and with al my worldly goodes I thee endow. In the name of the father, and of the sonne, and of the holy gost. Amen.

Then the man leuuing the ryng upon the fourth finger of the woman's lefte hande, the Ministre shal say,

¶ Let us praye.

O ETERNAL God, creatour and preseruer of all mankynd, geuer of al spiritual grace, the auctour of euerlastyng lyfe: Sende thy blessyng upon these thy seruauntes, this man and this woman, whom we blesse in thy name, that as Isaac and Rebecca liued faithfully together; so these persons maye surely perfourme and kepe the vowe and couenaunt betwixt them made, whereof this ryng geuen and receyued is a token and pledge: and maye euer remayne in perfecte loue and peace together; and lyue accordynge unto thy lawes; throughe Jesus Christe oure Lorde. Amen.

¶ Then shal the Priest ioyne theyr ryght handes together, and saye,

Those whom god hath ioyned together, let no man put asunder.

¶ Then shall the Ministre speak unto the people.

FORASMUCHE as *N.* and *N.* have consented together in holy wedlocke, and haue witnessed the same beefore god and thys company, and thereto haue geuen and pledged their troth either to other, and haue declared thesame by geuing and receyuing of a ryng, and by ioyning of hands: I pronounce that they bee man and wyfe together. In the name of the father, of the sonne, and of the holy gost. Amen.

¶ And the ministre shal adde thys blessyng.

GOD the father, god the sonne, god the holy gost blesse, preserue, and kepe you: the lorde mercyfully with his fauoure loke upon you, and so fyll you with all spirituall benediccion and grace, that you maye so lyue together in this life, that in the world to come you may haue lyfe euerlastynge. Amen.

¶ *Then the Ministers or Clerkes, going to the Lordes table, shall saye or syng this Psalme following.*

Beati omnes. cxxviii.

BLESSED are all they that feare the Lord : and walke in hys ways.

For thou shalt eate the labour of thy handes : O well is thee, and happy shalte thou be.

Thy wife shall be as the fruitfull vyne : upon the walles of thy house.

Thy chyldren lyke the Oliue braunches : round about thy table.

Lo, thus shal the man be blessed : that feareth the lord.

The lord from out of Sion shall blesse thee : that thou shalt see Hierusalem in prosperitie al thy lyfe longe.

Yea, that thou shalte see thy chyldrens chyldren : and peace upon Israel.

Glory be to the father, &c.

As it was in the, &c.

¶ *Or els thys Psalme folowinge.*

Deus misereatur. Psalm lxvii.

GOD be merciful unto us, and blesse us : and shew us the light of hys countenaunce, and be mercifull unto us.

That thy waye may bee knowen upon the earth : thy sauing health among al nacions.

Let the people prayse thee (O god :) yea, let al the people prayse thee.

O let the nacions reioice and be glad : for thou shalte iudge the flock righteously, and gouern the nacions upon the earth.

Let the people prayse thee, O God : lette al the people prayse thee.

Then shal the earth bring furth her encrease : and God, euen our god, shal geue us his blessing.

God shal blesse us, and al the endes of the world shall feare hym.

Glory be to the father, &c.

As it was in thee, &c.

¶ *The Psalme ended, and the man and the woman kneling afore the lordes table: the prieste standyng at the table, and turning his face towarde them, shall saye.*

Lorde, haue mercy upon us.

Aunswere. Christ, haue mercy upon us.

Ministre. Lorde, have mercye upon us.

¶ Our father which arte in heauen, &c.

And leade us not into temptacion.

Aunswere. But delyuer us from euyll. Amen.

Minister. O Lorde saue thy seruaunt, and thy hand-mayde.

Aunswere. Which put theyr trust in thee.

Minister. O Lorde, sende them helpe from thy holy place.

Aunswere. And euermore defende them.

Minister. Be unto them a towre of strength.

Aunswere. From the face of theyr enemye.

Minister. O Lorde, heare our prayer.

Aunswere. And let our crye come unto thee.

The Minister.

O God of Abraham, God of Isaac, God of Jacob, blesse these thy seruaunts, and sowe the sede of eternal lyfe in theyr mindes, that whatsoeuer in thy holy worde they shall profytably learne, they may in dede fulfyl the same. Loke, O Lord, mercyfully upon them from heaven, and blesse them. And as thou diddest send thy blessing upon Abraham and Sara to theyr great comfort; so vouchsafe to send thy blessing upon these thy seruaunts, that they obeying thy wyl, and alway being in safetie under thy proteccion, may abide in thy loue unto theyr liues' ende, through Jesu Christ our Lorde. Amen.

This prayer next folowing shalbe omitted where the woman is past chyld-birth.

O MERCIFUL Lord and heauenly father, by whose gracious gift mankind is encreased: we besече thee, assist with thy blessing these two persons, that they may both be fruiteful in procreacion of chyldren, and also lyue together so long in godly loue and honestie, that they may see their children's children, unto the third and fourth generacion, unto thy prayse and honour: through Jesus Christ our Lorde Amen.

O God, which by thy mighty power hast made all thinges of naught, which also after other thinges set in ordre didst appoynt that out of man (created after thyne owne ymage and similitude) womanne should take her beginning: and, knitting them together, didst teach that it should neuer be lawefull to put asunder those, whom thou by matrimonie hadst made one: O god, which hast consecrated the state of matrimonie to such an excellent misterie, that in it is signified and represented the spiritual mariage and unitie betwixt Christ and his church: Loke mercyfully upon these thy seruaunts, that both this man may loue his wife, according to thy worde, (as Christ did loue his spouse the church, who gaue himself for it, louing and cherishing it euen as his own flesh;) and also that this woman may be louing and amiable to her husband as Rachel, wise as Rebecca, faithful and obedient as Sara; and in all quietnes, sobriete, and peace, be a folower of holy and godly matrones: O Lorde, blesse them both, and graunt them to inheritie thy euerlasting kingdome, through Jesus Christ our Lord. Amen.

Then shal the Priest saye,

ALMIGHTIE god, which at the beginning did create our first parentes Adam and Eue, and did sanctifie and ioyne them together in mariage: poure upon you the riches of his grace, sanctifie and blesse you, that ye may please him bothe in body and soule, and lyue together in holy loue, unto your lyues' ende. Amen.

Then shal begin the Communion, and after the Gospel shal be sayd a sermon, wherein ordinarely (so oft as there is any mariage) the office of a man and wyfe shalbe declared according to holy scripture : or yf there be no sermon, the Minister shall reade this that foloweth.

ALL ye whiche be maried, or whiche entende to take the holy estate of matrimonie upon you: heare what holye scripture doeth saye, as touching the duetie of husbandes towarde theyr wyues, and wyues towarde theyr husbandes. Sainct Paule (in his Epistle to the Ephesians the fyfth Chapter) doeth geue this commaundementc to all maried men.

Ye husbandes, loue your wyues, even as Christ loued the church, and hath geuen himself for it, to sanctifie it, pourging it in the fountayne of water, throughe thy worde, that he might make it unto himself a glorious congregacion, not hauing spot, or wrinkle, or any such thinge; but that it should be holy and blameles. So men are bound to loue theyr owne wyues as theyr owne bodies. He that loueth his owne wife, loueth himself. For neuer did any man hate his owne flesh, but nourissheth and cherissheth it, euen as the Lord doth the congregacion; for we are membres of his body, of his fleshe, and of his bones.

For this cause shal a man leaue father and mother, and shall be ioyned unto his wyfe, and they two shalbe one fleshe. This mistery is great, but I speak of Christ and of the congregacion. Neuerthelesse, let euery one of you so loue his owne wyfe, euen as himselfe.

Likewise the same Sainct Paul (writing to the Colossians) speaketh thus to al men that be maried: Ye men loue your wyues and be not bitter vnto them. (*Coloss.* iii.)

Heare also what Sainct Peter the apostle of Christe, which was him self a maried man, sayeth vnto all men that are maried. Ye husbandes, dwel with your wiues according to knowledge: Geuing honour vnto the wyfe, as vnto the weaker vessel, and as heyres together of the grace of lyfe, so that your prayers be not hyndered. (1 *Pet.* iii.)

‣Hetherto ye haue hearde the duetie of the husbande towarde the wyfe.

Nowe lykewyse, ye wyues, heare and learne your duetie towardes youre husbandes, euen as it is playnly set forth in holy scripture.

Sainct Paul (in the forenamed Epistle to the Ephesians) teacheth you thus: Ye women submitte yourselues vnto your own husbandes as vnto the lord: for the husbande is the wyue's head, even as Christe is the head of the Church. And he is also the sauiour of the whole body. Therefore as the church, or congregacion, is subiecte vnto Christe, so lykewyse let the wyues also bee in subieccion vnto theyr owne husbandes in all thinges. (*Ephes.* v.) And agayne he sayth: Let the wyfe reuerence her husbande. And (in his Epistle to the Collossians) Sainct Paule geueth you this shorte lesson: Ye wyues, submit your selues vnto your own husbandes, as it is conuenient in the Lorde. *Coloss.* iii. (*sic*).

Sainct Peter also doth instruct you very godly, thus saying: Let wiues be subiect to theyr owne husbandes, so that yf any obey not the word, they may be wonne without the worde, by the conuersacion of the wyues, whyle they behold your chaste conuersacion, coupled with feare: whose apparel let it not be outward, with broyded heere and trimming about with gold, eyther in putting on of gorgeous apparel: but let the hyd man, which is in the heart, be without al corrupcion, so that the spirite be milde and quiet, which is a precious thing in the syght of God. For after this maner (in the olde tyme) dydde the holy women, whiche trusted in God apparel themselues, being subiect to their owne husbandes: as Sara obeyed Abraham callinge him Lord, whose daughters ye are made, doynge well and beyng not dismayde with any feare. (1 *Pet.* iii.)

The newe maried persons (the same daye of their mariage) must receiue the holy communion.

VISITACION OF THE SICKE.

¶ The Priest entering into the sicke person's house, shall saye.

Peace be in this house, and to all that dwell in it.

When he cometh into the sick man's presence, he shall saye, kneling downe.

REMEMBRE not, Lorde, oure iniquities, nor the iniquities of our forefathers. Spare us, good Lord, spare thy people, whom thou hast redemed with thy most precious bloud, and be not angry with us for euer.

Lorde, haue mercy upon us.
Christ, haue mercy upon us.
Lorde, haue mercy upon us,
Our father, which art in heauen, &c.
And leade us not into temptacion.
Aunswere. But delyuer us from euyll. Amen.
Minister. O Lord, saue thy seruaunt.
Aunswere. Which putteth his trust in thee.
Minister. Sende him helpe from thy holy place.
Aunswere. And euermore mightely defende him.
Minister. Let the enemie have none aduauntage of him.
Aunswere. Nor the wicked approche to hurte him.
Minister. Be unto him, O Lord, a stronge towre.
Aunswere. From the face of his enemie.
Minister. Lorde, heare oure prayers.
Aunswere. And let our crye come unto thee.

Minister.

O LORD, loke downe from heauen, behold, visite, and releue this thy seruaunt: Looke upon him with the eyes of thy mercy, geue him comforte, and sure confidence in thee: Defende him from the daunger of the enemye, and keepe him in perpetuall peace, and safetie: through Jesus Christ our Lord. Amen.

Heare us, almightie and most mercyful God and sauiour. Extend thy accustomed goodnes to this thy seruaunt, which is grieued with sicknes: Visite him, O Lorde, as thou diddeste visite Peter's wyue's mother and the Captayne's seruaunt. So visite and restore unto this sycke person his former health, (yf it bee thy wyl) or els geue him grace so to take thy vysitacion, that after this paynfull lyfe ended, he maye dwell with thee in lyfe euerlasting. Amen.

Then shall the Minister exhorte the sicke person after this fourme or other lyke.

DERELY beloued, know this: that almightie God is the Lord of lyfe and death, and ouer all thinges to them perteyning, as youth, strength, health, age, weakenes, and sickenesse. Wherfore, whatsoeuer your sickenesse is, know you certaynlye that it is god's visitacion. And for what cause soeuer this sickenesse is sente unto you: whether it be to trie youre pacience for the example of other, and that your fayth may be found in the day of the lord laudable, glorious, and honorable, to the encrease of glory, and endlesse felicitie: Or els it be sent unto you to correct and amend in you, whatsoeuer doeth offend the eyes of our heauenly father: know you certainly, that yf you truely repent you of your sinnes, and beare your sickenes paciently, trusting in god's mercye, for his dere sonne Jesus Christes sake, and rendre unto him humble thankes for his fatherly visitacion, submittinge yourself wholy to his wyll; it shall turne to your profit, and helpe you forward in the right way that leadeth unto euerlasting lyfe.

Yf the person vysyted be very sicke, then the curate maye ende hys exhortacion in this place.

¶ Take therefore in good worth the chastement of the Lorde. For whom the Lorde loueth, he chastiseth. Yea, (as Sainct Paul sayth,) he skourgeth euery sonne which he receyueth: yf you indure chastisement, he offreth him self unto you as unto his owne children. What sonne is he that the father chastiseth not? Yf ye be not under correccion (whereof all true children are partakers), then are ye bastardes and not children. Therfore seing that whan our carnal fathers do correcte us, we reuerentlye obeye them: shall we not now much rather be obedient to our spiritual father, and so lyue? And they for a fewe dayes dooe chastise us after theyr owne pleasure: but he doeth chastise us for our profyt, to the intent he may make us partakers of his holynes. These wordes, good brother, are God's wordes, and written in holy scripture for oure comfort and instruccion, that we shoulde paciently and with thankesgeuing beare our heauenly father's correccion, whansoeuer by anye maner of aduersytie it shall please his gracious goodnes to vysit us. And there should be no greater comfort to christian persons, then to be made lyke unto Christe, by sufferinge paciently aduersities, troubles, and sickenesses. For he himself went not up to ioye, but fyrst he suffered payne: he entred not into his glorye before he was crucifyed. So truely oure waye to eternall ioye is to suffre here with Christ, and our doore to entre into eternall lyfe is gladlye to dye with Christ, that we may ryse agayne from death, and dwel with him in euerlastinge lyfe. Now therfore taking your sicknesse which is thus profytable for you, paciently: I exhorte you in the name of God, to remember the profession which you made unto God in your Baptisme. And forasmuch as after this lyfe there is accoumpte to be geuen unto the righteous iudge, of whom all muste be iudged without respecte of persones: I requyre you to examine your self, and your state, both towarde God and man: so that accusing and condemning your self for your owne faultes, you may fynd mercy at our heauenly father's hande for Christ's sake, and not be accused and condemned in that feareful iudgement. Therfore I shall shortely rehearse the articles of our faythe, that ye maye knowe whether you do beleue as a Christian man should, or no.

¶ Here the Minister shal rehearse the articles of the faith, sayinge thus.

DOEST thou beleue in God the father almightie?

¶ And so forth, as it is in Baptisme.

¶ Then shall the Minister examine whether he be in charitie with al the world: Exhortinge him to forgeue from the bottome of his hearte al persons that haue offended hym: and yf he haue offended other to aske them forgeuenesse: And where he hath done iniurie or wrong to any man, that he make amendes to the uttermost of his power. And yf he haue not afore disposed hys goodes, let him then make his wyl. But men must be ofte admonished that they sette an ordre for theyr temporall goodes and landes whan they be in health. And also declare his debtes, what he oweth, and what is owing unto him, for discharging of his conscience, and quietnesse of hys executours.

¶ These words before rehearsed, may be said before the Minister beginne his prayer, as he shal see cause.

¶ The minister may not forgeat nor omitte to moue the sicke person (and that most earnestly) to lyberalitie towarde the poore.

¶ Here shal the sicke person make a special confession, yf he feele his conscience troubled wyth any weyghtie matter. After which confession the Priest shal absolue hym after thys sorie.

OUR Lord Jesus Christ, who hath left power to his Church to absolue al sinners, whiche truely repent and beleue in him, of his great mercy forgeue thee thine offences: and by his aucthoritie committed to me, I absolue thee from all thy synnes, in the name of the father, and of the sonne, and of the holy gost. Amen.

¶ And then the Priest shal saye the Collect folowinge.

¶ Let us praye.

O MOSTE mercyfull God, whiche according to the multitude of thy mercies doest so put away the sinnes of those which truely repente, that thou remembrest them no more: open thy eye of mercy upon this thy seruaunt, who most earnestly desyreth pardon and forgeuenes: Renue in him, most louing father, whatsoeuer hath been decayed by the fraud and malice of the deuyl, or by his owne carnal wyl, and fraylnesse: preserue and continue this sicke membre in the unitie of thy church, consider his contricion, accept his teares, asswage his paine, as shal be sene to thee most expedient for him. And forasmuch as he putteth his full trust onely in thy mercy; Impute not unto him his former synnes, but take him unto thy fauoure: through the merites of thy most derely beloued sonne Jesus Christe. Amen.

Then the Minister shal saye thys Psalme.

In te Domine speravi. Psal. xxi. (*sic*).

IN thee, O lord, haue I put my trust, let me neuer be put to confusion: but rydde me, and delyuer me, into thy rightousnesse; incline thyne eare unto me, and saue me.

Be thou my strong holde, (whereunto I may alway resorte) thou hast promised to helpe me, for thou art my house of defence, and my castell.

Deliuer me (O my God) out of the hand of the ungodly : out of the hand of the unrighteous and cruell man.

For thou (O Lorde God) art the thinge that I long for : thou art my hope, euen from my youth.

Throughe thee haue I been holden up euer since I was borne; thou art he that toke me out of my mother's wombe; my prayse shall alway be of thee.

I am become as it were a monstre unto many : but my sure trust is in thee.

O lette my mouth be fylled with thy prayse (that I may sing of thy glory) and honour all the daye longe.

Caste me not away in the tyme of age, forsake me not when my strength fayleth me.

For myne enemies speake agaynste me: and they that lay waite for my soule take their counsel together, saying : God hath forsaken him; persecute him, and take him, for there is none to delyuer him.

Goe not farre from me, O God : my God, haste thee to helpe me.

Let them be confounded and perishe that are against my soule : let them be couered with shame and dishonor that seke to do me euyll.

As for me, I wyll paciently abyde alwaye : and wyll prayse thee more and more.

My mouth shall daylye speake of thye righteousnesse and saluacion : for I knowe no ende thereof.

I wyl goe forth in the strength of the Lord God : and wyll make mencion of thy righteousnes onely.

Thou (O god) hast taught me from my youth up until now : therfore I wyl tel of thy wonderous workes.

Forsake me not (O God) in myne olde age, when I am graye headed, untill I haue shewed thy strength unto this generacion, and thy power to all them that are yet for to come.

Thy righteousness (O God) is very hygh : and great thinges are they that thou haste doone; O God, who is lyke unto thee?

O what greate troubles and aduersities haste thou shewed me! and yet diddeste thou turne and refreshe me : yea, and broughtest me from the depe of the earth agayne.

Thou hast brought me to greate honour : and comforted me on euery syde.

Therfore wyl I prayse thee and thy faythfulness (O God) playing upon an instrument of musicke, unto thee wyl I sing upon the harpe, O thou holy one of Israel.

My lippes wyl be fayne when I syng unto thee : and so wyll my soule whom thou hast deliuered.

My tonge also shall talke of thy righteousnesse al the daye longe, for they are confounded and broughte unto shame that seke to do me euyll.

Glory bee to the father, and to the sonne; and to the holye ghoste.

As it was in the beginninge, is nowe; and euer shall be; worlde without ende. Amen.

¶ Addinge this.

O Sauioure of the worlde, saue us, whiche by thy crosse and precious bloud hast redemed us, helpe us, we beseche thee, O God.

Then shal the Minister saye.

The almightie Lorde, which is a most stronge tower to all them that put their truste in him, to whom all thinges in heauen, in earth, and under earth, doe bowe and obeye: be nowe and euermore thy defence, and make thee know and feele, that there is no other name under heauen geuen to manne, in whom, and throughe whom, thou mayest receyue health and salvacion, but onely the name of oure Lorde Jesus Christe. Amen.

THE
COMMUNION OF THE SICKE.

Forasmuch as all mortal men be subiect to many sodayne perilles, diseases and sickenesses, and euer vncertayne what time they shal depart out of this lyfe: Therfore to thintent they may be alwayes in a readinesse to dye, whensoeuer it shal please almightie God to call them, the Curates shal diligentlye from tyme to tyme, but speciallye in the plague tyme, exhorte theyr parishioners to the oft receyuing in the church of the holye communion of the body and bloud of our sauiour Christ. Which (yf they do,) they shal haue no cause, in theyr sodaine visitacion, to be vnquieted for lacke of the same. But yf the sycke person be not hable to come to the church, and yet is desyrous to receyue the communion in hys house, then he must geue knowledge ouernyght, or els early in the morning to the Curate, signifyinge also howe manye be appoynted to communicate with hym. And hauing a conuenient place in the syke man's house, where the Curate maye reuerently minister, and a good nombre to receyue the communion wyth the sycke personne, with al thinges necessarye for thesame, he shall there minister the holye communion.

The Collecte.

ALMIGHTIE euerlyuinge God, maker of mankinde, which doest correcte those whom thou doest loue, and chastisest euery one whom thou doest receyue: we beseche thee to haue mercy vpon this thy seruaunt visited with thy hande, and to graunte that he may take his syckenesse paciently, and recouer his bodelye health (yf it bee thy gracious wyll), and whensoeuer his soule shall departe from the bodye, it maye bee without spotte presented vnto thee: through Jesus Christ our Lorde. Amen.

The Epistle. Heb. xii.

MY sonne, despyse not the correccion of the Lord, nether faynte when thou art rebuked of hym: For whom the Lord loueth, him he correcteth, yea and he scourgeth euery sonne whom he receyueth.

The Gospell. John v.

VERELY, verely I saye vnto you, he that heareth my worde, and beleueth on him that sente me, hath euerlasting lyfe, and shall not come vnto damnacion, but he passeth from death vnto lyfe.

¶ *At the tyme of the distribucion of the holy Sacrament, the Priest shal fyrst receyue the Communion himself, and after minister unto them that be appointed to communicate wyth the sycke.*

¶ *But yf any man either by reason of extremitie of syckenes, or for lacke of warning in due tyme to the Curate, or for lacke of company to receyue with him, or by any other iust impediment, do not receyue the Sacrament of Christes body and bloud ; then the Curate shal instruct him, that yf he do truly repent him of his synnes, and stedfastly beleue that Jesus Christ hath suffred death upon the crosse for him, and shed his bloud for his redempcion, earnestly remembring the benefites he hath therby, and gauing him heartie thanks therfore : he doeth eate and drinke the body and bloude of our Sauiour Christ, profytably to his soules health, althoughe he doe not receyue the Sacrament with hys mouth.*

¶ *When the sicke person is visited and receiueth the holi communion all at one tyme : then the priest for more expedicion shal cut of the forum of the visitacion at the Psalme. In thee, O Lord, haue I put my trust, and go streyght to the communion.*

¶ *In the tyme of plague, Swette, or suche other lyke contagious tymes of sycke-nesses or dyseases, when none of the parysh or neyghbours can be gotten to communicate wyth the syck in theyr houses, for feare of the infeccion, upon special request of the diseased, the minister may alonly communicate wyth hym.*

THE ORDRE FOR THE
BURIALL OF THE DEAD.

The Priest meting the corps at the Church style. shal saye. Or els the priestes and clerkes shal singe, and so go eyther unto the churche or towardes the graue.

I AM the resurreccion and the lyfe (sayeth the Lorde): he that beleueth in me, yea thoughe he were dead, yet shall he lyue. And whosoeuer lyueth and beleueth in me, shall not dye for euer. *John* xi.

I KNOWE that my redemer lyueth, and that I shall ryse out of the earth in the last day, and shalbe couered agayne with my skinn, and shall see God in my fleshe: yea, and I my selfe shall beholde hym, not with other but wyth these same eyes. *Job* xix.

WE brought nothing into this world, neither may we cary any thing out of this worlde. I *Tim.* vi. The Lord geueth, and the Lorde taketh awaye. Euen as it hath pleased the Lord, so cometh thinges to passe: blessed be the name of the Lorde. *Job* i.

When they come at the graue, whiles the corps is made ready to be layde into the earth, the Priest shall saye, or the priest and clerkes shall singe.

MAN that is borne of a womanne, hath but a shorte time to lyue, and is full of misery: he cometh up and is cut downe lyke a floure; he flieth as it were a shadowe, and neuer continueth in one staye. *Job* ix.

In the mideste of lyfe we bee in death: of whom may we seke for succour, but of thee, O Lord, which for our sinnes iustlye arte displeased? yet, O Lord God most holy, O Lord most mightie, O holy and moste mercyfull sauioure, delyuer us not into the bitter paines of eternal death. Thou knowest, Lord, the secretes of oure heartes: shutte not up thy merciful eyes to oure prayers: But spare us, lord most holi, O god most mightie, O holy and mercifull sauiour, thou moste worthy iudge eternall, suffre us not at oure last houre for any paynes of death to fall from thee.

Then whyle the earth shalbe cast upon the body, by some standing by, the priest shal say,

FORASMUCHE as it hathe pleased almightie God of his great

mercy to take unto himselfe the soule of our dere brother here
departed: we therefore commit his body to the ground, earth
to earth, asshes to asshes, dust to dust, in sure and certayne hope
of resurreccion to eternal lyfe, through our Lord Jesus Christ,
who shal chaunge our vyle bodye, that it maye bee lyke to his
glorious bodye, according to the mightie working wherby he is
hable to subdue all thinges to himselfe.

¶ *Then shalbe sayd or song,*

I HEARDE a voyce from heauen, sayinge unto me: Wryte from
henceforth, blessed are the dead which dye in the Lorde. Euen
so sayth the spyrite, that they rest from theyr laboures.

*Then shal folowe this lesson, taken out of the xv. Chapter to the Corinthians,
the fyrst Epistle.*

CHRISTE is rysen from the dead, and become the fyrst fruites
of them that slepte. For by a manne came death, and by a
manne came the resurreccion of the dead. For as by Adam all
dye, euen so by Christ shall all be made alyue, but euery man in
hys owne ordre. The fyrst is Christ, then they that are Christes,
at his comming. Then cometh the ende, when he hath delyuered
up the kyngdome to God the father, when he hath put downe all
rule and all aucthoritie and power. For he must reygne tyll he
haue put all hys enemies under his feete. The laste enemie that
shall be destroyed is death. For he hath putte all thinges under
his feete. But when he sayth all thinges are put under him, it is
manyfest that he is excepted, which dyd put all thinges under
him. When all thinges are subdued unto him, then shal the
sonne also himself be subiect unto him that put al thinges under
him, that God may be al in al. Els what doe they which are
Baptised ouer the dead, yf the dead ryse not at all? Why are
they then Baptysed ouer them? yea and why stande we alwaye
then in ieopardie? By our reioysing, whiche I haue in Christ
Jesu oure Lorde, I dye daylye. That I haue foughte with
beastes at Ephesus after the maner of men, what auantageth it
me, if the dead ryse not agayne? Lette us eate, and drinke, for
to-morowe we shall dye. Be not ye deceyued: euil wordes
corrupt good maners. Awake truely oute of slepe, and synne
not. For some haue not the knowledge of God. I speake this
to youre shame. But some man wyl saye: How aryse the dead?
with what body shal they come? Thou foole, that whiche thou
soweste is not quickened, excepte it dye. And what sowest
thou? Thou sowest not that body that shalbe; but bare corne
as of wheat, or of some other: but God geueth it a bodye at his

pleasure, to euery sede his owne bodi. Al fleshe is not one maner of fleshe: but there is one maner of fleshe of men, and other maner of fleshe of beastes, and other of fisshes, another of birdes. There are also celestial bodies, and there are bodies terrestriall. But the glorye of the celestiall is one, and the glory of the terrestrial is another. There is one maner glory of the sunne, and another glory of the mone, and another glory of the starres. For one starre differeth from another in glory. So is the resurreccion of the dead. It is sowen in corrupcion, it ryseth agayne in incorrupcion. It is sowen in dishonoure, it ryseth agayne in honour. It is sowen in weaknesse, it ryseth agayne in power. It is sowen a naturall bodye, it ryseth agayne a spyrituall bodye. There is a naturall bodye, and there is a spirituall bodye: as it is also written: the fyrst man Adam was made a lyuing soule, and the laste Adam was made a quickening spyryte. Howbeit, that is not fyrst which is spyrytuall: but that whiche is naturall, and then that whiche is spyrytuall. The fyrst man is of the earth, earthy: the second man is the Lord from heauen, heauenly. As is the earthy, suche are they that are earthy. And as is the heauenly, such are they that are heauenly. And as we haue borne the Image of the earthy, so shall we beare the Image of the heauenly. Thys say I, brethren, that fleshe and bloud cannot inherite the kyngdome of God: neyther doeth corrupcion inherite uncorrupcion. Beholde, I shewe you a mistery. We shall not all slepe: but we shall all be chaunged and that in a momente, in the twinkeling of an eie by the last trumpe. For the trumpe shall blowe, and the dead shall ryse incorruptible, and we shall be chaunged. For thys corruptyble must put on incorrupcion: and this mortall must put on immortalitie. When this corruptible hath put on incorrupcion, and this mortal hath put on immortalitie: then shalbe brought to passe the saying that is written: Death is swallowed up in victory: Death, where is thy styng? Hell, where is thy victorye? The styng of death is sinne: and the strength of sinne is the law. But thanks be unto God whiche hath geuen us victory, through oure Lorde, Jesus Chryst. Therefore, my deare brethren, be ye stedfaste and unmouable, alwayes riche in the worke of the Lorde, forasmuche as ye knowe that your labour is not in vayne in the Lorde.

The lesson ended, the priest shall saye.

Lorde, haue mercy upon us.
Christe, haue mercy upon us.

Lorde, haue mercy upon us.
Our father which art in heaven, &c.
And leade us not into temptacion.
Aunswere. But delyuer us from euill.   Amen.

The Priest.

ALMIGHTIE God, with whom doe lyue the spirites of them that
departe hence in the lord, and in whom the soules of them that
be elected, after they be deliuered from the burden of the fleshe,
be in ioye and felicitie: We geue thee hearty thankes, for that it
hath pleased thee to deliuer thys *N.* our brother out of the
myseryes of this sinneful world: beseching thee, that it maye
please thee of thy gracious goodnesse, shortely to accomplyssh
the noumbre of thyne electe, and to haste thy kingdome, that we
with this our brother, and al other departed in the true faith of
thy holy name, maye haue our perfect consummacion and blisse,
both in body and soule, in thy eternal and euerlastyng glory.
Amen.

The Collect.

O MERCIFUL God, the father of our Lorde Jesus Christe, who is
the resurreccion and the lyfe, in whom whosoeuer beleueth, shall
lyue though he dye; and whosoeuer liueth and beleueth in hym,
shall not dye eternally: who also taught us (by his holy Apostle
Paule) not to be sorye, as men without hope, for them that slepe
in hym: We mekely beseche thee (O father) to raise us from the
death of sinne unto the life of righteousnes, that when we shal
depart thys lyfe, we may reste in him, as our hope is thys our
brother doeth; and that at the general resurreccion in the laste
daye, we may be founde acceptable in thy syghte, and receiue
that blessing which thy welbeloued sonne shall then pronounce
to al that loue and feare thee, saying: Come, ye blessed children
of my father, receiue the kyngdome prepared for you from the
beginning of the world.   Graunt this we beseche thee, O merciful father, through Jesus Christ our mediatour and redeyemer.
Amen.

THE THANKES GEUING OF WOMEN AFTER CHILDE BIRTH,

COMMONLY CALLED

THE CHURCHYNG OF WOMEN.

The woman shall come into the churche, and there shall knele downe in some conueniente place, nighe unto the place where the table standeth : and the prieste standyng by her, shall say these wordes, or suche like, as the case shal require.

FORASMUCH as it hath pleased almightie God of his goodnes to geue you safe deliueraunce, and hath preserued you in the great daunger of childe birth: ye shall therefore geue harty thankes unto god, and praye.

Then shall the priest say thys Psalme.

I HAUE lyfted up myne eyes unto the hilles : from whence cometh my helpe.

My helpe cometh euen from the lord : which hath made heauen and earth.

He wil not suffre thy fote to be moued : and he that kepeth thee wil not slepe.

Beholde, he that kepeth Israel : shall neither slumber nor slepe.

The lorde hymselfe is thy keper : the lorde is thy defence upon thy right hande.

So that the Sunne shal not burne thee by daye : neyther the Moone by nyghte.

The Lorde shall preserue thee from al euil : yea, it is euen he that shal kepe thy soule.

The Lord shall preserue thy going out, and thy coming in : from this time furth for euermore.

Glory be to the father, and to the sonne, and to, &c.

As it was in the begynnyng, is nowe, and euer, &c.

> Lorde, haue mercy upon us.
> Christe, haue mercy upon us.
> Lorde, haue mercy upon us.
> Our Father, which, &c.
> And leade us not into temptacion.

Aunswere. But delyuer us from euill.   Amen.
Priest. O Lorde, saue this woman thy seruaunt.
Aunswere. Which putteth her trust in thee.
Priest. Be thou to her a strong tower.
Aunswere. From the face of her enemye.
Priest. Lorde, heare our prayer.
Aunswere. And let our crie come unto thee.

Priest.   ¶ Let us praye.

O ALMIGHTIE god, whiche hast delyuered this woman thy
seruant from the great paine and peryl of childe birth: Graunte,
we beseche thee, (most mercifull father,) that she through thy
helpe, maye both faythfully lyue, and walke in her vocacion,
accordyng to thy wyl in thys lyfe present; and also maye bee
partaker of euerlastinge glorye in the life to come: through
Jesus Christe our Lorde.   Amen.

The woman that cometh to geue her thankes, muste offre accustomed offer-
ynges : and if there be a Communion, it is conueniente that she receyue
the holy Communvon.

A COMMINACION AGAYNSTE SYNNERS,

WITH CERTAYNE PRAYERS TO BE USED DYUERS TYMES IN THE YERE.

¶ *After Mornyng praier, the people being called together by the ringing of a bell, and assembled in the Churche, the English Letany shalbe sayd after the accustomed maner : whiche ended, the Priest shall goe into the pulpite and saye thus*

BRETHREN, in the primatiue church there was a Godly discyplyne, that at the begynnyng of Lent suche persons as were notorious synners, wer put to open penaunce and punished in thys world, that their soules might be saued in the day of the lorde, and that others admonished by theyr example, myght be more afrayed to offende. In the stede wherof, untyl the sayd discipline may be restored againe, (which thing is much to be wyshed,) it is thought good, that at thys tyme (in your presence) should be read the general sentences of God's curssyng against impenitent sinners, gathered out of the xxvii. Chapiter of Deuteronomye, and other places of scripture: and that ye shoulde aunswere to euery sentence, Amen. To thintent that you, beyng admonished of the great indignacion of God agaynst synners, may the rather be called to earneste and true repentaunce, and may walke more warely in these daungerous daies, fleeing from such vices, for the which ye affirme with your owne mouthes the curse of God to be due.

CURSED is the man that maketh any carued or molten Image, an abhominacion to the Lorde, the worke of the handes of the craftes manne, and putteth it in a secrete place to worshyp it

And the people shall aunswere and saye,

Amen.

Minister. Cursed is he that curseth his father, and mother.
Aunswere. Amen.
Minister. Cursed is he that remoueth awaye the marke of hys neighbour's lande.
Aunswere. Amen.
Minister. Cursed is he that maketh the blynd to goe out of his waye.
Aunswere. Amen.

A Commination 431

Minister. Cursed is he that letteth in Judgemente the ryght of the straunger, of them that be fatherles, and of wydowes.

Aunswere. Amen.

Minister. Cursed is he that smiteth his neighboure secretly.

Aunswere. Amen.

Minister. Cursed is he that lyeth with his neighbour's wife.

Aunswere. Amen.

Minister. Cursed is he that taketh reward to slea the soule of innocent bloud.

Aunswere. Amen.

Minister. Cursed is he that putteth his trust in man, and taketh man for hys defence, and in hys hearte goeth from the Lorde.

Aunswere. Amen.

Minister. Cursed are the unmercifull, the fornicatours and adulterers, & the couetous persons, the worshyppers of ymages, slaunderers, drunkards, and extorcioners.

Aunswere. Amen.

The Minister. Nowe seeing that all they be accursed (as the Prophet Dauid beareth witnes) which dooe erre and goe astraye from the commaundementes of God: lette us (remembryng the dreadfull judgement hangynge ouer our heades, and beeyng always at hande) returne unto our Lorde God, with all contricion and mekenesse of hearte bewaylynge and lamentynge our synfule lyfe, knowledgyng and confessyng our offences, and seekyng to bring furth worthy fruites of penaunce (*Psa.* cxviii.). For nowe is the Axe put unto the roote of the trees, so that euery tree whiche bringeth not furth good fruite is hewen downe, and caste into the fyre (*Mat.* iii.). It is a fearfull thyng to fall into the handes of the lyuing God (*Heb.* x.): he shall poure down rain upon the synners, snares, fyre and brimstone, storme and tempest: this shalbe their porcion to drynke (*Ps.* x.). For loe, the Lord is comen out of his place, to visite the wickednes of suche as dwell upon the earth (*Es.* xxvi.). But who maye abide the daye of hys comyng? Who shalbe able to endure when he appereth? His fanne is in his hand, and he wil pourge hys floore and gather hys wheate into the Barne (*Mala.* iii.): but he wylle burn the chaffe with unquencheable fyre (*Mat.* iii.). The daye of the Lord cometh as a thefe upon the night; and when men shal say peace, and al thinges are safe, then shall sodenly destruccion come upon them, as sorowe cometh upon a woman trauailing with childe, and they shall not escape (i *Thes.* v.): then shall appeare the wrath of God in the daye of vengeance, which obstinate sinners, throughe the stubbernes of theyr hearte, haue heaped vnto themselfe, whiche despysed the goodnes, pacience, and long-sufferaunce of God, when he called them continuallye to repentaunce (*Rom.* ii.). Then shal they cal vpon me, sayeth the lord, but I wyll not heare: they shal seke me earlye, but they shall not fynd me, and that because they hated knowledge, and receiued not the feare of the Lorde, but abhorred my counsayle, and despysed my correccion: then shall it be to late to knock, when the dore shall be shutte, and to late to crye for mercy, when it is the time of Justice (*Proue* i.). O terrible voyce of moste iuste iudgemente, whiche shall be pronounced vpon them, when it shalbe sayd vnto them: Goe ye cursed into the fyre euerlasting, which is prepared for the deuill and hys Aungels (*Matt.* xxv.). Therefore, brethren, take we hede betime, whyle the day of saluacion lasteth, for the nyght cometh when none can worke (2 *Cor.* vi.): but lette us, whyle we haue the lyght, beleue in the lyght, and walke as the children of the lyght, that we be not cast into the vttre darkenesse, where is wepyng and gnashyng of teeth (*John* ix.). Let us not abuse the goodnes of God, which calleth us mercifully to amendemente, and of hys endlesse pitie promyseth us forgeueness of that whiche is paste, if (with a whole mynd and true heart) we returne vnto hym (*Matt.* xxv.): for though our sins be red as scarlet, they shall be as white as Snowe; and thoughe they bee lyke purple, yet shall they be as white as wolle (*Esai.* i.). Turne you clene (sayth the Lord) from all youre wyckednesse, and youre synne shall not be youre destruccion. Caste awaye from you all your ungodlynes that ye haue done, make you new heartes, and a newe spirite: wherfore wil ye die, O ye house of Israel? Seeyng that I haue no pleasure in the death of hym that dyeth? (sayeth the Lorde God.) (*Ezech.* xxviii.). Turne you then, and you shall lyue. Althoughe we haue synned, yet haue we an aduocate with the father, Jesus Chryste the ryghteous: and he it is that obteyneth grace for our sinnes (1 *John* ii.); for he was wounded for our offences, and smitten for our wickednes (*Esai.* liii.). Let us therefore returne vnto hym, who is the merciful receyuer of all true penytent synners, assuring our self, that he is ready to receiue us, and most wyllyng to pardon us, if we come to hym with faythfull repentaunce: if we wil submit ourselues vnto hym, and from hencefurth walke in hys wayes: if we wil take his easye yoke and light burden upon us, to folowe him in lowlinesse, pacience, and charitie, and be ordered by the gouernaunce of his holy spirite, seking alwayes his glory, and seruing him duely in our vocacion, with thankesgeuing (*Mat.* xi.). This if

we doe, Christ wil deliuer us from the curse of the law, and from
the extreme malediccion, whiche shal light upon them that shal
bee set on the left hand: and he wil set us on his ryght hand,
and geue us the blessed benediccion of his father, commaundyng
us to take possession of his glorious kyngdome; unto the which
he vouchesafe to bryng us all, for hys infinite mercy (*Matt.* xxv.).
Amen.

*Then shall they all knele upon their knees: and the Priestes and Clerks
kneling (where thei are accustomed to saye the Letany) shal saye this
Psalme.*

Miserere mei Deus. Ps. li.

HAUE mercy upon me, (O God,) after thy great goodnes :
accordyng to the multitude of thy mercies, do awaye myne
offences.

Wash me throughly from my wickednes, and clense me from
my sinne.

For I knowledge my faultes, and my synne is euer before me.

Againste thee onely have I synned, and done this euil in thy
syght : that thou mightest be iustified in thy saying, and cleare
when thou art iudged.

Beholde I was shapen in wickednesse, and in synne hath my
mother conceiued me.

But lo, thou requirest trueth in the inwarde parties, and shalt
make me to understande wisdome secretly.

Thou shalt purge me with Isope, and I shalbe cleane : thou
shalte washe me, and I shalbe whiter then Snowe.

Thou shalt make me heare of ioye and gladnesse, that the
bones which thou hast broken may reioyce.

Turne thy face from my synnes, and put out all my misdedes.

Make me a cleane heart, (O God) and renewe a right spirite
within me.

Cast me not away from thy presence, and take not thy holy
spirite from me.

O geue me the comforte of thy helpe agayne, and stablishe me
with thy free spirite.

Then shal I teache thy wayes unto the wycked, and synners
shalbe conuerted unto thee.

Deliuer me from bloud-guyltinesse, (O god,) thou that art the
god of my health : and my tongue shal sing of thy ryghteousnes.

Thou shalt open my lippes, (O lord) and my mouth shall shewe
thy prayse.

For thou desyrest no sacrifice, els would I geue it thee : but
thou delyghtest not in burnt-offeryng.

The sacrifice of god is a troubled spirite, a broken and a contrite heart, (O god,) shalt thou not despyse.

O be fauourable and gracious unto Syon, buyld thou the walles of Hierusalem.

Then shalt thou be pleased with the sacrifice of righteousnesse, with the burnte-offeryngs and oblacions : then shall they offer young bullocks upon thyne altare.

Glory be to the father, and to the sonne, &c.
As it was in the beginning, and is now, &c.

> Lord, haue mercy upon us.
> Chryst, haue mercy upon us.
> Lord, haue mercy upon us.

¶ Our father, which art in heauen, &c.
And lead us not into temptacion.

Aunswere. But deliuer us from euil.   Amen.
Minister. O Lorde, saue thy seruaunts.
Aunswere. Which put their trust in thee.
Minister. Sende unto them helpe from aboue.
Aunswere. And euermore mightely defende them.
Minister. Helpe us, O god our sauioure.
Aunswere. And for the glory of thy names sake deliuer us, bee mercifull unto us synners for thy names sake.
Minister. O Lorde, heare our prayers.
Aunswere. And let our crye come to thee.

Let us praye.

O Lord, we beseche thee mercifully heare our prayers, and spare all those whiche confess their sinnes to thee, that they (whose conscyences by synne are accused,) by thy mercyfull pardon maye be absolued : Through Chryste our Lorde.   Amen.

O most mightie god and mercyfull father, which hast compassion of al men, and hatest nothing that thou hast made: which wouldest not the death of a synner, but that he shoulde rather turne from synne and be saued: mercifully forgeue us our trespasses, receyue and comfort us, which be greued and weried with the burthen of our synnes. Thy property is to haue mercy; to thee only it apperteineth to forgeue sinnes: spare us therfore, good Lord, spare thy people whom thou hast redemed. Entre not into Judgemente with thy seruaunts, which be vile yearth, and miserable synners: but so turne thy yre from us, which mekely knowledge our vilenesse, and truely repente us of our faultes: so make haste to helpe us in thys worlde, that we maye euer lyue with thee, in the worlde to come: through Jesus Christe our Lord. Amen.

¶ *Then shal the people say this that foloweth, after the Minister.*

TURNE thou us, O good lorde, and so shall we bee turned: bee fauourable (O Lord) bee fauourable to thy people, whiche turne to thee in wepyng, fastyng and praying: for thou art a merciful god, ful of compassion, long suffering, and of a great pitie: Thou sparest when we deserue punishmente, and in thy wrath thinkest upon mercy. Spare thy people, good Lorde, spare them, and lette not thy heritage be broughte to confusion: Hear us (O Lord) for thy mercy is great, and after the multytude of thy mercyes looke upon us.

The fourme

and maner of makynge and consecratynge

Bishoppes, Priestes, and

Deacons.

Anno Domini, M.D.L.**II.**

THE PREFACE.

It is euident unto all men, diligently readinge holye Scripture, and auncient aucthours, that from the Apostles tyme there hathe bene these ordres of Ministers in Christ's Church: Bishoppes, Priestes, and Deacons: which Offices were euermore had in suche reuerent estimacion, that no man by his own priuate aucthoritie might presume to execute any of them, except he were first called, tried, examined, and knowen to have such qualities as were requisite for the same; And also, by publique prayer, with imposicion of handes, approued, and admitted therunto. And therfore, to the entent these orders shoulde bee continued, and reuerentlye used, and estemed, in this Church of England; it is requysite, that no man (not beyng at thys presente Bisshoppe, Priest, nor Deacon) shall execute anye of them, excepte he be called, tryed, examined, and admitted, accordynge to the forme hereafter folowinge. And none shalbe admitted a Deacon, except he be xxi yeres of age at the least. And euery man which is to be admitted a Priest, shalbe full xxiv yeres old. And euery man, which is to be consecrated a Bishop, shalbe fully thyrtie yeres of age. And the Bishop know-inge, eyther by himself, or by sufficient testimonye, any person to be a man of vertuous conuersacion, and wythoute cryme, and after examinacion and triale, fyndynge hym learned in the Latyne tongue, and sufficientlye instructed in holye Scripture, maye, upon a Sundaye or Holy daye, in the face of the church, admitte hym a Deacon, in suche maner and fourme as hereafter foloweth.

FOURME AND MANER

OF

ORDERINGE OF DEACONS.

Fyrst, when the daye appoynted by the Bishoppe is come, there shalbe an exhortacion, declaring the duetie and office of suche as come to be admitted Ministers, howe necessarye such Orders are in the Churche of Christe, and also, howe the people oughte to esteme them in theyr vocacion.

¶ *After the exhortacion ended, the Archedeacon, or his deputie, shal present such as come to the Bishop to be admitted, saying these wordes.*

REVERENDE Father in GOD, I presente unto you these persones present, to bee admitted Deacons.

¶ *The Bishoppe.* Take heede that the persones whom ye present unto us, be apte and meete, for theyr learning, and godlye conuersacion, to exercyse theyr ministrie duelye, to the honour of GOD, and edyfying of hys Churche.

The Archedeacon shall aunswere.

I haue enquyred of them, and also examined them, and thinke them so to bee.

¶ *And then the Bishop shall saye unto the people,*

BRETHREN, yf there bee anye of you, who knoweth anye impedimente, or notable crime, in any of these persones presented to bee ordered Deacons, for the whiche he ought not to be admitted to the same, lette hym come foorthe, in the name of GOD, and shewe what the cryme, or impedimente is.

¶ *And yf any great cryme or impediment be obiected, the Bishoppe shall surcease from ordering that person, untyl suche tyme as the partie accused shal trye himself clere of that cryme.*

¶ *Then the Bishop, commending suche as shalbe found mete to be ordered, to the prayers of the congregacion, wyth the Clerkes, and people present, shall saye or synge the Letany as foloweth wyth the prayers.*

THE LETANY AND SUFFRAGES.

O GOD the father of heauen : haue mercye upon us myserable synners.

O God the father of heauen : haue mercie upon us myserable synners.

439

O God the sonne, redemer of the worlde : haue mercye upon us myserable synners.

O God the sonne, redemer of the world : haue mercy upon us miserable synners.

O God the holy ghost, proceding from the father and the sonne : haue mercye upon us myserable synners.

O God the holy ghost, proceding from the father and the sonne : haue mercye upon us myserable synners.

O holy, blessed, and glorious Trinity, three Persons and one God : haue mercy upon us miserable sinners.

O holy, blessed, and glorious Trinitie, three persones and one God : haue mercye upon us miserable synners.

Remembre not, Lorde, our offences, nor the offences of oure forefathers, neyther take thou vengeaunce of our synnes : spare us, good lord, spare thy people, whom thou hast redemed with thy most precious bloud, and be not angry with us for euer.

Spare us, good Lord.

From all euyll and mischiefe, from synne, from the craftes and assaultes of the deuyll, from thy wrath, and from euerlastinge damnacion.

Good Lorde, deliuer us.

From all blyndnes of heart, from pryde, vayne glory, and hypocrisie, from enuie, hatred, and malice, and all uncharitablenes.

Good Lord, deliuer us.

From fornicacion, and all other deadlye synne, and from all the deceyptes of the worlde, the flesshe, and the deuyl.

Good lord, deliuer us.

From lighteninges and tempestes, from plague, pestilence, and famine, from battayle and murther, and from sodayne death.

Good lord, deliuer us.

From all sedicion and priuie conspiracie, from the tyrannie of the Bisshop of Rome, and all hys detestable enormities, from all false doctryne and heresy, from hardnes of hearte, and contempt of thy word and commaundemente.

Good lord, deliuer us.

By the misterye of thy holy incarnacion, by thy holye natiuitie and circumcision, by thy baptisme, fasting, and temptacion.

Good lord, deliuer us.

By thyne agonye and bloudy sweate, by thy crosse and passion, by thy precious death and buriall, by thy glorious resurreccion and ascencion, and by the comming of the holy Ghoste.

Good lorde, deliuer us.

In al tyme of our tribulacion, in al tyme of our welth, in the houre of death, and in the daye of iudgement.

Good Lord, deliuer us.

We synners doe beseche thee to heare us (O Lorde God), and that it maye please thee to rule and gouern thy holy Church uniuersally in the ryght waye.

We beseche thee to heare us, good Lorde.

That it maye please thee, to kepe EDWARD the sixth thy seruaunt, our Kyng and gouernour.

We beseche thee to heare us, good Lorde.

That it may please thee to rule his heart in thy fayth, feare, and loue, that he maye alwayes haue affiaunce in thee, and euer seke thy honour and glorye.

We beseche thee to heare us good Lorde.

That it maye please thee, to be his defendour and keper, geuing him the victorie ouer all his enemies.

We beseche thee to heare us, good Lord.

That it may please thee, to illuminate al Bisshops, Pastours, and ministers of the Churche, with true knowledge, and understanding of thy worde, and that bothe by theyr preaching and lyuing they may set it fourth, and shewe it accordingly.

We beseche thee to heare us, good Lorde.

That it may please thee, to blesse these men, and send thy grace upon them, that they may duelye execute the offyce, nowe to bee commytted unto them, to the edifyinge of thy Church, and to thy honour, prayse, and glorye.

We beseche thee to heare us, good Lorde.

That it maye please thee to endue the Lordes of the Counsaile, and al the nobilitie, with grace, wysdom, and understandinge.

We beseche thee to heare us, good Lorde.

That it may please thee, to blesse and kepe the Magistrates, geuing them grace to execute Justice, and to maynteyne trueth.

We beseche thee to heare us, good Lord.

That it may please thee, to blesse and kepe al thy people.

We beseche thee to heare us, good Lorde.

That it may please thee, to geue to all nacions unitie, peace, and concord.

We beseche thee to heare us, good Lorde.

That it may please thee, to geue us an hearte, to loue and dreade thee, and dyligentlye to liue after thy commaundementes.

We beseche thee to heare us, good Lorde.

That it maye please thee to geue all thy people encrease of grace, to heare mekely thy worde, and to receiue it with pure affeccion, and to bring forth the fruites of the spyryte.

We beseche thee to heare us, good Lorde.

That it maye please thee, to bringe into the waye of trueth all suche as haue erred and are deceyued.

We beseche thee to heare us, good Lorde.

That it maye please thee, to strengthen suche as doe stande, and to comforte and helpe the weake harted, and to rayse them up that fall, and finallye to beate downe Sathan under our feete.

We beseche thee to heare us, good Lorde.

That it may please thee, to succour, helpe, and comfort, all that be in daunger, necessitie, and tribulacion.

We beseche thee to heare us, good Lorde.

That it maye please thee, to preserue al that trauayle by lande, or by water, all women labouringe of chylde, al sycke persons, and yonge chyldren, and to shewe thy pytie upon all prysoners and captyues.

We beseche thee to heare us, good Lorde.

That it maye please thee, to defende and prouyde for the fatherles chyldren, and wyddowes, and all that bee desolate and oppressed.

We beseche thee to heare us, good Lorde.

That it maye please thee, to haue mercye upon all menne.

We beseche thee to heare us, good Lorde.

That it may please thee, to forgeue our enemies, persecutours, and slaunderers, and to turne theyr heartes.

We beseche thee to heare us, good lorde.

That it may please thee, to geue and preserue to our use the kyndly fruites of the earth, so as in due time we may enioy them.

We beseche thee to heare us, good lorde.

That it may please thee, to geue us true repentaunce, to forgeue us all our synnes, negligences, and ignoraunces, and to endue us with the grace of thy holye spirite, to amende oure lyues accordinge to thy holye worde.

We beseche thee to heare us, good Lorde.

Sonne of God: we beseche thee to heare us.

Sonne of God : we beseche thee to heare us.

O Lambe of god, that takeste awaye the synnes of the worlde.

Graunt us thy peace.

O Lambe of God, that takeste awaye the synnes of the worlde.
Haue mercie upon us.

O Christe, hear us.
O Christe, hear us.

Lorde, haue mercy upon us.
Lorde, haue mercy upon us.

Christ, haue mercy upon us.
Christ, haue mercy upon us.

Lorde, haue mercy upon us.
Lorde, haue mercy upon us.

¶ Our father, which art in heauen, &c.
And leade us not into temptacion.

But deliuer us from euill.

The versicle. O lorde, deale not with us after our sinnes.
The aunswere. Neither reward us after our iniquities.

Let us pray.

O GOD mercyfull father, that despysest not the syghinge of a contryte hearte, nor the desyre of suche as bee sorowefull, mercyfully assyste oure prayers that wee make before thee in all oure troubles and aduersities, whensoeuer they oppresse us: and graciously heare us, that those euyls, which the crafte and subteltie of the deuyll, or man, worketh agaynst us, be brought to naughte, and by the prouidence of thy goodnes they maye be dispersed, that we thy seruaunts, beyng hurte by no persecucions, may euermore geue thankes unto thee, in thy holy Churche: through Jesu Christe our Lorde.
O Lord, aryse, helpe us, and delyuer us, for thy names sake.

O god, we haue heard with oure eares, and oure fathers haue declared unto us, the noble woorks, that thou dyddeste in theyr dayes, and in the olde tyme before them.
O Lord, aryse, helpe us, and delyuer us, for thyne honour.

Glorye bee to the father, and to the sonne, and to the holy ghost. As it was in the beginning, is nowe, and euer shalbe, world without ende. Amen.
From our enemyes defende us, O Christe.
Graciously loke upon our affliccions.

Pitifully beholde the sorowes of our heart.
Mercifully forgeue the synnes of thy people.

Fauourably with mercy heare our prayers.
O sonne of Dauid, haue mercy upon us.

Both nowe and euer vouchesafe to heare us, O Christ.
Graciously heare us, O Christe.
Graciously heare us, O Lorde Christe.

The Versicle. O Lorde, let thy mercy be shewed upon us.
The Aunswere. As we do put our trust in thee.

Let us praye.

WE humbly beseche thee, O father, mercyfullye to looke upon our infyrmities, and for the glorye of thy names sake, turne from us all those euylles, that wee moost ryghteouslye haue deserued: And graunt that in al our troubles we maye put our whole trust and confidence in thy mercye, and euermore serue thee, in holynes and puresnesse of lyuing, to thy honoure and glory, through our onely mediatour and aduocate Jesus Christ our lorde. Amen.

ALMIGHTIE God, which haste geuen us grace at this tyme with one accorde to make our common supplicacions unto thee, and doeste promise, that when two or three be gathered in thy name, thou wylte graunt their requestes: fulfyl now, O Lord, the desyres and peticions of thy seruaunts, as maye be moste expediente for them, graunting us in thys worlde knowledge of thy trueth, and in the worlde to come lyfe euerlastyng. Amen.

Then shalbe sayd also this that foloweth.

ALMIGHTIE God, whiche by thy deuyne prouidence hast appointed diuerse Orders of ministers in the Churche, and diddest enspyre thine holy Apostles to chose unto this Ordre of Deacons the first Martyr sainct Stephin, with other: mercifully beholde these thy seruaunts, nowe called to the lyke office and administracion; replenishe them so with the trueth of thy doctrine, and innocencie of lyfe, that, both by wourd and good example, they may faithfully serue thee in this office, to the glory of thy name, and profyte of the congregacion, through the merites of our sauiour Jesu Christe, who lyueth and reygneth with thee, and the holy gost, now and euer. Amen.

Then shall bee song or sayed, the Communion of the daye, sauyng the Epistle shalbe read out of Timothe, as foloweth.

LIKEWYSE muste the ministers bee honeste, not doubletongued, nor geuen unto much wyne, neyther greedye of fylthy lucre, but holding the mistery of the faythe, with a pure conscience. And let them fyrst be proued, and then let them minister so that no manne be able to reproue them. Euen so must theyr wyues be honeste, not euyl speakers, but sobre, and faythfull in al thinges. Lette the Deacons bee the husbands of one wyfe, and suche as rule thyr chyldren well, and theyr owne housholdes. For they that minister well geat themselues a good degree, and a greate libertie in the fayth which is in Christe Jesu.

These thinges wryte I unto thee trustinge to come shortelye unto thee; but and yf I tarye longe that then thou mayest yet haue knowledge, howe thou oughteste to behaue thyselfe in the house of God, which is the congregacion of the lyuing God, the pyller and grounde of trueth. And withoute doubte greate is that misterie of godlynes. God was shewed in the flesshe, was iustifyed in the spirite, was seen amonge the Aungells, was preached unto the Gentyles, was beleued on in the worlde, and receyued up in glorye.

Or els this, out of the sixth of the Actes.

THEN the twelue called the multitude of the Disciples together, and sayde: It is not mete that we shoulde leaue the woorde of God, and serue Tables. Wherfore, brethren, looke ye oute amonge you seuen men of honeste reporte, and full of the holy ghost and wysdome, to whom wee maye committe thys busynesse. But we wyll geue ourselues continuallye to prayer, and to the administracion of the word. And that saying pleased the whole multitude. And they chose Stephin, a man full of fayth, and ful of the holy ghoste, and Philip, and Procorus, and Nicanor, and Timon, and Permenas, and Nicholas a conuert of Antioche. These they set before the Apostles: and, when they had prayed, they layde theyr handes on them. And the word of god increased, and the number of the Disciples multiplyed in Jerusalem greatly, and a great company of the priests, wer obedient unto the fayth.

¶ *And before the Gospell, the Bisshop sitting in a chair, shall cause the othe of the King's supremacie, and against the usurped power and aucthoritie of the Bisshop of Rome, to be ministred unto euery of them, that are to be ordred.*

¶ *The othe of the Kyng's Supremacie.*

I FROM hencefurth shall utterly renounce, refuse, relinquishe, and forsake the Bysshop of Rome, and hys authoritie, power, and iurisdiccion. And I shall neuer consent nor agree, that the Bysshop of Rome shall practise, exercise, or haue, anye maner of authoritie, Jurisdiccion, or power withyn thys Realme, or anye other the Kynges dominions, but shall resyste the same at all tymes, to the uttermoste of my power. And I from hence-foorth will accepte, repute, and take the Kynges Maiestie to be the onely Supreme head in earth, of the Churche of England: And to my connynge, witte, and uttermoste of my power, withoute guyle, fraude, or other undue meane, I will obserue, kepe, mayntayne, and defende, the whole effectes and contentes of all and synguler actes and Statutes made, and to be made within this Realme, in derogacion, extirpacion, and extinguish-ment of the Bishop of Rome, and his aucthoritie, and all other Actes and Statutes, made or to be made, in confirmacion and corroboracion of the Kynges power, of the supreme head in yearth, of the Churche of England: and this I wil doe agaynste all maner of persones, of what estate, dygnitie or degree, or condicion they be, and in no wise doe nor attempte, nor to my power suffre to be doone or attempted, directly, or indirectlye, any thing or thynges, prieuely or appertlye, to the lette, hinder-aunce, dammage, or derogacion therof, or any part thereof, by anye maner of meanes, or for any maner of pretence. And in case any othe bee made, or hath been made, by me, to any person or persones, in maintenaunce, defence, or fauoure, of the Bishoppe of Rome, or his authoritie, iurisdiccion, or power, I repute the same as vayne and adnichilate, so helpe me God through Jesus Christ.

¶ *Then shall the Bisshop examine euery one of them, that are to be ordered, in the presence of the people, after thys maner folowing.*

DOE you trust that you are inwardlye moued by the holye Ghoste to take upon you thys office and ministracion, to serue God, for the promoting of hys glorye, and the edifying of hys people?

Aunswere. I trust so.

The Bishop. Doe ye thinke, that ye truely bee called, accord-yng to the will of our Lorde Jesus Christe, and the due ordre of this realme, to the ministery of the churche?

Aunswere. I thinke so.

The Bishop. Doe ye unfaynedlye beleue all the Canonicall scriptures, of the olde and newe Testamente?

Aunswere. I doe beleue.

The Bishop. Will you diligently reade the same unto the people assembled in the Churche where you shalbe appoynted to serue?

Aunswere. I will.

The Bishop. It perteineth to the office of a Deacon in the

Churche where he shall bee appoynted to assist the Prieste in deuine seruice, and speciallye when he ministreth the holye Communion, and to helpe hym in distribucion thereof, and to reade holye scriptures and Homelies in the congregacion, and to instructe the youthe in the Catechisme, to Baptise and to preache if he be admitted thereto by the Bisshop. And furthermore, it is his office where prouision is so made to searche for the sicke, poor, and impotent people of the parishe, and to intimate theyr estates, names, and places where they dwell, to the Curate, that by hys exhortacion they maye bee relieued by the parishe or other conuenient almes: will you doe this gladly and willingly?

Aunswere. I will so doe by the helpe of God.

The Bishop. Will you applye all your diligence to frame and fashion your owne lyues, and the lyues of all youre familye, according to the doctrine of Christ, and to make both your selues and them, as much as in you lyeth, wholesome examples of the flocke of Christ?

Aunswere. I wyll so do, the Lorde beyng my helper.

The Bisshop. Wyll you reuerently obeye youre ordinary, and other chiefe Ministers of the Church, and them to whom the gouernement and charge is committed ouer you, folowing with a gladde mynde, and wyll theyr godly admonicions?

Aunswer. I wyl thus endeuour my self, the Lord being my helper.

Then the Bisshop layinge his handes seuerally upon the head of euery of them, shall saye,

Take thou aucthoritie to execute the office of a Deacon in the Churche of God committed unto thee: in the name of the father, the sonne, and the holy ghost. Amen.

Then shal the Bishop delyuer to euery one of them the newe Testamente, sayinge,

Take thou aucthoritie to reade the Gospell in the Church of God, and to preache the same, if thou be thereunto ordinarely commaunded.

Then one of them, appoynted by the Bisshop, shal reade the Gospel of that daye.

Then shal the Bisshop procede to the Communion. and al that be ordered, shal tarye and receyue the holy Communion the same daye wyth the Bisshop.

The Communion ended, after the laste Collecte and immediatly before the benediccion, shalbe sayd this Collecte folowynge,

ALMIGHTIE God, geuer of all good thynges, whiche of thy great goodnes hast vouchedsaufe to accept and take these thy seruauntes unto the Office of Deacons in thy church: make them, we beseche the, O Lorde, to be modest, humble, and constant in ther ministracion, to haue a ready wil to obserue al Spiritual discipline, that they hauing alwaies the testimonie of a good conscience, and continuyng euer stable and strong in thy sonne Christ, may so wel use themselues in this inferiour Office, that they may be founde worthy to be called unto the higher ministeries in thy Churche, through the same thy sonne our Sauiour Christe, to whome be glory and honour worlde without ende. Amen.

⁋ *And here it must be shewed unto the Deacon, that he must continue in that Office of a Deacon the space of an whole yere at the leaste (except for reasonable causes it be otherwise seen to his Ordinary) to thentent he may be perfecte, and wel expert in the thynges apperteinyng to the Ecclesiastical administracion, in executyng whereof if he be founde faithful and diligent, he may be admitted by his Diocesan to the order of Priesthode.*

¶ THE FOURME

OF

ORDERYNG PRIESTES.

When the exhortacion is ended, then shal folowe the Communion. And for the Epistle shalbe red out of the twentieth Chapiter of the Actes of the Apostles as foloweth.

FROM Mileto Paule sent messengers to Ephesus, and called the elders of the congregacion. Whiche when they were come to him, he said unto them, Ye know, that from the first daie that I came into Asia, after what maner I haue been with you at all seasons, seruyng the Lord with al humblenes of mind, and with many teares and temptacions whiche happened unto me by the layinges awayt of the Jewes; because I wold kepe back nothing that was profitable unto you, but to shew you, and teach you openly throughoute euery house: wytnessinge both to the Jewes, and also to the Grekes, the repentaunce that is towarde God, and the faythe whiche is toward our Lorde Jesus. And nowe beholde I go bound in the Spirite unto Jerusalem, not knowinge the thinges that shall come on me there; but that the holy ghost witnesseth in euery citye, sayinge, that bandes and trouble abide me. But none of these thinges moue me, neither is my life deare unto myself, that I might fulfyll my course with ioye, and the ministracion of the word which I haue receiued of the lord Jesu, to testifye the gospell of the grace of God. And nowe behold, I am sure that henceforth ye all, (through whom I haue gone preachinge the kingdome of God,) shall see my face no more. Wherefore I take you to record this day, that I am pure from the bloud of all men. For I haue spared no labour, but haue shewed you all the counsaille of God. Take hede therfore unto your selues, and to all the flocke emong whom the holg Ghost hath made you ouerseers, to rule the congregacion of God, whiche he hath purchased wyth hys bloud. For I am sure of this, that after my departing shall greuous wolues enter in emong you, not sparing the flocke: Moreouer of your owne selues shall men aryse speakyng peruerse thynges, to drawe disciples after them. Therfore awake and remembre, that by the space of three yeres, I ceassed not to warne euerye one of you nyght and daye with teares. And now, brethren, I commende you to God, and to the word of his grace, whyche is able to builde further, and to geue you an inheritaunce emong al them whych are sanctified. I haue desiered no man's siluer, golde, or vesture; Yea, you know your selues, that these hands haue ministred unto my necessities, and to them that were wyth me. I haue shewed you all thynges, how that so labouring ye ought to receue the weake; and to remembre the wordes of the Lorde Jesu, how that he said, It is more blessed to geue than to receiue.

¶ *Or els this thirde Chapter of the first Epistle to Timothe.*

THIS is a true saiying, If any man desire the office of a Bisshoppe, he desireth an honest worcke. A Bishop therfore must be blamelesse, the housbande of one wife, vigilant, sober, discrete, a keper of hospitalitie, apte to teache; not geuen to ouermuche wyne, no fighter, not gredy of filthy lucre, but gentle, abhorrynge fightinge, abhorryng couetousnes; one that ruleth well his owne house, one that hath children in subjeccion with all reuerence. For if a man can not rule his owne house, howe shall he care for the congregacion of God? He may not be a young skoler, leaste he swelle and fal into the judgemente of the euil speaker. He must also haue a good report of them which are without; least he fal into rebuke and snare of the euil speaker.

Likewise must the ministers be honest, not double-tongued, not geuen unto muche wyne, neither gredy of filthy lucre; but holdyng the ministery of the faith with a pure conscience; and let them first be proued, and then let them minister so that no man be able to reproue them.

Euen so must their wiues be honest; not euil-speakers, but sobre and faithful in all thynges. Let the Deacons be the housbandes of one wife, and suche as rule their children wel and their own householdes, for they that minister wel get themselues a good degre and great libertie in the Faith whiche is in Christe Jesu.

These thinges write I unto the, trusting to come shortly unto the, but, and if I tary long, that then thou maiest haue yet knowledge howe thou oughtest to behaue thy selfe in the house of God, which is the congregacion of the liuing God, the piller and ground of truth. And without doubte, greate is that mistery of Godlines. God was shewed in the fleshe, was iustified in the Spirite, was seen among the Aungelles, was preached unto the Gentiles, was beleued on in the worlde, and receiued up in glory.

After this shalbe redde for the Gospell a pece of the last Chapiter of Mathewe, as foloweth.

JESUS came and spake unto them, saying: All power is geuen unto me in heauen and in earth. Go ye therfore and teache all nacions, Baptisyng them in the name of the father, and of the Sonne, and of the holy Ghoste. Teachyng them to obserue al thynges, whatsoeuer I haue commaunded you. And loo, I am with you alwaie, euen untill the ende of the worlde. *Matt.* xxviii.

Or elles this that foloweth, of the x. Chapiter of Jhon.

VERELY, verely, I say unto you, He that entereth not in by the doore into the Shepe folde, but climbeth up some other way, the same is a Thefe and a Murtherer. But he that entreth in by the doore is the Shepeherde of the Shepe, to hym the porter openeth, and the Shepe heareth his voice, and he calleth his own Shepe by name, and leadeth them out. And when he hath sent furth his owne Shepe he goeth before them, and the Shepe folowe hym, for they knowe his voice. A straunger will they not folowe, but flye from hym: for they knowe not the voice of straungers. This Prouerbe spake Jesus unto them, but they understode not what thyngs they ware which he spake unto them. Then saide Jesus unto them againe, Verely, verely I say unto you, I am the doore of the Shepe. All (euen as many as came before me) are Theues and Murtherers: but the Shepe did not heare them. I am the doore, by me if any man entre in, he shalbe saufe, and go in and out, and fynde pasture. A Thefe cometh not but for to steale, kill, and to destroie. I am come that they might haue lyfe, and that they might haue it more aboundauntly. I am the good shepeherde: a good Shepeherde geueth his lyfe for the shepe. An hired seruaunt, and he which is not the shephearde (neither the shepe are hys own) seeth the wolfe coming, and leaueth the shepe, and fleeth, and the wolfe catcheth and scattereth the shepe. The hyred seruaunt fleeth, because he is an hyred seruaunt, and careth not for the shepe. I am the good shepehearde, and knowe my shepe, and am knowen of myne. As my father knoweth me, euen so knowe I also my father. And I geue my lyfe for the shepe. And other shepe I have, which are not of thys folde. Them also muste I bring, and they shall heare my voice, and there shalbe one folde and one shepehearde.

Or els this, of the xx. Chapter of John.

THE same day at night, which is the first day of the Sabbothes, when the dores wer shutte (where the disciples wer assembled together for feare of the Jews) came Jesus and stode in the middes, and sayed unto them, Peace be unto you.   And when he had so sayed, he shewed unto them hys handes and his side. Then wer the disciples glad, when they sawe the Lorde.   Then sayed Jesus unto them agayne, Peace be unto you.   As my father sent me, euen so sende I you also.   And when he had sayed those words, he breathed on them, and sayed unto them, Receiue ye the holy gost: whosesoeuers sinnes ye remitte, they are remitted unto them: and whosesoeuers synnnes ye retayne, they are retayned.

When the gospel is ended, then shalbe sayed or song.

COME, holy gost, eternall god, proceding from aboue,
Bothe from the father and the sonne, the god of peace and loue :
Visite our myndes, and into us thy heauenly grace inspyre,
That in all trueth and godlynesse we maye haue true desyre.
Thou art the very comforter, in all woe and distresse,
The heauenly gift of god most high, which no tongue can expresse,
The fountaine and the liuely spryng of ioye celestiall,
The fyre so bryght, the loue so clere, and Vnccion spirituall.
Thou in thy gyftes are manyfolde, whereby Christes Churche
    doth stande,
In faithfull heartes writing thy lawe, the fynger of God's hande.
Accordyng to thy promes made, thou geuest speache of grace,
That through thy helpe, the praise of god may sound in euery
    place.
O holy gost, into our wittes sende downe thyne heauenly lyght,
Kindle our heartes with feruent loue, to serue god daye and
    night,
Strength and stablishe all our weaknes, so feble and so fraile,
That neithere flesh, the world, nor deuill, againste us doe preuaile.
Put backe our enmie farre from us, and graunt us to obtaine,
Peace in our heartes with God and man, withoute grudge or dis-
    daine.
And graunt, O lorde, that thou being, our leader and our guide,
We maie eschewe the snares of sinne, and from thee neuer slide.
To us such plentie of thy grace, good lord, graunt, we thee praie,
That thou maiest be our comforter, at the laste dreadfull daye.
Of all stryfe and dissencion, O Lord, dissolue the bandes,
And make the knottes of peace and loue throughout all Christen
    lands.
Graunt us, O lorde, through thee to know the father most of
    myght,
That of his deare beloued sonne we may attaine the syght :

And that with perfect faith also we may acknowledge thee,
The spirite of them both alwaye, one god in persons three.
Laude and prayse bee to the father, and to the sonne equall,
And to the holy spirite also, one God coeternall :
And pray we that the onely sonne vouchesafe his spirite to sende,
To all that doe professe his name, unto the worlde's ende.   Amen.
And pray we that the onely sonne vouchesafe his spirite to sende,
To all tha doe professe his name, unto the worlde's ende.   Amen.

And then the Archedeacon shal present unto the Bisshop all them that shal receiue the order of Priesthode that daye.   The Archedeacon saying.

REVERENDE father in God, I presente unto you these persons present, to bee admitted to the ordre of Priesthode.   *Cum interrogatione et responsione, ut in ordine Diaconatus.*

And then the Bishop shal saye to the people.

GOOD people, these be they whom we purpose, God wyllyng, to receyue thys daye unto the holy office of Priesthode.   For after due examinacion, we fynde not the contrarye, but that they be lawfully called to their funcion and ministery, and that they be persons mete for the same: but yet yf there be any of you, which knoweth any impedimente, or notable cryme in any of them, for the whiche he oughte not to be receiued into this holy ministerie, now in the name of God declare the same.

¶ *And if any great crime or impedimente be objected, &c.*   Ut supra in Ordine Diaconatus usque ad finem Litaniæ cum hac Collecta.

ALMIGHTIE GOD, geuer of all good thinges, which by thy holy spirit hast appointed diuerse orders of Ministers in thy churche: mercifully behold these thy seruaunts, now called to the Office of Priesthode, and replenishe them so with the trueth of thy doctrine, and innocencie of lyfe, that both by worde and good example they may faithfully serue thee in this office, to the glory of thy name, and profite of the congregacion, through the merites of our sauiour Jesu Christ, who lyueth and reigneth, with thee and the Holy goste, worlde withoute ende.   Amen.

Then the Bishop shal minister unto euery of them the oath, concerning the kinges Supremacie, as it is sette oute in the Ordre of Deacons.   And that done, he shall saye unto them, whiche are appoynted to receyue the said Office, as hereafter foloweth.

You haue hearde, brethren, aswel in your priuate examinacion, as in the exhortacion, and in the holy lessons taken oute of the Gospell, and of the writinges of the Apostles, of what dignitie, and of how great importaunce thys offyce is, (whereunto ye be called). And now we exhorte you, in the name of our Lorde Jesus Chryste, to haue in remembraunce, into howe hygh a dignitie, and to howe chargeable an offyce ye be called, that is to saye, to bee the messengers, the watchemen, the Pastours, and the stewardes of the Lorde, to teache, to premonishe, to feede, and prouide for the Lordes familye: to seeke for Christes shepe that be dispersed abrode, and for his children, whiche be in the middest of this naughtye worlde, to be saued through Christ for euer. Haue always therfore printed in youre remembraunce, how great a treasure is committed to youre charge: for they be the shepe of Christ, whiche he boughte with his death, and for whom he shed his bloud. The churche and congregacion, whom you muste serue, is his spouse and hys bodye. And if it shall chaunce the same churche, or any membre thereof, to take any hurte or hinderaunce by reason of youre negligence, ye knowe the great-nesse of the faulte, and also of the horrible punishemente which wil ensue. Wherefore, consider with yourselues the ende of your ministery, towardes the children of God, towarde the spouse and body of Christe, and see that you neuer cease youre laboure, your care and diligence, untyll you haue done all that lieth in you, accordyng to your bounden duetie, to bryng all such as are, or shalbe committed to your charge, unto that agrement in faith, and knowledge of god, and to that ripenes, and perfectnesse of age in Christ, that there be no place left emong them, eyther for erroure in religion, or for visiousnesse in lyfe.

Then, forasmuche as youre offyce is both of so great excellency, and of so great difficultie, ye see with howe greate care and study ye oughte to apply youreselues, as well that you maye shew your-selues kynde to that Lorde, who hath placed you in so high a dignitie, as also to beware, that neyther you yourselues offende, neyther be occasyon that other offende. Howbeit be cannot haue a mynde and a wyll thereto of youreselues for that power, and abilitie is geuen of god alone. Therfore ye se howe ye oughte and haue nede, earnestlye to praye for his holy spirite. And seeyng that you cannot, by any other meanes, compass the doinge of so weightie a worke perteininge to the saluacion of man, but with doctryne and exhortacion, taken out of holy scripture, and with a life agreable unto the same, ye perceiue how studyous ye oughte to be in reading and in learnyng the holy scriptures, and in framyng the maners, both of yourselues, and of them that specially partein unto you, according to the rule of the same scriptures. And for this selfesame cause, ye see howe you oughte to forsake and set asyde (as muche as you way) all worldly cares and studyes.

We haue a good hope, that you haue well weighed and pondred these thynges with yourselues, long beefore thys time, and that you haue clerely. determyned, by Goddes grace, to geue your-selues wholy to this vocacyon, whereunto it hath pleased God to call you, so that (as muche as lyeth in you) you applye youre-selues wholy to this one thyng, and drawe all your cares and studies this waye, and to this ende. And that you wyll con-tinuallye praye for the heauenly assistaunce of the holy gost, from God the father, by the mediacion of our onlye mediatour and sauioure, Jesus Christe, that by daylye readinge and weigh-yng of the scriptures ye maye waxe riper and stronger in your ministerye. And that ye may so endeuoure yourselues, from time to time, to sanctifie the liues of you and yours, and to fashyon them, after the rule and doctrine of Christe, and that ye may be wholesome and Godly examples and paterns, for the rest of the congregacion to follow:

And that thys presente congregacion of Christe, here assembled, maye also understande youre mindes and willes, in these thinges: and that this your promes shall more moue you to doe youre dueties, ye shall aunswere plainly to these thinges, whiche we in the name of the congregacyon shall demaunde of you, touchyng the same.

Doe you thynke in your heart, that you be truely called, accordyng to the will of our Lorde Jesus Chryste, and the ordre of this Churche of Englande, to the ministerye of Priesthode?

Aunswere. I thinke it.

The Bishoppe. Be you perswaded that the holy Scriptures conteine sufficiently all doctryne, required of necessitie for eternall saluacion, through faith in Jesu Christ? And are you deter-mined with the sayd scriptures to instructe the people committed to your charge, and to teache nothing, (as required of necessitie to eternall saluacion,) but that you shalbe perswaded, maye be concluded, and proued by the scripture?

Aunswere. I am so perswaded, and haue so determined by Godde's grace.

The Bishoppe. Wil you then geue your faithful diligence alwaies, so to minister the doctrine, and Sacramentes, and the discipline of Christe, as the Lorde hath commaunded, and as thys realme hath receyued the same, accordynge to the commaundmentes of God, so that you maye teache the people commytted to youre cure and charge with al diligence to keepe and obserue the same?

Aunswere. I will so doe, by the helpe of the Lorde.

The Bishoppe. Wil you be ready with al faithful diligence to banishe and driue awaye al erronious and straunge doctrines, contrary to god's word, and to use both publike and priuate monicions and exhortacions, as wel to the sicke as to the whole, within your cures, as nede shall require and occasion be geuen?

Aunswere. I wil, the Lorde beyng my helper.

The Bishoppe. Wil you be diligent in prayers and in readynge of the holy scriptures, and in suche studies as helpe to the knowledge of the same, laying asyde the study of the world, and the fleshe?

Aunswere. I will endeuoure myselfe so to doe, the Lord beyng my helper.

The Bishoppe. Will you bee diligente to frame and fashion youre own selues and your families accordyng to the doctryne of Christ, and to make both yourselues and them (as muche as in you lieth) wholsome examples and spectacles to the flocke of Christe?

Aunswere. I will so apply myself, the Lord beyng my helper.

The Bishoppe. Will you maintein and set forwardes (as much as lieth in you) quietnes, peace, and loue emongs all christian people, and specially emong them that are or shalbe committed to your charge?

Aunswere. I wyll so doe, the Lord beyng my helper.

The Bishoppe. Wil you reuerently obeye your Ordnarie, and other chief ministers, unto whom the gouernement and charge is committed ouer you, folowynge with a glad mynd and wyll their Godly admonicion, and submittyng your selues to theyr Godly judgmentes?

Aunswere. I wyll so doe, the Lorde beeyng my helper.

Then shal the Bishoppe saye,

ALMIGHTIE God, who hath geuen you thys wyll to doe all these thyngs, graunt also unto you strength and power to performe the same, that he maye accomplishe his worke which he hath begon in you, untill the time he shall come at the latter daye to iudge the quicke and the dead.

After this the congregacion shalbe desired secretly in their praiers to make humble supplicacions to god for the foresaid thynges, for the whiche prayers there shall be a certain space kept in silence.

That doen, the Bishoppe shall praye in thys wyse.

¶ Let us praye.

ALMIGHTIE God and heauenly father, whiche of thy infinite loue and goodnes towardes us, hast geuen to us thy onely and moste deare beloued sonne Jesus Chryste, to bee our redemer and aucthoure of euerlastynge lyfe: who after he had made perfect our redempcyon of hys death, and was ascended into heauen, sente abrode into the world his Apostles, Prophetes, Euangelistes, Doctours, and Pastours, by whose laboure and ministerye he gathered together a greate flocke in al the partes of the worlde, to sette furth the eternall prayse of thy holy name: For these so greate benefites of thy eternall goodnesse, and for that thou haste vouchesafed to call these thy seruaunts here presente to the same offyce and ministerye of the saluacion of mankynde, we render unto thee moste hartie thankes, we woorshyp and prayse thee; and we humblye beseche thee by the same thy sonne, to graunt unto all us whiche either here or elswhere call upon thy name, that we maye shewe ourselues thankefull to thee for these and all other the benefites, and that we maye daily encrease and goe forwardes in the knowledge and faith of thee, and thy sonne, by the holy spirite. So that aswel by these thy ministres, as by them to whom they shal bee appointed ministers, thy holy name maye be always glorified, and thy blessed kyngdome enlarged: through the same thy sonne, our Lorde Jesus Christe: which liueth and reigneth with thee in the unitie of the same holy spirite world without ende. Amen.

¶ *When this prayer is done, the Bishoppe with the Priestes present shal lay theyr handes seuerally upon the head of euery one that receiueth orders : the receiuers humbly knelyng upon their knees, and the Bishop saying :*

RECIEUE the holy gost: whose sinnes thou doest forgeue, they are forgeuen: and whose synnes thou doest retayne, they are retayned: and bee thou a faithful dispensor of the worde of god, and of his holy Sacramentes. In the name of the father, and of the sonne, and of the holy gost. Amen.

¶ *The Bishop shal deliuer to euery one of them the Bible in his hande, saying.*

TAKE thou aucthoritie to preache the worde of God, and to minister the holy Sacramentes in this congregacion where thou shalte be so appointed.

¶ *When thys is doen, the congregacion shall syng the Crede, and also thei shal goe to the Communion, which al they that receiue orders shal take together, and remaine in the same place where the handes were layd upon them, untyl suche time as thei haue receiued the Communion.*

¶ *The Communion beyng doen, after the last Collecte, and immediatly before the benediccion, shal be sayd this Collecte.*

MOST mercifull father, we beseche thee, so to sende upon these thy seruaunts thy heauenly blessing, that they may be cladde

about with all justice, and that thy worde spoken by their
mouthes may haue such successe, that it may neuer be spoken
in vayne.   Graunt also that we maye haue grace to heare and
receiue the same as thy moste holy worde, and the meane of our
saluacion, that in al our wordes and dedes we may seke thy glory
and the encrease of thy kingdom, thorow Jesus Christ our Lorde.
Amen.

¶ *And if the Orders of Deacon and Priesthod be geuen both upon one day,
then shal al thinges at the holy Communion be used as they are appointed
at the orderyng of Priests.   Sauing that for the Epistle, the whole thirde
chapter of the first to Timothe shal be read, as it is sette out before in the
order of Priests.   And immediatly after the Epistle, the Deacons shal
be ordred.   And it shall suffice the Letany to be sayed once.*

THE FORME OF CONSECRATING

OF AN

ARCHEBISSHOPPE OR BYSSHOPPE.

¶ *At the Communion.*

The Epistle.

THIS is a true saying, If a manne desire the office of a Bisshoppe, he desyreth an honeste woorke. A Bisshoppe therefore muste bee blamelesse, the husbande of one wife, dilygente, sobre, discrete, a keper of hospitalitie, apte to teache, not geuen to ouermuche wyne, no fyghter, not greedy of filthie lucre, but gentle, abhorryng fightinge, abhorringe couetousnesse, one that ruleth wel his owne house; one that hath children in subieccion with all reuerence. For if a man cannot rule his owne house, how shal he care for the congregacion of God? he maye not be a young scholer, lest he swel, and fal into the judgement of the euil speaker. He must also haue a good report of them which are without, lest he fal into rebuke and snare of the euil speaker.

The Gospel. John iiii. (*sic*).

JESUS sayd to Symon Peter, Symon Johanna, loueste thou me more than these? He said unto him, Yea, lorde, thou knowest that I loue thee. He said unto hym, Fede my lambes. He said to him again the second time: Simon Johanna, louest thou me? He sayd unto him, Yea, lorde, thou knowest that I loue thee. He said unto him, Feede my shepe. He sayed unto hym the thirde tyme, Simon Johanna, louest thou me? Peter was sory because he sayd unto hym the third time, louest thou me? and he sayd unto him: lord, thou knowest al thynges, thou knowest that I loue thee. Jesus said unto him, fede my shepe.

¶ *Or els out of the tenth Chapiter of John, as before in thorder of Priestes.*

¶ *After the gospel and Credo ended, firste the elected Bishoppe, shall bee presented by two Bishoppes unto the Archebishoppe of that Prouince, or to some other Byshoppe appoynted by his commission : the Bishoppes that present hym sayinge.*

MOST reuerend father in god, we present unto you this godly and wel learned man to be consecrated Bishoppe.

459

¶ *Then shal the Archebishoppe demaund the Kyng's* mandate *for the con-secracion, and cause it to be read. And the othe touching the knowledge of the king's supremacie shalbe ministred to the person elected, as it is set oute in the Order of Deacons. And then shalbe ministred also the othe of due obedience unto the Archebishoppe as foloweth.*

¶ THE OTHE OF DUE OBEDIENCE
to the Archebishoppe.

In the name of god, Amen. I, *N*. chosen Bishoppe of the Churche, and sie of *N*. doe professe and promesse all due reuer-ence and obedience to the Archebishoppe and to the Metropoliti-call churche of *N*. and to their successours, so helpe me god throughe Jesus Chryste.

¶ *This othe shal not be made at the consecracion of an Archebishoppe.*

¶ *Then the Archebishoppe shal moue the congregacion present to praye, saying thus to them.*

Brethren, it is written in the gospell of Saincte Luke, that oure sauiour Christe continued the whole nighte in prayer or euer that he did chose and sende furth his xii Apostles. It is written also in the Actes of the Apostles, that the disciples which were at Antioche did fast and pray or euer they layed handes upon or sent furth Paul and Barnabas. Let us therefore, folow-ing the example of our sauiour Chryste and hys Apostles, firste fall to prayer or that we admit and sende furth thys person pre-sented unto us, to the worke whereunto we trust the holy gost hath called hym.

¶ *And then shalbe said the Letany as afore in the order of Deacons. And after this place :* **That it maye please the to illuminate al Bishoppes &c.** *he shal saye.*

That it maye please thee to blesse this oure brother elected, and to sende thy grace upon hym, that he may duly execute the office whereunto he is called, to the edifying of thy churche, and to the honoure, prayse and glorye of thy name.

Aunswere. We beseche thee to heare us, good Lorde.

¶ *Concluding the Letanye in the ende with this prayer :*

Almightie God, geuer of all good thinges, whiche by thy holy spirit hast appointed diuerse orders of ministers in thy Church: mercifully behold this thy seruaunt now called to the worke and ministery of a Bishoppe, and replenishe him so with the trueth of thy doctrine and innocencie of lyfe, that both by worde and dede he maye faithfully serue thee in this office, to the glorye of thy name, and profite of thy congregacyon: Throughe the merites of our sauioure Jesu Christ, who liueth and reigneth with thee and the holy gost, worlde without ende. Amen.

¶ *Then the Archebishoppe sitting in a chaire, shal saye this to hym that is to be consecrated.*

BROTHER, forasmuch as holy Scripture and the olde Canons commaundeth, that we should not be hasty in laying on handes and admitting of any person to the gouernement of the congregacyon of Chryste, whiche he hath purchased with no lesse price then the effusion of his own bloud: afore that I admit you to this administracion whereunto ye are called, I wyll examine you in certayne articles, to thend the congregacion presente may haue a trial and beare witnes howe ye be mynded to behaue your self in the church of god. Are you perswaded that you bee truely called to this ministracion accordyng to the wyll of oure Lorde Jesus Chryste and the ordre of thys realme?

Aunswere. I am so perswaded.

The Archebishoppe. Are you perswaded that the holy Scriptures conteine sufficiently all doctryne required of necessitie for eternall saluacion throughe the faith of Jesu Christ? And are you determined with the same holy scriptures to enstruct the people committed to your charge, and to teache or mainteine nothyng, as required of necessitie to eternall saluacyon, but that you shalbe perswaded may be concluded and proued by the same?

Aunswere. I am so perswaded and determined by god's grace.

The Archbishoppe. Will you then faithfully exercise yourselfe in the sayed holy scriptures, and call upon god by prayer for the true understanding of the same, so as ye maye be able by them to teache and exhorte with wholesome doctryne, and to withstande and conuince the gainsaiers?

Aunswere. I wyl so doe, by the helpe of god.

The Archebishoppe. Be you ready with all faithfull diligence to banishe and driue away all erronious and straunge doctrine contrarye to God's word, and both priuately and openly to call upon, and encourage other to the same?

Aunswere. I am ready, the Lord beyng my helper.

The Archebishoppe. Will you deny all ungodlynesse, and worldly lustes, and liue soberly, ryghteously, and Godly in this worlde, that you maye shewe yourselfe in all thynges an example of good woorkes unto other, that the aduersary may be ashamed, hauing nothing to laye agaynste you?

Aunswere. I wyl so doe, the lorde beyng my helper.

The Archebishoppe. Will you maintaine and set forwarde (as much as shal lie in you) quietnesse, peace, and loue, emonge al men? And such as be unquiete, disobedyent, and criminous within your Diocesse, correcte and punyshe, accordyng to suche aucthoritie, as ye haue by God's word, and as to you shall bee committed, by the ordinaunce of thys realme?

Aunswere. I wyl so doe, by the helpe of god.

The Archebishoppe. Wil you shewe yourself gentle, and be mercifull for Christ's sake, to poore and nedy people, and to al straungers destitute of helpe?

Aunswere. I wil so shewe myselfe, by god's helpe.

The Archebishoppe. Almightie god our heauenly father, who hath geuen you a good wil to doe al these thynges: graunte also unto you strength and power, to performe the same, that he accomplishing in you the good worke whiche he hath begon, ye maye be founde perfecte and irreprehensible at the latter daye: through Jesu Christ our Lord.   Amen.

Then shalbe song or sayd, Come holy gost, *&c. as it is set out in the Order of Priests.*

That ended, the Archbishoppe shal say.

Lorde, heare our prayer.
Aunswere. And let our crie come unto thee.

¶ Let us praye.

ALMIGHTIE God and moste mercyfull father, whiche of thy infinite goodnesse, hast geuen to us thy onely and moste dere beloued sonne Jesus Chryste, to bee oure redemer and aucthoure of euerlastyng lyfe, who after that he had made perfect our redempcion by hys death, and was ascended into heauen, powred down his giftes abundauntly upon men, makyng some Apostles, some Prophetes, some Euangelistes, some Pastours and Doctours, to the edifying and makyng perfecte of his con-gregacion: Graunte, we besche thee, to thys thy seruaunt such grace, that he maye euermore be ready to spreade abrode thy gospell, and glad tidings of reconcilement to god, and to use the authoritie geuen unto him, not to destroie, but to saue, not to hurt, but to helpe, so that he as a wise and a faithfull seruaunt, geuing to thy family meate in due season, may at the last daye be receiued into joye, throughe Jesu Christe our lorde, who with thee and the holy gost liueth and reigneth one God, worlde withoute ende.   Amen.

¶ *Then the Archebishoppe and Bishoppes present shal lay theyr handes upon the head of the elected Bishop, the Archebishoppe saying.*

TAKE the holy goste, and remember that thou stirre up the grace of God, which is in thee, by imposicion of handes: for god hath not geuen us the spirite of feare, but of powere, and loue, and of sobernesse.

¶ *Then the Archebishoppe shall deliuer him the Bible, saying.*

GEUE hede unto readyng, exhortacyon and doctryne.   Thinke apon these things conteyned in thys boke, be diligente in them, that the encrease comyng thereby maye be manifeste unto al men.   Take hede unto thyselfe, and unto teachyng, and be diligente in doyng them: for by doing thys thou shalte saue thyselfe and them that heare thee; bee to the flocke of Christ a shepeherde, not a wolfe, fede them, deuoure them not, holde up the weake, heale the sycke, binde together the broken, brynge agayne the outcastes, seke the lost: Be so merciful, that you be not too remisse, so minister discipline, that you forgeat not mercye: that when the chief shepeheard shal come, ye may receiue the immarcessible croune of glorye, through Jesus Christ oure Lorde.   Amen.

¶ *Then the Archbishoppe shal procede to the Communion, with whom the newe consecrated Byshoppe with other shall also communicate.   And after the last Collecte, immediatly before the benediccion, shalbe sayed this prayer :*

MOSTE merciful father, we beseche thee to sende down upon thys thy seruaunt thy heauenly blessing, and so endue him with thy holy spirite, that he preachyng thy word, may not only be earnest to reproue, beseche, and rebuke with al pacience and doctyrne, but also maye be to suche as beleue an wholesome example in worde, in conuersacion, in loue, in faith, in chastitie, and puritie: that faythfully fulfyllyng hys course, at the latter daye he maye receiue the croune of righteousnesse, layd up by the lord, the righteous iudge: who liueth and reigneth, one god with the father and the holy gost, worlde without ende.   Amen.

IMPRINTED AT LONDON

IN FLETE STRETE AT THE SIGNE

OF THE SUNNE OVER AGAYNSTE

THE CONDUITE BY EDVVARDE

WHITCHURCHE.

M.D.LII.

Cum privilegio ad imprimendum solum.